Reception and Communion Among Churches

edited by

Hervé Legrand

Julio Manzanares

and

Antonio García y García

Canon Law Department
Catholic University of America
Washington, D.C.

First published in English in *The Jurist*, Vol. 57 (1997), No. 1

Reprinted by permission

Printed in the United States of America

ISBN 0-9673864-0-3

CONTENTS

iii

III. Theological and Canonical Perspectives

IV. Closing Reflections

RECEPTION AND
COMMUNION AMONG CHURCHES

INTRODUCTION

The Salamanca Colloquia already have their short history. They began in 1988 with a theme which at that time had great urgency, episcopal conferences. The entire Church was involved in an in-depth study requested by the Extraordinary Synod of 1985 on two essential points: the theological "status," and the teaching authority of episcopal conferences. An international consortium of Catholic universities felt itself called to give its own contribution to the theme, organizing a colloquium with the participation of historians, theologians, canon lawyers, ecumenists, etc. The excellent welcome received by the acts, published in four languages (French, English, Italian, and Spanish) manifested quickly the appropriateness of the initiative.

Three years later, in 1991, a second experience with similar characteristics took place. The theme, suggested by the participants of the previous colloquium, was "The Local Church and Catholicity," also treated on this occasion in an interdisciplinary manner.

In Easter of 1996 we came to what has come to be known as "Salamanca III," with a theme which was also appropriate for the usual method in the colloquia: "Reception and Communion Among the Churches." Again, it dealt with an ecclesiological theme of great significance for the internal life of the Church (without reception the Church is not built) and with important consequences in the field of ecumenism.

The acts of this third colloquium bring together the presentations and remaining interventions as well as the results of reflections carried out in linguistic groups. The Spanish edition presents the texts in their original languages. We are seeking to respond in this way to those who have expressed the desire to be able to deal with the contribution of the authors in their own languages. However, to facilitate the spread of the results, we are also presenting editions in English, French, and Italian, as on previous occasions.

Ecumenical Dimension

Joined to the interdisciplinary theme and the inter-university and international level of the encounter, one characteristic appears especially worthy of mention in our "Salamanca III": ecumenicity.

The ecumenical dimension, a characteristic of the previous colloquia, was more present in "Salamanca III." Although in keeping with the intention of the organizers the colloquium always dealt with chapters in Catholic ecclesiology, we were very interested in the point of view of the other churches present, as well as the echo which our points of view and discussion raised for them. A good proof of this are the texts of the Orthodox Professor John Erickson and of the Anglican Professors Mary Tanner and Lionel Wickham.

Appreciation

We cannot fail to express our thanks for all those who made possible the good results of this colloquium. Above all, for the sponsoring universities which, by alphabetical order of the cities in which they are located, were the following: The Catholic University of Lisbon, the Catholic Institute of Paris, The Pontifical Gregorian University of Rome, The Pontifical University of Salamanca, The Catholic University of America in Washington, The Theological faculty of St. Georgen in Frankfurt a. Main, and the theological faculty of the north of Italy in Milan.

We express our thanks to the professors who prepared with painstaking care their interventions and accepted with good will the rather spartan discipline of the colloquium. A special mention and thanks are due to the episcopal conference of Spain for its unconditional support to the colloquium and for the attentive and warm presence of its president, His Excellency Elias Yanes, Archbishop of Zaragoza, who gave the inaugural address, and of its vice-president and the grand-chancellor of the university, His Excellency Fernando Sebastián, Archbishop of Pamplona, who honored us with the closing allocution. We express our gratitude as well for the Pontifical University of Salamanca who welcomed all and who gave its good wishes in the inaugural words of the Rector Magnificus, Professor Dr. José Manuel Sánchez Caro, and which placed its installations at the service of the colloquium.

We likewise express our appreciation to those who aided with their economic support: the episcopal conference of Spain, the Pontifical University of Salamanca, and the Council of Culture of the Junta of Castilla-León, and several other sources which prefer to remain anonymous.

In this list we cannot fail at least to mention the persons and institutions which in such a warm and cordial manner welcomed us during the colloquium: the Center of Spirituality Saint Vincent de Paul and the community of sisters which serve it, the Carmelite Convent of Segovia, and the diocesan bishops of Salamanca and Segovia. Gratitude, finally, is expressed to the members of the secretariat, always efficient and discreet, and in particular professors Marinano Sanz González and Julio Ramos Guerreira.

Toward the Future

The participants expressed their desires that the experience continue with characteristics similar to the colloquia which have already taken place. The work groups proposed a series of themes which would complement the rich theological vision of the preceding colloquia. Most expressed the wish to respond to the pope's desire given in solemn manner in his encyclical *Ut unum sint* of May 25, 1995. He asked that suggestions be offered about a possible exercise of the primacy which "without renouncing in any way to the essential of its mission, would be open to a new situation."

We are gratified to discern again the ecclesiological and ecumenical sensitivity of the participants in making this proposal. However, this is no more than an indication, but it does recommend itself by its coherence with the ecumenical commitment of the Catholic Church in whose heart resounds the words of Vatican II: "To promote the restoration of the unity among all Christians is one of the great proposals of the council."

Hervé Legrand
Julio Manzanares
Antonio García y García

A COLLOQUIUM ON RECEPTION:
GENESIS, OBJECTIVES, METHOD

Julio Manzanares*

In the solemn opening session, both Archbishop Elias Yanes, President of the Spanish Episcopal Conference, and Professor Gilles Routhier presented the theme which occupied us during the Colloquium as a living issue for our present time. It is not a museum piece; there is no doubt as to its urgency; rather it affects the very nucleus of ecclesiological renewal and the whole question of ecumenism, both of which are characteristic of this age we live in.

This would be enough to explain why *reception* has come to our colloquium, which, since its inception, has also been marked by a double and very keen interest in both ecclesiology and ecumenism.

It would not however be amiss, both for ourselves and for those who follow our work from further afield, to examine briefly the justification for our theme and to ask ourselves about the following three points: the genesis of the colloquium, its objectives, and its method.

Genesis of the Colloquium

Its first seed goes back to January 1988. In the colloquium we celebrated then on the topic of Episcopal Conferences we lived an experience whose result surpassed our expectations in a better understanding of "conferences" as an institution—a privileged sphere for the exercise of collegiality—and, at the same time, in a better understanding of the Church.[1]

The experience of interdisciplinary collaboration, strongly recommended by the legislation of the Church (cf. c. 820) and borne out by the good results, brought us to resolve to continue what we had lived, in

---

* Universidad Pontificia de Salamanca (Spain).
[1] *The Nature and Future of Episcopal Conferences*, ed. Hervé Legrand, Julio Manzanares, and António García y García (Washington: Catholic University of America Press, 1988); see also *The Jurist* 48 (1988) iii-412.

terms of both ambience and method, but on a new theme. But what theme? Two of the four language groups which could express themselves at that time highlighted the theme of reception. The German language group said: "We suggest that the concept of 'reception' of teaching of various ecclesial authorities be deepened. Does reception by the pope, by the college of bishops, and by the people of God mean in principle the same thing, or are there constitutive differences between them, and what are these?"[2] The English language group proposed with brevity: "Reception: as applied to actions of episcopal conferences; *sensus fidei*."[3]

In 1992 the Second International Colloquium took place on the theme "Local Churches and Catholicity," which at that time was considered a priority and which supposed a clarifying advance on important elements of the local church, on the theological value of its being rooted in each territory, and on the very image of the local church, far from passivity and without shrinking from Catholicity.[4]

Once again, alongside the specific theme, there was a passionate interest in the Church. And once again in all the participants the conviction was reinforced that we had taken the right path and that we needed to follow it. On what theme? "Reception as an ecclesial reality" asked the German group.[5] "The problem of reception" said the Spanish group; "To deepen it in the sense of the term and of its distinct meanings, as well as its theological and canonical dimensions."[6] The English language group recommended "an interdisciplinary study of reception, including the mutual reception among local churches, the reception of law, and the reception of doctrine."[7] Finally, the Italian group, among a wide range of themes, highlighted with few words, "reception."[8] Such an eloquent unanimity could no longer go unheeded by the organizers.

How did we get from the Acts of the two preceding meetings to the program for the new colloquium? The wide convergence already mentioned was not enough; a long road still had to be covered. Individual

---

[2] Ibid., 398.
[3] Ibid., 401.
[4] *The Local Church and Catholicity*, ed. Hervé Legrand, Julio Manzanares, and António García y García (Washington: Canon Law Department, Catholic University of America, 1992); see also *The Jurist* 52 (1992) 1-586.
[5] Ibid., 547.
[6] Ibid., 548.
[7] Ibid., 549.
[8] Ibid., 551.

meetings or group meetings with representatives from almost all the sponsoring institutions and with other experts gave definitive shape to our plan of work, also endorsed on this occasion by the two concerns, the ecclesiological and the ecumenical, given that—as Congar said—reception is a theme of as capital importance both from the point of view of ecumenism as from that point of view proper to a traditional and Catholic ecclesiology.[9]

What We Sought

We were not trying to write an "encyclopedia" on reception; nor did we seek to legitimate one or other process of reception, however much the efficient reference to concrete facts analyzed in the first part of our program helped us.

We sought to respond to what the two previous colloquia asked for: a deeper study of the meaning of the term and its different accepted usages, as well as its theological and canonical dimensions; to get down to the real life of the churches whose function is not merely passive but rather the active witness to the revealed message "with the public profession of their faith, with their liturgical sacramental activity, and with the same exercise of the active announcing of the revealed message";[10] to discover the soil into which reception put down its roots until that time when, as Congar says, it was all but eliminated when the ecclesiology of communion was substituted by a pyramidal theory of the Church: a mass determined and activated by its peak, in which and for which the Holy Spirit is considered as scarcely little more than the guarantor of the hierarchy's infallibility.[11]

As we know, reception is not identical with obedience; nor does it consist in the simple relationship of subordination to a legitimate authority. "It involves a collaboration of consent, eventually of judgment, where the life of a body which exercises its own original spiritual resources is expressed."[12] Does this mean that obedience would lose its place which

---

[9]   Yves Congar, "La 'reception' comme réalité ecclésiologique," *Revue des Sciences Philosophiques et Théolgiques* 56 (1972) 369.
[10]   Angel Antón, *El misterio de la Iglesia* (Madrid: Editorial Católica, 1987) 2: 1051.
[11]   Congar, 392.
[12]   Ricardo Blázquez, *La Iglesia del Concilio Vaticano II* (Salamanca: Sigueme, 1988) 15.

would then be taken by personal autonomy? Does reception however have anything to do with personal autonomy?[13] What would happen if a legitimately taken decision or a doctrine taught by the Magisterium were not received?[14] Would this be equivalent to a decision or doctrine which did not exist? Does the famous question of *rationabilitas legis* have anything to tell us on this issue?

If we apply reception to the papal magisterium do we clash with the famous clause of the constitution *Pastor aeternus* of Vatican I which stresses that the *ex cathedra* magisterium is of itself unchangeable, "of itself and not from the Church's consent" (*ex sese et non ex consensu Ecclesiae*)?[15] Are we not introducing something which could undermine unity and the legitimate exercise of the magisterium and the government proper to the ministry of the hierarchy?

But can we limit ourselves to mere questions of legal validity, thus forgetting the importance and the value of the *sensus fidelium*?[16] How can we ignore the famous *dictum* of Gratian: "Laws are instituted when they are promulgated, become firm when they are approved by the mores of those who use them" (*Leges instituuntur cum promulgantur, firmantur cum moribus utentium approbantur*)?[17] Congar, for his part, pinpointed that "non-reception does not mean a false decision; it means that the decision does not stir up any life force and therefore does not contribute to its own edification."[18]

---

[13] Ibid. He follows closely Congar's study cited above. See also Jacques Elisée Desseaux, "Paul VI et L'unité des Chretiens," in Istituto Paolo VI, *Notiziario* 5 (1982) 103.

[14] Congar, 385, displays his perplexity at some cases, indeed some recent ones, of non-reception on the part of a significant number of Catholics. Faced with these and similar facts, Blázquez, 403, adverts to the need to distinguish what proceeds from a legitimate responsibility which seeks to collaborate properly in the preservation and transmission of the faith, from what can take the form of pressure and by this road outside the limits of the exercise of power.

[15] *Conciliorum Oecumenicorum Decreta*, ed. Josepho Alberigo et al., 3rd ed. (Bologna: Istituto per le Scienze Religiose, 1973) 816.

[16] We refer to the quality of the subject on whom the grace of faith, of love, of the gifts of the Holy Spirit confer a capacity to perceive the truth of faith and to discern what is contrary to it. The *sensus fidei* is not the simple echo of the teaching of the pastors; it is not however resistant . . . to being discerned within the Church and to being recognized by the pastoral magisterium (cf. Blázquez, 359-404).

[17] Gratian, Pars I, D. IV, c. 3; ed. Friedberg, 1: 6.

[18] Congar, 399, quoting H. Bacht, recognizes that "la non-réception ne signifie pas que la décision portée soit fausse: elle signifie que cette décision n'eveille aucune force de vie, et donc ne contribue pas à l'edification."

Faced with this amalgam of questions and problems, it is small wonder that contemporary authors speak of reception as a "dangerous
topic";[19] or better said, a risky topic. Meanwhile many others, including
those who recognize its difficulty, consider it to be a pressing need of the
ecclesiology of communion and of the return to basics which is characteristic of our epoch and of all epochs of reform. "Reception based on a
societal and absolutely monarchical notion of the Church and expressed
in pure terms of authority and obedience, would be incompatible with the
model of Church as communion, such as was lived in the early Church
and which has revitalized itself in the ecclesiology and in the Church of
our days."[20]

To all we have said above, we must add the invitation which comes
from the ecumenical scene to deepen our understanding of the reality of
reception. It suffices to remember the call of the Nairobi Assembly in
1975 calling on the churches to "make a common effort to *receive*, appropriate and profess *together*, as concrete circumstances dictate, the
Christian truth and faith which have come down to us through the apostles and have been handed down through the centuries. Such an action,
which springs from free and constructive discussion under the authority
of the word of God accepted as such by all, has the double finality of clarifying and expressing the unity and diversity which are proper to the life
and mission of the Church."[21] On the other hand, within the same ecumenical scene, how do we get from the agreement among scholars to the
agreement of the people with their scholars?

What we said above turned the topic of reception into a question of
burning contemporary interest, as the introductory lecture told in a much
more detailed and complete fashion; it is even a question which could be
trivialized by extensive use, so that it ends up meaning nothing specific.

---

[19]   Cf. Congar, 370. Some authors involved in this colloquium take up this problem in
their writings: Wolfgang Beinert, "Die Rezeption und ihre Bedeutung für Leben und
Lehre der Kirche," in *Glaube als Zustimmung: Zur Interpretation kirchlicher Rezeption-
vorgänge* (Freiburg: Herder, 1991) 9; José Eduardo Borges del Pinho, *A recepção como
realidade ecclesial e tarefa ecuménica* (Lisbon: Didascalia, 1994) 111; Gilles Routhier,
La reception d'un Concile (Paris: Cerf, 1993) 15.
[20]   Angel Antón, "La recepción en la Iglesia y en la eclesiología, 1," *Gregorianum* 77
(1996) 68.
[21]   *Breaking Barriers, Nairobi 1975. The Official Report of the Fifth Assembly of the
World Council of Churches, Nairobi, 23rd November-10th December 1975*, ed. David N.
Paton (London: SPCK, 1975) 66; quoted by Antón, "La recepción," 69.

This was the task before us as we began our third colloquium: to clarify the concept, to make more precise its possibilities and its limits in the field of Catholic theology, to purify it of excessive applications which attempt to ignore a whole millennium of history in which the unity of the Church—and consequently the unity of the faith—has been achieved by another way: "the submission to a single head of the Church considered as a sort of single and immense diocese,"[22] however strange such an ecclesiology may seem to us. Neither should we forget the possibilities which reception offers us in the ecumenical sphere, as we had the opportunity of seeing throughout the days of the colloquium.

And as a guarantee of a satisfactory result, we had with us a good number of those names who have written and contributed most to the theme during the past two decades.

Method

We used the same method as that used in previous colloquia: interdisciplinary, participative, giving our Orthodox and Anglican brothers and sisters the opportunity to speak.

Each presentation was followed by a first reply entrusted to a professor from another discipline or cultural area, not as a "counterpresentation" but rather as a first reaction to the presentation, either with critical observations or broadening the horizon by coming at the theme from another specialty, or by raising questions for the consideration of working groups, a key piece in the methodology of our colloquia.

The subsequent reports from the working groups—summarized briefly—permitted us all to benefit from the contributions in the groups. And here, allow me to mention what we might well call the "spirit" of our colloquia in Salamanca: they seek to be inter-university meetings which bring together, generally by prior invitation, theologians, canonists, historians, and ecumenists who are particularly interested in handling ecclesiological questions in an interdisciplinary manner. We seek dialogue and scientific confrontation, committed to the search for truth and having as a goal the elaboration of instruments of reflection which can be such also for the Church of today.

---

[22] Congar, 394.

To conclude—a wish: we did not attempt to say the last word on a theme which is so complex and capable of such varied assessment; we did, however, seek to say a word that is serious, original and rigorous, a word that cannot be overlooked whenever anyone comes back to deal with this topic.

Translation by Denis E. Carlin

INAUGURAL ADDRESS

ELIAS YANES*

This third international colloquium proposes to study the theme "Reception and communion among the churches," and intends to develop four aspects: (1) a historic perspective; (2) the ecclesiological dimension; (3) the canonical dimension; (4) the ecumenical dimension.

It is a difficult and delicate theme. It holds a certain relationship with the themes studied in the previous colloquia, episcopal conferences and catholicity. Episcopal conferences constitute a field of the collegial exercise of the bishops' mission even though it does not deal in this case with the episcopal college in the strict sense. As to the local churches and catholicity, the local church is "in which and from which the one and unique Church exists" (*LG* 23). Reception is related both to the active and conscious faith life in local churches as well as to an ecclesiology which encounters in synodality one of its most significant expressions.

Most theologians, canonists, and historians who have studied this theme conclude in affirming that the reality and idea of reception has never been totally ignored in the Church. "Reception" was always present in a more or less explicit manner in the consciousness and life of the Church. With respect to "reception" one can affirm that life precedes theological and juridic reflection. In the writings of the New Testament itself the whole primitive Christian community shows a lively consciousness of being the community of those who have freely received faith and grace, the community of those who freely received from Christ and his Spirit the gifts of redemption to communicate them to all people by means of the distinct channels through which flows the life of communion in the new messianic community of salvation.

A noted Spanish Father, disciple of Vitoria, D. Martín Pérez de Ayala, Bishop of Segovia, expressed himself in this way at the Council of Trent: "There is a second way of apprehending the truth in doubtful matters;

---

*   Archbishop of Zaragosa (Spain); President of the Conferencia Episcopal Española.

11

namely, the received authority of all general councils by consent of the people's faith."

The idea of "reception" flourished in different contexts of the "Catholic reform" proposed by the Council of Trent, and then in the period of reception of Vatican Council I.

On the other hand, the use of the term "reception" as such entered into modern ecclesiology between the two world wars in certain publications related to the first ecumenical contacts thirty years before Vatican II. The diffusion of the term "reception" and the explanation of it has become more gradual since the Second Vatican Council, coinciding with the development of ecumenical dialogue between the Churches. It is a theme which has not lost its actuality.

For the study of "reception" a look at the past must not be left out, especially at the first millennium of our era when the undivided Church expressed in a spontaneous manner and with special vigor the ideals of its own being. Here we encounter the phenomenon of "reception" on the part of the ecclesial body to determine what was authentic Tradition and what was spurious, for building up the Church within apostolic continuity.

But an historical look is not enough. A theological reflection is required which will make it possible to determine the meaning and scope of "reception," the differentiation of the distinct elements in it, the analogical use of the concept of reception in the dogmatic and juridic fields. Questions of great importance are posed to us: how to determine the *sensus fidelium*; what repercussion does the active role of the faithful have in reception for a doctrine proposed by the magisterium; how do the apostolic ministry and the sense of the faith of the faithful complement one another in the transmission of the living tradition of the Church?

Theological reflection on "reception" cannot take place in an adequate manner without paying attention to the ecumenical repercussions of our reflection. The theological category of "reception" has constituted a theme of dialogue between the Catholic Church and the Orthodox Churches since the beginning of our century. But this dialogue has intensified with the development of the ecclesiology of communion beginning with Vatican II. The dialogue between Catholics and Anglicans over "reception" was begun in the last century by Cardinal Newman. He insisted on the idea that ecumenical reception is not possible if it is not situated in the context of already existing communion. For this the teaching of the

Second Vatican Council holds a special importance, which recognizes a true communion, even though imperfect, between all those who by the same baptism have been incorporated into Christ (cf. *LG* 15, *UR* 3).

The theological notion of reception is the object of research and analysis. On the concept of "reception" all the authors who treat it recognize the descriptive definition proposed by Yves Congar:

> By "reception" I understand (in the present article) the process by means of which a church (body) truly takes over as its own a resolution that it did not originate in regard to its self, and acknowledges the measure it promulgates as a rule applicable to its own life. Reception includes something more than what the Scholastics called "obedience." For the Scholastics it is the act by which a subordinate submits his will and conduct to the legitimate precepts of a superior, out of respect for the latter's authority. Reception is not a mere realization of the relation "secundum sub et supra": it includes a degree of consent, and possibly of judgment, in which the life of a body is expressed which brings into play its own original spiritual resources.[1]

Cardinal Willebrands proposed this notion of reception before a Lutheran audience in Toronto in 1980:

> It is a process thanks to which the people of God, in its structures (organization) differentiated and guided by the Holy Spirit recognizes and accepts new understandings, new witnesses of the truth and of its forms of expression with the *sensus fidei* of the whole Church. . . . In its full form, reception implies an official doctrine, its proclamation, liturgy, the spiritual and ethical life of the faithful, as well as theology as a systematic reflection on this complex reality. Reception also includes *kerygma*, *didaché*, and *praxis pietatis*.

According to Cardinal Willebrand's explanation, reception appears as a process of assimilation and progressive maturation of the faith in conformity with the "apostolic tradition" and the *sensus fidelium* of the whole believing community. To discern the authenticity of the new ele-

---

[1]   Yves Congar, "Reception as an Ecclesiological Reality," in *Election and Consensus in the Church*, ed. Giuseppe Alberigo and Anton Weiler, Concilium 77 (New York: Paulist, 1972) 45.

ments which enter in the process of reception he points to the criteria of apostolicity and catholicity in the setting of the Church's living faith:

> In as much as such witnesses of new understandings and experiences are recognized as authentic elements of apostolicity and of catholicity and they tend fundamentally to be accepted and included in the living faith of the Church.[2]

Father Angel Antón advises us that there still persists a tendency to use the term "reception"—itself complex and multidimensional—in a great many senses, including some rather marginal ones with the danger of losing the concept's theological substratum. But he indicates that it is not possible to trace a theological motion of reception by only a deductive manner, and even less, a priori.[3]

Theological reflection on "reception," when it seeks to establish criteria of action, cannot orient itself in a manner which would disvalue the specific authority of the magisterium ("under the leadership of the magisterium" *LG* 12) nor the communion of the faithful with their respective pastors ("the holy people gathered together with their pastors" *DV* 10). This does not decrease the scientific vigor of the method of historical investigation or of the demands of theological methodology. The action of the Holy Spirit which assists the magisterium assists as well the faithful in many ways before and after the magisterium makes a pronouncement. The same Spirit which inclines to obedience inclines as well to reflection which is directed toward an adequate understanding and intellectual acceptance of the Church's teaching. These processes of reception are frequently conditioned by highly differentiated historical, cultural, and political factors. Thus there is a responsibility of those who are called to exercise in the Church a sage and patient pedagogy and catechesis, in preaching, and in governing the Christian community, in theological reflection, in spiritual discernment, and in the application of the principle "in necessary things unity, in doubtful matters liberty, in everything charity" (*GS* 92).

The juridic aspect is also implied in the theme of "reception." Theological and juridical reflection, faithful to the principles of Catholic ec-

---

[2]   Cited by Angel Antón, "La recepción en la Iglesia y en la eclesiologia, 1," *Gregorianum* 77 (1996) 64-65.
[3]   Ibid., 79.

clesiology, have to flee two extremes: (1) on one side, Gallicanism, which sought to make the validity of the magisterial decisions of the Roman Pontiff dependent on the acceptance and positive reception on the part of local churches; and (2) on the other side, an excessive juridicism, which would limit itself to considering the legal validity of a council without paying attention to the processes of the slow, active, and conscious assimilation on the part of the Christian community of the conciliar teachings and decisions.

"Reception" creates neither legitimacy nor juridic force of obligation. But in the more secure Christian tradition, ministers who exercise authority never do it solo. "Reception" does not constitute the juridic quality of a decision; it does not confer validity on decisions. But it attests if this decision responds adequately or not to the good of the Church.

Father Sertillanges, in a chapter of his work *The Church* which dealt with the role of governors in the governance of the Church, said: "The Church is not . . . a machine; she is a living organism. And in an organism what is moved, that is the particular organs and even the most minute cells, is equally the mover, by reason of the body's organic solidarity." A little later on he says: "the divine Spirit which animates the hierarchy, in accordance with the Saviour's promise, also animates, in His name, those to whom it was said: 'Know you not that your members are the temples of the Holy Ghost?' "[4]

Be aware that the lessons of history, which show us tensions and unilateral affirmations which yet are completed and nuanced later after an initial rejection, speak to us about patience, about slow processes— sometimes a slowness of centuries—which assure an in-depth assimilation.

My desire is that the reflections of this third international colloquium will contribute to give an effective and fruitful impluse to the theological and juridical clarification of "reception." Perhaps there will be differ-

---

[4] A. D. Sertillanges, *The Church*, trans. A. G. McDougall (New York: Benziger Brother, 1922) 332. See also Yves Congar, "La 'reception' comme réalité ecclésiologique," *Revue des Sciences Philosophiques et Théologiques* 56 (1972) 369-403; idem, *Jalons pour une théologie du laïcat* (Paris: Cerf, 1953) ch. 5; Jean-Marie Tillard, *Church of Churches: The Ecclesiology of Communion* (Collegeville, MN: Liturgical Press, 1992); Antón, 57-95 (*supra*, note 2).

ences in the presentations and discussions, but I hope that they will al-ways be motivated by the desire for truth and to build up the Church. I am confident that the light of the Holy Spirit will not be lacking to any of those who participate in this colloquium, the Spirit which always guides us towards the full truth.

Translation by James H. Provost

RECEPTION IN THE CURRENT
THEOLOGICAL DEBATE

GILLES ROUTHIER*

Besides being distinguished for their multidisciplinary approach, the inter-university collaboration which they prompt, and the concern to integrate an ecumenical dimension in their work, the Salamanca colloquia are noted because they address ecclesiological themes which profoundly shape the consciousness and ecclesial life of our era. In this perspective, it is not surprising that the committee organizing the present colloquium chose the topic of reception. In effect the question of reception easily lends itself to a pluri-disciplinary treatment. Social history, literature, the arts, communications, law, and theology are disciplines which are interested in reception. However, the relevance of the topic notably exceeds the possibility of multiple approaches to the topic from the vantage point of different disciplines. Its true relevance is ecclesial properly speaking. From this point of view one can conclude that this question is not only the object of debates in the different Christian churches and at the heart of current ecumenical discussions, but is also of great importance for the life of the churches. The fact that the title of the colloquium has linked the terms "reception" and "communion among the churches" clearly indicates the high stakes of the current discussion on reception.

In effect one cannot believe that the revitalization of this topic during the past thirty years is merely a passing phenomenon which has generated temporary excitement. An examination of the rich and extensive bibliography of articles or works dedicated to this topic in the past thirty years leads me to conclude that this hardly represents a purely academic interest in a question without a real connection to the life of the churches. It indicates rather a growing interest in a question closely tied to the life of the churches at the end of the century.

*   Université Laval, Québec (Canada).

The distribution on a chronological graph of works or articles published on the subject in the course of the last three decades confirms a
hypothesis which it was easy to make, i.e., that the development of reflection on reception accompanies two events which have marked Christianity during the course of that period: the holding of Vatican II and the
acceleration of ecumenical dialogues. Commenting on the article of
Congar "La réception comme réalité ecclésiologique," André Birmelée
wrote recently that

> The objective of Congar was twofold. He noted on one hand the
> necessity for the Roman Catholic Church to reflect on and call
> for the reception of the texts and decisions of Vatican Council II.
> Furthermore he wished to draw attention to a fundamental and
> urgent task which is incumbent on the contemporary ecumenical
> movement if the churches do not wish to lose the benefit of the
> rapprochements of these last years.[1]

I have not been able to retrace in Congar's article such a formulation
of the objectives he pursued in writing it. However, such an interpretation
does not basically distort Congar's intent and his journey in developing
his reflections on reception. Hence I will maintain these two events as the
framework of analysis in my survey of the discussions on the notion of
reception in the current theological debate.[2] First I will address the question of reception in relationship to Vatican II and subsequently its treatment in the recent ecumenical dialogues.

VATICAN II AND RECEPTION

Today it is easy to confirm that the renewal of interest in the topic of
reception coincides with the convocation of Vatican II. We totally agree
with the judgment of William G. Rusch, who affirms that "de facto it is
in the convocation of the council in January 1959 by Pope John XXIII
that we find the first motivation of contemporary interest in reception."[3]
According to Wolfinger the convocation of Vatican II, its preparation, its

---

[1]   André Birmelée, "La reception comme exigence oecuménique," in *Communion et
réunion: Mélanges Jean-Marie Roger Tillard*, ed. Gillian R. Evans and Michel Gourges
(Leuven: Leuven University Press, 1995) 75.
[2]   The studies on reception in canon law are concentrated in two well-defined periods:
1975-1977, and 1989-1992.
[3]   William G. Rusch, *Reception—An Ecumenical Opportunity* (Philadelphia: Fortress
Press, 1988) 14.

development, and its conclusions have been equally for the other Christian churches an occasion to question themselves about the conciliar process and on the relevance of the reception of its conclusions for the other churches.[4] The return to the topic in theological studies is thus linked to a deepening of reflection on the conciliar nature of the Church and on relationships among the different local churches, a reflection that largely transcends the boundaries of the Catholic Church.[5]

Up to now the publications which have linked the study of the topic of reception to the conciliar event have done so especially in examining the process of reception of Vatican II. At the very least there has been an examination of the conciliar texts to find there some indications on the subject of reception. Finally and unfortunately, too little work has been done on the conciliar event itself and there has been a failure to analyze it from the angle of reception or as an exemplary locus of reception. I will gradually address these three aspects, focusing especially on the development of what has been neglected until now.

A. The Reception of Vatican II

1. "Application" of the Council

During the years following the closing of Vatican II, the thematic of reception did not surface initially in the Catholic world. The distribution on a chronological graph of articles and works addressing the question of reception of the council indicates that one must wait until the 1980's before that thematic forcefully entered the discourse of Catholic theologians. At the close of the council, the category of "application" was generally used in discussing the relationship between the conciliar teaching and the life of the local churches. The relation between the conciliar event and the life of the people of God was thus conceived following a schema which assigned a secondary role to practice in relationship to theology. In schematizing the situation one could structure the approach taken as follows: Vatican II gives us a definition of the Church; it is now to be implemented. Ecclesial practice will deduce the fundamental principles of-

---

[4]   See Franz Wolfinger, "Die Rezeption theologischer Einsichten und ihre theologische und ökumenische Bedeutung: Von der Einsicht zur Verwirchlichung," *Catholica* 31 (1977) 203.

[5]   On the conciliar nature of the Church see especially *Die ökumenischer Konzilien*, ed. Hans J. Margull (Stuttgart: Evangelisches Verlagswerk, 1961); English trans. *The Councils of the Church* (Philadelphia: Fortress Press, 1966).

fered by Vatican II. In this perspective practice follows the conciliar discourse to which one attributes the status of programmatic discourse.
After the council all one needs to do is "translate" it into action or apply
what has been articulated theoretically. A survey of the analytical index
of the *Documentation Catholique* reveals that the concept of "application" which one frequently finds in the conciliar corpus itself has been
commonly used to speak of the relationship between the ecclesial body
and the council during the postconciliar years. That is evident at the time
of the 1971 synod which evoked the fifth anniversary of the closing of
Vatican II.[6] It is even more true at the time of the outburst of the Lefebvre affair.[7] This concept was frequently used by Paul VI. It was also taken
up by John Paul I and John Paul II.[8]

It is not easy to escape this mechanical logic of application. For example, the 1983 apostolic constitution *Sacrae disciplinae leges* adopts a
view of law following from theology. In this perspective the code must be
considered as a

> significant effort to translate this same conciliar doctrine and ec-
> clesiology into canonical language. If, however, it is impossible
> to translate perfectly into canonical language the conciliar image
> of the Church, nevertheless, the Code must always be referred to

---

[6]   See especially the allocution of the secretary of the synod Msgr. Bartoletti, "La vie
de l'Eglise cinq ans après le Concile," *La Documentation Catholique* [*DC*] 68 (1971)
1113-1123. Only Cardinal Suenens spoke in terms of "reception." See Joseph Cardinal
Suenens, "Cinq ans après Vatican II," *DC* 68 (1971) 35-36.

[7]   On that occasion Paul VI conceptualized things in terms of a refusal "of the council
itself and its application." See Paul VI, "Les nominations de 20 nouveaux cardinaux," *DC*
73 (1976) 556-559. The same expression was used by the bishops of Fribourg and Paris.
See Georges Cottier, "L'enjeu d'Ecône," *DC* 73 (1976) 782 and "Lettre du Cardinal Marty
aux catholiques de Paris," *DC* 73 (1976) 819-820. However, the latter approaches the notion of "reception" without using the term in his homily at the Mass opening the school
year at the Institut Catholique of Paris. See idem, "Les bruyantes querelles autour du Concile," *DC* 73 (1976) 940-941.

[8]   For Pope Paul VI, see especially "Angelus du 11 decembre 1967," *DC* 64 (1967)
310; "L'application du concile," *DC* 64 (1967) 1287-1294; "Allocution au Sacré Collège,"
DC 68 (1971) 665-667; "La nomination de 20 nouveaux cardinaux," *DC* 73 (1976) 556-
559. For John Paul I, see "L'élection de Jean-Paul Ier: Son premier message au monde,"
DC 75 (1978) 801-805. Finally for John Paul II, see "Premier message au monde," *DC* 75
(1978) 902-905.

this image as the primary pattern whose outline the Code ought to express insofar as it can by its very nature.[9]

2. Theological Works Related to 1985 Synod

Even if the thematic of the reception of Vatican II appeared at the beginning of the 1980's, the year 1985 constituted a turning point. The extraordinary synod gave a new impetus to works on this theme. A series of publications surfaced during this period.[10] Between 1984 and 1988 there were at least twelve articles or works devoted to the reception of Vatican II. Different horizons were already uncovered by this first generation of studies on the reception of Vatican II. Europe especially attracts our attention but South America is well represented. The major work published under the direction of Giuseppe Alberigo, Jean-Pierre Jossua and Joseph Komonchak on the reception of Vatican II opened a new stage of research.[11] Even if it did not discuss the concept *ex professo*, the work offered a good number of valuable methodological indicators. Hence one moved from a problematic of application of the council which dominated

---

[9] English translation taken from *Code of Canon Law, Latin-English Edition* (Washington, CLSA, 1983) xiv. The development on the prior pages bears witness to the same logic. More recently the apostolic constitution *Fidei depositum* was not able to free itself from this "consecutive logic." See *Catechism of the Catholic Church* (Washington: USCC, 1994) 5.

[10] Angel Antón, "La recepción del concilio Vaticano II y de su eclesiologia," *Revista española de teologia* 48 (1988) 291-319; J. Miguez Bonino, "The Reception of Vatican II in Latin America," *The Ecumenical Review* 37 (1985) 266-274; Leonardo Boff, "Eine Kreative Rezeption des II. Vatikanums aus der Sicht der Armen: Die Theologie der Befreiung," in *Glaube im Prozeß*, ed. Elmar Klinger and Klaus Wittstadt (Freiburg: Herder, 1984) 628-654; Yves Congar, "Les lendemains des conciles" in *Le Concile Vatican II, son Eglise peuple de Dieu et corps du Christ* (Paris: Beauchesne, 1984) 99-106; idem, "Regard à l'occasion du 20ème aniversaire" in ibid., 66-72; *Venti anni di Concilio Vaticano II. Contributi sulla sua recezione in Italia*, ed. Severino Dianich and E. R. Tura (Rome: Borla, 1985); Avery Dulles, "The Reception of Vatican II at the Extraordinary Synod of 1985" in *The Reception of Vatican II*, ed. Giuseppe Alberigo et al. (Washington: The Catholic University of America Press, 1987) 349-363; Casiano Floristan, "La Iglesia después del vaticano II" in *El Vaticano II veinte años Despues* (Madrid: Ed. Cristiandad, 1985) 77-99; Elmar Klinger, "Der Laienkatholizismus — die Kirche der Laien. Das Problem der Rezeption des Konzils in Deutschland" in *Die Kirche der Laien: eine Weichenstellung des Konzils*, ed. Elmar Klinger (Würzburg: Echter, 1987) 15-24; Jean-Marie Tillard, "Did We Receive Vatican II?" *One in Christ* 4 (1985) 276-283; idem, "Final Report of the Last Synod," in *Synod 1985 — An Evaluation*, ed. Giuseppe Alberigo and James Provost, Concilium 188 (Edinburgh: T & T Clark, 1986) 64-77.

[11] *The Reception of Vatican II*, ed. Giuseppe Alberigo, Jean-Paul Jossua, and Joseph Komonchak (Washington: Catholic University of America Press, 1987).

the 1970's to a problematic of reception even if the conversion was not yet complete. There were the beginnings of an effort to appreciate the complexity and duration of the phenomenon. Twenty years after the close of Vatican II not everything had been implemented, and this was viewed as more complex than one would think in terms of the simple transposition of principles into action or the realization of theological statements. One was then forced to develop a more adequate conceptual instrument to reflect on and understand the process of assimilation of Vatican II by the churches and the impact of the conciliar teaching on the life of the local churches.

New distinctions emerged during this period, notably the distinction between the material reception of conciliar pronouncements and the reception of the conciliar dynamism itself. One finds this in Corecco and in Alberigo. One also discovers different types of reception of the council without being able to provide a systematic nomenclature. The question of the stages of the process of reception began to be refined. If this question was already posed, it still had not found a satisfactory response.

The works of the years 1985-1987 opened a new stage in the concept of reception in the Catholic Church and invited further research. It is at this time that one must situate the development of the most refined works on the reception of Vatican II. The works of the 1990's have benefitted from the research which preceded them. One could then expect that they will offer a first review of such reflections and a first synthesis of the research conducted up to then on the topic of the reception of Vatican II. These works of the last generation are distinguished especially by the fact that they concentrated on methodically analyzing the process of reception so as to uncover its constitutive elements, determining factors, stages, and actors. The publications of Unzuetta[12] and Routhier[13] reflected this tendency even if one can distinguish one from the other as

---

[12]   Angel Unzueta, *Vatikanum II und Ortskirche. Rezeption des Konziliaren Kirchenbildes in der Diözese Bilbao* (Bochum: University of Bochum, 1992). This doctoral dissertation was subsequently published under the same title in the collection Europäische Hochschulschriften, series 23 (Theologie), vol. 480 (Frankfurt-am-Main: Peter Lang, 1993). It has also been published in a Spanish translation under the title *Vaticano II e Iglesia Local. Recepción de la eclesiologia conciliar en la Diócesis Bilbao* (Bilbao: U. Deusto, 1994).

[13]   Gilles Routhier, *La réception de Vatican II dans une Eglise locale. L'exemple de la pratique synodale dans l'Eglise de Québec 1982-1987* (Paris: Cerf, 1991).

Joseph Famerée has carefully done.[14] The 1992 colloquium at Louvain-la Neuve was similarly oriented in opening the windows on Africa and South America.[15] The work in preparation on the reception of Vatican II in Belgium is also oriented in that direction. Reception is no longer only a general concept designating a complex and nearly imperceptible reality, as was customarily stated in prior decades, useful in representing the relationship between the council and the local churches. It becomes a better defined reality and an operative concept in analyzing precisely the historical development of the churches.

These resource materials which are concentrated on the particular facts of reception have permitted a considerable refinement of the general observations available until then on the unfolding of the process of reception, information which one drew until now from more global and more general analyses. These case studies have permitted a notable methodological refinement from which we can profit today. It is also necessary to take account of certain results of this research. They have notably highlighted factors which determine reception: socio-historical (the "peaceful revolution" in the case of Québec; the passage from Francoism to democracy in Spain; decolonization in the case of the Third World) and cultural (two minority cultures: francophone in the context of North America and Basque in the European context) which determine reception. Furthermore they have shown the importance of the agents (*Träger*) of reception, of the groups and the ecclesial processes in which the processes of reception are rooted. These studies have also shown that the hitherto available schematic chronologies regarding the reception of Vatican II need refinement. Above all it becomes evident that we are at the threshold of an understanding of reception if we remain at the level of a kerygmatic reception or if we are content with studying the developments on the plane of legitimate discourse. A history of mentalities which examines in depth the life of the people of God becomes indispensable if one wishes to attain the level of "Vollrezeption" or of practical reception. Hence these studies have permitted not only new advances

---

[14] Joseph Famerée, "Pour une histoire de Vatican II," *Revue d'histoire ecclésiastique* 84 (1994) 642.

[15] See Joseph Famerée's report, "Aspects de la réception de Vatican II: Journée d'étude organisée par le Centre *Lumen gentium*," *Revue théologique de Louvain* 23 (1992) 420-422. One must express a regret that until now, among the communications given at the colloquium, only that of Emmanuel Lanne has been published.

on a methodological level, but they have equally enabled us to achieve a broader understanding of this rich and original reality.

I am persuaded that the advance and deepening of reflection on reception still depends for the most part on an interdisciplinary study of the facts of reception. Until now, and keeping our focus on the reception of councils, it is known that historical studies, pursued in an ecumenical context, have largely clarified the reception of the Council of Chalcedon.[16] Other pertinent contributions of unequal depth have been relevant to the reception of the councils of the modern era, notably Trent and Vatican I.[17] The diversified approaches, even fragmentary ones, of the first generations (1970-1990) have permitted the highlighting of one or other element pertaining to the process of reception. The first monographs, often undertaken with a great deal of intuition, have constituted an invitation to a more systematic examination of the question. One does not generally find in this early literature the same methodological concern nor the same systematic treatment as one finds in the historians of law or in literary studies. Some studies are noteworthy, among which one must reserve a special place for those of Professor Grillmeier. The work of these pioneers has permitted those who follow to build on this capital and to be supported by these works in advancing the first syntheses which then transcend those works.[18]

It is not necessary to stop here on this productive path. Just as historians of law have been given a method to comprehend this reality and as literary experts have also proposed a way appropriate to their domain to study the facts of reception, so theologians in an interdisciplinary fashion

---

[16] See "Le Concile de Chalcédoine: son histoire, sa réception par les Eglises et son actualité," *Irenikon* 44 (1971) 349-366; Jean Coman, "The Doctrinal Definition of the Council of Chalcedon and its Reception in the Orthodox Church of the East," *The Ecumenical Review* 22 (1970) 363-381; Alois Grillmeier, "The Reception of Chalcedon in the Roman Catholic Church," *The Ecumenical Review* 22 (1970) 383-411; Edward R. Hardy, "Chalcedon in the Anglican Tradition," *The Ecumenical Review* 22 (1970) 412-423.

[17] For Trent see Giuseppe Alberigo, "La 'réception' du Concile de Trente par l'Eglise catholique romaine," *Irenikon* 58 (1985) 311-337. For Vatican I see above all Johannes Beumer, "Das Erste Vatikanum und seine Rezeption," *Münchener Theologische Zeitschrift* 27 (1976) 259-276, and Yves Congar, "Le Concile Vatican I en question. Recension d'écclesiologie conciliaire," *Revue des Sciences Philosophiques et Théologiques* 68 (1984) 452-456.

[18] The latest synthesis on the subject of which we are aware is that of José E. Borges de Pinho, "A recepçao como realidade ecuménica e tarefa ecclesial," *Didaskalia* 23 (1993) 389.

must fashion a method appropriate to study the process of reception in the Church. From my point of view, "case studies" still represent a price to pay if one wishes ecclesiological reflection on reception to become more profound, to move beyond generalities, and to avoid being simply repetitive. The methodical and systematic exploration of the phenomena of reception remains a necessary approach if one wants to advance. That constitutes a wish for our colloquium.

3. Reception at the 1985 Synod Itself

This breakthrough of the thematic of reception in the 1980's did not entirely abolish the tendency to conceptualize the relationship between the council and the life of the churches in terms of "application." This logic of application enters precisely into tension with the logic of reception at the time of the 1985 extraordinary synod. It is interesting to analyze in a more in depth fashion the breaks introduced into the semantic field constituted by the corpus containing the principal documents of this synod. The announcement of the event included the following lines: "Vatican II has always been . . . the constant point of reference for all pastoral action in the conscious effort to translate its directives for a concrete and faithful application at the level of each church and of the whole Church."[19] Furthermore, John Paul II indicated as the purpose of the initiative the exchange "of experiences and information on the application of the council at the level of the universal Church and the particular churches" and "the further deepening and constant insertion of Vatican II in the life of the Church, in the light also of new exigencies."[20] The letter of convocation addressed to the fathers by the secretary general Msgr. Tomko and the questionnaire which accompanied it were especially characterized by a logic of "application." In the four pages of these two documents, the word "application" is found four times. They also used synonymous expressions: "translate into act the prescriptions" or "the accomplishment of the prescriptions of the council." However, the perspective of reception is not entirely absent even if it does not inspire the document. The word is found in the wording of the first general question: "What has been done to make the council known, received and implemented?" Question three for its part places side by side the terms "interpretation" and "application."

---

[19] John Paul II, "Annonce du Synode extraordinaire," *Synode extraordinaire, célébration de Vatican II* (Paris: Editions du Cerf, 1986) 35.
[20] Ibid., 36.

The ensemble of the synod came to know the tension between the logic of application or translation of conciliar decisions and that of their reception, their appropriation, and their assimilation, problems akin to that of reception. In a significant fashion the presynodal reports of episcopal conferences made frequent use of the concept of reception even if the questionnaire focused their attention on the problematic of application. The second part of the initial report of Cardinal Daneels, who tried to summarize the situation twenty years after the council and which is structured on the basis of the input of the churches, is distinctly characterized by the problematic of reception. By contrast the final report is dominated by the perspective of application even if the vocabulary of reception is still found. Without wanting to be schematic, one can note easily that the problematic of reception is more present in the responses of the particular churches while that of application largely inspires the texts which emanate more immediately from the organized stages of the synod. That is a fact significant enough to be highlighted.

4. Relationship between Theology and Practice

The passage from a logic of "application" to a logic of "reception" does not depend solely on a deepening of theological themes relative to the local church, its synodal life, and communion among the churches. This passage is equally and largely linked to conceptions which one undertakes on the subject of the relationship between theology and practice. The adoption of the problematic of reception then equally entails a reexamination of the relationship between theology and practice, which is exceptionally reflected in the literature on reception which we have reviewed. I myself have addressed this question in my work on reception, but in an insufficient way which calls for a more in-depth approach.[21] The adoption of platonic schemata, according to which ecclesiology furnishes an image of the Church which is subsequently to be translated into reality, can hardly facilitate the understanding of the process of reception. In this perspective there can be only a deductive and consecutive relationship between the conciliar teachings and ecclesial practice.[22] This realizes more or less perfectly the ideas fixed in the conciliar pronouncements. Such a relationship can only go in one direction: from the council

---

[21]   *La réception d'un concile*, 183-187. See also Gilles Routhier, *Les pouvoirs dans l'Eglise* (Montréal and Paris: Editions Pauline & Médiaspaul, 1993) 343-347.

[22]   Hervé Legrand has studied this consecutive relationship between ecclesiology and law in "Grâce et instituion dans l'Eglise: les fondements théologiques du droit canon-

to practice. Hence it is not surprising that the letter of convocation of the 1985 synod and the questionnaire accompanying it were careful "to examine the application of the council" and the "accomplishment of the prescriptions of Vatican Council II."

On the contrary, if one engages in a hermeneutical paradigm, this leads naturally to the adoption of the problematic of reception. Thereby, according to the felicitous expression of Paul Ricoeur, one articulates the relationship between text and action.[23] In literature and in a general way in aesthetics, one constructs a theory of reception on the basis of hermeneutics. The evaluation of the preponderant role of the subject-reader emerges for us here from the relationship between theology and practice. For example, in the work of Hans R. Jauss, who constitutes one of the most illustrious representatives of this tendency, there is a precise taking of a position against "everything which reduces reality to imaginary substances, to presumably eternal essences."[24] The taking up of that literary theory by Wolfgang Iser following a slightly different conceptualization, that of "reader-response criticism" equally centers attention on the reader, the listener, the spectator, or on the act of reading which puts the text and reader together.[25] A conception of the work as a timeless substance is thus put aside in favor of another conception which at the same time encompasses the text and its reception or the text as correlative to its subject-readers. In this perspective the virtual structure of the text needs to be concretized, assimilated or actualized. These perspectives, today largely familiar in the domain of biblical exegesis, have until now remained largely foreign to theologians who have addressed the question of the reception of Vatican II.

With that being said, many Catholic theologians have taken up the problematic of reception without necessarily adopting explicitly the per-

---

ique," in *L'Eglise institution et foi*, ed. Jean-Louis Monneron et al. (Brussels: Facultés universitaires Saint-Louis, 1979) 139-172.

[23] Paul Ricoeur, *Du texte à l'action, essais d'herméneutique II* (Paris: Seuil, 1986); English trans. *From Text to Action* (Evanston, IL: Northwestern University Press, 1991).

[24] Jean Starobinski, "Préface," in Hans R. Jauss, *Pour une esthétique de la réception* (Paris: Gaillmard, 1978) 11.

[25] Wolfgang Iser, *The Implied Reader: Patterns of Communication in Prose Fiction from Bunyan to Beckett* (Baltimore: Johns Hopkins University Press, 1974); idem, *The Act of Reading: A Theory of Aesthetic Responses* (Baltimore: Johns Hopkins University Press, 1978); idem, *Prospecting: From Reader-Response to Literary Anthropology* (Baltimore: Johns Hopkins University Press, 1989).

spectives developed by hermeneutics but rather remaining anchored in the more classical framework of Aristotelian realism. For these theologians the Church is not a "reality of reason" according to the beautiful expression of Père de Lubac. Certainly a mysterious reality, or, according to the language of Vatican II, a *realitas complexa* (*LG* 8), a theandric reality, both social and spiritual, the Church has a concrete existence; it lives in history. Ecclesiology is thus presented as the systematic understanding of this reality which belongs to our world. It is especially the theologians who are familiar with history and the social sciences who until now have been interested in the reception of Vatican II. Several are heirs of the French Dominican and Franciscan ecclesiological tradition marked by the great contemporary figures such as Chenu and Congar. Others are more attached to the perspectives opened by Bernard Lonergan.

5. Three Influences

Three remarks are necessary before drawing conclusions at the end of this first section. All three intend to indicate factors which have contributed to the adoption of the problematic of reception during the post-conciliar period. The first has treated the development of communications theories which have described a 180 degree turn during the last fifty years, passing from the "theory of the projectile" to that of communications considered as an "act of sharing." The theory of the projectile corresponded to an era marked by propaganda in the Eastern countries and in the fascist movements in the 1930's, and still utilized by the belligerents during the Second World War. According to the theory of the projectile, the listener is a fixed target towards which one aims a "magical shot" which would be capable of transferring ideas or information.

Gradually, the idea of a passive hearer was abandoned and replaced by that of the activity of the hearers. These manipulated messages rather than being manipulated by them. Different studies had in effect undercut the credibility of the projectile theory. The in depth studies of Lasswell and several others on the effect of propaganda have shown that certain listeners refused to be overwhelmed or indeed that the propaganda sometimes provoked undesirable effects or even was counterproductive. Subsequently studies in the domain of advertising have indicated that there are different categories of listeners. Persons react differently depending on their intellectual ability, academic background, experience, social class, etc. The audience is very segmented, and one should not think that communications is an act by which one can transfer information or ideas from a transmitter to a passive receptor. If indeed something happens between the two, the intermediary stages of the process are less simple than one formerly thought.

More and more communications began to be conceived as a relationship, an act of sharing between two subjects, equal partners in the exchange, for the listener is extremely active and selective in this exchange enterprise. A survey of different models of communications from Lasswell to Watzlavick shows well the whole change operative in theorizing about and developing models of communications.[26]

One can guess that reception cannot be accommodated to every communications model. The evolution of theories of communications, especially during the 1960's, probably influenced the evolution of the thematic of reception during the postconciliar period even if it is not explicitated in the literature on the subject. All the more so, it would be advantageous for theologians and pastors to be aware of their a priori attitudes regarding the models of communications which they use and favor. It would be unfortunate to lump together certain representations of revelation with mechanistic or one-directional models of communications. Even if they are unaware of it, their references on the level of models of communications determine their understanding of reception. Furthermore, one can ask if the Church has sufficiently taken account of the research of the past fifty years in the domain of communications or if the faithful are employing the same model of communications as theologians and pastors. One may conclude that the introduction of concepts of exchange and dialogue in ecclesial discourse have changed the former equilibrium, but the positions still remain ambiguous in this domain.

My second remark concerns the affirmation of the local churches especially in the 1970's. Undoubtedly this fact is underestimated in the Church. Even if there is general agreement that the conception and procedures of the Roman synods are defective, it is true, more and more, that the local churches find there a locus of expression which was formerly not available to them. The Church becomes more and more conscious of its diversity as well as the customs of different churches and more and more diversified theological traditions. The trips of Paul VI and John Paul II have had the unforeseen effect of highlighting and mediating this

---

[26] For an initial survey of different models of communications, see *La communication modélisée. Une introduction aux concepts, aux modèles et aux théories*, ed. Gilles Willet (Montreal: ERPI, 1992); Denis McQuail and Windahl Swen, *Communication Models for the Study of Mass Communications* (London: Longmans, 1981).

diversity of local churches. Finally the holding of local, regional, or continental synods have indicated still more the specificity of these churches. Despite everything the Catholic Church appears less and less like a European or Roman church. These noteworthy events, whose symbolic effect is important, have shaped the Christian consciousness. One no longer represents the Church simply as a great society with its affiliates in various countries. Evidently one is confronted with churches as distinct subjects relating to one another in bonds of communion. This new ecclesial consciousness makes it possible henceforth to adopt a perspective of reception.

My third remark deals with the development of the concept of inculturation beginning in 1974-1975 and its more and more generalized usage in Catholicism both in official texts and in the theological literature. This led the Church to reflect even more on the relationship between faith and culture. This deepening of perspectives has rendered ever more vital the consciousness of the fact that this relationship is complex and especially that it is not a unique reality.

6. Some Initial Conclusions

The return of the concept of reception at the beginning of the 1980's manifests, witnesses, and accompanies an ever more vital consciousness that one has of the very reality of reception, which, hidden as it was for centuries, has always subsisted in the Church and has profoundly affected the ecclesial body during the postconciliar period.

Furthermore, it has been seen rather clearly that the adoption of the perspective of reception is due not only to dogmatic factors. The epistemological factors are far from being innocent. They determine not only one's conception of ecclesiology but they permit one to address (or not to address) the relationship between a council and the life of the churches according to the problematic of reception.

The models of communications within the context of which one functions condition equally broadly the possibility or not of adopting the problematic of reception. The growth of exchanges among the churches, the affirmation of their specific character, and the possibility of mediating these realities equally shape the Christian consciousness and lead it to review its ways of understanding the relationship between a council and the churches or the relationships among the churches themselves.

Finally the conceptual instruments which one uses to consider the faith-culture relationship correct the overly inadequate ways of envisioning the relationship between a dogmatic teaching and cultures.

B. Reception in the Conciliar Texts

1. References to Reception in the Council Texts

The overview of the conciliar documents regarding the topic of reception remains rather limited. One does not find a systematic treatment of the question of reception in the conciliar documents. The word is certainly found, but the real problem was not posed. Furthermore, when the subject was addressed, it was done in a very unsatisfactory fashion. For Olivier Clément, in the light of the expressions of Vatican II, "the question of reception is expressed, despite everything, in terms of obedience rather than of synergy (cf. *LG* 25). The supernatural sense of the faith of the whole people can be manifest only in the consent of which the dogmatic constitution speaks (*LG* 12)."[27] These two texts in effect do not provide the desired clarity, and their interpretation and usage in the Church today is not of such a nature as to dissipate all the ambiguities and eliminate all the reservations on the subject expressed in ecumenical circles.

The analysis of the texts of Vatican II regarding the topic of reception cautions us to be attentive to a consideration not sufficiently emphasized until now: the Church as a place of welcome or reception of the visit of God. If one wishes to explore this topic somewhat systematically, we need to address the material references to the verb *recipere*. First, note that the Vatican II redactors used more often the verb *accipere* (90 occurrences) than *recipere* (35 occurrences) to designate the action of welcome or reception as is the case in the Latin versions of the New Testament (1 Cor 11: 23; Gal 1: 9-12). It is worth noting that in *Dei verbum* 7-8 the verb *accipere*, not *recipere*, is used correlatively with the verb *tradire*. Thus in no. 7: "the apostles transmitted (*tradierunt*) . . . what

---

[27]   Olivier Clément, "Après Vatican II: Vers un dialogue théologique entre catholiques et orthodoxes," *La Pensée Orthodoxe* 13 (1968) 46. See Hermann Pottmeyer's treatment of these two texts in his reflection on the conciliar texts: "Rezeption und Gehorsam — Aktuelle Aspekte der wiederentdeckten Reälität 'Rezeption,'" in *Glaube als Zustimmung. Zur Interpretation kirchlicher Rezeptionsvorgänge*, ed. Wolfgang Beinert et al. (Freiburg: Herder, 1991) 81-84. See also Francis A. Sullivan, *Magisterium, Teaching Authority in the Catholic Church* (New York: Paulist, 1983) 119ff.

they had received (*acceperant*) from the mouth of Christ." One finds a comparable structure in no. 8 which contains the phrase: "the apostles transmitting (*tradentes*) what they themselves had received (*acceperunt*)." Number 14 of the declaration on religious liberty takes as a point of departure the same terminology: "The heritage (*tradita*) transmitted by the apostles has been received (*acceptata*) in different ways." A systematic examination of vocabulary leads us to conclude that often the two verbs are interchangeable, and there is a certain confusion about their meaning. The acceptance of the Word and a mission is expressed both by *accipere* and *recipere*. Vatican II preferred the verb *accipere* to *recipere* when it wanted to speak of the action of welcoming and receiving, i.e., where we speak today of the process of reception. Thus to describe the exchanges (gift and acceptance) which happen in meetings among peoples, Vatican II used the verb *accipere*. This plurality of terms to approach the phenomenon of reception in Vatican II corresponds well to what we find as well in the New Testament where this reality is expressed in a differentiated fashion.[28]

The conciliar texts speak of the Word of God (*LG* 12, 37; *SC* 6; *PO* 13), the gospel (*LG* 16, 19; *GS* 57; *AG* 27; *NA* 4), the books of the Old Testament (*DV* 15), revelation (*LG* 25; *NA* 4), doctrine (*DH* 12), truth (*DH* 14), or the heritage of the apostles (*UR* 14), which are received in the Church. The Church and the faithful receive God (*GS* 32), the Spirit (*SC* 6, 11), sanctification (*LG* 40), grace (*LG* 12, 13; *SC* 11, 33, 59; *PO* 12; *AA* 3), varied gifts and charisms (*LG* 43; *DV* 8; *PO* 6, 10; *AA* 4). Among these gifts one distinguishes faith (*LG* 11; *AG* 14, 41; *DH* 14). Finally the Church and the faithful also receive their mission (*LG* 5, 17, 24; *GS* 34; *PO* 1; *AA* 11, 25), their vocation (*PO* 12), and the invitations of the Spirit (*GS* 92 §3). Thus the Church is a community which has received the gift of God.

This is not far from what one finds in the New Testament; the faithful are given and receive the gospel of Christ (1 Cor 15: 1; Gal 1: 9-12), his word (Mk 4: 20; Acts 2: 41; 8: 14; 11: 1; 17: 11; 1 Thes 2: 13-14), his Spirit (Jn 7: 39; 14: 17; 20 : 22; Acts 1: 8; 2: 38; Rom 8 :15; 1 Cor 2: 12), the Kingdom (Mk 10: 15; Heb 12: 28); the grace of God (2 Cor 6: 1) and ultimately Christ himself (Jn 1: 11; Col 2: 6). Several authors have indi-

---

[28] For an indepth study of the terms *lambanein, paralambanein, dechesthai, doche, apodoche, apodechesthai, bebaioun*, consult the article by Gerhard Delting in *Dictionary of the New Testament*, ed. Gerhard Kittel, vol. 4 (Grand Rapids: Eerdmans, 1964) 5-15.

cated that all the other processes of reception observed in the Church ought to be rooted in this primary fact of reception.[29] One can then speak of reception, using the terminology of Hans Dombois, as a fundamental, original, and originating structure of Christian activity.[30] The Christian faith is essentially an act of reception of what has been transmitted. The Church is constituted in this act of exchange; i.e., the gift of God and its reception, the proclamation of the Word and the response to that proclamation. It is only at this depth that we can understand what is reception in its fullness in the Christian dispensation. The other facts of reception participate in this much broader and fundamental paradigmatic fact of reception, which is described in the New Testament.

What must be noted here is the difficulty experienced by Vatican II in passing from evoking this fundamental fact of reception to other processes of reception at work in the ecclesial body. That is mentioned only occasionally. Thus *Lumen gentium* 22 indicates that a council ought to be received (*receptum*) by the successor of Peter. He also can receive (*recipiat*) a collegial act of the bishops dispersed throughout the world (*CD* 4). Only once does Vatican II mention the reception of its teaching by the people of God, i.e., paragraph 24 of the decree on the means of social communications.[31] However, the council receives the common teaching of the Church[32] and receives the teaching of the councils which

---

[29]   On the question of reception in the New Testament, see Rusch, 35-36 (*supra*, note 3); Wilmer Küppers, "Reception, Prolegomena to a Systematic Study," in *Councils and the Ecumenical Movement* (Geneva: WCC, 1968) 78; Ulrich Kühn, "Reception: An Imperative and an Opportunity," in *Ecumenical Perspective on Baptism, Eucharist and Ministry*, ed. Max Thurian (Geneva: WCC, 1983) 165-167; Nikolaus Nissiotis, "The Meaning of Reception in Relation to the Results of Ecumenical Dialogue," *The Greek Orthodox Theological Review* 29 (1985) 151-152; Jean-Marie Tillard, *Church of Churches: The Ecclesiology of Communion*, trans. R.C. De Peaux (Collegeville, MN: Liturgical Press, 1992) 113 ff, 126; John D. Zizioulas, "The Theological Problem of Reception," *Bulletin Centro pro Unione* 26 (1984) 4-5.

[30]   Hans Dombois, *Das Recht der Gnade* (Witten: Luther Verlag, 1969) 816.

[31]   The text reads as follows: "For the rest, this synod has every confidence that its presentation of undertakings and norms will be willingly received and faithfully observed by all members of the Church." Translation from *Decrees of the Ecumenical Councils*, ed. Norman P. Tanner (London and Washington: Sheed and Ward and Georgetown University Press, 1990) 849*.

[32]   *GS* 91: "what is proposed here is ... the received doctrine of the Church (*doctrinam iam in Ecclesia receptam*)."

preceded it (*LG* 51).[33] The teaching of Vatican II stops there except for some other indications which cannot be classified or categorized; i.e., *Gaudium et spes* 44 and 45 referring to what the Church receives from the world.[34] These references undoubtedly are weightier than one might have believed initially. In any event they are linked to the thought of John Zizioulas, who develops the idea that the Church receives the world and is received there like Christ "who not only receives vertically (the mission of his Father), but also horizontally, i.e., the history of the people of Israel to whom he belongs as a man."[35] Unfortunately this perspective is neglected in the ensemble of literature on our subject.

2. Indirect Influence of Council Texts on Theology of Reception

It is not necessary to limit the Vatican II contribution to the discussion of reception to certain references. Several authors have noted that Vatican II puts in place an ecclesiological framework within the context of which it becomes possible to consider the question of reception: a theology of tradition, the beginnings of a theology of the local church, which is accompanied by a reevaluation of the value of communion among the churches and the adoption of a more noticeable pneumatological perspective. For Congar it is a question of a theological environment within which one can develop a theology of reception.[36] Indeed Vatican II marks precise advances in these different domains by reintegrating these different elements. However, its reflection remains still incomplete in different aspects. It has often been noted that the theology of the local church still remains minimally elaborated in the conciliar texts.[37] The council's

---

[33]   "This venerable faith of our ancestors . . . the holy council receives (*recipit*) with great piety; it proposes again the decrees of the holy councils: Nicea II, Florence, and Trent."

[34]   See *GS* 25 for the same meaning.

[35]   Zizioulas, 3. In the same sense Vatican II four times cites the passage from the hymn of the epistle to the Philippians which emphasizes Christ's acceptance (*accipit*) of the human condition.

[36]   Yves Congar, "La reception comme realité ecclésiologique," *Revue des Sciences Philosophiques et Théologiques* 56 (1972) 392.

[37]   This judgment is largely shared by specialists on this question. See Adrien Nocent, "The Local Church as Realization of the Church of Christ and Subject of the Eucharist," in *The Reception of Vatican II*, 219 (*supra*, note 10); Joseph Komonchak, "The Church Universal as the Communion of Local Churches," in *Where Does the Church Stand?*, ed. Giuseppe Alberigo and Gustavo Gutiérrez, Concilium 146 (New York: Seabury Press, 1981) 32; idem, "The Local Realization of the Church," in *The Reception of Vatican II*, 77; Emmanuel Lanne, "Chiesa locale," in *Dizionario del Concilio Ecumenico Vaticano Secondo*, ed. Salvatore Garofalo (Rome: UNEDI, 1969) coll. 818-819; idem, "L'Eglise lo-

pneumatology still is deficient,[38] and the theology of communion among the churches does not occupy the place which it ought to. That being said, Vatican II lays the foundations for subsequent developments.

---

cale et l'Eglise universelle: Actualité et portée du thème," *Irenikon* 43 (1970) 487; Hervé Legrand, "Inverser Babel, Mission de l'Eglise," *Spiritus* 43 (1970) 323.

[38] The pneumatology of the conciliar texts is judged deficient not only by the Orthodox but also by Catholics. For the Orthodox see Nikos Nissiotis, "The Main Ecclesiological Problem of the Second Vatican Council and the Position of the Non-Catholic Churches Facing It," *Journal of Ecumenical Studies* 2 (1965) 31-62; idem, "Report on the Second Vatican Council," *Ecumenical Review* 18 (1966) 193-200; idem, "Rapport au Comité Central du Conseil oecuménique des Eglises," *Istina* 11 (1966) 249-252; idem, "La pneumatologie ecclésiologique au service de l'unité de l'Eglise," *Istina* 12 (1967) 324-325 (here the author remarks that in *Lumen gentium* the Spirit is subordinated to Christ); Oliver Clement, "Quelques remarques d'un orthodoxe sur la constitution 'de Ecclesia,'" *Oecumenica* 1 (1966) 97-116. For a Protestant viewpoint see A. Roux, "Le décret sur l'activité missionaire de l'Eglise," in *Points de vue de théologiens protestants: études sur les décrets du Concile Vatican II*, Unam Sanctam 64 (Paris: Cerf, 1967) 112-114; Vilmos Vajta, "Renewal of Worship: De sacra Liturgia," in *Dialogue on the Way*, ed. George Lindbeck (Minneapolis: Augsburg, 1965) 107; Lukas Fischer, "L'Eglise, communauté de l'Esprit. Reflexions sur la seconde session du concile du Vatican," *Lumière et Vie* 67 (1964) 45; Gaston Westphal, *Vie et foi du Protestant* (Paris: Centurion, 1967) 134 (according to this latter author there is only a slight sprinkling of pneumatology in *Lumen gentium*). For the opinion of Catholics see Bernard Lambert, "La constitution du point de vue catholique de l'oecuménisme," in *L'Eglise de Vatican II*, ed. Guilherme Baraúna (Paris: Cerf, 1966) 1268; Bertulf van Leeuwen, "La participation universelle à la fonction prophetique du Christ," ibid., 450; Jean Tillard, "L'Eucharistie et le Saint Esprit," *Nouvelle Revue Théologique* 90 (1968) 363-364; Louis Bouyer, *L'Eglise de Dieu, corps du Christ et temple de l'Esprit* (Paris: Cerf, 1970) 209.

Gerard Philips, the principal redactor of *Lumen gentium*, addressed these critiques. After mentioning the place attributed to the Spirit in the constitution, he concluded: "How can one affirm that the council has attached little or no importance to pneumatology?" See Gerard Philips, *L'Eglise et son mystère au IIe Concile du Vatican* (Paris: Desclée, 1966) 1: 232; 2: 32-33. Yves Congar also showed a sensitivity to such critiques and challenged them in a way that reduces their import. See Yves Congar, "Les implications christologiques et pneumatologiques de l'ecclésiologie de Vatican II," in *Les Eglises après Vatican II*, ed. Giuseppe Alberigo (Paris: Cerf, 1980) 117-130; idem, "Une pneumatologie ecclésiologique," in *Initiation à la pratique de la theologie*, ed. Bernard Lauret and François Refoulé (Paris: Cerf, 1983) 1: 493-502; idem, *I Believe in the Holy Spirit* (New York: Seabury, 1983), esp. chapter 10, "The Pneumatology of Vatican II," 1: 167-173. See the important contribution of A. M. Charrue, "Le Saint-Esprit dans *Lumen gentium*," *Ephemerides Theologicae Lovanienses* 45 (1969) 358-359; Henri Cazelles, "Le Saint-Esprit dans les textes de Vatican II," in *Le mystère de l'Esprit Saint* (Paris: Mame, 1968) 161-186.

A simple synoptic reading of the different schemata of *Lumen gentium* shows that as marginal as was the affirmation of the role of the Spirit in the first version, it gained ground progressively in succeeding versions.

a. Theology of the Local Church

The elaboration of a theology of the local church certainly constitutes one of the most significant contributions of the postconciliar period.[39] In effect one cannot reflect on reception apart from a movement of communications among the churches. Otherwise reception is reduced to the judgment passed by each individual believer on the teaching of the pope alone. All of a sudden the churches disappear, and one is left with relationships among individuals. Reception is often invoked today to speak of the possibility offered to the faithful to be linked with or separated from the teaching of their pastors. Reception is thus understood as the faculty attributed to each believer to express agreement or disagreement. The appeal to the *sensus fidelium* apart from its organic link to the ecclesial body poses difficulties. Reception considered as an "ecclesial reality" entails the rehabilitation of the local churches. One can reflect on reception only with difficulty if one does not view the whole Church from the perspective of local churches living in communion one with another, a communion nourished, stimulated, protected, and safeguarded by bonds of communication established among them and with the church of Rome.

Vatican II certainly took steps in that direction even if its heritage still remains ambiguous on this matter. A study of Vatican II in the perspective of reception forces us to reexamine all the passages where the issue of the relationship among the churches is addressed (notably *LG* 13 and 23), those recognizing the existence of churches enjoying their proper traditions, particular discipline, specific liturgical usages, or proper spiritual and theological patrimony (notably *OE* 3, 5-6; *UR* 14-16), and those which try to elaborate the "links and bonds" which permit exchanges among the churches and the development of this communion of the churches. Number 14 of *Unitatis redintegratio* is particularly significant. Without using the term, it indicates that the Latin Church has received many elements of liturgy, spiritual tradition, and law from the treasury of the Churches of the East.

One cannot limit the theology of the local church to passages which indicate a recognition of it or to developments which bring about the promotion of exchanges among the churches in the communion. The effec-

---

[39]   For a thorough bibliography on the subject see Gilles Routhier, "'Eglise locale' ou 'Eglise particulière': querelle sémantique ou option theologique?" *Studia Canonica* 25 (1991) 277-324. See also Jean-Marie Tillard, *L'Eglise locale. Ecclesiologie de communion et catholicité* (Paris: Cerf, 1995).

tive rehabilitation of the local churches leads to a genuine concern for the fullness of the Church, to use the beautiful expression of the Orthodox Church.[40] The 1988 Salamanca colloquium already noted that if the relationships among the churches were envisaged only through the prism of episcopal collegiality they did not engage us in the direction of a healthy theology of reception.[41] Following the tradition in that regard, episcopal collegiality must be situated within the context of the communion of churches, which in turn engages the synodal life of the local churches.[42] The testimony of Cyprian is noteworthy on that point.[43] The subject churches are equally churches of subjects, which engages a theology of the Holy Spirit who distributes charisms to all the members of the people of God. To reread Vatican II in the perspective of reception supposes equally that one revisits its teaching on the various gifts dispersed among the ensemble of the members of the Church and on the active participation of all the faithful in the life of the local church. One is thus led to examine attentively all that Vatican II advanced on the level of the synodality of the local church. That is not expressed solely by the creation of the pastoral council (*CD* 27) and the presbyteral council (*PO* 7) but also in everything which is affirmed regarding listening, exchange, and dialogue in the Church.[44] Reception is constructed on the basis of these concrete processes.

b. Importance of Culture

However, this theology of the local church does not stop there. For our subject what must be noted is the new interest in cultures which appears in the conciliar texts. With Vatican II we witness a veritable discovery of

---

[40] On the subject see Alexandros Papaderos, "Quelques réflexions sur la réception sans laisser de côté la vie et le plérôme de l'Eglise," *Proche Orient Chrétien* 33 (1983) 186-189.

[41] See especially the reports of the group discussions. Episcopal collegiality, the synodality of the churches, and reception are constantly linked. See *The Nature and Future of Episcopal Conferences*, ed. Hervé Legrand, Julio Manzanares and Antonio García y García (Washington: Catholic University of America Press, 1988); also *The Jurist* 48 (1988) iii-412.

[42] See the remark to that effect of Nikolaus Nissiotis, "Die Ekklesiologie des zweiten vatikanischen Konzils in orthodoxer Sicht und ihre ökumenische Bedeutung," *Kerygma und Dogma* 10 (1964) 157-158.

[43] See in particular his letters 19/2: 2 and 34/4: 1. He articulates perfectly the internal synodality of his church, the communion of churches, and the collegiality of bishops.

[44] See Gilles Routhier, "La synodalité de l'Eglise locale," *Studia Canonica* 26 (1992) 111-161.

culture. In effect the idea of culture enters forcefully into the conciliar documents even if the problematic of inculturation is absent and even if there is often a resistance to integrating this datum of culture in the elaboration of a theology of the local church.[45] Hervé Legrand, Joseph Komonchak, and Jean Tillard[46] are perhaps the contemporary Catholic theologians who have best articulated the lin5ing of theological and socio-historical factors in the constitution of the Church.[47] Hervé Legrand affirms that "theologically the particularity of a church stems from its relation to the world."[48] Joseph Komonchak links theological and socio-historical principles ("generative principles" and "individuating principles") while emphasizing that the two are essential to the emergence of a local church.[49]

Vatican II is the first council to address the thematic of culture, and the importance attributed to it is noteworthy. One can judge this by the simple fact that the word "culture" appears 91 times in the conciliar documents. In the conciliar corpus the term "adaptation" was the conceptual instrument which served to examine the relationship between the gospel, the Church, and cultures. One finds it frequently in the constitution on the liturgy and in the decree on the missionary activity of the Church. The question of culture was equally treated in the document on social communications and especially in *Gaudium et spes*, which devoted a whole chapter of its second part to a systematic exposition on culture.

For our purposes we will highlight three fundamental affirmations of Vatican II on culture. First the recognition of the diversity of cultures (*GS*

---

[45] Certain theologians affirm that the local/particular church rests essentially on theological criteria: the episcopate, the Holy Spirit, the gospel, and the Eucharist. Yet this neglects the first element: this portion of the people of God, shaped by its culture, proper traditions and customs. For the debate on this question see Gilles Routhier, "'Eglise locale' ou 'Eglise particulière,'" 277-334 (*supra*, note 39).

[46] See *L'Eglise locale*, 15-16, 51-56, where the author develops the relationship between a church and its human space and culture.

[47] I am conscious that this way of speaking is inadequate. In effect it is not correct to affirm that socio-historical elements have nothing to do with theology. Besides it is no longer correct to think that the episcopate, the proclamation of the gospel, etc., are not conditioned by socio-historical factors.

[48] Hervé Legrand, "The Revaluation of Local Churches: Some Theological Implications," in *The Unifying Role of the Bishop*, ed. Edward Schillebeeckx, Concilium 71 (New York: Herder and Herder, 1972) 60.

[49] Joseph A. Komonchak, "The Local Church and the Church Catholic: The Contemporary Theological Problematic," *The Jurist* 52 (1992) 416-447.

53), which is found in *Lumen gentium* as well as in *Gaudium et spes* and in the decree on the missionary activity of the Church. There are *cultures*, which presupposes that the gospel and the Church must be rooted in the human terrains which they encounter. The local churches, "gatherings of the faithful, endowed with the cultural riches of their own nation, must be profoundly rooted in the people" (*AG* 15). Subsequently Vatican II reflected on the question of the emergence of new cultures. Thus the constitution *Gaudium et spes* affirmed that "the conditions of life of modern people have been profoundly transformed from the social and cultural point of view so that one can speak of a new age of human history" (*GS* 54). An ensemble of socio-historical factors contributes today to "creating new forms of culture . . . from which result new ways of thinking, acting and using leisure time." It is thus that "little by little a new type of civilization is prepared." Finally Vatican II recognized that the proclamation of the gospel is strictly linked to culture. It is on the basis of these three points that one subsequently affirms the necessary adaptation of the Church to different cultures.

These three facts, the recognition of the plurality of cultures, the fact of the emergence of new cultures, and the affirmation of the link between culture and the expression of the message of Christ, led the conciliar fathers to envisage new frontiers for the Church: a dialogue with new cultures, the adaptation of the communication of the teaching of Christ in a culturally relevant language, and the renewal of the ecclesial image. The conciliar reflection on culture built upon the openness of John XXIII in his inaugural allocution, which emphasized the fact that the expressions of the faith are culturally influenced while indicating the importance to be accorded to different cultures if one wanted to express the gospel in an "adapted" fashion. Paragraphs 44-58 of *Gaudium et spes* are undoubtedly the most important passages on this issue. In following the teaching of Vatican II, one is brought to the realization that, far from constituting a threat to the proclamation of the gospel or jeopardizing the vitality of the faith (*GS* 62), the emergence of new questions can "prompt a more precise and profound understanding of the faith." This new understanding of the faith, which will require new research on the part of theologians, "constitutes an invitation to seek unceasingly the most appropriate way of communicating doctrine to their contemporaries" (*GS* 62). It then becomes necessary:

> that in every great socio-cultural region . . . theological reflection should be encouraged. By means of this, in the light of the tradi-

tion of the universal church, the deeds and words revealed by
God, recorded in sacred scripture and explained by the fathers
and the teaching office of the church, are to be subjected to a
fresh investigation. In this way, it will emerge more clearly in
what ways the faith can be understood in terms of the philosophy
and wisdom of these peoples, and how their customs, their attitude to life and their social structure can be reconciled with the
way of living proposed by divine revelation. As a result, avenues
will open up for a more profound adaptation in the entire area of
christian life.[50]

To achieve this Vatican II suggested the need to highlight episcopal
conferences, which in each significant socio-cultural territory would be
able to pursue the adaptation necessary so that "the particular traditions
with their proper qualities enlightened by the light of the gospel of each
family of nations may be assumed into Catholic unity" (*AG* 22). It also
proposed an increase of exchanges between the Church and different cultures. To do this the Church must first of all count on the contribution of
the laity well integrated in the culture. Thus *Gaudium et spes* 44 insisted
on the fact that "to expand such exchanges the Church . . . particularly
needs the contribution of those who live in the world, who know the different institutions, the different disciplines and embrace the different
ways of thinking, whether it be believers or unbelievers." According to
Vatican II (*AG* 21) the laity constitute the privileged interfacing between
the gospel and culture even if this understanding of cultures is also necessary for missionaries (*AG* 16), pastors, and theologians, whose task is
to "scrutinize, discern and interpret the multiple languages of our times
and to judge them in the light of the divine word in order that the revealed
truth can unceasingly be better perceived, better understood, and presented under a more adapted form" (*GS* 44).

Indeed these texts did not adopt the perspective of inculturation. However, they constitute a step which oriented the Church in this direction.
They especially accented the fact that the communicator must encode the
message with a respect for different audiences. This corresponds to the
state of theories of communications at the beginning of the 1960's.
Hence the fact of reception was considered even if it is not there in its
fullness. One becomes attentive to the one receiving. Even more, certain
texts began to describe a living process of exchange between the Church

---

[50]   Tanner, 1030-1031.

and cultures. All of this teaching on culture is not neutral in relationship to our question of reception in Vatican II. This point has been too little highlighted until now.

One sees that the teaching of Vatican II has put in place several elements which will permit the Church subsequently to consider the processes of reception. At a distance we are led to think that the theology of tradition and its interpretation, which was a point of controversy at the council, remains the weakest link in that ensemble. The difficulty in recapturing the dynamic inaugurated by Vatican II on the subject indicates that there was not a sufficient maturation of ideas during the conciliar period.

C. The Council as an Event of Reception

It has often been noted that Vatican II arrived at an elaboration of a theory of collegiality on the basis of a practice of collegiality. Moreover, the common celebration of the Eucharist according to the different liturgical traditions operative in the Churches of the East and West permitted the council fathers to broaden their understanding of the mystery of the Church and the communion of the Churches duly respectful of their diversity and proper traditions. Hermann Pottmeyer wisely notes that "a practice and an experience of communion are necessary if a corresponding ecclesiology can develop and be accepted. The formation of a communion-ecclesiology in the midst of the conciliar event is an excellent example of the intimate union between practice and the experience of communion on the one hand and the theoretical reflection and formulation of it on the other hand."[51]

Likewise it is only in experiencing communion that the Christian consciousness is able to grasp and understand the local church as a communion of persons and the Church as a whole as a communion of sister churches. This experience will permit it to achieve an ever clearer consciousness of the process of reception which animates it and makes it grow in communion. This relationship between ecclesial life and the conceptual rediscovery of this experience restates an idea dear to Congar. Already in 1937 he emphasized that "it is in realizing itself as universal

---

[51] Hermann Pottmeyer, "Continuité et innovation dans l'ecclésiologie de Vatican II. L'influence de Vatican I sur l'ecclésiologie de Vatican II et la nouvelle réception de Vatican I à la lumière de Vatican II," in *Les Eglises après Vatican II*, 93 (*supra*, note 37).

that the Church has become conscious of its universality."[52] Further on in the same text he added this remark:

> We have there an order of things which is not understood only in texts and pronouncements but is understood itself in the very becoming . . . the life of the Church as such is a necessary "theological locus." . . . A strictly bookish and academic way of envisaging things would want only to examine the texts although the institution explains itself and is understood itself only in living.[53]

In a notice placed at the beginning of the 1941 edition, he further developed this viewpoint:

> It is necessary to justify in showing . . . that the reality of the Church transcends one's consciousness of it, one's expression of it . . . that things are truly part of the essence of the Church which are not in the texts . . . . It is necessary to show that it is not so much the text which explains the reality of the Church, that it is this reality which enlightens and enables one to understand the text; that thus the life of the Church for its part enables us to enter into the revelation of its mystery.[54]

One can endlessly examine the texts of Vatican II to draw from them certain teachings or points to support one's view on the subject of reception. That is certainly useful but it should not lead us to neglect the conciliar event itself which constitutes a central event of reception in the Church. That point has been much too neglected until now.

The study of Vatican II as an event of reception has led to several areas of inquiry.[55] The first treats the profoundly spiritual character of the conciliar life, which is a hearing of the word of God in docility to the Spirit. In a council the Church puts itself in a situation of receiving and welcoming what has been transmitted to it. The studies pursued on the conciliar nature of the Church during the 1960's and 1970's highlighted this dimension. Vatican II has also been examined in terms of its reception of

---

[52]   Yves Congar, "Vie de l'Eglise et conscience de la catholicité," in *Esquisse du mystère de l'Eglise*, 2nd ed. (Paris: Cerf, 1953) 121.

[53]   Ibid., 126.

[54]   Ibid., "Avertissement," 8.

[55]   See Gilles Routhier, "Orientamenti per lo studio del Vaticano II come fatto di ricezione," in *L'Evento e le decisioni. Studi sulle dinamiche del concilio Vaticano II*, ed. Maria Teresa Fattori and Alberto Melloni (Bologna: Il Mulino, 1997) 465-499.

Scripture, the liturgical and patristic tradition, the teaching of pastors and doctors, papal teachings of the last century, and modern councils. Some elements of this research are already available. For example, there is the data gathered by Dionne on the reception of papal teachings of the last century in the conciliar document on the missions.[56]

It is even more important to consider how Vatican II received what was developing in the life of the churches during the years preceding it. Such an enterprise does not refer simply to a minute study of *vota*,[57] an important but insufficient task undertaken during the last few years. It entails an examination of reception by Vatican II of the rich and varied contributions of the different episcopates gathered in Rome and of the theology elaborated during the postwar years. However, such a study also points us in the direction of the reception of the aspirations of the members of the people of God formulated during different preconciliar consultations.[58] Such an assessment of the life of the people of God in the different local churches would permit a better articulation of the collegiality of bishops and the conciliarity of the churches.

Congar has always been attentive to this life of the Church, which makes an imprint on all theological elaboration leading up to the work of councils. He has often noted this with regard to past ecclesiology, marked by the struggle against Gallicanism and Modernism. He has also noted this regarding contemporary ecclesiology: "Still more profoundly than in theological work, it is in the life of the Church itself that today we

---

[56] J. Robert Dionne, *The Papacy and the Church. A Study of Praxis and Reception in Ecumenical Perspective* (New York: Philosophical Library, 1987) 288.

[57] See the studies on the *vota* of the bishops from Belgium, Bavaria, Spain, Italy, the Netherlands, Switzerland, and the Eastern churches in Mathijs Lamberigts and Claude Soetens, *À la veille du Concile Vatican II. Vota et réactions en Europe et dans le catholicisme oriental* (Louvain: Bibliotheek van de Faculteit der Godgeleerdheid, 1992) 277. For South America see the analyses of the *vota* of the bishops of Argentina, Chile, Paraguay, Colombia, and Venezuela as well as Central America, Mexico, and the Caribbean in José Beozzo, *Cristianismo e iglesias de America Latina en visperas del Vaticano II* (San José, Costa Rica: DEI, 1992) 216. See the *vota* of the French, Italian, and English bishops published in the acts of a colloquium organized in 1986 by the French School of Rome under the title *Le deuxième Concile du Vatican (1959-1965)* (Rome: Ecole française de Rome, 1989) 867. To that one can add the study of A. G. Aiello, "I 'vota' dei vescovi siciliani per il Vaticano II," in *A venti anni dal Concilio. Prospettive teologiche e giuridiche* (Palermo: Edizioni OFTeS, 1983) 93-106. See also Joseph Komonchak, "U.S. Bishops' Suggestions for Vatican II," *Cristianesimo nella Storia* 16 (1994) 313-372.

[58] We are currently researching the preconciliar consultations of the laity in the dioceses of Quebec. Up to now we have focused on seven dioceses.

witness a transformation whose developments or consequences we cannot predict."[59] These lines written in 1937 are amply developed in his introduction to *Vraie et fausse réforme dans l'Eglise.*[60] A study of Vatican
II as an event of reception must then equally attempt to measure what the
Church receives from the life of the churches and the contemporary
world on this occasion.

The study of the reception internal to the conciliar event also directs
our attention to what the council did not wish to receive. One thinks immediately of the seven schemata elaborated by the preparatory commissions and sent to the fathers in July 1962. These are not the only examples of the phenomenon of non-reception internal to the conciliar event.
A good understanding of the positions the council did not wish to adopt
is central to a correct interpretation of the conciliar teaching. As one
knows, reception always involves a certain selectivity. It constitutes a
judgment on the appropriateness of such and such an affirmation.

Finally the study of Vatican II as an event of reception prompts an examination of the internal reception of conciliar intuitions from one document to another. One could easily state at what point the constitution on
the liturgy embryonically contains various points which will be developed in other schemata. Already *Sacrosanctum Concilium* affords an understanding of the local church (*SC* 41-42). Paragraphs 22 §2 and 63b
oriented the conciliar deliberations toward subsequent developments on
episcopal conferences. The constitution on the liturgy also developed the
notion of the people of God, the unique subject of the celebration within
which one situates the diversity of orders and functions and the effective
participation of all (*SC* 26). There one also finds an affirmation regarding
the equality of rites (*SC* 3), which was developed subsequently, and regarding the promotion of the active participation of the faithful, which
was subsequently extended to all domains of ecclesial life.

RECEPTION AND THE ECUMENICAL MOVEMENT

As in the Catholic Church, it was at the same time at the beginning of
the 1960's that the topic of reception was put on the agenda of the ecumenical movement. Prescinding from any effort at a chronology, one can
consider different facets of the evolution of the thematic of reception in

---

[59]   Yves Congar, "L'Eglise et son unité," in *Esquisse du mystère de l'Eglise*, 54.
[60]   Yves Congar, *Vraie et fausse réforme dans l'Eglise* (Paris: Cerf, 1968) 47-51.

the ecumenical movement. Initially the question seemed to be posed only at the moment when different agreements from the bilateral or multilateral dialogues were forwarded to the churches. In fact the completion of the work of certain commissions entailed a new interest in the topic of reception.

However, reception was above all presented within the context of reflection on the conciliar life of the churches, and it was subsequently linked to discussions on authority in the Church. Only following that was the focus on reception of the agreements arising from the dialogues. Finally the adoption of the perspective of reception has certainly affected the method according to which the ecumenical dialogues are conducted.

A. Reception and the Conciliar Life of the Church

In the ecumenical movement the question of reception surfaced within the context of a study of the councils of the early church initiated in New Delhi in 1961 at the general assembly of the World Council of Churches. This study was then entrusted to the Faith and Order Commission. This group met in Oxford in 1963 and 1964 and at Bad Gastein (Austria) in 1965 and 1966. In the words of a participant, these last two meetings constituted "the very first occasions when this question began to emerge on the ecumenical horizon."[61] These consultations led to the publication of a final report which marked a turning point in the reintegration of the concept of reception in the ecumenical context.[62] The resumption of dialogues between the Orthodox Churches and the neo-Chalcedonian Churches accelerated this movement.[63] In effect the option of considering as a whole the Councils of Chalcedon, Ephesus and Constantinople presupposed the notion of reception. In this perspective the councils were viewed as stages in the same development which engages us to undertake a continuous hermeneutics.

The decision of the Faith and Order Commission (Bristol 1968) to examine the reception of the decisions of the Council of Chalcedon constituted a turning point.[64] There the approach to reception in terms of a con-

---

[61] Zizioulas, 3 (*supra*, note 29).

[62] *Councils and the Ecumenical Movement* (*supra*, note 29).

[63] For an account of the unofficial discussions at Aarhus, August 11-15, 1964 see *The Greek Orthodox Theological Review* 10 (1965) 14-15.

[64] To implement this research the commission organized a colloquium at Geneva from August 31 to September 9, 1969. The principal contributions to this colloquium are found

crete case permitted the establishment of some important directions from
a methodological standpoint. I have drawn from that a significant teaching for the study of the reception of a council. This approach to reception
in terms of the conciliar life of the churches also raised very important
questions. In a number of them one would pose the question of the link
between the validity of a dogmatic decision and its reception; the reception by the fullness of the Church as a constitutive element of conciliar
life; the question of the receivability of certain decisions or the evaluation of non-dogmatic factors.[65]

B. Reception and the Question of Authority in the Church

In 1985 Roger Greenacre published an article in *Irenikon* posing two
problems for Anglicans raised for the reception of doctrine in the reception of texts from the dialogues.[66] He indicated clearly that in an ecumenical context the question of reception was not posed simply at the
end of the discussions when the agreed texts are forwarded to the
churches but that reception itself was a subject of lively discussion
among the churches. First posed in the 1970's when work was being
done on the councils of the early church, the question of reception, situated in the more general context of the exercise of authority in the
Church, arose again in the 1980's in the course of dialogues between An-

---

in *The Ecumenical Review* 22 (1970). See especially the articles by Mesrob Ashjian, "Acceptance of the Ecumenical Councils by the Armenian Church," with special reference to
the Council of Chalcedon; Jean Coman, "The Doctrinal Definition of the Council of Chalcedon and its Reception in the Orthodox Church of the East," 368-381; Alois Grillmeier,
"The Reception of Chalcedon in the Roman Catholic Church," 383-411; Edward R.
Hardy, "Chalcedon in the Anglican Tradition," 412-423. See also *Faith and Order Louvain 1971: Study Reports and Documents*, Faith and Order Paper 59 (Geneva: World
Council of Churches, 1971) 23-24, 224-229. For the final report see "Le Concile de Chalcédoine: son histoire, sa réception par les Eglises et son actualité," *Irenikon* 44 (1971) 349-
366.

[65]   The problem of receivability has been posed by Harding Meyer, "Les présupposés
de la réception ecclésiale ou le problème de la 'recevabilité.' Perspectives lutheriennes."
Irenikon 59 (1986) 5-19. There is an abundant bibliography on the question of the assessment of non-doctrinal factors in reception. See the recent research listed in the revue *Istina*
38 (1993) 227-252.

[66]   Roger Greenacre, "La réception des textes des dialogues et la réception de la doctrine: deux problèmes pour les anglicans," *Irenikon* 56 (1985) 471-491.

glicans and Catholics.[67] The link between these two questions is so evident that it does not need to be explored in depth here. However, what must be noted is the striking convergence between the solutions advanced in the different agreed texts. In the final report of the international Anglican-Catholic dialogue this convergence is expressed in terms of the concept of primacy, conciliarity, and synodality.[68] Still more systematically the members of the International Lutheran-Catholic Commission articulated the relationship between personal responsibility, the synodality of the local churches, and the conciliarity of the churches.[69] This actually restates what had been advanced at Lausanne in 1927 at the time of the world conference of Faith and Order on ministry in the Church, which was later affirmed in BEM.[70]

A second element of this convergence resides in the recourse to the reality of *koinonia* as a general framework within which to describe relationships among persons and churches. This reality is central to all the developments relative to the exercise of authority in the Church in the final report of ARCIC. Paragraph 4 of the introduction is not simply being rhetorical when it affirms that "the concept of *koinonia* (communion) is fundamental to all the declarations." One finds the same forceful conviction in the Lutheran-Catholic document in its affirmation of the fact that the Church is a communion.[71]

That is linked to a third element of this impressive convergence: the local church. The Venice document gives a good description in number 8, which introduces section III entitled "Authority in the Communion of Churches." A similar affirmation is found in number 5 of the document

---

[67] See especially number 16 of the 1976 Venice document on authority in the Church and number 3 of the "Elucidations" and number 25 of the 1981 declaration on "Authority in the Church II." For a collection of these texts see *Growth in Agreement*, ed. Harding Meyer and Lukas Vischer, Ecumenical Documents 2 (New York and Geneva: Paulist and WCC, 1984) 61-129.

[68] See "Authority in the Church," nn. 9, 19-23; "Elucidation," n. 5; "Authority in the Church II," nn. 28, 31.

[69] See especially "Facing Unity," nn. 112-114, in *Facing Unity: Models, Forms and Phases of Catholic-Lutheran Fellowship* (Geneva: Lutheran World Federation, 1985).

[70] See Faith and Order, *Proceedings of the World Conference, Lausanne* (New York: G. H. Doran, 1928) 469. See n. 26 of BEM in *Baptism, Eucharist and Ministry*, Faith and Order Paper 111 (Geneva: WCC, 1982).

[71] See "Facing Unity," nn. 5, 27-30, 41-45.

"Facing Unity": "Thus the Church itself is a communion (*communio*) constituted by a network of local churches."

These three elements of convergence in the documents issued by the international Anglican-Catholic and Lutheran-Catholic Commissions are completely consonant with what we find in the Orthodox contributions to the discussion on reception, contributions elaborated in the context of studies on the councils of the early church or at the time of the forwarding to the churches of the Lima Document for an official response. There is an insistence on communion which is expressed concretely by the conciliarity of the local churches and synodal life within them. This integrates the central elements of Vatican II even if, as we have seen, it did not draw all the consequences for a theology of reception of its affirmations on communion, the conciliar life of the Church, the local church, and the revitalization of its synodal life. What the ecumenical discussions contribute then is very much in agreement with the conciliar developments, which, however, remain in tension with a more centralized way of envisaging things.

C. Reception of the Results of the Ecumenical Dialogues

A first result of the ecumenical dialogues was to give a powerful thrust to discussions on reception. Early in the 1980's the results of several dialogues were submitted to different churches for their evaluation. This was the case for the bilateral dialogues between Catholics and Anglicans. In 1976 in its Venice declaration, the international commission asked the two churches to examine the agreements and explore their implications.[72] The necessity of this evaluation was recognized by the common declaration of Paul VI and Dr. Coggan on April 26, 1977.[73] The publication of the final report in 1982 was to open a new stage in the dialogue. The authorities of the different churches were asked to ascertain if the agreements contained in that report were "consonant" with the respective faith of the churches. A long process engaged each of the two churches. On the Catholic side, at the invitation of the Secretariat for Christian Unity, the episcopal conferences rendered a judgment on these texts; some published their response to the agreements undertaken by the

---

[72]   Venice declaration, n. 26.
[73]   "Common Declaration," April 29, 1977, in *Called to Full Unity: Documents on Anglican-Roman Catholic Relations 1966-1983*, ed. Joseph W. Witmer and J. Robert Wright (Washington: USCC, 1986) 158 (the end of n. 4).

members of the mixed commission. The question of reception occupied a significant place in the long and challenging debate which was then beginning.[74]

Some years later the discussions between Catholics and Lutherans followed the same path. In 1984 the document "Facing Unity" asked the churches to "examine," "correct," or "complete" and give authority to the conclusions of the Commission.[75] The bilateral dialogues undertaken at the national level themselves followed the same path and reached the same destination. Hence in its common declaration the members of the Lutheran-Catholic study group in the United States submitted their agreement to their respective churches in the hope of finding a favorable response.[76] That also inaugurated an examination process engaging a judgment on the agreements reached and a response proportionate to that judgment. The discussions between Lutherans and Catholics have also addressed the question of reception; however, it did not assume so much importance as in the Anglican-Catholic dialogues.

The same phenomenon occurred in the multilateral dialogues.[77] In 1982 the Faith and Order Commission asked the churches to prepare an official response to the 1982 Lima document, *Baptism, Eucharist and Ministry*.[78] This invitation to the churches to prepare an official response to these texts which express "substantial theological agreement" or "significant theological convergence" stimulated a great deal of activity in the different churches engaged in these discussions.[79] One could speak

---

[74]   See, for example, "Réponse de la Conference episcopale française aux questions du Secretariat pour l'unité des chrétiens," *DC* 82 (1985) 867-875 and "Réponse de la Conference episcopale d'Angleterre et du pays de Galles aux questions du Secretariat pour l'unité des chrétiens," ibid., 876-881. See also the observations of the Congregation for the Doctrine of the Faith in *Origins* 11/47 (May 6, 1982) 753-756. In March 1983 Cardinal Ratzinger published an article on the Anglican-Catholic dialogue in which he considered the question of reception. See "Anglican-Catholic Dialogue: Its Problems and Its Hopes," *Insight* 1/3 (March 1983) 2-11, esp. 4.

[75]   *Face à l'unité: tous les textes officiels (1972-1985)*, ed. Hervé Legrand and Harding Meyer (Paris: Cerf, 1986) 297.

[76]   "Justification by Faith," 1984, in *Building Unity*, ed. Joseph A. Burgess and Jeffrey Gros, Ecumenical Documents 4 (New York/Mahwah, NJ: Paulist Press, 1989) 274.

[77]   For a review of the bilateral dialogues see *Growth in Agreement: Reports and Agreements of Ecumenical Conversations on a World Level*, ed. Harding Meyer and Lukas Fischer (New York: Paulist, 1984).

[78]   *Baptism, Eucharist and Ministry*, x.

[79]   For the responses of the churches see *Churches Respond to BEM*, ed. Max Thurian, Faith and Order papers, 6 vols. (Geneva: World Council of Churches, 1986-1988). For the

of the decade of BEM given the considerable enthusiasm prompted by the text. This text, translated into 32 languages, was discussed by thousands of groups throughout the world.

These events have broadly influenced the life of the churches[80] and contributed to the "democratization" of the concept of reception. Between 1981 and 1987 at least 48 articles or chapters of collective works appeared, directly linked to the theme of the reception of the results of the ecumenical dialogues, of which 12 are directly related to BEM.[81] All the significant churches are involved. From April 12-14, 1983, 150 theologians, pastors, and leaders of more than 20 "churches" gathered at a congress in Chicago to discuss the theme of "reception."[82] In preparation for this conference its organizers had sent to the different churches or confessions a questionnaire seeking information on the practice of reception operative in each of the churches.[83] The same year the Secretariat for Promoting Christian Unity organized a discussion on the theme of reception. The working paper, still unpublished, prepared by Emmanuel Lanne was entitled "Les résultats des dialogues théologiques bilatéraux." Henceforth the concept is no longer limited to specialized reviews, and its usage is not limited to expert theologians. It has become a fashionable concept with all the risks that entails.

This first result of the ecumenical dialogues, whose results were in turn submitted to the judgment and evaluation of the churches, has also permitted a more in depth understanding of the notion of reception, especially a more precise awareness of the relationship between the reception and the

---

July 21, 1987 response of the Catholic Church prepared by the Secretariat for Christian Unity and the Congregation for the Doctrine of the Faith see *Origins* 17/23 (November 19, 1987) 401, 403-416.

[80]   In 1985 Cardinal Willebrands treated the impact of the ecumenical dialogue in the life of the churches. See "The Impact of Dialogue," *Origins* 14/44 (Apirl 18, 1985) 720-724.

[81]   See the bibliography in Routhier, *La réception*, 243-261 (*supra*, note 13).

[82]   The essentials of the conferences are published in the *Journal of Ecumenical Studies* 21 (1984). A condensed version of the works of this congress appeared in "Baptism, Eucharist and Ministry Conference: April 12-14, 1983, Chicago, Illinois," *Mid-Stream* 25 (1986) 322-329.

[83]   For a synthesis of 27 of these responses see Rastko Trbuhovich, "Summary of U.S. Churches' BEM Reception Processes," *Journal of Ecumenical Studies* 21 (1984) 22-33.

truth of a statement.[84] There is also a more precise distinction between reception and related notions such as the recognition of the churches and official responses. The international Catholic-Lutheran Commission most clearly distinguished "reception" from "recognition."[85] The distinction between "official response" and "reception" is most clearly articulated in the introduction to BEM, the official response being a first stage which can eventually lead to a veritable process of reception.

This first half of the 1980's, largely dominated by the question of the reception of the results of the ecumenical dialogues, contributed in another way to a deepening of the discussion on reception. There was more and more of a preoccupation with the impact of the official dialogues in the ecclesial body. The more the dialogues advanced, the more one perceived that the agreements reached by the commissions will achieve their full impact and authority only if they are broadly shared among the faithful of the churches which have entered into dialogue. One quickly saw the risk of ecumenical breakthroughs which remain without effect in the real life of the churches.

The entrance into a new stage, the asking for an official response which opens the door to a veritable process of reception, permitted something of an advance on another level, that of procedures, participants, modalities, stages, and phases of the process of reception. Who in each of the churches is authorized to respond officially to the agreed texts? What is the modality and the rhythm whereby these texts can be disseminated throughout the ecclesial body and be assimilated by believers in the different churches? The appeal to official responses, indeed to reception, no longer sufficed. One must be preoccupied with the modalities of reception and the instruments of animation and the steps which accompany it. From that time new preoccupations arose: a renewed interest in synodal procedures in each of the churches, a new interest in religious teaching which is ecumenical in character, and in new advances on the liturgical plane in each of the churches.

D. Reception as a Method of Ecumenical Dialogue

The appearance of the problematic of reception is certainly one of the elements which has contributed to the evolution of the method imple-

---

[84] See the "Elucidations" (1981) added to the ARCIC document (n. 25) on authority in the Church, *Called to Full Unity*, 264-270. See the position of the Sacred Congregation for the Doctrine of the Faith in *Origins* 11/47 (May 6, 1982) 754-755.

[85] See *Face à l'Unité*, 321f.

mented in the ecumenical dialogues. For the partners engaged in the dialogue, it is a question not of comparing term by term the propositions advanced during the discussions with their respective confessional statements, but of elaborating formulations apt to express the faith received from the apostles. The abandoning of the comparative method at Lund (1952) called for new in-depth approaches regarding the method to be followed in the ecumenical dialogues. The problematic of reception situated differently the different partners in the discussion: not one group facing the other but all submitted to the one Word of God, which they receive in the linguistic and cultural conditioning of their respective traditions.

CONCLUDING REFLECTIONS

A survey of the evolution of the topic of reception in the theological literature of the last three decades indicates a close relationship between theological reflection and ecclesial life. It is above all the life of the churches which has put the question of reception on the agenda. It is also ecclesial life which has permitted a deepening of reflection on the topic and the methodological advances on this question. By the same token, the deepening of reflection on reception has contributed to the refinement of practice, notably the revitalization of synodality in the local churches and the development of new ways of assuring communion among sister churches.

The reevaluation of the ecclesial reality of reception is dependent on the significant ecclesiological themes on which it depends: a theology of communion and of tradition, a theology of the local churches, which includes the relationship between a church and its setting, a development of the synodal life of this church, and a theology which strikes a balance between the generative principles and the principles of identification of the Church. It is closely linked to a deeper theological understanding of the conciliar life of the Church and to an ecclesiological perspective which sufficiently integrates pneumatology. However, we must not neglect the fact that reception is also partly linked to a proper theological appreciation of culture.

Finally, the highlighting of reception also depends on non-dogmatic factors to the extent that one retains a conception of the relationship between ecclesial practice and theology, and of the fact of communications or the process of inculturation. One sees that the study of reception obliges us to be attentive not only to developments in the historical sciences or in literature but also to the philosophical sciences, to the sciences of language and communications, and to anthropology.

Translation by Thomas J. Green

RECEPTION IN THE EARLY CHURCH: FUNDAMENTAL PROCESSES OF COMMUNICATION AND COMMUNION

EMMANUEL LANNE, O.S.B.*

By "reception" we understand here, in the broad sense, the manner in which a teaching or a doctrinal or a disciplinary decision was welcomed in a given Christian community in such a way that the teaching or decision became part of the life of this community.[1] There would certainly be a place to distinguish, as is done today, "reception" from "response," this latter being a reaction of the concerned community to the teaching or to the decision which was proposed to it or imposed for its "reception," without the teaching or decision becoming part of the life of this community. One must also distinguish, as we shall see, different levels of reception for a teaching or a decision.

As temporal limits for the "early church" we take the Church before the peace of Constantine or before Nicea. In effect, outside the ecumenical council, all the principal structures of the Church were already in place by the end of the third century. By structures we understand what in English is understood as "order."[2] The term could embrace not only ecclesial institutions but also the instruments which permit the transmission of the Christian faith and its spread, such as, for example, the canon of Scriptures or the profession of faith. As to the essentials, all that had been acquired before the beginning of the fourth century: episcopate and three-fold ministry, synodal life, canon of the Scriptures, ritual for the celebration of baptism and of Eucharist, etc.

One might think that our presentation ends too early because for historians "early church" goes as far as the Council of Chalcedon, or, with

---

*   Abbaye de Chevetogne (Belgium).

[1]   On the theme of "reception" in the early church, see Gilles Routhier, *La réception d'un concile*, Cogitatio fidei 171 (Paris: Cerf, 1993) 43ff. For bibliography, see 16, note 7; 38, note 73; and 243ff.

[2]   For example, in the "Faith and Order" movement (which the French call "Foi et Constitution").

Duchesne up to the fourth century. It seems, however, that the field of reception is already sufficiently vast if one ends the presentation at the dawn of the fourth century. In any case, as we shall see, it is our conviction that the first three centuries furnish a sufficient field of inquiry. Within the limits of this presentation it will not be possible, moreover, to do more than to touch several points which we think are decisive. We shall attempt to examine sufficiently closely several more concrete examples of the mechanism of reception. At the end we will examine an example taken from the fifth century which could clarify, by contrast, the true dimensions of reception.

RECEPTION AT CORINTH

To open the question of reception in the early church and of the fundamental processes of communication and communion implied by reception, it is best to begin the documentation with the New Testament and in first place with what Paul says about it in a major text. In fact, two passages of the first letter to the Corinthians dealt directly with reception in the early church. These are even the earliest texts which do this: 1 Cor 11: 23ff on the institution of the Eucharist, but especially 1 Cor 15: 1ff on the gospel which Paul transmitted to the Corinthians.[3]

One must begin by re-reading the second passage. We will see to the first later. In 1 Cor 15 Paul recalled the gospel which he announced to the Corinthians and his point was Christ's resurrection. In these verses there are not only two but even three stages of reception, although normally we are attentive only to two of the more evident ones announced by the words: "you have received" (παρελάβετε, v.1) "that which I myself have received" (παρέλαβον, v. 3). But it must be noted that these two receptions, by the Corinthians and by Paul, suppose an earlier stage of reception, which is signified by "according to the Scriptures" (κατὰ τὰς γραφάς), a formula repeated twice in verses three and four. The gospel of Jesus Christ received, announced, and transmitted by Paul, and received

---

[3]   One could also mention 1 Thes 2: 13 (ὅτι παραλαβόντες λόγον ἀκοῆς παρ᾽ ἡμῶν τοῦ Θεοῦ, ἐδέξατε οὐ λογον ἀνθρώπων ἀλλὰ καθώς ἐστιν ἀληθῶς λόγον Θεοῦ) but the process of reception appears here with less clarity. Moreover, in an article on the reception of the results attained in the dialogue of the Anglican-Catholic Commission, Henry Chadwick raises the question of reception and of the "recognition" in regard to Jews and Gentiles in the primitive church (Gal 2): "Reception," in *Communion et Réunion. Mélanges Jean-Marie Roger Tillard*, ed. Gillian R. Evans and Michel Gourges (Leuven: Leuven University Press, 1995) 95-107.

by the Corinthians, supposes a logically prior reception, that of the Jewish Scriptures. Certainly in Luke 24: 27-44, the risen Jesus twice established explicitly the connection between the Scriptures and his redemptive work. But Paul's reference is much earlier than the redaction of Luke. That Paul received the Jewish Scriptures is not surprising. But that he recognized in them the announcement of the "death of Christ for our sins," then that of his "resurrection on the third day," is perhaps more so. But the most remarkable thing in the verses is that the Corinthians themselves, who for the most part, it is thought, were not of Jewish origin, must in their turn "receive" these Scriptures to welcome the gospel of Jesus Christ, his death and his resurrection. Moreover, following what Paul wrote to the Corinthians, the Church in general has always held that the gospel of Jesus Christ supposes in order to be received correctly that it be interpreted according to the Jewish Scriptures. Such was the basis for the struggle against Marcianism. It does not matter here to what passages in the Jewish Scriptures Paul intended to refer when he announced the kerygma "according to the Scriptures." What is important is that on the one hand he himself received this message "according to the Scriptures"—that is, without denying his Judaism but, on the contrary basing himself on it—and on the other, in his turn, he transmitted it to the Corinthian community in this setting required for the reception of the gospel: the Scriptures. There is therefore a preliminary reception of the Jewish Scriptures in order to be able to welcome the gospel and this goes both for the Church at Corinth as well as for the first community of Jesus' disciples.

Quite correctly Tillard has written, "The first Christian generations 'received' the Old Testament in spite of the knowledge that they have something that surpasses this by the Word and in the Passover of Christ Jesus, and despite the Jewish opposition and even hatred. In the Spirit, they understand that everything is accomplished 'according to the scriptures.'"[4]

In this text of 1 Cor 15 one also notes that the process of reception is preceded necessarily by a transmission, a "tradition" (παρέδωκα γὰρ ὑμῖν). This tradition is even the essential step in the passage on the Eu-

---

[4]   Jean-Marie R. Tillard, *Church of Churches: The Ecclesiology of Communion* (Collegeville, MN: Liturgical Press, 1992) 121-122.

charist of 1 Cor 11,[5] Παρέδϖκα ὑμῖν, which supposes here also that the Corinthians have received—but they have received poorly and Paul is going to correct them—while Paul on his side affirms he received (παρέλαβον) this rite from the Lord.

Reception is thus not a secondary element with regard to the life of the Church. It is situated in its heart. The gospel must be announced ("evangelized": ἐυαγγελισάμην: two times, vv. 1 & 2) and received, and first of all the Scriptures of the first Testament must be received as the foundation for this gospel "according to the Scriptures." The Eucharist must itself be received, and that such as Paul himself has received it from the Lord and has passed it on. Reception is thus constitutive of the life of the Church,[6] and the Church is the community of those who have "received," that is, of those who have made their own the message which was announced to them and as it was announced to them.

One can thus apply to the new reception, which the Church at Corinth must carry out, the implications of eucharistic celebrations and of those of the gospel announced by Paul, what the metropolitan of Pergamum Jean Zizioulas said: "Reception is a process by which the Church received the person of Christ as a gift offered by God for the life of the world in re-receiving in a new and historical context [here, that of Corinth] and in the Holy Spirit (that is, in and by the communion which involves all the members of the Church) the 'faith transmitted to the saints one time for all' (Jude 3) in and by an act (or acts) of confession and participation in the event by which this gift offered by God took place, as it is recorded in the Scriptures."[7] Reception supposes a going back even to the person of Christ and to his salvific acts.

The example of the two passages of the first letter to the Corinthians which we have taken to open this study is particularly significant in this regard. The paschal mystery of Christ announced by Paul is at the center of the two texts. Paul transmitted here what he himself had received. But Christ is at the center also because he fulfilled the Jewish Scriptures

---

[5]   Gordon D. Fee, *The First Epistle to the Corinthians*, 2nd ed. (Grand Rapids, MI: Eerdmans, 1991) 548 recalls that the verbs "receive" and "transmit" in the two passages are technical terms from Paul's Jewish heritage. For "receive" he cross references also to 1 Thes 2: 13, 4: 1, and to other passages in the pauline letters. For "transmit" he cross references to v. 2, commented (pp. 499 ff.).

[6]   Here are some other passages on reception in Paul: 2 Cor 11: 4 (the Spirit); Gal 1: 9-12 (the gospel; cf. Phil 4: 9); Col 2: 6 (the Lord). See also, later, 1 Tim 1: 15; 4: 9.

[7]   From the intervention of John Zizioulas at the 1985 Chevetogne colloquium on "La 'reception' des résultats des dialogues par les Églises," *Irénikon* 58 (1985) 538.

which must then be received inseparably from the paschal mystery of Christ. Both for the eucharistic celebration and for the faith in the resurrection, the Corinthian church must re-receive what was transmitted and announced to it by Paul.

The trajectory, however, is not terminated with this re-reception by the Corinthians evangelized by Paul of what he had announced to them and which they have not correctly or entirely grasped. This trajectory must be followed in this same church at Corinth. The letter of Clement to the Corinthians of the following generation testifies to this. Usually this letter is dated between 95 and 98.[8] For some today, however, the date of Clement's writing would be much earlier to what is normally admitted.[9] Whatever, this text preceded the later writings which were retained in the New Testament canons. We are here in the presence of a re-reception of the Pauline letters, as indicated by the explicit references of 1 Clem 47 which refers to 1 Cor 1-4, and the unequivocal allusion to 1 Cor 13 in 1 Clem 49-50. The re-reception which the Corinthians must carry out of the first letter which Paul addressed to them no longer bears directly on the theology of the Eucharist of chapter 11 nor the gospel of the paschal mystery of the Lord of chapter 15, but rather to the doctrine of the whole of the letter. In effect, it is because of the divisions which took place in Corinth that Paul wrote his letter "under the inspiration of the Spirit" (1 Clem 47: 3), as well as what he himself clearly indicates in the first chapters and as is evidenced by the "hymn to charity" of chapter 13. The Corinthians who had earlier "refused" the inspired message of the apostle must work a new global reception of his teaching on fraternal relations, especially with regard to presbyters (1 Clem 47: 6).

For Corinth, then, it is a question of a new process of reception. But one must note also that Paul's letter had been "received" not only at Corinth. It was also received by the Roman community of which Clement is the spokesperson and it is Paul's teaching that 1 Clem makes its own as a matter of course, well known both at Rome and at Corinth.

There is further witness to the reception of the first letter of Paul at Corinth in the letter of its bishop Dionysius to Pope Soter less than a century later, but at the same time of the reception which had also been the object at Corinth of the letter of Clement as well as the letter of Soter to

[8]   Annie Jaubert, "Introduction," to Clement of Rome, *Épître aux Corinthiens*, Sources chrétiennes 167 (Paris: Cerf, 1971) 20.
[9]   See Joseph Ysebaert, *Die Amtsterminologie im Neuen Testament und in der alten Kirche. Eine lexikographische Untersuchung* (Breda: Eureia, 1994) 211ff.

which Dionysius replied. One knows, in effect, what Dionysius wrote according to the witness of Eusebius: "In the same letter, he (Dionysius) refers to Clement's *Epistle to the Corinthians*, proving that from the very first it had been customary to read it in church. He says: 'Today being the Lord's Day, we kept it as a holy day and read your letter, which we shall read frequently for its valuable advice, like the earlier letter which Clement wrote on your behalf.'"[10]

This example, on which we have paused a bit, is remarkable because it helps us to see the multiple trajectory of reception: reception of the doctrine transmitted by Paul in his preaching and which the Corinthians must receive anew; reception itself based on that of the Jewish Scriptures; new re-reception of the doctrine of the first letter to the Corinthians at the time of the letter of Clement; reception by the Corinthians of this letter of Clement, which was read during the Sunday synax and which also implies the re-reception of the first letter of Paul to the Corinthians; reception, finally, and on the same basis as that of 1 Clem, of Soter of Rome's letter by this same Corinthian community.

As we have discerned in 1 Cor 11 and 15, reception implies the communication of the essential gospel message and communion in it. Communication is done first by Paul's preaching, in the present case to the Corinthians, a preaching in which he announced Jesus Christ in basing himself on the Jewish Scriptures; he himself received orally from the primitive community what he transmitted to them and which they have received. The communication is then made by letters, those of Paul to the Corinthians, then that of Clement which suggests to receive anew that of Paul, then the one from Soter to which Dionysius of Corinth responds, finally by the Sunday assembly during which, in order that they might be received always anew, one reads Clement's letter and, certainly, Paul's, to which was then added that of Soter. In these same Sunday assemblies one can presume that they commenced by reading certain passages of the Jewish Scriptures which alone would make intelligible Paul's preaching.

This communication in different stages and at different levels had for its purpose communion: communion between Paul and the Corinthians, then between the community of Rome of which Clement is the spokesperson and that of Corinth troubled by dissensions, and finally that of

---

[10]   Eusebius, *The History of the Church*, trans. G.A. Williamson (New York: Penguin Books, 1989) 132, bk. 4: 23.

Soter of Rome and of Dionysius. This communion at each of these stages was manifested by the public reading and renewal of these letters in the Sunday assembly.

Yet communion is not limited to these ecclesial relations. Its purpose is the very mystery of Christ and the sacrament of his paschal sacrifice. It is a communion in the faith and in sacrament, as is already indicated by chapter 10 of the first letter to the Corinthians. And beyond the event of Christ, there is communion with the entire plan of God which the Jewish Scriptures make known and which Christ came to complete in his death and resurrection. Such is Paul's teaching in First Corinthians, but that is also implied in Clements' letter and the response of Dionysius to Soter. This leads one to think of the great "eucharistic" prayer which ends Clement's letter (ch. 59-61), and to the fact that these letters were read in the Sunday assembly.

The letters are thus a privileged instrument of communication and of communion,[11] and their content must always be anew the object of a reception, first by their recipients, but also by the other churches, as is the case at Rome (but also at Lyons or at Smyrna) since Irenaeus uses 1 Clem with regard to the apostolicity of the Roman Church.[12]

Finally, it was thanks to the extremely rapid diffusion of Eusebius' *History of the Church* during the fourth century, that the chain of reception of the Corinthian documents from the first letter of Paul up to the exchange of letters between Dionysius and Soter knew a reception in the entire Christian world, a model of reception, if one can say so, which then is applied to the whole of the canon of Scripture. But one must keep in mind a reservation which will be noted below.

RECEPTION OF THE CANON OF SCRIPTURE

The history of the reception of the canon of Scripture has been the subject of a considerable literature and is still today in full research.[13] Yet

---

[11] On the importance of the exchange of letters at this period see Pierre Nautin, *Lettres et Ecrivains chrétiens des IIe et IIIe siècles* (Paris: Cerf, 1961), and Ludwig Hertling, *Communio und Primat*, Miscellanea Historiae Pontificiae 7 (Rome: Pontifica Università Gregoriana, 1943); English translation *Communio—Church and Papacy in Early Christianity*, trans. Jared Wicks (Chicago: Loyola Univesity Press, 1972).

[12] Irenaeus, *Adversus Haereses* 3: 3: 3; see Eusebius, 5: 6.

[13] See *The New Testament in Early Christianity: La réception des Ecrits néo-testamentaires dans le Christianisme primitif*, ed. Jean-Marie Sevrin et al., BETL 86 (Leuven:

one can suppose certain observations which make it possible to reflect on reception during the first centuries of the Church.

How is it, in fact, that Clement's letter, as widely distributed as it was, was not finally received into the canon of New Testament writing? It was received at Corinth and the criterion of this reception was that it was regularly read in the Sunday assembly. But was it always welcomed at Rome and elsewhere, with the same type of reception? Eusebius says, in effect, with regard to this: "I have evidence that in many churches this letter was read aloud to the assembled worshippers in early days, as it is in our own. That it was in Clement's time that the dissension at Corinth broke out is plain from the testimony of Hegesippus."[14] Implicitly, Eusebius leads one to understand that in his time it was not received among the Scriptures which were read at church in all the communities and, consequently, that it did not become part of what became the canon. Moreover, when he recapitulated "the New Testament writings already referred to,"[15] he indicated the four gospels, the acts of the apostles, Paul's letters, the first letter of John and the first letter of Peter, and "if it is thought proper,"[16] the apocalypse. These are the "recognized books," to which are opposed the "disputed books," such as the letter of James, that of Jude, the second of Peter, the second and third of John. Finally, a third category: the apocrypha, of which the inventory is more uncertain as it eventually contained a book considered by others as "recognized," the apocalypse, and which elsewhere he also calls "disputed."

The letter of Clement is absent from all these books. Apparently it is not even contested. Or, rather, it was known that is was certainly from Clement, but it did not enter—or rather, it no longer entered—in the list of writings which from then on counted in the New Testament canon, even if it was still read in the assemblies of certain communities and if the

---

Leuven University Press, 1989); the special number of *Istina* 36 (1991) 129-201, with contributions of Bernard D. Dupuy, Henri Cazelles and Bernard Sesboüé; Yves-Marie Blanchard, *Aux sources du canon, le témoinage d'Irénée*, Cogitatio Fidei 175 (Paris: Cerf, 1993); Jean-Noël Aletti, "Jésus-Christ fait-il l'unité du Nouveau Testament?" in *Jésus et Jésus-Christ* 61 (Paris: Desclée, 1994). See also Mauro Pesce's observations, "La trasformazione dei documenti religiosi: dagli scritti protocristiani al canone neotestamentario," *Vetera Christianorum* 26 (1989) 307-326.

[14]   Eusebius, 80, Bk. 3: 16.

[15]   Eusebius, 88, Bk 3: 25, 1:ἀνακεφαλαιώσασθαι τὰς δηλωθείας τῆς καινῆς διαθήκης γραφάς.

[16]   Ibid.: ἔι γε φανείη.

two Clementine writings were still retained by certain lists of books of Scripture, such as canon 85 of the Apostolic Constitutions which concludes with the list of the canonical collection.[17] A decanting is thus underway. How did it happen and according to what criteria? Is not the fact that a letter has been read in the Sunday assembly and that it still is in certain places not a definitive criterion of reception?[18]

It is easy to remark that Irenaeus did not cite as Scripture that writing (ἱκανοτάτην γραφήν) which the Roman church addressed to the Corinthians under Clement. Moreover, there are some problems in the kind of resume which he gives of it.[19]

In any case, it is indeed with Irenaeus that a distinction is clearly at work between the Scriptures received by the Church and those which were propagated by heterodox sects. At Book Three of his "Detection and Refutation of the Knowledge Falsely So Called"—the *Adversus Haereses*—he ties the reception of the four Gospels which we call canonical to the notion of apostolic tradition which he presented at the beginning of this section (3: 3, 1ff.). In passing, he first mentions Paul's witness (3: 6, 5f.). He then comes with insistence to what he calls the "fourfold gospel," the gift of the Logos (3: 11, 8),[20] and he then pauses on the witness of Peter and the disciples and again on that of Paul, especially

---

[17]   The fact that Clement's two letters as well as the text of the Apostolic Constitutions themselves are included in canon 85's list of Scriptures is naturally explained by the fact that the Apostolic Constitutions are attributed to Clement. Yet it would be unlikely that Clement's writings would be mentioned in the list of received books if they were not the object of a public reading in the assemblies which the list's author knew.

[18]   Tillard has recently written on this point: "There is, therefore, a very complex history behind this slow 'reception' of the books which make up the rule of faith itself. Three points must be raised. The 'reception' of some books and the 'non-reception' of others seems at the start less as the fruit of a theological reflection than as a state of fact, the consequence of the consciousness of a sort of internal evidence by which a particular book asserted itself and another one did not. What is at stake here is an instinct about the faith. Elsewhere, this instinct is manifested in the lives of the communities. Finally, the definitive list is established thanks only to the interplay of relationships between Churches, certain ones sharing with others their own richness. The process is one of communion." Tillard, *Church of Churches*, 124.

[19]   See note 1 of Adelin Rousseau and Louis Doutreleau to *Adversus Haereses* 3: 3, Sources chrétiennes 210 (Paris: Cerf, 1974) 237, which refers to Bernard Botte, "Saint Irénée et l'Épître de Clément," *Revue des Études Augustiniennes* 2 (1956) 67-70.

[20]   ἔδωκεν ἡμῖν τετράμορφον τὸ εὐαγγέλιον. As the Oxyrhynque papyrus 405 evidences, this text was known in Egypt shortly after its composition by Irenaeus. See Doutreleau's commentary in the critical edition of *Adverses Haereses* 3: 126ff. See *infra*.

on the Acts of the Apostles, then on the Pauline letters. Since the time of Hardey's edition (1857), people have contested the inventory of New Testament books that Irenaeus knew and which come quite close to our canon.[21] In fact, if Irenaeus also knew the *logia* of the Lord, and perhaps some collections of *logia*, the essential of his demonstration is based especially on a collection of writings which we call neotestamentary and which he is the first to oppose in block to the writings vindicated by the heterodox. The tie established at Book Three between the apostolic tradition, the apostolic churches, and these apostolic writings is even more remarkable.

But one must go higher. For Irenaeus the idea of reception is more englobing than this simple application to the apostolic writings or to others which the heretics claim are such. One encounters, in effect, at the beginning of the *Adversus Haereses*, a very significant use of the verb "received" (παραδέχομαι, *recipere*). It is found on the page where Irenaeus compares the use that the heretics make of the texts of Scripture to a cento of verses from Homer or to the stones of a mosaic of the king which the heretics have made into a fox: "One who keeps in himself, without bending it, the rule of truth which he received by his baptism, . . . recognizes the stones of a mosaic (the parables of Scripture) but he does not *receive* as a portrait of the king the silhouette of the fox" (1: 9, 4).

In relation with John 1: 11, "and his own did not receive him" (3: 11, 2),[22] Irenaeus situated the rejection of the gospel of John and parting with the prophetic spirit by the Aloges, and added "it is normal that such people also do not receive the apostle Paul, for, in the letter to the Corinthians, he spoke with precision about prophetic charisms" (3: 11, 9).

To all that he opposed, on a celebrated page in Book Four, the "true spiritual disciple." The passage is worth recalling here because it includes several domains of reception and because the Scriptures occupy a special place here.

---

[21]   Cf. Blanchard, 122ff. Indeed, the indices of the editions of Irenaeus must not mislead, even when they try to distinguish clearly between a citation and a real or supposed citation. This is even true for the remarkable *Biblia Patristica* from the Centre d'Analyse et de Documentation Patristiques de Strasbourg. For Irenaeus, see vol. 1 (Paris: CNRS, 1975).

[22]   See 3: 19, 1: "Not having received the Word of incorruptibility, they remain in their mortal flesh." Yet note that the verb used by John 1: 11 and cited by Irenaeus in this context is παραλαμβάνω, λαμβάνω (as in 1 Cor 11: 23 and 15: 1), and not παραδέχομαι.

The truly spiritual disciple "is not judged by anyone" (1 Cor 2: 15) since for him, everything possess an unbreakable firmness: with regard to the one all-powerful God, "from whom all things come" (1 Cor 8: 6), it is a total faith; with regard to the Son of God, Jesus Christ our Lord, "through whom all things come," and his economies by which the Son of God became man, it is a firm conviction; with regard to God's Spirit who procures the knowledge of truth, which puts the economies of the Father and Son before the eyes of human beings, according to each generation, as the Father wishes, it is a true gnosis. This gnosis includes the teaching of the apostles; the original organism of the Church spread throughout the entire world; the distinctive mark of the Body of Christ consisting in the succession of bishops to whom the apostles handed over each local church; an immutable preservation of the Scriptures come down even to us, implying:[23] an integral count of these without addition or subtraction, a reading exempt of fraud and, in keeping with the Scriptures, a legitimate interpretation, appropriated, exempt of danger and of blasphemy; finally, the preeminent gift of love, more precious than knowledge, more glorious than prophecy, superior to all other charisms (4: 33, 7-8).[24]

This well-known text calls for several observations. In the first place it begins with the rule of Trinitarian faith which is the basis for faith, conviction, and true gnosis.

Then comes the content of the true gnosis: (1) the apostles' teaching; (2) the universal "original organism" (ἀρχαῖον σύστημα) of the Church; (3) the succession of bishops in local churches; (4) the preservation of the Scriptures with its three conditions.

The four elements of this content of true gnosis are the object of a reception, if one can call it that, by the truly spiritual disciple, just as the rule of faith in three members, but also the three characteristics of an authentic preservation of the Scriptures: all the Scriptures and nothing but them, internal coherence of the whole of the Scriptures, the correct interpretation of these.

One sees then that if Irenaeus does not use the term reception, this is implied by the diverse elements listed. The Scriptures must be preserved

---

[23]   This is a rather obscure passage in Latin, and the Greek version is lost. The Armenian translation clarifies it; cf. the French edition in Sources chrétiennes 100, 820, and note 270-3.

[24]   Slightly modified from Rousseau's translation.

according to the indicated criteria, which signifies that they have already been received by the Church. This reception and this safeguarding of the Scriptures is in direct relationship with three first facts of true gnosis: the apostles' teaching, the original organism (σύστημα) of the Church, that is its primitive structure, and the succession of bishops in local churches, the mark of the true Body of Christ. These are also necessarily "received" in the life of the Church.

It was noted above that here it is a question of the arrival point of reception: the truly spiritual disciple as "judge in the Church." All this chapter 33 is given over, in effect, to an explicitation of 1 Cor 2: 15. It passes in review the different categories of heretics and schismatics on which the truly spiritual disciple gives his judgment. But this judgment, founded on the reception of the rule of faith and of the components of true gnosis, is handed down in the ecclesial context of apostolic tradition. One is led thus to a perspective which is quite similar to that which opens the First Book of *Adversus Haereses* and which follows the image of the mosaic of the king recomposed into a fox. The figure of the fox has been composed with the help of stones from the image of the king which are the different texts of Scripture. Irenaeus begins by opposing to these degrading speculations, the baptismal faith (1: 9, 4)[25] which is that of the Church and which each Christian must hold onto. It is the rule of truth[26] which the content of the baptismal creed enunciates (1: 10, 1). This text is one of the first developed presentations of the profession of faith. This (apostolic) preaching and this faith have been "received" (παραλαμβάνω) by the Church spread through all the world and have been safeguarded by it with diligence. Then Irenaeus passes from the unique Church spread throughout the world to the diverse churches founded in Germany, among the Iberians, among the Celts, in the East, in Egypt, in Libya, at the center of the world: they have no other faith nor any other Tradition (1: 10, 2). But what bears on the rule of truth received at baptism and thus received and transmitted by all the churches, is first of all the Scriptures and their interpretation. The context is very much the same as in the passage of Book Four on faith and the true gnosis of the spiritual disciple. The rule of faith is founded on Scripture, and both the one and the other are the object of the

---

[25]   One who preserves in himself the rule of truth which he received by baptism.

[26]   On the rule of faith, see Emmanuel Lanne, "'La Règle de la verité.' Aux sources d'une expression de saint Irénée," in *Lex orandi Lex credendi. Miscellanea in onore di P. Cipriano Vagaggini*, ed. Gerardo Békés and Giustino Farnedi, Studia anselmiana 79, Sacramentum 6 (Rome: Editrice anselmiana, 1980) 57-70.

unique act of reception on the part of the Church across the entire world. Reception passes, then, from the one Church across the world to each of the particular churches, and from these in the same process to each of the truly spiritual disciples. But the reception of the Scriptures is concomitant with that of the rule of faith, and at the same time with the tradition received from the apostles and with the succession of bishops, as the first chapters of Book Three have shown. Such is at least the manner in which Irenaeus represents the process of reception by the entire Church disseminated throughout the world.

It is by such writings as those of Irenaeus, or by the lists set down by Origen[27] or by Eusebius himself, that a canon of Scriptures was spread throughout all the churches well before a synod such as that of Laodicea toward 360 started to fix the norms which must apply to all.[28] But—and one cannot insist on this too much—the reception of New Testament writing is indissolubly bound to that of the rule of the apostolic faith and to that of the ecclesial structure which supposes also the transmission of a common interpretation of Scripture opposed to that of the heretics. The Scriptures of this canon are first of all destined to be read in the Sunday assembly and are thus in strict connection with the eucharistic celebration of which they form the first part, the Liturgy of the Word.

Synodal Practice and the Reception of a Single Feast of Easter

A classical study on reception in the early church ought to begin with synods or councils, since the concept first had its origin in conciliar practice. The Church, nevertheless, lived without synods or councils during the first generations, although, as we have seen, the work of reception goes back as far as its origins: Paul received the kerygma and transmitted it in order that it might be received and, eventually, received always anew.

Moreover, to speak of the synodal practice of reception evokes first of all, naturally, reception of the great councils which have been called ec-

---

[27] Eusebius, 6: 25.

[28] We will not mention here canon 85 of the Apostolic Constitutions, for even though this collection dates from around 380, there is less assurance on the date of the collection of the eight-five canons which conclude it. The festal Letter 39 of Athanasius of 367 also gives our canon (*PG* 26: 1437).

umenical, from Nicea to Chalcedon and beyond.[29] The subject is henceforth well-known and in the setting of the present study it would be difficult to suggest new elements which would stimulate this colloquium's
reflections. Also, we believe it to be more useful to go back to the first
synods which we know historically, the synods of the paschal controversy.[30]

"Even if the first synods we know about dealt effectively with the date
of Easter, the existence of such synodal meetings is not necessarily tied
to the paschal controversy," Éric Junod remarks.[31] Even while questioning whether the meetings concerning Montanists in the second century
were (or were always) synods of bishops of local churches, Junod is of
the opinion, with good reason, that the signing by the first bishops of the
documents which circulated is an indication of an "inter-communitary
procedure"[32] and consequently of a reception of these documents by
those responsible for the diverse communities to which they were communicated. There could be here a reception exercised by the bishops
without their being gathered together in synod. According to Junod this
is the case with the letter of Serapion, bishop of Antioch, against Montanism and with other writings against the new prophecy "which carried
the personal signatures of a great number of other bishops."[33] These signatures indicated that the dispersed churches had "received" a document
which was sent to them by the bishop of another church.

At the end of the second century there was thus a synodal phenomenon
evident. Even if for the condemnation of Montanism it is not certain that
synods of bishops of several churches gathered, as Junod indicates,[34] on
the other hand for the paschal controversy Eusebius has a rather abundant documentation concerning diverse episcopal synods. It is apparently confirmed by Tertullian who presents them as the usage of the East
which seems not yet common enough in the Africa of his time:

[29]   See Jean-Marie R. Tillard, *L'Église locale. Ecclésiologie de communion et
catholicité*, Cogiatio Fidei 191 (Paris: Cerf, 1995) 431-452.
[30]   See Tillard, *L'Église locale*, 412.
[31]   Éric Junod, "Naissance de la pratique synodale et unité de l'Église au IIᵉ siècle,"
Revue d'Histoire et de Philosophie religieuse 68 (1988) 164.
[32]   Ibid., 172. See also Hilaire Marot, "Conciles anténicéens et conciles oecuméniques," in *Le concile et les conciles, contribution à l'histoire de la vie concilare de
l'Église* (Chevetogne-Paris: Éditions de Chevetogne & Éditions du Cerf, 1960) 19-43, and
Emmanuel Lanne, "L'origine des synodes," *Theologische Zeitschrift* 27 (1971) 201-222.
[33]   Eusebius, 5: 19.
[34]   Junod, 166ff.

> In the Greek countries (he wrote) there are held in certain deter-
> mined places these assemblies (*Illa . . . concilia*) formed of all
> the churches, where one deals in common with the most impor-
> tant questions, and which are celebrated with great solemnity as
> the representation of everything with the name Christian.[35]

The synods held on the occasions of the paschal quarrel and apparently at the request of Pope Victor, became finally the object of a solemn
reception of the decision taken.[36] Eusebius, who informs his readers of
diverse features of the dossier in his possession, begins by indicating that
it is a very important question and he explains in what the difference consisted between the Quatrodeciman practice of "all the Asian dioceses,"
and that of the churches of the "rest of the world." These, "in accordance
with apostolic tradition . . . preserved the view which still prevails, that it
was improper to end the fast on any day other than that of our Saviour's
resurrection."[37]

We should note right away that what is at play is an "apostolic tradition" which is opposed to a "very ancient tradition," itself also apostolic,
which held to the fortieth lunar day observed by the Quatrodecimans.
From one side as well as from the other the reference is to history: the
passover of the Savior, the day of his resurrection; and to an apostolic tradition. It is clear that this must have been Victor's argument in basing
himself on the succession of Peter and Paul at Rome, but for Polycrates
of Ephesus, the head of the Quatrodecimans, the usage which he defended was also of apostolic tradition.

After having explained in what the discord consisted, Eusebius continues: "Synods and conferences of bishops were held on the subject."
Eusebius goes right on to tell us the resolution of the controversy. All the
bishops' synods "without a dissentient one, drew up a decree of the
Church, in the form of letters addressed to Christians everywhere, that
never on any day other than the Lord's Day should the mystery of the

---

[35] Tertullian, *De jejuniis* 13: 6, in Tertullian, *Opera*, Corpus Christianorum 1-2, 2 vols.
(Turnholt: Brepols, 1954) 2: 1272. Historians are quite divided on these *concilia*. Were
they Catholic or Montanist? The allusion to the paschal fast at the beginning of this chapter 13 moves in the direction of Catholic synods held on this occasion. Yet see Marot,
"Conciles anténicéens," 25, note 7.

[36] See Joseph A. Fischer, "Die Synoden im Osterfeststreit des 2. Jahrhundert," *Anua-
rium Historiae Conciliorum* 8 (1976) 15-39 (with bibliography).

[37] Eusebius, *History of the Church*, 171; 5: 23, 1: Ζητήσεῶς . . . οὐ, σμικρᾶς.

Lord's resurrection from the dead be celebrated, and that on that day alone we should observe the end of the Paschal fast."[38]

The synods which were held to resolve this question are only clearly attested to for Palestine, Pontus, and Osroene, and of course for Asia, the place where the dispute originated. For Rome and for Corinth it is disputed to know if it could be a question of episcopal synods in the sense of assemblies of bishops. For Gaul it could hardly be a question of this.[39] According to Eusebius there was a unanimous and universal decision (πάντες τε μιᾷ γνώμῃ... τοῖς πανταχόσε). In other terms, after the different synods and the exchange of letters which resulted from them, there was a unanimous reception of the decision which had been made. Such is Eusebius' opinion and such is probably the reality at the moment in which he wrote his *History of the Church*. In his time the Quatrodecimans were only a weak sect.

Now let us go back to the facts such as Eusebius' dossier reports them. For him, the debated question was not without importance. Victor of Rome considered it to have been vital for the Church since he "attempted at one stroke to cut off from the common unity all the Asian dioceses, together with the neighbouring churches, on the ground of heterodoxy, and pilloried them in letters in which he announced the total excommunication of all his fellow-Christians there."[40]

Eusebius has not passed on to us Victor's letters: those to Polycrate of Ephesus where he ordered him to observe the Roman usage, those supposed where he called for the meetings of synods everywhere about the question, those where he excommunicated the churches of Asia and their neighbors. The fact is that this excommunication raised an outcry. Even those who received the paschal usage of the Romans "very sternly rebuked Victor." They did not receive Victor's manner of proceeding and counseled him to "turn his mind to the things that make for peace and for unity and love toward his neighbours."[41] Here intervenes the long letter of Irenaeus of Lyons in favor of tolerance. He did not consider the question of the paschal fast to be without importance. He himself "held that the mystery of the resurrection of the Lord must be celebrated only on the day of Sunday." The question was not new, Irenaeus said. The presbyters, that is, the bishops of Rome who preceded Victor, were well aware of this

---

[38]   Ibid.
[39]   See Junod, 176ff.
[40]   Eusebius, 172.
[41]   Ibid.

difference in usage for the paschal celebration, and nevertheless they "used to send the Eucharist to Christians from dioceses" who observed the Quatrodeciman practice.[42] The question was raised between Polycarp and Anicetus. This did not impede the communion between them, "and in the church Anicetus made way for Polycarp to celebrate the Eucharist."[43] One will note the connection between the debated question and the celebration of the Eucharist, which is the other side of the excommunications pronounced by Victor. Irenaeus—who carried well his name, Eusebius said—added that Polycarp and Anicetus "parted company in peace, and the whole Church was at peace, both those who kept the day and those who did not." More than that, for Irenaeus "the divergence in the fast emphasizes the unanimity of our faith."[44] What is important is to safeguard peace with one another and this peace is expressed in the sharing of the Eucharist.

From this controversy and the synods which were held on its occasion we can retain the following points:

1. The two practices, Quatrodeciman and Sunday, intended to base themselves on an apostolic tradition, and thus "to receive" and keep such a tradition alive.

2. The paschal celebration touched the heart of the Christian mystery and is in direct connection with the Eucharist. To receive the apostolic tradition of each of these two practices was connected to what Paul, according to the first letter to the Corinthians, had himself received by tradition, transmitted, and written in order that this tradition might be correctly received anew.

3. The local synods which were held were unanimous in confirming, and thus receiving, the practice of the Sunday celebration of the paschal mystery, but the bishops and their synods did not receive the excommunication pronounced by Victor against the Quatrodecimans because his motives were badly based.

4. After Irenaeus' intervention peace was reestablished between the Churches. Peace in Irenaeus' terms is a higher good which is attached to

---

[42]   Ibid., 173.
[43]   Ibid.
[44]   Ibid.

the work of salvation and to Christ's presence in his Church, and which the sharing in the Eucharist expresses. It must always be received anew.[45]

5. After all is said and done, reception happens at the level of each local church for which the bishop is responsible. Solidarity functions between the churches, but the final responsibility of reception is found in the local community.[46] It is not enough that the bishops "receive" either in council or by letters. It is necessary that this reception also be that of the clergy and of the people who are confided to them by God and who are the carriers with him of living tradition.

The meeting of synods on the paschal quarrel, the first which are clearly attested, is exemplary for the different aspects of reception. One could also analyze the African synods and the exchange of letters on the occasion of the question of rebaptism: Rome, Carthage, Caesarea in Cappadocia, Alexandria. Here, as in the case of the Quatrodecimans, one is in the presence of two opposed practices. Their apostolic foundation is less clearly affirmed by the protagonists. There was also a double reception; that of the Roman usage and of the theory on which it was based. Augustine, at the moment of the Donatist quarrel, elaborated the theology which was missing and which was received by the Church of the West. The African practice, defended also by Firmilien of Caesarea, was received by St. Basil and, through him, by the Greek East even up to today.

In the working of synods there is thus a place to distinguish at least two levels of reception: the doctrine or the practice which the synods received, i.e., which they defended against the contrary doctrines or practices; and the synodal decisions—creeds or tomes, or doctrinal or disciplinary canons—which had to be received by the churches and by their faithful.

CONCLUSION

The history of the early church teaches us about the reception of letters read in Sunday assemblies of the communities, about the progressive reception of books which would form the canon of the New Testament, and about reception in the first episcopal synods. On the other hand, it tells us very little about two capital domains in ecclesial life which have been the

---

[45]   Dom Bruno Reyders, who was a specialist on Irenaeus, showed at one time, and not without verisimilitude, that Irenaeus alluded to Victor's attitude in the paschal controversy, in the passage of the *Adversus Haereses* cited above (4: 33, 7); see already 4: 26, 3. Bruno Reyders, "Premières réactions de l'Église devant les falisifications du dépôt apostolique: Saint Irénée," in Olivier Rousseau et al., *L'Infallibilité de l'Église* (Chevetogne: Éd. de Chevetogne, 1962) 48-50, note 45.

[46]   See the fine remarks in this regard by Tillard, *L'Église locale*, 448-451.

object of reception on the part of the whole Church: the structure of the eucharistic celebration and the triple ministry of bishop, presbyter, and deacon. This last is already attested to by Ignatius of Antioch, but when and how was it received by the ensemble of the churches? There is a lot of incertitude on this matter.

The same goes for the structure of the eucharistic celebration. In this regard one can observe three facts: (1) all the Churches accepted the bi-partite structure of the celebration of the Word of God which precedes that of the sacrificial memorial of the Lord; (2) the order of Scriptures is always and everywhere one which goes from an eventual reading of the Old Testament to New Testament writings and to the terminal and culmi-nating point which presents the reading of a Gospel pericope; (3) the complexity of the primitive history of the eucharistic prayer itself. The recitation of the institution in Paul (1 Cor 11: 23ff) and in the Synoptics already has a liturgical tone, but how did its reception come about in the celebration of diverse churches and how did it happen that certain tradi-tions, such as that of the *Didachè* 9 and 10, were not integrated into the eucharistic prayer? There are many hypotheses, as is known, and here is not the place to discuss them.

Our overview has thus led us from reception such as it is formulated by Paul in the first letter to the Corinthians, across the later stages of recep-tion at Corinth, but also at Rome and elsewhere. Naturally this has led to reflection on the process of reception of the New Testament writings of which Irenaeus remains a privileged witness, and finally to reception of the apostolic tradition or apostolic traditions across the synods of the paschal controversies and the intervention of the same Irenaeus. This in-tentionally limited inquiry permits several observations to be made:

1. Reception takes place at different levels: that of the Christians of a local church (some can "receive" and others reject; this is the case of the Corinthian Christians to whom the letter of Clement was addressed); the level of this local church as such; the level of the grouping of local churches.

2. Reception covers at the same time and simultaneously several areas of ecclesial life: proclamation of the gospel, canonicity of Scripture, ministry in the apostolic succession (a question already posed by 1 Clem 42-44), communication and communion between the churches by the ex-change of letters and synods, but also—and first—by the Eucharist.

3. The ultimate criterion of reception is the gospel transmitted since the apostles and coming from the apostolic tradition. Christ's mystery

and the Spirit's action are at the root of all acts of reception, and the eucharistic celebration (or the sharing in the Eucharist) is the sign of communion in this reception.

4. Local churches can have contrary traditions in the reception of an apostolic tradition; this is the case of the Quatrodecimans whose tradition was opposed to the majority of churches, who held for dominical celebrations of the paschal mystery. This would also be the case in the baptismal question at the third century. Nevertheless, a choice is at work within the same communion; one of the two traditions would be definitively received, the other abandoned. If two practices, each considered as *the only* valid one, were maintained, it is because the communion was compromised if not broken. The breadth of Irenaeus' view who preferred peace, that is canonical and sacramental communion, to uniformity, from at a time when the peace of the faith was safe, is scarcely found during the course of the first centuries of the Church's history. A pope such as St. Leo would require of Dioscorus of Alexandria that he follow the Roman liturgical usages, from which those received at Alexandria (eucharistic fast, time of ordinations, Sunday celebrations) could not diverge, and that at a time where there was no doctrinal disaccord yet separating the two churches, in 444, that is, five years before the "robber council" of Ephesus.[47] According to St. Leo, the Roman usages were received from St. Peter who handed them on to St. Mark. There had thus been at Alexandria a poor reception which must be corrected immediately. Such was the beginnings of the relations between Leo and Dioscorus. It is known how later on this latter refused to "receive" the Roman Christology of Leo's tomes which appeared to him unfaithful to that of St. Cyril.

The example of 444 has led us beyond the temporal limits which we fixed for ourselves. But if we have permitted this derogation it is in order to highlight by contrast Irenaeus' attitude, two centuries and a half earlier, on what it is essential to receive.

Translation by James H. Provost

---

[47]   Or 445. Leo, *Ep.* 9, *PL* 54: 624A: "Cum enim beatissimus Petrus apostolicum a Domino acceperit principatum, et Romana Ecclesia in ejus permaneat institutis, nefas est credere quod sanctus discipulus ejus Marcus qui Alexandrinam primus Ecclesiam gubernavit, aliis regulis traditionum suarum decreta formaverit: cum sine dubio de eodem fonte gratiae unus spiritus et discipuli fuerit et magistri, nec aliud ordinatus tradere potuerit, quam quo ab ordinatore suscepit. Non ergo patimur, ut cum unius nos esse corporis et fidei fateamur, in aliquo discrepemus; et alia doctoris, alia discipuli instituta videantur."

RESPONSE TO EMMANUEL LANNE

Angel Antón-Gómez*

Faced with the description by Emmanuel Lanne of some processes of reception in the early Church, a systematic theologian has to be faithful to the hermeneutical need to return to the theological source of all reception in the Church, which is itself essentially a community of reception. I begin therefore by highlighting from the point of view of systematic ecclesiology the intimate connection between the theological foundations of reception in the Church at all times, and its processes which are always active at various levels in the life of the ecclesial community.

The Theological Source of Reception

In the *paralambanein* (1 Cor 11: 23; 15: 1-3) and, respectively, *dechesthai* (1 Thes 2: 13; 2 Cor 6: 1) of the New Testament, the ecclesiologist discovers a double dimension to reception. From the anthropological point of view, it is a reality which man cannot do without, destined as he is by his Creator to live with and for other men and, as such, to develop his human existence in a constant give and take; from the theological point of view, all reception in the Church goes back to the same source, the free and gratuitous self-communication of God which culminates in the eschatological and unrepeatable Christ event, and requires that man receive it, giving his personal and free response in the act of faith. Precisely because both dimensions always go together, are indeed inseparable, the ecclesiologist uses the term "reception" in its primordial sense in order to indicate the human act of Christian faith which has its origins in God granting his gifts to man, while man receives them and communicates them to other believers. In the Church the believer, at the same time as he relives the dimension of communion with other believers, must deepen his own faith in a way which is ever more profound and personal. The affirmation also is valid in reverse: that the re-reception of his faith in the personal sphere of the believer brings with it a re-vitalization of his faith so far as he is a member of the believing community. The term re-

* Università Gregoriana, Rome (Italy).

ception, then, which *in recto* describes a strictly theological-anthropological reality, also includes *in obliquo*, because of the principle of unity between the orders of creation and redemption, the human living out of the faith of the believer with the other members of the ecclesial community and of each of these communities with the other local and/or regional churches within the *communio ecclesiarum*.

Reality of Reception Precedes Theological Reflection

Just as the reality of the Church precedes all theological reflection about itself, so reflection in the Church has its theological protology which applies in its multiple historical processes.[1] It should come as no surprise that the writings of the New Testament should echo reception, not attesting to it by a formal act, but rather in so far as its reality belongs essentially to the being and acting of the Church. The community of the first disciples of the Risen Lord had a real and living awareness of having received the *euaggelion tou Theou* and/or *tou Xristou* and of being witness and herald of this eschatological message of salvation, to make it present efficaciously so that it might be received by all peoples and all generations. Right from the start it is necessary to emphasize that the historical processes of reception are not just results of a deductive elaboration of abstract principles of ecclesiology. The nexus which obtains between doctrine and life, reflection and ecclesiological praxis—the outline of the three concrete processes of reception in Lanne's presentation bears this thesis out—and, finally, between the development of the Church and of ecclesiology by means of the existential channel of its concrete and historical reality and the doctrinal channel of theological reflection on the Christian message of saving truth and grace, has always been a relation of mutual and reciprocal enrichment.[2] The desired synthesis is not achieved by a merely inductive analysis of the data which historical and sociological science offers us on the multiple processes of reception in the life of the Church, nor by means of a merely deductive reflection on the most original in the theological protology of the ecclesial reality in the richness of its mystery. This synthesis can only be reached as the result of a work of systematization capable of bringing together in itself the data afforded by the sciences involved in the examination of the multiple historical

[1]   Angel Antón, *El misterio de la Iglesia. Evolucion historica de las ideas eclesiologicas*, 2 vols. (Madrid: Editorial Católica, 1986-1987) 1: 14-23.
[2]   I reaffirm this thesis in Angel Antón, "La 'recepcion' en la Iglesia y eclesiología. 1: Sus fundamentos teológicos y procesos históricos en acción desde la epistemologia y eclesiología sistemática," *Gregorianum* 77 (1996) 57-96.

processes of reception which, emanating from the common source of all reception in the ecclesial sphere and coursing through its own proper channels, flow together in the abundant torrent of reception of the Church which is essentially a "community of reception."[3]

The Notion of Reception from the Perspective of Systematic Ecclesiology

Faced with the rich and polyvalent reality which includes the phenomenon of reception in contexts as diverse a those Lanne sketched out, it is imperative that my reply begin by outlining a notion of reception which can be adopted as a basis for further theological reflection. It is only descriptive because reception, belonging as it does to the very essence of the Church, is no more given to a "real definition" in the strict sense than is the Church itself. The speaker takes as his starting point a notion which he qualifies as "broad" and paradoxically which I take to be too limited to the three processes of reception analyzed in his presentation.

From the point of view of systematic ecclesiology and having understood reception in its protological and global sense, one can describe it as:

> a (complex and slow) process by means of which a Christian community differentiated in itself (pastors and faithful all: *cum and sub*[4]) and different from others in the interecclesial ambit (given the necessary differentness within the communion of churches) with the help of the Holy Spirit, recognizes as good for itself and accepts new understandings of the Christian message contained in Scripture and in the living Tradition of the Church as authentic elements of the catholic and apostolic faith.

Reception includes therefore, in its global sense, all that the Church "is and believes" (cf. *DV* 8a): the *depositum fidei*, its authentic proposition by those who possess the charism of truth in the Church, and other manifold forms of expression of and witness to the Christian message which are fruit of the *sensus fidei* of the faithful as a whole and which are transmitted in ecclesial institutions, liturgical sacramental practice, theological reflection and doctrine, the example of Christian life, etc.[5]

---

[3] Cf. Jean-Marie R. Tillard, *Church of Churches: The Ecclesiology of Communion* (Collegeville, MN: Liturgical Press, 1992) 118-140. Idem, "Reception-Communion," *One in Christ* 28 (1992) 314-318.

[4] "... plebs sancta Pastoribus suis adunata," *Dei verbum* 10; "sub ductu sacri Magisterii," *Lumen gentium* 12.

[5] This notion gathers and synthesizes those elements which I take as essential to describe the theological reality of "reception" and on which there is a consensus among theologians on the various notions proposed by them. I would like to highlight three such here

This descriptive notion of reception, whose grade of effectiveness is deducible only to the thread of analysis of each one of its multiple historical processes and using the method of the sciences involved in them, is based on the concepts of revelation-transmission of the Christian message expounded in *Dei verbum*, which understands its perennial transmission in and through the Church more as *paradosis* of the truths of the faith, as a vital making present of the event of grace communicated *eph'hapax* to humanity in Christ.[6]

It is very necessary to accept here that the notion proposed embraces, since the early Church, a great variety of concrete processes of reception.

1. As it has as its object all that the Church is and believes, there are processes of reception with the aim of transmitting the Word of God, the *depositum fidei*, liturgical sacramental practices, institutional structures and organisms, ethical norms, disciplinary and doctrinal decisions, etc.

2. Churches at local and/or regional levels of the *communio ecclesiarum* in the catholic and ecumenical ambit are in the category of subjects of reception. Trying to be more precise about the exogeneity between subjects of reception in the communion dynamism of mutual giving and receiving, which every process of reception brings with it, I have problems in admitting that there is enough at the level of diocesan churches. The danger of theoretically and practically absolutizing local elements and of narrowing the horizon of catholicity is little short of unavoidable. The processes of reception in the early church were at the level of ecclesial units made up of the local and/or regional churches around the great cultural centers with their own spiritual, liturgical, theological, juridical, and sociocultural heritage.[7]

3. With regard to the process of reception, slow and complex in itself, this goes far beyond the pure act of obedience or a mere passive accep-

for their outstanding paradigmatic value: Yves Congar, "La 'reception' come realité ecclésiologique," *Revue des Sciences Philosophiques et Théologiques* 56 (1972) 369-403, esp. 370; Jan Willebrands, "The ecumenical dialogue and its reception," *One in Christ* 21 (1985) 217-225, from 222; Karl Rahner, "Ekklesiologische Grundlagen," in *Handbuch der Pastoraltheologie. Praktische Theologie der Kirche in ihrer Gegenwart*, ed. F.X. Arnold, Karl Rahner, et al. (Freiburg: Herder, 1964) 1: 119.

[6] Cf. Angel Antón, "La comunidad creyente, poradora de la revelación," in *La Palabra de Dios en la historia de los hombres. Commentario temático a la Const. Dei Verbum*, ed. Luis Alonso-Schökel and A. M. Artola (Bilbao: Mensajero, 1991) 285-291, 302-310.

[7] Alois Grillmeier, "Konzil und Rezeption. Methodische Bemerkungen zu einem Thema der ökumenischen Diskussion der Gegenwart," *Theologie und Philosophie* 45 (1970) 324-332.

tance.[8] Reception supposes within the believing community an activity of discernment and maturation in faith which also includes "the act of consent and, as far as possible, of judgement on whether the object proposed for reception is for the common good."[9] Reception does not guarantee the legitimacy of a doctrinal or disciplinary decision handed down by the competent authority;[10] neither does nonreception with nothing further deny its legitimacy. Such a decision, however, when it has been proposed in a non-definitive way, can decay progressively, if it is not ratified by reception. Further, "the definitive decision of faith needs reception, given that without reception, it would not integrate itself in the living reality of the Church."[11]

Theological Elements Implied in the Process of Reception

The descriptive notion of reception proposed above contains the theological-ecclesiological elements which are indispensable in the theology of reception. We can deduce these from the three processes of reception analyzed in the presentation.

1. The Church essentially a "community of reception." This goes back in the History of Salvation to the fount of all reception, the supreme self-communication of God in Christ to humanity (*Ecclesia fructus salutis*). The primitive Christian community was very conscious of this, its *kairos*, or of having received from Christ and from his Spirit all the benefits of redemption, to transmit them to men through the various channels through which flows the stream of life and communion in the new messianic community of salvation (*Ecclesia medium salutis*).

---

[8] Cf. Edward J. Kilmartin, "Reception in History: An Ecclesiological Phenomenon and Its Significance," *Journal of Ecumenical Studies* 21 (1994) 36-37. Harding Meyer observes correctly that the term "reception" can suggest an attitude of passivity which would obscure the element—essential in every process of reception—of the active participation in some way of the whole believing community: "Les présupposés de la réception ecclésiale ou le problème de la 'recevabilité': Perspectives luthériennes," *Irénikon* 59 (1986) 12-13.

[9] Ibid.

[10] On the other hand, Thomas Rausch is right when he affirms that "in the early Church disciplinary or doctrinal ecclesiastical decisions only acquired normative value for the later Church when they had been received by the communion of the churches and, in the last instance, by the Christian faithful themselves." Thomas P. Rausch, "Note. Reception, past and present," *Theological Studies* 47 (1986) 501-502.

[11] Andreas M. Wittig, "Konzil und Rezeption. Die Annahme von Glaubensentscheidungen eines Konzils durch das Kirchenvolk als Akt des geschuldeten Glaubensgehorsams oder als Beitrag zur Gultigkeit der Entscheidung," *Annuarium Historiae Conciliorum* 20 (1988) 246.

2. *Sensus fidei - consensus fidelium* and reception. This *sensus fidei* or capacity and instinct to discern and know the realities of faith—more intuitive than deductive, more experiential than noetic—is always a factor of capital importance involved in the concrete processes of reception in the early church and in the Church at all times.

3. *Paradosis* - reception. The study of the processes of reception in the early church bears out the affirmation of Yves Congar which includes a solid theology of tradition among the theological elements of reception.[12] *Dei verbum* starts from the original source of reception-tradition in the Church, the revelation and self-giving of God which reached its fullness in the Word made flesh. The primary receiver and subject carrier of this divine self-communication is the People of God in its totality. When *Dei verbum* presents the factors in Tradition it begins by mentioning reflection on and study of the words and institutions by the faithful and concludes the summary with the contribution of the pastors in the task entrusted to them of proclaiming the Christian message. The ultimate guarantor of fidelity in the whole process of tradition and/or reception on the part of the whole people of God is the action of the Spirit (*DV* 8). Reception is an indispensable component of paradosis which highlights the subjective aspects of the same. Just as revelation is inconceivable without a subject to receive it, Tradition would cease to be Tradition without the reality of "reception."

4. Ecclesiology of communion and reception. The lived experience of *koinonia* (cf. Acts 2: 1-47; 1 Cor 10: 16-17) was in the primitive community the warm humus in which the flowering of the processes of reception sketched out by the speaker flourished.[13] The rediscovery of communion as a central reality always living in the double channel (doctrine and practice), through which flows the great tide of the benefits of redemption which the Church has received and still receives without ceasing from Christ, is decisively stimulating an awakening of new consciousness and practice of reception in the different aspects of the life of

---

[12] Cf. Congar, 392.

[13] Cf. Tillard, 66-76, 186-216; Pier C. Bori, *Chiesa primitiva. L'imagine della comunità degli origini—Atti 2, 42-47; 4, 32-35 nella storia della Chiesa antica* (Brescia: Paidea, 1974); Josef Hainz, *Koinonia. "Kirche" als Gemeinschaft bei Paulus* (Regensburg: Pustet, 1982); idem, "Koinonía, koinoneo, koinonos", in *Exegetical Dictionary of the New Testament*, ed. Horst Balz and Gerhard Schneider (Grand Rapids, MI: Eerdmans, 1990-1992) 2: 303-305.

the Church today and in the intra- and inter-ecclesial ambit of the communion of the churches.

5.   Theology of the local / regional church and reception. The speaker has demonstrated that in the early church there was an intense exchange of spiritual goods through the vital processes of reception at the local and/or regional level between different churches of the *communio ecclesiarum*. Each one of these had a living consciousness of being an active subject in the total process of reception in the Church of Christ. Any reflection therefore on any determined process of reception, whichever one it may be, in order to be valid, must necessarily start from the analysis of the data which the ecclesial units contribute on the concrete reality of reception, within the sufficiently broad spatio-temporal and socio-cultural coordinates which permitted a greater degree of differentness or exogeneity than obtains today between diocesan churches.

6.   Synodality/conciliarity and reception in the Church. It is an acquired datum—the speaker analyzes it in the third process of reception—that the stimuli which most intensely built up the praxis of *koinonia* and reception in the early church simultaneously developed the synodal and/or conciliar element which is a spontaneous expression of both in the life of the Church at local and/or regional levels. Further, the multiplicity of forms of synods and councils and of their respective reception processes in the ambit of communion between the local and/or regional churches manifested that synodality and/or conciliarity was a structural dimension of the early church and of the Church at all times.

7.   Reception, guarantee of catholicity. I take catholicity in *Lumen gentium*'s sense, as in two passages of paradigmatic value: first, it speaks of catholicity referring to the unity of the plurality of local and/or regional churches (*LG* 23); second, of the catholicity which, taking on the legitimate peculiarities of the local churches, contributes to unity achieving its fullness (*LG* 13). Unity and catholicity are a gift of Christ to his Church which brings with it the task of daily making them present in a more perfect way, intensifying the communion dynamism of mutually giving and receiving the spiritual goods, which each church has as its own particular goods, through a series of processes of reception in the multiplicity of aspects of ecclesial life.

8.   Reception, reality and action of the Spirit. It would be an unpardonable omission to close this summary of the theological foundations of reception in the Church, without highlighting the action of the Spirit included in each one of its many processes in the life of the Church. As

the Spirit is the constitutive principle and source of life in the Church and because reception is something which belongs essentially to its constitution and mission, it must be affirmed that this is a reality maintained by the action of the Spirit in all its historical processes. It is not possible to trace a theology of reception without an adequate development of pneumatology. Nor is it by chance that one proves in the history of ecclesiological ideas that when pneumatology was relegated to a secondary level in ecclesial understanding and praxis, the living space for reception was also reduced, so that it could not develop and ended up being identified with the mere act of obedience to hierarchical authority and non-reception was identified with the rejection of this obedience.[14]

Conclusion

In concluding my reply to Abbé Emmanuel Lanne, I insist once more on the nexus between the theological-ecclesiological foundations of reception and the concrete processes of reception in the Church. There have been three stages in my reply: first, the point of departure has been to trace a descriptive notion of the reality of reception in the Church and, more concretely, from the point of view of systematic ecclesiology, gathering up the elements of greater convergence among ecclesiologists; second, the notion presented was not deduced from abstract principles nor from a merely theoretical ecclesiology with pretensions of imposing itself on the practice and life of the Church, but rather it is the result of the analysis of the concrete processes of reception sketched out in the presentation; third, in an attempt at theological reflection I have tried to highlight the theological-ecclesiological elements involved in the reality of reception.

Translation by Denis E. Carlin

---

[14] Cf. Antón, *El misterio de la Iglesia*, 242-245, 302-305, 526-527, 548-550, 920-923, 961-963 (*supra*, note 1).

MOST IMPORTANT QUESTIONS
CONCERNING RECEPTION

After the introductory presentations (Professors Routhier and Manzanares) gave an orientation to the colloquium and the historical perspectives were initiated (Professors Lanne and Anton), the working groups formed on the basis of common languages were asked to determine the most important problematic questions regarding the general topic of the colloquium. Their contributions on April 9, 1996 were the following.

Spanish Language Group

1. Reception in relation to modern theories and techniques of communications. Undoubtedly theories and techniques of communications have repercussions in the theological process of reception. This leads naturally to a deepening understanding of the nature of the faith, to an actualizing of the function of the magisterium and its normative character in the life of the Church, and therefore, also in the processes of reception, to fostering a climate of freedom under the guidance of the Spirit. In other words, it is necessary to disclose in greater depth the specific function of the magisterium as a witness and guarantee of the Church's fidelity to the apostolic tradition. At the same time it is necessary to offer channels for the *sensus fidei* to guarantee real processes of reception.

2. Reception and inculturation. It is necessary to pursue in depth the Church's self-consciousness as a "community of reception." Accordingly one perceives the great relevance of inculturation. How does the Church receive and assimilate contemporary culture in its pluralism? How does it dialogue with and integrate the great diversity of cultures? To what extent are historical or socio-cultural factors determinative for reception?

3. Reception and failed receptions. Past and present history reveal possible examples of non-reception or of problematic receptions. Would not its recognition, analysis, and evaluation shed light on theological reflection on reception? Given possible cases of non-reception, are we not required to revise both the modalities of consultation and decision-making as well as the methods of perceiving reception?

French Language Group

From the exchange among the participants, four questions seem particularly important.

1. An effort at conceptual clarification of what is meant by "reception." For that it would be necessary to have a minimum consensus on the different elements of the definitions which are proposed, in specifying the modalities, levels, forms, and juridic structures such as councils, assemblies, and diocesan synods which permit a non-juridic practice. It would also be appropriate to place the concept of reception in relationship with other realities which are related to it: inculturation, appropriation, *recognitio*, and the *sensus fidelium*. Is there a transformation of what is received in the process or the very act of reception?

2. A certain number of questions linked to a "reduced" or "deficient" practice of reception in today's Church. Reception cannot be reduced to an "authority-submission" model. It is not a one-way process but rather a two-way or circular process among partners who may be unequal. Yet it seems that we have not truly moved beyond an "authority-submission" model. This datum explains in part the current difficulty in developing a theology of reception which is based on the experience which the churches have of reception. As one participant emphasized, "One tries to articulate a theology of what one does not have."

3. Some present difficulties relative to the practice of reception:

a. the very problematic functioning both of councils within the local churches and of the synod of bishops as well as the absence of ecclesial places of discernment both within the local church and among the local churches;

b. the apparent absence of reception at the grassroots level, i.e., with the local churches as the point of departure; the difficulty for a bishop to be the witness of the faith of his people; the absence of intermediary instances of reception between the local churches and the Roman center;

c. the difficulty experienced by the local churches in situating themselves as "subject churches" and in developing a particular law or practicing a horizontal reception between local churches;

d. the absence of particular councils where one would find not only bishops, but also the lay faithful with priests and deacons; in some sense episcopal conferences seem to have taken the place of particular councils so that in a certain sense laity, priests, and deacons have been excluded from the debates.

4. Other questions linked to the cultural dimension of the process of reception. Can one link a "crisis" of reception in the Church with a "crisis" of socialization or of democracy in the global society? What is the weight of cultural and contextual factors in the process of reception? Historically they seem to have played a great role; will it be the same today in the reception of ecumenical agreements?

English Language Group

1. Contemporary culture poses questions for reception. What is handed on is not always heard in the same way; it is difficult to grapple with differences between local churches in what is being received.

Even the very idea of "receiving" a message runs counter to how people today think religious or moral truths are to be arrived at; for many contemporary people, religion is something private, a matter of "my opinion." When reception implies receiving something from an authority, it runs into the contemporary crisis of authority; or at least, it suffers from the way in which authority has acted in handing on the tradition.

2. Reception has a necessary aspect of "tradition," in the sense both of content and of the process of handing on. We tend to focus on the end product, but reception is a lengthy, on-going process, discerning where the faithful are, then the voice of authority, then reception (i.e., an open process, not just automatic). Yet where this process has been attempted, as with the extensive listening process the U.S. bishops conducted before their pastoral letters on peace, and on the economy, it does not seem to have helped the "reception" of the letters appreciably within the local churches which constitute the *ecclesia americana*.

This points up the need for people to have the basics in order to be able to receive. The process for tradition and reception is illustrated by the process of Christian initiation through which one is formed to be able to say "I believe" (rather than "these are the various opinions"). Reception requires re-reception of one's own patrimony. There can be a temptation to respect received positions without exploring, discovering new aspects of one's own heritage.

If reception is related to tradition, what type of theology of Tradition is at work? Some bishops consider themselves delegates of the pope, which is not the Tradition. How does reception operate at the center of the communion of churches? The consultation process and structures have improved (e.g., consultative bodies, the Roman Synod of Bishops), but the candid exchange of views seems to suffer, especially when "authorities" consult only those whose positions they already know to be in harmony with the judgments of those same authorities.

3. Reception involves the community. An example is in the role of the community in the ordination of new ministers. The community has a role in the formation of the candidate, and during the ceremony has a role in attesting that this candidate has the community's faith, is prepared to be a person who can articulate the tradition and pass it on both within the community and to the world at large.

The "passivity" dimension of reception has to be counterbalanced by the sense of the local church as a subject-church. The most important concepts of "communion" and "collegiality" have been providentially recovered, but are often understood in terms of a communion of bishops rather than the communion of the churches which they head and for which they speak—much less the communion within the local church.

4. Models of communication are pertinent. Today we have the paradox of vastly superior communications media, yet so much passivity. Instead of a greater discernment of tradition, many since the council have stopped short at a level of what they learned in catechism rather than doing the work to discern the authentic tradition. Moreover, communication has been focused on the word, without attending to the pneumatological dimension.

5. What is "dangerous" about reception (which is how Congar characterized it)? Would Catholics be split apart if local churches became actively engaged? What are the dangers in reception?

Is reception being used to cover up our past mistakes which have become the "received way of doing things," even though they may be wrong, and so we are not willing to change?

6. There are some fundamental questions about the meaning of terms. What is the relationship between reception, acceptance, recognition, etc.? Should we be speaking more of a "critical" reception? Reception implies "non-reception," but can we speak of a process really resulting in non-reception? Can one distinguish "receiving" or "non-receiving" as part of the process which may lead to reception? Can one distinguish "recognition" (acknowledge something as potentially good) and "reception" (accept something as my own)? Does non-reception mean, at times,

that "this does not relate" to our situation, but this non-reception is not necessarily a rejection?

Italian Language Group

1. The subject of reception-transmission. From the reports emerges the multiplicity of subjects: pope, council, local church, etc. Today, when one speaks of reception, to what subject(s) is one referring? If reception occurs on the part of diverse subjects, what importance do they assume in relationship to reception itself?

2. The role of authority. Professor Lanne has developed the topic of the reception of the gospel in Corinth. The texts cited (especially 1 Cor 11 and 1 Cor 15) suggest the role of authority regarding reception-transmission. In confronting a mistaken reception, Paul invites a re-reception. Today, when we speak of reception, to what authority are we referring? What is the role of authority regarding reception and non-reception or the necessity of a re-reception?

3. Language. At times the language of documents bespeaks a past theological framework which does not help reception; in fact it often provokes a reaction of resistance or distancing. The "reduction" of Christian truth to the "doctrinal" dimension precludes entrance into the dynamic of a broader communication.

4. Reception in the first millennium is linked to tradition. The concept of reception-tradition is distinguished vis-à-vis that of authority-obedience from pure obedience and from the idea of arbitrariness. The tradition in fact is formed through a progressive reception, and this in turn happens in the context of tradition.

5. How express the concept of reception in canonical terms and how does this modality of expression differ in respect to other formulations?

Translation by Thomas J. Green

RECEPTION OF COUNCILS FROM NICEA TO CONSTANTINOPLE II: CONCEPTUAL DIVERGENCES AND UNITY IN THE FAITH, YESTERDAY AND TODAY

BERNARD SESBOÜÉ*

Reception, considered as a human and social phenomenon and not as a juridic act, is a reality which happens before it is reflected upon. This aspect applies especially to the reception of the early councils, which present this particular trait without presenting us with any concept of reception. From Nicea to Constantinople II we are in a period where it is the ensemble of the theology of an ecumenical council which is developing and where the phenomenon of reception lives its first and painful rebounds.

It would therefore be dangerous to impose too rigorously a concept of reception developed in the light of twenty centuries of not only ecclesial but also juridic tradition, to a time where the facts preceded the words. However, it is not possible to search without having some idea of what one is looking for. I am therefore obliged to use a hypothetical concept of reception, sufficiently workable to permit me to determine the object of my research.

The term "reception" is absent from the major theological dictionaries, at least in France. On the other hand, a number of articles or recent books have sketched a definition of reception. I believe it would be useful, at the beginning of this report, to cite some of these which correspond more to what will be the object of my research.[1]

* Centre Sévres, Paris (France).
[1] General bibliographic indications: Joseph Hefele—H. Leclercq, *Histoire des conciles d'après les documents originaux*, vol. 1-3/1 (Paris: Letouzey et Ané, 1907-1909); *Le concile et les conciles. Contribution à l'histoire de la vie conciliaire de l'Eglise* (Chevetogne: Éd. de Chevetogne, 1960); *Problems of Authority*, ed. John M. Todd, (Baltimore: Helicon, 1962); Alois Grillmeier, "Konzil und Rezeption. Methodischer Bermerkungen zu einem Thema des ökumnenischer Diskussion," *Theologie und Philosophie* 45 (1970) 321-352; Yves Congar, "La 'réception' comme réalité ecclésiologique," *Revue des sciences philosophiques et théologiques* 56 (1972) 369-403 (bibliography); Wilhelm de

Some Definitions of Reception

Here is the definition which Yves Congar proposed in an article he wrote on this subject in 1972:

> By "reception" I understand here the process by means of which an ecclesial body makes its own a determination which it did not give in regard to itself, in acknowledging in the measure promulgated as a rule applicable to its own life. Reception includes something quite other than what the Scholastics call "obedience." . . . Reception . . . relation includes a relationship proper to consent, and eventually of judgment, in which the life of a body is expressed which brings into play its own original spiritual resources.[2]

This definition situates reception as an ecclesial reality on its own level. It is a process, thus it takes time; a process of acceptance, of consent, of assimilation by infiltration of a doctrinal determination received from legitimate authority. This process is distinguished from formal obedience because it is active and it even includes a "judgment" on the thing received.

Jean-Marie Tillard's definition in 1982 is close to that of Congar:

> What is meant . . . by reception? Simply the course by which the ecclesial body, judging that it *recognizes* its faith in it, *makes its own* a rule of faith, a doctrinal precision, a norm which a church instance has determined. It is not a pure and simple acquiescence, but the welcome which justifies harmony between what is proposed and what one "knows" of the faith (often more by instinct than by explicit science).[3]

The International Anglican-Roman Catholic Commission (ARCIC) has reflected a lot on the ecclesial notion of reception. Here is its definition from 1981:

> By "reception" we mean the fact that the people of God acknowledge such a decision or statement because they recognize in it the

---

Vries, *Orient et Occident. Les structures ecclésiales vues dans l'histoire des sept premiers conciles oecuméniques* (Paris: Cerf, 1974); Heinrich J. Sieben, *Die Konzilsidee der Alten Kirche* (Paderborn: F. Schöningh, 1979); Gilles Routhier, *La réception de Vatican II dans une Eglise locale* (Paris: Cerf, 1991).

[2]   Congar, 370.

[3]   Jean-Marie Tillard, in *Initiation à la pratique de la théologie*, ed. Bernard Lauret and François Refoulé (Paris: Cerf, 1982) 1: 165-166.

apostolic faith. They accept it because they discern a harmony between what is proposed to them and the *sensus fidelium* of the
whole Church. As an example, the creed which we call Nicene has
been received by the Church because in it the Church has recognized the apostolic faith. Reception does not create truth nor le-
gitimize the decision: it is the final indication that such a decision
has fulfilled the necessary conditions for it to be a true expression
of the faith. In this acceptance the whole Church is involved in a
continuous process of discernment and response.[4]

The commission gives an important weight to reception in the process
of validating a conciliar determination. Reception does not take the place
of the legitimate authority which made a decision. Nevertheless, it appears
necessary for the full guarantee that the determination in question is an
authentic expression of the faith. The ultimate truth of a council becomes
clear in this perspective by a process of coming and going between doctrinal authority and the *sensus fidei* which resides in the Christian people.[5]

Another definition can be taken from a document of the French episcopal commission for Christian unity in response to questions from the
Roman Secretariat in 1985:

Reception . . . is a factual datum which is proven after the fact.
Generally it goes beyond the setting of one generation because it
enters progressively into the life and thought of the Church. It
speaks the concrete meaning that the people of God at the same
time recognize and confer on the definition, in its manner of passing into the flesh and blood of ecclesial life. Reception enters into
the concrete sense of a definition. Certainly it does not contradict
it, but it enriches it, discloses the implications but also manifests
its limits and shows what needs to be completed or recovered.
This process engages the entire church body and enters into what
ARCIC has well-described as an exchange between doctrinal authority and the Christian people.[6]

---

[4]   International Anglican-Roman Catholic Commission, *Final Report 1981*, in *Growth
in Agreement*, ed. Harding Meyer and Lukas Vischer, Ecumenical Documents 2 (New York
and Geneva: Paulist Press and World Council of Churches, 1984) 102.

[5]   On this point see the great reticence of the Congregation for the Doctrine of the
Faith in its response on behalf of the Holy See to the *Final Report* of ARCIC I (1982). See
"Vatican Response to ARCIC I Final Report," *Origins* 21/28 (December 19, 1991) 444.

[6]   Commission épiscopale française pour l'Unité des chrétiens, "À propos de l'évalu-
ation du Rapport final de l'ARCIC I," *Documentation Catholique* 84 (1985) 875.

This description of reception underlines well all the newness brought by this process to a dogmatic definition. Reception declares itself, it is not decreed. It is not manipulated or provoked in any way. It engages the *sensus fidelium* in what is vital to it. But the document does not say that reception pertains to the validation of the moment of truth implied in the definition. A non-received definition does not remain any less true.

Finally, there is the conception of reception proposed by Gilles Routhier in his 1993 book:

> Reception is the spiritual process by which the decisions proposed by a council are welcomed and assimilated in the life of the local church and become for it a living expression of the apostolic faith.[7]

"Spiritual process" means a process of concrete faith with regard to a fact which is "a good to be received." It involves spiritual affectivity and an experience in the order of existence. I would complete this definition only on two points: the "spiritual" process is also a doctrinal process; on the other hand, if reception goes by local churches, it also becomes a fact of the universal Church, at least in the case where it succeeds.

Reception and Roman Confirmation

It is important to distinguish clearly the reception described here from the confirmation of a council by the pope, and from any juridic act of recognition of a council's authority. This distinction of the two concepts is to be maintained all the more because with the course of time confirmation became more and more a formally juridic act, while at the beginning the act of the bishop of Rome was at first understood as an act of reception. Roman confirmation is one element of the complex process of reception, but it is quite far from taking it over completely. In any case, if it appears to be necessary it is far from being sufficient. For the fact of reception cannot be reclaimed by any positive law. According to P. Fransen, it is an organic fact, not a juridic one. Yet it becomes law in itself but without ever taking on the form of law.

Reception: Distinct but Inseparable from its Attestation

But here we have come full circle: how to catch up with the living fact of reception without passing through its attestation? And how to avoid

---

[7]   Routhier, 69.

confusing the former with the latter? The problem here is the same as for tradition, to which reception pertains in some manner: tradition as a theological reality of the Church's life is something other than the monuments of tradition. Yet we cannot reach it in truth without passing through the "monuments of tradition." Likewise it is only through written or institutional witnesses that we can come to the fact of reception.

But if these witnesses can be found in liturgy and catechetics, they are more numerous among theologians, bishops, and in documents of a magisterial or juridic character. Reception spontaneously takes on juridic expressions, which are not external to it since they attest to it across time. Globally, documents issued by lay people are rare; what has come to us through historians are certain events where the people reacted according to the spontaneity of their faith: those listening to Arius at Baucalis did not receive his preaching, nor did Eusebius of Dorylée those of Nestorius. But these are events of refusal and conflict; they leave more tracks than acceptance, which of itself is largely silent. Who does not say anything, consents!

We are thus in the presence of a subtle dialectic whose two poles must be respected. We touch there the reason for the evanescence of the theology of reception—not of its fact—in Catholic tradition. This has a spontaneous horror for what appears to it to be flux and cannot be enclosed in clear formulas, or which does not rest on authorized documentation. This is why, even as it has a tendency to reread the monuments of ancient tradition in seeing there any number of expressions of the magisterium, it has simply put off reception to the juridic confirmation on one hand, and to the duty of obedience on the other. This attitude is connected with what concerns the Catholic position vis-à-vis the *sensus fidelium*; one praises it in the texts, but one is reluctant to interrogate it and to listen to it on certain delicate points in order to make it a competitor to magisterial reflection. Newman was right in saying: "Though the laity be but the reflection or echo of the clergy in matters of faith, yet there is something in the "pastorum et fidelium *conspiratio*," which is not in the pastors alone."[8]

A Case Study: Reception of the Scriptures

As a preview to the study of the first council I would like to evoke a reception, as generally forgotten as it was fundamental, by its object and its

---

[8]   John Henry Newman, cited by John Coulson, "Le magistère de l'Eglise et son rapport au sensus fidelium," *Concilium* [French edition] 108 (1975) 107.

antiquity: that of the canon of Scriptures. The process of the reception of the Scriptures speaks clearly the very nature of reception.

The canon of the Scriptures was "received" during the second century according to a process which totally escapes us, since we can only catch up with its result. It is clear that this process is very anterior to the first formal written attestations which we have of it, and even more to the first conciliar determinations, infinitely much later. What is equally remarkable, across even the hesitations concerning the belonging of a particular book to the canon of the New Testament, is that the idea of the canon preceded its concrete determination. Irenaeus is a privileged witness of this anteriority. Later on, the term "reception" took on an official value to express the relationship of different councils both with regard to the confession of faith as well as to the holy books: "received and venerated," Trent said.

***

These indications on reception are sufficient to give a general direction to my research. My task thus is to uncover by means of diverse attestations which we can reach, the concrete phenomenon of the reception of the early councils up to Constantinople II. This is a very rich history but it could be extended even further.

RECEPTION OF NICEA I AND THE BIRTH OF CONCILIAR THEOLOGY[9]

The theology of an ecumenical council did not pre-exist the first experience of such a council, as Sieben has clearly shown. One can say that the development of conciliar theology happens in the very movement where the council was received. The attestations of the one are the attestations of the other. Conciliar theology's progress is that of Nicea's reception.

Yet before Nicea the meetings of local and regional councils had already led—other than the law of unanimity of decisions taken—to the practice of sending synodal letters to the bishops of the region who were absent, in order that they might subscribe to the decisions which had been taken. There thus began to develop a manner of episcopal reception which one could call, with Alois Grillmeier, "exogenous." Sometimes the syn-

---

[9]   See Monald Goemans, *Het agemeen Concilie in de vierde Eeuw* (Nijmegen-Utrecht: Dekker & Van de Vegt, 1945); Ignacio Ortiz de Urbina, *Nicée et Constantinople* (Paris: l'Orante, 1963).

odal letters were sent beyond the region with a view toward ecumenicity.[10] This supposed that the bishop is in the Church and the Church is in the bishop, according to Cyprian's expression. The episcopal college is a microcosm of the whole Church. The authority of the first councils was largely received, to the extent that not only did the bishops feel themselves bound by their decisions, but that a new synod did not dare to change them.

The Council's Self-Awareness

To what degree did the fathers of Nicea have an awareness of the novelty of this conciliar reunion with regard to previous synods? It was called by the emperor, which gave it a solemnity and a particularly strong stake; it gathered bishops of East and West; it thus went beyond the category of earlier regional councils. It called itself "The Great and Holy Council,"[11] which constitutes a new manner of expression; it attributed to itself a particular authority because it took binding disciplinary decisions concerning vast regions, such as the Schism of Meletius at Alexandria; it issued disciplinary canons concerning the universal Church and the Sees of Alexandria, Antioch, Jerusalem, and Rome. No council had dared to take such measures concerning the universal Church.

The same was true in doctrinal matters. "In the awareness of the Fathers, the decision of the council had a definitive and irrevocable character. It was taken expressly 'in the name of the Catholic Church.' "[12] A real threshold was crossed in the awareness of the authority of a council, but a threshold of degree, crossed on the basis of the conviction of the authority which the earlier councils enjoyed. We must not read too quickly here an awareness of an "infallibility." The continuation of the history will show that the ensemble of churches was far from sharing these convictions.

Papal Confirmation?

Can one speak of "confirmation" by Sylvester? This is generally affirmed, but Ortiz de Urbina does not even make an allusion to it. In fact, it is deduced more often than attested by documents contemporary with

---

[10]   Cf. Hilaire Marot, "Conciles anténicéens et conciles oecuméniques," in *Le concile et les conciles*, 39-41. This view of things, inspired by Eusebius' witness, has been questioned by Allen Brent, *Hippolytus and the Roman Church in the Third Century* (Leiden: E. J. Brill, 1995).

[11]   Cf. de Vries, 17-18.

[12]   Ibid., 18.

Nicea. It is known that the documents which overstate Nicea's confirmation by Sylvester are false.[13] Historically this pope remained passive and exterior to the whole business carried on by Constantine. He declined the invitation to come to Nicea, we are told, "because of his great age"; but in fact he lived ten years longer. On the other hand, his absence constituted a precedent; it is undoubtedly the origin of the institutional practice according to which the pope does not assist personally at the deliberations of an ecumenical council.

That being said, Pope Sylvester was certainly in agreement with what his legates did and signed at Nicea. Otherwise he would have reacted. But does this fact have the juridic value of the confirmation which will be revindicated by Rome in the second half of the fourth century and which will be verified beginning with Chalcedon? The question seems anachronistic. Sylvester *received* Nicea without difficulty, but it is impossible to say if he did this as Patriarch of the West, or if he saw in it an exercise of his primacy, and in this case what sense he gave to the position he took. Modern day historians are always tempted to interpret a retroactive normalization of the conditions for the meeting at Nicea, in the light of rules which would be established later.

Pope Julius I, Sylvester's successor, was of the opinion in 335 that the Council of Nicea was on the same level as that of Antioch in 269. According to Sieben, he seemed to think that the judgment issued against the Arians was subject to revision.[14] De Vries is not convinced: "But after all, it must be said that what made the singularity of the Council of Nicea also did not appear very clearly in Pope Julius' letter."[15] The same pope wrote in 341 that Sylvester's legate had confirmed the true faith at Nicea,[16] but he said nothing specifically of an act by his predecessor.

Fifty Years of Conflict for Reception

The awareness that the council might have had of itself was far from being shared at the time by the ensemble of churches. It was not evident to everyone's eyes that Nicea was a radically new case in relationship to the earlier councils. The opposition appeared quite early because of the

[13] Cf. Hefele-Leclercq, 1/1: 627-631. The authors hold, however, that Sylvester's confirmation of Nicea was asked and obtained. But their arguments remain quite out of date.
[14] Sieben, 31-34.
[15] De Vries, 22-23.
[16] Ibid., 33.

additions to the creed taken from philosophical vocabulary. The Nicene Creed scandalized a number of people because it "innovated," and the pejorative connotation to such a term in ancient language is well known. It is useless to give here the list of the many synods which were held in the East and which marked the oscillations of position for or against Nicea. The reception of Nicea began, thus, in the East by a rather massive "non-reception" and continued for fifty years of bitter doctrinal conflicts, marked by numerous reversals. It was the object of a debate in which the council's authority was progressively recognized in the facts and of a same theologizing movement in law.

The conclusion of these debates took place at the First Council of Constantinople in 381. "The faith of Nicea," Congar wrote, "was 're-ceived'—and totally—only after 56 years of strife punctuated by synods, excommunications, exiles, interventions, and imperial violence. . . . The Council of Constantinople marked the end of these quarrels."[17] We do not know exactly what form this "reception" took, since the acts of this council have been lost. But we verify it by means of the Constantinopolitan Creed which takes up the highly disputed term of "consubstantial." Also, the first canon affirmed that one must "not abrogate the profession of faith of the fathers united at Nicea in Bithynia."[18] Finally, the letter of 382 to Pope Damasus witnesses that "for the evangelical faith, ratified by the 318 fathers at Nicea of Bithynia, we have held well."[19] This seems to echo the repeated efforts of Basil of Caesarea in his correspondence to make as the only conditions for return to ecclesial communion the acceptance of the Nicean faith and the confession that the Spirit is not a creature. Nicea's reception by Constantinople I is in fact the conclusion of the conflictual process of reception which preceded this council. Moreover, this latter, despite the tensions which it also knew, was a council of reconciliation which sought to bring about religious peace in the East. The conciliar decision of 381 constitutes a conclusive witness to the reception of the Nicene Creed.

Athanasius' Role

The council's authority was defended by Athanasius who was an active agent for its reception. But Sieben has shown that Athanasius him-

---

[17]   Congar, 372.
[18]   *Conciliorum Oecumenicorum Decreta [COD]*, ed. Josepho Alberigo et al., 3rd ed. (Bologna: Istituto per le scienze religiose, 1973) 31.
[19]   *COD*, 28.

self knew an evolution in his manner of appreciating Nicea.[20] With time he gave it an increasingly greater authority. At the beginning, the legitimacy of Arius' condemnation did not appear evident to him. The formula of faith did not yet have an absolute authority. He sought to refute the Arians by Scripture and reason, and not by invoking the council. Then, in 356, Nicea constituted a summary of orthodoxy. The council became for him the faith of the Catholic Church as such, without speaking of its absolute authority. Finally, in 363, he said that the Nicene Creed is as "the word of God which lives eternally." As to the "infallibility" of Nicea according to Athanasius, Sieben makes the following judgment:

> If one understands by "infallibility of councils" an impossibility of being mistaken tied, one might say, automatically to the realization of certain conditions, then one must affirm that Athanasius did not know such an infallibility. He knew certainly the criteria to which one could measure the legitimacy and the relative value of synods, but not such that they could justify an absolute pretension to the truth.[21]

De Vries thinks that Sieben is a bit of a minimalist here. The vocabulary of infallibility is evidently not that of the time. But Athanasius made some very strong affirmations: "Eternal rock placed at the frontier"; "engraved stone erected for always against all heresy"; "word of God which lives eternally."[22] These expressions go in the direction of the council's absolute authority.

Athanasius also appealed to reception as an argument in favor of Nicea: "All the *oikoumene* gave its agreement (to Nicea's faith) and now that many synods have been held, all, whether in Dalmatia, Dardanis, Macedonia, Epiria, Greece, Crete and the other islands, as well as Egypt and Libya and the majority of Arabia, recall it."[23]

It is thus manifest that Nicea's reception as an ecumenical council with an irreformable authority was, according to Athanasius, the fruit of a journey during which the elements of the problem were progressively clarified. He moved from the observation/conviction that the Council of Nicea renewed the faith of the apostles, to the conclusion that it could not

[20] Sieben, 25-67.
[21] Ibid., 63; trans. in de Vries, 237.
[22] Athanasius, *Epistola ad Afros, Patrologia Graeca [PG]* 26: 1032A, 1048A.
[23] Ibid., *PG* 26: 1029; cited in Congar, 375.

have been otherwise, since the council represented the universality of the Church safeguarded by the Spirit in the faith. From there, the council became by right a reference point and the formal characteristics of its reunion became the references for later discernment of the ecumenicity of councils. This reflection contributed to the reception of the council at the same time that it is based upon it. According to Goemans, Athanasius thought that the following conditions must be met in order that a council might be ecumenical: all the universe must be represented there; the decision was taken unanimously; the decree was in conformity with Scripture, the teaching of the apostles, and the tradition of the holy Fathers. He does not mention the need for a participation by the bishop of Rome.

From Reception in Fact to Legal Doctrine

Later, in the conflict between Cyril and Nestorius, the Council of Nicea became a touchstone for understanding the Incarnation. The conflict between the two men rested on the basic agreement that their debate must be judged on the conformity of their thought to the council's teaching. This is a capital act of reception.

Nicea is an excellent example of the passage from a factual authority to a legal authority. To the degree that with the passage of time and the discernment exercised on the conflicts provoked by Nicea, one perceives that the council confirmed the faith of the apostles, that it is faithful to the Scriptures, and that it is effectively received by the largest number of churches, one affirms that it spoke in a definitive manner and one ties that to its ecumenical character; it is the unanimity of the Church which is expressed there. Now, the Church which is expressed there cannot err in the faith. Thus the great vicissitudes of Nicea's reception were the crucible in which was developed the awareness of the decisive and definitive authority of an ecumenical council.

THE RETROACTIVE RECEPTION OF CONSTANTINOPLE I[24]

An Eastern Synod

The case of Constantinople I is particularly interesting since this is an Eastern synod, received sometime later as an ecumenical council. Con-

---

[24] See Ortiz de Urbina (*supra*, note 9); Adolf M. Ritter, *Das Konzil von Konstantinopel und sein Symbol* (Göttingen: Vandenhoeck & Ruprecht, 1965); *La signification et l'actualité du II concile oecuménique pour le monde chrétien d'aujourd'hui* (Geneva: WCC, 1982).

stantinople I was convoked by Emperor Theodosius. This is without doubt the reason for which the letter of 382 to Pope Damasus, drawn up by the fathers present at the council in the previous year, spoke of the "ecumenical" Council of Constantinople.[25] Use of the term shows its still imprecise character which does not correspond to the "trademark" which we give it today: it was a council of all the East. If it had been truly ecumenical, Damasus would not have the idea of celebrating a new one in Rome so soon. But he sought to have a voice of the West heard in the matter.[26] Moreover, the acts of the council were communicated to Rome not for approval, but in a spirit fraternal communication.[27] This is perfectly coherent with the non-ecumenical character of the council and shows that the question of papal confirmation was not raised until Ephesus.

A Mysterious Silence

From then on, mystery reigns around Constantinople whose acts have been lost, a grand silence during three quarters of a century. We have only certain allusions of Theodore of Mopsuest to this council and to its creed in his catechetical homilies,[28] which Theodore himself refers to as the Nicene Creed. Constantinople's Creed seems unknown or forgotten at the time of Ephesus, since it is the Nicene Creed to which Cyril and Nestorius refer in their conflict. One could say that the Constantinopolitan Creed was not received until Chalcedon. The Council of Ephesus observed the same silence; it referred officially to the Nicene Creed and even forbade the composition of any confessions of faith other than that one.[29] At the Robber Council of Ephesus in 449, the Council of Constantinople I and its creed are also ignored. But Nestorius, then Eutyches,

---

[25] *COD*, 29.

[26] The interpretation of the awareness of the council's ecumenicity given by Chr. S. Konstantidinis, in *La Signification et actualité*, 78-80, seems unduly inflated. It is based on a unique use of the term "ecumenical," and underestimates the massive fact of the West's absence.

[27] Ortiz de Urbina, 224. But Photius would later much speak of an approval of Constantinople I by Damasus; see Hefle-Leclercq, 2/1: 41.

[28] Theodore of Mopsuest, *Homélies catéchétiques*, 9: 1 and 14, ed. Raymond Tonneau and Robert Devreesse (Vatican City: Biblioteca Apostolica Vaticana, 1949) 213-215 and 235-237. Konstantidinis, 81, holds that the Constantinopolitan Creed was already in use for baptisms in the last decades of the fourth century, and cites several authors as witnesses to this creed during this initial period. We cannot verify these affirmations, which lack references.

[29] *COD*, 65.

lived for at long time at Constantinople and they should normally be the witnesses for a synod held in that city.

The Reception by Chalcedon

Constantinople I was received by Chalcedon as ecumenical beginning with the reception of its creed. It seems that it was the imperial commissioners who, in their desire to have a formula of faith adopted at Chalcedon, brought out of their archives the Constantinopolitan Creed.[30] They had it read before the fathers, after that of Nicea. The creed is then received by acclamation. In Chalcedon's definition we see the appearance of the recapitulating process by which a new council refers to the preceding ones. The text of the definition says in its prologue:

> We have renewed the unerring creed of the fathers. We have proclaimed to all the creed of the 318; and we have made our own those fathers who accepted this agreed statement of religion— the 150 who later met in great Constantinople and themselves set their seal to the same creed.

> . . . we decree that pre-eminence belongs to the exposition of the right and spotless creed of the 318 saintly and blessed fathers who were assembled at Nicea when Constantine of pious memory was emperor; and that those decrees also remain in force which were issued in Constantinople by the 150 holy fathers in order to destroy the heresy.[31]

The council then cites the two creeds of Nicea and Constantinople, putting them in this way on the same footing and considering them as the expression of the same faith. The second is considered as the complement and confirmation of the first. There is here undoubtedly the concern not to contravene the decision of Ephesus forbidding the formulation of any new confession, since the Constantinopolitan Creed was anterior to that council.

We have here an act of reception of one council by another. The term "we define," must not be surcharged semantically by its later usage. It designated an act of authority, while the act of Chalcedon was at the same

---

[30]   This initiative thus came from lay people present at the council.

[31]   COD, 83-84; English trans. from The Decrees of the Ecumenical Councils, ed. Norman P. Tanner (London and Washington: Sheed & Ward and Georgetown University Press, 1990) 83-84.

time an act of authority and of submission. It was not for Chalcedon to confirm Nicea which had already been received; it proclaimed that it "received" it, in order to inscribe its own teaching in a tradition which was already authoritative. It does recognize that the faith of Constantinople I was defined by that council. It then received it in the same terms as that of Nicea, but this time with the double meaning of submitting itself to it as to a norm, of recognizing it, but also of giving it an authority which it did not have up until that time. The reception of the Constantinopolitan Creed by Chalcedon brought about from then on a process of reception in the churches of which it is a major step.

Note that Chalcedon did not feel the need to define formally the ecumenicity of Constantinople I.[32] But its act of reception and proclamation of the creed of 381 had the effect that Constantinople I would from then on be recognized and received in the list of ecumenical councils. "It is a sort of consensus of the Church," Camelot writes "which recognized after the fact this character (of ecumenicity) to a council which had nothing ecumenical in its intention or in fact."[33]

Reception in the West

From the end of the fifth century the Gelasian decree counted Constantinople I among the "ecumenical" councils.[34] In 519 Pope Hormisdas tacitly recognized this council in receiving the confession of faith of Patriarch John.[35]

There remains the question of the canons of Constantinople I of which the third, which dealt with the primacy of honor of this city and ushered in canon 28 of Chalcedon, caused difficulty at Rome. At Chalcedon the Roman legates reacted against this third canon as they did for that of Chalcedon. Leo, later, said that these canons had never been transmitted to Rome.[36] But here we are leaving the domain of reception to regain that of confirmation.

Later the creed was received in a liturgical manner in the Sunday celebration of the Eucharist. Peter the Fuller, a Monophysite opposed to

---

[32]   Ortiz de Urbina, 239, speaks too juridically and anachronistically when he refers to an "ecumenization" which would be a sort of *sanatio in radice* of Constantinople I.

[33]   Pierre-Thomas Camelot, in *Le concile et les conciles*, 73 (*supra*, note 1).

[34]   Ortiz de Urbina, 234.

[35]   Congar, 372.

[36]   Ortiz de Urbina, 236-237.

Chalcedon, introduced the custom of reciting the Nicene-Constantinop-
olitan Creed at all solemn Masses. Thus marked his rejection of Chalcedon. The Chalcedonians followed his example, then the West.

The teaching of the reception of Constantinople I is thus an original
fact. It shows us the unpredictable character of reception, so unpredictable that it could have a retroactive force on the manner of considering a council. It underlines again how facts engender law and how the juridic dimension of the conciliar act of Chalcedon engendered in its turn a
new fact of reception.

EPHESUS (431)[37]

The "True" Council of Ephesus

With regard to Ephesus the first question is to know where the true
council is to be found: on the side of Cyril, or of John of Antioch? In the
midst of the vicissitudes of what Duchesne has called "this lamentable
and complicated tragedy," where two assemblies of bishops mutually
anathematized each other, it was quite difficult to make a valid discernment. But at their arrival the Roman legates joined Cyril's assembly and
were in solidarity with him, bringing him the adherence of the West, a
central point for the ecumenicity in the genesis of the council. Moreover,
even in the East, no one claimed the formal legitimacy of the rival synod
held by John of Antioch. Finally, Celestine, who from the beginning of
the debate was on the side of Cyril against Nestorius and who gave certain delegations to the former before the conciliar meeting, rejoiced in
the re-establishment of orthodoxy by diverse letters to Cyril and to the
church of Constantinople.[38] He died on July 26, 432, and was succeeded
by Sixtus III who took an analogous position in diverse letters, but also
intervened in favor of reconciliation by asking that John of Antioch and
his partisans be received in communion if they condemned what the
Council of Ephesus had condemned.[39] But before 433 one must say that
the entire matter remained in suspense. The pope and Emperor Theodo-

---

[37] See Pierre-Thomas Camelot, *Ephèse et Chalcédoine* (Paris: l'Orante, 1962); J.
Liébart, s.v. "Ephèse," *Dictionnaire d'Histoire et de Géographie Ecclésiastiques* 15
(1963) 554-579; Ch. Fraisse-Coué in *Histoire du christianisme*, ed. Jean-Marie Mayeur et
al., 2: *Naissance d'une chrétienté (250-430)* (Paris: Desclée, 1995) 499-550.

[38] *Acta Conciliorum Oecumenicorum [ACO])*, ed. Eduard Schwartz (Berlin and
Leipzig: W. de Gruyter, 1927-1932) 2/2: 88-101.

[39] Cf. Hefele-Leclercq, 2/1: 385.

sius were aware of this and worked by various initiatives for peace. All were persuaded that matters could not stay where they were. Moreover, in such a short lapse of time, one could not yet speak of reception.

The Act of Union of 433

It would not have been possible to get out of the impasse without the Act of Union of 433 which gives to Ephesus a necessary condition for its ecumenicity: unanimity among the conciliar fathers by means of the common recognition of a same doctrine between the leaders of the two camps. The Act of Union became part of Ephesus on the same basis as the letters of Cyril to Nestorius. What is remarkable in this union is that Cyril recognized the dogmatic legitimacy of a confession of Christological faith expressed in the Antiochian language, while John separated himself from Nestorius and recognized the *theotokos*. This Act of Union is a major dogmatic text because it essentially takes up the confession of faith of John of Antioch's synod and it makes it the matrix for the Chalcedonian definition. John's synod launched a formula destined to be received ecumenically. Newman made a good diagnosis of the value of the Act of Union which gained the adherence of the opposing parties. He judged that the subsequent reception by the proponents complements the council and is an integral part of it.[40] It is thus on the basis of the Act of Union that the Council of Ephesus was received in the East—but not universally—which it used in reference to Chalcedon, as this council's Christological formula shows, and entered into the series of ecumenical councils.

The Pope and the Council at Ephesus

Camelot, and then de Vries, have shown that one should not speak too quickly of a Roman "confirmation" of the Council of Ephesus. At Ephesus the legates read the letter of Celestine. This was acclaimed and thus "received." But a real ambiguity remained in the understanding of this reception by the participants. The legates could consider that the council lined up behind, perhaps "submitted" to, Celestine's request and doctrine. The priest Philip said this: "The members are joined to the head." The council on its side thought it had recognized the agreement of Celestine with its own decision: "Celestine, in agreement with the council!"

---

[40] Congar, 375, citing Newman on the subject of rallying the opposed sides of Vatican I to the dogma of papal infallibility.

We see here that "reception" means something entirely different from "obedience." Camelot correctly emphasizes: "One must not see here a 'confirmation' in a formal sense of the word, the act of a higher instance sanctioning definitively the decisions of an assembly, which do not until then have the force of law. There are not two distinct authorities here, subordinate the one to the other, the council and the pope. There is the council deliberating and deciding with the pope, present and acting by his legates."[41] Likewise, one must not give to Celestine's letters rejoicing in the decision at Ephesus a juridic value of confirmation. Camelot says again with great clarity: "The documents do not leave us any trace of a formal confirmation by Sylvester, Damasus, Celestine, or Leo of the decrees of Nicea, Constantinople, Ephesus, or Chalcedon. The texts where some see an intervention of this sort are without authority or try to say something else."[42]

Sixtus III, however, Celestine's successor, recalled in a letter addressed to Cyril that John of Antioch and his followers must "be admitted again into the communion of priests if they were ready to reject all that the holy synod rejected *with our confirmation*."[43] For a long time people concluded that this is a confirmation by the pope. De Vries judges rather that it is simply a reference to the agreement given by the legates at the Council of Ephesus: "To understand a 'solemn confirmation' in the style which is understood today appears to us, especially at this time, to be a pure anachronism."[44]

The question is thus very complex. It seems that at Ephesus there was an underlying difference at work with regard to the relationship of authority between the pope and the council. This difference reappeared at Chalcedon. It was without gravity in the immediate context because it bore upon the interpretation of a consensus. But it is the carrier of a heavy ambiguity for the future.

The Nestorian Church

The agreement between Cyril and John of Antioch was not universally "received." The Nestorian movement remained in the region of Edessa. Some bishops refused the Act of Union and "joined with the Syrian

---

[41]   Camelot, 70.
[42]   Ibid., 69.
[43]   *ACO* 1/1 7: 144; cited by de Vries, 81.
[44]   De Vries, 81.

church of Persia which in 486 at the Synod of Seleucia, officially adopted Nestorianism. . . . Thus the Nestorian Church separated at the same time from the Church of Constantinople and from the Byzantine Empire. The Nestorianism of the Persian Church was affirmed in the most complete fashion at the Synod of 612 which adopted the clearly heterodox formulas of Babai the Great."[45] A part of the Nestorian Church was later reconciled with Rome in the 16th century. But there still exists a "Holy Apostolic and Catholic Assyrian Church of the East," more commonly called the "Assyrian Church of the East." Its current Catholicos-Patriarch Mar Dinkha IV asked that this Church no longer be called "Nestorian" given the pejorative connotation of the adjective. On November 11, 1994 this patriarch signed with Pope John Paul II a "Common Christological Declaration," a text closer to the Act of Union and to the definition of Chalcedon than the language of Ephesus. But it clearly expresses the incarnation of the son of God in the womb of the Virgin Mary. The *theotokos* gives place to two types of expressions: "Mary, Mother of Christ our God and Savior," from the Assyrian; "Mother of God" and "Mother of Christ" from the Catholic side.[46]

It is thus the Council of Ephesus which occasioned the first lasting schism in the Church, and not Chalcedon as is often claimed. There are no Arians anymore, nor any Pneumatomachians, but there is still a Church in the Nestorian tradition. The non-reception of a council is thus capable of creating a millenary schism. This point will be verified again in history; such is the decisive role of reception.

On the other hand, one cannot call this agreement a reception of Ephesus by the Assyrians, and still less a "re-reception" of this reception by the Catholic side. It is a new agreement, which has taken a necessary step back with regard to the conflicts of the past and in a certain degree with regard to their vocabulary. It is this agreement in itself which will from now on be submitted to the process of reception.

The Robber Council of Ephesus (449)

This council merits an entire study by itself because it constitutes a model example of "non-reception." The causes are clear: the violence which dominated the debate; the partisan spirit of the Monophysite ten-

---

[45] Pierre-Thomas Camelot, "Nestorius-Nestorianisme-Eglise nestorienne," in *Catholicisme* 9 (1982) 1172.

[46] Text in Pontifical Council for Christian Unity, *Information Service* 88 (1995/1) 2-3.

dency; the refusal to listen to the Tome of Leo to Flavian; and the decisions which were taken. Such a council is at the opposite extreme of the rule of unanimity. The legates could only speak their disagreement.

Leo I called it a robbery and with the Roman Synod united around him he "condemned all that took place by Dioscorus against the canons, in tumult and for secular hatreds."[47] Must one say that this council was "broken" by Leo, in a juridic sense which would be the inverse of confirmation? This does not seem to be the case. For Leo this robbery did not exist as a council, since the voice of the West was not listened to there.

But it was not received in the East, either. Chalcedon began its work by "washing the dirty linen" of the synod of 449. Its members were in the position of the accused. A firm agreement reigned to say that this gathering had been scandalous. Afterwards, no one dared to invoke it during the hundred years of discord around Chalcedon.

CHALCEDON (451)[48]

The Reception of Chalcedon in the East and in the West

If the Council of Nicea experienced fifty years of conflict before its reception, that of Chalcedon, for a long time considered as "damned" by some, had a century of them in the East before being recognized, and then not by everyone. This history is known with great details after the volume by Grillmeier completely dedicated to the ups and downs of "reception and opposition."

We observe first of all the political stakes, evident at the time, in the reception of a council bearing on a point of faith. This is why the emperors were very closely involved. But one also sees that the first concern of the emperors was not for the authenticity of the faith but for unity and peace in the empire, for which religious peace was a necessary element. The succession of dogmatic edicts of the emperors always had for their pur-

---

[47]   *ACO* 2/4: 28; cited by Camelot, *Ephèse et Chalcédoine*, 112.

[48]   See *Das Konzil von Chalkedon. Geschichte und Gegenwart*, ed. Alois Grillmeier and Heinrich Bacht, 3 vols. (Würzburg: Echter Verlag, 1951-1954); Faith and Order Commission, "Le concile de Chalcédoine: son histoire, sa réception par les Eglises et son actualité (1969)," *Irenikon* 44 (1971) 349-366; Alois Grillmeier, "The Reception of Chalcedon in the Roman Catholic Church," *The Ecumenical Review* 22 (1975) 383-411; idem, *Le Christ dans la tradition chrétienne. 2/1: Le concile de Chalcédoine (451): réception et opposition* (Paris: Cerf, 1990).

pose to reestablish this unity around the ecclesiastical pole which they judged to be the majority. Hence a series of reversals which went from the condemnation of Chalcedon (Encyclical of Basiliscus), to its discreet abandonment (Henoticus), even to a turn around in its favor, unstable with Anastasius but firm with Justin. In the West, reception was spontaneous and did not raise any problems. But the crisis in the East involved a schism of thirty-three years between the two parts of the Church, a sinister omen.

At the beginning of this process, Emperor Leo organized a vast inquiry concerning Chalcedon among the bishops, which enables us to estimate the degree of the council's reception in the East at this time. The replies divided into two groups: for the first, Chalcedon is only the confirmation of Nicea. The second is more attentive to the proper authority of Chalcedon because of the divine assistance of which the Fathers of 451 were the object. One moves thus from a relative assent to an absolute assent.[49]

It is language which at first sight was the basis for the conflict; some said "one nature" in fidelity to Cyril; others said "two natures" in keeping with the definition of Chalcedon and the Tome of Leo. The conflict is thus for a large part a "schism of language." The Severian Monophysites did not hold the rude doctrine of Eutyches at all. This feature carries an openness to reconciliation, since it was the same "dogmatic" Christ that was received but across two linguistic spaces.

The imperial manipulations did not finally impede the slow process of a majority recognition of Chalcedon. Across time and a number of twists and turns, the council made its way and was received by the greater number of the bishops, and one can think that they were the witnesses of the faith of their people. The West also enjoyed its role in this reception. However, Chalcedon continues to pose difficult hermeneutic problems.

The Council and the Pope

From Ephesus to Chalcedon the relationship of the pope to the council was modified in favor of Leo. The difficulties which remained after Ephesus, and even more the problems raised by the Robber Council of Ephesus, several times put the pope in the position of arbitrator. Chal-

---

[49]   Cf. Grillmeier, *Le Christ dans la tradition chrétienne*, 281-334.

cedon is the first council with regard to which the pontifical primacy was formally exercised.

However, the ambiguity discerned with regard to Ephesus coming from the divergence of understanding of the relationship between the pope and the council remained. When the fathers of Chalcedon acclaimed Leo's letter and proclaimed their accord with Cyril, what did they do? From Paschasinus' point of view, they accepted it and submitted to it. From the point of view of the Eastern fathers, they recognized the agreement of Leo with Cyril, judged it orthodox, and on this basis "received" his letter. De Vries has clearly shown that the East and the West did not have the same interpretation of the event.[50] Nevertheless, the debate concerning canon 28 on the primacy of honor of Constantinople after Rome put the council in a state of dependance with regard to Rome.

The pontifical legates refused to ratify this canon 28 of Chalcedon. This is why the council drafted a very reverential letter to the pope to ask him to confirm only this litigious canon. According to de Vries this leads us to suppose that for the rest of the conciliar decisions the legates' adherence was enough.[51] A little later, the emperor and Anatol, the Archbishop of Constantinople, made the same request. Leo took his time in replying, but only to the emperor, to Anatol, and to Pulcherius. He only replied on the question raised on canon 28. He formally refused to confirm it. In the letter to Pulcherius he said: "As to the decrees adopted by the bishops contrary to the rules established by the holy canons of Nicea, in union with the piety of your faith, we annul them, and, via the authority of the blessed apostle Peter, we definitively break them (*cassamus*)." We are henceforth in the presence of a juridic decision concerned with juridic texts, on the part of someone who judged himself to have the full authority to do this.

But Leo did not reply to the letter of the council. Now the Monophysites argued from this fact that the pope had not confirmed Chalcedon. The emperor wrote again in 453 to ask the pope to confirm the Christological confession. He asked him to "ratify" (*bebaiôsthai*) the council's decision. Leo then replied to the conciliar fathers on March 21, 453. He proclaimed that he gave his adherence to the decisions of the council, but only in mat-

---

[50] De Vries, 126-149.
[51] Ibid., 124.

ters of faith (*in sola fidei causa*).[52] We can consider that we have here the first confirmation of a council by the pope in the formal sense of the term, a confirmation which was paradoxically requested by the East. But in his reply, Leo made clear the full awareness of his authority. This confirmation thus enters into the much larger process of reception, which in the East was carried on in a rather independent manner.

Time having settled things down, Gregory the Great (590-604), when the First Council of Constantinople was still a poor relation in the conciliar series, dared to compare the four first ecumenical councils to the four Gospels: "I receive the four synods of the holy universal Church as the four books of the holy Gospel."[53]

Non-reception and the Pre-Chalcedonian Churches

It remains that the council was not received by a certain number of Churches and provoked a lasting schism of Copts, Armenians, and Jacobites. Non-reception was translated by a schism, which remains a fairly frequent law in the history of councils. Those who do not accept the last council make a schism in the name of its predecessors.

In these last decades Popes Paul VI and John Paul II have signed a series of Christological confessions with the patriarchs of various pre-Chalcedonian Churches. The guiding intention for this is the following: the new document tries to follow closely the affirmations of Chalcedon but does not use the language of two natures and accounts by means of another vocabulary for the distinction between the divinity and the humanity of Christ. Such a doctrinal reconciliation is very important because it shows that in the affirmation of the faith the reality which is aimed at takes precedence over the language which is used, the second being at the service of the first. The Catholic Church shows itself in this way capable of reconciling on fundamentals, in passing beyond the language canonized by the most celebrated conciliar definition there is.

Must one then speak in this regard of a "new reception" of Chalcedon? It is towards this which a document of Faith and Order is directed.[54]

---

[52] *ACO* 2/1 2: 158-163; cf. Camelot, *Ephèse et Chalcédoine*, 172.
[53] *Patrologia Latina [PL]* 77: 613B.
[54] Faith and Order, "Le concile de Chalcédoine: son histoire, sa réception" (*supra*, note 48).

Congar refers to it in writing: "In the setting of contemporary Christological research, which begins much more with the man Jesus of the Synoptics, one speaks of 're-reception' of Chalcedon. Chalcedon is already acquired and is not in question, but in a new context of Christological vision, and also of ecumenical research, one must proceed to a new reading of its history and of its deep intentions and thus 'receive' it anew."[55] In the same setting Congar evokes a "re-reception" of Vatican I.

I am very reserved about this vocabulary of "re-reception." First, it presupposes that a "re-reception" could be the work of a reflective and concerted action, and of official agreements between Churches. All of history shows that "reception" has never functioned this way. A "re-reception," to be worthy of its name, must function in the same manner. On the other hand, the problem of historical distance is inevitably raised. The process of reception took place across a space of time where the Churches were still concretely united in the problematic and vocabulary being used. Beyond this limit one can no longer speak of reception. This goes for the ancient councils. In fact, their authority does not address us in the same way as it did their contemporaries.

Finally, the acceptance of the language and confession of the Chalcedonian Christological formula was not required of the participants. These would undoubtedly be very surprised to learn that they "received" Chalcedon or participated in its "re-reception." The problem is one of conciliar hermeneutics. Historical distance permits us to discern better the aim of the affirmation and its language. The first is not necessarily united with the second. The Catholic Church thinks only that its signature on the new confession of faith is in keeping with its reception of Chalcedon. This is, in my view, the ecumenical approach which is to be followed for Trent and Vatican I. The non-Catholic partners should not be asked to subscribe to them, but to subscribe to new documents which the Catholic Church for its part would consider to respect the aim of its own councils. Perhaps it is the absence of a sufficient historical distance which currently keeps this type of approach from being used in Western ecumenical dialogue. These new documents are then submitted, through force of circumstances, to a new process of reception.

---

[55]   Congar, 375 (*supra*, note 1).

Constantinople II[56]

The Second Council of Constantinople (553) presents a first-rate dossier with regard to reception. The troubled conditions in which it was held are well-known, based on the quarrel between Justinian and Pope Vigilius. The violence of the first with regard to the second has even led some to question the council's freedom and thus its validity.

This council promulgated two documents: a sentence of condemnation of the Three Chapters, a long polemic text which we have retained only in Latin (except for the introduction). There then follows a series of fourteen anathemas whose title says that they are directed "against the Three Chapters." But the ten first canons constitute an interpretation of the Chalcedonian definition in reference to the affirmations of Ephesus, and do not speak of either the Three Chapters or their authors. The eleventh canon condemns Origenism, Justinian's bête noire, and the three final are directed formally against Theodore of Mopsuest, Theodoret of Cyrrhus, and Ibas of Edessa.

Constantinople II took its time in joining the pack of recognized and received ecumenical councils. The first four councils were compared to the four Gospels: was this not a closed number? And yet Constantinople II was placed progressively on their level and counted eventually as one of the seven councils—another perfect number—recognized by both the East and the West.

Throughout this century contemporary researchers have looked into the multiplicity of problems posed by Constantinople II. Can one consider as an ecumenical council an assembly which anathematized the pope and held the bulk of its sessions at odds with him, and which even

---

[56] See Robert Devreesse, *Le cinquième concile et l'oecuménicité byzantine* (Vatican City: Biblioteca Apostolica Vaticana, 1946); A. Amann, s.v. "Vigile," *Dictionnaire de Théologie Catholique* 15/2 (1950) 2994-3005; idem, "Trois Chapitres (Affaire des)," ibid., 1868-1924; Charles Moeller, "Le chalcédonisme et le néochalcédonisme en Orient de 451 à la fin du VIᵉ siècle," in Grillmeier-Bacht, 1: 637-720; idem, "Le cinquième concile oecumènique et le magistère ordinaire au VIᵉ siècle," *Revue des sciences philosophiques et théologiques* 35 (1951) 413-423; R. Janin, s.v. "Constantinople (II concile de)," *Dictionnaire d'Histoire et de Géographie Ecclesiastiques* 13 (1953) 754-766; Ignacio Ortiz de Urbina, "Quali sententia 'Tria Capitula' a sede romana damnata sunt?" *Orientalia Christiana Periodica* 33 (1967) 184-209; Francis X. Murphy and Polycarp Sherwood, *Constantinople II et Constantinople III* (Paris: l'Orante, 1974).

held a "conciliarist" thesis? How can it be that a series of popes confirmed a council which excommunicated their predecessor? In requiring
the acceptance of the condemnation of the Three Chapters, did they not
explicitly accuse Vigilius of heresy, who in his *Constitutum I* refused to
do this? Can one finally hold that there is nothing in Constantinople II
which is opposed to Chalcedon?[57]

These studies are focused on the problem of the diverse confirmations
of Constantinople II by the popes. Their reflection develops on a juridic
level and has a blind spot, for they do not ask about reception, a sign that
this question was outside the awareness of Catholic theology. The paradox of Constantinople II holds to a radical divergence between confirmation and reception: what was confirmed is no longer received because
it has become obsolete; what was not confirmed has been received as a
common good of the Church.

Confirmation by the Popes

Pope Vigilius, after a final reversal of position, confirmed the council's
canons in his *Constitutum II* of February 23, 554. But this confirmation
was addressed specifically to the canons on the Three Chapters and did
not mention the ten dogmatic canons which constituted an interpretation
of Chalcedon.[58]

His successor, Pelagius I (556-561), who accused Vigilius for the condemnation of the Three Chapters, did a U-turn himself and condemned
what he had defended up until then. Pelagius had difficulty in being admitted at Rome. In the West, several bishops became defenders of the
Three Chapters and did this even to the point of schism.

Gregory the Great (590-604), who "received with great devotion and
kept integrally the first four councils," added "I likewise venerate the
fifth," because the condemnation of the three Antiochean doctors did not
contradict the teaching of Chalcedon.[59] He even thought that the council

---

[57]   De Vries, 166-167.
[58]   "Quant à la portée des condamnations conciliaires, on notera que le pape Vigile n'a
pas eu un mot pour les dix premiers canons et que le Constitutum de 553, en soi irré-
formable, interdit de condamner les trois personnes incriminées." Murphy and Sherwood,
127.
[59]   *Epistulae*, 3: 25; 3: 10; 9: 52; *PL* 77: 478B, 613B, 985B. Cf. Murphy and Sherwood,
128.

"was not concerned at all with the faith, but uniquely with questions about persons."[60]

In short, papal confirmation and the struggle over Constantinople II concerned exclusively the Three Chapters, "not the whole dogmatic work of the council,"[61] and was contented with showing that this condemnation did not constitute in any way a denial of the Council of Chalcedon.

The Struggle Concerning Reception by Bishops

In the East, Justinian sent the acts of the council to the absent bishops, asking for their signature and obtaining it "practically without difficulty."[62] The only refusal came from the monks of the new anchorite monastery in Palestine. But the Monophysite bishops were not at all reconciled; hence, they did not receive it.

In the West, the Roman deacon Rusticus and the African Abbot Felix of Gillitanum refused the decrees against the Three Chapters. The Western bishops reacted in their regard in a very negative way, especially in Africa, in north Italy, and in Gaul. A certain number of them wrote a memorandum to Justinian to declare "very energetically that the condemnation of the Three Chapters was without any basis."[63] Under the pontificate of Pelagius I, the Church of Aquilea (Pauline) used this as the motive for a schism which lasted until the end of the seventh century. Facundus of Hermiana in Africa was also opposed to the council. Gregory the Great in his turn attempted to reconcile the schismatic Church of Aquilea but remained discreet with regard to the council's reception.

Western authors were slow to count Constantinople II among the number of ecumenical councils and many Greek sources of the seventh century seem to have only a vague idea of its work.[64]

---

[60] De Vries, 172.

[61] Ibid.

[62] Hefele-Leclercq, 3/1: 133.

[63] Ibid., 143.

[64] "On sait que cinquante années après sa célébration, Constantinople II ne jouissait pas de l'autorité reconnue au concile de Chalcédoine, dont il apparaissait comme un complément. En Orient, la tradition est si flottante qu'on hésite sur ce qui fut son principal objectif. Tandis que certains le limitent à la condamnation des monophysites survenue en 536, d'autres estiment que sa tâche fut de stigmatiser les erreurs origénistes. D'autres encore voient le V° concile oecuménique dans les sessions de 553 qui condamnèrent les Trois Chapitres." Murphy and Sherwood, 127.

Charles Moeller cites in this regard the little work *De sectis*,[65] attributed to Theodore of Rhaïtou (end of sixth century). The author, a Chalcedonian, replied to the classical objection on the condemnation of the Three Chapters which he expressed in this way: "Either they were good, then why condemn them? Or they were bad, then why did Chalcedon not condemn them? And how can you at the same time condemn them and receive Chalcedon?" He replied that Justinian did this "by economy" to bring about the union of the Monophysites. Moeller judges that for the author the council was not ecumenical.

Patriarch Eulogius of Alexandria, a neo-Chalcedonian, recognized "the blessed fifth ecumenical council." This latter is like the others, "divinely inspired."[66] But he only noted the condemnation of Origen without mentioning that of the Three Chapters. The process of reception is thus slow, but in this it does not stand out with regard to the reception of the earlier councils.

Reception of the Doctrinal Work of Constantinople II

In what we have discussed up to now the first ten canons of Constantinople II seem to have remained outside of preoccupation. Papal confirmation did not take them into account. Yet at the Roman Council of the Lateran of 649, under Martin I (649-653), which constituted the first taking of a position against Monothelism and which announced the Third Council of Constantinople, canons two and five repeat certain theological formulas of Constantinople II.[67] This act of reception would have remained implicit if it were not accompanied by a canon prescribing to confess the doctrine of the five ecumenical councils "up to one summit" (*usque ad unum apicem*).[68] Likewise, Constantinople III (680-681) declared that it "received the five councils which preceded it,"[69] in that they confessed the same Christological and trinitarian faith. In these two cases there is no longer question of the Three Chapters business but of the exactitude of the Christological confession. It should be noted that these two councils teach the two wills of Christ, which goes more in the sense of Chalcedon than in that of Constantinople II. In the following centuries Byzantine theologians oriented their Christology in the direc-

---

65 Moeller, "Le cinquième concile oecuménique," 417-419.
66 Ibid., 420.
67 DS 502 and 505; cf. de Vries, 169-170.
68 DS 517.
69 DS 554.

tion of Constantinople II. It was the same in the West up until modern times.[70]

Debate Among the Moderns (Amann, Moeller, DeVreesse)

Some authors judge that the council's decisions were not canonically valid because the council was not in communion with the pope at the moment of their promulgation and that only the condemnation of the Three Chapters was accepted by Vigilius and his successors.

The article we have already cited by Charles Moeller on Constantinople II studied this from the point of view of pontifical confirmation. He argued from the fact, known since Baluze in the seventeenth century, that the council was no longer in communion after the sixth session, to conclude that the decrees of the eighth session "are rendered null." They were thus not approved except to the exact degree in which they were taken up in the *Judicatum* of February 23, 554, where Vigilius aligned himself with the decisions of Justinian's council. "But the *Judicatum* does not breathe a word of the ten first anathemas of June 2, 553. The neo-Chalcedonian Christology *is thus not raised to the level of a dogma of faith*. If it retained its value as speculative theology, it cannot in any manner claim the infallible authority of the Church."[71]

Aligning himself with the positions of Amann, Moeller judges that the only valid document of Vigilius is the *Constitutum* of 553, declared "irreformable" by the pope, and not the *Judicatum* of 554 which contradicts it. The council must be judged in light of this text and retain only what is not in disagreement with it. The ecumenicity of a council is discerned beginning with the "ordinary magisterium" of the Church.

There are several remarks to be made here. First, Moeller is clearly anti-neo-Chalcedonian, his sympathies are toward the school of Antioch. His argumentation has for its purpose to deny any conciliar value to the ten canons of Constantinople II, an attestation of what is called "neo-Chalcedonianism." Something other than a simply historical motive un-

---

[70] "Cette théologie influencera le développement ultérieur de l'intelligence par l'Eglise du mystère de l'incarnation; aussi est-il légitime de se demander si Vigile a réellement accepté la formulation doctrinale, étant donné que le concile n'était pas en communion avec le pape quand ces anathèmes furent décidés. La question devient toutefois superflue si l'on se rappelle que, dans les cinq anathèmes du I° Constitutum, Vigile s'est contenté de réaffirmer la doctrine 'néochalcédonienne.'" Murphy and Sherwood, 129.

[71] Moeller, "Le cinquième concile oecuménique," 414.

derlies the vigor and insistence of his affirmations, at the very time that he pretends to report only historical facts which are above discussion.

Then, he lets himself follow an unconscious anachronism in applying to the period of the sixth century the modern categories which come from Vatican I concerning the Magisterium (an expression unknown at the time), infallibility, etc.[72] His argumentation seeks to be truly juridical and forgets the importance of the "reception" of Constantinople II by the following councils and its entry into the group of the "seven first ecumenical councils." It is a typical example of the misunderstanding of the idea of reception.

Doctrinal Reflections on this Road of "Reception"

1. All the debate which followed Constantinople II was directed to the question of the Three Chapters. This was confirmed by successive popes. But in the West they were "received" only slowly and with difficulty.

2. With time, however, Constantinople II was counted among the number of ecumenical councils and became part of the group of seven. This is explained by means of its "reception" by later councils, which are the witnesses of general consideration. This "reception" was global and did not enter into details with regard to the council's canons.

3. On a longer term, one perceives that the affair of the Three Chapters fell increasingly into obsolescence. It is no longer current and has even lost its meaning. It would be good to follow the steps of this progressive forgetfulness. Can one say that the condemnation of the Three Chapters has any value today? The question of the orthodoxy of Theodore of Mopsuest, of Theodoret of Cyrrhus, and of Ibas of Edessa has henceforth been abandoned to historians and theologians, who judge it according to completely different criteria from Justinian's dogmatic criteria. The magisterium no longer intervenes. In fact, no theologian is held any longer by these three canons to the condemnation of the men. One can hold the contrary with de Vries: "the authoritative judgment of a council recognized by the pope concerned a 'dogmatic fact' and thus,

---

[72]   He even misuses these categories since he speaks of the "ordinary magisterium" of the pope, which according to Vatican I does not exist, this council knowing only an "ordinary and universal" magisterium.

in fact, has become obsolete. The orthodoxy of Theodore of Mopsuest is today an open question on which specialists can debate in full liberty."[73]

4. On the other hand, one perceives that the first ten canons, which constitute a small Christology, became progressively a jurisprudence in the interpretation of Chalcedon. A fact of reception is at play there, in particular at the doctrinal level. Constantinople II is not considered as a council which brought anything truly new to Christology, but as one which furnished an "authentic" interpretation of Chalcedon. It is at this title that this council still "lives" today in the Church. One should thus not argue from the non-confirmation of Constantinople II's canons by the popes to conclude to their lack of any doctrinal normativity, as does Moeller.[74] Their authority comes from the fact of a double reception: insertion of Constantinople II in the list of ecumenical councils, and the lasting influence which they have had on the understanding of Christological dogma. We are thus in the presence of a paradox; these are the canons which were not confirmed by the pope who received them, while the confirmed canons have fallen into obsolescence.

FINAL REFLECTIONS

At the end of this journey it is only possible to draw some limited conclusions. It would be good to make the assessment of the reception of all the councils which followed Constantinople II and to draw from them the lessons of a systematic comparison of the different processes. It is possible, however, to make some reflections beginning with the five case studies which have the unique advantage of having in some way seen the creation of the process of reception.

1. Reception is truly an "event" which took place or did not take place, which can even be selective in regard to the decisions of one or another council. It is always a surprising and unpredictable event in its duration and its modalities. Even when reception is sought and willed by political or religious authority, in fact it escapes them as to its essential. In its process the relationship of the Church to the world plays a major role, for reception always takes place in a determined cultural sphere.

2. Reception is an event which takes place in a more or less long time period. It always goes through a debate, often conflict. A council needs to

---

[73] De Vries, 179.
[74] And to some degree, de Vries.

grow old in order to be received. It "improves" as a wine does which is taken from the bottle and decanted, that is, the vicissitudes of its meeting fade in favor of its message. After a certain lapse of time people no longer fight against it because they become aware—sometimes better than it would have thought itself—of the element of truth which it promotes. Nicea, after having divided, reunited. Chalcedon was a condemned council for a long time, but after Constantinople II it entered into the series of four councils compared to the four Gospels.

3. Reception is an event which has an end. At the end of a complex process, which includes reversals, the council becomes the object of "peaceful possession" by all those who have received it. When the cultural world which saw its meeting is transformed, the council and its reception make a single piece as a unit which belongs to the deposit of faith, but no longer addresses believers in the same manner. A council will always be the object of a hermeneutic, it is no longer truly an object of reception. The churches which received it remain free to propose new documents of faith for the reception of their faithful. They remain free to conclude ecumenical accords on the points engaged by the ancient councils, without for this having to require their partners to receive these councils. It thus appears less happy to speak of a continuous process of reception or of the "re-reception" of a council. It is not fitting, moreover, to call everything reception; this would empty the concept of its content.

4. Reception is a fact which engages the faith of the Christian people, a people structured in each local church under the presidency of its bishop. It is a process of exchange between Christian people and hierarchical authority. In this sense it transcends its witnesses. However, the episcopal and theological witnesses belong to the process of reception and are indispensable for us to catch up with it.

5. Reception produces something new: it is creative. It constitutes a "gift of meaning" which was not foreseen at the beginning. On this basis it constitutes an important element of conciliar hermeneutic. Undoubtedly this meaning does not contradict the original meaning, but it goes beyond it. Reception must thus not be confused with the obedience commanded to put a council to work. "One insists on (obedience)," Congar writes, "when one sees the Church as a society under a hierarchical authority; and on reception-consent, when one sees the Church universal as a communion of churches."[75] Obedience arises from a "jurisdictional un-

---

[75]   Congar, 394.

derstanding of the Church," while reception arises from an "organic understanding." Reception can only be highlighted in an ecclesiology of communion. It is completely in keeping with the centralizing ecclesiology of the Catholic Church in modern times to have given no place to it.

6. If one takes into consideration the nature of reception, one can never make it the object of a project or a strategy. It is not the question of knowing if one should receive or "re-receive" a council. Reception cannot be commanded; it is a fact which is recorded. Undoubtedly it is on this basis that it is a sign of the Spirit's action. From this point of view the ARCIC commission employs a faulty expression when it speaks of the "duty of deferring to reception" in certain cases.[76]

7. Reception is thus a fundamentally different reality from confirmation by the pope. Reception and confirmation cannot coincide. But this difference is concealed by two facts. In the first case there is an ambiguity on the real meaning of the pontifical act. At the beginning, this seems to be only a reception (Nicea and even Ephesus), before becoming a formal confirmation (beginning with Chalcedon), at least in the conviction of the Roman Pontiffs. On the other hand, papal confirmation enters most often as one element among others in the vast process of reception.

Translation by James H. Provost

---

[76]   ARCIC, "Authority in the Church II," n. 29, in *Growth in Agreement*, 114 (*supra*, note 4).

RESPONSE TO BERNARD SESBOÜÉ

Lionel R. Wickham*

Many far-reaching considerations have emerged from Bernard Ses-boüé's careful analysis. I point to the most obvious, indeed banal feature of the history it reveals: that the tale of the reception of the first five ecu-menical councils is a tangled one, full of ambiguities and paradoxes. As he rightly shows, the basic plot remains constant: a contentious issue, an assembly of bishops, an agreed text. Next comes disagreement, to be fol-lowed by eventual acceptance after the personal issues have been forgot-ten and a modicum of historical myth has been allowed to blur the actu-alities. Such is the general pattern.

But there are notable variations, so much so that you might perhaps wonder whether either "ecumenical council" or "reception" could be an univocal concept. The large assembly presided over by Constantine at Nicea, the much smaller group at Constantinople in 381, Cyril of Alexan-dria's caucus at Ephesus in 431, the prestigious council of Chalcedon (so large, so divisive, so unreceived by so many!), and the devious Justin-ian's carefully staged showpiece are the entities which, though their def-initions overlap, fall, only with difficulty, into a single class.

And that brings me to another point. Whatever it is, an ecumenical council is not like a sacrament; it is not valid in virtue of its form and mat-ter. Whoever convokes an ecumenical council takes the risk that it may be a complete flop. Like Shakespeare's Glendower, in Henry IV part one, you may call spirits from the vast deep: "but will they come when you do call for them?"—as Hotspur puts it skeptically. Something beyond formal correctness is required both for the efficacy and the validity of ecumeni-cal councils; namely, the assent of the Church's heart and mind. Indeed, "assent" may not be the right word, for it hints too much at constrained obedience. The reception of a council occurs, and the council becomes an ecumenical council in the full sense, when, and only when, the teaching it has given is taken up and presupposed in Christian faith and discourse.

* The Divinity School, Cambridge (England).

Reception is an intuition of truth, an intuition whose conditions cannot be prescribed. Debate has always taken place before that intuition happens. But happen it does. There is a process of receiving, but a stage is reached at which the process is complete. Bernard Sesboüé emphasizes the point that the process has a terminus: "Reception is truly an "event" which took place or did not take place." If we talk of a continuous process of reception, or of "re-reception," we evacuate the concept (so he says) of its meaning.

I think a process of reception is required on my part here, for I do not think that I entirely follow him. I will revert to the matter later. It is a point he makes as the first of his final reflections, with almost all of which I find myself in full agreement. Perhaps I should wish to nuance a little of what is said about the novelty produced by reception (reflection no. 5), but not much for it is finely balanced. As for the matter of papal confirmation (no. 7), we verge upon the moot and are in danger, perhaps, of addressing to the ancient Church questions and distinctions which simply did not occur to it. Is it the pope or the Church of Rome (to make an awkward distinction) that we are talking about? In any event, though, it is clear that without the concurrence of Rome there could in antiquity be neither ecumenical council nor reception.

It is not my place to open up fresh considerations which may get in the way of addressing the fundamental points in Bernard Sesboüé's paper. Perhaps though I may be allowed to draw attention to some features he has only lightly touched upon. He has mentioned non-reception. It will help, if we pause to reflect on those other councils, failing in the period, which so far as their convoking was concerned had at least the appearance of being ecumenical. I think of Sardica (342 or 343 - the date is disputed), the double council of Rimini/Seleucia of 359 which melted into a council at Constantinople in the months following, and the so-called *Latrocinium* or Robber Council of 449. Why did they fail to be received? They were summoned, as were the others, by imperial command. That was part of the rationale of an ecumenical council. For it always bore relation to the need of the Roman state to know the body with which it had to deal: who was in charge, who had a right to the buildings, what bishops were competent to hear petty lawsuits. The state provided the means to collect together the bishops, laid down part of the agenda and exercised pressure, more or less severe, to secure discipline in the assembly and to give effect by legal sanctions to the decisions of the majority.

I say "of the majority," but it was not a parliamentary system. No continuing opposition was allowed: loss of office and exclusion from the Catholic Church followed upon disagreement with the dominant will. The tale of the failure of these councils, especially those convened under Constantius, makes sad reading. So much waste. So much unhappiness. The documents are filled with accounts of misery, torture, and violence. Particularly depressing is the story of Liberius, Bishop of Rome. A good man, much harassed, perhaps too easily overawed and certainly not of the heroic caste, he betrayed the trust reposed in him and repudiated the creed of Nicea—how sharply is a matter of dispute. But he was not the only one to lapse or to experience painful trials in the process whereby Nicea was received, other councils were repudiated, and the Church's mind was disclosed.

If I talk in this way of "disclosing the Church's mind," I speak the language of the Christian theologian. But it is a language close to that in which people at the time expressed themselves. For, in theory at least, both for the Emperor Constantius and for the bishops of the Church, there was a given truth, and a given consensus as to the truth, which required to be made apparent to them. Christianity was a religion of revelation, its content not the creation of the human mind which, by divine grace, discerns it. Fact and theory, I believe, coincided. Nobody wanted to follow Arius and his triad of unequal deities, nobody wanted to follow Marcellus and his expanding godhead and still less Fotinus: the Son of God was for all, or at least the great majority, God begotten. The negatives were louder than the affirmations, no doubt. It was clear that to speak of Christ, at the level of God and before his manifestation in the flesh, as created or merely temporary, was disloyal both to the Bible and to tradition; much less clear, that to use the unscriptural term *usia* to expound the notion of God begotten was legitimate.

Constantius, convinced, apparently, that it was this word *usia* which divided the Church, and determined too to be rid of Athanasius, attempted to force upon the Church a "disinvention" of the term. The Church of the East did not care for Athanasius, either his character or his association with Marcellus. The council of Sardica failed because it simply revealed the split between East and West over the unevenly yoked pair. The councils of 359 were wrecked upon the attempt to abolish the use of the term *usia*. The issues of doctrine, of personalities, and of church-political rights became so entangled that it took far longer to resolve them than one might have thought necessary. And so far as doctrine was concerned it was the evident fact that by banning mention of *usia* and by substituting "likeness" between Father and Son, a foothold was given to the people who affirmed a dissimilarity of *usia*. This last invited, indeed compelled, an acceptance of the Creed of Nicea. Nicea was received because those who thought about the issues saw that if a council could express the Church's mind (and it could) Nicea had done so. Rimini/ Seleucia was the *demonstratio ad oculos* of the path the Church could not go down; Nicea remained the viable alternative.

What about the *Latrocinium* of 449? That council suffered from the opposite defect of too little imperial control. Theodosius II's policy of disengagement left too much scope to the pope of Alexandria, who rebuffed the legates of the pope of Rome. Even if we set aside, as mostly hypocritical excuses, the claims made at the Council of Chalcedon by bishops present at the *Latrocinium* that blank papers had been signed and coercion employed, Dioscorus of Alexandria behaved in a high-handed manner. Moreover, he backed a foolish cause. It was absurd to give his patronage to Eutyches who had refused the agreed formula of reunion of 433 with its affirmation of Christ's double consubstantiality with the Father and with us. Dioscorus eventually dropped him, as everybody else did, but it was too late. Eutyches and Nestorius function somewhat like Arius and Marcellus in the fourth century debate: they are positions recognized as intolerable. But in the fifth there was no equivalent of the Council of Nicea to guide in *oeconomia* as Nicea had guided in *theologia*. Chalcedon affirmed the validity of the proceedings at Ephesus in 431, but it could not repeat its creed, for there was none. It had to take to heart the words of Leo's *Tome* and make a fresh start in defining the Faith. The subsequent councils of East and West together (the fifth, sixth and seventh ecumenical councils) are but extensions of the fourth: sessions, as it were, which were held in different places and with different personnel but having essentially the same agenda. And has the fourth council been truly *received*? Well, certainly until the ancient Oriental Churches receive the council (until the Greek kalends?), we cannot reckon its reception complete.

And that brings me to some questions that arise, I suggest, from Bernard Sesboüé's paper. First, would he agree with me that one may take too romantic a view of reception as a free act of assent by the Church? Reading the history disinclines me to think quite that way. The re-instatement of Chalcedon in 518 was a messy business. A great deal of coercion was employed. What bearing does he think that has upon the nature of reception? Second, I think I am in agreement with him about reception's finding its terminus. But if we cannot fix a terminus because that would be to assimilate reception to something juridical, when can we know that it has occurred? Might it not be better to think of ecumenical councils as privileged interpreters of tradition, received once and yet ever being received? Finally, is there such a thing as reception of substance coupled with rejection of form? I mean, can we allow for a case where a council is officially rejected, but its teaching tacitly acknowledged or acknowledged in a different form of words? Would we be justified in calling such acknowledgement "reception"? These, though are only some of the issues that arise out of a thought-provoking analysis which it has been a particular pleasure to respond to.

THE GREGORIAN REFORM
AND THE BEGINNING OF
A UNIVERSAL ECCLESIOLOGY

KLAUS SCHATZ*

The original topic for this study was "Gregory VII and the Beginning of a Universal Ecclesiology," but I have changed it somewhat. Gregory VII certainly stands at the center of my subject. Like few other popes, he influenced the Church of his time through his personal characteristics, his thought, his charisma, as well as his instability. But that does not mean it would be appropriate to center everything around him personally. He stands within the so called "Gregorian Reform." He did not start the reform even though he did hasten it by the force of his personality. He was carried by the reform movement of his time, one that would later bear his name. He advanced the ideas that came before him, molding them according to his own personality. But this personal coloring of ideas did not always have a lasting influence. There are differences of opinion and divisions within the ranks of Gregorian scholars regarding the questions of primacy and the Church. There is no monolithic block of opinion on these matters, and the thought of Gregory himself has not always prevailed.

The decisive break in ecclesiology, the ecclesiological shift, is found in the Gregorian reform of the eleventh century. Congar was primarily responsible for pointing out the new understanding of Gregory.[1] The novelty is that papal primacy became, in a way hitherto unknown, the central and pivotal issue of the understanding of the Church, at least with regard to its institutional aspects. Papal primacy was no longer simply a support for ecclesial unity, and defined by reason of the unity itself;

---

* Theologische Fakultät St. Georgen, Frankfurt-am-Main (Germany).

[1] Yves Congar, "Der Platz des Papsttums in der Kirchenfrommigkeit der Reformer des 11. Jarhhunderts," in *Sentire Ecclesiam*, ed. Jean Dan<sup>iélou and Herbert Vorgrimler (Freiburg: Herder, 1961); idem, *Die Lehre von der Kirche von Augustinus bis zum abendländischen Schisma*, trans. Hans Sayer (Freiburg: Herder, 1971) 53-68.

rather, ecclesial unity was now defined from the viewpoint of the primacy of the Roman church. This occurred, as Congar has further emphasized, through an extensive transformation of traditional terms, partly those of the papacies of Damasus to Leo the Great, partly those of Nicholas I, and finally, through a variety of uses of the pseudo-Isidorian decretals of the ninth century. The individual terms are not new; but their frequent and concentrated use provides an overall picture in which primacy changes from *centrum unitatis* to *caput* on which the entire life of the Church depends. That is, the Church becomes a *regnum* or *imperium* governed by the pope.

The individual elements of this basic outline must now be distinguished. The questions are:

1. What precisely do the individual key notions and ideas mean? What was the relationship between the Roman church and the other churches? In response, the following points should be emphasized:

a. that, as with other questions (such as the precise relationship between temporal and spiritual power or the special controversy concerning the validity of simoniacal ordinations), the Gregorian reform movement did not form an absolutely homogenous unity; rather, it contained remarkable nuances.

b. that not all key notions and ideas attributed to the Gregorian reformers were actually carried out by them. Some gained acceptance only in the twelfth and thirteenth centuries in the wake of the more legal way of thought prevalent then.

2. The achievement of a universal image of the Church seen in the light of primacy did not preclude that other central notions of the Church survived, gaining new impetus during the Gregorian era, and testifying to a fundamentally different image of the Church. This is especially evident in the notions of episcopal elections and spiritual marriage.

3. If one asserts a universal notion of the Church, at least on the level of the relation between the Roman church and other churches, one must then ask whether this notion is identical in all aspects to the idea of an absolute papacy. In fact, it will be shown that out of the difference between the *Ecclesia Romana* on the one hand, and the pope on the other, dialectical consequences arose that were fully developed in late medieval con-

ciliarism, and that gave renewed importance to reception on a universal basis.

I. CENTRAL NOTIONS

The central terms with which the reformers described the Roman church's relationship to other churches were: hinge *(cardo)*, head *(caput)*, mother of all the churches *(mater omnium ecclesiarum)*, source *(fons)*, summit *(vertex)*, foundation *(fundamentum)*, and *basis*. Gregory VII himself preferred the expressions *mater (omnium ecclesiarum)* and *magistra*.[2] These expressions were in no way new. The terms *caput* and *cardo* were derived from the vocabulary of the Pseudo-Isidore.[3] There they already had a brilliant but ambiguous meaning. This was even more so when the terms were used by the Gregorian reformers. On the one hand, they signified the normative character of the Roman church for the other churches. The Roman church is the anchor, the head, mother, because all churches are oriented toward it and accept it as normative. Furthermore, it is the "source" since it expresses and safeguards unerringly the apostolic tradition of the faith and the ecclesial discipline going back to Peter. It is a norm that is not strictly limited to the sphere of faith. Rather, as the Anglo-Saxon reformers during the Carolingian era already recognized, it extends to the entire sphere of correct practices in the life of the Church, both in law and especially in the liturgy. In light of this principle, Gregory VII succeeded in having the Roman liturgy accepted in the Spanish kingdoms, and in combating the ancient Spanish liturgy which he considered to have been infected with arian and priscillian influences.[4] The "petrine obedience" was especially important to Gregory because he saw in it a concentration of the obedience due God and Jesus Christ. It signified for him an alignment toward the norm of the Roman church that "was founded by Peter and Paul on the solid rock of Christ and consecrated through his blood."[5] Peter Damian already saw the Church as the *mater et fons* since it was the teacher and model for all churches. It is *mater omnium Ecclesiarum, magistra et fons caelestis*

---

[2] For Gregory's notion of primacy, see especially, Leo Meulenberg, *Der Primat der römischen Kirche im Denken und Handeln Gregors VII* (Den Haag, 1965); also, Klaus Ganzer, "Das Kirchenverständnis Gregors VII," *Trier Theologische Zeitschrift* 78 (1969) 95-109.

[3] Congar, "Der Platz des Papsttums," 199, and note 14.

[4] Especially Reg 1: 64, *Das Register Gregors VIII*, ed. Erich Caspar (Berlin: Weidmannsche Buchhandlung, 1920) 93; cf. Meulenberg, "Der Primat," 39f.

[5] Ibid.

sapentiae out of which the light shines in so far as the Church is the *caput ecclesiasticae disciplinae* that enlightens the entire body of the Church.[6]

From here there is but a small step to the next wide-ranging notion, that the Roman church is not only a norm for the other churches in teaching and life, but also their origin, such that the other churches owe their very existence as churches to the Roman church.[7] Thus the Roman church becomes the source from which all churches have their origin. They are not simply subordinate to the Roman church, which always enjoys a certain independence, but also comprise its "members." This is clear from the Pseudo-Vigilius, a text from the Pseudo-Isidorian collection which was later appropriated into the *Collectio canonum* of Anselm of Lucca who became Pope Alexander II (1061-1073): "No correct believer does not know that there is no doubt . . . that the Roman church is the foundation and source of the churches, from which all churches take their origin."[8]

Life, well-being, and health flow out from the Roman church to all the other churches. This central idea is developed in fragment A of the *De sancta Romana ecclesia* (until recently attributed to Humberto of Silva Candida and dated at 1053/1054)[9] with all its tragically cryptic dimensions. For the author, dependence on the Roman church has both a positive and negative side, one that brings well-being, and one that brings harm. The health of the entire Church depends on the Roman church. If the Roman church flourishes, so blooms the entire Church. If it languishes, then the rest of the Church sickens to the point that human beings wander in droves into hell. And it is tragic that men and women can do nothing about it. This is not the naively optimistic idea of nineteenth

---

[6] As is indicated in the *Praefatio des Liber Gomorrhianus, Patrologia Latina [PL]* 145: 161 A.

[7] The titles, *cardo, caput, mater, fons, fundamentum, basis*, "qualify this Church as the decisive element from which the entire Church is built"; Congar, "Das Platz des Papsttums," 202.

[8] "Nulli . . . dubium est, quod ecclesia Romana fundamentum et sors sit ecclesiarum, a qua omnes ecclesias principium sumpsisse nemo recte credentium ignorat." Paul Hinschius, *Decretales Pseudo-Isidorianae et Capitula Angilramni* (Leipzig: B. Tauchnitz, 1863) 712; Anselm of Lucca, *Collectio canonum* 1: 9, ed. Friedrich Thaner (Innsbruck: Libreriae Academicae Wagnerianae, 1906) 10.

[9] The text is found in Percy E. Schramm, *Kaiser, Rom, Renovatio. Studien und Texte zur Geschichte des römischen Erneuerungsgedankens vom Ende des Karolingischen Reiches bis zum Investiturstreit* (Leipzig: Wissenschaftliche Buchgesellschaft, 1929) 2: 128f.; for a treatment of the author and historical context, see 120-133.

century Ultramontanism, that the Holy Spirit guarantees in every case that the Church will flourish through the papacy. Apparently, it is the terrible experiences of the Dark Ages (*saeculum obscurum*) and the dominion over the Roman papacy that led the author to these thoughts. No other author expressed the ambiguity of dependence on the Roman church so thoroughly, brutally, and bluntly. If the Roman church is sick and corrupt, then for Humberto there is no human remedy. For according to the fundamental principle, *Prima sedes a nemine iudicatur*,[10] the pope judges all people and is judged by no one but God alone. There is but one exception: *Nisi forte deprehendatur a fide devius*. This is the classic heresy clause to whose meaning and impact we will return. Otherwise, the only remedy is prayer for the Roman church since the health of the faithful depends on its well-being. The fact that every situation that Humberto apparently had in mind was actually remedied from outside the Church, through the intervention of the empire under Henry III, is not reflected in his theory.

A similar passage from "norm" to "source" is found in the idea that the Roman church alone of all the churches was "the only one founded by the Lord" (*a solo Domino fundata*). This is the well-known first and guiding sentence of the *Dictatus papae* of Gregory VII.[11] Now the question becomes: Who founded the other churches? Peter Damian answered that those churches were not founded by the Lord, but by emperors or kings.[12] Therefore, they are of human origin, not divine. The consequence for Peter Damian of the fact that the Roman church comes from such an essentially higher level is that the Roman church is normative for the other churches, for example, in the liturgy. But the fact that many churches owe their legitimate origin to the establishment by kings and emperors, something that did not touch on the lay investiture controversy, was evidently acceptable. In the measure that the investiture question became a problem and a contentious issue in the establishment of a church, things could no longer remain as they were. It is no wonder, then, that first Anselm of Lucca and then Cardinal Deusdedit would cite a version altered by Peter Damian, one according to which all other churches

---

[10] For a history of this principle, see Salvatore Vacca, *Prima sedes a nemine iudicatur. Genesi e sviluppo storico dell'assioma petrino al Decreto di Graziano* (Rome: Editrice Pontificia Universitas Gregoriana, 1993).

[11] *Dictatus papae* [*DP*]: Reg. 11 55 a, ed. Caspar, 201-208.

[12] *PL* 145: 68 B and 91 B-D.

were founded by the Roman church, which was itself alone founded by the Lord.[13] In order to arrive at this conclusion, it was necessary to transfer an already current Roman notion applicable to all Western churches to "all the churches together." This was the (historically false) idea found for the first time in 416 in Innocent I. He maintained that all the Western churches had to have been founded directly or indirectly by Peter or his successors since no other apostle had worked in the Western regions of the Church. It follows, then, "that they observe the customs of the Roman church from which they doubtlessly had their origin."[14] From this arises the assertion—now hardly to be understood in precise historical terms— that "all the churches" were founded by the Roman church. From the notions of the superior level of the Roman church and its normative nature, both derived from Peter Damian, the transition is made to the Roman church as being the original source from which the others are derived.

However, an idea corresponding to that of the Church as "source," namely, that all ecclesial power, even that of bishops, comes from the pope and is ultimately delegated by him, is found only in isolation and sporadically among the Gregorian authors. It is found in the *Apologeticus* of Bernold of St. Blase after 1076. He was an author who distanced himself from the other Gregorians by his strict papalist ideas,[15] which is also the reason he is not a representative author. Speaking of the strict obedience owed the pope, Bernold told bishops that if they tolerated disobedience against the pope they themselves cut off the branch of their own authority, for all ecclesial power emanated from the pope.[16] For Bernold, papal obedience stood above all other types of obedience, even above that due one's own bishop, an obedience that bound only in a reserved fashion. With this in mind, Bernold presented a comparison that already appeared in the first

---

[13] Anselm of Lucca, *Collectio canonum* 1: 63, ed. Thaner, 31f.: "Quod Romana ecclesia omnes instituit dignitates ecclesiasticas, ipsam autem verbum illud fundavit, per quod creata sunt omnia." This was then developed as follows: all dignities of patriarchs, metropolitans and bishops were instituted by the Church, and it alone was founded by Christ.

The same is found in Deusdedit, *Collectio canonum* 1: 167, ed. Victor Wolf v. Glanvell (Paderborn: F. Schöningh, 1905) 106f.

[14] *PL* 20: 552 B.

[15] See Heinrich Weisweiler, "Die päpstliche Gewalt in den Schriften Bernolds von St. Blasien," *Studi Gregoriani* 4 (1952) 129-147.

[16] "Videat autem quilibet prelatus, quia sibi reverentiam a subditis exigat, nec eam Romano pontifici denegare velit, a quo omnis ecclesiastica potestas procedit"; *Monumenta Germaniae Historica* [*MGH*] *LL* 2 (Hannover: Hahn, 1837) 161, 37-39.

letter of Pope Leo IX to Patriarch Michael Cerullarius of Constantinople;[17] namely, the comparison of the papal church to a kingdom: "A
bishop does not have so much power over the flock committed to him as
the apostolic prelate, who although he has divided his care among the individual bishops, in no way is deprived of his universal and principal
power, just as a king does not diminish his royal power even though he divides his kingdom among divers dukes, counts, or judges."[18]

However, other authors did not follow Bernold's line of thought, not
even Gregory VII. Certainly, the Gregorian authors maintained numerous times that the Roman church should call all churches *in pariem sollicitudinis* such that the *plenitudo potestatis* remains in it alone. They
base themselves on the text already cited from Pseudo-Isidore which asserts that all churches have their *principium* in the Roman church.[19]
However, if one takes into account the context, the text does not speak of
the relation between the Roman church and episcopal churches as such,
but between the Roman church and patriarchal, primatial, and especially
metropolitan churches.[20] Thus, every "supra-diocesan" power and ecclesial structure is also conferred by the pope and shares in the papal power.
For Gregory VII as well, the metropolitan structure was instituted by the
Apostolic See.[21] The application of these two notions (*plenitudo potestatis—in partem sollicitudinis*) to the relationship between pope and
bishops was made in passing for the first time by Bernard of Clairvaux,[22]
and resolutely by Innocent III. He interpreted the notion of the church of
Rome as *caput* in the sense that in the head would be the fullness of life

[17] All *sacerdotes* (bishops) have the Roman church as head, "sicut omnes iudices
regem"; *PL* 143: 751 B.

[18] "Quilibet episcopus nec super gregem sibi commissum tantam potestatem habet,
quantum presul apostolicus, qui licet curam suam in singulos episcopos diviserit, nullo-
modo tamen se ipsum sua universali et principali potestate privavit, sicut nec rex suam re-
galem potestatem diminuit, licet regnum suum in diversos duces, comites sive iudices diviserit"; ibid., 88: 1-6.

[19] Hinschius, 712.

[20] In the context it is a question of the text from Pseudo-Isidore on the right of bishops
threatened with deposition by a provincial synod to appeal to Rome at any time. The
"other churches," then, are first of all the metropolitan churches. Their power is a "participation" in the power of the Roman church and no power of its own right.

[21] ". . . sedes apostolica . . . per diversas provincias et regna praesules archiepiscopos
et primates ordinavit"; Reg 6: 35; Caspar, 450.

[22] *De consideratione* 2: 8; *PL* 182: 752 B/C. The expression here obviously does not
mean the derivation of episcopal power from papal power; rather, the contrast between
local and universal power is intended.

and senses (*plenitudo sensuum*) which would emanate to the members. Thus one could also say of the pope (after Christ): "We have received all things from his fullness."[23]

There was another way in which the Gregorian authors did not come to an "absolutist" conclusion, one that would not be clearly advanced for the first time until the thirteenth century, above all by Innocent IV (1243-1254): namely, that the pope stands above the canons, that is, above all canon law which receives its legitimacy as "papal law" through him alone.[24] In order to realize such an idea, it was necessary not only to concentrate all ecclesial power in the pope, but also to achieve a clearer distinction between *ius divinum* and *ius ecclesiasticum* as well as the transfer of the (late) Roman law idea of the *princeps legibus solutus* to the pope as sovereign of the Church. One may be slightly tempted to take the following phrase from the *Dictatus papae* in this sense: *Quod illi soli licet pro temporis necessitate novas leges condere*.[25] However, this phrase does not actually envisage sovereign power over all church law. The conservative legal notion is still that of the early medieval period: The law, both in the Church and state, is not "made," but "handed down" and "discovered." Divine and ecclesial law form one binding Tradition of the Church to be faithfully safeguarded. Moreover, and this is what is meant by the *novae leges pro temporis necessitate*, the law was to be made current in a flexible manner, prudently applied and defended. The pope, too, is a witness to the laws handed down, but he himself does not make the law. Even with Gregory VII papal legislative acts, as with the teaching office, were not creative, but interpretive: they differentiate and formulate the authentic and true Tradition of the Church over against a possible abusive penetration of pure *consuetudo* as, for example, lay investiture was for Gregory.[26]

---

[23]   Klaus Schatz, "Papsttum und partikularkirchliche Gewalt bei Innocenz III," *Archivum Historiae Pontificiae* 8 (1970) 61-111. The text mentioned can be found in two places: Reg 1: 320, in Othmar Hageneder and Anton Haidacher, *Die Register Innocenz III* (Graz-Cologne: H. Bohlaus, 1964) 465; and 6: 188, in *PL* 215: 205.

[24]   See especially Ludwig Buisson, *Potestas und Caritas. Die päpstliche Gewalt im Spätmittelalter* (Cologne: Bohlau, 1958) 82-86.

[25]   *DP* 7.

[26]   Meulenberg, "Der Primat," 102-107; also idem, "Une question toujours ouverte: Grégoire VII et l'infallibilité du Pape," in *Aus Kirche und Reich. Studien zu Theologie, Politik und Recht im Mittelalter*, ed. Hubert Mordek (Sigmaringen: J. Thorbecke, 1983) 166-170. Gregory once quashed a monastic privilege granted by his predecessor Alexander II because it was "contra sanctorum patrum instituto"; Reg 7: 24; Caspar, 504.

However, for the majority of the Gregorian authors the pope did not stand over, but under the canons.[27] Generally speaking, the Gregorian authors could not recognize, especially in the polemical treatises surrounding the problem of lay investiture, a total papal control over the canons and over the entire authentic legal tradition of the Church. Their concern was that in the past there were many papal decisions regarding the investiture question or, more generally, regarding temporal power, that could be used against them and which they could not easily refute. Thus they were compelled to allow for limitations on papal power as well as the overstepping of its usual competence. This was especially true for Deusdedit for whom the decree on the papal election of 1059 was against the Fathers of the Church.[28] Only Bernold of St. Blase provided for an exception: for him even conciliar canons receive their authority from the pope. Thus, for Gregory the Great, the reverence due the first four councils as well as the Gospels was *a fortiori* due the decrees of the Apostolic See.[29] For him the pope is the *auctor canonum*.[30] Otherwise, the pope would be bound by the canons. This explains the Church's resistance to the *Privilegium* of Paschal II of 1111 as well as the protests at the Lateran Synod of 1123 against the concessions in the concordat of Worms (1122). With this concordat a place was opened in the churches for reception or non-reception. Decisions that were in conflict with canons were not to be received. On the other hand, it is also clear that the actual reception through the other churches, or their large majority, could not be an ultimate criterion for the Gregorians, for the consent of the other churches did not constitute a forum of appeal against the Roman church. Their conduct could reflect the actual *nefanda consuetudo*, that is, the mere adaptation of ecclesial norms in the political and societal spheres as it did in the investiture controversy. And even if the Roman church did at times pay its tribute to the spirit of the age and its *consuetudo*, the other churches were not so well protected against it. If there is an institutional criterion here, it is the reception on the part of the *Ecclesia Romana* which embodies the authentic Roman tradition in the face of errors or erroneous decisions on the part of individual popes. But more on this later.

Finally, a key notion must be investigated whose further implications will concern us toward the end. This notion is the connection or, more

---

[27] Carl Mirbt, *Die Publizistik im Zeitalter Gregors VII* (Leipzig: J.C. Hinrichs, 1894) 555-557.
[28] *MGH LL* 2: 309-313.
[29] Ibid., 62f.
[30] Ibid., 140f.

precisely, identification of *Romana* and *universalis*. The word *universalis* was torn from its reference to verification through the consent of the other churches and to reception through the entire world. Instead, it was connected only to Rome. This is evident in the denomination of the Roman church and the pope as *universalis*, and in the new concept of the *Concilium universale*. *Universalis* no longer meant, "generally recognized and received"; rather, it meant for the most part being significant and normative for all people and all the world. Therefore, the phrase *Romana universalis ecclesia*[31] does not mean that the Roman church is itself the entire Church, but that the Roman church is meaningful and normative for all churches. Gregory attests to this when, in the second sentence of the *Dictatus papae* (immediately after the statement that the Roman church was founded by the Lord alone), he declares that the Roman bishop alone is rightly called *universalis*.[32] It is the relation of the head to the body, an image that would later be used in the correspondence of 1199 between Innocent III and Patriarch John Camateros of Constantinople as an explanation of the "universal" character of the Roman church.[33] A letter of Leo IX to an African bishop in 1053 speaks to this. He says there can be no *universale concilium* without the Roman bishop.[34] This is not the Roman (and partly Eastern) notion of the first centuries, that the Roman bishop must cooperate with other bishops at the ecumenical synods, and that without him there can be no question of universal reception. For here there was no question of a world-wide council, but of a synod of only five African bishops. Through the approval of the pope, and only through it, would such a council receive a "universal" dimension and ultimate binding character. This becomes all the more clear in cases where the celebration of a *universale concilium*

---

[31]   For example, in the decree of papal election of 1059: "obeunte huius Romanae universalis ecclesiae pontifice"; *MGH Const.*, n. 382 (Hannover: Hahn, 1893) 1: 539, 21.

[32]   *DP* 2.

[33]   Innocent was responding to the patriarch's difficulty in understanding the description of the Roman church as *Ecclesia universalis*. Naturally, as a single church, the Roman church could not be the entire Church. As a particular church it was a part of the *Ecclesia universalis*, even if obviously the first and most admirable, as the head in the body, "quoniam in ea plenitudo potestatis existit, ad coeteros autem pars aliqua plenitudinis derivatur." It could be called *universalis* in so far as all other churches are subordinate to it (*sub se continet*). Reg 2: 209; *PL* 214: 763; *Die Register Innocenz III*, ed. Othmar Hagender et al. (Rome: Biblioteca Apostolica Vaticana, 1979) 2: 387f.

[34]   *PL* 143: 728 C; Johannes D. Mansi, *Sacrorum conciliorum nova et amplissima collectio* 19 (Venice, 1759) 657. Cf. *DP* 16: "Quod nulla synodus absque praecepto ejus debet generalis vocari."

was paralyzed by the deposition of a bishop. In either case, the definitive sentence was possible only together with Rome.[35] The real, world-wide dimension of the Church was replaced with the Roman alone. This corresponded to the new reality of the universal or general council since the twelfth century at which the presence of the pope became the decisive element.[36]

II. ANOTHER IMAGE OF THE CHURCH

The Gregorian reform also transmitted and cultivated ideas and concepts that were derived from another image of the Church, and that actually stood in contrast to a purely universalistic conception of the Church centered around the pope. One encounters them especially in the context of episcopal elections by the Church, a notion promoted by the reformers during the investiture controversy. For Gregory VII, that bishop alone can enter the sheepfold through the door, that is, through Christ the bridegroom, if he becomes a bishop through canonical election.[37] The theory of spiritual marriage between a bishop and a church corresponds to this. It was developed by the Gregorian polemicists against simony and lay investiture. They emphasized that simony was spiritual prostitution, and that lay investiture was abduction and rape.[38] An ecclesiology of the particular church, rather than a universal ecclesiology, lay at the root of this. The "spousal" consent with his particular church gives the bishop legitimacy. As custodian of the canons, the pope certainly had the task of supervising the functioning of this "marriage," as well as to judge cases in which there was a disputed election. But his decision did not take the place of the election, or did so only in highly exceptional cases. It is noteworthy that Innocent III did not use his *plenitudo potestatis* to justify his

---

[35]   "Hoc autem nolo vos lateat, non debere praeter sententiam Romani pontificis universale concilium celebrari aut episcopos damnari vel deponi; quia, etsi licet vobis aliquos episcopos examinare, diffinitivam tamen sententiam, absque consulto Romani pontificis, ut dictum est, non licet dare"; ibid.

[36]   Franz J. Schmale, "Systematisches zu den Konzilien des Reformpapsttums im 12. Jahrhundert," *Annuarium Historiae Conciliorum* 6 (1974) 21-39.

[37]   Citations: Reg 4: 11; 5: 5; 6: 5b, 12; 9: 36 (Caspar, 310, 353, 404, 414, 629); cf. also, Reg 5: 11 (Caspar, 364). This does not preclude that Gregory also named bishops in individual cases. This seldom happened and only when those charged with the election did not present a candidate or presented someone canonically unsuitable.

[38]   See Gerd Tellenbach, *Libertas. Kirche und Weltordnung im Zeitalter des Investiturstreits* (Stuttgart: W. Kohlhammer, 1936) 155-157; Robert Benson, *The Bishop-Elect: A Study in Medieval Ecclesiastical Office* (Princeton: Princeton University Press, 1961) 121-149.

claim of papal jurisdiction in the removal and transfer of bishops. Nor did he justify it by asserting that bishops cannot of their own accord resign their offices since they were called by him *in partem sollicitudinis*. Rather, he argued that the spiritual marriage was in itself indissoluble, and could be dissolved only by the pope as vicar of God.[39] In this case, in both theory and practice, another line of tradition was at work. It would only be repressed with the systematic reservation of episcopal elections on the part of Rome from the fourteenth century on. It gained acceptance again, in another form, at the Council of Trent in the discussion over the *ius divinum* of the residential bishops.

III. THE POPE AND THE ROMAN CHURCH

Naturally, the concentration of the *Ecclesia universalis* into the *Ecclesia Romana* had unexpected consequences which Horst Fuhrmann referred to in a short, but worthwhile article.[40] At first the *ecclesia Romana* gained more and more of a universal dimension. On the other hand, it was not necessarily absolutely identical in every aspect with the pope, even though for the Gregorian reformers the two entities were normally interchangeable. But it is surprising that Gregory VII, precisely in the *Dictatus papae*, where he speaks penetratingly and constantly of the pope alone (*solus papa*), apparently intentionally deviates in three places and speaks of the *Romana ecclesia*. Apart from the first phrase, which speaks of the founding of the Roman church by the Lord alone, the other phrases concern first the unerring character, not of the pope, but of the Roman church.[41] And the second sentence speaks of the fact that one cannot be a Catholic without being in agreement with the Roman church.[42] Thus the actual and ultimate guarantee of truth does not lie with the pope as such, but in the *ecclesia Romana*.[43] Among all the Gregorian writers, Deusdedit, who most strongly allows for erroneous papal

---

[39]   Schatz, 98-111; see also Wilhelm Imkamp, "Pastor et sponsus. Elemente einer Theologie des bischöflichen Amtes bei Innocenz III," in *Aus Kirche und Reich*, 285-294 (*supra*, note 26).

[40]   Horst Fuhrmann, "Ecclesia Romana—Ecclesia Universalis," in *Rom im hohen Mittelalter. Studien zu den Romvorstellungen und zur Rompolitik vom 10. bis zum 12. Jahrhundert. Festschrift für R. Elze*, ed. Bernhard Schimmelpfennig and Ludwig Schmugge (Sigmaringen: J. Thorbecke, 1991) 41-45.

[41]   "Quod Romana ecclesia nunquam erravit, nec in perpetuum, Scriptura testante, errabit"; *DP* 22.

[42]   "Quod catholicus non habeatur qui non concordat Romanae ecclesiae"; *DP* 26.

[43]   See Meulenberg, "Der Primat," 38-48; and idem, "Une question."

decisions, sees most clearly the Roman church as the true bearer of the primacy conferred by Christ on Peter.[44] This means that one must allow for at least a theoretical possibility of a *papa haereticus*. As we have seen, according to Humberto of Silva Candida, the *nisi devius a fide deprehendatur* was limited by the immutable principle, *Prima sedes a nemine iudicatur*. And his formulation made its way into the *Decretum Gratiani*.[45] There were a few historical examples of heretical popes. Among them was not yet included the famous case of Honorius, which had been forgotten by the Middle Ages. Rather, there were the (unhistorical) cases of Pope Anastasius II (496-498) who supposedly communicated with a member of the Acacian schism; and of Pope Marcellinus (296-304) who was supposed to have abjured the faith and handed over the sacred books during the Diocletian persecution.

Ultimately, the *ecclesia Romana* alone was infallible in the faith. But what is the Roman church? Where is it concretely manifest, if not in the Roman bishop? It was obvious to understand the Church as the concrete Roman tradition in teaching and customs. The personal bearer of these was normally the pope, but so too were the Roman clergy (that is, the cardinals), should the occasion arise. The question was handled on several occasions by the "Decretalists," the canonists who interpreted the *Decretum Gratiani* from 1150 to 1250.[46] They essentially sifted two answers out of the *Decretum*. The first identified the *ecclesia Romana* with the Roman particular church; practically speaking, with the pope, the curia, and the cardinals. The other answer was a logical consequence of the universalization of the *ecclesia Romana*. According to it, the *ecclesia Romana* is fundamentally identical with the *ecclesia universalis* which as a whole cannot err. Such an interpretation appears for the first time in the summa *Et est sciendum*, written sometime between 1180 and 1185 in the ecclesiastical province of Reims.[47] It is a brief passage and written al-

---

[44] See Uta Renate Blumenthal, "Rom in der Kanonistik," in *Rom im hohen Mittelalter*, 29-39.

[45] *Decretum Gratiani* I, D 40 p. 3 c. 11. Gregory VII himself believed, of course, that no pope had ever been a heretic.

[46] See Brian Tierney, *Foundations of Conciliar Theory: The Contribution of the Medieval Canonists from Gratian to the Great Schism* (Cambridge: Cambridge University Press, 1955) 36-46; idem, *Origins of Papal Infallibility 1150-1350: A Study of the Concepts of Infallibility, Sovereignty and Tradition in the Middle Ages* (Leiden: E. J. Brill, 1972) 36-38.

[47] "... nomine romana ecclesia accipitur interdum universalis ecclesia"; cited by Tierney, "Foundations," 41.

most in passing. But it does indicate that this interpretation had already been used in numerous instances. Things were clearer around 1188 with Huguccio of Pisa, the teacher of Innocent III, the pope who promoted the image of the *ecclesia Romana* and *universi fideles*.[48]

In this way, a sudden, dialectical change occurred with grave consequences. The identification of the universal Church with the Roman church resulted in the ultimate relaxing of the absolute normative character of the Roman particular church, and gave the last word to reception by the universal Church, at least with regard to matters of faith. A place was now given to reception that would not have been granted it by Gregory VII who reduced everything to the *oboedientia Sancti Petri et Romanae ecclesiae*. It is no wonder, as Brian Tierney has proven,[49] that William of Ockham, of all people, depended directly on Huggucio of Pisa for his assertion "That Roman church which cannot err is the universal Church."[50] The last inheritance of this development (with its background in the historical experiences of the great papal schism and the Avignon papacies) was conciliarism. The ecclesiology of conciliarism is universal. Its notion of a council, like the concrete structure of the late medieval councils, contains a universal ecclesiology: the council as similar to general states of kingdoms, to "an assembly of the kingdom of Christianity and its states," rather than to merely an assembly of singular local churches represented by their bishops. But this was already the case with the "papal" councils of the thirteenth century. They were the assemblies of "Christianity," whose participants were selected by the pope according to their importance.

Translation by Ronny E. Jenkins

---

[48] Tierney, "Foundations," 42 ("in romana ecclesia intelligitur universitas fidelium"); idem, "Origins," 37, n. 1.

[49] Brian Tierney, "Ockham, the Conciliar Theory, and the Canonists," in idem, *Church Law and Constitutional Thought in the Middle Ages* (London: Variorum Reprints, 1979) 40-70.

[50] "Illa autem Romana ecclesia quae errare non potest est universalis ecclesia"; ibid., 66.

RESPONSE TO KLAUS SCHATZ

MIGUEL MARÍA GARIJO GUEMBE*

Professor Klaus-Schatz has presented the central lines of the beginning of a universalist ecclesiology, which he has called "the Gregorian reform." Gregory VII took up again ideas which had already been formulated before his time, and drew them into a synthesis in which the primacy of the Roman See was expressed in a form which, up to a certain point, was new. The primacy appears not only as a center of unity (*centrum unitatis*) of a common agreement of Churches, but also as head (*caput*) of the Church, beginning with which life in ecclesial unity must be explained. The terms with which relations were established between Rome and the other Churches are *cardo, caput, mater (omnium ecclesiarum), fons, fundamentum, basis*. These terms, as Schatz indicates, are not new. They are already found in Pope Nicholas I (+867) and have earlier roots in Rome.

My purpose is to establish the differences between the Roman and Byzantine understandings. I am only dealing with this from a purely historical level. The current interest of the theme for the dialogue between the Catholic Church and the Orthodox Churches is evident. Note that Orthodox theology today thinks with the same characteristics as in the past.

The Break of 1054 and Its Expressions

The date of 1054 is found in our period. It has a symbolic character in terms of the break between Rome and Byzantium. An ensemble of factors, also of a political order, where behind the break between the papal legate, Cardinal Humberto of Silva Candida, and Patriarch Michael Cerularius. The Roman demand for the return of Illiricum to its jurisdiction, as well as all the contention over southern Italy, as well as the fact that Rome accepted an emperor in the West and the presence of Normans in the south of Italy, are factors which influenced negatively on the peaceful relations between Byzantium and Rome. The rupture between

* Katholische-Theologische Fakultät, Münster-im-W. (Germany).

Cardinal Humberto and Patriarch Cerularius appear as the culmination of measures by one side and counter-measures by the other in relationship to liturgical uses, Greek or Latin or vice-versa. The occasion of the dispute was the writing of Leo, Greek Archbishop of Ocrida, to the Latin bishop of Trani. At the insistence of Patriarch Cerularius, Leo of Ocrida defended the Greek rite by attacking Latin usages, especially the use of unleavened bread for the eucharistic celebration. Cardinal Humberto rose up in defense of the Latin tradition. By means of the petitions and letters of Humberto—sometimes as texts of the pope himself—the Byzantines came to see the ecclesiological principles of the reform movement which had taken over Rome with the election of Leo IX (1049-1054). At that moment the issue was the legitimacy of the Roman liturgical usage. The Roman response argued from principle, that is, from the Petrine foundation of the Roman Church. The texts of Mt 16: 17-19 and Lk 22: 32 were cited. The conclusion was clear: all heresy has been repelled by the see of the prince of the apostles, the Roman church, which has maintained the faith of Peter, while on the Greek side there have arisen so many heresies. The Petrine argument was used as well to place the Churches of Alexandria and Antioch ahead of Constantinople. Likewise rejected was that Cerularius named himself the Ecumenical Patriarch. Finally, from the claim of Rome to be the head and mother of Churches (*caput et mater ecclesiarum*) it was deduced that any see which dissented from Rome could no longer be called a church, but was simply a little council of heretics (*conciliadulum haereticorum*), a little convent of schismatics (*conventiculum schismaticorum*), and the synagogue of Satan (*synagoga Satanae*).

Here we have to ask ourselves if Pope Leo IX and his Cardinal Humberto were innovators, or if on the contrary they did nothing but repeat again the Roman thesis. The reference that the church of Rome had never erred in the faith is a theme which appears often in history. An example of it is the well-known profession of faith of Pope Hormisdas which he sent to Constantinople to be signed and by which he put an end to the schism of Acaciano (DS 363). Rome, Congar writes, appears as a model, being the Church of Peter, the first to confess Christ in an exemplary way. The use of the Petrine texts is likewise traditional. Finally, it is traditional in Rome to see the dignity of Alexandria and Antioch in connection with Peter, for they are petrine sees. This appeared in the Gelasian decree (DS 351), a document cited by Pope Nicholas I as *De libris recipiendis et non recipiendis*. In his reply to the question from the Bulgars (*Responsa ad consulta Bulgarorum*) Nicholas I indicated that the patriarchs in a strict sense are only those of Rome, Alexandria, and Antioch. The authority of Constantinople and Jerusalem was inferior to the other patriarchates. Nicholas thus took up again the argumentation of Pope Leo the Great against canon 28 of the Council of Chalcedon. The pope underlined the principle of apostolic and petrine origins of the sees. Because of this he held that Rome, Alexandria, and Antioch were ahead of Constantinople. The first three were tied to Peter—Alexandria by means of St. Mark, disciple of Peter—while the title of Constantinople was only that of being the city where the emperor resided; it was not an apostolic see. Canon 28 of Chalcedon was later integrated in canonical collections, including Latin ones, but of a private character. The assumption of Constantinople in the order of sees after Rome and before Alexandria and Antioch became standard practice with Novella 131 of Emperor Justinian.

A new basis of discussion arose when in Rome it was perceived that the archbishop of Constantinople was calling himself the ecumenical patriarch. Pope Pelagius II (579-590) was scandalized by this usage. His successor, Gregory the Great, protested again. In Constantinople this title was traditional by the beginning of the sixth century. It is the title which Justinian used when he referred to the pope and the other patriarchs. In Dvorniak's opinion, the title "does not mean more than the supreme power exercised by a patriarch within the limits of his patriarchate." For Gregory the Great the title cast suspicion upon the power of the other bishops and contradicted the Petrine origin of the patriarchates of Alexandria and Antioch. The pope's reaction had no effect. Worthy of interest, however, is the indication in the *Liber Pontificalis* that Pope Boniface II, the second successor of Gregory, obtained from emperor Focas "the confirmation that the apostolic see of the blessed apostle Peter was ahead of all the Churches, because the Church of Constantinople was bragging that it was the first of all the Churches."

The title of ecumenical patriarch was denied to the bishop of Constantinople by Pope Leo IX. On this occasion he referred to the decisions of Popes Pelagius II and Gregory, as well as averting that St. Leo the Great did not accept this title which was offered to him, and that none of his successors had accepted it.

Having reached this point we can ask whether these documents of Pope Leo IX and Cardinal Humberto left out any central successes in the relations between Byzantium and Rome. Really, they do call attention to the fact of the ineffectiveness of the document signed between Pope John

VIII and the patriarch of Constantinople Phocius on the occasion of the synod of 879-880. Cardinal Deusdedit did refer to it later. In this synod it was accepted that each see—Rome, Constantinople, and the other sees of the East—held the right to maintain the traditions which they possessed from antiquity. Patriarch Phocius emphasized several times that the sees could maintain legitimate traditions within the identity of the same faith. But in his polemic against the Romans, Patriarch Cerularius hardly held on to this same principle.

Two Ecclesiologies or Conceptions concerning the Roman Primacy

The Roman ecclesiology experienced a development with Popes Leo IX and Gregory VII. Such an ecclesiology is already found, although only in germinal form, in Pope Nicholas I two centuries before. It can even be affirmed that this ecclesiology was already *in nuce* in St. Leo the Great (on the occasion of the Council of Chalcedon). With the *dictatus papae* of Gregory VII such an ecclesiology acquired the following concrete expressions:

Only the Roman Church has been instituted by the Lord (1).

The Roman Church has not erred nor will err as Sacred Scripture attests (22).

Only those can be considered Catholic who are in agreement with the Roman Church (26).

Only the pope can be called, with good right, universal.

In indicating that only the Roman Church has been instituted by the Lord the pope refers to a characteristic of the Roman Church. It is the see of the apostles Peter and Paul, a reality all recognized. When the Romans speak of Rome only as the see of Peter, the Byzantines add "and of Paul." In the pope's judgment all the other instances in the Church—metropolitans, patriarchs—are creations of the pope who calls them to participate in his universal care. Gregory VII's thesis is linked with the understanding that Nicholas I already had of the patriarchate; they are, certainly, sees of the apostles, but Nicholas I reduced the patriarchs to Peter: his presence in Alexandria by means of his disciple Mark, his presence for a time in Antioch, and his definitive and always actual presence by means of his successor in Rome.

The Byzantines had profound difficulty with these ideas, above all because historical patriarchates are realities established by ecumenical councils. In the eighth and ninth centuries in Constantinople the idea of the pentarchy had put down deep roots. The agreement of the five patriarchates on a doctrine was a sign of truth in the Church. Thus was expressed the universality of the Church! In the expression of Theodore Studites, the five patriarchs are successors of the apostles. The idea of a pentarchy appeared expressly in the council for Ignatius of 869-870. Anastasius the librarian witnessed to its acceptance in Rome. The idea of the pentarchy presupposed on one side the autonomy of the patriarchs and in consequence the acceptance of the legitimate differences in expression of Phocius, and on the other a type of collegiality. Each patriarch was related to the others in maintaining the universal faith. In this way of thinking Rome held the first place, and there is no doubt of this. Without papal approbation of the acts of a council they did not have the character of an ecumenical synod. That Rome accepted a synod as ecumenical had a special character in relation to the approval on the part of the other patriarchs.

These are facts attested to by the history of ecumenical councils. However, it must not be forgotten that Roman decisions, as for example the Tome of Leo, were analyzed in ecumenical councils to see if they were in accord with the faith transmitted by the Church. According to *Dictatus Papae* 16, "without the approval of the pope no synod can be termed general," that is, to have a definitive character. Express Roman approval was necessary. The autonomy to which Byzantium was accustomed and which was a principle of life in the *koinonia* of the churches, was thus put into question.

The consequence of all this was the identification *romana* with *universalis*. For this reason only the pope could be called universal. With the identification of *romana* with *universalis* the Roman church acquired a normative character for all the churches.

Here there was already a step which could wind up being very dangerous. To say the Roman church is *caput et mater* of all the churches had the danger of isolating it from the other churches, of not valuing the *koinoia* of the churches in ecclesial life. At least this is how it appeared to the Byzantines in the later polemic against the primacy, and to contemporary orthodox theologians.

Translation by James H. Provost

RECEPTION IN THE FORMATION OF CANON LAW WITHIN THE FRAMEWORK OF EXCHANGES BETWEEN CHURCHES DURING THE MIDDLE AGES

Antonio García y García[*]

This theme will be developed in five sections: preliminary concepts; reception before the 12th century; reception in the Decree of Gratian (1140-1150); reception in councils and canonical collections in the 12th-14th centuries; recapitulation.

I. Preliminary Concepts[1]

1. We take as given the distinction between canon law as the ordering or juridical system of the Church as a whole; canonical collections which contain canons and which are sometimes private (made by private au-

---

* Universidad Pontificia de Salamanca (Spain).

1 The following abbreviations will be used in this study:

BMCL NS = *Bulletin of Medieval Canon Law*. New Series.

CCQL = *Constitutiones Concilii quarti Lateranensis una cum commentariis glossatorum*, ed. Antonio Garcia y García, Monumenta iuris canonici, Series A: *Corpus glossatorum* 2 (Vatican City: Biblioteca Apostolica Vaticana, 1981).

COD = *Conciliorum Oecumenicorum Decreta*, ed. Josepho Alberigo et al., 3rd ed. (Bologna: Istituto per le Scienze Religiose, 1973).

Coll. = *Collectio.*

Coing = Helmut Coing, dir., *Handbuch der Quellen und Literatur der neueren Europäischen Privatrechtsgeschichte*, 1: *Mittelalter (1100-1500). Die Gelehrten Rechte und die Gesetzgebung* (1973); 2/1-2: *Neure Zeit (1500-1800). Das Zeitalter des Gemeinen Rechts* (Munich: Beck, 1976 and 1977).

Fournier-Le Bras = Paul Fournier and Gabriel Le Bras, *Histoire des collections canonique en Occident* 1-2 (Paris: Sirey, 1931-1932; Aalen: Scientia, 1972).

Friedberg = Aemilius Friedberg, *Corpus Iuris Canonici*, 2 vols. (Leipzig: B. Tauchnitz, 1879; Graz: Akademische Druck- u. Verlagsanstalt, 1959).

HDC = Antonio García y García, *Historia del Derecho Canónico*, 1: *El Primer Milenio* (Salamanca: Impr. Calatrava, 1967).

thors, which have no more juridical value than what each legal text has independently of its inclusion in any determined canonical collection) while other collections are public or authentic (with binding juridical force, issued by the competent ecclesiastical authority); *canonistic* or canonical science, either an author or a school elaborating juridical doctrine; and jurisprudence or the practice of the ecclesiastical courts.

Canonical collections not only contain normative ecclesiastical texts but also elements of secular law, along with theological, biblical, liturgical, and other texts which do not always necessarily contain canonical norms but which also serve as a framework or context for such normative material.

2. As to the concept and classes of canonical reception, we will call "reception," in the juridical field, the fact of accepting as binding in one's own legal system the whole or some part of norms from another, different system. In our concrete case, this consists in the acceptance by one church of all or part of what is canonically normative from another church or from other churches.

3. As well as the reception of norms from another church or from several other churches, we also have the reception of secular laws as binding in the ecclesiastical sphere or, said in other words, we have the reception of secular law into the canon law of the Church.

Medieval canon law is based before and above all on roman law which is, from the juridical point of view, the *ratio scripta* and the matrix of all Western law systems not only in the Middle Ages but right up to the end

---

JL = Philippe Jaffé et al., *Regesta pontificium romanorum ab condita Ecclesia ad a. post Christum natum MCXCVIII*, 1-2 (Leipzig: Veit, 1885-1888; Graz: Akademische Druck- u. Verlagsanstalt, 1956).

Maassen = Friedrich Maassen, *Geschichte der Quellen und der Literatur des canonischen Rechts*, 1: *Die Rechtssammlungen bis zur Mitte des 9. Jahrhunderts* (Graz: Leischner & Lubensky, 1870; Graz: Akademische Druck- u. Verlagsanstalt, 1956).

MGH = Monumenta Germaniae Historica.

PL = Patrologia Latina.

REDC = Revista Española de Derecho Canonico.

Savigny = Friedrich C. von Savigny, *Geschichte des römischen Rechts im Mittelalter*, 2nd ed., 1-7 (Heidelberg: Mohr, 1834-1851; Bad Homburg: Gentner, 1961).

SH = Synodicon hispanum, 1-7, dir. Antonio García y García (Madrid: BAC, 1981-1997).

ZRG Kan. Abt. or *Rom Apt. = Zeitschrift der Savigny Stiftung für Rechtsgeschichte. Kanonistische Abteilung* or *Romanistische Abteilung.*

of the second millennium and the beginnings of the third.[2] On the other hand, the reception of roman law and roman canon law was not identical right down to the last detail in every kingdom and church, but rather varied from one situation to another, being much wider in some cases than in others.[3]

4. From the 13th century onwards, we have a further reception of common roman canon law in the juridical systems of the European kingdoms of the late Middle Ages, a reception which went on until the end of the ancien régime at the end of the 18th century.

5. We also have reception of medieval roman canon law in the churches born of the Protestant Reformation (particularly among the Lutherans, Calvinists, and Anglicans), even though this medieval canon law is eminently pontifical. Although the basis for this reception is explained with somewhat different nuances in each case, all these churches coincide in relating it to its solid foundation in natural law.[4]

6. Apart from both types of reception (of canonical norms and civil norms), we also have "use," that is, using concepts and categories from secular law in a canonical text or system. In this case however, the juridical texts have no more binding force than what the ecclesiastical legislator gave them. In this last sense we cannot speak of the reception of roman law into canon law before the 9th century but only of its simple use.

7. We use the terminology of "universalization of reception" when normative material which hitherto belonged only to local churches is received into the universal Church. In line with this, we call "universalist" those collections which receive norms from all or from the majority of

---

[2] Benedict XV, constitution *Providentissima mater Ecclesia*, May 27, 1917, on the promulgation of the 1917 *Codex Iuris Canonici*, spoke thus of roman law: "ipsum quoque Romanorum ius, insigne veteris sapientiae monumentum, quod *ratio scripta* est meritum nuncupatum, divini luminis auxilio freta, tempera correctumque christiane perfecit." Roman law is moreover a subject which is still studied in all faculties of both secular and canon law. On the reception of roman law from the Middle Ages up to the end of the ancien régime see Coing.

[3] See on this point the different authors of each chapter of vol. 1 of the manual directed by Coing.

[4] *Canon law in Protestant Lands*, ed. Richard H. Helmholz, Comparative Studies in Continental and Anglo-American Legal History 11 (Berlin: Duncker & Humblot, 1992). The geographical areas specially studied by the authors of this volume are Germany, Holland, France, Switzerland, Northern Ireland, and the former British colonies in America.

local churches. In view of the fact that these were the collections which had the greatest circulation and acceptance, their legislation tended to universalize itself.

8. Let us now look briefly at the attitudes toward reception, and the arduous path which reception followed in this respect, given that a division of opinion was produced in the Church on this point from the highest authorities right down to private authors who dealt with this material. Some examples will help us better to take on board the intellectual climate in which both the use and the acceptance of roman laws took place.

In the Roman Synod of Pope Agatho (679) there is an implicit quotation from the Digest of Justinian.[5] St. Gregory the Great spoke of principles which "legibus canonibus conveniunt."[6] Pope Eugene III was reproved in these terms by his friend Bernard of Clairvaux: "quotidie perstrepunt in palatio tuo leges, sed Iustiniani non Domini."[7] Pope John VIII, in a text which passed into the Decree of Gratian,[8] spoke of roman laws "divinitus per ore principum promulgatae."[9]

A prestigious bishop such as Atto of Vercelli (mid-10th century) expressed himself in an ambivalent way about roman laws; "etiam nobis sacerdotibus in multis convenit observare."[10] Another great bishop as well as legislator, Yves of Chartres expressed himself in these terms: "dicunt enim Instituta legum novellarum, quas commendat et servat Romana Ecclesia";[11] ". . . leges saeculi quas catholici reges composuerunt et ex auctoritate Romanae ecclesiae catholicis populis servandas tradiderunt."[12]

To this chorus we must add the voice of the councils. As early as the year 511 canon 1 of the Council of Orleans said: "id constituimus observandum quod ecclesiastici canones decreverunt et lex Romana consti-

---

[5]   See Stephan Kuttner, "An implied reference to the Digest in Pope Agatho's Roman Synod of 679," in *ZRG Rom. Abt.* 107 (1990) 382-384.

[6]   St. Gregory the Great, Ep. 2: 28 (*MGH* ep. 2. 1. 125).

[7]   Federico Patetta, "Opere attribuite ad Irnerio e la scuola di Roma," *Bolletino del Istituto di Diritto Romano* 8 (1895) 78.

[8]   C. 16 q. 3 c. 17.

[9]   See JL 2247; Anselmus Lucensis, *Collectio canonica* 4: 45; *Coll. trium partium* 1.63.4. (cf. Friedberg, *Decretum*, col. 745-746).

[10]   Savigny, 2: 282, note a.

[11]   Ep. 280 (*PL* 162: 281).

[12]   Ep. 244 (?).

tuit."[13] The Council of Pavia of 1022, for its part, spoke in these terms of Justinian's law and of ecclesiastical (Nicene) law: "legant denique vel si legere fastidiunt, legentem intelligent Iustiniani Augusti, viri christianissimi . . . longo oculo vir Iustinianus . . . merito iustus . . . si ergo hoc concedit saecularibus propter utilitatem et necessitatem. . . . Secundum ecclesiasticam regulam . . . sed neque secundum humanas leges . . . et nostris regulis et mundanis legibus concordantibus."[14] The pseudonymous author who hides behind the name of Benedict Levite, in his *Capitularia* (847-857) described "Lex romana omnium humanarum legum mater."[15] Cardinal Deusdedit (1083-1087), in the midst of the Gregorian reform of the 11th century, affirmed in the introduction to his canonical collection that he was editing it "ex variis sanctionibus patrum et christianorum principum auctoritatibus potioribus . . . presens defloraui opusculum."[16]

One would be mistaken if one thought that these voices were totally unanimous. Lactantius affirmed that the Romans' "legibus etiam sibi nomine iustitiae iniquissimas iniustissimasque sanxerunt."[17] St. Jerome contrasted the law of Christ and that of Caesar, the precepts of God and those of Papianus.[18]

In the eleventh century some even came to admit that roman laws bind in the Church by their own authority. The rest of canonical tradition, however, does not hold with this but rather "canonizes" roman or other secular laws in each case and so is conscious than such laws do not bind of themselves.

Gratian posed the question of collision between roman and canon laws and he concluded that roman laws "ecclesiasticis legibus post ponendae sunt."[19] Popes Honorius III and Innocent IV (1219 and 1254) banned

[13] *Concilia Galliae*, ed. Carolus de Clercq, Corpus Christianorum, Series Latina 148A (Turnholt: Brepols, 1963) 4.

[14] Cf. Johannes D. Mansi, ed., *Sacrorum concilorum nova et amplissima collectio* 19 (Venice, 1774) 357-358, where there is something similar though not quite the same; cf. Maassen, 204.

[15] Edition in *MGH LL* 2/2 (Hannover: Hahn, 1837) 156, 17ff.; *PL* 97: 698 ff. Cf. Horst Fuhrmann, *Einfluss und Verbreitung der pseudoisidorischen Fälschungen vor ihrem Auftauchen bis in die nuere Zeit, MGH SS* 24/1-3 (Stuttgart: Hiersmann, 1973) 822.

[16] *Die Kanonessammlung des Kardinal Deusdedit*, ed. Victor Wolf von Glanvell (Paderborn: F. Schöningh, 1905; Aalen: Scientia, 1967) 2.

[17] Lactantius, *Divinae institutiones* 5: 6 (*PL* 6: 567).

[18] St. Augustine, *Sermo* 355: 4 (*PL* 39: 1572); St Jerome, Ep. 77 *ad Oceanum* (*PL* 22: 690).

[19] D. 10 dpc.6.

clerics from studying roman law. The reason for this ban lay not in any possible incompatibility but rather in an attempt to forestall clerical jurists neglecting their pastoral work in favor of their more economically rewarding dedication to the civil law courts. A political motivation for such bans is also commonly admitted, given that the popes had no wish to encourage imperial pretensions. The tension between the Empire and kingdoms on the one hand and ecclesiastical power on the other created a climate of opposition between the *leges* and the *canones*. But in fact the popes never at any time opposed the teaching of roman law in the Universities.

As a conclusion to this first section it is opportune to highlight that the concept and applications of reception in the field of law in general and in the Church in particular have aspects in common with reception in the theological sense; however, it also presents important aspects which make it different, such as the role which roman law played, as this is the model for all Western law systems both secular and canonical. It is owed, among other factors, to the circumstance that law harbors less risks than does theology of heading into a collision with the dogmas of the Church. Another aspect to bear in mind in this regard is that the perfection of roman law has not been surpassed by any other juridical tradition, past or present, so much so that even today the most advanced legal systems are based in large measure on roman law.

II. Antecedents of Reception in Gratian

Until the sixth century there were no canonical collections properly so-called, but rather just mixed collections which contained liturgical and catechetical texts, etc., as well as normative ones. Such is the case of the so called Pseudo-Apostolic Collections.[20]

It should be noted that the most receptive collections were those of a universalist tendency, with the single exception of the collections of the Gregorian reform, as we shall see later. These two concepts of universality and receptivity superimpose themselves one upon the other.

In the East the first canonical collections appeared in the 4th century, and in each one of them the councils of each particular church were received into a common corpus, as happened with the *Syntagma canonum*

---

[20]   See *HDC* 1: 43-49, where there is a summary of this theme with an essential bibliography on it.

or *Corpus Canonum Orientale* (second half of the 4th century), *Collectio Trullana* (691), etc.[21] These collections received texts from different Eastern Churches, but not from the Latin Church, with the exception of the African Church. With regard to the attitude of the Easterners to pontifical letters, their reception does not necessarily signify that they were received from the pope as such, but can rather be understood as the reception of letters from the Patriarch of the West, which relativizes the value of this reception.

In the West there was a first period (4th -5th centuries) of regional and local collections (Africa, Iberian Peninsula, Gaul, Italy) until in the time of Pope Gelasius (492-496) this movement became centered in Rome, being known in current historiography as the "Gelasian Renaissance," after the pope of this name whom we have just mentioned. The main protagonist of this compilation activity in Rome was Dionysius Exiguus, a monk of Escitia, versed in Greek and Latin, who first compiled the ecumenical and particular councils of the East and West, and then the pontifical letters or decretals; the collection of both these elements is known as the *Collectio Dionysiana*.[22] This collection was private; it did not have the approval of any pontifical authority nor of any other ecclesiastical authority, but rather each text maintained the binding force it had because it belonged to a general or particular council or was a pontifical decretal. We have here, therefore, a very wide reception of law from every particular church, which was universalized in this *Collectio Dionysiana* thanks to the great spread of the work of Dionysius, but not thanks to any new approval by any authority, and so each text keept the force it had at its inception and which was accepted de facto in the other churches.

In the image and likeness of this dionysian experience, similar collections were formed in each of the germanic kingdoms which emerged in the territories of the former Roman Empire. Among these collections the principal ones are those of a universalist stamp, imitating in this regard that of Dionysius Exiguus insofar as they received texts from other churches and from Rome, or from their own church. The principal ones,

---

[21] See Alphonsus M. Stickler, *Historia iuris canonici latini*, 1: *Historia fontium* (Turin: Pontificium Athenaeum Salesianum, 1959) for bibliography, editions, and other details on these and other Eastern collections.

[22] Edition in *PL* 67: 9-230 (councils) and 229-316 (decretals). Critical edition of the registers in Hubert Wurm, *Studien und Texte zur Dekretalensammlung des Dionysius Exiguus* (Bonn: Röhrscheid, 1939; Amsterdam: P. Schippers, 1964) 62 ff.

which constitute an obligatory point of reference, are these: *La Hispana*,[23] the *Vetus Gallica*,[24] and the *Dacheriana*.[25] It is worth drawing attention to the recognition or reception which the *Collectio Hispana* made of the decretals of the popes in these words: "Maneant in suo vigore conciliorum omnium constituta, simul et synodicae sanctorum praesulum Romanorum epistolae."[26] Although the three collections which we have just mentioned were conceived for local churches, the materials received in them are characterized by their universality, which means that these collections in their turn received a warm welcome in churches different from those for which they had originally been conceived.

Parallel to these collections of universalist stamp already mentioned, the literary-normative genre of the penitentials sprang up with vigor from a celtic anglo-saxon background, and from there spread onto the Continent. These penitentials were formed in the main from apocryphal texts, particularist, ajuridical in character, and somewhat unilateral, given that they were centered almost exclusively on tariffed penance. Born in the island church in the middle of the 5th century, they spread with vigor into the churches of the Continent in the following centuries.[27]

During the Carolingian period, in addition to the genuine collection known as the *Dacheriana* mentioned above, apocryphal collections also sprang up. Among these the so-called *Decretales Pseudoisidorianas* stand out as a collection of universalist character whose universalism

---

[23] Study and critical edition by Gonzalo Martínez Díez and Félix Rodriguez, *La Colección Canónica Hispana*, 1-5 (Madrid: CSIC, 1966-1992), which comes as far as the 10th Council of Toledo. For the part not covered in this edition, see the edition of Franciscus A. Gonzalez, *Collectio Canonum Ecclesiae Hispaniae* (Madrid: Typographia Haeredum D. Joachim de Ibarra, 1808).

[24] Hubert Mordek, *Kirchenrecht und Reform im Frankreich*, Beitrage zur Geschichte und Quellenkunde des Mittelalters 1 (Berlin and New York: W. de Gruyter, 1975); study on 1-338 and critical edition on 339-666.

[25] A fairly imperfect edition in L. d'Achery, *Veterum aliquot scriptorum spicilegium* 11 (Paris, 1669) 1 ff., with a second Paris edition of 1723, 509 ff. Haeni is currently preparing an edition. Cf. *HDC* 1: 295-296.

[26] Third Council of Toledo (589), c. 1 toward the end. *Concilios visigóticos e hispanoromanos*, ed. José Vives et al. (Barcelona and Madrid: CSIC, 1963) 125. The text of the visigothic councils is only known because of their tradition or reception in the *Colección canónica Hispana*.

[27] See *HDC* 187-189, 292-293, where sources and relevant bibliography are indicated.

came from the *Hispana*, despite its apocryphal character, given that the falsifying was built on another previous falsification of a codex of the above collection.[28]

Dependent on the Carolingian reform and of special importance for its later influence are the collection of Regino of Prüm (c. 906)[29] and that known as *Collectio Anselmo dedicata*, written by an unknown author *circa* 882 and dedicated to Anselm, bishop of Milan.[30] Outstanding for their width and universalism among the collections which preceded the Gregorian reform are the *Decretum* of Burchard of Worms[31] and its recension widely known as the *Collectio duodecim partium*.[32]

The collections of the Gregorian reform made a careful selection of what had gone before, looking for what was in tune with the aims of the reform, creating a new recension or editing of the most recent principal collection which was the *Decretum* of Burchard of Worms; they also put other new ones into circulation, the principal ones being: *Breviarium Cardinalis Attonis*,[33] *Dictatus Papae* (of Gregory VII),[34] *Collectio 74 tit-*

---

[28]   *Decretales Pseudo-Isidorianae et Capitula Angilrami*, ed. Paul Hinschius (Leipzig: B. Tauchnitz, 1863; Aalen: Scientia, 1963), where other critical editions are indicated.

[29]   Critical edition by F. G. A. Wasserschleben, *Reginonis Abbatis Prümiensis libro duo de synodalibus causis et disciplinis ecclesiasticis* (Leipzig, 1840; Graz: Akademische Druck- u. Verlagsanstalt, 1964) (first recension), and *PL* 132: 175-484 (second recension taken from Étienne Baluze, Parisian edition of 1671).

[30]   Not edited as such, but preface and a summary provided in Angelo Mai, *Nova Patrum Biblioteca* 7, Part 3 (Rome: Spithover, 1854) and in *PL* 134: 9-52.

[31]   Unsatisfactory edition in *PL* 140: 537-1058. Critical edition in the care of Otto Meyer, to appear in the *Sectio Conciliorum* of the *MGH*. Cf. Otto Meyer, "Überlieferung und Verbreitung des Dekrets des Bischofs Burchard von Worms," *ZRG Kan. Abt.* 24 (1935) 141-183.

[32]   Jörg Müller, *Untersuchungen zur Collectio Duodecim Partium*, Münchener Universitätsschriften-Juristische Facultät, Abhandlung zur rechtswissenschaftlichen Grundlagenforschung 73 (Ebelsbach: Gremer, 1989).

[33]   Edition by Angelo Mai, *Scriptores veterum nova collectio* 6/2 (Rome: Typis Vaticanis, 1832) 60-120.

[34]   Critical edition by Erich Caspar, *Das Register Gregors VII*, in *MGH Epistolae selectae* 2 (Berlin: Weidmannsche Buchhandlung, 1920-1923) 202ff. There is a Spanish translation in Bernardino Llorca et al., *Historia de la Iglesia Catolica*, 2: *Edad Media* (Madrid: BAC, 1963) 319-320.

ulorum,[35] *Collectio Anselmi Lucensis,*[36] Cardinal Deusdedit,[37] *Liber de vita christiana Bonizonis,*[38] and the *Collectio Britannica.*[39] Throughout this series of collections there was a lot of emphasis on pontifical authority, celebration of councils, defense of the ecclesiastical immunity of churches and monasteries, coercive power of the Church, while at the same time the abuses of Nicholaism, simony, and lay investiture were combatted.[40] In order to have an idea of the extent and depth of the romanistic reception of canon law in the Gregorian era, it suffices to remember that around a hundred texts of roman law were received in the so-called *Collectio Britannica.* As is known, roman law contains not a few elements useful to the centralization for which the Gregorian reform pushed hard.

Although it may appear strange today, as does the fact that the German emperors felt themselves the successors of the Roman emperors, popes and jurists admitted, although with certain limitations, the validity of roman law in the field of the canon law of the Church. Thus Frederick I of Germany declared in 1165: "Nos igitur, praedecessorum nostrorum divorum imperatorum magni Constantini videlicet et Iustiniani et Valentiani, nec non Karoli et Ludovici, vestigiis inherentes, et sacras leges eorum tanquam divina oracula venerantes imitari non erubescimus Constantinum imperatorem de sacrosanctis ecclesiis et rebus et privilegiis eorum constituentem."[41] Because of this Dante Alighieri put into the mouth of Justinian that his codification was inspired by God: "Tosto che con la Chiesa mossi i piedi, a Dio per grazia plaque di spirarmi, l'alto lavoro e tutto 'i liu mi diedi."[42]

Meanwhile, all through the eleventh century the rediscovery and use of Justinian's roman law was happening in Ravenna and Tuscany, first of

---

[35] Critical edition by John T. Gilchrist, *Diuersorum patrum sententiae siue Collectio in LXXIV titulos digesta,* Monumenta Iuris Canonici, series B: Corpus Collectionum, vol. 1 (Vatican City: Biblioteca Apostolica Vaticana, 1973).

[36] Edition by Friedrich Thaner, *Anselmi episcopi Lucensis collectio canonum una cum collectione minore* (Innsbruck: Libreria academicae Wagnerianae, 1915; Aalen: Scientia, 1965).

[37] Critical edition by Wolf von Glanvell (*supra,* note 16).

[38] Edition by Ernest Perels, *Liber de vita christiana* (Berlin: Weidmannsche Buchhandlung, 1930).

[39] Edition of the letters and rubrics in Paul Ewald, "Die Papstbriefe der Brittische Sammlung," in *Neues Archiv* 5 (1880) 277-414 and 501-596.

[40] Cf. ibid., 160-191.

[41] *MGH LL* 2: 139 (*Constitutio de bona clericorum decedentium*).

[42] *Parad.* 6: 22-24.

all in notarial acts and then in court activity. The learning process of the same took place first of all in the teaching of the liberal arts and even more in the schools of notaries. The school of Bologna founded at the end of the eleventh century concentrated its activity primarily on roman law and later also on canon law. With this, both laws acquired university status and the example of Bologna was followed by the universities of juridical tradition in Italy, France, Spain, Portugal, and later by the university centers of the rest of Europe.[43]

III. Reception in Gratian's Decree

A triple renaissance was produced in the thirteenth century: of Aristotelian philosophy, of roman law, and of canon law. These disciplines were not only reborn but their study acquired scientific and university status in the recently founded universities of Paris and Bologna and in the other universities which were founded following their example.

From what we have seen already of the antecedents it is clear that by the end of the twelfth century all was prepared for an extensive and profound reception of the canonical norms of the churches of the first millennium into the classic medieval canonical system. This was done principally although not exclusively in the Decree of Gratian or the *Concordia discordantium canonum*,[44] which constitutes the first piece of the *Corpus Iuris Canonici*. Note that the Decree is a private collection as were all previous ones in the Church; and texts did not acquire greater juridical value by the mere fact that they were included and formed part of the Gratian's *Decretum*. Despite this, its author is considered to be the father of canon law as a science,[45] and no other collection has had such an important impact in the history of ecclesiastical discipline. Gratian gathers together in his work many disciplinary sources of very different value

---

[43]   Ennio Cortese, *Il rinascimento giuridico medievale* (Rome: Bulzoni, 1992), where he offers a good exposition of the theme along with an updated reference to sources and bibliography.

[44]   Around a thousand manuscripts of the Decree are preserved, 48 incunable editions and 164 which are later than 1500. Cf. Erich Will, "Decreti Gratiani incunablia," *Studia Gratiana* 6 (1959) 280; Aldo Adversi, "Saggio di un catalogo delle edizioni del 'Decretum Gratiani' posteriori al s. XV," ibid., 281-453. In 1582 the Roman edition was published, the best of the ancient ones. Friedberg's edition is not critical enough, but it continues to be the necessary point of reference until we have something better at our disposal. See Friedberg, 1: *Decretum Magistri Gratiani*.

[45]   Stephan Kuttner, "The Father of the Science of Canon Law," *The Jurist* 1 (1941) 2-19.

from the first millennium: Holy Scripture, natural law, *Canones Apostolorum*, canons from general and particular councils, papal decretals, texts from the Fathers and from other ecclesiastical authors, normative material from the celtic anglo-saxon penitential books and from their spread through the continent of Europe, local customary law, episodes from ecclesiastical and civil history, along with roman law, germanic law, constitutions of medieval kings and emperors, jurisprudence, and doctrine. In all this multicolored amalgam what stands out above all the rest are the canons of councils, papal decretals and patristic texts and, to a lesser degree, civil law, historiography, liturgy, etc. As we know, Gratian copied the relevant texts in a literal way, taking them from the collections of the carolingian reform, many of which we have already mentioned, and from these the following stand out: *Collectio Anselmo dedicata*, *Reginonis Prümiensis libro duo de synodalibus causis et disciplinis ecclesiasticis*, *Decretum Burchardi Wormatiensis* and its expanded version known as *Collectio duodecim partium*, *Collectio Anselmi Lucensis*, *Collectio Cardinalis Deusdedit*, *Polycarpus* of Cardinal Gregory of St. Chrysogonus, *Collectio Caesaraugustana*, *Liber de misericordia et justitiae* of Alger of Liège, etc.[46] An even heavier influence on Gratian than the collections mentioned above was that exercised by the three collections of Yves, Bishop of Chartres from 1091-1116, *Tripartita*,[47] *Decretum*,[48] and *Panormia*.[49]

Gratian, however, was much more than a compiler of other people's texts because he introduced a dialectic into them, interrogating them with great efficiency, posing the questions that emerge from these texts, while adding the reasons for and against each one of the solutions. With this canon law acquired a scientific status, as did its contemporary and parallel work, the Sentences of Peter Lombard; but Gratian's had an even more widespread historical effect, given that the Decree of Gratian formed part of the law of the Church until the Code of Canon Law of 1917. In addition to editing an introduction to each section along with rubrics and inscriptions, Gratian made his own commentaries known as the *dicta Gratiani* and with these he introduced the dialectic method into

---

[46] For information on these collections, see thematic index in *HDC*.
[47] Edition of preface in Augustin Theiner, *Disquisitiones criticae in antiquas iuris canonici collectiones* (Rome: Typis Vaticanis, 1836) 154-155.
[48] Edition in *PL* 161: 59-1022, which reproduces an old edition of P. Fronteau (1647).
[49] Edition in *PL* 161: 1045-1344, which reproduces the edition of Melchior de Vosmédian (1557).

the treatment of the canonical sources of the first millennium.[50] We can therefore describe the reception of Gratian as "critical," given that he did not limit himself to receiving texts and authorities but rather subjected their value to rigorous scrutiny.

IV. RECEPTION IN MEDIEVAL COUNCILS
AND CANONICAL COLLECTIONS (12-14 CENTURY)

A. *The Church's Conciliar and Compilation Activity*

If the Church's compilation activity up to Gratian is noted, among other aspects, for being the work of private authors, beginning with the middle of the twelfth century this activity was also the work of popes, without impeding the surfacing of private collections of great impact, which reached the exalted number of two hundred.[51]

A first manifestation of this phenomenon is the celebration of the general councils in the West in the late Middle Ages: Lateran I (1123), II (1139), III (1179), and IV (1215); Lyons I (1245) and II (1274); Vienne (1310); etc. Their constitutions were brought in to form part of the collections of the *Corpus Iuris Canonici*, as Gratian (1140), Gregory IX (1234), Liber VI (1298) and Clementine (1217). These councils were not called ecumenical, but general or universal,[52] which meant at that time that they were presided over by the pope or his legate, or simply that the Roman Pontiff ordered their convocation, as in the East such councils were called "ecumenical" because the emperor was the lord of the *ecuméne*. But these conditions were also fulfilled in various councils

---

[50]   For a more detailed description of Gratian's Decree, see Stickler, 200-216 (*supra*, note 21); Jacqueline Rambaud in *L'âge classique: 1140-1378*, ed. Gabriel Le Bras et al, Histoire du droit et des institutions de l'Eglise en Occident 7 (Paris: Sirey, 1965) 52-129; Antonio García y García, "El derecho canónico medieval," in *El dret comú i Catalunia. Actas del II Simpio Internacional, Barcelona, mayo-1 de junio de 1991*, ed. Aquilino Iglesias Ferreirós (Barcelona: Fundació Nogura, 1992) 17-51.

[51]   On each of these collections see Walther Holtzmann, *Kanonistische Ergänzungen zur Italia Pontificia* (Tübingen: M. Niemeyer, 1959), which appeared later in *Quellen und Forschungen aus italienischen Archiven und Bibliotheken*, 37-38: *Decretales ineditae saeculi XII from the papers of the late Walther Holtzmann*, ed. and rev. Stanley Chodorow and Charles Duggan, Monumenta Iuris Canonici, Series B, Corpus Collectionum 4 (Vatican City: Bibliotheca Apostolica Vaticana, 1982); *Studies in the Collections of Twelfth-Century Decretals from the Papers of the Late Walther Holtzmann*, ed., rev., trans. Christopher R. Cheney and Mary G. Cheney in the same series, vol. 3 (Vatican City: Bibliotheca Apostolica Vaticana, 1979).

[52]   See the citations *infra*, note 54.

which have not passed into history as ecumenical, such as happened, for example, with those of Rheims in the years 1119, 1131, and 1148. These councils appear to have value for the churches represented in them by their respective bishops. Logically, it should follow that an ecumenical council is a general council with representation from the majority of the bishops of all the peoples of Christianity, which amounted to Latin Christianity, while Eastern representation was quite small. In any case, the expression "ecumenical" was applied to councils convened by the emperor's mandate, who was the lord of the *ecuméne*, while the expression "general" alluded to a generality without precising in what it consisted. This explains the vacillations which occurred, evident for example in the fact that Merlin's edition moved from the last council in the East to that of Constance. This did not create many problems for the medievals, since many councils of East and West, whom no one held as ecumenical, acquired a universal value in the Latin Church by the fact that they entered into canonical collections which were authenticated by the Roman Pontiff or simply admitted by the canonical science of the period.[53]

Another problem related to reception of ecumenical and general councils is their number. This theme was recently studied by Vittorio Peri,[54] whose argument can be synthesized as follows, based on his numerous

---

[53] See *HDC* 1: 283-287 with the sources and bibliography cited there.

[54] Vittorio Peri, "Il numero dei concili ecumenici nella tradizione cattolica moderna," *Aevum* 37 (1963) 430-501; idem, *I concili e le Chiese* (Rome: Studium, 1965); idem, "C'è un concilio ecumenico ottavo?" *Annuarium Historiae Conciliorum* 8 (1976) 53-79; idem, "Postilla sul Concilio ecumenico ottavo," *Revista di storia e letteratura religosa* 14 (1978) 208-213; idem, "Concilium plenum et generale. La prima attestazione dei criteri tradizionali dell'ecumenicità," *Annuarium Historiae Conciliorum* 15 (1983) 41-78; idem, "Il Concilio di Firenze. Un appuntamento ecclesiale mancato," *Il Veltro: Rivista della civiltà italiana* 27 (1983) 197-217; idem, "I concili ecumenici come struttura portante della gerarchia ecclesiastica," in *The 17th International Byzantine Congress. Major Papers, Dumbarton Oaks/ Georgetown University, Washington, D.C., August 3-8, 1986* (New Rochelle, NY: A.D. Caratzas, 1986) 59-81; idem, "Vent'anni dopo. Ancora sul numero dei concili ecumenici," *Revista di storia e letteratura religosa* 23 (1987) 289-300; idem, "L'ecumenicità di un concilio come processo storico," *Annuarium Historiae Conciliorum* 20 (1988) 216-244; idem, "La letteratura del Concilio di Firenze nella prospettiva unionistica romana," in *Christian Unity: The Council of Ferrara-Florence 1438/39 - 1989*, ed. Giuseppe Alberigo, Bibliotheca Ephemeridum Theologicarum Lovaniensium 97 (Leuven: Peeters, 1991) 593-611; idem, "Le Chiese nell'Impero e le Chiese 'tra i Barbari.' La territorialità ecclesiale nella riforma canonica trullana," in *The Council in Trullo Revisited*, ed. George Nedungatt and Michael Featherstone (Rome: Pontificia Istituto Orientale, 1995) 199-213.

studies on this topic. In order for a council to be said to have been received it is necessary that it become part of the faith and life of the universal or local church, according to the type of council. The seventh
council of the East (Nicea II, 787) established that, aside from the canonical fact of reception of a council as ecumenical with a universal validity
and public recognition, this is concretized by assigning it a number
which corresponds to it in the series, as happened with Nicea II, assigning it the number seven. The last council in which this rule was observed
was Florence, assigning it the number eight,[55] because, as is known, the
Easterners recognized only what took place in Florence itself as ecumenical, while not what took place in Ferrara, in order to conclude later
their admitting the decree in this council. The Catholic Church declared
the Council of Trent to be ecumenical and, of course, Vatican I and II,
without requiring among the conditions for this declaration the prior reception of the council in question. In other words, for the Easterners only
the subsequent council can declare if the preceding one was ecumenical
or not. For the Latin Church, reception is a later reality, which does not
affect the declaration of a council's ecumenicity. The current numbering
of councils, which includes the medieval ones as ecumenical, is commonly attributed to Robert Bellarmine in 1595.[56]

In the *Corpus Iuris Canonici* official papal letters or "authentic" ones
(Gratian, Gregory IX, Liber VI, and Clementine) coexist pacifically with
what lacks pontifical authorization, remaining as the work of private authors (the *Extravagantes* of John XXII, and the *Extravagantes com-
munes*) where each text has only the juridic value which it held before becoming part of the collection, and with it, of the *Corpus Iuris Canonici*.

Now we can see what texts were received in these collections of
the *Corpus Iuris Canonici*. Aside from texts of the general councils in the
Middle Ages already mentioned, and the decretals of popes from the
twelfth to the fourteenth centuries already alluded to, into the collection
of the Decretals of Gregory IX were received ancient texts of Eastern col-

---

[55]   Meanwhile Constantinople IV (869-870), recognized by Pope Adrian II as ecumenical, was not so recognized by the Easterners.
[56]   José Goñi Gaztambide, "El número de los concilios ecuménicos," in *Ecclesia Militans. Studien zur Konzilien und Reformationsgeschichte Remigius Bäumer zum 70.
Geburtstag gewidmet*, ed. Walter Branmüller, 1: *Zur Konziliengeschichte* (Paderborn: F.
Schöningh, 1988) 1-21 shows that the current numeration of councils is due to the French-
man Arnaud Pontac, twenty years before Bellarmine.

lections such as the Apostolic Canons,[57] Eastern councils (Sardica and Chalcedon), African councils of Carthage, the *Statuta ecclesiae antiquae*,[58] Visigothic councils, Gallican councils which go from Arles II in 353 to Touron in 1163, Germanic councils from the *Concilium germanicum* of 742 to the Salegunstadt Council of 1022, and five Roman councils.[59]

Not lacking either are texts from Greek and Latin Fathers: Hermas, Hilary, John Chrysostom, Jerome, Augustine, Fulgentius of Ruspe, and Isidore of Seville; ecclesiastical writers such as Bede, Hincmar of Rheims, Anastasius, John the Deacon; sources from roman law (*Pauli Sententiae, Novellae, Codex Theodosianus*), the *Lex Romana Visigothorum*, capitularies of French kings, penitential books, etc.[60] Great changes were introduced in each step, but there is also evident a coherence with the previous period's way of proceeding, as we have just seen.

Thus, the reception of texts understood at times for the universal Church and at others for particular churches continued, being received into the authentic and official collections approved by the popes in the twelfth to fourteenth centuries. The difference with the previous period is based in the fact that, contrary to what took place with the preceding collections, there is a much larger dose of texts from the medieval popes themselves than were received in earlier periods, in which much more was received and very little new was created. Now it is the reverse: what is received is relatively little in comparison with what is created.

The phenomenon of reception in the period we are dealing with did not depend only on the juridic logic applied at that time, but also and above all on the relationship between Eastern and Western Christianity, which had chilled prior to the break which took place in 1054 between the Church of Byzantium and that of Rome, and which had as immediate protagonists the prominent personage of the Gregorian Reform, Humbert of Silvacandida, and the Patriarch Michael Cerularius. Episodes such as the fourth crusade, which instead of conquering Palestine con-

---

[57]   Edition in Franciscus X. Funk, *Didascalia et Constitutiones Apostolicae* 2 (Paderborn: F. Schöningh, 1905; Turin: Bottega d'Erasmo, 1959) 40-50.
[58]   Edition in Charles Munier, *Les Statuta Ecclesiae Antiqua: édition, études critiques* (Paris: PUF, 1960).
[59]   Friedberg, 2: x-xii.
[60]   Friedberg, 2: xvii-xviii.

quered Constantinople and established a Latin Empire there, created a climate more favorable to the separation between the two churches than to reception between them. As a result, it should not be surprising that the official conversations looking to the reestablishment of unity of the two churches produced hardly any results during these centuries.

The intention that the Easterners take part in the general councils of the West did not have more constructive results, either. This question was not even raised seriously for the first three of these councils (Lateran I-III).

In any case, the Easterers were hoping for help from the West against the Turks, for which they promised in exchange a representation from the Greek Church in a future council which Innocent III could call, while the Westerners were preoccupied with the union of the two Churches. In this context a correspondence was begun with letters between the Emperor of Byzantium, Theodore Lascaris (with his seat in Nicea, because Constantinople was occupied by the Latins of the fourth crusade), and the Patriarch of Constantinople, John X. Kamateros, on one side, and Pope Innocent III on the other. In this correspondence neither of the parties achieved what they wanted.[61] The Greek Church did not send any representatives to Rome for Lateran IV in 1215, in which, aside from the representation of the Latin Church established in the Latin Empire of Constantinople, there is mentioned only the somewhat marginal presence of the Maronite Patriarch Jeremiah,[62] a deacon representing the Melkite Patriarch of Alexandria Nicholas I, and the Jacobite Patriarch John XIV, who is said to have attended personally. The thesis which Innocent III maintained in the correspondence mentioned above and the thesis held in Lateran IV in 1215 were the same, namely, that the Easterners first had to submit an unequivocal obedience to the Church of Rome, and then the rest of the pending questions could be dealt with.[63]

---

[61] On this correspondence and on the position of Innocent III and Lateran IV with respect to the Greek Church, see Antonio García y García, "La Iglesia griega y el Concilio IV Lateranense de 1215," *Diálogo Ecuménico* 13 (1978) 121-144. See also G. Haguedorn, "Papst Innocenz III. und Bizanz am Vorabend des Vierten Kreuzzugs (1198-1203)," *Kirchliche Studien* 23 (1978) 3-20, 105-136; Giorgio Fedalto, *La chiesa latina in Oriente*, 3 vols. (Verona: Ed. Mazziana, 1973).

[62] *Bullarium Maronitarum*, ed. Tobias Anaissi (Rome: Max Bretschneider, 1911) 2-5.

[63] "Chronicon Montis Sereni" ("Chron. de Lautenberg"), *MGH SS* 23 (Hannover: Hahn, 1874) 186, and "Chronica Albrici Monachi Trium Fontium" (Aubrey de Trois Fontaines), ibid., 23: 886.

The agreements which were made with the Easterners in the Councils of Lyons II (1274) and Florence (1439) unfortunately remained dead letters for the same or similar reasons as the dialogue in the time of Innocent III to which we have just alluded.

B. Reception in Provincial Councils and Diocesan Synods

We are now going to examine the system for the reception of norms from the universal Church and from each ecclesiastical province. Lateran IV mandated the celebration of provincial councils on an annual basis, preceded by a visitation of the dioceses of the corresponding ecclesiastical province which would serve as the basis for the measures which the provincial council would consequently decide.[64] This institution of the provincial council had already been fixed by canon 5 of Nicea I (325) as once per year,[65] then by canon 19 of Chalcedon (419) as two times per year,[66] and by canon 6 of Nicea II (787) again as one time per year.[67] Canon 6 of Lateran IV (1215) referred to these ancient councils with the phrase, "as is known to have been instituted by the holy fathers in times past" (*Sicut olim a sanctis patribus noscitur institutum . . .*). The norms of the provincial councils were to be applied by each of the province's bishops in his respective diocese by means of a diocesan synod which was to be held annually, under penalty of suspension from office for bishops who did not comply with this statute. As is known, diocesan synods were held with more or less frequency in the High Middle Ages, this being the first norm of common canon law which prescribed its celebration.

One of the more interesting characteristics of Innocent III's legislation consisted in taking up again the existing legislation, but imprinting his personal seal on some apparently small changes, but which had important practical results. In fact, this chaining together of general council, provincial council, and diocesan synod was the touchstone of putting the ecclesiastical reform of 1215 into practice.

---

[64]   Lateran IV, c. 6: *CCQL*, 53.
[65]   *COD*, 8.
[66]   *COD*, 96.
[67]   *COD*, 132.

France[68] and England[69] observed rather well the general lines of Pope Innocent III's norms, and with this the Lateran reform was realized there to a good extent.

In regard to France, the synodal statutes of Eudes de Sully were taken up and adapted in many dioceses of the French ecclesiastical provinces: dioceses of Angers, Tours, Nantes, and Le Mans (Province of Tours); Orleans (Province of Sens); Rouen, Bayeux and Lisieux (Province of Rouen); Poitiers (Province of Bordeaux); Nîmes (Province of Narbonne); Dax (Province of Auch); Clermont Ferrand and Rodez (Province of Bourges); etc.[70]

Eudes de Sully's synodal statutes not only inspired a good deal of the French synodal legislation, but were also copied more or less literally in such distinct and distant places as the rest of the French dioceses, Lisbon, Italy, Mainz, etc., thus giving a reception between local churches, some closer and others more distant.[71] This reception sometimes was indirect

---

[68]   *Les statuts synodaux français du XIIIe siècle précédés de l'historique du synode diocésan depuis ses origines*, 1: *Les statuts de Paris et le Synodal de l'Ouest (XIIIe)*, ed. Odette Pontal, Collection des documents inédits sur l'histoire de France 9 (Paris: Biblioteque Nationale, 1971); 2: *Les statuts de 1230 à 1260*, ed. Odette Pontal (Paris: CTHS, 1983); 3: *Les statuts synodaux angevins de la seconde moitié du XIIIe siècle, précédés d'une étude sur la législation synodale angevine*, ed. Joseph Avril (Paris: CTHS, 1988); 4.: *Les statuts synodaux de l'ancienne province de Reims (Cambrai, Arras, Noyon, Soissons et Tournai)*, ed. Joseph Avril (Paris: CNRS, 1985); *Les Conciles de la Province de Tours / Concilia Provinciae Turonensis (s. XIII-XV)*, ed. Joseph Avril (Paris: CNRS, 1987). See also a census of the synodal statutes of French dioceses in André Artonne, Louis Guizard, and Odette Pontal, *Répertoire des statuts synodaux des diocèses de l'ancienne France du XIIIe à la fin du XVIIIe siècle*, 2nd ed. (Paris: CNRS, 1969). The simple citation of the detailed bibliography of these and other authors on the medieval French councils and synods beginning with the thirteenth century would far exceed the space available here.

[69]   For the immediate application of the Lateran legislation in England, see *Councils and Synods with other documents relating to the English Church*, 2: *A.D. 1205-1313*, 1-2, ed. Frederick M. Powicke and Christopher R. Cheney (Oxford: Clarendon, 1964). See also Christopher R. Cheney, *English Synodalia of the thirteenth century* (Oxford: Oxford University Press, 1968).

[70]   In addition to the works already cited by Pontal and Avril, see Odette Pontal, "Les plus anciens statuts synodaux d'Angers et leur expansion dans les diocéses de l'Ouest de la France," *Revue d'Histoire de l'Eglise de France* 46 (1960) 54-67, and above all, idem, "Naissance et évolution des législations synodales dans les diocèses du Nord et de l'Ouest de la France (1200-1250)," *ZRG Kan. Abt.* 72 (1986) 152-249.

[71]   For Mainz, see Peter Johanek, "Der Pariser Statuten des Bischofs Odo von Sully und die Anfänge der kirchlichen Statutengesetzgebung in Deutschland," in *Proceedings of the Seventh International Congress of Medieval Canon Law. Cambridge 23-27 July 1984*,

through some intermediary, as happened with the *Liber sinodalis* of Gonzalo de Alba, promulgated in Salamanca in 1410,[72] in which there are verbatim pieces from the synod published by the diocese of Nîmes in 1252 by the canonist Pierre de Sampzon, who for his part made great use of the *Synodal de l'Ouest*. In turn, the *Liber sinodalis* of the Dominican bishop Gonzalo de Alba was adopted also by the diocese of Cuenca by the likewise Dominican bishop Lope de Barrientos, and by the diocese of Segovia in 1440.[73]

In England the statutes of Richard Poore, Bishop of Salisbury (1217-1221) and those of Robert Grosseteste, Bishop Lincoln (1240-1243) were likewise the object of derivations or receptions in other dioceses.[74]

Reception and application in the dioceses of the Empire was uneven, undoubtedly due to the heterogeneous character of the different dioceses in the extensive imperial territories. Neither is there a comprehensive study for the whole thirteenth century, but only for the years 1216-1245.[75] A relatively high number of councils and synods were held, very unevenly spread in time and space. Reception and application of the Lateran reforms was likewise uneven. The very frequency of councils and synods was not uniform, as can be seen from the tables offered by Pixton.[76] They add up to 37 provincial councils and more than a hundred synods, but most of them lack any true sense of reform. The factors which impeded a greater reception and practical implementation of the Lateran legislation were due to the fact that many bishops were involved

---

ed. Peter Linehan, Monumenta Iuris Canonici C, vol. 8 (Vatican City: Biblioteca Apostolica Vaticana, 1988) 327-347. For Lisbon, see I. da Rosa Pereira, "Sínodos da diocese de Lisboa," *Lumen* 25 (1961) 385-398. The Synod of Lisbon alluded to here was celebrated around 1240 and edited in *SH* 2: 285-297.

[72]   *SH* 4: 67-293.

[73]   See *SH* 6: 381-382, where we indicate how Lope de Barrientos adopted for Segovia the Spanish text of this *Liber synodalis* promulgated for Salamanca by Gonzalo de Alba. It must be added that the prologue and the first canon of the synod of Barrientos for Segovia in 1440 (*SH* 6: 385-387) were also copied from the text of the 1410 synod of Gonzalo de Alba for Salamanca. For fuller information on this subject see Bernardo Alonso Rodríguez, Francisco Cantelar Rodríguez, and Antonio García y García, "El *Liber synodalis* salmantino de 1410," *REDC* 41 (1985) 347-364.

[74]   See Cheney (*supra*, note 69).

[75]   Paul B. Pixton, *The German episcopacy and the implementation of the decrees of the Fourth Lateran Council 1216-1245: Watchmen on the tower* (Leiden: E. J. Brill, 1995).

[76]   See Pixton, 438-440, where he offers a list of diocesan synods of the dioceses of the Empire from 1216-1245. Mainz, Cologne, and Trier stand out for their higher numbers.

in diplomatic and political activities, becoming consequently more involved in temporal activities and business than in the proper pastoral office of their charge. Many of these bishops were at the same time men of
government in the Church and in secular politics.

In the Iberian peninsula the reception and application of Lateran IV
during the thirteenth century is sufficiently notable in the territories of
the Kingdom of Aragon, but weaker in the Kingdom of Castille.[77] On the
other hand, beginning with the legantine Council of Valladolid in 1322[78]
matters were reversed to a certain point, in the sense that the Church of
Castille tended toward a reform which culminated in the time of the
Catholic Monarchs, while in the Church of Aragon the opposite occurred.

A characteristic of this period from the twelfth to the fourteenth centuries is the flourishing of a weighty activity in the juridical faculties
scattered through various countries: Bologna and other Italian universities, Salamanca, Coimbra, Montpellier, Toulouse, Avignon, and more to
the North that of Orléans, and those of Oxford and Cambridge. All of the
other medieval juridical faculties are after the start of the fourteenth century. Within this context the relationships between schools and the
Roman pontificate and, as appropriate, the bishops, were important.
Some historians, especially in dealing with theological formation, give a
pejorative impression of canon law and of canonical science in the sense
that, according to these authors, they produced an excessive juridiciza-
tion of the Church at the expense of its theological elements. Perhaps it
would be opportune to recall that one ought not to confuse true science
with the possible caricatures of it; a legislator or a jurist is not the same
as a legalist. And this observation is valid for canon law as much as for
theology. There are some clarifying examples for this question, which it

---

[77]   Peter Linehan, *The Spanish Church and the Papacy in the Thirteenth Century*
(Cambridge, England: Cambridge University Press, 1971), with some additions in the
Spanish translation: *La Iglesia española y el Papado en el siglo XIII* (Salamanca: Universidad Pontificia, 1975). For the application foreseen through provincial councils and synods, see *SH* 1-7, where there is a critical edition of the synods of Portugal and the present
territories of Galicia, Asturias, León, Extremadura, and Old Castille. Through the appara-
tus of the *fontes* one can see well to what extent the pontifical legislation on reform in the
Church was received and applied in the dioceses of the Kingdom of Castille. In future vol-
umes it is planned to conclude this work for the rest of the Iberian peninsula.
[78]   See Antonio García y García, "Las constituciones del Concilio legatino de Valladolid (1322)," in *Ecclesia militans*, 109-131 (*supra*, note 56).

is enough to signal, leaving to the corresponding bibliography without detaining ourselves to develop this theme more fully.

Gratian laid down the basis for the future doctrine of the "custom contrary to law" (*consuetudo contra legem*), that is, of the custom of the people which, clothed in certain qualities, can acquire binding force.[79]

V. RECAPITULATION

To recapitulate what has gone before in this short study, it is appropriate to underline in greater detail the more important characteristic phenomena regarding the theme of reception. For this we distinguish two historical moments: from the beginning to the Gratian's Decree, and the following stage which includes from the middle of the twelfth century to the conclusion of the formative process for classical medieval canon law, which terminated in the middle of the fourteenth century, stages which we will denominate briefly under the two following headings.

A. Reception in the First Millennium of Canon Law

1. Above all, this was a time of a *more ample reception* due to the quantity of patristic texts, conciliar texts, and texts of another nature which were received, and for the diversity of provenance from the universal Church and the different local churches of East and West. In the editions, especially the more recent ones, which we have cited for each of the numerous canonical collections of each period it is usual to indicate, not only each of these provenances, but also the recension or textual form which was received.

2. All of this immense mass of texts is *generally of a normative character*, but also not a few of a theological, liturgical, etc., character. Thus their study is interesting not only for the Church's juridical dimension, but also for its theological, liturgical, etc., reality. It must not be forgotten that Gratian's Decree is not only a canonical collection, but also a treatise on the Church's law with important theological statements.

3. This reception was *spontaneous and active*, at least in most cases, not passive or under the pressure of competent ecclesiastical authorities, in the sense that it was carried out by private authors, without restraints

---

[79] See Antonio García y García, "Antecedentes medievales sobre la problemática moderna sobre la costumbre," *Congresso Internazionale sulla consuetudine. Università di Napoli, 30-31 maggio 1997* (in preparation).

or mandate from these authorities. They accepted and received because they believed what was genuine discipline, and took it not only from the universal Church but also from local churches. These cases were influenced especially by the communion in the same faith joined with other factors already mentioned, which moved the reception of a same discipline and vice-versa. In any case, unity of faith did not necessarily carry a unity of discipline. The first was urged both at the level of the universal Church as well as in local churches. The second admitted a notable variety according to the different local churches, although their initiatives were increasingly limited beginning especially with the canonical collections which were declared authentic by the popes. The first canonical collection declared by a pope (Innocent III) as obligatory for all the Church was the *Compilatio III Antiqua* of 1210.[80] This was followed by the *Compilatio IV Antiqua* (1216), the *Liber Extra* of Gregory IX (1234), the *Liber VI* of Boniface VIII (1298), the *Decretales Clementinae* (1317), etc.

4. This reception was *more horizontal than vertical*, in the sense that most of what was received came from local churches and not from the universal Church properly so-called. Consequently, it was more ascending than descending, and more horizonal than vertical.

5. It was *universalizing*, in that it resulted in unifying to a great extent, in a work such as that of Gratian, the discipline of all the local churches of the West. This process was achieved by means of collections of a universalist character (*Dionisius Exiguus, Hispana, Vetus Gallica*, etc.) and not by those of a particularist character, such as the apocryphal ones which occurred in four waves (pseudo-apostolic collections, the Symmachian apocrypha, carolingian apocrypha, and celtic anglo-saxon penitentials).[81]

6. Most of the receptions in canonical collections generally took place *in view of reform* of the local church to which they referred, or of

---

[80]   Edition by Antonio Agustín, *Antiquae Collectiones Decretalium* (Lérida, 1576), with other editions of lesser quality since his death. See Stephan Kuttner, "Antonio Augustin's edition of the Compliationes Antiquae," *BMCL NS* 7 (1977) 1-14. In de Luca's 1769 edition, the *Compilatio III Antiqua* is found in 4: 424-608.

[81]   On all this apocrypha see the bibliography in *HDC* 1: 43-47, 330-331.

the universal Church in collections which, at least de facto, were diffused and received at this latter level.

7. Both the canonical collections of private authors as well as those which were declared authentic, i.e., with legal force by the popes, were driven in the debate to justify the legal innovations which they introduced by their conformity or at least coherence with Sacred Scripture, as well as councils and earlier church norms. This criteria implied conformity, real or supposed, with the past and, consequently, reception of the past by later norms.

8. Reception *was not then and is not now the same as a real application of the received norm*. In the past as well as today, there is the phenomenon that a good deal of what is contained in any canonical collection, medieval or the present code, is a dead letter from the very day the text came to light publicly, fulfilling the famous Spanish proverb, "I respect it, but I don't carry it out" (*Se acata, pero no se cumple*).

9. This reception *was not only conciliar*, as is frequently said, but refers to many other sources, as has already been explained. At least since Dionysius Exiguus, it included as well a good deal of pontifical decretals, patristic texts, and texts of other types.

10. *The more centralized collections* or the more authoritative ones, which are undoubtedly those of the Gregorian reform, *were never promulgated by any pope as obligatory for the universal Church*, but once again were the work of private authors, without any explicit endorsement of ecclesiastical authority, aside from what each of the included texts had by reason of its origin. This gave way only for the first time in 1210, as already explained.

11. Both the diffusion and the reception of canonical collections in the first millennium *were governed by the law of supply and demand*, since no ecclesiastical authority attempted to impose them on the universal Church.

12. Many of these canonical collections were the *work of bishops*, who redacted them or had them redacted for their local churches, but *in fact they were received but much wider settings* in the breadth and width of Western Christianity, as happened, among others, with the *Decretum* of Burchard of Worms, the collections of Ivo of Chartres, etc. In these cases there was a type of reception of law conceived by one local church

in many other local churches, becoming universalized by this means, sometimes in an ascending manner and for others in a horizontal sense.

B. Reception in the Late Middle Ages

1. Reception was *more vertical than horizontal*, in the sense that it was much more what the local churches received from Rome than vice-versa.

2. The texts received were *less expository and more normative or decisive*.

3. Inversely to what happened in the previous period, *it was more a descending than an ascending reception*, or, in other words, it was much less the particular legislation which became universal, and more the universal destined to be received by the local churches.

4. It followed the process described in numbers 6-8 of the summary of the first millennium, although in this one it happened always with greater papal initiative and intervention.

5. The proportion of conciliar texts was now less than that of pontifical decretals.

6. The more important canonical collections were now promulgated by the popes, contrary to the first period in which all were the work of private authors up to 1210. Without losing the appearance of private collections, some of these were included within the *Corpus Iuris Canonici* (*Extravagantes* of John XXII and the *Extravagantes Communi*), but this happened precisely when the pope's power began to decline in the historical horizon of the encounters between the pope and Philip the Fair of France, and other less notable similar cases.

7. There was a strict collaboration between the schools of canonical science which spread out from Bologna, in greater or lesser extent, through all of Europe, while in the first millennium the schools did not exist and the popes intervened much less in the creation and reception of law.

8. The bishops now had to receive and apply pontifical law, principally through provincial councils at the metropolitan level, and diocesan synods at the diocesan level. Curiously, law created in this way came to

be received in other dioceses, so much so that the margin of creativity now was much less.

To sum up in a few words what has been presented, we can say that in the first millennium private initiative dominated, without annulling pontifical legislative activity whose letters or decretals were a channel for reception of earlier law, and were also channels of creation of new norms which were widely received in the canonical collections made by private authors. In the Late Middle Ages, the papal initiative, which moved to the first place, was not insensitive to the reception of law coming from lower instances which preceded it, but the decretals of medieval popes, as with their general councils, were drawn up more to be received than to receive.

From these conclusions on reception in the Late Middle Ages it could appear that the papal power was really unlimited, and this is a very widespread cliche among non-experts in this field. To be convinced that it lacks a foundation, it is enough to recall some examples, which we cannot develop here, so we must limit ourselves to offering some recent, select bibliography on it.

Under the inspiration of jurists in this period in which we find ourselves, there was a tendency to limit the absolute authority of the pope or of the bishops, on the one hand, and of the emperor, kings and other temporal authorities, on the other.[82] According to Pennington, the break toward absolutism began in the secular field with Nicolò Machiavelli, and not with Jean Bodin as is usually claimed, who is closer to what was often said to be the positions of classical medieval jurists.

Since the Second World War, modern investigations have become aware with respect to relations between ecclesiastical and secular power, that classical medieval canonical science declared itself more for the du-

---

[82] See Brian Tierney, *Religion, Law, and the Growth of Constitutional Law, 1150-1650* (Cambridge, England: Cambridge University Press, 1982); Kenneth Pennington, *Pope and Bishops. The Papal Monarchy in the Twelfth and Thirteenth Centuries* (Philadelphia: University of Pennsylvania Press, 1984); idem, *The Prince and the Law, 1200-1600: Sovereignty and Rights in the Western Legal Tradition* (Berkeley, CA: University of California Press, 1993).

alist theory than for hierocratic monarchy, which bears a certain limitation on ecclesiastical power.[83]

On the other hand, some of the more remote sources of modern democracy are rooted in the adoption of the formula from Roman public law: "What touches all the same way, is to be approved by all" (*Quod omnibus similiter tangit, ab omnibus comprobetur*),[84] applied by the medievals not only to the field of public law, but also in the area of private law. Neither were canonists insensible to the rediscovery of the books of Aristotle's *Politics*. Moreover, while the system of government of the medieval church was not democratic in its general lines, such as the term is understood today, nevertheless it was such from a certain point of view, in certain areas within the Church, such as the chapters of canons, councils, the mendicant orders, universities, etc., where final decisions were taken according to the principle of the "greater and healthier part" (*maior et sanior pars*), that is, by majority vote.[85]

Translation by Denis E. Carlin and James H. Provost

[83]   See Antonio García y García, "Sacerdocio, Imperio y Reinos," *Cuadernos informativos de derecho histórico público, procesal ye de la navegación* 2 (1987) 499-552
[84]   Cod. 5. 59. 5. 2.
[85]   Lateran IV (1215) c. 24: ". . . ut is collatione adhibita eligatur in quem omnes vel maior vel sanior pars capituli consentit" (*CCQL*, 70).

RESPONSE TO ANTONIO GARCÍA Y GARCÍA

Joseph Avril*

This communication is not properly speaking a "response" to the magisterial presentation of Antonio Garcia y Garcia, but rather some complementary remarks which can be made by an historian versed in the publication of councils and synods, and also in the study of diocesan supervision and parish institutions. More than "reception" or "communion" in the strict sense, it deals with exchanges, complementary relations, adaptations or modifications made in dioceses to the decrees of general councils or to those of provincial assemblies. In fact the different decrees were never the object of a full and entire reception in the Middle Ages, any more than in other epochs.

To work out the problems briefly and more closely, we will begin this study with some preliminary remarks before following a chronological order in tackling successively the end of Christian antiquity (i.e., the time of the barbarian kingdoms), then the Carolingian period, the post-Carolingian centuries, and at the end, the Gregorian reform. We will end with what can be called the classical age, that is, the time of the great councils of the thirteenth and fourteenth centuries with prolongations up to the Council of Trent. This division corresponds to a certain understanding of the history of pastoral life with its successive moments: the Carolingian pastoral, theoretically remaining in force up to the thirteenth century; then the directives promulgated in the conciliar times orienting the ministry of priests up to the sixteenth century.[1] The examples will be chosen especially from what is now France and the countries surrounding it.

Preliminary Remarks

Between the different churches a level of regulation was established in the fourth century by the councils of Nicea and Antioch, namely, the met-

*   Centre National de Research Scientifique [CNRS], Paris (France).

[1]   Joseph Avril, "De la pastorale carolingienne à la pastorale conciliaire du XIIIᵉ siècle: L'*Admonitio synodalis* et les statuts synodaux de l'évéque de Paris, Eudes de Sully," in *La christianisation des campagnes, Actes du Congrés International d'Histoire ecclésiastique comparée, Liége 25 - 28 août 1994* (in preparation).

ropolitan bishop. Placed at the head of a province calculated on the administrative organization of the Roman Empire, this prelate presided at episcopal elections, convoked councils, and supervised his suffragans.[2]

But quite rapidly this system showed its limitations. In effect, metropolitan power remained imprecise, poorly defined, especially since it had to take into account a reality which was already probably in place, the diocese. Each bishop was the sole master of a church which possessed its own individuality, which was translated by a series of "customs."[3] In effect it was custom which determined, for example, the powers of archdeacons, as affirmed in the synodal statutes of Liège in the eighth century.[4]

Moreover, the same councils defined the rules for the functioning of assemblies, but, if there were some truly provincial councils from the beginning, the gatherings went beyond the cadre initially forseen.[5]

Finally, it should be recalled that a council did not have for its first mission to legislate in matters of doctrine or discipline; it was first of all a court of justice charged with arbitration, settling conflicts, and pronouncing sentences. Aside from situations of some import, with a view to repressing abuses or making earlier decisions more precise, councils were quite naturally conducted to elaborate the decrees theoretically received in the dioceses of the bishops who were present.

Finally, before the Carolingian period, decisions which were properly diocesan were quite rare. Certainly, at the time of the creation of rural churches, the diocesan synod replaced the ancient *presbyterium*. But, as with the council, it was a judiciary institution controlling the clergy and

---

[2]   Jean Gaudemet, *L'Eglise dans l'Empire romain (IVe-V^e siécle)*, Histoire du Droit et des Institutions de l'Eglise en Occident 3 (Paris: Sirey, 1958) 380-383.

[3]   Bernard Delmaire, *Le diocése d'Arras de 1093 au milieu du XIVe siécle. Recherches sur la vie religieuse dans le nord de la France au Moyen Age*, Mémoires de la Commission départementale d'Histoire et d'Archéologie du Pas-de-Calais (Arras: CDHAPdC, 1994) 405.

[4]   *Les statuts synodaux de Jean de Flandre, évêque de Liège*, ed. Emile Schoolmeesters (Liège: Cormaux, 1908) 51.

[5]   Gaudemet, 451-456.

deciding the foundations of churches or monasteries; the synod kept this function for a long time.[6]

The Merovingian Period

With some exceptions such as the province of Arles, the councils of this period can be defined as inter-regional assemblies called at the initiative of princes and destined to reestablish peace and unity. During the rise and decline of this period, meetings were convoked in the context of kingdoms.[7] The bishops' role and even that of metropolitans was essential, while the interventions of the Roman Pontiff remained exceptional.

Yet an analysis of their prescriptions surfaces a real progression. Councils began to make the earlier canons more precise and to refine them, as appears from a research of the sources they used. Thus a certain number of decisions of the Council of Epaône took up those of the Council of Orleans of 511. Then the canons of the same Council of Epaône were transcribed at Arles in 524 which was also inspired by the statutes of Agde (506).[8] One also finds Epaône at Clermont in 525, whose canon 15 is constructed from the decisions of Arles and Vaison. It would be possible to continue to show the influence of this assembly of Clermont on the councils gathered at Mâcon in 581-583 and in 585. Most of the renewed, developed, or modified prescriptions concerned the powers of bishops over priests, the status and discipline of clergy, and, as at other times, a defense of ecclesiastical patrimony.

A unique example concerning diocesan legislation has been preserved from this period, namely, the statutes drawn up in 585 by the bishop of Auxerre for his clergy. The synod proceeded to an adaptation of recent councils, relative not only to ecclesiastical discipline, but also to liturgy

---

[6]   Joseph Avril, "L'évolution du synode diocésain principalement dans la France du nord, du Xᵉ au XIIIᵉ siécle," *Proceedings of the Seventh International Congress of Medieval Canon Law. Cambridge, 23-27 July 1984*, ed. Peter Linehan, Monumenta Iuris Canonici C, vol. 8 (Vatican City: Biblioteca Apostolica Vaticana, 1988) 305-325. See *Les statuts synodaux français du XIIIᵉ siècle*, 1: *Les statuts de Paris et le synodal de l'Ouest*, ed. Odette Pontal, Collection de documents inédits sur l'histoire de France 9 (Paris: Biblioteque Nationale, 1971) xxvi-xl.

[7]   *Les canons des conciles mérovingiens (VIᵉ-VIIᵉ siècles)*, ed. Jean Gaudemet et Brigitte Basdevant, Sources chrétiennes 353, 2 vols. (Paris: Cerf, 1989); Odette Pontal, *Histoire des conciles mérovingiens* (Paris: Cerf, 1989).

[8]   *Les canons des conciles mérovingiens*, 93-95.

and the sacraments.[9] This is the first attempt at codification and popular-
ization for the usage of a clergy which had become rural.[10]

The Carolingian Reform

The accession of the Carolingians marked a provisional end to dividing up the territory and the establishment of a certain unification. This
was a time of an intensive legislative activity at all levels.[11] This legislation proceeded not only from the episcopal hierarchy, but especially from
the sovereigns. These latter legislated personally in promulgating reforming texts (*capitularia*), of which the *Admonitio generalis* of 789
constitutes the fundamental charter.[12] Moreover the same doctrines were
taken up and adopted by councils convened undoubtedly at the initiative
of the political power, but for the greater profit of the Church. In addition,
in the ninth century, bishops drew up for their clergy some reforming decisions (*capitula*).[13] For the rest, with the weakening of imperial power,
the bishops took up the initiative for renewal and completed the earlier
decisions, as appears from an analysis of the canons of the Council of
Mainz of 847.[14] However, despite the reinforcement of the ecclesiastical
hierarchy, the metropolitans were not successful in affirming their power
over their suffragans. Quite the contrary, in the instability and insecurity
of the end of the ninth century, these latter consolidated their power as is
attested by the development of the False Decretals,[15] and at the same

---

[9]   Ibid., 486-505.
[10]   Pontal, *Histoire des conciles*, 251-279; see Pierre Imbart de la Tour, *Les paroisses
rurales du IVᵉ au XIᵉ siécle* (Paris: A. Picard et fils, 1900); Élie Griffe, *La cité chrétienne*,
La Gaule chrétienne à l'époque romanaine 3 (Paris: Letouzey et Ané, 1965).
[11]   Wilfried Hartmann, *Die Synoden der Karolingerzeit im Frankreich und in Italien*
(Paderborn: F. Schöningh, 1989); Pierre Riché, "Le christianisme dans l'Occident car-
olingien (milieu VIIIᵉ-fin IXᵉ siècle)," in *Evêques, moines et empereurs (610-1054)*, ed.
Jean-Marie Mayeur, *Histoire du Christianisme* 4 (Paris: Desclée, 1993); Jean-François
Lemarignier, *Institutions ecclésiastiques*, vol. 3 of *Histoire des Institutions Françaises*,
ed. Ferdinand Lot and Robert Fawtier (Paris, PUF, 1962) 12-32.
[12]   *MGH Leges* 2/1 (Hannover: Hahn, 1837; Stuttgart: Anton Hiersmann, 1965) 52-56.
[13]   Peter Brommer, "Les capitula de Theodulf d'Orléans," *Zeitschrift der Savigny
Stiftung für Rechtsgeschichte, Kanonistische Abteilung* [*ZRG KA*] 70 (1974) 1-120; *MGH*,
Capitula episcoporum, 1, ed. Peter Brommer (Hannover: Hahn, 1984).
[14]   *MGH, Concilia* (Hannover: Hahn, 1924) 3: 158.
[15]   *Decretales Pseudo-Isidorianae et capitula Angilramni*, ed. Paulus Hinschius
(Leipzig: B. Tauchnitz, 1863; Aalen: Scientia, 1963). See Horst Fuhrmann, *Einfluss und
Verbreitung der pseudo-isidorischen Fälschunge*, *MGH SS* 24/1-3 (Stuttgart: Hiersman,
1972).

time, the Apostolic See began to free itself from the imperial power and to regain a certain influence.

These decisions, joined to the ancient councils, were collected in compilations which were somewhat crude at the start, the canonical collections. At a lower level, in the spirit of the councils and the *capitula*, the Carolingian legislation inspired the manual for pastoral visits of Regino of Prüm.[16] Such guides became indispensable in a time when churches and chapels multiplied, and the diocesan hierarchy was being put in place (archdeacons, archpriests, deans, *kalendes*).[17] This movement culminated in the publication of the *Admonitio synodalis*, contemporary with Regino.[18] One can never emphasize enough the importance of this pastoral directory; in effect, introduced quite early into the synodal liturgy, the *Admonitio* was transcribed throughout the Middle Ages even to the sixteenth century.[19]

The Post-Carolingian Period and the Gregorian Reform

This was again a period of disorganization and instability during which the initiative of reform passed first to the monks, who were only indirectly involved in our topics. But, during a time, Carolingian legislation was taken up by certain prelates such as Atto of Vercelli or Rathier

---

[16]   *Reginonis abbatis Prumiensis. Libri duo de synodalibus causis et disciplinis ecclesiasticis*, ed. F. G. A. Wasserschleben (Leipzig, 1840; Graz: Akademische Druck- u. Verlagsanstalt, 1964).

[17]   Joseph Avril, "La 'paroisse' dans la France de L'An Mil," in *Le roi de France et son royaume autour de L'An Mil* (Paris: Picard, 1992) 203-218.

[18]   Rudolf Pokorny, "Nachmals zur Admonitio synodalis," *ZRG KA* 71 (1985) 20-51. A critical edition was published by Robert Amiet, "Une Admonitio synodalis de l'époque carolingienne. Etude critique et édition," *Medieval Studies* 26 (1964) 12-82. The liturgical version of the pontifical is preferable: *Le pontifical romano-germanique du dixième siécle*, ed. Cyrille Vogel et Reinhard Elze, 2 vols., Studi e Testi 226-227 (Vatican City: Biblioteca Apostolica Vaticana, 1963) 1: 286- 289. A thirteenth century version appears in *Les statuts synodaux français du XIIIe siècle*, 6: *Les statuts du Midi*.

[19]   Joseph Avril, "Sources et caracteres du livre synodal de Raimond de Calmont d'Olt, évêque de Rodez (1289)," *Cahiers de Fanjeaux* 29 (1993) 215-243; idem, "Les Instructions et Constitutions de Guillaume Durand, évêque de Mende," *Guillaume Durand, évêque de Mende (v. 1230-1296)* (Paris: CNRS, 1992) 73-74. The *Admonitio* was even transcribed in Poland in 1521 by Andrew Lipski, Bishop of Luck, in "Les synodes du diocése de Luck et leurs statuts," in *Concilia Poloniae. Etudes critiques et sources*, ed. J. Sawicki (Warsaw, 1949) 3: 101.

of Verona, and also in several councils.[20] However, the problems of an epoch marked by feudalism are revealed in the formulations of a provincial council held at Bourges in 1031.[21] But if the conciliar and synodal systems seemed to function more or less regularly, their activities were principally of a juridic or administrative order (reestablishing peace, status, and possession of churches and monasteries).[22]

Yet certain provinces such as Rouen maintained their cohesion and acquired a legislation which was new in its expression; thus the councils of Rouen (1072) and of Lillebonne (1080).[23] But from then on, the initiative for change came from the Apostolic See by the intermediary of legates, or directly from the Roman Pontiffs. Continuing in the line traced by his predecessors since Leo IX, Urban II convoked at Clermont in 1095 a council charged with organizing the crusade, but this assembly also published a series of canons of a disciplinary and sacramental order.[24] For the rest, one can follow the diffusion of these measures in later assemblies (Councils of Nîmes and Rouen, 1096; councils of Paschal II),[25] or even in the preambles of charters (*Redemptio altarium*, for example).[26]

Later, during the course of the twelfth century, divers indices announced new legislations.[27] There is first the small collection of *precepta* of Bernard, Bishop of Saintes (toward 1140-1150) where the prelate forbade monks to live alone in their priories (cf. Lateran III, c. 10) and imposed the presence of a priest for matrimonial unions (cf. Lateran IV, c.

[20]   For example, the Council of Trosly in 909; see Odette Pontal, *Les conciles de la France capétienne jusqu'en 1215* (Paris: Cerf, 1995) 49- 52. The texts came from canonical collections.

[21]   Johannes D. Mansi, *Sacrorum conciliorum nova et amplissima collectio* 19 (Venice, 1759) 503-506; see Avril, "La 'paroisse' dans la France de l'An Mil."

[22]   Avril, "L'évolution su synode diocésain" (*supra*, note 6).

[23]   Mansi, 20: 33-40, 559-564.

[24]   Robert Somerville, *The Councils of Urban II*, 1: *Decreta Claromontiensia*, Annuarium Historiae Conciliorum (Amsterdam: Hakkert, 1972).

[25]   Mansi, 20: 931-937, 921-926.

[26]   Joseph Avril, *Le gouvernement des évêques et la vie religieuse dans le diocèse d'Angers (1148-1240)* (Lille-Paris: Cerf thèses, 1984) 152.

[27]   *Le troisième concile du Latran (1179). Sa place dans l'histoire*, ed. Jean Longère (Paris: Etudes augustiniennes, 1982).

51).[28] Moreover, the regulation of Leprosaria (cf. Lateran III, c. 23) was rooted in part in the acts of foundation of these establishments.[29]

But after the Third Council of the Lateran of 1179, the movement of renewal intensified. Examples are the Council of Rouen of 1190 with its decrees dealing with residence or the behavior of clergy,[30] the Council of Avignon (1209) dealing with priests' garb,[31] and the legislation of Legates (Galon, Robert de Courçon) largely exploited by the bishops.[32] A comparable evolution appears from the reading of the English councils of the twelfth century; Westminster 1102 (clerical garb, publicity of marriages), Westminster 1200.[33] An analysis of the sources of Lateran IV would undoubtedly render an account of this evolution and different exchanges; "reception" is not only descending but also ascending.

Conciliar Times

The Lateran Council of 1215 renewed by modifying the traditional discipline concerning provincial councils and diocesan synods; an entire mechanism of reception was foreseen.[34] Evoking first the ancient prescription,[35] the decree obliged metropolitans to call councils with a view to correcting excesses and reforming mores, notably those of the clergy. For this purpose the archbishops were to refer to the canonical norms, notably to those of the present council. With a view to elaborating reforms judged indispensable, the prelates were to entrust capable persons ahead of time with the task of researching what must be corrected and reformed in order to report to the metropolitan and his suffragans during the following council. This assembly would then take the necessary de-

---

[28] Jean Leclercq, "Les décrets de Bernard de Saintes," *Revue du Moyen Age latin* 2 (1946) 167-170.

[29] Joseph Avril, "Le IIIe concile du Latran et les communautés de lépreux," *Revue Mabillon* 60 (1981) 21-76.

[30] Council of Rouen, cc. 5, 8, in Mansi, 22: 582-583.

[31] Council of Avignon, c. 18, in Mansi, 22: 781.

[32] Decree of Galon, in *Les statuts synodaux français*, 1: 98-99; councils of Paris, Rouen, in Mansi, 22: 818-854, 897-924.

[33] *Councils and Synods with Other Documents relating to the English Church*, 1: *AD. 871-1204*, ed. Dorothy Whitelock, M. Brett and Christopher N. L. Brooke (Oxford: Clarendon, 1981).

[34] Fourth Lateran Council, c. 6, in *Conciliorum Oecumenicorum Decreta*, ed. Josepho Alberigo, 3rd ed. (Bologna: Istituto per le Scienze Religiose, 1973) 236-237.

[35] D. 18 c. 5, 6 §1, 10, 12.

cisions destined to be published by the bishops at the moment of their annual synod.

Once again, the system functioned only partially. The council of 1215 established a close bond between provincial canons and synodal statutes; in fact, there were none or hardly any. Certainly, some provinces during the course of the thirteenth century did hold legislating conciliar reunions, but never according to the rhythm foreseen by Lateran IV.[36] Moreover, during the fourteenth and fifteenth centuries provincial gatherings became still rarer. During the thirteenth century important legislation was promulgated in certain provinces such as Rouen, Tours, Bordeaux, and even Bourges. It was not the same at Rheims, Sens, Lyons, or at Vienne: for these two latter provinces, one can even speak of limited pastoral initiatives.[37] Provincial prescriptions were inserted in synodal books, but this was not the exclusive source of these diocesan legislations, such as there were.

The reasons for these declines are already known to us: weakness of the metropolitan power contrasting with the solidity and efficacy of the diocese. Certain archbishops, those of Tours for example, frequently convened their suffragans and with their consent took on a number of decisions which were later really received in the dioceses and codified; one could speak in this case of a true collegiality.[38] But archbishops were often too absorbed by the government of their own diocese, and also by the missions commanded by Rome or by the sovereigns.[39] Finally, in confiding to legates the care of calling interprovincial councils such as Bourges (1276),[40] the Apostolic See intervened outside the established institutional system.

It is especially evident that if the decree of 1215 had been deviated from its first meaning, even ignored, it is because, even before its promulgation, it was in competition with a procedure developed by the bish-

---

[36] *Les conciles de la province de Tours/Concilia provincias Turonensis*, ed. Joseph Avril, Sources d'Histoire médiévale publiées par l'Institut de recherche d'Histoire des Textes (Paris: CNRS, 1987).

[37] Bruno Galland, *Deux archevéchés entre la France et l'Empire. Les archevéques de Lyon et les archevéques du milieu du XIIᵉ siécle au milieu du XIVᵉ siècle*, Bibliothéque des Ecoles françaises d'Athénes et de Rome (Rome: Ecole française de Rome, 1974) 625.

[38] Avril, *Les conciles de la province de Tours*, 66-68.

[39] Galland, 579-624, 657-694.

[40] Mansi, 24: 164-180.

ops which was much more pastoral. In effect, in the first decade of the thirteenth century, the Bishop of Paris, Eudes de Sully, published in synod his *precepta* responding to the new conditions of parish ministry.[41] These decisions constituted the first version of a new type of manual, dealing with the administration of the sacraments, the celebration of the liturgy, the behavior of priests, and the government of parishes. They took into account new regulations, notably in penitential and matrimonial disciplines.[42]

After 1215 this little collection served as a model and framework, and experienced a striking success. One can find its influence with certain additions and modifications at Albi, Bordeaux, Narbonne, Noyon, Soissons, Metz, and likewise in Portugal and in Germany.[43] Then toward 1225-1240 it received, in addition to the decrees of Lateran IV, implicit liturgical and doctrinal complements. Thus was drafted the "Synodal of the West" later adopted not only in the province of Tours (Angers, Le Mans, Tours, Nantes),[44] but also at Rouen, Bayeux, Orléans, Poitiers, Saintes, Clermont, and Sisteron.

Under a less developed form the Parisian statutes were utilized in the first *precepta* of Cambrai and in the synodal books of a "Nordic" type (Arras, Tournai, Cologne, and Sweden).[45] Moreover, the synodal codification of Nîmes, later taken up at Bézeirs, Lodève, Uzès, Arles, and Carcassonne, came from this same legislation redone according to the tech-

---

[41] Pontal, *Les statuts de Paris et le synodal de l'Ouest*, vol. 1 (*supra*, note 6).

[42] Joseph Avril, "Naissance et évolution des législations synodales des diocèses du nord et de l'ouest de la France (1200-1250)," *ZRG KA* 72 (1986) 162-249.

[43] *Les statuts synodaux fraçais du XIIIᵉ siècle*, 2: *Les statuts de 1230 à 1260*, ed. Odette Pontal, Collection de documents inédits sur l'histoire de France 15 (Paris: Biblioteque Nationale, 1983), iii; *Les statuts de l'ancienne province de Reims (Cambrai, Arras, Noyon, Soissons et Tournai)*, ed. Joseph Avril, Collection de documents inédits sur l'histoire de France 23 (Paris: Biblioteque Nationale, 1995); Nicolas Roussel, *Histoire ecclésiastique et civile de Verdun*, 2 vols. (Bar-le-Duc: Contant-Laguerre, 1863-1864) 1-40; *Synodicon Hispanum*, 2: *Portugal*, ed. Antonio García y García (Madrid: BAC, 1982) 285-300; Peter Johanek, "Die Pariser Statuten des Bishofs Odo von Sully und die Anfänge der kirchlichen Statutengesetzgebung in Deutschland," *Proceedings of the Seventh International Congress of Medieval Canon Law*, 327-347 (*supra*, note 6).

[44] Pontal, *Les statuts synodaux français*, vols. 1, 2, 3; Avril, "Naissance et évolution."

[45] Pontal, *Les statuts synodaux français*, vol. 4.

niques of canonical science.[46] Finally certain prelates, such as the bishops of Rodez, Mende, and Dax, borrowed from several synods to compose original manuals, often of good quality.[47]

This synodal activity built up in the fourteenth century and later with the elaboration of new collections (Rheims, Tréguier, Chartres)[48] or with the addition of supplements (Angers, Cambrai).[49] One could also follow in England the transformations which affected the oldest statutes, those of the Archbishop of Canterbury, Stephen Langton, a contemporary of Eudes de Sully.[50]

With the success of these synodal books, it was the diocese which took precedence over the province. One must recognize that the synodal constituted a manual of easy usage, while provincial councils promulgated canons on such diverse subjects as the defense of ecclesiastical privileges and monastic observance.

Moreover, other declines intervened, since certain councils elaborated legislations of a synodal type receivable in all the dioceses of a province (Vienne 1289)[51] or several provinces (Lavaur 1368).[52] Finally, some bishops modified conciliar decrees taking into account ancient practices; for example, in certain places, the obligation of annual Communion did

---

[46]   Pontal, *Les statuts synodaux français*, vol. 2. Note the originality of Carcassonne's statutes (*Les statuts synodaux*, vol. 6, in preparation).

[47]   Joseph Avril, *Sources et caracteres du livre synodal de Raimond de Calmont d'Olt* (*supra*, note 19); idem, "Les Instructions et Constitutions de Guillaume Durand" (*supra*, note 19); idem., "Sources et caracteres et contenu du livre synodal de Dax (1283)," *Pyrénées, terres frontiéres. Actes du IIIe congrés des sociétés historiques et scientifiques. Pau 25-29 octobre 1993*, ed. Christian Desplat (Paris: CTHS, 1996) 1-8.

[48]   Th. Gousset, *Les actes de la province ecclésiastique de Reims* 2 (Rheims, 1843) 534-575; Edmond Martène, *Thesaurus novus* (Paris: Delaulne et al., 1717) 4: 1097-1113; Maurice Jusselin, "Statuts synodaux et constitutions synodales du diocése de Chartres au XIVe siècle," *Revue d'Histoire de Droit Français et Étranger* 8 (1929) 69-109. At least Grenoble, Troyes, and Mirepoix could also be added.

[49]   Pontal, *Les statuts synodaux français*, vols. 3 and 4.

[50]   *Councils and Synods with other documents relating to the English Church, 2: AD. 1205-1313*, ed. Frederick M. Powicke and Christopher R. Cheney (Oxford: Clarendon, 1964).

[51]   *Un concile provincial au treizième siècle. Vienne 1289. Eglise locale et société*, ed. Louis Boisset, Théologie historique 21 (Paris: Beauchesne, 1973).

[52]   Mansi, 26: 473-548.

not suppress the ancient discipline of three confessions and three Communions.[53]

This last example is also revelatory of the preponderance of local usages, of "customs." Bishops kept full liberty in the elaboration of their prescriptions and superior authorities took into account local decisions. Exchanges were thus never in only one direction; thus provincial councils were inspired by synodal constitutions.[54] Moreover, these "receptions" were selective, often taking up partially the decrees of general and provincial councils, integrating more or less completely other synodal books, finally, elaborating their own presciptions. Yet, despite the diversity of presentation and content, there exists an authentic "communion" around an understanding of pastoral ministry, which is shown by the diffusion of the *Admonitio synodalis* and the use of the *precepta* of Eudes de Sully. Finally, despite inevitable ossification, evolution had to continue; certain Iberain synodal books of the fifteenth and sixteenth centuries already announced Tridentine Catholicism (Badajoz, Coria, Plasencia).[55]

Translation by James H. Provost

---

[53]   Joseph Avril, "Remarques sur un aspect de la vie religieuse paroissiale la pratique de la confession et de la communion du Xe au XIVe siècle," *L'encadrement religieux des fidèles au Moyen Age et jusqu'au concile de Trente. Actes du IIIe congrès national des Sociétés savantes. Dijon 1984* (Paris: Ministère de l'Éducation Nationale, 1985) 345-463. Cambrai's statutes mentioned Communions for Easter, Pentecost, All Saints, Christmas, of the dedication, and of the patron saint (Gousset, 2: 485-486).

[54]   Council of Tours 1282, c. 5: Avril, *Les statuts de la province de Tours*, 282 (*supra*, note 36).

[55]   *Synodicon Hispanum*, 5: *Extremadura: Badajoz, Coria-Cáceres y Plasencia*, ed. Antonio García y García (Madrid: BAC 1990).

THE EPISTEMOLOGY OF RECEPTION
(To Yves Congar, In Gratitude)

JOSEPH A. KOMONCHAK*

In *Communionis notio*, its letter to the world's bishops on "Some Aspects of the Church Understood as Communion,"[1] the Congregation for the Doctrine of the Faith (CDF) criticized as "ecclesiological onesidedness" the view "that every particular church is a subject complete in itself and that the universal church is the result of a reciprocal recognition on the part of the particular churches" (n. 8). Against the view that the universal Church is either "the sum of the particular Churches," "a federation of particular Churches," or "the result of their communion," the CDF stated that "it is a reality that is *ontologically* and *temporally* prior to any *single* particular church."

> For, *ontologically*, the Church which is mystery, the one and only Church, according to the Fathers precedes creation and gives birth to the particular churches as daughters, expresses herself in them, is the Mother and not the product of the particular churches. *Temporally*, the Church manifests herself on the day of Pentecost in the community of the 120 gathered around Mary and the twelve Apostles, representatives of the single Church and future founders of the local Churches, who have a mission orientated toward the world: already then is the Church *speaking all languages*.

For this reason the CDF felt it necessary to amend the language of Vatican II:

> From this Church, universal in origin and manifestation, have begun the various local Churches, as particular realizations of

---

* The Catholic University of America.
[1] *Acta Apostolicae Sedis* [*AAS*] 85 (1993) 838-850; the CDF has also published the text, with Italian translation and commentaries, in *Lettera "Communionis Notio" su alcuni aspetti della Chiesa intesa come comunione (28 maggio 1992)* (Vatican City: Libreria Editrice Vaticana, 1994) 16-49.

the one and single Church of Jesus Christ. Arising *in* and *from* the universal Church, they have their ecclesial character in and from her. For this reason the formula of Vatican II: *The Church in and from the Churches* (*ecclesia in et ex ecclesiis*) is inseparable from this other formula: *The Churches in and from the Church* (*ecclesiae in et ex ecclesia*) (n. 9).

These statements provoked a good deal of critical comment both in the Catholic Church and outside it, which led to the publication a year later on the first page of *L'Osservatore Romano* and over three asterisks of an authoritative clarification of the CDF's "Letter."[2] If nothing is formally retracted in the article, several matters are explained more fully. One thing not clarified, however, is the "Letter's" repudiation of the idea of "reciprocal recognition," a term close enough to the theme of this symposium as to suggest that it might be useful to undertake an investigation of it.

Some may regard my title as odd: "The Epistemology of Reception." If this phrase will not seem strange to anyone acquainted with the literature on the hermeneutics of reception, it is rare for "epistemology" to appear in the titles of articles or books on ecclesiology.[3] Churchmen and theologians seem more at home with words like "ontology" and seldom give much attention to the epistemological grounds of statements about ontology and to the fact, on which I wish to concentrate, that the specific ontology of the Church is of a peculiar kind to which issues of epistemology are by no means secondary. I shall argue that reception is constitutive of the Church and that therefore an epistemology of reception provides a way into an ontology of the Church as concretely realized. I shall begin with a reflection on some common theological language about the Church, argue that this language requires explication in terms of reception, defend the hypothesis that the Church's concrete reality is "onto-

---

[2]   "La Chiesa come Comunione," *L'Osservatore Romano*, June 23, 1993; this text is now available in *Lettera "Communionis Notio,"* 81-90; in the Preface to this volume, Alberto Bovone, Secretary to the CDF, states that "L'articolo . . . ha un carattere autorevole" (p. 6).

[3]   See Severino Dianich, "Il difficile statuto epistemologico dell'ecclesiologia," *Teoria* 7 (1987) 27-49. Addressing the issue in an entire book, Dianich comments: "mentre moltissimi teologi hanno scritto tantissimi libri ed articoli sulla chiesa, non molti e solo raramente hanno scritto qualcosa sull'ecclesiologia." *Ecclesiologia: Questioni di metodo e una proposta* (Turin: Ed. Paoline, 1993) 7, with the bibliography given in the note.

logically subjective," and end by returning to the position of the CDF as clarified in the subsequent article in *L'Osservatore Romano*.

REFERENTS OF THE WORD "CHURCH"

We may begin by asking to what does the word "Church" refer. In his *Vraie et fausse réforme dans l'Eglise*, Yves Congar distinguished among four meanings of the word "Church." The first refers to the Church "in her formal and constitutive principles which come from God as his gifts," enumerated as the grace of salvation, the deposit of faith, the sacraments, and the apostolic ministries: the *Ecclesia de Trinitate*. A second meaning refers to the Church in terms of its "material principle," the people who constitute the community of the faithful, the *Ecclesia ex hominibus*. A third meaning refers to those believers who are invested with hierarchical authority, who may act *in persona Ecclesiae*. But there is another sense to the word:

> Finally, in a fourth and last sense, one may designate by "the Church," not merely the formal elements that proceed, pure, from the gift of God nor solely the human matter that sociologically constitutes the People of God, but the conjunction of the two, the union of the divine formal principle and of the human material principle, the divine-human reality that is born of this union. The word then takes on its full sense and synthetically designates the concrete Church in its totality: a Church made of people, but insofar as these people have received from Christ and actualized a new principle of being, of organization, and of activity: the Body of Christ, humanity insofar as, thanks to the energies and realities instituted for this by Jesus Christ, it has a new existence in him. . . . The *Ecclesia ex Trinitate* and the *Ecclesia ex hominibus* meet and form one thing in the *Ecclesia in Christo*, the Church of the Incarnate Word, the Body of Christ. This meaning includes and synthesizes all the others.[4]

Of these four meanings the first two and the last are most pertinent to our purposes, the third being dependent on and unintelligible outside the other three. Congar's analysis might be taken as a sort of "ontology" of the Church, an effort to distinguish and to relate the basic causes or principles of this unique being. Only the last meaning envisages the Church in its concrete actuality, as realized. The first two are derived by an ab-

---

[4]   Yves Congar, *Vraie et fause réforme dans l'Eglise*, 2 ed. (Paris: Cerf, 1965) 94-97.

straction that identifies and distinguishes the form and matter that constitute its essence, which still needs the act of existence in order to be. And, of course, in discourse about the Church the question is whether or not it is only of the full, existent reality that predications of being and action can be made.

On the level of this abstract analysis, one may make an observation or two about the "formal" and "material" principles of the Church. The first is to note that Congar later revised his views when he nuanced his description of the "institutional" elements of the Church by recognizing that "the Spirit did not come simply in order to animate an institution that was already fully determined in all its structures, but that he is really the 'co-instituting' principle." He illustrated this claim by describing briefly the Church's part in the constitution over time of its sacramental system and the forms of apostolic ministry, to which one might add the formation of the canon of the Scriptures.[5] What is remarkable here is that the "co-instituting" work of the Spirit is illustrated by the activity of *the Church*, by the long and complex process by which the actual historical community (communities) of faith was (were) led to the set of decisions—canon of the Scriptures, rule of faith, sacramental system, forms of apostolic ministry—which defined it as the *Catholica* and which subsequent generations accept as formal, normative, and constitutive principles of its distinctive existence.

This makes the important point that the formal elements of the Church are never found in their "purity," "as they flow from God," but only as received by the Church which was and is under the Spirit's guidance, the active agent of what might be called *self-constitutive reception*, the process by which the Church defines itself by defining the divine gifts and norms by receiving which in faith and obedience it was and is to live. The Church, the receptive community, was and is a "co-instituting principle" even of its formal element.[6]

Something similar must be said when one considers the actual constitution of the Church in the full sense of this term. In this event, people are not simply the material element (*ex quibus*) from which the Church is constructed by reception of the revealed faith and instituted sacraments

---

[5]   Yves Congar, *Je Crois en l'Esprit Saint* (Paris: Cerf, 1979) 2: 19-21; English translation, *I Believe in the Holy Spirit*, 3 vols. (New York: Seabury, 1983) 2: 9-10.

[6]   This, of course, is why the issue of "ius divinum" is so complex. See Yves Congar, "Ius divinum," in *Eglise et papauté* (Paris: Cerf, 1994) 65-80.

by which, as Aquinas said, the Church is constituted, fabricated, built up. Along with the objectivated sense of the *fides quae*, there is also the *fides qua* intended when Aquinas says that "faith is as the foundation from whose strength the whole structure of the Church derives its strength."[7] Similarly, the sacraments are sacraments *of faith* and do not exist apart from faith; the Eucharist, for example, is dynamically constitutive of the Church: its *res*, its purpose and result, is the *unitas Corporis Christi*, realized when the many eat the one bread that is the one Body of Christ and become by their faith and love the Body they eat.[8] And there surely is great and wider ecclesiological significance in what Aquinas said about the Scriptures: "Even the letter of the Gospel would kill unless there is present within the healing grace of faith."[9] In all of these respects, then, the active believing participation, the subjectivity, of its members is co-constitutive of the Church. As we shall see, this raises the question whether the Church may be said really to precede its members.

Some later remarks of Congar offer another approach to the theme. In one of his last major works he spoke of the Church as born and living in virtue of the two "missions" of the Word and of the Spirit:

> That the Word and the Spirit *come* does not mean that they move. It means that *they make a creature exist in a new relationship with them*. This means that the procession that situates them in the eternity of the Uni-Trinity culminates freely and efficaciously *in a created effect*. . . . The Church, as an organism of knowledge and love, is entirely dependent on these missions. It is the fruitfulness, *outside God*, of the Trinitarian processions.[10]

---

[7]   Thomas Aquinas, Commentary on Colossians, ch. 1, l. 5 (Marietti n. 57): "Fides est sicut fundamentum, ex cuius firmitate tota firmatur ecclesiae structura." See his comment on Ephesians, ch. 4, l. 2 (Marietti n. 199); ch. 2, l. 6 (Marietti n. 131): "ipsam ecclesiam, quae tunc construitur quando homines ad fidem convertuntur"; see also ch. 4, l. 4 (Marietti n. 214): "et quantum ad hoc dicit 'in aedificationem Corporis Christi,' id est ut convertantur infideles, ex quibus aedificatur ecclesia Christi, quae est corpus eius."

[8]   See *Summa theologica*, 3, q. 73, a. 4: "Aliam autem significationem habet [Eucharistia] respectu rei praesentis, scilicet ecclesiasticae unitatis, cui homines congregantur per hoc sacramentum. Et secundum hoc dicitur *communio* vel *synaxis*. Dicit enim Damascenus . . . quod 'dicitur communio quia communicamus per ipsam Christo; et quia participamus eius carne et deitate; et quia communicamus et unimur ad invicem per ipsam.'"

[9]   *Summa theologica*, 1-2, q. 106, a. 2.

[10]   Congar, *Je Crois en l'Esprit Saint*, 2: 17; emphasis added. See also, after a discussion of the *communio* the Spirit effects, the insistence that all this takes place "in the con-

This brief remark rests upon a Thomist notion of the relations between God and creatures. Aquinas denied that God had a real metaphysical relationship with creatures; real relations were utterly on the side of the creature. God does not change by becoming a Creator; creatures come to exist and their existence is the reality that makes it true that God is Creator. Bernard Lonergan elaborated on this the thesis that all contingent predication about God requires as the condition of its truth the existence of something contingent. This does not mean, of course, that the contingent reality is the *cause* or even the condition of the divine act that brings it into existence; but it does mean that if something contingent is predicated of God, then something contingent must exist as the consequence of God's activity and as the condition of the truth of that predication.[11]

These metaphysical and epistemological considerations give rise to some interesting questions. If a creature must exist for it to be true that God is Creator and Lord,[12] then for God to be Revealer, there must exist believers, for God to be Savior, there must exist people freed from their sins, for God to will the Church, there must be a concrete People of God, a *congregatio fidelium*.[13] Claude Welch made a similar point:

> The church may be fully dependent on God's act, but it is not simply God acting. It is a people believing, worshipping, obeying, witnessing. Thus we can and must make fast at the outset our understanding of the church as a body or community of human beings, albeit existing in response to the activity of God. In this

---

crete, everyday life of believers": "What is most concrete, most ordinary is part of what is most sublime" (English translation, 22; French, 35).

[11]   Bernard Lonergan, *De constitutione Christi ontologica et psychologica* (Rome: Gregorian University Press, 1961) 51-53; see also idem, *De Deo Trino*, 2, *Pars Systematica*, 3rd ed. (Rome: Gregorian University Press, 1964) 217-219, 226-235; idem, *Insight: A Study of Human Understanding* (New York: Longmans, Green and Co., 1958) 661-662.

[12]   Compare Lonergan's remark: "non prius concipitur Deus ut Creator quam concipiatur Dei creatura" (*De constitutione Christi*, 53) with Aquinas' statement: "Licet igitur Deus sit prior creaturis, quia tamen in significatione Domini clauditur quod habeat servum, et e converso, ista duo relativa, Dominus et servus, sunt simul natura. Unde Deus non fuit Dominus, antequam haberet creaturam sibi subiectam" (*Summa theologica*, 1, q. 13, a. 7, ad 6m).

[13]   See Clement of Alexandria: "Just as the will of God is an act and is called the world, so his intention is the salvation of men and is called the Church." *Pedagogue*, 1, 6, cited by Henri de Lubac, *Catholicisme: Les aspects sociaux du dogme*, 4 ed. (Paris: Cerf, 1947) 45; English translation, *Catholicism: Christ and the Common Destiny of Man* (San Francisco: Ignatius Press, 1988) 70.

sense, the ontology of the church means in the first instance the humanly subjective pole of the relationship.[14]

It may strike some people as odd to say that the *ontology* of the Church entails a "humanly *subjective* pole." Many people want the ontological to be something more solidly "objective" than this, and they are encouraged in this by the long history and massive institutional bulk of the Catholic Church and perhaps also by the tendency of sociologists since Ernst Troeltsch almost to define the ideal-type of a "Church" primarily by "objective" criteria. But it may also be that the seemingly unsubstantial character of subjectivity and intersubjectivity leads theologians, while rightly insisting, for example, that the Church is more than the sum of its members, to have recourse, when explaining this "more," mainly to her transcendent divine principles, or even to propose that she has "a supernatural subsistence which presupposes and transcends the natural subsistence of the individual persons who are her members."[15] It also may be that legitimate criticism of the notion of the Church as a *societas perfecta* has led some ecclesiologists to fear the application to the Church of any sort of social theory elaborated elsewhere. They neglect the acute observations of Congar that the problem with the societal ecclesiology was, first, the philosophical poverty and sociological datedness of the idea of *societas* employed and, second, its concentration on efficient and final causality and neglect of intrinsic causality; but he argued that a more theological notion, such as "communion," "would have to adopt the valuable contributions not only of sociology, but of interpersonal ontology and of the philosophy of personalism."[16]

For whatever reasons, the emphasis in ecclesiology today falls mainly on distinctively theological notions such as "mystery" and "communio," often to the disparagement of notions such as "People of God," which is suspected of tempting people to be content with a "merely" sociological

---

[14]   Claude Welch, *The Reality of the Church* (New York: Charles Scribner's Sons, 1958) 48.

[15]   Jacques Maritain, *De l'Eglise du Christ: La personne de l'Eglise et son personnel* (Paris: Desclée de Brouwer, 1970) 39; Maritain's thesis is contextualized and acutely criticized in Yves Congar, "La personne 'Eglise,'" *Revue Thomiste* 71 (1971) 613-640, who points not only to theological problems but to the questionable notion of "subsistence" presupposed by Maritain.

[16]   Yves Congar, "Peut-on définir l'Eglise? Destin et valeur de quatre notions qui s'offrent à le faire," in *Sainte Eglise*, Unam Sanctam 41 (Paris: Cerf, 1963) 21-44. To these aids might be added a more critical social theory than that supposed when one counterposes "institution" and "event."

approach to the Church.[17] If distinctively theological notions must govern any adequate ecclesiology, exclusive attention to them tends to abstract the Church out of history and out of those quite concrete particular realizations that are the individual churches assembled locally, that is, in particular times, places, and cultures, with distinctive historical tasks to undertake.[18] The Church is thought to be so unique and transcendent in its origin that it can be described adequately solely in terms of its divine generative principles.[19] This tendency is also reflected when predications about God are confused with predications about the Church and when predications about the Church are thought to have substantial meaning without reference to any created body of spiritual creatures. But if all contingent predications about God—such as his intention of the Church—require as the simultaneous condition of their truth the existence of something contingent, in the case of the Church on earth this means the actual existence of the community of faith. The simple question is this: Are there any predications made about the Church—from the *totus Christus*, the *ecclesia ab Abel*, and the eschatological *communio sanctorum* to the most prosaic descriptions of its activity in the world—that do not require to be verified in some concrete created community?

On Not Reifying the Church

Bernard Lonergan once criticized theologians who "seem to have thought of truth as so objective as to get along without minds."[20] One

---

[17] For an example, see the debates at and the "Final Report" of the 1985 Synod of Bishops. It would be useful to extend an investigation of the common suspicion of sociology illustrated by André Rousseau, "Emploi du terme 'sociologie' dans les textes du Magistère central de l'Eglise," *Social Compass* 17 (1970) 309-320.

[18] For similar reservations about exclusive attention to the notions of "mystery" and of "communion," see Giuseppe Colombo, "Il 'Popolo di Dio' e il 'mistero' della Chiesa nell'ecclesiologia post-conciliare," *Teologia* 10 (1985) 97-169, and Dianich, *Ecclesiologia*.

[19] Langdon Gilkey makes a remark pertinent here when he criticizes the "category mistake" made when "symbols expressing the *relation* of God to the life of the existing churches have been mistaken for the substantial *elements* out of which the Church is itself composed." The "concrete historical institution made up of visible people" is often neglected in favor of biblical symbols such as "koinonia" or "People of God." But "unless . . . empirical description supplements theological categories, the actual human beings who make up the ecclesia, with all their cultural habits, activities, and goals, not to mention their weaknesses and sins, are left completely out of the picture, and quite holy but unactual abstractions result." *How the Church Can Minister to the World Without Losing Itself* (New York: Harper & Row, 1964) 134.

[20] Bernard Lonergan, *The Subject*, The Aquinas Lecture 1968 (Milwaukee: Marquette University Press, 1968) 5. Lonergan liked to cite Aquinas' argument that truth is eternal

may ask if there is not a parallel and related problem when people imagine a Church, a "communion of life, charity and truth" so objective that it does not need to be embodied in people and communities, in "that messianic people" which may be only a "little flock" (see *LG* 9). When Charles Journet, echoing Maritain, proposed as a solution to a famous problem that "the Church is not without sinners, but is itself without sin," Congar was moved to ask, "Is this not to reify a formal point of view?"[21]

Reification has been much studied in the social sciences, where it refers to a tendency to misrepresent the distinctive ontology of social relations and institutions. Because we encounter already existing and powerful social realities when we enter this world, we almost inevitably reify them, that is, apprehend them as non-human, assign them the same kind of reality as other things in this world, "bestow on them an ontological status independent of human activity and signification."[22] This "ontological" status may be derived from cosmological or divine causality: this is

---

only because there is an eternal divine mind: "Unde si nullus intellectus esset aeternus, nulla veritas esset aeterna." *Summa theologica*, 1, q. 16, a. 7. For the force of the argument see how he replied to the sophisms urged in the fourth objection of this question: "quia intellectus noster non est aeternus, nec veritas enuntiabilium quae a nobis formantur, est aeterna, sed quandoque incoepit. Et antequam huiusmodi veritas esset, non erat verum dicere talem veritatem non esse, nisi ab intellectu divino, in quo solum veritas est aeterna. Sed nunc verum est dicere veritatem tunc non fuisse. Quod quidem non est verum nisi veritate quae nunc est in intellectu nostro; non autem per aliquam veritatem ex parte rei."

[21] "Mais n'est-ce pas là réifier un point de vue formel?"; Yves Congar, *L'Eglise: Une, sainte, catholique et apostolique* (Paris: Cerf, 1970) 136-137. See also, in the same volume, 259: "on ne peut, à moins de verser dans l'idéalisme, séparer l'institution du peuple des fidèles." The contrast between tortured modern approaches to the question of the holiness of the Church and the ease with which St. Thomas moved from the "Ecclesia" to the "nos" of its members says a great deal about what has happened in ecclesiology: "dicendum quod esse Ecclesiam 'gloriosam, non habentem maculam neque rugam' est ultimus finis ad quem perducimur per passionem Christi. Unde hoc erit in statu patriae, non autem in statu viae, in quo 'si dixerimus quia peccatum non habemus, nosmetipsos seducimus' (1 Jn 1: 8)"; *Summa theologica*, 3, q. 8, a. 3, ad 2m.

[22] For the analysis of reification, see Peter Berger and Thomas Luckmann, *The Social Construction of Reality: A Treatise in the Sociology of Knowledge* (Garden City, NY: Doubleday Anchor Books, 1967) 89-92; it would appear to be identical to the temptation "to think of *social objects* as independently existing entities on analogy with the objects studied by the natural sciences. . . . In the case of social objects, however, the grammar of the noun phrases conceals from us the fact that, in such cases, process is prior to product. Social objects are always . . . constituted by social acts; and, in a sense, *the object is just the continuing possibility of the activity*." John R. Searle, *The Construction of Social Reality* (New York: Simon & Schuster, 1995) 36.

what "nature" demands or what "God" wills. Examples are not hard to find, even outside ecclesiology.

But in fact social realities, even if they derive from "natural law" or are said to be divinely instituted, are the products of human intentionality. Their genuine reality in the world, their "objectivity," is constituted by subjectivity; they are, as John Searle puts it, "ontologically subjective."[23] One might also say that they are subjectively ontological: in the broad realm of what exists "objectively," that is, may be truly said to exist, there is a basic difference between things that are not constituted by meaning and value and things that are so constituted.[24] To catch what is meant, one might reflect on the difference, in ontology, between a facial tic and a wink, between a piece of flint and an arrowhead, between a pride of lions and a human family, between a bee-hive and a city. In all four cases, while the first of the pairs is fully intelligible without having to take human intentionality into account, meaning is constitutive of each of the second, and this difference ought to ground a difference in method between the *Naturwissenschaften* and the *Geisteswissenschaften*.

Consider, for example, this international colloquium on "Reception and Communion among the Churches." This now exists, "objectively"; but its "ontology" was constituted first by the shared intentionality of the group that conceived it, assigned it a theme, drew up its program, and invited its participants; and, since their effort has happily met a better fate than poor Bella Fleace did (who gave a party to which no one came),[25] its "ontology" is now being constituted by the shared intentionality of all of us now engaged in this conversation. Various differentiations among us are also constituted by common assumptions, expectations, agreements, responsibilities as, for example, in organizers, speakers, chairs of sessions, other participants, etc. And this particular event takes place against sets of larger common intentionalities definable in terms of a common Christian faith, interest in ecumenism, concern about the life of the Church, standards of courtesy, scholarship, rational argument, etc. It

---

[23] See Searle, 9-12.
[24] These latter constitute what Lonergan called "the world constituted by meaning." See Bernard Lonergan, *Method in Theology* (New York: Herder and Herder, 1972), the index on meaning as constitutive of community.
[25] See Evelyn Waugh's short story, "Bella Fleace Gave a Party," in *Tactical Exercise* (Boston: Little, Brown and Company, 1954) 15-27.

might take a book to set out all the dimensions of the intersubjectivity that makes this meeting what it is.

We would think oddly of anyone who would maintain now that it is not taking place or later that it never took place. Because the phrase is often invoked as if it were true only of the Church, it should be noted also that what exists is more than the mere sum of all of us participants or even of our individual intentions. Lonergan describes that "more" as the set of common meanings and values that constitute "the substance of a community" as distinct from a mere aggregate of people. Searle means largely the same thing when he uses such terms as "collective intentionality," "collective agreement," "we-intentions," a "system of expectations."[26] For both authors, the "objective," "substantive" reality of what is happening here is subjective and intersubjective, and no other "subsistence" is needed to make one's analysis "ontological."

As I write these lines, two months before the colloquium is to meet, Salamanca III is little more than a bright idea in the minds of us who planned it and invited people to it. What we planned was an intersubjective encounter for a particular ecclesial and scholarly purpose. What will become real and afterward be known as "Salamanca III" is, of course, the set of intersubjective encounters and conversations that, God willing, will occur between the 8th and the 14th of April, 1996, when the idea or plan is realized. But as I write, it does not yet have "objective" existence.

To propose this as an analogy for the constitution of the Church can claim good Thomist grounds. In his commentary on Ephesians Aquinas asked how it could be that to angels, who know all things in God, "the manifold wisdom of God" was said by the Apostle to have been made known "through the church." His final answer was that the Church is one of those mysteries hidden in God that even the angels know only as they are unfolded in effects, in this case when the mysteries "hidden in the divine mind were unfolded (*explicatas*) in the Apostles. Just as a house which exists in the mind of the builder or in the concept of the house that is to be built cannot be known as long as it is hidden in his mind except only to God, who alone reads minds; but after the concept has been unfolded in the extrinsic effect when the house is built, then anyone can be

---

[26] Lonergan, *Method in Theology*, 50; Searle, passim. Another effort to address the question is Margaret Gilbert, *On Social Facts* (Princeton, NJ: Princeton University Press, 1992).

instructed about the already built house, not by the house but in the house."[27]

The point, of course, is that the house which is the Church that God intends (see 1 Pt 2: 5) is the great *communio sanctorum* which will gather all of humanity into the Body of Christ. The initiating subjectivity here is wholly God's, but what it intends is something that is to be unfolded only in and as the transformed subjectivity and intersubjectivity of spiritual creatures. The divine plan began to become real *in statu legis* as the people of Israel, already looking to Christ in hope (a *congregatio sperantium*); it has its present reality *in statu viae* as the Church (the *congregatio fidelium*); it will be fully realized only *in statu patriae* when faith is transformed into sight (the *congregatio comprehendentium*).[28] At every point, what God intends and what comes to exist by his efficacious will is a community of spiritual creatures united by the free spiritual operations of faith, hope, and affection. It is all gloriously concrete, and what is concrete is ontologically subjective and intersubjective, constituted in its successive moments by hope, by faith, and by beatifying sight.

Consider its original genesis. Christians believe that in the fullness of time "God was in Christ reconciling the world to himself." A man named Jesus of Nazareth appeared, announced the in-breaking of the Kingdom of God and the repentance it requires, and gathered disciples. A new social phenomenon appeared: call it the "Jesus Movement," if you wish: an itinerant rabbi and some people following him around—not the first, notice, without the second. When the leader is arrested and executed, the nascent community is dissolved, their hopes that he would be the one to redeem Israel disappointed (see Lk 24: 21). But then they become convinced that he has been raised from the dead and by this conviction they are reconstituted as a community. They start to gather together regularly to remember him, to confess him as Lord, to celebrate the new life which he has given them to share, and to await his return. And they begin now to proclaim, first to their fellow Jews and then to Gentiles also, that the

---

[27] Aquinas, *Comment on Eph*, ch. 3, l. 3 (Marietti n. 160).
[28] See St. Thomas: "Ecclesia secundum statum viae est congregatio fidelium; sed secundum statum patriae est congregatio comprehendentium"; *Summa theologica*, 3, q. 8, a. 4, ad 2m. I have added the phrase "congregatio sperantium," which I think reflects St. Thomas' view of Israel.

one who had been crucified has been made Lord and Christ (see Acts 2: 36).

A new social phenomenon, increasingly different from any other, even from Israel, gradually becomes unmistakable: individuals now being called "Christians," a community now calling itself the *Ekklesia*, the Church. Note that it is utterly dependent upon God's presence and action in Christ and in Christ's Spirit. But what is thus utterly dependent is a new this-worldly community, constituted by the acts of faith, hope and love towards God that his action enables them to perform and by their own transformed intersubjectivity under God and in Christ. The *koinonia* with God in Christ and the Spirit is embodied in their *koinonia* among themselves.[29] If the latter is impossible without the former, the former does not exist except in the latter. As with the itinerant rabbi and his disciples, so here also Christ and Church make a single event. The emergent Church *is* the event of the reconciliation with God Christ effected, and without the Church nothing in the world is different because Jesus of Nazareth once lived.[30] The Church is the historic—that is, history-affecting, history-shaping—significance of Jesus Christ, and apart from the significance he has obtained in the Church he would not be the object of more than antiquarian interest.

This Church embodies itself in the many churches which are born from the originating event. In every case of the generation of a new individual Church, the originating event is repeated. So that their joy may be complete, those who already believe and live in the new communion proclaim what they have seen and heard and thereby invite new people into the communion with them that is also communion with God and with his Son Jesus Christ (1 Jn 1: 1-4). A new Church arises when this invitation is received in faith, hope and love, so that the originating principles of the first community now originate and constitute a new community, new and distinct because comprised of new members, but the same original community because gathered in the same Christ and animated by the same Spirit. The earlier communities rejoice and give thanks when the word of an apostle, whose gospel comes "not only in word, but also in power and in the Holy Spirit," is not preached "in vain," but is received "not as the

[29]   See John Reumann, "Koinonia in Scripture: Survey of Biblical Texts," in *On the Way to Fuller Koinonia*, ed. Thomas F. Best and Günther Gassmann, Faith and Order Paper no. 166 (Geneva: WCC Publications, 1994) 37-69.
[30]   This is a major theme in the work of the late John Knox; see especially his *The Early Church and the Coming Great Church* (London: Epworth, 1957), esp. ch. 2.

word of men but as what it really is, the word of God, which is at work in [those] who believe" (1 Thes 1-2).

We see here the structure of ecclesiogenesis as it has taken place across cultures and across generations and as it continues to take place today: "Every day the Church gives birth to the Church."[31] The apostolic Gospel comes with the power of the Spirit and is received by faith, and where this event of communication takes place, the Church is born again. Where this event does not take place, where the Gospel is preached in vain, no Church arises. Where the Gospel ceases to be believed, the Church ceases to exist. The whole ontology of the Church—the real "objective" existence of the Church—consists in the reception by faith of the Gospel. Reception is constitutive of the Church.

It is so constitutive of the Church that everything else depends on it. "Faith is as the foundation from whose strength the whole structure of the Church derives its strength" (Aquinas). There is no fellowship with the preaching Church of one generation if a believing Church does not arise in the next. The sacraments are sacraments *of faith*, ineffective apart from it. Succession to apostolic office presupposes succession to the apostolic faith.[32] All of the massive institutional power of the Church, all of the varied articulation of its life in traditions, dogmas, relations, institutions, roles, liturgies, devotions, movements, etc., exists and functions as preparation, mediation, or explication of the founding and generating event of communication and reception of the word and grace of God.[33] For all these reasons, the most basic definition of the Church, presupposed as their referent by all other designations, is that of the *congregatio fidelium*.

Where the Church differs from all other intersubjective communities is not to be found in the alleged claim that it alone is "more than the sum of its members" and therefore must possess some mysterious "supernatural subsistence." Its unique and transcendent substance is constituted by

---

[31]   See Henri de Lubac, *The Splendour of the Church* (New York: Sheed and Ward, 1956) 74, quoting the Venerable Bede, *Explanatio Apocalypsis*, Bk. 2: *Nam et Ecclesia quotidie gignit Ecclesiam*; *PL* 93: 166d.

[32]   See Yves Congar, "Apostolicité de ministère et apostolicité de doctrine: Essai d'explication de la Réaction protestante et de la Tradition catholique," in *Ministères et communion ecclésiale* (Paris: Cerf, 1971) 51-94; note the methodological significance of the medieval discussion of a heretical pope (79-80).

[33]   This is an effort to give broader ecclesial significance to what St. Thomas said about the "new Law" of the new Covenant; *Summa theologica*, 1-2, q. 106, a. 1.

the free and initiating subjectivity of God, communicating himself in Christ and the Spirit, and by the free and receptive subjectivity of those who by his grace become by that Spirit the Body of Christ, his members and members of one another. The ontology of the Church is subjective, but the subjectivity is both divine and human: God's freedom liberating human freedom, God's loving intending of us evoking our loving intending of God.

One might even say that the ontology of the Church consists precisely in this reciprocal recognition. The Church as a whole is the group of people who in the words of men recognize and receive the Word of God, the Gospel of and about Christ. That reciprocal recognition, by which individual believers know God and are known by him (see Gal 4: 9), generates the reciprocal reception by which they are to "receive one another as Christ has received you" (Rom 15: 7), love one another as Christ loves them, recognize one another as members of one Body, as one person, in a unity compared to which the divisions between slave and free, male and female, Jew, Greek, barbarian and Scythian are as nothing (Gal 3: 26; Col 3: 11).

As no individual Church exists except by the reciprocal recognition between believers and God and by the reciprocal recognition by which they receive one another as brothers for whom Christ died (see Rom 14: 15), so also the many churches constitute one Church because of their reciprocal reception whereby, for example, "the churches of God in Christ Jesus which are in Judea" recognize themselves in the Church of God which has emerged in Thessalonica (see 1 Thes 2: 14). If what makes the Church the Church in one place is what makes the Church the Church in other places, the many churches are one Church, and one Church because they recognize that Christ is not divided (see 1 Cor 1: 10-14).

ON NOT REIFYING AUTHORITY

Nothing has been said so far about structures of authority in the Church, one of the main concerns of the CDF's Letter.[34] I had several reasons for this. First, emphasis on the prior constitutive role of faith seems appropriate at a time when, on the one hand, many people are tempted to think that the Church has some existence apart from its com-

---

[34] See n. 8, which refers to notions of the particular church which weaken the concept of the unity of the Church "in its visible and institutional dimension."

munity of faith as, for example, in some amorphous "culture" of "fellow-feeling," and, on the other hand, others think that the best way to address this crisis is a simple assertion of institutional authority. Both groups perhaps need to recognize that the real challenge is to promote the transformation of subjectivity and intersubjectivity that is the conversion of freedom evoked by the Gospel and motivated by the Spirit.

Second, many discussions of authority neglect the fact, first, that an authority-relationship itself is constituted by shared intentionalities and, second, that these presuppose a prior community of intentions, in our case the community of faith. Sacramentally, ordination presupposes the primordial sacrament of faith that is baptism. Intentionally, without sharing the Church's faith Peter is not a rock and the apostles and prophets are not the Church's foundation. Even in the Apostles, their being *fideles* precedes their being *episcopoi*.

Third, the subjective character of the Church's ontology may help avoid a not uncommon tendency to reify authority. To say that God wills certain structures of authority in the Church is to describe a divine intention; but what exists by that will is a set of social relationships and institutions that, however normative they are, have substantive existence only in the shared intentionalities of the members of the Church. If God wills that some members of the Church be recognized by other members to have authority from him to teach and to lead, this divine will is not realized in some reified realm of divinely empowered "objective" authority, but only when that authority is recognized and received by others. An authority existing *in se*, that is, not acknowledged by anyone else, would be, to echo Newman, as silly as a Church without the laity.[35] In that respect, paradoxical as it may appear, church-authority is co-constituted by the trusting expectations of those subject to it. A teaching-authority, for example, exists concretely when people expect to learn from it, and it is concretely effective when, as Newman put it, it is regarded with "admiration, trust, and love,"[36] and that condition is the consequence, not sim-

[35] To the rather dismissive question, "Who are the laity?" Newman replied that "the Church would look foolish without them"; *Letters and Diaries of John Henry Newman* 19 (London: Nelson, 1969) 141.
[36] Responding to a possible objection that a new convert was "putting himself under a sort of intellectual tyranny by doing an act which he is not allowed to reverse," Newman made some profoundly true remarks: "The ecclesiastical prohibition to doubt and inquire, is not so much a practical rule as a scientific principle, which is laid down to make the theological system logically consistent with itself. A Catholic is kept from scepticism, not by any external prohibition, but by admiration, trust, and love. While he admires, trusts, and

ply of the formal authority of an office, but of the work of the Holy Spirit.[37]

For these reasons, one may question the adequacy of a distinction that sometimes is made, as, for example, when Congar claims that "reception does not bestow their legitimacy upon a conciliar decision and an authoritative decree: they obtain their legitimacy and their obligatory value from the authorities which have supported them."[38] This I find as difficult to accept as the idea that truth can exist outside of minds.[39] "Legitimacy" and "obligatory value" describe characteristics assigned by and within a certain community to certain actions, and they can no more exist outside of that community than truth can exist outside of minds. What would be the "legitimacy" of an enactment that *no one* received? The attitude and response of those for whom the enactment is made is constitutive of its real authority. Otherwise the enacting authority will find itself in the embarrassing situation of an unfortunate who claims to be Napoleon but has no armies behind him.

It may be prudent here to insist that this is not to surrender the idea of a divinely legitimated authority within the Church in favor of a purely empirical, statistical notion of authority. Certainly it is true that many modern notions of "legitimacy" identify it with de facto acceptance or re-

---

loves our Lord and His Church, those feelings prohibit him from doubt; they guard and protect his faith; the real prohibition is from within. But suppose those feelings go; suppose he ceases to have admiration, trust, and love, of Our Lord and His Church; in that case, the external prohibition probably will not suffice to keep him from doubting, if he be of an argumentative turn.

"Thus it avails in neither case; while he loves and trusts, it is not needed; when he does not love and trust, it is impotent"; *Letters and Diaries of John Henry Newman* 20 (London: Nelson, 1970) 430. See also 425: "You cannot make men believe by force and repression."

[37]   Perhaps this is a way of making sense of the statement in *Lumen gentium* 25: "To these definitions the assent of the Church can never be lacking because of the action of the same Holy Spirit by which the whole flock of Christ is preserved and makes progress in the unity of faith." To which the Doctrinal Commission added the gloss: "Principium unitatis fidei est *assistentia Spiritus Sancti*"; *Acta Synodalia*, 3/8 (Vatican City: Libreria Editrice Vaticana, 1976) 92.

[38]   Yves Congar, "La 'réception' come réalité ecclésiologique," in *Eglise et papauté*, 259 (*supra*, note 6).

[39]   Compare Congar's statement to the syllogism in which Lonergan found a fallacy: "What God has revealed is true. God has revealed the mysteries of faith. Therefore, the mysteries of faith are true"; *The Subject*, 4 (*supra*, note 20).

ception, so that a power is considered "legitimate" when it can and does in fact impose its will on others. But to find this notion analytically and descriptively useful need not entail abandoning the classical and normative notion of legitimacy by which one may truly say, for example, that a particular office exists in the Church by divine institution and that, therefore, people truly *ought to* trust and obey it. But that "ought to" is a judgment, and judgments do not occur outside of minds.

Finally, if there is a crisis of authority in the Church today, it is crucial that in order to resolve it, we not indulge the view that authority exists in order to relieve people of the burden of personal authenticity in the exercise of their own intelligence, reason, and freedom. Divine authorization does not substitute for conversion in those who occupy offices in the Church,[40] nor will it be acknowledged by the unconverted, who tend to admire, trust, and love people they should not and not to admire, trust, and love people they should. To resolve any crisis that may exist will have to entail the restoration of the full context of the existence and good functioning of authority, and that is the community of intersubjective relations that authority must presuppose but cannot by itself guarantee.

RECEPTION AND THE COMMUNION OF THE CHURCHES

We may now return to the question with which we began, whether the universal Church may be considered to be the result of the reciprocal recognition of the particular churches. Against this, recall, the CDF argued for the ontological and historical priority of the universal Church to any single particular church. This issue of priority had been posed by the statements in *Lumen gentium* 23 that while the particular churches are "formed in the image of the universal Church," it is "in them and out of them that the one and single Catholic Church exists" (*LG* 23). The first statement suggests a priority of the one Church to the many churches; the "ex quibus" formula in the second suggests a priority of the many churches. Perhaps because it here ignores the first statement, the CDF's

---

[40] Discussing the question of pluralism and unity, Lonergan wrote: "But the real menace to unity of faith . . . lies in the absence of intellectual or moral or religious conversion," which becomes "particularly perilous" "when the absence of conversion occurs in those that govern the church or teach in its name." *Method in Theology*, 330 (*supra*, note 24). The body of literature on this subject is not large.

Letter proposes balancing the second by a new statement of its own: that "the Churches exist only in and out of the Church."

Properly understood, this new formula could be acceptable, although one may wonder if it is really needed. The main point, however, is that to take either of the conciliar statements apart from the other is to upset the council's careful balance. With regard to the first statement, Congar is correct that the universal Church "does not pre-exist them [the particular churches] as a concrete reality might pre-exist other concrete realities: it pre-exists them in the plan of God as their defined ideal, their rule, or their absolute essence."[41] Agreeing with Hervé Legrand, who warns against a Platonic reification of this "image,"[42] one might say that the "image" of the one Church refers to the normative pattern that must be realized in any concrete community if it is rightly to be called the Church. This pattern might be spelled out in terms of what Congar called the divine generative principles, a list of which might be derived from the texts of Vatican II: the call of God, the word of Christ, the grace of the Spirit, the sacraments, the apostolic ministry. These pre-exist any particular church only in the fashion in which the divine intention pre-exists the Church *tout courte* or in which a "form" may be said to pre-exist the matter in which it is received; but this reception is precisely what is needed for a concrete reality called the Church to exist, and this happens only in the churches.

The CDF, on the other hand, appears to have reified the universal Church, when, to defend its *ontological* priority, it says that it exists before creation as mystery and gives birth to the particular churches as a mother does her daughters. In response to critics, the article in *L'Osser-*

---

[41] Congar, "La consécration épiscopale et la succession apostolique, constituent-ils chef d'une Eglise locale ou membre du collège?" in *Ministères et communion ecclésiale*, 131 (*supra*, note 32). In a private letter circulated in response to the CDF's Letter *Communionis notio*, Congar repeated this view: "En quoi consiste et oú existe cette Eglise universelle que le cardinal [Ratzinger] dit antérieure chronologiquement et ontologiquement aux Eglises particulières? Il est certain que quand saint Paul parle de l'Eglise qui séjourne à Corinthe, il entend l'Eglise purement et simplement, à savoir une unique Eglise potentiellement universelle. Mais celle-ci n'existe concrètement que dans l'unité et la communion de foi des Eglises particulières." Earlier in the same letter, he said: "Il me semble que le texte du cardinal, s'il honore bien le '*in quibus*', efface trop le '*ex quibus*, à partir d'elles.'"

[42] Hervé Legrand, "La réalisation de l'Eglise en un lieu," in *Initiation à la pratique de la théologie*, ed. Bernard Lauret and François Refoulé, 3 (Paris: Cerf, 1983) 152n.

vatore Romano rightly pointed out that many had overlooked the emphasis in the Letter that the priority claimed for the universal Church was with respect to any *single* particular church, not to *all* the particular churches. But it passed over the issue of "ontological" priority except to appeal to its biblical basis in the Epistles to the Colossians and to the Ephesians. Instead it concentrated on the claim of an historical priority of the universal Church and offered a defense that is worth quoting in full:

> Perhaps the reason why the *chronological priority* which the Letter attributes to the universal Church has not been understood is that all too frequently the universal Church is considered as an abstract reality opposed to the concrete reality of the particular Churches. On the contrary, in this sentence about priority, the Letter considers the universal Church in the most concrete and at one and the same time the most mysterious way. The universal Church it speaks of is the Church of Jerusalem on the day of Pentecost. There is nothing more concrete and localized than the 120 gathered there. However, the unique originality and the mystery of the 120 consists in the fact that the *ecclesial structure* constituting the Church is *the very structure of the universal Church*: here there are the Twelve, with Peter at their head, and in communion with them the whole Church which grows—the 5,000— and speaks all languages, in a moment of unity and universality which is at the same time as local as can be, without being—in that it is the Church of Pentecost—an *"individual* particular Church" in the sense given to that term today. At Pentecost there is no "mutual interiority" between universal and particular Church, because these two dimensions are not yet distinct. There is the Christological *ephapax* (cf. Heb 7: 27), an eschatological anticipation of the Church, of the Body of Christ *tout court*.[43]

This very useful clarification explicitly excludes what many commentators saw in the Letter, that is, the idea of "an abstract reality opposed to the concrete reality of the particular Churches." It states that the Church that is prior to any [other] particular church is the "concrete and localized" "Church of Jerusalem on the day of Pentecost." That "the unique originality and the mystery of the 120" should be identified with the presence there of the universal Church's "structure"—itself, it seems, reduced to Peter and the other Apostles—is unfortunate; surely this primal

---

[43] *Lettera "Communionis notio,"* 84.

and originating instance of the Church deserves a fuller, more substantive, and more vital definition. But the point being made here is legitimate: that the already universal Jerusalem Church of Pentecost is particular in a unique sense, not verified in other particular churches. (The CDF does not mention the possibility, not in principle impossible, that the day could come when the universal Church is again reduced to a single particular Church.)

But the insistence on the very concrete and localized particularity of the Pentecost Church is surely in a certain tension with the Letter's claim, not greatly clarified in the article, that it is the Church as mystery existing since before creation that "gives birth to the particular churches as her daughters" (n. 9). Two considerations give one pause before this explanation of the "ontological priority" of the pre-existent "universal Church." First, it is difficult to understand how the "universalis discipulorum Domini communitas," as the CDF's Letter nicely defines the universal Church (n. 7), can be said to pre-exist creation. Only God really pre-exists creation, and if his intending of the one and universal Church can be said also to pre-exist creation, that intending has still to be realized in fact and in time and until it begins to be realized, it is surely difficult to conceive how it can be said to do anything, much less generate daughter-churches. This begins to happen only when, to use Aquinas' phrase, the Church God intends begins to be "explicated in the Apostles."

Second, when one looks for an historical existent and agent of the birth of the other particular churches, what does one find except that Jerusalem Church which is at once universal, speaking all languages, and particular, that is, precisely those 120 in Jerusalem from whom would go out those who by their preaching would bring other and distinct communities into the mystery of Christ? It is not a pre-existent "universal Church" that is the Mother Church; it is the Jerusalem Church to which the churches of all other places and times are bound by concrete ties of origin and kinship (*koinonia*) which St. Paul tried vigorously to maintain and which it would be very dangerous to weaken.

Congar's comments on the Spirit as "co-instituting principle" allows one to keep the divine priority historically concrete: what stands over and against any new generation is a divine "institution" that has taken its apostolic and catholic form in an historical process guided by the Spirit. In this sense what stands over and against a new generation of the Church is not simply God, Christ, and the Spirit, but the Church that was born out of the active and now normative faith, hope, love, and determinations of previous generations of believers and, in particular, of the apostolic Church. All this is pertinent to an understanding of certain apparently paradoxical linguistic usages such as the one, already cited, of the Venerable Bede: "Every day the Church gives birth to the Church." What meaning can be assigned to these two uses of the same word? The Church that is born anew everyday refers to the *congregatio fidelium*, the *Ecclesia congregata*, that is born whenever the word and grace of God are received in faith and love. The Church that is the generating Mother of this new-born Church, the *Ecclesia congregans*, is the concrete believing community of an earlier generation and in particular that first believing community of the apostles. It is, in other words, a concrete and actual Church that gives birth everyday to a concrete and actual Church. "Mother Church" is the one, holy, catholic, and apostolic Church, already realized in Jerusalem on Pentecost and also already realized in that concrete and actual Church which now, as its continuing apostolic generating act (see 1 Cor 4: 15; Gal 4: 19), hands on what it itself has received. It is the *historically* prior Church that is *ontologically* and generatively prior.[44]

The CDF's criticism of the idea of "reciprocal recognition" is not clarified in the *L'Osservatore Romano* article. It seems to have been aimed against the idea that the universal Church is simply the sum of the particular churches or the result of some federation among them. The CDF is not wrong to oppose these ideas. The "sum" of all the churches is simply the material totality; communion adds constitutive internal relations. "Federation" implies a second moment and perhaps some degree of externality, as if the particular churches existed first in themselves and became the universal Church by some subsequent act. But "reciprocal recognition" need not be understood in this fashion, but rather as an act which, as it is *constitutive* of the very reality of any individual church as the redeemed *community* of faith is simultaneously *constitutive* of the *community* of all communities of faith that is the one Church. Similarly, the one Church is not simply the result of the communion among the many churches; it *is* that communion.

---

[44] See the helpful and blessedly concrete discussion of the "Ecclesia Mater" theme in Louis Bouyer, *L'Eglise de Dieu: Corps du Christ et Temple de l'Esprit* (Paris: Cerf, 1970) 655-662. Reflect also on Aquinas' interpretation of the Pauline "quae sursum est Ierusalem . . . quae est mater nostra," which could mean "vel illam per quam generamur, quae est ecclesia militans; vel illam matrem in cuius filios generamur, quae est ecclesia triumphans" (Comment on Galatians, ch. 4, l. 8; Marietti n. 264). Note that the actively generative Church here is the *Ecclesia militans*.

When, to use the CDF's example, "the 5000" were added to the Church on that Pentecost day, how were they added except by faith, that is, by reception of the apostolic kerygma? That particular Church was now constituted by a much larger number of people who had become one in their faith. And when churches arose elsewhere, how were they known to be churches, accepted as churches, by that first Church and other later-born churches, except by a reciprocal recognition that knew them all not to be different churches but, even in their multiplicity and variety, *one and the same* Church? What have schisms ever been, on either side, but the refusal to recognize the other as the same true Church? If the CDF's Letter and the later clarification can say that the *una Catholica* is present in the Orthodox Churches,[45] what is this but an act of "recognition"; and what is hoped for as the goal of ecumenical conversation but that one day the Orthodox (and other Christian communities) and Catholics may reciprocally recognize that we are all one Church, and that in and because of that reciprocal recognition we will all become one Church? Much will have to happen before that reciprocal recognition can be given, but when, pray God, it is given, it will be an ontological constituent of "full communion."

Finally, one may ask whether the sorts of considerations proposed in this essay might not also help to give some concrete meaning to a phrase often invoked in order to explain the relationship between the one Church and the many churches: that of "mutual interiority." "Objective" grounds for this are often set forth, and not inappropriately: as, for example, the formal elements of one faith, baptism, the Eucharist, the episcopate, the Petrine ministry, etc. But these do not unite any single Church and do not unite all the churches together apart from their reception and vital appropriation in the people and communities in which the Church is realized. It is because the same Word is received in faith, the same Christ incorporates all into his living Body, the same common life is lived within a hierarchical communion, that the many churches are one Church. "Mutual interiority" exists in the concrete realities of communities that know and rejoice in their common origin, center and goal.

In this lies the importance of Pope John Paul II's use of the related, if not identical, phrase: "mutual inclusion." In his address to the Roman

---

[45]   See *Communionis notio* n. 17 and the comments in the *L'Osservatore Romano* article in *Lettera "Communionis Notio,"* 87.

Curia on December 21, 1984, the pope used this phrase, not to refer to the relation between particular churches (which in this context referred, not to dioceses, but to groupings of dioceses, as in *LG* 13) and the universal Church, but to refer to the relations *among the particular churches themselves*:

> In fact among the individual particular churches, there is an ontological relationship of mutual inclusion: every particular church, as a realization of the one Church of Christ, is in some way present in all the particular churches "in which and out of which the one and unique catholic Church has its existence." This ontological relation must be translated on the dynamic level of concrete life, if the Christian community does not wish to be in contradiction with itself: the basic ecclesial choices of believers in one community must be able to be harmonized with those of the faithful in the other communities in order to allow that communion of minds and hearts for which Christ prayed at the Last Supper.[46]

This is nicely concrete: the "ontological" relationship, which may be taken to refer to the relationship grounded in the divine gifts given to all the churches, has to be realized "on the dynamic level of concrete life" at which believers in each community make their "basic ecclesial choices"; otherwise there is no "communion of *minds and hearts*." In other words, Christ's prayer remains unrealized without the freedom of the believers who constitute the particular churches both in themselves and in their divinely willed communion with one another. Once again, then, the concrete "ontology" of the many churches as one Church requires the subjectivity of believers, receiving one another because all have received the same divine gifts.

[46]   See *AAS* 77 (1985) 506.

RESPONSE TO JOSEPH KOMONCHAK

José Eduardo Borges de Pinho*

In Professor Komonchak's reflection we are presented not only with a consistent foundation for reception as a structural dimension for the life and action of the Church, but he also defends the point that an epistemology of reception opens the road to an ontology of the Church in its existing concrete theology. Thus he shows that the Church—in its original constitutive phase as well as in the whole process which generates it ever anew throughout time as a community of faith, hope, and love— cannot cease to be a community of reception in the freely realized conjuncture of divine initiative and human response. This vision clarifies where certain fundamental topics are intimately joined together: the antecedent constitutive role of faith and the perception of an ontological subjectivity which constitutes the reality of the Church; the affinity which shows itself here with a dialogical structure of revelation and of faith; the inseparability of the divine and human elements in the Church; the reciprocal recognition of believers and local churches between themselves as an original ontological fact of a Church which is communion; the role of ecclesial authority and the responsibility of all the believing people relative to the truth of the faith; the question of concrete conditions necessary for the Church to realize itself effectively as a community of reception. I propose here to make a brief reference to some of these aspects.

In attending to the Church such as it appears to us concretely realized, there emerges above all the fact that in it is manifested and actualized— in what constitutes, moreover, the most profound root of reception—the dialogical structure which characterizes the events of revelation and faith. The gratuitous initiative of God who, by the mediations of a living tradition and by the force of the Holy Spirit, arouses faith, summons free persons called to be the subjects of their own faith history: revelation is a dialogical event in the concrete reality of history. It is not independent of the affirmative human word which welcomes it; it exists only concretely

* Universidade Catolica de Lisboa (Portugal).

as a revelation "heard and believed" (Karl Rahner). In this communicative interpersonal encounter the human response is not, in effect, accidental or simply posterior to the event of revelation itself; it must above all be understood as a co-constitutive element of revelation insofar as it actualizes itself and is made present throughout history. Inasmuch as revelation is not a pure and simple communication of a fixed knowledge before all else, but includes simultaneously the action of God in history and the believing experience of the people of God translated into an interpretive expression of this action, so this experience and its interpretation belong essentially to the event of revelation.[1] This means that the "word of God" is not perceptible without the mediation of the "human word," the gifts of God arrive only in the signs which give them concrete historical form. The circumstances which clothe the human experience of the welcome of God are mediations of his revelation for us.

In this light Komonchak corroborates how the normative and structural elements of the Church have been, from the beginning, co-instituted by it in an attitude receptive of God's gifts, in a process of discernment which can be characterized—as he does—as being an "auto constitutive" reception. But this dimension of active envelopment of the believing community is valid at no matter what moment of ecclesial life. In the most diverse registers of the Church's living faith the human subject pole, the subjectivity of the members of the Church, plays a co-constitutive role. In the concrete reality of the Church, we are always faced with a creative subjectivity, fruit of the encounter of the divine with the human as dimensions which cannot be separated.

This consciousness of the inseparability of the divine and human elements in the concrete reality of the Church is a structural given in an epistemology of reception. Because it is always present, there is a risk of falling back into an idealist vision of the Church, which, losing the sense of its real historicity, would hardly help believers in their ecclesial attitude nor make more believable the witness of the Church in the world. In this regard one must consider that maintaining the tension between two poles, as *Lumen gentium* 8 indicates, represents a point of no-return in the role of seeing the mystery of the Church which cannot be abstracted

---

[1] See Edward Schillebeeckx, *Experience humaine et foi en Jesus Christ*, French ed. rev. J. Dor (Paris: Cerf, 1981) 30; idem, *Menschen. Die Geschichte von Gott* (Freiburg: Herder, 1990) 52, 58-61 and 67-71. See also Max Seckler, "Der Begriff der Offenbarung," in *Handbuch der Dogmengeschichte*, ed. Walter Kern et al. (Freiburg: Herder, 1985) 2: 64-67.

from its concrete historical realizations in time, space, culture, immediate challenges, etc.

It is well known how the idealist visions of the Church lead to insoluble theological problems, with repercussions visible in the ecumenical field. For example, there is the way in which the question of sin in the Church is addressed traditionally.[2] The ecumenical question of divine law is situated in this same context of the problem.[3] Attention to reception indicates to us that one cannot make certain structures so absolute that, however definitive they may be, they scarcely appear as always also a human expression. These are the realities co-instituted by the receptive apostolic community, and marked by the receptive actualization throughout time under historically conditioned forms. A lot is missing to understand all the consequences which result—for ecumenical problems of the episcopacy and primacy, for example—from the creative role of the people of God in giving form in fidelity to the Holy Spirit to the life of faith beginning with its historical cultural situation. In an epistemological perspective, reception deepens the sense of the historicity of faith and of the Church. It raises the question of the concrete conditions implicated in the process of the affirmation of truth in the Church.

The task of welcoming the truth of the faith and of witnessing to it pertains to the entire community. In view of the Holy Spirit's action which endows each of the faithful with the *sensus fidei*,[4] the whole Church is the subject which carries the faith; all the people of God are called to discern the truth of the faith, to express it with coherence, and to come up with the most correct ways for its witness. Corresponding to this elementary conviction of what the Holy Spirit does on all the faithful is an awareness

---

[2]   See "Commentaire sur les Observations de la Congregation pour la doctrine de la foi sur le document de l'ARCIC II," in *La Documentation Catholique* 1976 (1989) 72 ff.; Gemeinsame römisch-katholische/evangelisch-lutherische Kommission, *Kirche und Rechtfertigung. Das Verständnis von Kirche im Licht der Rechtfertigungslehre* (Paderborn-Frankfurt: Lembeck, 1994) 81-87, 148-165.

[3]   See "Amt und universale Kirche. Unterschiedliche Einstellungen zum Päpstlichen Primat," in *Papstum und Petrusdienst*, ed. Günther Gassmann et al. (Frankfurt: Lembeck Verlag, 1975) 109, n. 30; José Eduardo Borges de Pinho, "O ministerio de Pedro como problema ecuménico," *Didaskalia* 19 (1989) 166-171.

[4]   See Wolfgang Beinert, "Die Bergrundung des Glaubenssinnes als eines dogmatischen Erkenntniskriterium," *Catholica* 25 (1971) 271-303; idem, "Der Glaubenssinnes der Gläubigen in Theologie und Dogmengeschichte. Ein Überblick," in *Der Glaubenssinn des Gottesvolkes—Konkurrent oder Partner des Lehramts?*, ed. Dietrich Wiederkehr (Freiburg: Herder, 1994) 66-113.

that the specific authority which belongs to certain services in the Church does not mean a privileged possession, self-sufficient or exclusive of the criteria for discerning the truth. If there were a sense to speak of a certain "epistemological privilege" in questions of the faith, it could only concern those who, in fidelity to God's Spirit and faced with limit situations of life's opacity (poverty, marginality, the silence of God) are capable of discovering how God in his mystery continues to envelop human beings and this history with his love, in giving them a meaning and a future even in the absence of meaning in concrete situations of life.

In effect, what is involved in reception is the value which is attributed to the whole of believers in the understanding and recognition of the faith in all its aspects. The subjectivity which ontologically constitutes the ecclesial community must make itself objective, on the part of the faithful and in the concrete experience of ecclesial life, as a sensibility at work in all that concerns the welcome, the explication, and the witness of truth. It is an irreplaceable role, with even a transcendent meaning for the transmission and actualization of the faith, in light of the experiences of concretization and innovation which believers are called to make in normal situations of life.[5] An epistemology of reception must, thus, wonder with regard to the meaning of the discovery of truth which pertains to Christian practice.[6] That is, it becomes necessary to go beyond the tendency of only following deductive schemes in the perception of truth in order to know how to evaluate better the cognitive contents which result from the faith as lived. It is not a question of opposing an epistemology which begins "from on high" to an epistemology which begins "from below." Simply, and without breaking the dialectical tensions existing here, it is important to recognize the believing experience as an authentic theological locus from which arise the essential impetus to Christian existence, and authentic expressions of faith which carry an undeniable authority.

The plurality of authorities which emerges here does not challenge the purpose for a proper charism of discernment and of authorized expressions of the faith in doctrinal matters in the Church. But the awareness of

---

[5] See José Eduardo Borges de Pinho, *A recepção como realidade eclesial e tarefa ecuménica* (Lisbon: Didascalia, 1994) 157-167. Also confer, despite a certain equivocation which the title could suggest, the contributions contained in *The Teaching Authority of Believers*, ed. Johannes Baptist Metz and Edward Schillebeeckx, Concilium 180 (Edinburgh: T & T Clark, 1985).

[6] See Schillebeeckx, *Menschen*, 225-227.

plurality recalls that, in the Church, it is never enough to have an authority based on simple formal criteria.[7] And, especially, it makes evident that doctrinal authority in the Church cannot be understood without the contribution of believers, their active reaction, their witness. Authority in the Church presupposes—in keeping with this subjective character of the ontology of the Church—an active attitude of reception. The magisterium's authority as a fundamental instance of interpretation and decision must be included in the ensemble of diverse elements which structure and form the faith of the believing community.

In this order of ideas the process of reception appears as something which is in close correlation with the representative character—both in a Christological perspective and in an ecclesiological one—which provides the foundation and qualifies the magisterial authority in the Church. Magisterial authority in the Church can be understood correctly only in the setting of a task truly representative of the faith of all the believing people. This means that the faithful recognize in it a qualified form of witness to the truth—above all, because of the service which, by God's gift, the magisterium is called to carry out, but not less because, by fidelity to the signs of the Spirit acting in the life of the believing community, it is capable of integrating all the elements of discernment of the faith and of welcoming what believers experience and express as an authentic living of the faith. There is no doubt that the full insertion of the exercise of the magisterium in the awareness of the faith of all the people of God and the corresponding recognition of the doctrinal authority of the faithful is a theological and practical question which is still far from having received the reflection and maturation which are needed.

In the necessary interdependence of people, charisms, and functions in the Church, in the concomitant recognition of the spiritual and doctrinal authority which pertain also to simple faithful, there emerges the question of the indispensable convergence of diverse factors in the process of clarifying the truth of the faith. An epistemology of reception must be particularly sensitive to the contribution that several moments, criteria, and factors are called to play in this process. None of the criteria or instances of discernment and of fidelity in the faith—whether they be the written word of God, tradition, liturgy, magisterium, theology, the *sensus fidei*, prophecy, holiness of life, individual conscience—can become ab-

---

[7]   See Joseph Komonchak, "Reflexiones teologicas sobre la autoridad doctrinal de la Iglesia," *Concilium* [Spanish edition] 117 (1976) 91-103.

solute as if it were the final indubitable criterion, totally valid independent of a process of collective search for the truth. All these criteria and
instances depend on the daily welcome of the word of God in the power
of the Spirit, directed so that it might be possible to maintain Christian
identity within the historicity of knowledge and human living. The truth
in the faith can only be welcomed, affirmed and witnessed, in effect, in
an open relationship of envelopment, of convergence and of complementarity, not only of all the members and groups in the Church, but also
of the diverse moments or "theological places" as specific configurations
by means of which the Church articulates in its very being the transmission of the faith.[8] Thus the epistemological question of reception is
knowing how to evaluate the relative weight and the conditions for the affirmation of diverse instances which intervene in the process of the clarification of the faith, a process in final analysis conducted by the Spirit.

In this perspective, the knowledge of the truth in the Church and the
persistence of the Church in the truth appear as a dialogical event. In the
awareness that our perceptions and expressions of truth are always fragmentary, dialogue both in the internal ecclesial sphere as well as outside
it appears as an indispensable epistemological presupposition for the discovery of the truth.[9] Dialogue in and directed toward the faith possesses,
thus, a fundamental theological meaning: motivated by the search for
truth to an encounter with the other, dialogue is an existential form of
love of God and of neighbor. In this light one can understand how ecclesiastical authority must be exercised in an ever more dialogical and communicative manner, how believers must grow in the culture of listening
to each other in their differences, how the Church in its ensemble must
develop collective processes for searching the truth of the faith.

An epistemology of reception must confront, in effect, the decisive
problem of the conditions which permit Christians to enjoy a role which
pertains to them in the process of the understanding and expression of
truth. The decisive elements for that are a sense of the historicity of the

---

[8] See Peter Hünermann, "Tradition—Einspruch und Neugewinn. Versuch eines
Problemaufrisses," in *Wie geschiet Tradition? Überlieferung als Lebenprozess der Kirche*,
ed. Dietrich Wiederkehr (Freiburg: Herder, 1994) 62.
[9] In this context see Lothar Üllrich, "Dialog und Identität. Philosophische und theologische Aspekte," in *Denkender Glaube in Geschichte und Gegenwart*, ed. Wilhelm Ernst
and Konrad Feiereis (Leipzig: Beno Verlag, 1992) 320-335; Karl Lehmann, "Eine
Lebensfrage für die Kirche. Bischof Karl Lehmann zum Dialog als Form der Wahrheits-
findung," *Herder Korrespondenz* 49 (1995) 29-35.

believing path in deepening the truth and the attentive sensibility to concrete forms of how the ecclesial community articulates itself in the process of reception. But no less important is an awareness of the continuing weight—by their institutional consequences, but also by the interiorization which has been made of them—of past factors in the manner of how to proceed in the search for the truth in the Church. If in a Church which knows how to be called to realize itself as a communion of believers there continues to be a difficulty in understanding and in giving concrete expression to what is evident (that is, the participation of all in everything which concerns them), it is because we are still under the effects of historical developments which have deformed the basic realities of Christian existence in the Church.[10]

The sense of the "subjectivity" which constitutes the Church as an historically realized community must become explicit, in effect, in a rigorous self-critique of the concrete conditionings—of global mentality, of structural order, of elementary human character, of Christian spirituality—which in ecclesial life foment or hinder, accelerate or retard, the active contribution of believers in the process of the discernment of the truth. The epistemological problem of reception has to deal decidedly with the practical aspects relative to the form of how one understands and structures the relationship magisterium-faithful, with the conditions which surround dialogue in the Church, with the indispensable freedom of opinion, with respect toward legitimate pluralism, with the sense of the inalienable place of one's own conscience. The great task which persists is that of going beyond these epistemological obstacles, these intellectual and practical resistances which make a necessary renewal very difficult or even render it impossible—in what concerns, for example, synodality and the practice of co-responsibility, openness to the forms of democratic life, to the place of public opinion in the Church, to sensibility to the signs of non-reception and of dissent, to the meaning which the really lived experience of Christians in each place possesses.[11]

It is my conviction that it is not possible to go beyond the impasses which are borne out in this setting without a new ecumenical awareness which can sense the limitations in the perception of the truth of the faith and in Christian witness resulting from the division of Christians. Re-

---

[10]   See Borges de Pinho, *A recepção*, 58-74.
[11]   Ibid., 283-320.

ception as an internal ecclesial process and ecumenical reception are not two separate realities, but are quite interpenetrating. This is why an epistemology of reception cannot fail to be open to the questions which arise from the personal experience and ecclesial reality of other Christians.

Translation by James H. Provost

ARE CURRENT APPROACHES TO RECEPTION
CONFIRMED OR QUESTIONED
BY CHURCH HISTORY?

After the historical vision of the topic of "reception" was completed (Professors Sesboüé, Wickham, Schatz, Garijo, García, and Avril) and the theological reflection had been initiated (Professors Komonchak and Borges de Pinho), the working groups were asked on April 10, 1996 to contribute by clarifying the concept and specifying the conditions which would permit a reasonable process of reception. These were the responses.

Spanish Language Group

1. It is necessary to clarify the concept of reception, which is not univocal, but rather analogous and very complex since there are various interwoven dimensions. What is the minimum common denominator enabling one to speak of reception?

2. The passage of time is of great importance for reception; it is a question of a slow and patient process. Therefore it would be necessary to determine historical criteria so as to know when it is verified and when it is concluded and to be able to evaluate if it is situational or irreversible.

3. Currently reception takes place in new conditions by comparison to the recent past due to the influence of factors such as secularity, pluralism, the simultaneous diffusion of the knowledge or the conditions proper to any decision.

If we summarize the contribution of the Spanish language group in light of its reflection on history, it is clear that we need (1) a more adequate clarification of the concept and (2) to determine the criteria for an historical evaluation of reception while we emphasize the unique features of the current processes.

French Language Group

Following the conferences and responses devoted to historical perspectives, the participants of the French working group noted the following.

1. As regards the clarification of the concept of reception, the group identifies certain points to be specified. The presentations, especially those of Fathers Lanne and Sesboüé, lead us to distinguish levels of reception as regards its content. Thus it is not exactly the same thing to receive the canon of the Scriptures as foundational texts linked to the apostolic church, or the normative texts of the faith as in the case of the first four councils, or the normative texts of the subsequent councils as in the case of the medieval councils, considered ecumenical by the Catholic Church but which defined themselves as general councils. In addition to this difference of levels, it is noted that it is equally necessary to clarify the forms of reception or their juridical procedures. Finally, how is the *sensus fidelium* manifest in the process of reception or non-reception?

2. As certain historical examples presented in the Wednesday conferences have taught us, we ask ourselves about the conditions for the realization or production of reception.

In this regard it is evident that certain ecclesiologies can favor or delegitimize reception. The gregorian ecclesiology, of which the *Dictatus papae* constitutes an unequivocal expression, completely disqualifies any process of reception, the pope being situated "alone" vis-à-vis the Church. Moreover, a so-called ecclesiology of communion, conceived unilaterally according to a juridical and hierarchical model, substantially reduces reception in bringing it back to an "authority-submission" schema. Hence ecclesiologies are not neutral as regards reception.

English Language Group

1. History demonstrates that reception has been a long process, often quite controversial. Would it be possible to take such a long time today, given the communications media now available (almost instantaneous with the Internet or fax)? Would even such a long and contentious process be tolerated?

All the conflict and emotion were part and parcel of reception, and we should not be surprised to find it taking place today. The issues may not be the same, but they are expressed often in the same kind of practical slogans and images which were involved in the past controversies (e.g., today it is over liturgy, role of women, etc.) which point to deeper issues of our relationship with God. We may be trying to avoid the tension by appealing to "pluriformity," but there are some issues for which people are not willing to compromise.

From history we need to learn that reception cannot be managed from on high; the process cannot be forced. History also tells us how not to carry on the process; e.g., no premature anathemas, but rather the need for civil conversation between people on all sides. There needs to be a passion for truth, respect for the fact that it often entails conflict, but also a willingness to experience the other's pain in order to search out the truth.

Catholics are coming out of a time of great concern about doctrinal division. If reception takes time, we may need to be less concerned about specifics and more respectful of the fact that people are at different stages in the process. While diversity does not seem to work on some issues (e.g., abortion), are these always "communion dividing" issues? Perhaps the key to the process is conversion: how open is each one to accepting the need for one's own conversion? This is a basic epistemological stance, and takes some time. Seeking an objective understanding of all sides is a difficult process, but central to developing an understanding in the midst of tensions and conflict.

We are in a better position than previous ages to see the historical, the political, and other factors, in order to analyze the processes of reception. Some past factors are no longer a problem (we don't have an emperor to worry about), but there are still external factors which impinge on the openness of the process of reception.

2. Can there be "re-reception"? The issue was raised by Sesboüé's paper. Re-reception, which is in current usage in ecumenical discussions, means rereading and reapplying to one's situation, accepting the substance without being too tied to the form. It is not a question of reopening whether we should still receive something which has already been received, but a question of the meaning of the doctrine.

Sesboüé saw this as hermeneutics rather than re-reception. But what of a situation between two churches, one of which has received something and the other has not? Then it would seem appropriate to speak of both churches reexamining the issue, and perhaps coming to a re-reception.

Italian Language Group

1. Historical analysis arising from the reports confirms the questions posed earlier on the subject(s) and on authority in relationship to reception.

2. One may affirm in a simplified way that in the first millennium of church history there was an accentuation of reception on the part of central authority and of the instances arising from the local churches, while in the second millennium reception seems to follow a reverse movement, i.e., from the center to the local churches.

We ask ourselves if this dual flow ought not find today a greater correspondence of reception in a double sense, i.e., on the part of central authority and the local churches. Cannot the places of this correspondence be strengthened, i.e., the various forms of synodality at various levels, universal and local?

Translation by Thomas J. Green

THE *PLENA ET SUPREMA POTESTAS IURISDICTIONIS* OF THE POPE AT THE FIRST VATICAN COUNCIL AND *RECEPTIO*

HERMANN J. POTTMEYER*

Without a doubt, this topic is a focal point of contemporary ecclesiological discussion. The current interest in reception and consent has to do with the concern of describing the Church as the people of God, as the *communio ecclesiarum* and *communio fidelium*. Many people, relying on the changes brought about by the Second Vatican Council, maintain that such a Church is no longer separated into those who merely teach and lead and those who are merely taught and obey. Rather, all people— whether as shepherds and teachers or as members of the Church without an official office—are in a mutual relationship of giving and receiving in which they witness to one another about the Word of God and its vitality, and so they come to a mutual understanding about how the gospel should be lived out in today's world. When mutual dialogue replaces one way communication, the form of transmission and reception also changes. And when theology seeks to understand transmission and reception as events in the life of the Church which have taken on various forms in the course of church history, then it is ultimately up to the Church to find and recommend that form which can best serve the preaching and appropriation of the gospel today. Theology assists in this endeavor by pursuing the causes of those disturbances in communication that are presently obstacles to the life of the Church and to effective preaching.

A certain view and exercise of papal primacy, often described as absolute, seeks to reduce the reception of papal decrees or pronouncements on the part of local churches to unconditional obedience. In reaction to the growing number of incidences of non-reception of Roman decisions, the demands for obedience have increased and intensified. However, the essential source of the growing lack of reception has not been a spirit of contradiction or disobedience. Rather, it has been the fact that the local churches and their bishops have been given an ever decreasing share in

* Universität Bochum (Germany).

the preparation of decrees and decisions directed at the universal Church. This has been the case even though in our day the means of mutual communication are not difficult to coordinate. Those who neglect consultation, or who listen only to one side, make the reception of a decision difficult, particularly when the local churches are under the impression that their interest in the matter has received little consideration. The situation becomes all the more difficult when it concerns decisions in the area of faith and morals.

The First Vatican Council's definition of papal primacy in jurisdiction and teaching has continuously been held responsible for the so-called absolutist view and exercise of papal primacy. Either a relapse behind the Second Vatican Council is deplored, or the point has been made that the Second Vatican Council changed nothing about the criticized view of the primatial authority of the pope as it was defined at the First Vatican Council.

Consequently, the question in the background of the current discussion is whether the First Vatican Council actually defined the pope's jurisdictional and doctrinal primacy in such a way as to acknowledge reception as an event in the life of the Church with its own meaning or to exclude it altogether or reduce it to mere obedient compliance. Our thesis is that despite their one-sided orientation and evaluation, both definitions of the First Vatican Council neither exclude reception nor reduce it in a compelling way to a mere matter of obedience. The council dealt with reception only in a limited sense.

Two Different Viewpoints

The First Vatican Council dealt with reception in conjunction with the definition of the infallibility of the extraordinary magisterium of the pope. It still contained a reference to the jurisdictional primacy of the pope, for according to the definition, the *plena et suprema potestas iurisdictionis* of the pope applied to questions of faith and morals as well as to the discipline and governance of the Church.[1] The ensuing definition spoke only of the charism of infallibility of the pope's teaching office and his *ex cathedra* decisions in questions of faith and morals.[2] Without going into the disputed area of the power of jurisdiction and the

---

[1]　DS 3064.
[2]　DS 3074.

teaching office,[3] it follows from the connection of both definitions that the special perspective of the council on *ex cathedra* papal pronouncements concerned his judicial and legislative activity as well as the exercise of papal jurisdiction in questions of faith. According to this perspective, the council declared reception to be subsequent approval by consent of the universal Church. But the council rejected this form of reception as a legally required condition for the validity of papal *ex cathedra* pronouncements. It was in this sense that the council established that papal definitions were irreformable "of themselves, not however from the consent of the Church" (*ex sese, non autem ex consensu Ecclesiae*).[4]

In contrast to the council's limited view on reception, stood the far broader perspective of the minority. They were concerned not only with the legal aspects of reception, but also saw papal pronouncements on the faith as well as their reception as witnesses to the faith of the Church. Therefore, the minority was also interested in the council discussing the process leading to consent regarding the process for discovering the truth and coming to decisions, a process that must precede a papal doctrinal decision and in which bishops should take some part. The minority certainly saw the connection between consultation by the pope in the preparation of a decision regarding the faith, and the subsequent consensual reception of that decision. The more expressly the entire Church would be included in the process of decision making, all the more credible would be the right of a papal doctrinal pronouncement to witness to the faith of the universal Church. And the more clearly the credibility of this claim is apparent to all, the more generally will the reception of a doctrinal decision by the faithful come about as they attest to its truth. It is evident that a distinct picture of the Church was at work behind the different view of the minority. Its character was determined by the original view of the Church as a "communion of churches" (*communio ecclesiarum*). According to this view, consent of the particular churches and their bishops is the fundamental witness to the faith of the universal Church. Therefore contentious questions of faith would normally be decided at the level of the universal Church by means of a council.

After this outline sketch of the different points of view in which reception was considered at the council, our thesis will be substantiated in what follows by means of a few characteristic facts and statements.

---

[3]   See Hermann J. Pottmeyer, *Unfehlbarkeit und Souveränität. Die päpstliche Unfehlbarkeit im System der ultramontanen Ekklesiologie des 19. Jahrhunderts* (Mainz: Matthias-Grünewald, 1975).

[4]   DS 3074.

RECEPTION AND THE FOURTH GALLICAN ARTICLE

From the beginning of the council, Pius IX and an influential group of cardinals and bishops had two key concerns: the solemn confirmation of the syllabus, the list of modern errors, and the solemn condemnation of Gallicanism which was undermining the defensive power of the Church through its view of papal primacy.[5] Both concerns were tightly connected. The episcopate was hindered by the state churches from warding off the influence of modern errors on the Church. Thus it was necessary to strengthen the papacy, and so to strengthen the primacy of jurisdiction and the infallible teaching authority of the pope. Behind both concerns stood the painful history of the Church at the end of the eighteenth and nineteenth centuries as well as the two-fold experience that liberalism adopted the state churches in order to disperse its modern ideas, and that the papacy proved itself to be the strongest mainstay against the state churches. No less at work was a growing movement in church politics that sought to oppose the moderns by restoring a closed, Christian society.

The fourth article of the so-called "Declaration of the Gallican Clergy" (*Declaratio cleri gallicani*) of 1682 stated clearly that the pope was the highest authority in questions of faith. But his judgment was not irreformable so long as it lacked the agreement of the Church.[6] The relevance of an explicit or factual reception by the entire Church as a necessary condition of the infallible authority of papal magisterial decisions was still not present in the second half of the nineteenth century. The additional consent of the bishops counted more as a means of bringing the fact that there had been a papal *ex cathedra* pronouncement to the awareness of the faithful.[7] For first through the consent of the bishops, who witness to the faith of their local churches, would it become clear to all that the pope witnesses to the faith of the entire Church by means of a solemn doctrinal pronouncement. While classical Gallicanism concerned itself with protecting the collegial responsibility of the bishops who were seen as judges in matters of faith with and under the pope, semi-Gallicanism of the late nineteenth century placed less emphasis on

---

[5]   See Klaus Schatz, *Vaticanum I. 1869-1870*, 3 vols. (Paderborn: F. Schöningh, 1992-1994).

[6]   DS 2284; see Louis Châtellier, s.v. "Gallikanismus," in *Lexikon für Theologie und Kirche*, 3rd ed., 4: 277.

[7]   See Schatz, 1: 23f, 106-108, 208.

the level of authority and right, and more on the level of witnessing. Here again, to speak of "Gallicanism" or "Semi-Gallicanism" certainly reveals the polemical language of some Infallibilists.

For reasons other than those concerns already mentioned, on the eve of the council Rome and the Infallibilists still considered Gallicanism to be dangerous. In the intensifying polemic over papal infallibility, differences were no longer tolerated, and those positions intent on achieving a balance were suspected of being incipient forms of extreme Gallicanism. Thus the first council since 1682 had to condemn Gallicanism through the definition of papal infallibility.[8] Furthermore, numerous regimes before and after the French Revolution had continued to use gallican arguments in order to bring the Church under state influence. The Jansenists had done the same in order to bring into doubt the binding character of papal pronouncements. Finally, moderate gallican positions found a renewed influence in reaction to the increasing ecclesial politics of restoration, and out of a concern to reconcile the Church with modern society.

An example of this is found in the work published in 1869 by Bishop Henri Maret, entitled *Du concile général et de la paix religieuse*. In opposition to Joseph de Maistre and other ultramontane thinkers who presented the Church as an absolute monarchy, Maret wanted to understand the Church as a "moderate monarchy," moderate due to the collegial joint responsibility of the bishops.[9] What concerns our topic is that, from the fact that councils had scrutinized papal doctrinal teachings, Maret concluded that even outside of councils bishops enjoyed the right to consent to papal decisions in matters of faith after they had adequately scrutinized them. This would cease to be a binding, necessary condition only when the pope had consulted the bishops in a proper way before the decision. Even if only a few members of the minority went so far as Bishop Maret, the necessity of prior consultation of the episcopacy was to play a great role at the First Vatican Council. Pius IX described Maret as a "true heretic."[10]

Thus from the beginning, the subject of reception stood at the council in the shadow of the four gallican articles and their intended condemnation. This was already apparent in the preparatory commission for doc-

---

    [8] Ibid., 248, 273.
    [9] Ibid., 250-259; see Hermann J. Sieben, *Katholische Konzilsidee im 19. und 20. Jahrhundert* (Paderborn: F. Schöningh, 1993) 80-100.
    [10] Schatz, 2: 238-241.

trine. The commission criticized a draft by the Jesuit Clemens Schrader of a decree on papal infallibility, claiming that he did not repudiate Gallicanism sufficiently. The commission insisted that it must be clearly expressed that the pope is infallible even before the consent of the Church is given.[11]

Along the same lines are a number of statements on the *Caput addendum* on papal infallibility, the first presentation of this subject before the council. This draft deliberately abstained from inserting a phrase along the lines of the later *non autem ex consensu ecclesiae*.[12] This abstention was criticized by many council fathers. According to some opinions the desired anti-gallican emphasis would lead to the isolation of the pope from the Church; papal decisions in matters of faith would be infallible, "even when preceded or followed by no consent of the Church or the bishops."[13]

DÖLLINGER AND THE QUESTION OF RECEPTION

On account of the new procedural rules, both within and outside of the council a controversy arose which likewise concerned the necessity of *consensus unanimis*. Ignaz von Döllinger stepped into the discussion with an article.[14] In it he also took a position on the significance of reception for the Church. It remains an open question, however, whether or not he understood the whole of the faithful as a higher authority or whether he saw reception by the entire Church as merely a confirming witness to the truth of doctrinal pronouncements. On the one hand, he wrote: "The authority or the witness of the entire Church must stand over every council as decisive and confirmatory."[15] On the other hand, he wrote in a footnote: "The Church attests to councils (not only authority) just as it attests to single books of the bible through its biblical canon. Naturally, when it attests to the bible the inner authority of the canon does not flow out of the Church. In this way the Church is *testis, non auctor fidei.*"[16]

---

[11] Ibid., 157.
[12] Ibid., 180.
[13] Ibid., 208.
[14] *Collectio Lacensis* 7: 1499-1506; see Klaus Schatz, *Kirchenbild und päpstliche Unfehlbarkeit bei den deutschsprachigen Minoritätsbischöfen auf dem I. Vatikanum* (Rome: Università Gregoriana, 1975) 180-183.
[15] *Collectio Lacensis* 7: 1505a.
[16] Ibid., 1502, n. 2.

This article, which triggered a controversy and subsequent Roman measures, was greeted by the minority German bishops as a support. Though they too expressed thoughts, as for instance Bishop Hefele did, against the view that reception by the Church should be a final criterion of the validity of a council; yet a short time later Bishop Hefele seems to have agreed with Döllinger's position.[17] At the council, this latter position was found only in Bishops Kenrick[18] and Ramadié.[19] Archbishop Scherr, on the other hand, saw in Döllinger's article a disapproving "appeal from a council to the people."[20]

THE SPEECH OF CARDINAL GUIDI

Without a doubt, the speech of Cardinal Guidi, the Archbishop of Bologna, belongs among the high points of the conciliar debate on infallibility. He belonged to the Dominican order and claimed to represent the position of the school of Thomas Aquinas.[21] The defining point of his talk was the requirement of the pope to consult before issuing a definition of faith. Since it was necessary that such a definition include within it the "prior, concomitant, and subsequent sense of the Church" (*sensus ecclesiae praecedens et concomitans et subsequens*), the pope had to be certain beforehand of the "sense of the whole Church" (*universalis ecclesiae sensus*) and the Tradition in the particular churches. In this way, it would be evident to everyone that the pope was defining the faith of the Church and so the required reception could be given without delay. By relying on important witnesses to Tradition, Guidi was able to reject both the gallican position as well as the opposite view, that in questions of the faith the pope must be able to proceed independently of the *consensus ecclesiae antecedens, concomitans et subsequens* in order to be infallible *ex sese*.

It was stated most clearly in Guidi's speech that the entire process of coming to a true decision about the definition of papal infallibility (even to its subsequent reception by the Church) represented a lively coherence

---

[17]   Schatz, *Vaticanum I*, 2: 238-241.

[18]   See Peter R. Kenrick, *De Pontificia infallibilitate qualis in Concilio Vaticano definienda proponitur* (Naples, 1870).

[19]   Johannes D. Mansi et al., *Sacrorum conciliorum nova et amplissima collectio*, 51 (Arnhem and Leipzig: Hubert Welter, 1925) 996 D.

[20]   Schatz, *Kirchenbild*, 183.

[21]   Ulrich Horst, *Unfehlbarkeit und Geschichte. Studien zur Unfehlbarkeitsdiskussion von Melchior Cano bis zum I. Vatikanischen Konzil* (Mainz: Matthias-Grünewald, 1982) 164-213; see Schatz, *Vaticanum I*, 3: 99-109.

of reciprocal communication in which the pope can not operate isolated from the Church, and especially from the bishops. Guidi distinguished more clearly than did most of the infallibilists and some minority bishops (such as Maret) between the level of legal authority and the level of witnessing. According to the Domincan's ecclesiological tradition, he allowed no conditions or restrictions to be put on the jurisdiction of the pope since his power came from God alone without any mediation through the Church. However, he placed clear conditions on the means of discovering truths of the faith. A "due diligence" (*debita diligentia*) and "consultation" (*consultatio*) had to be carried out in order for a definitive decision in matters of faith to witness to the *universalis ecclesiae sensus*. Otherwise, one risked accepting a new and special revelation from the pope. Moreover, history showed that the popes did in fact act de iure and de facto in the same way that the dogmatic definition of 1854 would require.

THE REACTION OF THE DOCTRINAL COMMISSION

The impression that this speech made on the council fathers was so forceful that it appeared to pave the way for a turn in the debate on infallibility; namely, for a coalition between the minority and the moderate wing of the majority. This was prevented by the sharp reaction of Pius IX who, in contrast to Cardinal Bilio, the president of the commission on doctrine, no longer wanted a balanced solution.[22] Bilios' expert opinion, prepared by some members of the doctrinal commission, stated that Guidi was correct in maintaining that the solemn judgements of the pope should always follow the consent of the Church. But the statement that infallibility had to have the *consensus antecedens et concomitans* as a necessary prerequisite was gallican. Indeed, this assertion even went beyond the gallican position which required only the Church's subsequent *consensus tacitus*.[23] When Guidi maintained that the mother (Rome) is not without her daughters (the particular churches), and the teacher not without her students,[24] he used the teacher-student relationship between the pope and bishops in an opposite sense. Whoever even speaks of conditions of infallibility denies that the pope is *ex sese* a subject of infallibility, a position that everyone would take for heretical. Here he inten-

---

[22] See Schatz, *Vaticanum I*, 3: 102-106.
[23] See Horst, 195-201.
[24] See Mansi, 52: 742 D.

tionally ignored what Guidi had stated, that the *ex sese* must not refer to the pope, but to his definitions.

An essential cause of the misunderstanding and the criticism of Guidi's position was this: Guidi distinguished thoroughly between the power of jurisdiction and the teaching office, and therefore considered the uncovering of the *universalis ecclesiae sensus* as an internal element of the infallible decision. Thus Guidi was able to find support in a long, theological, and always orthodox tradition. Even the pre-Revolutionary absolutist teaching of the state (in order to enlist this comparison) likewise distinguished between legitimate and capricious acts of the absolute monarch. Naturally, Guidi's opponents also wanted to avoid denying that the pope necessarily had to take great care in coming to a decision, something that bound his conscience. But since they did not make a distinction between the functions of the primacy of jurisdiction when applied to discipline and to teaching, they conceived of every condition merely as a limitation or denial of the pope's power of jurisdiction which came from God alone. Therefore, they also understood reception as obedience in the face of the unconditional power of the pope to command, and they feared that the introduction of conditions would weaken this type of immediate reception. Examples of such fears could be found in the Jansenist attempts to deny the binding character of papal decisions by claiming that the necessary conditions for their infallibility had not been met. However, now we know, thanks to what both history and the present day teach us, that a lively reception is not to be forced by requiring obedience; rather, it needs convincing appropriation.

Bishop d'Avanzo presented the official reply of the commission on doctrine.[25] It corresponded to Bilios' expert opinion. Still, it deserves attention since it showed that the doctrinal commission could barely counter Guidi's reference to the testimonial character of a definition of faith. D'Avanzo first considered the reproach that Guidi was more gallican than the Gallicans themselves. Then he discussed the fourth article of the *Declaratio cleri gallicano*. In order to counter the image of the separation of the head and the members, he promoted the "preceding and express consensus" (*consensus praecedens et expressus*) of the bishops as a condition. Where Guidi took this for an inner condition and the agreement of the content of the infallible decision with the faith of the Church, d'Avanzo took it for a legal condition that limited the ability to exercise

----

[25]   Ibid., 760C-767C.

the primacy of jurisdiction. It is this purely legal point of view with which the council treated reception as subsequent consent.

D'Avanzo replied to Guidi's argument that even Bellarmine taught that the pope was bound by the bishops' attesting to tradition, by stating that this was an "ordinary fact" (*factum ordinarium*). Obviously, the pope had to take the necessary care to inform himself about the truth of the faith, and possibly by seeking the opinion of the Roman Church and bishops through a synod or council. Consequently, such a reference to the meaning of the consent of the bishops could certainly be included in the corresponding chapter for it was a general teaching that the magisterium arises from the pope together with the bishops. But in the definition neither prior nor subsequent consent could be inserted as a condition. As the endless struggle with the Jansenists over the bull *Unigenitus* showed, one condition would then follow another in order to delay the reception of an unpopular decision.

There was also extensive agreement concerning the pope's duty to consult as well as his being bound to the witness of the faith of the Church and even to the consent of bishops in making decisions. What divided the positions was the limited view of the one side that considered only the jurisdictional element of the papal teaching office, and who were led by the endeavor to forge an effective weapon for an efficient protection of the unity of the faith and only generally to strengthen papal authority. According to d'Avanzo, the definition of papal infallibility was the clearest response to the modern denial of the supernatural order whose incarnation was the pope.

THE SPEECH OF BISHOP GASSER

D'Avanzo's speech already permitted the recognition that Guidi's remarks, despite their failure, contributed to a clarification and deepening of the question. This became even more evident in the final *relatio* of Bishop Gasser as spokesman for the doctrinal commission on the chapter on infallibility.[26] In contrast to d'Avanzo, Gasser abstained from any polemics, and attempted to demonstrate that the legitimate concerns of Guidi and the minority should be considered. The fact that Gasser's statement constantly referred to the *consensus ecclesiae* and the *consensus episcoporum* proved that the council recognized the concerns of the minority as well as the entire tradition as legitimate. Since the pope was

---

[26] Ibid., 1204A-1230D.

not infallible by way of some type of inspiration he should not and could not be separated "from the cooperation and concourse of the Church" (*a cooperatione et concursu ecclesiae*). Certainly, however, the claim to do this had to be left to the pope and his conscience. There was no doubt about the relative necessity of consultation. One needed faithful trust that along with the promised assistance in making infallible decisions the pope also was given the corresponding means to witness to the *consensus ecclesiae*. As Gasser asserted, we also believe that his definitions will never lack the agreement of the Church. For the *corpus episcoporum* could not be separated from its head, and the entire Church cannot err in matters of faith. Since Peter was given the special promise to strengthen the brothers in the faith and to protect it, the definitions of the pope must be infallible *ex sese*. And therefore no other conditions besides those already in the text could be introduced for an *ex cathedra* decision.

Gasser then dealt with two concerns of the minority that had not yet been considered. The minority saw the relation between the pope and bishops as a mutual relationship in which the bishops, as co-responsible for the teaching office and witnesses to the Church's faith, should be considered as cooperating subjects, and it should not be left to the whim of the pope whether to allow bishops to participate. Principally, this coresponsibility can appear in the form of prior consultation as well as subsequent consent. Gasser's response is noteworthy. Talk of mutuality was only an *oratio figurativa* that did not enjoy the force of an argument. Lay people and priests too did not have a say in ultimate pronouncements even though they also were members of the Church. And the bishops were related to a pope defining a matter of faith as students to their teacher for it was a matter of strengthening the brothers. This was also evident in the decrees of a council which received infallible character only by virtue of papal confirmation.

Despite this response, Gasser had to distance himself from the extreme infallibilist position which held that the Church received its infallibility only through the Petrine office. Actually, Christ gave the infallibility of the teaching office to Peter along with the other apostles. Of course, Peter additionally received the special promise. Still, Gasser's response was obviously inadequate. Whoever takes both his examples seriously cannot describe the bishops as "students" since that would not correspond with the active role the bishops received through the promise and the responsibility that came with it. Gasser sought to limit their active role to subsequent agreement which always had to occur by virtue of the common promise received by Peter and the apostles. This was compatible with the student-teacher relationship and implied no mutuality.

The second concern of the minority was supported by the conviction shared by everyone that Peter was promised infallibility only in his relationship to the Church. This fact also appeared in the definition of infallibility as one of the conditions for an *ex cathedra* statement. The minority then raised the issue that this relationship constituted an indisputable *relatio publica*. Since according to the Catholic view the Church was also a visible entity, this *relatio publica* had to appear visibly and publicly, and needed visible signs to do so. The internal actions of the pope's conscience did not fulfill this requirement. At best the requirement was fulfilled by the *manifesta consensio* of the bishops which could appear following prior consultation of the bishops. Gasser replied that whoever maintains that the pope is dependant on the *manifesta consensio* of the bishops in making infallible pronouncements is necessarily representing the false principle that all the pope's dogmatic pronouncements are in and of themselves insufficient and reformable if the consent of the Church does not accompany them. Here again the limited, legal viewpoint becomes evident. Finally, Gasser mentioned that there certainly would be a *manifesta consensio* of the bishops; namely, in the form of subsequent consent by the bishops and the entire Church.

It became once more apparent what central significance was accorded Gasser's statement that the infallible pronouncements of the pope would never lack the subsequent consent of the Church. This statement appeared to connect three theological facts together: the infallibility of the faith of the universal Church, the infallibility of the entire teaching office of the pope and bishops, and the infallibility of the papal teaching office. Besides, the bishops as well as the universal Church appeared to be given an active role, if only in the form of subsequent consent. On the other hand, this statement protected the sovereignty of the pope and permitted the understanding of the relationship between a pope defining a matter of faith and the body of bishops to be that of teacher to students. It also allowed reception to be understood as a form of obedience.

Gasser's phrase represented only an apparent reconciliation of opposing views. It did not represent the true concerns of Guidi and the minority, which were: (1) to understand the process of coming to a true papal decision, and then achieving subsequent reception as a living unity of mutual communication and witnessing within a Church understood as *communio*; (2) to take seriously the collegial responsibility of bishops in doctrinal decisions that touch the universal Church and define the faith of the Church to which the bishops are also called to be authentic witnesses; (3) and finally, to make known to everyone in some way the *consensio* of the bishops to the decision so that the reception of it would occur not merely in the form of obedience to the jurisdictional authority of the pope, but also by reason of the conviction arising out of the power of persuasion or authority of the definition.

In view of its problematic meaning as an apparent reconciliation of opposing views, it was not by chance that this phrase of Gasser was appropriated by the Second Vatican Council: "These definitions can never lack the consent of the Church due to the work of the same Spirit, through whom the entire flock of Christ is preserved in the unity of faith and progresses" (*LG* 25). The special character of this sentence corresponds exactly to the special character of the ecclesiology of the Second Vatican Council. Even in the most recent council the ecclesiological differences were not settled. Therefore this council appears to us today ever more clearly as a transitional council that made truly important steps forward in an understanding of the Church as *communio ecclesiarum* and *communio fidelium*, but which did not succeed in integrating the one-sided dogma of the First Vatican Council.

THE SURVIVING POSITION OF RECEPTION AND ITS CRITERIOLOGICAL SIGNIFICANCE

Finally, evaluating the debates and conclusions of the First Vatican Council, we find our thesis confirmed. At the insistence of the minority, the council paid great attention to the consent of faith of the Church and the doctrinal consent of the bishops, both as an actual prerequisite for a papal definition and its reception, and as an approving response through the consent of faith and teaching of the entire Church in the form of successful reception. The high position the council attributed to reception based on the assertion that the Church's consent of faith was infallible, went uncontested. The doctrinal commission's assurance that the infallible definitions of the pope would never go without the approving consent of the Church was understood in light of the dogma of infallibility itself. But the council did not address the concerns of the minority. Above all, it left open the question of the criteriological significance of reception and non-reception, a question that was always discussed in the tradition both in relation to papal as well as conciliar definitions. Is reception due its own significance as a reliable witness not only to the truth of a definition, but also to the definition's suitability for addressing a problem, its choice of formulation or its reconciling and pacifying force? Should complete or partial non-reception have a critical significance, either in the case of an heretical pope or in the case of a definition which is not suitable?

Without in any way calling the doctrine of infallibility into question, indeed, on the foundation of the dogma, theologians raised the question left open by the First Vatican Council during the period after the Second Vatican Council. Joseph Ratzinger stated: "Where neither unanimity of the universal Church exists or a clear witness to the sources is given, a binding decision is not possible. If it were formally pleasing, its conditions would still be lacking and so the question about its legitimacy would be raised."[27] Avery Dulles made a similar statement: "If in a given instant the assent of the Church were evidently not forthcoming, this could be interpreted as a signal that the pope had perhaps exceeded his competence and that some necessary condition for an infallible act had not been fulfilled."[28] Or Walter Kasper: "The pope can be infallible only insofar as the Church recognizes him as the mouthpiece and witness to its own infallibility. If the Church were to refuse him this recognition (not to be confused with the rejection by Vatican I of subsequent consent to an *ex cathedra* decision by which it would first obtain its juridically binding character) then the pope would be in the extreme case heretical or schismatic, and so would no longer be pope at all."[29]

Actually, the addition of *non ex consensu ecclesiae,* with which the council in its waning hours clarified the *ex sese,* did not thoroughly settle the criteriological question. Concerning this, Gasser stated that the addition clarified only negatively what the *ex sese* expressed positively.[30] In this sense, and continuing Gasser's commentary, the Second Vatican Council clarified the addition; papal definitions "need no confirmation through others and tolerate no appeal to another judgment" (*LG* 25). In order to condemn the fourth gallican article, and the limited legal view of reception contained in it, the council wanted to exclude subsequent consent of the universal Church as a necessary condition for the binding character and so for the truth of papal *ex cathedra* pronouncements. This

[27] Joseph Ratzinger, *Das neue Volk Gottes. Entwürfe zur Ekklesiologie* (Düsseldorf: Patmos, 1969) 144.
[28] Avery Dulles, *A Church to Believe In. Discipleship and the Dynamics of Freedom* (New York: Crossroad, 1987) 139.
[29] Walter Kasper, "Zur Diskussion um das Problem der Unfehlbarkeit," in *Fehlbar? Eine Bilanz,* ed. Hans Küng (Zurich: Benziger, 1973) 84.
[30] Mansi, 52: 1317 AB.

exclusion was justified. For the condition understood as it was, stood in opposition to the teaching of the council that the papal definitions were infallible (and thus *ex sese*) due to the promise made to Peter, and the infallible faith of the Church. The gallican view raised the universal Church to the level of a superior appellate and decision making authority above that of the primacy of the papal teaching office. But the council expressly did not want to reject the notion that there were other instances of infallible witnessing to the faith of the Church besides that of the pope, even the consent in faith of the universal Church.

Apart from the juridical question, the gallican position is guilty of an actual theological error of reasoning. That is, it explains consent of the Church with the notions of *regula fidei* or norm of faith. Be that as it may, these phrases contain linguistic ambiguities, and can lead to a misunderstanding. Such an undesirable ambiguity is also found in Gasser: "It is true that the consent of the present preaching of the whole magisterium of the Church, united with its head, is the rule of faith even for the pontiff's definitions."[31] However, neither the consent of the universal Church nor the teaching office are the *regula fidei* or the norm of the faith, but the gospel alone, that is, the content of revelation or the Word of God in the witness of Scripture and Tradition. The diachronic and synchronic consent of Tradition and the magisterium, the formal authoritative acts of a council or a pope, or the formal consent of the universal Church offer merely criteria of recognition *quoad nos*, whether something belongs to the binding content of the message of revelation.[32]

The misunderstandings originating from the ambiguity mentioned above appear to have played no role whatsoever in the controversy between the Gallicans and the Infallibilists. For some gallican theologians, consent had only the formal quality of a criterion of knowledge. It is the same case with Guidi and the minority bishops when they count the investigation involved in consent among the *media humana* which the pope must use in the preparation of a definition. Other theologians shift the meaning of prior or subsequent consent in the direction of the normative dimension of the content of conciliar or papal magisterial pro-

---

[31] Mansi, 52: 1216 D: "Verum est quod consensio praedicationis praesentis totius magisterii ecclesiae unitae cum capite sit regula fidei etiam pro definitionibus pontificis."
[32] See Hermann J. Pottmeyer, "Normen, Kriterien und Strukturen der Überlieferung," in *Handbuch der Fundamentaltheologie*, ed. Walter Kern and Hermann J. Pottmeyer (Freiburg: Herder, 1988) 4: 139-150.

nouncements. This was the same for Döllinger who understood the representation of the Church through the bishops at the council in a parliamentarian sense. "The conclusion was obvious, that the faith, which the bishops must witness to, did not have a normative dimension based on Scripture and Tradition, but had simply the factual, ordinary faith of the members of the Church. That such a shot had to backfire against the minority was thoroughly noted by their opponents. For many minority bishops, especially in France, did not represent the faith of their infalliblist clergy and church members."[33] The same misunderstanding is noticeable today in some demands for a democratization of the Church.

Conversely, and involving the same confusion of norm and criterion of knowledge, some opponents of infallibility as well as some extreme infallibilists also misunderstood papal infallibility as inspiration or new revelation from the pope. This was the case for Döllinger[34] or for those infallibilists who considered the use of *media humana* by the pope to be irreconcilable with the *ex sese* of his infallibility, understanding it as an habitual, ontological quality of the pope which automatically made the pope infallible. Supported by tradition, Guidi demonstrated that the charisma of infallibility concerned an *auxilium actuale* or *lux transiens* which applied to the correct exercise of his office in the case of a solemn definition as well as to the use of *media humana*.[35]

The notion of the pope as endowed with inspiration was also expressly rejected by the council as a misunderstanding. This was used after the council by the opponents of papal infallibility as an objection against the dogma. It was also manifest in an inaccurate manner of speaking that described the pope as infallible in himself. "The *ex sese* was related to the pope (instead of the definitions), to the causal foundations of infallibility (instead of to the foundation of the irreformability), a fundamental mistake, that obviously is disseminated even today among theologians."[36]

The confusion of norm and criterion of knowledge still can play a role today among those who cite Vatican I, and oppose themselves to the theologians mentioned above, Ratzinger, Dulles, and Kasper, to deny reception and especially non-reception of papal *ex cathedra* pronouncements any characteristic criteriological significance. Actually, non reception of a papal *ex cathedra* pronouncement is not consistent with the dogma of

---

[33] Schatz, *Vaticanum I*, 3: 238.
[34] See ibid., 229.
[35] Mansi, 52: 741 CD.
[36] Schatz, *Vaticanum I*, 3: 243.

infallibility. By setting up conditions for the occurrence of an *ex cathe-dra* pronouncement, this dogma gave the faithful the right and the duty to examine the fulfillment of these conditions in the case of a well-founded doubt. The theologians cited above say nothing else. It is important to hold on to this possibility in order to counter the assertion of Hans Küng[37] and others that the First Vatican Council actually taught the a priori infallibility of the pope, an infallibility which demanded blind obedience. The conciliar acts as well as later clarifications of the dogma show that this assertion is untenable.[38]

RECEPTION AND OBEDIENCE

The frequent impressions of more recent times of the "religious obedience of the mind and will" due the authentic papal magisterium have contributed to the wide spread opinion that reception is to be equated with unconditional obedience.[39] Now, obedience as a consensual response to a binding instruction of the magisterium is certainly one means of reception, just as the element of jurisdictional authority to issue instructions belongs to the authentic magisterium. According to the theological tradition, the activity of the hierarchical magisterium encompasses both the presentation of the content of faith through authentic witnessing as well as the jurisdictional protection of the faith through religious laws that condemn or command.[40]

But did the First Vatican Council not actually contribute to the impression that reception consisted first and foremost in obedience? Now, what the dogma of infallibility demanded was that obedience to the faith be directed at the revealing God whose message was infallibly interpreted in a solemn papal definition. Consequently, it cannot be denied that the council did actually convey the impression that reception of a papal interpretation came about especially through obedience to the authoritative teaching of the pope. The reason is the repeatedly mentioned weak dif-

---

[37] See Hans Küng, *Infallible? An Inquiry* (Garden City, NY: Doubleday & Company, 1971).

[38] Schatz, *Vaticanum I*, 3: 207-300; Hermann J. Pottmeyer, "Das Unfehlbarkeits-dogma im Streit der Interpretationen," in *Das Petrusamt*, ed. Karl Lehmann (Munich: Schnell and Steiner, 1982) 89-109.

[39] See Hermann J. Pottmeyer, "Rezeption und Gehorsam," in *Glaube als Zustimmung. Zur Interpretation kirchlicher Rezeptionsvorgänge*, ed. Wolfgang Beinert (Freiburg: Herder, 1991) 51-91.

[40] See Pottmeyer, *Unfehlbarkeit*, 298-329, 381-388 (*supra*, note 3).

ferentiation between the pope's power of jurisdiction in the sphere of discipline and in the sphere of teaching, something continuously criticized by the minority. Consequently, the element of witnessing to the faith retreated too far into the background. One of the reasons for this was the gallican and Jansenist traumas that resulted in a struggle for certainty. One consequence of this was that "doctrinal controversies should be resolved in each case expeditiously without too much time lost on them."[41] The conciliar majority was thinking of an exceptional situation in which both the episcopacy and the Church were hopelessly torn, or in which the episcopacy was unable to act for other reasons, such that ecclesial consent could be reestablished only by means of a commonly recognized infallible magisterial decision of the pope. The minority usually proceeded from the unexceptional cases of the discovery and transmission of ecclesial Tradition. Thus they saw the pope as acting within, and related to, the entire ecclesial structure. The majority, on the other hand, proceeded from the extreme case scenario mentioned above and so emphasized unilaterally the jurisdictional primacy of the pope.

The concern to strengthen the power of the papal magisterium fit in with another reason for the unilateral evaluation of the jurisdictional side of the magisterium. It was the influence of Mauro Capellari (later Gregory XVI) and Joseph de Maistre on the ultramontane advocates of papal infallibility.[42] Both transferred the modern notion of sovereignty, defined by unconditional independence and undivided dominion, to the pope and fused the primacy of jurisdiction insolubly with infallibility as its essential and legitimating property for executing the papal power to command. The influence of these thinkers was continuously felt in the council. It is thanks to the influence of the minority and the insight of the theologically independent minded members of the majority that this idea was not accepted and dogmatized. Had this occurred, the council would have actually reduced the reception of papal pronouncements to pure obedience.

The Second Vatican Council expressed the fact that reception is more than mere obedience in this way: "The understanding of things and words handed down grows through the reflection and study of the faithful who consider them in their heart (cf. Lk 2: 19, 51); by means of an inner insight that arises out of their spiritual experience; and through the

---

[41] Schatz, *Vaticanum I*, 3: 308.

[42] See Horst, 78-120 (*supra*, note 21); Hermann J. Pottmeyer, "Ultramontanismus und Ekklesiologie," *Stimmen der Zeit* 117 (1992) 449-464.

preaching of those who have received the sure charism of truth after succeeding to the office of bishop" (*DV* 8).

Finally, it can be stated that the First Vatican Council neither denied reception the place of a significant, vital process in the Church nor did it reduce reception to mere obedience. Vatican I acknowledged reception only marginally as an expression of the infallible consent of faith of the Church. In its hostile stance to the gallican position, the council confined itself to rejecting the approving consent of the Church as a cause or necessary condition of the truth or binding character of papal *ex cathedra* pronouncements.

Translation by Ronny E. Jenkins

RESPONSE TO HERMANN POTTMEYER

ALFONSO CARRASCO ROUCO*

The process of reception of Vatican I's teaching on the petrine ministry (and, in particular, its two dogmatic affirmations on the primacy of jurisdiction and papal infallibility) had a decisive moment in Vatican II's constitution *Lumen gentium*.

In effect, *Lumen gentium* took up and affirmed again with great care all the fundamental ideas of *Pastor aeternus*;[1] but situated them in a new ecclesiological context, which implied for the doctrine on the primacy a double decentralization: toward Christ (who acts in the Spirit), across the radically sacramental consideration not only of the Church,[2] but also of the episcopal ministry in the concrete;[3] toward the Church itself, programmatically situating this ministry in service to the people of God.[4]

The Successor of Peter in the Horizon of a New Reflection on Ministry

1. In the context of a renewed reflection on the "hierarchical constitution of the Church," Vatican II made a major effort to complete

---

* Facultad de Teología San Dámaso, Madrid (Spain).

[1] See, for example, *LG* 18, 22, 23, 25, 27. *Pastor aeternus'* teaching on the primacy of jurisdiction was expressed in a synthetic and particularly clear manner at the beginning of the decree *Christus Dominus (CD* 2).

[2] Already the first document of Vatican II presented the Church as an admirable sacrament, born from the side of Christ on the Cross: *Sacrosanctum Concilium* 5. Cf. Alois Grillmeier, "Commentary," in *Commentary on the Documents of Vatican II*, ed. Herbert Vorgrimler, 1 (New York: Herder and Herder, 1967) 141; Gérard Philips, *L'Église et son mystère au deuxième Concile du Vatican*, 1 (Paris: Desclée, 1967) 72-73, 338-342; finally, see Josef Meyer zu Schlochtern, *Sakrament Kirche: Wirken Gottes im Handeln des Menschen* (Freiburg: Herder, 1992) 38-60.

[3] See *LG* 21.

[4] See *Relatio generalis ad cap. III*, in *Acta Synodalia Sacrosancti Concilii Oecumenici Vaticani II [Acta Synodalia]*, 3/1 (Vatican City: Typis Polyglottis Vaticanis, 1973) 210.

the doctrine about the primacy with an ample teaching on the episcopacy.[5]

In this regard, *Lumen gentium*'s radical newness does not consist in the affirmation that the bishop is a true pastor, successor of the apostles, endowed with his own proper, ordinary and immediate power,[6] nor in the affirmation that the "episcopal college," united with the pope and never without him, is likewise a subject of the Church's full and supreme power;[7] it lies more in the teaching on the sacramentality of the episcopacy, which places ordained ministry and its relationship with the Church in a new light.

The great relevance of this affirmation for the reception of the doctrine on the primacy of jurisdiction is already evident initially in its consequences for the understanding of the power of governance (*potestas regiminis*): taking a step beyond Vatican I,[8] *Lumen gentium* 21 teaches that its origin is sacramental[9] and at the same time emphasizes that it can be exercised only in the hierarchical communion of the episcopal college and, as such, in communion with the successor of Peter.

This teaching of Vatican II on episcopal ministry constituted a fundamental contribution at the time to confronting precisely the major challenge on the way to the reception of the teaching of *Pastor aeternus*: the

---

[5] *LG* 18: "Quam doctrinam de institutione, perpetuitate, vi ac ratione sacri Primatus Romani Pontificis deque eius infallibile Magisterio, Sacra Synodus cunctis fidelibus firmiter credendum rursus proponit, et in eodem incepto pergens, doctrinam de Episcopis . . . coram omnibus profiteri et declarare constituit."

[6] Cf. the famous paragraph *Tantum autem abest* of *Pastor aeternus* 3 (Johannes D. Mansi et al., *Sacrorum conciliorum nova et amplissima collectio* 52 [Arnhem and Leipzig: Hubert Welter, 1926]: 1332 CD).

[7] Cf. the *Relatio* of Bishop Zinelli: "concedimus lubenter et nos in concilio oecumenico sive in episcopis coniunctim cum suo capite supremam inesse et plenam ecclesiasticam potestatem in fideles omnes" (Mansi, 52: 1109 C).

[8] Vatican I did not adopt any teaching in this regard. While Bishop Zinelli denied during Vatican I that it was necessary to affirm the derivation of papal power from episcopal jurisdiction (cf. Mansi, 52: 1109 C, 1110 D), during Vatican II some thought this was the only possible solution; see the intervention of Anicetus Fernández [Master General of the Dominicans] (*Acta Synodalia*, 3/1: 708-709) and, in a similar manner, Fransicus Franic's *Relatio* (*Acta Synodalia* 3/2: 196-197).

[9] There is quite a discussion over the meaning of this text and, in particular, over the significance of the term *munus*; the reasons for the affirmation made here can be seen in Alfonso Carrasco Rouco, *Le primat de l'évêque de Rome* (Fribourg: Ed. Universitaires, 1990) 51-64.

assumption of the jurisdictional dimension of the primacy in an ecclesiology of communion.

2. *Lumen gentium* 21 teaches that the bishop receives in his consecration the fullness of the sacrament of orders, a sacred gift which enables him to work *in persona Christi*, priest, prophet, and king. In keeping with the sacramental theology common to the Western Church, of Augustinian tradition, the council then presents ministry as service, as an instrument of Christ who, by means of his Spirit, is the true subject who works in the Word and the sacraments, so they might constitute the Church in history.

The "instrumental" nature of this service, by which Jesus Christ is the true subject of the action, implies that the minister situates him at the center of his person; then he cannot pretend to be the principle of new life for the faithful, substituting himself for the Spirit of Christ. In the same way, neither can he pretend to determine the nature of the service to which he is called and of the communion which he is to serve. On the contrary, in the exercise of his ministry, his intention must be to "submit to the principal agent; that is, to seek to do what Christ and the Church do."[10]

If the bishop remains in full communion, his special service to the Word and the sacraments is a necessary instrument for the presence of the Church in history, to such an extent that communion with him becomes the condition of remaining in the Church for the Christian faithful. This dependence is not imposed, evidently, with respect to the bishop insofar as a private person, but insofar as he fulfills his ecclesial mission. It has to do with remaining in the unity of the faith which he proclaims and with the reality of communion, fruit of the sacraments and especially of the Eucharist.

Thus is manifested the basis for the dimension of authority of his special service within the Church, of his power of governance (*munus regendi*). In the words of *Lumen gentium*, "the faithful . . . must adhere to their bishop, as the Church does to Christ and as Jesus Christ does to the Father, so that all may agree together in unity and abound to the glory of God" (*LG* 27). That is, all the faithful are called to live the diversity of

---

[10] Thomas Aquinas, *Summa theologiae* 3, q. 64, a. 8, ad 1.

graces, services, and activities given by the Spirit in the unity of the children of God, for building up the Body of Christ.[11]

Thus, thanks to the structural dependence with regard to Christ and the Church, by which the minister surrenders himself to the work of the Other and not to the construction of a project which he himself determines, each one of the bishops can be called "the visible principle and foundation of unity in his particular church" (*LG* 23); a true principle, even though characterized as "visible" or, in other similarly traditional terms, as "secondary," for the primary principle of the Church's unity and of all spiritual gifts is Jesus Christ, who surrenders himself to human beings in the Spirit.

3. In the horizon of a sacramental understanding of the Church and the episcopate, likewise the successor of Peter finds himself in the context of a reality originated by the action of Christ and his Spirit, not determined by himself and to whose service he is called.[12]

Lumen gentium goes on to summarize synthetically the significance of his ministry, saying that Jesus Christ "instituted in him for always the perpetual and visible principle and foundation of the unity of the faith and of communion."[13] Consequently, in order not to separate themselves from full communion, all the faithful, among whom are to be included obviously the ordained minsters, are called to live out their own gifts, their vocation and mission, remaining in unity with the successor of Peter.

Now, as has already been observed in regard to the episcopacy, likewise the bishop of Rome is called to carry out this mission according to a precise modality. He is the "principle of unity," but in a "visible" and "secondary" manner.[14] Thus in no way is he the one who institutes

---

[11]   *LG* 32; see also *LG* 7, 12, 30. In this sense, the 1983 Code of Canon Law, after affirming the fundamental equality of all the faithful in building up the Body of Christ, presents the first duty of all Christians: "The Christian faithful are bound by an obligation, even in their own patterns of activity, always to maintain communion with the Church" (c. 209 §1).

[12]   Of special importance in *Lumen gentium* is the reflection on the situation of the pope in the episcopal college; yet this teaching is itself in a wider context of the teaching on the hierarchical structure of the people of God.

[13]   *LG* 18, recalling the teaching of *Pastor aeternus, Proemium*.

[14]   Vatican I explicitly used the distinction between the primary principle of unity, which is Christ, and the secondary principle which he instituted in the pope; see Bishop Leahy's *Relatio*, Mansi, 52: 638 B - 639 D.

by himself the faith, the sacraments, or the unity of the Church, which are the work of the one Lord and of the one Spirit. Yet, communion with the successor of Peter is the criterion of remaining in hierarchical communion, in full communion, but not because he constitutes it but rather because he, in fact, is the visible and objective sign of its presence in history.

This fundamental fact, which makes his particular ministry in the Church possible, is not the result of the power of the individual called to such a mission; it does not originate in his personal conscience, in the perfection of his faith, or in a model and morally irreprehensible way of carrying out his responsibilities as a minister. No human being—not even the apostles—has been called by Christ to be placed above the Word and the Church, and to determine in what the true faith consists, but rather to listen to the gospel, to participate freely in the communion opened by Christ and to give his witness with the grace of the Spirit. This is likewise verified in the case of the successor of Peter; only the Spirit, without which no one can say "Jesus is Lord," can guarantee that his witness remains in the truth.

The objective significance which the petrine ministry has in its relationship with the universal Church is made possible by the special assistance of the Holy Spirit (the charism of infallibility), thanks to which the successor of Peter, in exercising his essential ministry,[15] is not separated from the universal Church. Thanks to the gift of this remaining in the truth of Tradition, the petrine ministry can be a visible sign for all the faithful of the presence in history of the "full communion" (*communio plena*).

The Spirit of God thus makes possible the objectivity of the Church's presence and, as such, of the Word and the sacraments *Dei et ecclesiae*, which are not left to any one's discretion, not even that of the bishop of Rome. So the Christian faithful, to live in the unity of the Church, do not

---

[15]   Defining *ex cathedra* a doctrine *de fide et moribus*. See the brief explanation of Bishop Gasser: "Proinde reapse infallibilitas Romani pontificis restricta est ratione 'subiecti,' quando papa loquitur tanquam doctor universalis et iudex supremus in cathedra Petri, id est, in centro, constitutus; restricta est ratione 'obiecti,' quando agitur de rebus fidei et morum; et ratione 'actus,' quando definit quid sit credendum vel reiiciendum ab omnibus Christifidelibus." Mansi, 52: 1214 B-C.

depend on the subjective interpretation of the faith and of communion which nobody can give, not even an ordained minister.

In this way, starting with the gift which safeguards the objectivity of his permanence in the unity of the Church, in the center of the petrine ministry there is no form of human power, but rather a particular "spiritual gift" which makes possible the mission of Peter's successor. In effect, this special assistance of the Spirit qualifies the position of the bishop of Rome in the Church in such a manner that unity with him is the condition of remaining in the *communio*; thus it is possible to understand his special function of governing (*munus regendi*), whose theological value has been described precisely in such terms with regard to ordained ministry.[16]

In the same way it is clear in this perspective that to affirm the primacy of the bishop of Rome absolutely does not mean that the Church's life depends on his capacities and activities. His ministry is not important, in the first place, because he is a model of pastoral action, capable of acting in different circumstances with perspicacity and intelligence. History itself shows us that the significance of his service for the Church does not depend on his disposing of a more developed theology or a more effective "politics," nor that he make frequent use of his "infallible magisterium."[17] Rather, it is rooted in the fact that the presence of Peter's successor is the objective and visible criterion of "full communion," so that the faithful can be certain that united with him, they remain in the true unity which comes from Christ's Spirit.[18]

One can thus understand the fundamental dogmatic affirmations of Vatican I on the ministry of Peter's successor.

One on hand, the special "gift" of infallibility serves as a guarantee of the *extra nos*, of the objectivity of revelation;[19] it does not respond sim-

---

[16] See *LG* 27, and *supra*.

[17] See, for example, Klaus Schatz, "Welche bisherigen päpstlichen Lehrentscheidungen sind 'ex cathedra'? Historische und theologische Überlegungen," in *Dogmengeschichte und katholische Theologie*, ed. Werner Löser et al. (Würzburg: Echter, 1985) 404-422.

[18] See, for example, Ludwig Hertling, "Communio und Primat. Kirche und Papsttum in der christlichen Antike," *Una Sancta* 17 (1962) 122-123; also Klaus Schatz, *Vaticanum I: 1869-1870*, 3 (Paderborn: F. Schöningh, 1994) 306-308.

[19] See Schatz, *Vaticanum I*, 304.

ply to the human search for security,[20] but more profoundly, to the necessity that the presence of the divine work in history be safeguarded in its otherness with regard to human subjectivity.[21]

On the other hand, the "primacy of jurisdiction" does not appear simply as a question of "sovereignty" or of a monarchical or absolutist constitution of the Church,[22] but in reference to the truth of the presence in history of the *communio* which comes from Christ. It is possible to say, therefore, that in the origin of the petrine ministry the principle contrary to absolutism is at work, that is, that "truth, not authority makes the law": in this case, the truth of the abiding of Peter's successor in full communion.

Reflection on Some Fundamental Dimensions of the Petrine Ministry:
Infallibility and Jurisdiction

1. Vatican II made a particular effort to show how this special assistance of the Spirit to Peter's successor in the chair of the Church of Rome does not situate him outside the Church, but on the contrary, inserts him in all the dynamism proper to life in the unity of faith and communion.

So, *Lumen gentium*, following Vatican I's teaching, explains clearly that this particular assistance of the Spirit is not given to Peter's successor so that he can have new revelations, but to guarantee a fidelity essential to the faith of the Church. The chrism of infallibility, consequently, does not mean in any manner a special privilege which would make it

---

[20] Which is sometimes emphasized somewhat unilaterally; see, for example, Ulrich Horst, *Unfehlbarkeit und Geschichte* (Mainz: Matthias Grünewald, 1982) 255.

[21] See, for example, Peter Eicher: "Das neuzeitliche Offenbarungsdenken kann dabei im wesentlichen als der Versuch gesehen werde, die Alterität und soteriologische Gratuität des kirchlich vermittelten Evangeliums alt- und neutestamentlicher Art angesichts seiner historische Aufklärung und seiner atheistischen Überzeugungen in ideologiekritische Begründungszusammenhänge zu wahren. . . ." Peter Eicher, *Offenbarung. Prinzip neuzeitlicher Theologie* (Munich: Kösel, 1977) 584.

[22] This is not to deny at all the historical context in which the definition of the primacy and infallibility were prepared; see on this point, Hermann J. Pottmeyer, *Unfehlbarkeit und Souveränität* (Mainz: Matthias Grünewald, 1975).

possible for the bishop of Rome to dispose at will of the Word and the sacraments.[23]

This special assistance of the Spirit is not to be understood as inspiration, either; every Christian is called to listen to the revelation proclaimed by the apostles, which the Church preserves, transmitting down through history "all that she herself is, all that she herself believes" (*DV* 8). The bishop of Rome, likewise, cannot rely on special inspirations, but must seek to be faithful to the Church's tradition, applying his efforts to this and using appropriate means.[24] The Spirit's assistance is not given to avoid the proper work of life in the Church's communion, in all its dimensions and indeed limitations; it does guarantee, however, that given the case of a "definition *ex cathedra*" Peter's successor will not separate himself from the Church's faith.[25]

The *ex sese*, therefore, is not to be understood as an absolutist affirmation of the pope's power relative to the Church, but a reference to the precedence of the gift of the Holy Spirit as foundation and principle of the possibility of his ministry;[26] of course, this is not an attempt to describe all the dimensions of the relationship of the bishop of Rome with the universal Church.

In this sense, there is further weight to the teaching of *Lumen gentium* 25 which explains this expression, saying that such definitions do not need any other approbation nor are they subject to appeal,[27] because they enjoy the assistance of the Holy Spirit. For the same reason, they are ex-

[23]   In this sense it is possible to understand the traditional hypothesis about a heretical pope, which Gratian himself took from earlier canonical tradition: the pope "can be judged by no one, unless he is found to deviate from the faith" (D. 40, c. 6). On this theme see Ludwig Buisson, *Potestas und Caritas* (Cologne: Böhlau, 1982) 166-215.

[24]   *LG* 25. In the conciliar acts it is affirmed, with Gasser, that the Roman Pontiff and the bishops in issuing a definition, *eosdem habet fontes quales habet ecclesia* (Mansi, 52: 1216 D) and that they strive to use adequate means (Mansi, 52: 1213); see *Acta Synodalia* 3/1: 253.

[25]   Gasser spoke in this sense: "nil timendum, ac si per malam fidem et negligentiam pontificis universalis ecclesia in errorem circa fidem induci posset. Nam tutela Christi et assistentia divina Petri successoribus promissa est causa ita efficax, ut . . . si reapse pontifex ad definitionem deveniat, illa infallibiliter vera existat" (Mansi, 52: 1214).

[26]   Recognizing the teaching on the nature of this gift and, therefore, on the conditions which delimit its exercise, not only shows that the minister cannot use this gift arbitrarily, but also underlines that it is really the Lord's Spirit which safeguards the Church in truth.

[27]   Even to another judgment of the Roman Pontiff himself; see the *Relatio* to n. 25: *Acta Synodalia* 3/1: 252.

empt of error and are considered irreformable. Following in the steps of Vatican I, *Lumen gentium* also affirms that because of the assistance of the same Spirit, the assent of the Church to this special exercise of the magisterium cannot be lacking, for it is certainly in agreement with revelation.[28]

Thus is explained an aspect of the teaching on the charism of infallibility given to the pope, thanks to which, in fact, he is not separated from the Church's faith. Consequently, infallible definitions and the Church's assent to them are affirmed as two sides of the same reality: Christ's Spirit safeguarding the Church in the truth.[29]

For both Vatican Councils it is unthinkable that the exercise of this supreme magisterium by the successor of Peter and by the episcopal college would not receive the Church's assent; *Lumen gentium* explicitly recognizes this teaching in its number 25. Nothing is said, of course, about the time and the path of welcome, about the process of reception implied in such assent. In this respect, the history of conciliar definitions amply demonstrates the difficulties which can be encountered and the efforts which can be necessary within the Church's life in order to arrive at full reception.[30]

For its part, the conciliar affirmation that the "consensus of all the faithful" (*consensus universalis fidelium*) shows the special property of the people of God by which it cannot err in the faith (*LG* 12), does not introduce a variation on this teaching. For it does not pretend to constitute an instance which would permit to discern after the fact the infallible exercise of the magisterium. In effect, it is not possible to contrast the magisterium with the rest of the faithful in this consensus, for in it is evident the faith of "all the people of God, including the hierarchy."[31] This consensus, on the other hand, has only a positive sense;[32] its existence witnesses infallibly the Church's faith, while on the contrary, the absence of the consent of the *universitas fidelium* receives no criteriological value in *Lumen gentium*. Such "consent of all the faithful" can be realized precisely as the fruit of a whole historical process of reception, in which it

---

[28]   *LG* 25; cf. Mansi, 52: 1214 A.

[29]   See the response to *modus* 175 commenting on this assent: "Principium unitatis fidei est assistentia Spiritus Sancti" (*Acta Synodalia* 3/8: 92).

[30]   See, in this regard, Heinrich J. Sieben, *Die Konzilidee der alten Kirche* (Paderborn: Schöningh, 1979).

[31]   *Relatio* to n. 12: *Acta Synodalia* 3/1: 198; the text of *LG* 12 itself is clear.

[32]   Gasser said something similar: Mansi, 52: 1217.

cannot be guaranteed there will be no problems, and which also does not exclude that a schism could take place.

Consequently, to the teaching about the charism of infallibility is tied the affirmation of the fact of the Church's assent. Neither the texts nor the intention of both Vatican councils give to this assent a criteriological value, as a later instance by which one can discern the existence or not of a magisterial teaching *ex cathedra*.[33]

This teaching does not surreptitiously convert the episcopal or papal magisterium into a new source of revelation, nor claim to constitute the truth of the faith; it simply affirms that the Spirit safeguards its witness in fidelity to the Lord, in a way that it can truly be "witness to divine and catholic faith" (*divinae et catholicae veritatis testes— LG* 25).

2. The mission of the bishop of Rome, as "visible principle of unity in faith and communion," is not based on subjective human capacities of will, intelligence, or religiosity. It is made possible by Christ's promises and by the gift of the Spirit; thus, it is not at his disposition to determine the nature of his service,[34] of his special relationship with the Church whose fundamental feature, which makes it possible to understand his mission, is already determined: Peter will not separate himself from the Church, nor this from Christ.[35]

The perspective opened by the council, in which the ministry does not appear as a power over the Church but structurally as service to Christ and to his work of communion in the Spirit, offers a solid basis for a process of reception also of the "full and supreme jurisdiction" of the bishop of Rome.

---

[33]   Schatz observes that similar ideas, which do not reflect so much the council's content as what some desired it might contain, found some small echo after Vatican I. They can be found in some letters of Maret and of Dupanloup, and were publicly defended by Aemil Ruckgaber, *Die Irrlehre des Honorius und das vaticanische Decret über die päpstliche Unfehlbarkeit* (Stuttgart: Cotta, 1871); the book was put on the Index. See Schatz, *Vaticanum I*, 3: 293-294 (*supra*, note 18).

[34]   He cannot change it in an essential way, for example, eliminating or introducing the need to remain in unity with him even in his private theological opinions.

[35]   In this sense, Gasser presented to the conciliar aula the meaning of the Church's tradition on Peter's primacy: "Nam communicatio cum cathedra Petri erat et habita fuit communicatio cum ecclesia et cum ipso Petro, proinde etiam cum veritate a Christo revelata aequiparabatur; . . . Petrus, constitutus fundamentum ecclesiae, ab ipsa ecclesia . . . nunquam possit separari." Mansi, 52: 1207, 1208.

For this, the better way seems to be that of understanding and development of all that is implied in this "objective" relationship of the bishop of Rome with the universal Church. One can thus think of forms for exercising the primacy adequate to the new historical situation, without the need for reinterpretations which question what is essential in his mission.[36]

In effect, to affirm the abiding of Peter's successor in the truth of the Church does not mean, even jurisdictionally, that he is situated above it, but rather in it. In fact, it is common doctrine that, for his ministry, the pope is not above the Word of God (*DV* 10), which is manifested in the rule of faith, in the teachings of ecumenical councils, included in the "general state of the Church" (*status generalis Ecclesiae*), or, in a word of juridical flavor, in divine law (*ius divinum*). In this context it is traditional likewise to recall that authority in the Church is given "for building up and not for destruction" (2 Cor 10: 8).

Consequently, Peter's successor is called to exercise his ministry living fully the dynamic of communion proper to the Church.

This means, above all, that he has to receive and serve the Word and the sacraments which come from God and are conserved and transmitted by the Church; therefore, neither its substance nor the binding dimensions which derive from it (with juridical value) are at his disposition. By way of example can be mentioned the reality of the self-same bishop, who receives the fullness of the sacrament of order, called by Christ to be successor of the apostles and proper pastor of a particular church; but likewise the episcopal college, itself a reality which is not instituted by the pope and whose existence, nature, or ecclesial mission he cannot deny.

In a word, neither the constitution nor the life of the Church are originated by the bishop of Rome; as all the Christian faithful, he lives in the first place a dynamic of reception, which also embraces the binding dimensions proper to its fundamental features: the *ius divinum*.

To understand adequately this relationship of Peter's successor with the Church can be of great importance in facilitating ecumenical relations. The bishop of Rome is called to recognize all the real dynamic of com-

---

[36] See John Paul II, encyclical *Ut unum sint*, May 25, 1997, n. 95. See also Ludwig Hertling, 122 ff, and Congar's reflections, proposed again recently in the volume *Eglise et papauté* (Paris: Cerf, 1994).

munion, the Word and the sacraments, the proper features of the ecclesial constitution, which each Church or separated community conserves.[37]

The awareness the Church has of its current situation has led it, in like manner, to pay special attention to the dynamic of life proper to each Christian faithful; thus it is clear that the awareness of the people of God does not lead it to fulfill its mission in the world without exercising the common priesthood and the *sensus fidei*, in that each of the faithful receives and lives in the first person the Word and the sacraments.[38] Its welcome in each of its dimensions, likewise binding, in historically and theologically adequate forms, can certainly aid a better understanding and reception of what is proper to each ordained ministry and, in particular, of the petrine ministry, and to an experience of greater concord and richness in the Church's life.

The Code of Canon Law has taken important steps in this direction, for example with the recognition of the "Christian faithful" as the primary subject of the Church's life, and with the development of a catalogue of the faithful's rights and duties. The absence in the code, on the other hand, of dimensions such as charisms, to which *Lumen gentium* dedicated ample space, undoubtedly shows that there are more steps to be taken.[39] In effect, charisms, which the Spirit gives to the faithful to build up the Church and which habitually bear a collective dimension, are truly paradigms of this dynamic of reception to which ministry in the Church is called.[40]

---

[37] Even though, in the same measure in which there is separation from the bishop of Rome, it is a question of a realization of not-full communion. On the idea of different grades of remaining in hierarchical communion see Wilhelm Bertrams, "De gradibus communionis in doctrina concilii Vaticani II," *Gregorianum* 47 (1966) 286-305; Richard Potz, "Die Grade der Communio im katholischen Kirchenrecht," *Kanon* 8 (1987) 51-64.

[38] See the importance of chapter 2 of *Lumen gentium*, especially nn. 10-13.

[39] See, for example, Eugenio Corecco, "Aspects of the Reception of Vatican II in the Code of Canon Law," in *The Reception of Vatican II*, ed. Giuseppe Alberigo et al. (Washington: The Catholic University of America Press, 1987) 249-296; likewise Frank Ochmann, "Kirchliches Recht in und aus dem Leben der Communio—Zur 'Rezeption' aus kanonistischer Sicht," in *Glaube als Zustimmung. Zur Interpretation kirchlicher Rezeptionsvorgänge*, ed. Wolfgang Beinert (Freiburg: Herder, 1991) 123-163.

[40] See Eugenio Corecco, "Carisma," in *Digesto della Discipline Pubblicistiche*, ed. Rodolfo Sacco et al., 2 (Turin: UTET, 1988) 504-508; Libero Gerosa, *Carisma e diritto nella Chiesa* (Milan: Jaca Book, 1989); Rinaldo Bertolino, "*Sensus fidei*, carismi e diritto nel popolo di Dio," in *Antropologia, fede e diritto ecclesiale*, ed. Libero Gerosa (Milan: Jaca Book, 1995) 57-96.

In this perspective, on the other hand, the proper authority of Peter's successor does not exist at all in the Church as a purely extrinsic authority, having as its only basis the relationship of power as one who is superior to others, and can impose his will. Thus it always appears, according to its nature, as a sign of remaining in the Church's full communion. This is the reason why the Christian can respond with "a religious *obsequium* of intellect and will" (*LG* 25).

Even if there are always conflicts, and history teaches us about how harsh they can strike within the Church, ruptures come only when the horizon of the Church's communion disappears as the real foundation of relationships. The recognition of the authority of Peter's successor thus does not exclude possible divergences or debates; but it excludes that a personal interpretation of things could be a point of departure sufficient to establish another objective criterion for remaining in the Church's unity.

Extreme conflict or rupture, however, is not normal. In the daily life of communion, the proper authority of Peter's successor is assumed in the Church for its meaning as the principle of unity in faith and communion, that is, with "religious *obsequium*," which, of course, admits diverse grades, according to the different modes for the exercise of his authority by the minister.[41]

Peter's successor, for his part, is called to exercise his ministry with the clear intention of service for building up the people of God; that is, searching out those forms, means, and pastoral modes which will better serve a fruitful and active "reception" by the faithful. The bishop of Rome has no guarantee in this, neither for the right thing to say nor for the outcome; yet, striving to show the natural truth of his service for the universal Church, he will make in any case an important contribution to the reception on the part of each of the faithful of his special mission in favor of the universal Church.

In conclusion, it can be said that the Second Vatican Council constitutes a decisive and determinant moment in the process of reception of the "full and supreme jurisdiction" affirmed by Vatican I, and in the first

---

[41] See the explanation given concerning *LG* 25 in the *Relatio* to n. 25, *Acta Synodalia* 3/1: 251.

place thanks to the fundamental perspectives of its presentation of the Church and of ministry. The task, already begun, continues of deepening and developing this promising sense of direction for theological investigation.

Translation by James H. Provost

THE ADOPTION OF THE PRINCIPLE OF CODIFICATION: ECCLESIOLOGICAL SIGNIFICANCE WITH SPECIAL REFERENCE TO RECEPTION

CARLO R. M. REDAELLI*

To introduce the topic of this report it is important above all to clarify what is meant by the "principle of codification." This expression means not only the use of the technical legislative instrument called a "code" but also and above all juridical concepts which are at the origins of its conceptualization and have subsequently accompanied its development.

THE PRINCIPLE OF CODIFICATION IN THE CONTEXT OF EUROPEAN JURIDICAL THOUGHT

The context in which the idea of a code was born was that of the Enlightenment and the affirmation of the absolute state in the 18th century.[1] The emphasis on the centrality of human reason which characterized the Enlightenment was translated juridically by what has come to be called the "natural law school" into a concept which holds that it is possible to arrive at a universally and absolutely valid natural law, taking reason and not the context of faith as the point of departure. Such a law should be formulated properly in a way which is rational, systematic, global, simple, and clear: hence the code.

---

* Facoltà Teologica dell'Italia Settentrionale, Milan (Italy).

[1] To reconstruct the development of codification see, with the bibliography cited there, Guido Fassò, *Storia della filosofia del diritto. 3: Ottocento e Novecento* (Bologna: Il Mulino, 1970) 11-30; Adriano Cavanna, *Storia del diritto moderno in Europa. 1: Le fonti e il pensiero giuridico*, 1 (Milan: Giuffrè, 1982) 197-200, 237-295; idem, *Dal diritto comune alla codificazione. Appunti dalle lezioni di esegesi delle fonti del diritto italiano* (Milan: Giuffrè, 1991); Piero A. Bonnet, "De momento codificationis pro iure Ecclesiae," *Periodica* 70 (1981) 303-368, esp. 309-339.

Between the end of the 1700's and the beginning of the 1800's, this theoretical approach confronted the practical exigencies of bringing order out of the confusion and uncertainty of juridical norms resulting from the degeneration of the common law as well as responding to changing socio-economic situations. This approach was also prompted by the political exigency of the absolutist states of the Enlightenment[2] to reduce the juridical order (*diritto*) to the law (*legge*) and a law in itself rational, absolute, and complete so as to guarantee their own centralized power and to realize a government based on rationality and, there-fore, securely (in their view) directed to the good of the people. Thus normative intermediary instances were eliminated between the sover-eign and the citizen (which had generated, for example, the citizen and corporation statutes) as well as all other sources of law such as custom, jurisprudential precedents, and the opinions of the juriscon-sults. Only the sovereign, or the state, therefore became the rational legislator, and the interpretation of the laws was reserved to him alone. Legal theory could only comment on the laws, and the judge could only apply them, addressing *lacunae* in the legislative corpus by referring to the general principles of the code and to norms governing analogous cases.[3]

This cluster of motivations led to the birth of the codes, especially the Napoleonic *Code civil* of 1804, which became the model for every sub-sequent codification. It is observed that the codes do not present for the most part a new law; rather, they broadly restate the preceding common law, rationalizing it through a typically code-like formulation: brief, clear, without reference to a motivation. The newness of codification,

---

[2]   But even the liberal states emerging after the French Revolution would have the same exigencies.

[3]   These dispositions are contained in the Prussian code (*Allgemeines Landrecht fur die Preussischen Staaten, Einleitung*, par. 46); the similarity with canon 18 of the 1917 code is striking. In the same line the dispositions of the *Code civil* are very sig-nificant: "Art. 4. The judge who refuses to judge under pretext of the silence, obscurity or inadequacy of the law can be prosecuted as guilty of denying justice. Art. 5. Judges are forbidden to decide by way of general regulatory disposition on cases which are sub-mitted to them." As regards the redaction of article 4 of the *Code civil*, see Fassò, 22-25; Cavanna, *Dal diritto commune*, 67. During the various drafts there was a development from an initial deference to natural law and equity, therefore with an area of discretion re-served to the judge, to a strict linking of his activity to the positive law envisioned in the definitive text.

therefore, is not so much a matter of content but of methodology and an underlying concept.[4]

Codification entailing the rationalization and systematization of all the law in one legislative instrument[5] inevitably gave rise at the theoretical level to the school of exegesis (*école de l'exégèse*).This refers to a current of thought that holds that all law is reduced to the code. In fact it is the supreme and definitive instrument to express rational natural law; therefore the only thing to do is comment on it and explain it without any need to refer to other principles or other disciplines.[6]

Parallel to the affirmation of an exegetical approach to the code and because of its absolute centrality, there was also a movement from a natural law approach to one of juridical positivism and voluntarism. De facto the code was produced by the legislator with the intent of codifying the rational and absolute natural law; therefore the will of the legislator is in a certain sense subordinated to the rationality of the law. But once the code is realized, it is recognized as absolute and one forgets what grounds it. The will of the legislator is understood in itself as rational without any reference to a reality transcending it, and therefore as the sole source of the rationality and juridical character of the code. One has recourse to the will of the legislator for interpretation purposes without the possibility of referring to principles which are considered meta-juridical and therefore outside the proper field of law.

Without wishing here, even in a sketchy fashion, to follow the evolution of juridical doctrines in the 19th and 20th centuries, it seems important for its relevance to canonical theory to recall two developments of

---

[4] The recovery of the preceding law was further favored by the fact that at the time the private initiative of students and the attempts at partial legislation by sovereigns had fostered a rationalization and systematization of Roman law rethought in the light of an ideal of rational perfection. There was a similar rationalization and systematization of the operative law, purified, however, and unified by the principle of rationality. See Fassò, 14-16; Cavanna, *Storia*, 252-295.

[5] In reality only the Prussian code embraced much more than civil law and was not accompanied by other codes, while in the French sphere the *Code civil* was quickly followed between 1806 and 1811 by the *Code de procédure*, the *Code de commerce*, the *Code pénal*, and the *Code d'instruction criminelle*. Something analogous happened in other states which followed the French example.

[6] As a result, in French law schools in the period immediately following the code, any teachings about the natural law and the theory of law were suppressed. See Fassò, 27, who refers to Julien Bonnecasse, *L'école de l'exégèse en droit civil*, 2nd ed. (Paris: Boccard, 1924).

modern juridical thought linked to the principle of codification. The first is that of the so-called juridical dogmatics which concerns the articulation of a general theory of law (*allgemeine Rechtslehre*), i.e., a system constructed on the basis of principles drawn from positive norms considered as dogmas.[7] The second development is more recent and, more than a theory, is the clarification of the fact of the failure not only of the ideal or, if you will, of the myth of codification, but of the very practical relevance of codes in the context of contemporary juridical systems to such an extent that the code vis-à-vis special legislation can be seen even as a residual law and no longer as the axis undergirding any juridical construction.[8]

THE PRINCIPLE OF CODIFICATION AND ECCLESIAL CODIFICATION IN 1917 AND IN 1983-1990

A.   A Methodological Premise

The picture which has just been delineated and which has enabled us to follow the rise, development, and decline of the principle of codification permits us now to see its relevance in the canonical arena. We do this not abstractly in relation to a hypothetical codification of the law of the Church, but in relation to the *fact* of the codification of 1917 and its revival in 1983 (*CIC*) and 1990 (*CCEO*), taking cognizance synthetically of the cluster of factors which sets such events apart and shapes them within the framework of the life of the Church.[9]

B.   The 1917 Codification

1.   The Preparation and Work of Redacting the Code

The process of shaping the 1917 code has been studied in depth in its various phases: the first efforts at new collections of sources of law after

---

[7]   Fassò, 217-230.

[8]   See the reflections of Natalino Irti, *L'età della decodificazione* (Milan: Giuffrè, 1979). On the idea of codification today and on its more or less authentic renaissance see *Renaissance der Idee der Kodifikation*, ed. Franz Bydlinski et al., Schriften zur Rechtspolitik 5 (Vienna: Bohlau, 1991). On our topic see also Johannes W. Pichler and Karim J. Giese, *Rechtsakzeptanz*, Schriften zur Rechtspolitik 6 (Vienna: Bohlau, 1992).

[9]   The need to refer to the concrete experiences of codification is accentuated by the decision to highlight the theme of reception, which by definition refers to the concreteness of ecclesial life.

the Council of Trent,[10] the emergence of a request for codification at Vatican I,[11] the subsequent debate in canonical circles with the elaboration of private attempts at codification,[12] and finally the genuine and proper efforts at codification.[13]

Synthesizing the results of the research, one can note especially that at Vatican I, even in the preparatory phase, there was a prevailing emphasis on practical exigencies leading to a reform of the law of the Church. It was a question of surmounting the inconveniences arising from a legislation that was vast, contradictory, mixed in character, and left to the whim of the

---

[10] Adam Vetulani, s.v. "Codex Iuris Canonici," 1. "Les essais de codification du XVIᵉ au XIXᵉ siecle," in *Dictionnaire de Droit Canonique [DDC]* (Paris: Letouzy et Ané, 1942) 3: 910-917, esp. 910-914; Alfons Stickler, *Historia iuris canonici latini Institutiones academicae,* 1: *Historia fontium* (Turin: Apud Custodiam Librariam Pontif. Athenaei Salesiani, 1950) 362-366.

[11] See the following works and the bibliography they cite: Mario Falco, *Introduzione allo studio del "Codex iuris canonici,"* ed. Giorgio Feliciani (Bologna: Il Mulino, 1992) 94-97; Vetulani, 914-915; Giorgio Feliciani, "Il Concilio Vaticano I e la codificazione del diritto canonico," *Ephemerides Iuris Canonici* 33 (1977) 115-143, 269-289; Winfried Aymans, "Die Quellen des kanonischen Rechtes in der Kodifikation von 1917," in *La norma en el Derecho Canonico Actas del III Congreso Internacional de Derecho Canonico: Pamplona 10 a 15 de octubre de 1976* (Pamplona: EUNSA, 1979) 1: 487-503, esp. 488-490; Augustin Motilla, "La idea de la codificación en el proceso de formación del Codex de 1917," *Ius Canonicum* 28 (1988) 681-720, esp. 684-687, 690-698. Certain opinions expressed by various episcopates at Vatican I are also reported by Cardinal Gasparri in his preface to the code. On the 1917 codification in its entirety see Pietro Gasparri, "Storia della codificazione del Diritto canonico per la Chiesa Latina," in *Acta Congressus Iuridici Internationalis VII saeculo a Decretalibus Gregorii IX et XIV a Codice Justiniano, promulgatis, Romae 12-17 Novembris 1934* (Rome: Libreria Editrice Vaticana, 1937) 4: 1-10.

[12] Falco, 97-102; Vetulani, 915-917; Stickler, 366-370; Motilla, 698-704. Among these attempts recall those of De Luise, Colomiatti, Pillet, Deshayes, Pezzani, Russo. Partial efforts were made by Périès, Cadena y Eleta, and Hollweck.

[13] Falco, 103-118; Vetulani, s.v. "Codex Iuris Canonici," 2: "L'initiative de Pie X"; 3. "Les travaux préparatoires du Codex," in *DDC* 3: 917-935; Motilla, 704-719; Stickler, 371-384; Romeo Astorri, *Le leggi della Chiesa tra codificazione latina e diritti particolari* (Padua: CEDAM, 1992) 9-85; Giorgio Feliciani, "Mario Falco e la codificazione del diritto canonico," in Falco, 13-35; Antonio García y García, "Las codificaciones y su impacto en la Iglesia a través de la historia," in *Temas fundamentales en el nuevo Codigo,* XVIII Semana Española de Derecho Canónico (Salamanca: Universidad Pontificia, 1984) 50-56. For several years the codification archives have been available. See the research directed by Giorgio Feliciani on the canonical codification, which uses material from that archive. Besides the text of Astorri see Maria Vismara Missiroli and Luciano Musselli, *Il processo di codificazione del diritto penale canonico* (Padua: CEDAM, 1983); Francesco Falchi, *I chierici nel processo di formazione del Codice piano-benedettino* (Padua: CEDAM, 1987). Reference is also made to material in the archives by Stephan Kuttner, "The Code of Canon Law in Historical Perspective," *The Jurist* 28 (1968) 129-148.

interpreter: the uncertainty of the law, its ineffectiveness, the refusal to study it. These are problems that can bring us back to the theme of reception: the people of God were no longer in a position to receive and even more to perceive the shape of a discipline which would give certainty to ecclesial life and to the rights and duties of individuals. The modalities suggested by the council fathers to cope with this situation were extremely varied and did not all follow the pattern of codification.[14] In any event the characteristics of their requests[15] for an intervention on canonical legislation (such as completeness, comprehensibility, an organic character, a systematic character, brevity) make one think of at least an implicit reference to state codification even if this is not entirely evident.

However, in the debate at Vatican I, there seemed to be neither a consciousness of the specificity of church law vis-à-vis civil law nor a real understanding of the possible risks for canon law of an accentuation of uniformity and the *lex scripta*, which would happen with the assumption of the method of codification. From an ecclesiological standpoint there seemed to be a discounting of any reference to the doctrine of the *societas perfecta*,[16] a doctrine reaffirmed by those engaging in private efforts at codification after Vatican I.[17]

---

[14]   The proposals advanced were synthetically: a revision of the *Corpus Iuris Canonici* or a new redaction of it, the compilation of a new codification to be added to those already existing, the abandoning of the traditional legal approach to use that of codification for some parts (especially procedural and penal law) or for the whole body of canon law. See Motilla, 685-686.

[15]   Apart from the fathers favorable to an organic reform of the ecclesial legal system, there was de facto at the council also a minority position which did not see the need for any intervention in the operative legislation. See Feliciani, "Il Concilio Vaticano I," 142-143. Also significant was the fact that some called for a codification, or at least a systematization, of Eastern law. See ibid., 121-122.

[16]   See what was expressed by Bishop Salzano: "who after praising the codification undertaken by various states complained that such was entirely lacking in ecclesiastical . . . society, which is a true society, despite the fact that the very State of the Church was provided with a code of procedure." See Feliciani, "Il Concilio Vaticano I," 137. Therefore, there does not seem to be a great difference between the Church and the "State of the Church"; both are a *societas* and as such must have a law redacted in the form of a code according to the opinion cited.

[17]   These show a substantial acceptance of the technique of codification, but (and this is very significant from an ecclesiological standpoint) they abstract it from a reference to a rationalist ideology of Enlightenment origin and situate it in a theoretical context of the school of public ecclesiastical law. See Camillo Tarquini, *Iuris ecclesiastici publici institutiones*, 2nd ed. (Rome: Typographia Polyglotta, 1908); Felice Cavagnis, *Institutiones iuris publici ecclesiastici*, 4th ed. (Rome: Desclée, Lefebvre et cie., 1906). Such an approach highlighted the notion of the Church as a *societas perfecta* like the states even if it were superior to them in virtue of its mission. See Motilla, 701-702, who refers to the works of Pillet, Deshayes, and Pezzani.

Finally the genuine and proper work of codification was initiated with the publication of the motu proprio *Arduum sane munus* on March 19, 1904, which was accompanied especially in the early years by a wide ranging debate in canonical circles. It is interesting to note that the idea of codification in a modern vein was not very evident in the motu proprio itself, although in reality it was present from the beginning as is witnessed by the draft of the pontifical document, drawn up by Cardinal Gennari, and the report accompanying it. This was also true subsequently in the letter of Cardinal Gasparri to Catholic universities (April 6, 1904) and in the norms for the work of redaction (April 11, 1904). The practical motivation for the codification, derived from Vatican I, was always present but by then the reference to the "myth" of codification and the legislation of states was ever more prevailing notwithstanding some resistance on the part of those who saw the risk of jeopardizing continuity with the canonical tradition and the special character of church law.[18]

2.   The Principle of Codification in Official Documents

To assess the role of codification in the legislative work of 1917 and its impact on an ecclesiological understanding and on reception, it is very important to refer to the official and explicit self-understanding of the Church regarding the code expressed in various documents.

A first text to be considered is the apostolic constitution *Providentissima Mater Ecclesia*, by which Benedict XV promulgated the code on Pentecost May 27, 1917.[19] An attentive reading leads to the following observations. There is lacking any reference to state codification or even

---

[18]   This was the position of Ojetti, Wernz, and De Luca. However, the majority position within the code redaction commission was expressed very significantly by what Lega maintained, that "motivating the request that the norms contain 'only the will of the legislator without giving any reason' is the observation that 'all the civil codes are forged using that method.'" See also Latini, who "notes that to treat 'promiscuously' the 'dispositive' part and the 'procedural' part would expose the commission to ridicule, as if they did not want to take into account the ideas on codification prevalent in all civil nations." See Feliciani, "Mario Falco," 23. Even the debate in canonical circles did not seem to question this approach, but was skeptical about the possibility of the success of the codification undertaking, referring above all to certain distinctive characteristics of the canonical system (e.g., its relationship to moral theology), to the centrality of the papacy, and to the then extremely delicate problem of relationships with states, a problem which could have been aggravated, according to these authors, if public ecclesiastical law were codified, indeed with reference to the Syllabus. On the thought of these different authors (Friedberg, Ruffini, Calisse, Sägmüller, etc.) see Astorri, 13-42.

[19]   *AAS* 9/2 (1917) 5-8.

to the principle of codification with which it might be compared or by which it might be inspired.[20] The qualification of the Church as a perfect society justifies not only the code but rather the legislative power of the Church in general, which is therefore native and proper and not dependent on the states. The value of church law is vindicated also as a form of civilization, in particular in the specific juridical arena. The legislative intervention has an eminently practical purpose: to surmount the limitations of the operative law so that church law can be known and achieve its proper purpose. It is not explained how this result will be achieved by the drafting of a code, but it is taken as an implicit given.

Much more unbalanced regarding the code is a document which can be seen as a typical expression of the myth of codification, i.e., the motu proprio *Cum iuris canonici* of September 15, 1917.[21] With such a provision the pope wished to preclude jeopardizing the *stabilitas* of the code either by way of private interpretation or by an increase in the number of laws. Therefore with very significant consequences the following points were determined. The Commission for the Authentic Interpretation of the Code was established, the activity of interpretation was reserved to it. The Roman congregations were prohibited from issuing general decrees with the sole possibility of issuing instructions implementing the code.[22] If it were necessary to issue a new general decree, then once it was approved by the pope, it had to be transmitted to the commission, which was to redraft one or more canons and indicate what canons were to be substituted or what new canons were to be introduced, to be numbered *bis*, *ter*, etc. regarding the preceding canon (even the numbering of the canons was sacred!).[23]

One might situate in the same line two instructions of the Sacred Congregation for Seminaries and Universities of Studies. The first, issued on

---

[20]   The word "code" itself is used only toward the end of the document.
[21]   This was published in *AAS* 9 (1917) 483-484 and inserted in official editions of the code.
[22]   It was emphasized that it must be evident that these were only explanations and complements of the canons.
[23]   In subsequent years de facto only some marginal changes were actually introduced in the code; e.g., the abrogation of the second comma of paragraph 2 of canon 1099 because of the motu proprio *Ne temere* of August 1, 1948 (*AAS* 40 [1948] 305). Such indications are given in the work of Vincenzo Del Giudice, *Nozioni di diritto canonico*, 12th ed. (Milan: Giuffrè, 1970) 57-58.

August 7, 1917,[24] took as its point of departure the fact that from the day the code took effect it would be the authentic and only source of canon law. Accordingly the instruction determined that the code alone was to be used in implementing ecclesial discipline, be it judicial or in schools (*eo uno utendum esse*). Moreover, in the so-called *schola textus*, the code was to be explained analytically canon-by-canon, following the numerical succession scrupulously (*religiosissime*). Furthermore it was indicated that the code was the only book the students needed; if the teacher wished to use another textbook, it ought to be adapted to the code and not vice-versa. The second instruction, dated October 31, 1918, concerned examinations.[25] In accord with the indications given for schools, even on exams the students were to expound the "exegesis" or the "interpretation" of the canons of the code taken individually or related to one another. As is evident, we are fully in the exegetical school (*école de l'exégèse*) were it not for the fact that the first instruction envisioned the exposition of the origin and development of individual institutes on the part of the teacher (but it seems only orally since there existed, as it were, only the code); and therefore the second instruction indicated such an exposition as material for examinations.

A last document to consider (even if it is only semi-official) is Cardinal Gasparri's Preface (to the code). Its intent is evident from the first few words: to demonstrate through history that the Church has always intended to collect in one source all the sacred canons (*propositum . . . ut sacri . . . canones in unum colligerentur*) and therefore the promulgation of the code is in continuity with the traditional line. Given this intent it is interesting to note that when Gasparri emphasizes the request presented to the Holy See to rework and reorder canon law on the model of the more recent states (*capto a recentioribus omnibus civitatibus*), the reference to the modern codification is immediately justified by a parallel to the work completed by Gregory IX in imitation of the *Corpus* of Justinian.[26] Therefore the codification would not constitute a break with ecclesial tradition.[27]

---

[24]   *AAS* 9 (1917) 439.

[25]   *AAS* 10 (1918) 19.

[26]   "Quemadmodum Gregorius IX Iustinianum imitari non dubitaverint."

[27]   The last part of the Preface is noteworthy regarding the theme of codification; it recalls in particular the norms given to the consultors and collaborators. Among them: the code must deal solely with discipline even if it may contain principles of natural law or references to the faith itself. The discipline is drawn from different sources, beginning with

3. The Choices Underlying the Adoption of the Technique of Codification in the Concrete Configuration of the 1917 Code

After examining the ecclesial self-understanding concerning the adoption of the principle of codification explicitated by official or semi-official documents, it can be useful to see what choices were entailed by the adoption of such a principle in the concrete redaction and promulgation of the 1917 code. It is not a matter of considering the contents of the code; in certain respects these prescind from the technique of codification. For example, the almost absolute preeminence of clerics is evidently not due to the choice of codification. Rather it is a question of illustrating what are the options at the level of the understanding of church law and of its reception which inevitably flow from the adoption of a technique of codification.

A first consequence above all is the formal break with the canonical tradition notwithstanding the effort at giving evidence of continuity with its sources and the substantial continuity of the code with the preceding law.[28]

A second aspect is the accentuation of the text of the law, in particular that of the code, as the only source of rights; certainly all of custom is not cancelled; and in the case of *lacunae* in the law there is an allusion to recourse to the general principles of law "observed with canonical equity" (*cum aequitate canonica servatis*) as well as to the "stylus" and practice of the Roman Curia and to the common and constant understanding of canonical doctrine (cf. c. 20). However, it is striking that reference is made to a notion as central to the canonical tradition as equity only in the context of a norm which of its very nature is residual, regarding hypothetical cases of a *lacuna* in the law. In keeping with the absolute sovereignty of the law, it remains clear that judicial activity cannot create the law but only interpret it authentically in an individual case (cf. c. 17 §3).

In its concrete configuration, however, one must recognize that the Pio-Benedictine code attenuates the character of exclusivity typical of state codes, as emerges clearly from the first canons (cc. 1-6).[29] The pre-

---

the *Corpus Iuris canonici*, but the canons ought to contain only the dispositive part and be brief and clear. Besides, they can introduce innovations to be formulated as canons wherever it is necessary. As regards the emphasis on the practical character of the choice of codification, on which the Preface insists, see Motilla, 718, who does not give evidence of this point being taken up in post-code canonical theory.

[28] Vidal could reedit the *Ius Decretalium* of Wernz after the promulgation of the code. See Franciscus Wernz-Petrus Vidal, *Ius canonicum ad Codicis normam exactum* (Rome: Apud Aedes Universitatis Gregorianae, 1923-1937).

[29] Despite the title of the code, the Eastern Church is preserved, and therefore implicitly its legislation (c. 1); room is left for liturgical laws (c. 2), agreements with states (c. 3),

eminence of the code and therefore of the supreme legislator in the Church is, however, never put in doubt.

Another effect implied in the adoption of codification is the accentuation of the principle that the law is valid in itself and not because of its motivation, which furthermore is not expressed. Indeed the will of the legislator suffices for there to be law as such; it is not necessary to have recourse to external principles to justify it (meta-juridical principles). It is the inevitable opening to positivism parallel to what happened following the promulgation of the state codes: if the code by definition is rational (while custom must demonstrate this: cf. c. 27, §1), there is no need to have recourse to a *ratio* to justify it; it is self-evident.[30]

4. The Effective Reception of the 1917 Code and its Influence on Canonical Theory and the Life of the Church

In addition to what has already been expounded, to appreciate the importance of the adoption of the principle of the 1917 codification regarding the way of conceiving the Church and its law, it is necessary to consider how the Pio-Benedictine code was concretely received in the Church and, in general, in society and culture, and what has influenced such reception positively and negatively.

A first observation is positive: the code with its brevity, clarity, comprehensibility, and logical character achieved the dual purpose of rendering ecclesial discipline understandable and therefore applicable, thereby placing it at the service of pastoral action in the Church and of the consolidation of its structures.[31] However, the reception of the canonical

---

vested rights, privileges, and indults (c. 4), customs in a limited measure (c. 5), laws at least implicitly contained in the code itself (c. 6, 6°), the legislative power of instances below the Roman Pontiff (plenary and provincial councils, cc. 281-292; diocesan bishops, c. 335 §1), and the proper law of religious (c. 489). One may not forget the somewhat frequent appeal to divine law, generally understood as a reality contained in canon law (c. 6, 6°) and not as a superior and distinct source. However, in the context of the canonization of civil law in matters of contracts, canon 1529 refers generically to an eventual contradiction of divine law.

[30]   Another aspect linked partially to the adoption of the principle of codification is the systematic organization of the code. In reality the division into five books is not immediately referred to the principle of codification, but arises from Roman law through the mediation of the *Institutiones* of Lancelotti. Even the *Code civil* takes from Roman law the tripartite structure (*res, personae, actiones*), reading it in relationship to the three fundamental civil rights of freedom, property, contracts. See Cavanna, *Dal diritto comune*, 62.

[31]   On the pastoral interpretation of the 1917 code and on its continuity and service of the program of pastoral renewal of Pius X, see Astorri, 54-59.

normative system was on the whole passive; it descended from on high and was put in place through a principle of authority.[32]

Another practical exigency linked with codification was the possibility of studying the law of the Church, be it from within the Church or outside it.[33]

It is not necessary to insist on the other side of the coin of this diffusion of the study of canon law; i.e., on the limits of a canonical science which became for the most part code-oriented, to use the noted expression of Stutz,[34] based mainly on exegesis and forgetful of history,[35] detached from a link with theology (even because of a deficiency of the latter, still incapable of articulating a satisfactory ecclesiology and often, after the code, characterized by an uncritical assumption not only of the contents but also of the very code system as happened in the realm of moral theology[36]). However, when one refers to the manuals in use at the time of

[32]   In the social context of Europe during the first half of this century, reception by way of authority did not create a great problem. This was because that context was characterized globally by what might be described as a favorable predisposition toward authority and law, and it was an ecclesial context where both ecclesiology and, even more strongly, the *sensus fidelium* were globally oriented to exalt the role of the Supreme Pontiff.

[33]   According to the preface of Cardinal Gasparri, up to that point the study of canon law was reserved to a few clerics attracted to such study by nature and above all endowed with leisure (*otium*) and a great number of books (*magna librorum copia*). Now, according to the instructions of the Sacred Congregation for Seminaries and Universities, it was enough, in fact it was supposed to be enough, to have one book to study all of canon law. On the canonistics of this period see Georg May and Anton Egler, *Einführung in die kirchenrechtliche Methode* (Regensburg: Pustet, 1986) 86-99.

[34]   Ulrich Stutz, *Der Geist des Codex Iuris Canonici. Eine Einführung in das auf Geheiß Papst Pius X. verfasste und von Papst Benedikt XV. erlassene Gesetzbuch der katholischen Kirche* (Stuttgart: F. Enke, 1918) 169. On a non-negative reading of the expression of Stutz, on his mode of judging the 1917 code, and on his concept of the separation between history and the system of canon law (a separation to be understood for the advantage of the development of a genuine historical understanding of canon law) see Astorri, 42-85; idem, "'L'introduzione' del Falco nel dibattito sulla codificazione," in Falco, 51-79.

[35]   But the 1931 apostolic constitution *Deus scientiarum Dominus* sought to provide a remedy. See *AAS* 23 (1931) 241-262. See also the attached *Ordinationes* of the Sacred Congregation for seminaries and Universities of Studies in *AAS* 23 (1931) 263-284.

[36]   There were not lacking manuals of moral theology whose titles referred to the Code of Canon Law; some were organized according to the five books of the code. See Aldo Gorini, "Dal giuridismo preconciliare alla pastoralità postconciliare: spunti di analisi," in *Ius in Vita et in Missione Ecclesiae. Acta Symposii internationalis iuris canonici occurrente X anniversario promulgationis Codicis iuris canonici diebus 19-24 aprilis 1993 in Civitate Vaticana celebrati [Ius in vita]* (Vatican City: Np, 1994) 107-117.

the code, one aspect bears emphasizing. That is the absence of an in-depth understanding of the notion of canon law, reduced to a complex of laws, and therefore of its foundation.[37]

The dependence of this approach on codification is evident; the centrality of the code could only lead to the accentuation of the positive law and the identification of the law with it.

The picture of canonical science sketched thus far naturally needs to be nuanced. A global negative judgment regarding the canonical science subsequent to the 1917 code is not only extremely simplistic but also unjust. One cannot forget the developments at an historiographic level, the attention given to pastoral and theological problems,[38] and in the area of canonical exegesis itself the valuable contributions to the study of various institutes, e.g., matrimonial matters. The so-called lay Italian school of canonical science merits particular mention. Such a canonical current could exist only because the code was promulgated. This was because in a context characterized by a positivistic, statist, dogmatic conception of law such as was true for Italy in the first half of this century, only a code similar to those in use in the states could justify the juridical character of canon law, the possibility of a scientific study,[39] and the application to it of the methodology of juridic dogmatics. Lay Italian canonical science then led to an apparently paradoxical outcome. It maximally developed the potentialities inherent in codification and above all in the method of juridic dogmatics, without forgetting to evaluate properly the juridic character and the specificity of the canonical system. However, it also highlighted all the limits of a theory, which, taking the positive character

---

[37] One has the impression of a homogeneity of manuals in this regard. The schema is always the same: an etymological explanation of the concept of law, a reference to justice, a distinction between subjective and objective law and the prevalence of the latter, a definition of canon law as a "complexus legum sive a Deo sive ab ecclesiastica potestate latarum, quibus constitutio atque regimen et disciplina Ecclesiae catholicae ordinatur" (Wernz-Vidal, 1: *Normae generales*, 2nd. ed. [Rome: PUG, 1952] 68-69). See also the manuals of Blat, Cappello, Naz, etc. Even Eichmann-Mörsdorf is not free from this approach, at least in part. See Carlo Redaelli, *Il concetto di diritto della Chiesa nella riflessione canonistica tra Concilio e Codice* (Milan: Glossa, 1991) 60-62.

[38] This was true above all in German canonical science stimulated by the challenge of Protestant canon law, be it at the level of an understanding of church law or at the level of theological reflection on the law which concentrated on the law-gospel relationship. See, for example, the thought of Gottlieb Söhngen, articulated on the eve of Vatican II: *Grundfragen einer Rechtstheologie* (Munich: Anton Pustet, 1962).

[39] It should not be forgotten that one of the problems of lay Italian canonists was justifying their proper presence in faculties of jurisprudence in Italian universities.

of law as a point of departure, could only relegate to the level of the meta-juridic what is instead at the center of the ecclesial juridical reality.[40]

Another aspect favored by codification was that of relationships with states in particular through the instrumentality of the concordat. The fact that the code wisely avoided codifying public external law[41] and had aligned certain aspects of canonical legislation with that of modern states, permitted a structuring of the relationship with the states through a translation of the concept of *societas perfecta*, typical of heretofore tra-ditional ecclesial reflection, into a more current concept of a primary ju-ridical order, thereby in a certain sense rendering state and church com-parable in the context of modern international law.[42]

Finally, as regards the relationship between code law and particular law, it must be observed that the code did not signal the end of the pro-duction of this latter type of law. One needs think only of the continuation of the phenomenon of the celebration of diocesan synods and plenary and provincial councils, which experienced an increase after the middle of the 19th century.[43] De facto, however, the attraction exercised by the code and

[40]   On lay Italian canonical science see Giorgio Feliciani, "La scuola canonistica laica italiana dal dogmatismo giuridico al post-Concilio," in *Scienza giuridica e diritto cano-nico*, ed. Rinaldo Bertolino (Turin: G. Giappichelli, 1991) 61-80.

[41]   Notwithstanding the merited fears of some canonists (Ruffini, Sägmüller, Fried-berg). See Falco, 108-111. This gave a certain prominence to what has been defined as the "spiritualization" or "de-temporalization" of the law of the Church (Stutz). See Astorri, "'L'introduzione' del Falco," 61-66.

[42]   See Astorri, *Le leggi della Chiesa*, 87-294. The effect of codification on concordats cannot be overemphasized and is to be seen in relationship to radical changes occurring in the post-World War I period. As always in the area of church history but also in history as such, juridical elements are never detached from the concrete unfolding of events. In rela-tionship to concordats and codification Astorri has clarified how the post-1917 code con-cordats had two interesting effects in terms of the reception of ecclesial law: its acceptance in the arena of state legal systems and, what can seem strange at first, the development of particular canon law at least in some cases. Because of their attention to the local situation, including its ecclesial aspects, the concordats have in fact many times been the occasion for developing particular norms or certain particular institutes (e.g., Catholic associations) not given freedom because of the rigidity of the code. However, one must not also forget that on other occasions concordatary norms had the effect of homogenizing particular laws vis-à-vis the code law.

[43]   Eugenio Corecco, *La formazione della Chiesa Cattolica degli Stati Uniti attraverso l'attività sinodale con particolare riguardo al problema dell'amministrazione dei beni ec-clesiastici* (Brescia: Morcelliana, 1970); René Metz, "Organismes collegiaux et moyens de gouvernement," *Histoire du droit et des institutions de l'Eglise en Occident*, 17: *Le droit et les institutions de l'Eglise catholique latine de la fin du XVIIIème siècle à 1978* (Paris: Cujas, 1982) 120-124, 138-142.

the prevalence of centralist orientations led the local legislator to repeat, sometimes literally, the approach and content of the code.[44] Something analogous can be said regarding the influence of the code on the adaptation of the proper law of existing religious orders and congregations and on the shaping of the norms of those founded after 1917.[45]

C. The Codification of 1983-1990 for the Latin Church and the Eastern Churches

We spent time on the 1917 codification because the principle of codification played an extremely significant role in it. Even in the very phases which preceded and followed the promulgation of the code there are impressive parallels with the phenomenon of codification in the European states mentioned at the beginning: the imposing of a rationalistic character on practical exigencies and theoretical visions, the first public and private attempts at reform, the redaction of the code text which de facto restated the operative law but in the totally new context of codification, the inevitable outcome in exegesis and in a positivist vision.[46] Certainly, and we have seen this, there are distinct characteristics of canonical codification. But it is the very way of conceiving the Church as a *societas perfecta* which offers an ideological option only apparently very different from what guides state codification. In reality such a theory, putting the Church and State on the same level, offers an optimal bridge for an uncritical assumption of the principle of codification, even for the myth itself of codification.

1.   The Directive Principles of 1967 (*CIC*) and 1974 (*CCEO*) and the Issues in Canonical Science between the Council and the Code

The principles for the revision of the code were presented and discussed at the first synod of bishops in October 1967.[47] As was affirmed in

---

[44]   Sergio Ferrari, "I sinodi diocesani del post-Concilio," *Aggiornamenti sociali* 39 (1988) 362.

[45]   A legal system *praeter Codicem* that continued to develop even after 1917 was that of so-called missionary law. See Raymond Naz, s.v. "Missions (Le droit des)," in *DDC* 6: 908-916.

[46]   Eugenio Corecco, "I presupposti culturali ed ecclesiologici del nuovo 'Codex,'" in *Il nuovo Codice di diritto canonico*, ed. Silvio Ferrari (Bologna: Il Mulino, 1983) 44-45. See also Hervé Legrand, "Grâce et institution dans l'Église: les fondements théologiques du droit canonique," in *L'Église: institution et foi*, ed. Jean-Louis Monneron et al. (Brussels: Factultés universitaires Saint-Louis, 1979) 142-155.

[47]   For the text of the principles, the report (*relatio*) and the responses of Cardinal Felici, and the synodal voting see *Communicationes* 1 (1969) 77-100.

the preface to the 1983 code, which synthesizes them, they were effectively the guidelines for the whole succeeding work of the consultors.[48] An analogous function was served by the directive principles for the revision of the Eastern Code of Canon Law[49] approved in 1974 even if they were only partly restated in the respective preface.[50] Therefore, with due regard for certain necessary distinctions, they can be considered together in relationship to the topics which interest us.

First of all the decision emerged that the two codes be one for the two spheres. While for the Eastern Churches this was justified by a desire for greater unity but also a concrete guarantee for the preservation of the proper discipline of each Church, for the Latin Church the fifth principle explicitly rejected the hypothesis of particular statutes at the national level.[51] There was thus a fear that the unity of ecclesiastical discipline could be broken (even as to "legislative tecniques" [*quoad technicam legislativam*]) in favor of national churches, even if provision is made for particular legislation.[52]

The juridical nature of the two codes is thereby fixed and justified. Upon further reflection it seems strange that we have to emphasize the juridic nature of a code, which is never doubted in state law. The fact that it was necessary to reaffirm it for canon law indicates that at the beginning

[48]   "Ac re vera his principiis consultores in novo Codice textu elaborando veluti manu ducti sunt." *Praefatio*, in *Codex Iuris Canonici* (Vatican City: Libreria Editrice Vaticana, 1983) xxiii.

[49]   They are published in various languages in *Nuntia* n. 3 (1976) 3-24.

[50]   *Praefatio*, in *Codex Canonum Ecclesiarum Orientalium* (Vatican City: Libreria Editrice Vaticana, 1990).

[51]   "Statuta peculiaria . . . quae veluti formam praebeant specificam legibus ecclesiarum nationalium."

[52]   One can be a bit surprised that this space is justified by an appeal to the principle of subsidiarity, which is operative in any society and hence even in the Church, and not instead in reference to the mystery of the Church and therefore to the nature of the particular churches and the *communio ecclesiarum*. However, it must be kept in mind that the obvious conceptual system was that of centralization; in a certain sense decentralization was justified concretely by appealing to the principle of subsidiarity in the ecclesial arena through the mediation of the nature of the society proper to the Church. In the Eastern directive principles the reference to the principle of subsidiarity is made in a context in which the specificity of the discipline of each particular Church is highly emphasized, taking as a point of departure the concrete situation of the particular Churches. On the principle of subsidiarity see Joseph Komonchak, "Subsidiarity in the Church: The State of the Question," in *The Nature and Future of Episcopal Conferences* (Washington: Catholic University of America Press, 1988; also *The Jurist* 48 [1988]) 298-349 (with rich bibliographical notations).

of the reform efforts the parallelism between the canonical code and the civil codes was no longer operative in the self-consciousness of the people of God. In other words, one could not simply presuppose that "code" meant automatically a systematic, rational, complete collection of norms based on the will of the legislator.[53] The Western and Eastern directive principles therefore felt obliged to emphasize the juridic nature (of the codes) not so much in reference to the principle of codification or their similarity to modern state codes, but rather in terms of an appeal to the societal nature of the Church (with the necessity of regulating rights and duties)[54] and, in the first principle for the Latin code, in terms of the power of jurisdiction given by Christ to the hierarchy.

To speak of the juridical nature of the two codes today means rejecting the hypothesis that the principal purpose of the code is to propose a rule of faith and morals (*regula fidei et morum*) and that it has a dogmatic character. However, what is striking is that all the other directive principles insist on emphasizing the pastoral character of the code, its orientation to a supernatural purpose, the necessity of providing room for the sphere of the internal forum, the appropriateness of the norms being tempered by equity and not being overly rigid, the advisability of minimizing the number of norms when indications, exhortations, suggestions, etc. suffice. The underlying mindset is clear: the fact that the Church is a society means that it has a juridic element, which is qualified by a whole series of specific factors that differentiate it from juridic elements in civil societies. One may ask if it is proper to consider what is specific to the Church as an exception with regard to the juridic element in general or whether it is much more fruitful to do the opposite: to take as a starting point what is proper to the ecclesial juridic reality in defining it with a reading of the ecclesial juridic phenomenon based on internal criteria.[55]

---

[53] For Lombardía the emphasis on the juridical character of the code is motivated by opposition to anti-juridical currents and to the imperfect legislative technique in the post-conciliar documents. In his view the code succeeded in this purpose while conceding something to pastoral concerns and being less rigorously juridical. See Pedro Lombardía, "Técnica jurídica del nuevo Código (una primera aproximación al tema)," in *Temas fundamentales en el nuevo Código*, XVIII Semana Española de Derecho Canónico (Salamanca: Universidad Pontificia, 1984) 159-160.

[54] The ninth principle of the Latin codification refers to the societal nature of the Church as the justification for the presence of penal law in the Church to the extent that it is a *societas perfecta*.

[55] Endogenous rather than exogenous criteria, to use terminology dear to Remigiusz Sobański, "Modell des Kirche-Mysteriums als Grundlage der Teorie des Kirchenrechts," *Archiv für katholisches Kirchenrecht* 145 (1976) 22-24.

In other words, is "sociality" in the Church equivalent to other types of "sociality" even given its specificity, or is it something else, concretely *communio*? And therefore, is church law a law equivalent to that of civil societies even given its proper character or is it something to be defined in terms of ecclesial communion? In this sense ought it not be a *regula fidei et morum*? All these themes began to be discussed in postconciliar canonical science along with the reform of the code,[56] yet their solution is probably still to be developed.

However, it is interesting that from the directive principles there emerged a shift in the canonical debate from the problem of codification to the problem of the nature and the meaning of law in the Church. This does not mean that there were no proposals regarding individual points of the new legislation or reflections on modalities of the same,[57] but the question was why and for what reason does law exist in the Church.[58]

2.   The Project of the *Lex Ecclesiae Fundamentalis*

The project of drawing up a *Lex Ecclesiae fundamentalis*, practically initiated with the effective beginnings of the work of reforming the 1917 code and officially abandoned only on the eve of the promulgation of the current Latin code, merits particular attention in reference to the topic we

---

[56]   For a framework of fundamental questions debated between the end of the council and the promulgation of the code see Redaelli, above all the bibliography on pp. 299-325. He also examines the contributions of currents of thought or individual authors not belonging to the three schools studied in the volume.

[57]   Among the other proposals recall Peter Huizing, "The Reform of Canon Law," in *Pastoral Reform in Church Government*, ed. Teodoro Jiménez Urresti et al., Concilium 8 (New York: Paulist, 1965) 95-128; the articles contained in *The Revised Code of Canon Law: A Missed Opportunity?*, ed. Piet Huizing and Knut Walf, Concilium 147 (Edinburgh: T & T Clark, 1981); Bonnet (with an ample bibliography); Francesco Finocchiaro, "La codificazione del diritto canonico e l'ora presente," in *La Chiesa dopo il Concilio. Atti del Congresso internazionale di diritto canonico Roma 14-19 gennaio 1970* (Milan: A. Giuffrè, 1972) 2: 647-667. Of interest is the view of Cardinal Felici, the president of the Commission for the Revision of the Latin code, who was dogmatically in favor of codification but was also conscious of the dangers connected with it. See *Communicationes* 5 (1973) 249.

[58]   See the title of an essay by Peter Krämer which indicates the fundamental question for post-code canonistics: *Warum und wozu kirchliches Recht? Zum Stand der Grundlagendiskussion in der katholischen Kirchenrechtswissenschaft* (Trier: Paulinus, 1979).

are treating. It is not certain that this is the place to analyze the successive schemata or the work of the Commission[59] or even the various interventions of scholars.[60] It is interesting to recall that the ambiguity surrounding the proposal and understanding of a fundamental law has on the one hand set aside the project and the very idea of it—and this can be considered as something positive or negative depending on one's viewpoint. On the other hand it has constrained both scholars and public ecclesial opinion in general to focus attention on certain decisive issues for the law of the Church (given the broad resonance which the problem of the fundamental law occasioned).

The ambiguity was due to the fact that the fundamental law was understood in very different ways.[61] This led to multiple problems which went beyond the question of the fundamental law. Does law in the Church make sense? What is law in the Church? What is the relationship between ecclesiology and canon law? Whether and how a dogmatic fact can be translated into juridical language? Whether and under what conditions certain juridical techniques originating in an extra-ecclesial context can be applied to the reality of the Church? It is a matter of questions and corresponding responses which are mutually interrelated and connected.[62]

---

[59] To reconstruct them one will find very helpful the indices published in *Communicationes* 19 (1987) 304-308.

[60] For an initial orientation, consult the following collective works which offer a broad panorama of different positions: *Legge e vangelo. Discussione su una legge fondamentale per la Chiesa* (Brescia: Paideia, 1972); *Lex fundamentalis Ecclesiae. Atti della Tavola Rotonda, Macerata, 12-13 ottobre 1971*, ed. Attilio Moroni (Milan: Giuffrè, 1973); *De lege Ecclesiae fundamentali condenda. Conventus canonistarum Hispano-Germanus Salmanticae diebus 20-31 ianuarii 1972 habitus* (Salamanca: Instituto "San Raimundo de Peñafort," 1974); *El proyecto de Ley Fundamental de la Iglesia. Texto y analisís critico* (Pamplona: Redacción Ius Canonicum, 1976).

[61] For example, as a common code containing the *ius constitutivum* of the Church and valid for the Latin Church and the Eastern Church, each endowed with its own code (this was the initial hypothesis of Paul VI, manifest already in 1965 to the members and consultors of the commission. See *AAS* 57 [1965] 985-989); as the opportunity to translate into juridical language the ecclesiology of Vatican II; as an operation of restoration of an old juridical and authoritarian ecclesiological conception as opposed to the ecclesiology of Vatican II; as the application to the Church of the technical details of constitutional law, articulated in relationship to states even for a better protection of the rights of the faithful.

[62] It is evident that if there is no reason to speak of law in the Church, all other problems are radically resolved. Or to give another example: if law in the Church is formally identical to the law of the state and is differentiated only in terms of the material, one automatically resolves affirmatively the problem of adopting techniques from the world of civil law, and besides such techniques, the *ideologies* underlying them.

Hence the question of the fundamental law was an important moment in posing, if not resolving, a series of fundamental questions. One can say, at least in part, that in this case, although perhaps it may hardly be noticed, the very problems posed by the adoption of the principle of codification are represented more than fifty years after the adoption of modern constitutional law.

But the episode of the fundamental law is interesting even from a final perspective: that of reception. The manifest refusal of the idea of the fundamental law, even outside academic circles, be it conditioned and in part emphasized by a series of contingent factors,[63] shows very well that one cannot discount the reception by the people of God of something developed outside a common ecclesial sensibility even with the best of intentions.

3.   The Apostolic Constitutions Promulgating the Two Codes and the Orientations of John Paul II

Particular attention is directed to the two apostolic constitutions *Sacrae disciplinae leges*[64] and *Sacri Canones*[65] by which the two legislative texts were promulgated. This is to determine the interpretation of the recent and double task of codification by the same legislator and to understand the factors of an ecclesiological character even in reference to reception.

If one compares the two documents, they reveal a significant diversity of concepts. The first constitution insists above all on two themes: the continuity and instrumentality of the code vis-à-vis the council and the justification of its necessity for the Church. The second, however, underscores three points: the continuity between the code and the patrimony of *sacri canones* typical of the Eastern Churches, the role and the necessity of particular law, the relationship with the Latin code and the constitution on the Roman Curia *Pastor bonus*.

---

[63]   In an ecclesial context already suspicious of Rome and characterized by a negative prejudice toward whatever could smack of the juridical and of authority, even a certain secrecy regarding the *schemata* and the skillful journalistic violation of such with the publication and divulging of what was *sub secreto*, contributed to focusing attention on the topic of the fundamental law not only of those involved in the work but also of the faithful in general.

[64]   January 25, 1983: *AAS* 75/2 (1983) vii-xiv.

[65]   October 18, 1990: *AAS* 82 (1990) 1033-1044.

The difference in content, however, reflects an identical intention: to address the most discussed problems in the two contexts, i.e., those therefore that presumably could create the most difficulties for its reception. In the Latin Church effectively the problem was faithfulness to the council and its not being distorted by using canonical language—one thinks of the eruption of this question on the occasion of the fundamental law project—and, moreover, the justification of a role of law in the Church. In the context of the Eastern Churches, however, the problem was to justify a complete and unique legislation of common discipline while also safeguarding the disciplinary identity of the individual Churches.

As regards the problem of codification as such, it seems interesting to note that while in *Sacri Canones* it does not play a particular role except in the sense indicated, in *Sacrae disciplinae leges* there is a notable emphasis on the code.[66] Such an emphasis is explained by the substantial identification of the code and canon law. From the moment that the code is viewed as the "primary legislative document of the Church" (*primarium documentum legiferum Ecclesiae*), there are applied to it all the motivations customarily employed to justify the meaning of law in the Church. Despite a reference to the "doctrine whereby the Church is viewed as a communion," the fundamental motivation is based on the fact that the Church is a society and therefore "needs norms," i.e., the code.[67] It is also justified in relationship to its specific content reflecting the ecclesiology of Vatican II.[68] The question is hardly raised about

---

[66]   "Codex eo potius spectat, ut talem gignat ordinem in ecclesiali societati, qui praecipuas partes tribuente amoris, gratiae atque charismatibus, eodem tempore faciliorem reddat ordinatam eorum progressionem in vita sive ecclesialis societatis, sive etiam singulorum hominum, qui ad illam pertinent. . . . Instrumentum, quod Codex est, plane congruit cum natura Ecclesiae. . . . Ac revera Codex Iuris Canonici Ecclesiae omnino necessarium est." *AAS* 75/2 (1983) xi-xii.

[67]   On the conception underlying *Sacrae disciplinae leges* regarding the nature of canon law, see Adolfo Longhitano, "Chiesa diritto e legge nella Costituzione Apostolica 'Sacrae disciplinae leges,'" in *A venti anni dal Concilio. Prospettive teologiche e giuridiche* (Palermo: OFTeS, 1984) 109-140.

[68]   However, an examination of the effective contents of the code leads to the conclusion that a societal concept of the Church prevails over a *communio* ecclesiology. See Remigiusz Sobański, "Rechtstheologische Vorüberlegungen zum neuen kirchlichen Gesetzbuch," *Theologische Quartalschrift* 163 (1983) 178-188; idem, "L'ecclésiologie du nouveau *Code de droit canonique*," in *The New Code of Canon Law: 5th International Congress of Canon Law* [*The New Code of Canon Law*] (Ottawa: St. Paul University, 1986) 1: 259-260; Eugenio Corecco, "Aspects of the Reception of Vatican II in the Code

whether it is correct to identify church law with the code, nor is the choice of codification an issue. Unless I am mistaken, the only allusion is in the preface to the Latin code in connection with the choice made of codification instead of compilation at the time of the 1917 code.

Three other interesting topics in the promulgating constitutions, in this case in relationship to the topic of reception, are the emphasis in both on the collegial character of the revision effort (which for the Eastern code means that the "Easterners themselves have carried it out"), the accent placed on the necessity that it be observed and "felicitously translated into the activities of everyday life" (phrase of Paul VI restated in *Sacri Canones*), and the relation of each code to the council, of the codes among themselves and with the law on the Roman Curia.

This last point was developed by John Paul II in two discourses given at the official presentation of the new Latin code[69] and the new Eastern code.[70] In the first the pope proposed the image of a triangle with Sacred Scripture at the base (centered on the gospel) and above it the acts of the Second Vatican Council and the code, linked, however, at the base by sides representing respectively the magisterium of the councils throughout the centuries and the centuries-old patrimony of juridic wisdom.[71] In the second, however, the supreme pontiff indicates the two codes and the apostolic constitution *Pastor bonus* as constitutive of the unique and new *Corpus iuris canonici*.[72]

4. The Reception of the 1983 Code in the Life of the Church and in Canonical Reflection

Limiting our attention to the 1983 Latin code and with an awareness of our inability to avoid simplifications, one can indicate certain directions on the topic of its reception. Above all one must recognize a substantially favorable reception on the part of canonists, which is characterized not

---

of Canon Law," in *The Reception of Vatican II*, ed. Giuseppe Alberigo et al. (Washington: The Catholic University of America Press, 1987) 249-296.

[69] *Communicationes* 15 (1983) 9-16.
[70] *Nuntia* n. 31 (1990) 10-16.
[71] See n. 9, *Communicationes* 15 (1983) 16.
[72] See n. 8, *Nuntia* n. 31 (1990) 13.

by a naive attitude but rather by one that is cognizant of the values but also of the limitations of the legislative effort of 1983.[73]

It does not seem that there are particular difficulties in receiving the new legislation as a whole on the part of the people of God: it has already become part of everyday ecclesial practice.[74] In this sense the positive aspects of the instrument of the code, already present in the 1917 codification and substantially linked to its practical character, continue to exist.[75] Besides it is recognized that the 1983 code, with due regard for its limitations, de facto contributes to the translation of the contents of the council into ecclesial consciousness and practice, above all at the level of structures. One thinks of the various organisms of participation.

One should also consider the fact that even in general terms the code has not blocked but in certain respects has favored a development of particular law, at the level of the episcopal conferences or at the level of dioceses. The first application of the code actuated in particular by episcopal conferences,[76] even with its limitations, can also be considered as a

---

[73] See, for example, the reflections proposed by Eugenio Corecco in "Aspetti della ricezione: i presupposti culturali ed ecclesiologici"; idem, "Theological Justifications of the Codification of the Latin Canon Law," in *The New Code of Canon Law*, 69-96.

[74] For the reception of the code in different cultural settings see for Germany: Winfried Schulz, "Problem der Reception des neuen Codex Iuris Canonici in der Bundesrepublik Deutschland," in *Recht als Heilsdienst. Matthäus Kaiser zum 65 Geburtstag gewidmet von seinen Freunden, Kollegen und Schülern*, ed. Winfried Schulz (Paderborn: F. Schöningh, 1989) 144-159; Richard Puza, "L'attuazione del nuovo codice di diritto canonico in Germania," *Quaderni di Diritto e Politica Ecclesiastica* 1994/1: 159-178; for Spain: Agustin Motilla, "Aplicación y desarrollo del Código de Derecho Canónico en España," ibid., 179-194; for France: Jean Paul Durand, "Echos de la mise en oeuvre en France du nouveau Code latin de droit canonique par la Conférence des évêques," ibid., 195-217; for the United States and Canada: James H. Provost, "L'applicazione del Codice del 1983 in Canada e negli Stati Uniti," ibid., 219-228.

[75] It is a question of the following characteristics: organic and systematic presentation of the law of the Church, possibility of easy knowledge, understandable and recognizable modality of juridical expression even outside the ecclesial arena (thus it is possible, for example, that new concordat agreements can make easy reference to the legislation of the Church). See the citation of the 1983 code in the premises of the Agreement on the Revision of the Lateran Treaty, stipulated February 18, 1984 between the Holy See and the Italian state.

[76] To have an idea of the development of what can be described as "complementary law," developed by the episcopal conferences, see the collection: José T. Martín de Agar, *Legislazione delle conferenze episcopali complementare al C.I.C.* (Milan: Giuffrè, 1990) and for the Italian experience alone Mario Marchesi, *Diritto complementare italiano. La normativa della CEI* (Bologna: Dehoniane, 1992).

first promising step toward a normative pluralism, more attentive to the developing life of the Church.[77] The impression of a certain disorganized character in particular legislation and of a lack of formal precision is due among other things to the fact that the scope attributed to particular law in the code is more a matter of a specific reference to it on individual points rather than an organic provision for such even if it is formally coordinated with the instrumentality of the code. In other words the code does not envision a type of "code" at the local level coordinated with the universal level. It can be an advantage not to tie particular law to a suffocating formality since by definition it is more attentive to the pluralism and changeableness of different situations of ecclesial life. But it can also be a sign at a formal level of a *lacuna* in the way of conceiving the autonomous and organic juridic responsibility of the particular churches.

An aspect of non-reception of the code is instead its marginalization at the level of the magisterium, public ecclesial opinion, and theological reflection. This is a question of evidently different but mutually related phenomena which should be studied in an analytical fashion. Remaining at the level of impressions and subject to correction, one can affirm that often magisterial interventions, even on matters certainly linked to what can be considered church law, do not take due account of the provisions in the code or ignore its existence—even while citing extensively the conciliar texts but not the code texts derived from them, or attributing a marginal role to the latter.[78] Public ecclesial opinion, in turn, while it is not inattentive to individual aspects of the ecclesial legal system,[79] seems to consider the juridical in general as a reality of secondary importance

---

[77]   At the diocesan level what seems particularly interesting is the recovery of the synodal phenomenon. Even in this case it is a question of an experience which manifests evident limitations at the level of procedure, efficiency (often the time and commitment linked to the synodal event appear disproportionate to the ultimate influence of the final documents on the concrete life of the Church), normative precision (the unresolved relationship between law and pastoral practice and the continuing prejudice regarding disciplinary aspects of the Church do not help in this regard). See Ferrari, "I sinodi diocesani," 351-363 (*supra*, note 44).

[78]   A particularly noteworthy case is the March 25, 1992 post-synodal apostolic exhortation *Pastores dabo vobis*, dedicated to the topic of priestly formation. If I am not mistaken, it cites the code only three times in a footnote (notes 111 and 230) but *never* a canon from the extensive and, in the judgment of scholars, well done part which the code dedicates to the formation of clerics (cc. 232-264). See Francesco Coccopalmerio, "La formazione al ministero ordinato," *La Scuola Cattolica* 112 (1984) 219-251.

[79]   One thinks of matrimonial topics or those regarding the parish or organs of participation.

even if it is somewhat tolerable.[80] Finally one can say that theological reflection in general ignores ecclesial law or discounts it frequently as reflecting a positivist conception. Ecclesiology itself seems to have noticed only recently the need to engage in a reflection on the juridical dimension of the Church and to initiate a dialogue with canonical thought.[81] There are interesting indications in this regard; however, for the moment they are at the level of good intentions.[82] What is the reason for this non-reception, which in reality attacks not just the code but the juridical dimension of the Church? The reasons can be multiple; e.g., the incapacity of canonical thought to make itself understood, the minimal dialogue among the disciplines, the permanence of an anti-juridic prejudice in the Church and in today's culture. The most genuine and profound reason, however, seems to be the uncritical acceptance of an identification of the code and ecclesial law with the acceptance, even if entirely implicit and unconscious, of an underlying positivistic conception of ecclesial law based on the fact that the Church is a society and not instead a communion. Until we overcome such a canon law-norm (code) identification or express ourselves with other concepts, the identification of institutional law with legislative law,[83] and unless we have a "theologically" satisfac-

---

[80] For what can be a sign of the ecclesial relevance of disciplines and not of concrete persons, consider the different ecclesial esteem reserved to the exegete, the theologian, the pastoral expert, and the sociologist vis-à-vis the canonist.

[81] See Louis Bouyer, *L'Église de Dieu. Corps du Christ et Temple de l'Esprit* (Paris: Cerf, 1970) 228ff; Angel Antón, "Postconciliar Ecclesiology," in *Vatican II. Assessment and Perspectives Twenty-Five Years After (1962-1987)*, ed. René Latourelle (Mahwah, NJ: Paulist, 1988) 1: 424.

[82] Of some significance are the reflections of Tullio Citrini in a recent course of ecclesiological updating promoted by the Italian Theological Association: "The recognition of the theological nature of canonical science has led more theologically inclined canonists to develop a theological ecclesiology useful for their purposes, sometimes incorporating fragments of ecclesiology found in the work of systematicians. . . . It is not entirely the fault of canonists. . . . The more ecclesiologists disdain law or neglect its legitimate appeals, the more canonists construct their own ecclesiology (those, it is understood, who do not decide to do without it entirely). . . . In reality systematic ecclesiology has its own exigencies and methods; carefully pursued according to its originality and verified in a closed debate among systematicians, they can be valuable for ecclesial law provided they are not short-circuited." Tullio Citrini, "Questioni di metodo dell'ecclesiologia postconciliare," in *L'ecclesiologia contemporanea*, ed. D. Valentini (Padua: EMP, 1994) 21-22.

[83] On the distinction between law and norm, see Francesco Coccopalmerio, "Diritto ecclesiale e norma canonica. Appunti per una riflessione su distinzione e rapporti tra due realtà," *La Scuola Cattolica* 110 (1982) 404-515 (also in *Diritto, persona e vita sociale. Scritti in memoria di Orio Giacchi* [Milan: Giuffrè, 1984] 258-269). As regards the distinction between institutional law and legislative law, see Legrand, 139-172, esp. 155-167 (*supra*, note 46), who takes up again the theories of Dombois.

tory understanding of the juridical dimension of the Church, we cannot have a real and correct reception of law in the Church even if other difficulties were overcome.

Finally another question is noted which is always linked to the conception of ecclesial law: what are the sources of law in the Church? In other words how are the codes and other normative documents to be coordinated with the conciliar texts, certainly frequently restated verbatim in the code texts,[84] and with other texts, unequivocally containing the law for the Church?[85] The allusion of John Paul to a new *Corpus Iuris Canonici* constituted by the two codes and *Pastor bonus* can perhaps indicate a way to overcome the dichotomy between the code norms and other expressions of the juridical nature of the Church without thereby losing the positive benefits acquired by the use of the technique of codification.[86]

CONCLUSIONS

The principle of codification, as it has been developed in the context of European juridical thought, has not been simply the proposal of the adoption of a technique. A double ideology lies behind it: a rationalist natural law ideology at the outset, and then a positivistic state ideology.

In the technique of codification the Church has found practical help in resolving problems which in certain respects were analogous to those of

---

[84]   It seems reductionist in the interpretation of code provisions to view the preeminent role of the council, authoritatively proposed by the Supreme Pontiff, solely in terms of a recourse to the mind of the legislator (*mens legislatoris*), which canon 17 of the code (cf. *CCEO* c. 1499) presents as a subsidiary and not the principal criterion of interpretation. For a reflection on the juridical relevance of the council, see Pietro Gismondi, *Il diritto della Chiesa dopo il Concilio* (Milan: Giuffrè, 1973) 35-58.

[85]   For example, one thinks of the criteria of "ecclesiality" for lay groupings presented by *Christifideles laici*. Undoubtedly one is dealing with criteria having a juridical relevance, determining the relationship between such lay groupings and the ecclesial *communio* in view of judging and recognizing them ("ad discernendas et agnoscendas huiusmodi laicales aggregationes": *Christifideles laici*, n. 30). Based on the conciliar teaching, these criteria are not present in the two codes, which seem to be concerned only with the phenomenon of associations in the strict sense and not with groupings in general. Nor are such criteria expressed with the usual technical juridical formalities, but rather they are manifestations of an ecclesial juridic character. See regarding a document of the Italian bishops on lay groupings, Carlo Redaelli, "Le aggregazioni laicali nella Chiesa. Una recente nota pastorale della CEI," *Quaderni di Diritto Ecclesiale* 6 (1993) 441-453.

[86]   Another case of minimal coordination between juridic sources is the so-called liturgical law. Canon 2 of the Latin code and canon 3 of the Eastern code refer respectively to

states; e.g., dispersion and multiplicity of norms, inability to know them and implement them, etc. But in the contemporary period the Church has also absorbed the ideology, even if mediated through its referral to the concept of the perfect society. The reception of the principle of codification on the part of the Church therefore has not been ideologically neutral nor without pertinent and particularly serious consequences. It has accentuated a positivistic vision of canon law; it has based the rational and obligatory character of the norm on the principle of authority; it has led to the marginalization of what was and is specific in the canonical tradition; it has emphasized ecclesial centralization.

The lack of an ecclesiology articulated in a satisfactory fashion even in reference to the juridical dimension of the Church and the comparable lack of a convincing definition and understanding of church law in canonical circles has precluded the assumption of the principle or at least the technique of codification from finding in the consciousness of the Church intra-ecclesial critical instances capable of filtering the ideological presuppositions connected with codification.

If this were true for the 1917 code, the legislative endeavor leading to the 1983 code and to a certain extent the 1990 code thought that it resolved the problems by calmly using a *technique*, indeed already widely praised in 1917, detached from the *ideology* of codification (given the deficiencies of the *myth* of codification even in extra-ecclesial juridical thought).[87] It was thought that the limitations of the 1917 code at the level of its systematic basis and its content could be overcome as much as possible by drawing on the council. This has been more evident in reference to the Eastern codification where the myth of codification played a marginal role, different from the Latin codification,[88] where a signifi-

---

the liturgical laws and the prescriptions of the liturgical books; but then both codes, especially the Latin code, treat extensively of the *munus sanctificandi*, referring many times to elements which remain abstracted from a more profound consideration as regards those presented in the liturgical books. However, the literary genre of the liturgical *praenotanda* seems particularly effective in situating normative prescriptions in a broader context which permits an interpretation and observance of them which is not rubrically but ecclesially significant.

[87] A parallel between the crisis of law, and in particular of codification, in the state legal orders and in the canonical order has been drawn by Finocchiaro (*supra*, note 57).

[88] For a precise specification of the difference between the two codifications and for the historical and ecclesiological substratum which justifies them in different ways, see Ivan Žužek, "Incidenza del 'Codex Canonum Ecclesiarum Orientalium' nella storia moderna della Chiesa universale," in *Ius in vita*, 675-735.

cant heritage of the myth has remained present through the precedent of the 1917 code if not otherwise.[89]

In reality the recent codification activity has not resolved the fundamental questions. Among other things this is demonstrated by the problematic of the fundamental law, set aside but not resolved.[90] As regards the technique of constitutional law, this problematic has reproduced the same problems referred to codification and has uncovered the fragility of the ecclesial understanding of canon law and its inadequacy in dealing with the juridical world. This is evidenced also in the unsatisfactory understanding of church law present in the directive principles and in *Sacrae disciplinae leges* itself, with its tendency to identify the code and canon law and with the societal, and therefore extrinsic, justification of the juridical dimension of the Church, be it in general or in relationship to its specific aspects.[91] This is underscored also by the lack of a technical but primarily theoretical coordination of the sources of church law in an organic *Corpus*.[92]

In conclusion one can still ask if the format of codification would have been possible in a theologically correct context reflective of a satisfactory understanding of the Church and its law. One need not respond negatively. As such, all its juridical techniques in principle can be useful in

---

[89]   For a comparison between the two Latin codifications see René Metz, "Les deux codifications du droit de l'Église," in *Vitam impendere vero. Studi in onore di Pio Ciprotti*, ed. Winfried Schulz and Giorgio Feliciani (Vatican City: Libreria Editrice Vaticana, 1986) 185-207; Alfons M. Stickler, "Der *Codex iuris canonici* von 1983 im Lichte der Kodifikationsgeschichte des Kirchenrechts," in *The New Code of Canon Law*, 1: 97-104. See also Piero A. Bonnet, "La codificazione canonica nel sistema delle fonti tra continuità e discontinuità," in Francesco Coccopalmerio, Piero A. Bonnet and Nicola Pavoni, *Perché un Codice nella Chiesa* (Bologna: Dehoniane, 1984) 57-125.

[90]   Eugenio Corecco justifies the choice of the 1983 codification as if it were a *surrogate* for the fundamental law. That is, the code would be explained as a constitutional framework within which the juridic expression of the particular churches could be developed with a certain security within the bond of the *communio ecclesiarum*. See "Theological Justifications," 69-96.

[91]   The justification of patrimonial, penal, and procedural law offered by the 1983 code is unequivocally based on the fact that the Church is a society. See Eugenio Corecco, "Aspects of Reception," 256-263.

[92]   In this regard the idea of a fundamental code will surface again, purified of all the misunderstandings that emerged in the debate on the fundamental law as a framework-law or an index-law, which offers the context for articulating the development of and coordinating the various normative levels (Latin Church and Eastern Churches, groupings of particular churches, and individual church, etc.) and normative areas (e.g., the liturgical law), expressed, if it be the case, also with different juridical formalities.

expressing the Church's juridical reality. But on a double condition. Above all that they are viewed as *techniques* and not *ideologies*, and do not introduce, even surreptitiously, extraneous—much less damaging—elements into the understanding of the Church. Naturally this requires a work of filtering and rethinking of the techniques themselves in relation to an ecclesial context, often very different from the one in which they originated, a work which can be difficult and demand a long maturation period.[93] The second condition is that such juridical techniques be effectively useful in expressing ecclesial reality and that they be able to be adapted to it and in turn not force it into reductionist and distorted categories. The principle of usefulness determines the consideration of each technique, even the most refined and suggestive, as a technique and not as a myth. This entails also the contingent character of each technique; it is used to the extent that it serves the goals for which it is employed.[94]

Is a codification still useful today for the Church? Weighing the advantages and disadvantages, one could say yes.[95] Will this be true in the

[93] It will be neither easy nor immediate even at the level of juridic techniques to compare the canonical tradition, linked to a Roman-Germanic juridical conception, and other juridical conceptions. See Jean Imbert, "Le Code de Droit Canonique de 1983 et le Droit Romain," *L'Année Canonique* 28 (1984) 1-12. However, it will be inevitable, above all at the level of the particular churches, and it will be addressed in a correct fashion to avoid the errors of the past. See Remigiusz Sobański, "Diritto canonico e cultura," in *Scienza giuridica e diritto canonico*, 121-150; Philippe Antoine, "Le code de droit canonique face aux exigences de l'inculturation," *L'Année Canonique* 34 (1991) 175-204.

[94] One may take as a point of departure the 1996 discourse of the pope to the Rota (see *L'Osservatore Romano* [January 22-23, 1996] 6), which emphasizes the public nature of the marriage process (the scope is to ascertain the objectivity of an ecclesial status) and notes the incongruity of applying to it procedural norms not in keeping with its purpose. If one does so, one can hypothesize a more specific shape of the canonical marriage process, abstracting from the context of the ordinary contentious trial. Or even more radically one can envision that the clarification of the status of a believer can be achieved in a way different from the current procedure.

[95] Eugenio Corecco, for example, emphasizes among its contributions the maintenance of the *catholicity* of the Church, overcoming the centralization of the 1917 code, however without losing its positive features. See "I presupposti culturali ed ecclesiologici," 39-43. René Metz offers another example in stating that "the new code is far from perfect, but it does not close the door to the future; it contains the seeds of a possible adaptation to the changes which are manifest in society today and which await those of tomorrow. This is not the least of its qualities." See Metz, 207 (*supra*, note 89).

future? It may be. The real problem is the Church succeeding in expressing its juridical dimension correctly tomorrow, indeed in a more satisfactory way than today. The how is secondary.

Translation by Thomas J. Green

RESPONSE TO CARLO REDAELLI

PETER KRÄMER*

Since Redaelli's statements merit approval, for the most part, this article will express some additional, partly critical comments.

Multiple Levels in the Legal System as a Prerequisite for Reception

Law and legal development are always integrated into a cohesive socio-cultural region. A worldwide law that ignores this would be ineffective and lose its force. It follows, for the codification of ecclesiastical law, that a worldwide code must have factors built into it that are able to regulate the application of the law to a particular region. Otherwise, the adoption and further development of the law will be rejected by the particular churches and particular regions. The short life of the 1917 code is an eloquent witness to this: the former code lost its viability after only sixty-five years, and even before that it had already lost some of its effectiveness through non-observance.

A multilevel structure is more clearly recognizable in the 1983 code. This is true in so far as the current code contains several areas understood as skeleton law that must be filled in by particular legislation; for example, the promotion of ecumenical concerns (c. 755 §2), regulation of lay preaching (c. 766), and the establishment of a local rite of marriage (c. 1120). The principle applicable here is that a universal law will not derogate from a particular law (on the level of a particular church or a conference of bishops) unless the universal law expressly provides otherwise (c. 20).

A multilevel structure in the legal system has been restored inasmuch as the office of bishop has risen in value and a decentralization in the ecclesial legal system has been successfully achieved. Thus, according to a provision of the Second Vatican Council (see *CD* 8), a bishop possesses

* Katholische Universität Eichstätt (Germany).

comprehensive and legislative power over the particular church entrusted to him. Of course, an exception to this is whatever is expressly reserved to the highest authority or another authority in the Church (c. 381 §1).[1] And the conference of bishops was established as a true, constitutional authority possessing legislative competence in certain areas over the particular churches that belong to it (see *CD* 37-38; cc. 447-459).[2]

If the multilevel structure of the legal system constitutes a prerequisite for the process of reception, then it should be implemented more thoroughly. In the course of the post-conciliar reform of church law it was originally planned to introduce an ecclesial constitution, a *Lex ecclesiae fundamentalis (LEF)*.[3] The ecclesial legislator was not satisfied with a unified code for the entire Catholic Church or with two codes, one for each sphere of church law. Rather, a constitution was to be drafted, which would have broken with the previous system of codification, so that the common elements binding the Eastern and Western traditions together could be provided for in a constitutional form. Such a constitution, which would have been placed above both partial codes, would have had but one purpose, to assist in achieving a stronger decentralization in the ecclesial legal order, and to guard at the same time against a division in the legal system that would obscure the nature and mission of the Church.[4] The project of an ecclesial constitution has been set aside for the time being. Its concerns, however, remain current.

By concentrating on constitutional principles that are binding on the whole Church, an ecclesial constitution could make room for an independent legal tradition in the individual, particular churches and regions. Such a constitution would be suitable, "for circumscribing the parameters of a different legal development for the particular churches and regions that have to this point belonged to the Latin Church, but which have had difficulty with the legal culture surrounding them and the Western legal tradition out of which the law of the Latin Church arose. In this connection, the young churches of Africa and Asia should be considered

---

[1]   Hubert Müller, "Zum Verhältnis zwischen Bischofskonferenz und Diözesanbischof," in *Die Bischofskonferenz. Theologischer und Juridischer Status*, ed. Hubert Müller and Hermann J. Pottmeyer (Düsseldorf: Patmos, 1989) 236-255.

[2]   Peter Krämer, "Das Verhältnis der Bischofskonferenz zum Apostolischen Stuhl," in *Die Bischofskonferenz*, 256-270.

[3]   *Communicationes* 1 (1969) 36-42, 114f.

[4]   See Heribert Schmitz, *Auf der Suche nach einem neuen Kirchenrecht* (Freiburg: Herder, 1979) 72-79; Peter Krämer, "Lex Ecclesiae Fundamentalis," in *Lexikon für Theologie und Kirche*, 3rd ed., 6: 870-871.

first."[5] Obviously, the goal is to achieve a multilevel legal system that greatly surpasses the present gradations. It certainly cannot be denied that the development of this goal would be extremely beneficial to a lively process of reception.

Reception in the Framework of Codification

The concept *receptio* is used only four times in the 1983 code. It is given a twofold meaning: (1) the reception of sacraments (cc. 276 §1; 777, 2°; 841); and (2) the reception of members into an ecclesial association (c. 307 §1). If one considers the verbal form (*recipere, receptus*), two further meanings are discovered: (1) reception into the Catholic Church after baptism had already been received in another community (cc. 11; 1086 §1; 1117; 1124), and (2) the adoption of laws or the acceptance of legally relevant decisions (cc. 6 §1, 3; 25; 40; 197).[6]

From the foregoing, it is apparent that reception as an ecclesiological reality is either not significant or not directly significant to the present legal framework of the Church. This is true also for the code of the Catholic Eastern Churches (*CCEO*) when one considers its corresponding use of the notion. Nevertheless, the question must be examined more closely to what extent the matter itself is discussed in the code. With regard to this question, two things should be noted.

First of all, the 1983 code brought about a significant change in perspective. Previously, a clerical office holder was considered the only legitimate person able to carry out ecclesial business.[7] Now the Christian faithful (*christifidelis*) is recognized as the central subject of the ecclesial legal order. This "breaks, at least in principle and despite possible inconsistencies, with the constitutional hegemony the hierarchy has always

---

[5] Winfried Aymans, "Das Projekt eine Lex Ecclesiae Fundamentalis," in *Handbuch des katholischen Kirchenrechts*, ed. Joseph Listl et al. (Regensburg: F. Pustet, 1983) 70.

[6] See Xavier Ochoa, *Index verborum ac locutionum Codicis Juris Canonici* (Rome: Libreria Editrice Lateranense, 1983) 368-370. Similarly, prior to the 1983 code, see Rudolf Köstler, *Wörterbuch zum Codex Juris Canonici* (Munich: J. Kösel and F. Pustet, 1927) 298.

[7] Even though canon 87 of the 1917 code stated that all the baptized were bearers of rights and duties, the statement did not have any formative influence in the code. See, Georg Gänswein, *Kirchengliedschaft: Vom Zweiten Vatikanischen Konzil bis zum Codex Juris Canonici. Die Rezeption der konziliaren Aussagen über die Kirchenzugehörigkeit in das nachkonziliare Gesetzbuch der Lateinischen Kirche* (St. Ottilien: EOS Verlag, 1995) 5f, 214-216.

enjoyed in canon law."[8] The change in perspective comes to light immediately in canon 204 §1 as well as in the beginning of the second book on
the people of God, where the category of the *christifidelis* is introduced,[9]
a category that goes beyond the notion of clerics and lay people. Henceforth all the faithful have a share in the priestly, prophetic, and kingly office of Christ and in the mission entrusted to the Church in the world.[10]
This participation must not be derived from ecclesiastical ministry or the
sacrament of orders. Rather, it is founded directly on the sacramental
event of baptism and is thus an expression of what binds all the faithful
in the Church together. Therefore, the faithful should not be seen as (passive) receivers of ecclesial legal decisions arising out of canon law;
rather, they are included in the process of reception itself.

On the other hand, this change in perspective has not always been incorporated into either the codification of 1983 or that of 1990. For example, a definition of the faithful as bearers of the common priesthood (*sa-
cerdotium commune*: *LG* 10), and the *sensus fidei* at work in the people of
God (*LG* 12) was not a priority. And the code was content with a succinct
statement that the determination of an ecclesial law comes about through
promulgation (see c. 7; and *CCEO* c. 1488). The basis for this defect rests
not with the abstract manner of codification or in the idea of codification
as such, but in the inadequate reception of the Second Vatican Council.

Outcome and Outlook

As Redaelli rightly emphasizes,[11] the Church found in the technique
of codification a practical means to overcome poorly arranged law. The
principle of codification is useful to the ecclesial legal order if it has a
built in "filter" to keep alien influences at a distance, influences that can
be damaging to the Church's self-understanding. Moreover, the principle
of codification proves useful when it is helpful in expressing the ecclesial
reality in a legal fashion. "Is a codification still useful to the Church
today?" Redaelli answers cautiously: "Weighing the advantages and dis-

---

[8]   Eugenio Corecco, "Aspects of the Reception of Vatican II in the Code of Canon
Law," in *The Reception of Vatican II*, ed. Giuseppe Alberigo et al. (Washington: The
Catholic University of America Press, 1987) 265.
[9]   See Peter Krämer, *Kirchenrecht II. Orstkirche-Gesamtkirche* (Stuttgart: Kohlhammer, 1993) 21-23.
[10]   *CCEO* c. 7 §1 makes the same provision.
[11]   Carlo Redaelli, "The Ecclesiological Significance of the Principle of Codification
with Special Reference to Reception," *supra*, 274-275.

advantages, one could say yes."[12] I would answer less cautiously: "One would have to say yes, if one does not want to fall back into previous shortcomings." This assumes, however, that the codification of church law will not lead to the ossification of law, but that it will positively appropriate the reforms and reform movements of the Second Vatican Council, updating them according to pastoral requirements. In this way, a greater significance will be awarded to the process of reception.

Consequently, all individual considerations lead to the question of how a reception of the Second Vatican Council is actually to be accomplished. It seems that a problematic development in this area has occurred during the post-conciliar period. Various ecclesiological approaches have dismantled the council into a communitarian, communal, and social understanding of the Church, the latter being marked by a stronger juridic tone. It has been asserted that the conciliar texts themselves reached the level of empty formulations of compromise, with this or that statement being acceptable according to one's own theological position. In this way, the Second Vatican Council has actually been devalued. For no reception in the line of the council will be pursued according to the meaning discernable in the texts themselves. Rather, the unity achieved after so many struggles has dissolved and given way to indifference. One cannot easily forget that this point of view goes back to the controversial canonist Hans Barion (1899-1973), whose acrid critique of Vatican II received great attention.[13] According to Barion, the conciliar texts could only be understood as dim compromises that obscure Catholic doctrine and distort the Church's legal form. In this way, Barion attempted, with the help of the 1917 code, to lessen the importance of the conciliar reforms. However, by doing so he betrayed an appalling positivistic attitude that was promoted at the time of the 1917 codification as well as since then, and which Redaelli rightly deplores.[14] Canonical science is in danger of contenting itself with the interpretation of positive norms, and of thus becoming too tied to the codified form of law. Nor can it be denied that insufficient justifications are given in official documents that refer to the promulgations or presentation of the 1983 code and the 1990 Code of Canons of the Eastern Churches.[15] For

---

[12] Ibid., 277.
[13] See Peter Krämer, *Theologische Grundlegung des kirchlichen Rechts. Die rechtstheologische Auseinandersetzung zwischen H. Barion und J. Klein im Licht des II. Vatikanischen Konzils* (Trier: Paulinus, 1977) 97-104.
[14] See Redaelli, 255-262.
[15] Ibid., 263-270.

example, the "legal character" of the code is emphasized,[16] but how that character relates to the pastoral sphere remains unclear. Or a one-sided presentation of the social nature of the Church is used to justify the necessity of an ecclesial legal culture. In this way, the impression is given that the Church is understood theologically as a community (*communio*), but legally as a society (*societas*).

Two points are to be made in response to the foregoing observations:

1. If the legal character of the code is emphasized, it should not be directed against the theological foundation and pastoral orientation of ecclesiastical law. Rather, the aim should be to bring out the binding character of canonical norms in order to prevent the code from being broken down into a collection of non-binding advice and recommendations.[17]

2. In official documents one often discovers a poorly balanced comparison between *communio* and *societas*. This criticism is directed even more strongly at theology, and within theology at the canonical sciences which have yet to succeed at reaching a sufficient consensus in the matter. Even today the positions that seek to provide a foundation for church law are too disparate.

It would indeed be too schematic and simplistic to play *communio* and *societas* off against one another.[18] Certainly in the wake of the Second Vatican Council and the post-conciliar codification, various ecclesiological approaches have taken hold. Frequently no success has been met with in balancing these statements with one another. Indeed, a fundamental problem lies behind this failure: as a *communio* the Church is a "complex reality" (*LG* 8), a taut combination of diverse elements. In order to avoid polarization, and to make a true process of reception possible, it is necessary to keep in mind the relationship between divergent elements. In this sense, the relation between *communio* and *societas* is to be understood in such a way that the social structure of the Church represents a partial view of the spiritual-visible community.

Translation by Ronny E. Jenkins

---

[16] "Principia quae Codicis Iuris Canonici recognitionem dirigent," in *Communicationes* 1 (1969) 77-100 (principles 1 and 9).

[17] See Ludger Müller, "Theologische Aussagen im kirchlichen Gesetzbuch. Sinn-Funktion-Problematik," *Münchner Theologische Zeitschrift* 37 (1986) 33-35.

[18] See Peter Krämer, "Theologische Grundlagen des kirchlichen Rechts nach dem CIC/1983," *Archiv für katholisches Kirchenrecht* 153 (1984) 392-394.

THE *CODE OF CANONS OF THE EASTERN CHURCHES*: A DEVELOPMENT FAVORING RELATIONS BETWEEN THE CHURCHES?

JOHN H. ERICKSON*

"When this code appears, every Orthodox who takes note will cry out: 'Yes, truly, this is our code, this is our law, this is the voice of our fathers.'" With these words Cardinal Massimo Massimi, president of the Pontifical Commission for the Oriental Code, expressed to Melkite Patriarch Cyril IX and the bishops with him his hopes for the *Codex Iuris Canonici Orientalis (CICO)* then in preparation.[1] While not using the word reception (it had not yet entered the theological lexicon), the cardinal did suggest that the new code would at the very least result in an important prerequisite for reception: recognition. In the new code the Orthodox would recognize their own heritage; they would see the code as an authentic expression of the discipline and order that flow from their own apostolic faith.[2]

Of course, the cardinal was speaking in 1939. Since that time the context for possible recognition and reception has changed dramatically. The code of which he spoke was never promulgated in integral form. Only four of its twelve sections were issued, in the form of apostolic letters *motu proprio*, by Pope Pius XII. Continuation of the Eastern code project was interrupted by that pontiff's death (1958) and by the veritable ecclesiological revolution which ensued with Vatican II (1962-1965). With its ecumenical openness and concern for the renewal of church life, the postconciliar church has been very different from the church of 1939. This changed context raises some hope that the new 1990 *Codex Canonum Ecclesiarum Orientalium (CCEO)* will not be an obstacle but rather will advance the cause of Christian unity in general and, in particular, the goal of

* St. Vladimir's Orthodox Theological Seminary, Crestwood, NY.
[1] Cardinal Massimo Massimi, quoted in Archbishop Peter (Medawar) of Pelusium, "On Safeguarding the Rights of the Oriental Church," trans. from the French in *The Unity of the Churches of God*, ed. Polycarp Sherwood (Dublin: Helicon, 1962) 21.
[2] On the relationship between reception and recognition see Jean-Marie Tillard, "Reception—Communion," *One in Christ* 28 (1992) 307-322.

full communion of all the Eastern Churches with the Catholic Church[3]—
a hope that possibly we Orthodox in some way will be able to recognize
and receive it as "our code," "our law," "the voice of our fathers."

But here it is useful to keep in mind the scholastic maxim *Quidquid recipitur ad modum recipientis recipitur*—whatever is received is received
according to the manner of the recipient. Orthodox Christians pride
themselves on their fidelity to tradition, and no doubt rightly, but Orthodoxy is not an unchanging monolith. Since 1939 the external circumstances of the Orthodox Churches have changed in many significant
ways. No less important, though certainly less conspicuous, has been internal Orthodox reflection and debate on ecclesiological issues. The context for possible reception has changed.

The promulgation of the *CCEO*, therefore, raises for the Orthodox a
whole series of interrelated questions not all of which would have occurred to them in 1939. Most obvious, of course, would be the question
of whether the *CCEO* does indeed have the "Eastern character" called for
in the "Guidelines for the Revision of the Code of Oriental Canon Law."[4]
Is it truly Eastern, or is it simply the 1983 *Codex Iuris Canonici (CIC)* in
an Eastern guise? Before "receiving" the *CCEO* in any manner, the Orthodox would ask to what extent the *CCEO* itself receives the ancient
canonical patrimony preserved to this day among the Orthodox
Churches. But most Orthodox would grant that the *CCEO* quite legitimately seeks and claims to be more than an exercise in archeology, an exotic ornament for a museum church. It should be "capable of responding
to present-day demands," and so some recourse to "other sources of ecclesiastical law" (such as the *CIC*) may not be inappropriate.[5] In addition, while the *CCEO* is intended to be Eastern, its main purpose is to
translate Vatican II's theological and ecclesiological vision into juridical
norms. This raises further questions: How in fact does the *CCEO* receive
Vatican II? And how might the Orthodox receive Vatican II?

A few decades ago, when a Great and Holy Council of the Orthodox
Churches still seemed imminent and projects for the codification of Or-
thodox canon law were being advanced, the appearance a new Eastern
Catholic Code of Canon Law might have prompted a lively response

---

[3] Cf. John Paul II, apostolic constitution *Sacri Canones*, October 18, 1990: *AAS* 82
(1990) 1033-1044, promulgating the *CCEO*.

[4] In English translation in *Nuntia* n. 3 (1976) 19.

[5] Ibid.

among the Orthodox. Questions like the above might have been posed and discussed. Thus far, however, the 1990 *CCEO* has been greeted with polite silence. The Orthodox have not commented on it extensively, nor have they shown signs of incorporating any elements of it into their own life, of plagiarizing it, as it were, for their own purposes after the fashion of Peter Moghila in the 17th century. This silence, this lack of response may itself be significant. Quite possibly the Orthodox at this point find the new code irrelevant to their own needs and circumstances, rendering moot the question of reception in any form. On the other hand, Eastern Catholics, whom the code necessarily affects in a direct manner, have been much more vocal and, in some cases, quite critical.

After a superficial glance at the *CCEO*, the disinterested Orthodox observer might be inclined to sympathize with its Eastern Catholic critics. It does seem odd to have a common code for some twenty very disparate ecclesial entities, which draw on five major liturgical traditions (Alexandrian, Antiochian, Armenian, Chaldean, and Constantinopolitan/Byzantine), whose traditional homelands range from Ethiopia to Russia, from Italy to India, and whose faithful now can be found in practically every corner of the world, for whom no common designation could be found save the practically untranslatable "Church *sui iuris*"; to have a code whose official language is Latin and whose very name, *Code of Canons of the Eastern Churches*, when placed alongside that of its Latin counterpart, *Code of Canon Law*, suggests that the "Eastern" represents an exception to the Latin norm for church order and life. Of course, these peculiarities can easily be explained and even justified. Latin not only has a venerable history of legal use; for the Eastern Churches in question, it also is a "neutral" language. While in principle it might be preferable for each of the Eastern Catholic Churches to have its own code rather than a generic Eastern one, in fact many of the Churches in question are extremely small, in some cases comprising only a few thousand faithful, and lack the resources necessary for such an undertaking.[6] And, as the "Guidelines" for the preparation of the code note, "The legal heritage of the Oriental Churches is to a great extent founded on the same ancient canons that are to be met with in almost all Oriental canonical collections and on common traditions."[7] (Of course, it should be noted that the "an-

---

[6]   A convenient presentation of historical background and current statistical estimates for all the Eastern Churches—Orthodox, Catholic, and "other"—is provided by Ronald G. Roberson, *The Eastern Churches: A Brief Survey*, revised 5th ed. (Rome: Pontificio Istituto Orientale, 1995).

[7]   *Nuntia* n. 3 (1976) 19.

cient canons" referred to here also are to be met with in virtually all the most ancient Western canonical collections; they are in fact common to the universal Church, not just to the East.) As for the name of the code, once the designation *Codex Iuris Canonici* with no geographical or ecclesial specification had been preempted by the 1983 Latin code, few alternatives remained; under the circumstances, the oriental code commission had to make do as best it could.[8]

More problematic is the term "Church *sui iuris*." Like the name for the code, it in effect was adopted by default. *Orientalium Ecclesiarum* 2 had used the term *ecclesia particularis seu ritus* to refer to the Eastern Catholic Churches. The use of the designation *ritus* was regrettable, since the general thrust of *Orientalium Ecclesiarum* was to recognize them precisely as Churches, not simply as exotic rites within the one Roman Catholic Church. The term *ecclesia particularis*, on the other hand, ecclesiologically richer, was preempted by the Latin code commission (following the vocabulary of *Christus Dominus* and *Lumen gentium*) to refer to the diocese. Diverse other proposals were studied and found unsatisfactory. For example, the technical terms most commonly in use among the Orthodox, autocephalous and autonomous, quite correctly were recognized as describing entities significantly different from the Eastern Catholic Churches. Meanwhile, the 1983 *CIC* adopted the term *ecclesia ritualis* or *ecclesia ritualis sui iuris* to refer to the Eastern Catholic Churches. The oriental code commission dropped the problematic *ritualis*, leaving—by a process of elimination—*ecclesia sui iuris*. No doubt it is fortunate that any lingering temptation to regard the Eastern Catholic Churches simply as rites was thus resisted. One of the great achievements of the *CCEO* is that for the first time Church and rite are clearly distinguished, the latter being appropriately understood as "the liturgical, theological, spiritual and disciplinary patrimony, culture and circumstances of history" manifested in the former (c. 28, §1).[9]

But this clarity came at a price. The term *ecclesia sui iuris* may be a convenient juridical designation for these various ecclesial entities, but it is a term singularly lacking in theological resonance and ecclesiological depth. In effect, the code says that an *ecclesia sui iuris* is an entity which

---

[8]   On the title of the code see especially George Nedungatt, "The Title of the New Canonical Legislation," *Studia Canonica* 19 (1985) 61-80, and also his book *The Spirit of the Eastern Code* (Rome and Bangalore: Centre for Indian and Inter-religious Studies, and Dharmaram Publications, 1993) 42-44.
[9]   Cf. Nedungatt, *Spirit of the Eastern Code*, 60-75.

the supreme authority of the Church recognizes as an *ecclesia sui iuris*.[10] Here we touch upon a difficult issue which has preoccupied not only Eastern Catholics but also Latin Catholics and Orthodox: What is the ecclesiological significance (if any) and therefore also the juridical authority of ecclesial entities more comprehensive than the episcopal diocese/eparchy but less comprehensive than the universal Church—of such intermediary entities as patriarchal Churches and metropolitan Churches but also episcopal conferences?

As this brief initial foray into the *CCEO* suggests, its critics have called into question not only details relating to its title and terminology but also its fundamental ecclesiological orientation and principles, as expressed especially (though not exclusively) in Titles III-IX. Is the *CCEO* in this respect a mere derivative of the Latin *CIC*, as some critics have charged? To such ecclesiological issues we must return, since they impinge most directly and profoundly on Orthodox-Catholic relations. First, however, it might be useful to examine other aspects of the *CCEO*, taking into account the views of those, both Eastern and Latin Catholic, who have regarded it in a more favorable light. We should not neglect, for example, the studies now appearing which, on the basis of detailed comparison of specific sections of the two codes, have detected subtle differences of religious mentality, revealing the distinctiveness yet complementarity of East and West.[11] And in fact, in many sections of the *CCEO* elements can be discerned which we Orthodox Christians could truly consider "our own," elements which therefore might be classed as "Eastern."

Particularly striking in this connection is Title XXVII ("Penal Sanctions in the Church") along with Title XXVIII ("The Procedure for Im-

---

[10] Cf. c. 27: "A group (*coetus*) of Christian faithful joined together by a hierarchy according to the norm of law, which is expressly or tacitly recognized as *sui iuris* by the supreme authority of the Church, is called in this Code a Church *sui iuris*." For a criticism of the circular nature of this statement see Antony Valiyavilayil, "The Notion of a *Sui Iuris* Church," in *The Code of Canons of the Eastern Churches: A Study and Interpretation. Essays in Honour of Joseph Cardinal Parecatil . . .*, ed. Jose Chiramel and Kuriakose Bharanikulangara (Alwaye, India: St. Thomas Academy for Research, 1992) 60, n. 9, cited by Andrew T. Onuferko, "The New Code of Canons of the Eastern Churches: Ecclesiological Presuppositions," *Logos* 35 (1994) 147.

[11] See, for example, Rose M. McDermott, "Two Approaches to Consecrated Life: The *Code of Canons of the Eastern Churches* and the *Code of Canon Law*," *Studia Canonica* 29 (1995) 193-239; Thomas J. Green, "Penal Law in the *Code of Canon Law* and in the *Code of Canons of the Eastern Churches*: Some Comparative Reflections," *Studia Canonica* 28 (1994) 407-451; and Aurelie A. Hagstrom, "Canon 207 (CIC) and Canon 399 (CCEO): A Comparative Analysis," *Logos* 34 (1993) 622-638.

posing Penalties"). The tone is set by its initial canon 1401 (which has no counterpart in the *CIC*):

> Since God employs every means to bring back the erring sheep, those who have received from Him the power of loosing and binding are to treat in an appropriate manner the illness of those who have committed offenses, by correcting, reproving and appealing, never failing in teaching and in patience, and are even to impose penalties with a view to healing the wounds caused by the offense, so that on the one hand the offender is not driven to the precipice of despair nor on the other hand is free rein given unto dissoluteness of life and contempt of the law.[12]

As in the Eastern tradition generally, penalties are understood as medicinal in nature rather than vindictive or expiatory. Absent is the natural law theme of restoration of justice, so conspicuous in the 1917 Latin code and still present to some extent in the 1983 *CIC* (e.g., in c. 1341, which has no counterpart in the *CCEO*), and the equally alien concept of coercive power (see *CIC* cc. 1311-1312, which also have no counterpart in the *CCEO*). Absent as well are penalties *latae sententiae*.

"Eastern" elements, sometimes very self-consciously introduced, may be noted at many other points as well. For example, monasticism, so central to the life of the Christian East over the centuries, introduces the presentation of institutes of consecrated life in Title XII, in effect serving as a standard and point of reference for what follows. In another obeisance to Eastern sensibilities, the code specifies that valid marriage requires "a sacred rite, in the presence of the local hierarch, local pastor, or a priest who has been given the faculty of blessing the marriage . . ." (c. 828).

Such examples of the *CCEO*'s "Eastern character" could be multiplied, and no doubt we should be thankful for them. A few words of caution may be in order, however. While the *CCEO* does contain a number of "Eastern" elements, it also ignores or excludes many others which the attentive reader of the "ancient canons" might expect to find. For exam-

---

[12]   Here as elsewhere I have freely modified the Canon Law Society of America translation of the *CCEO*, *Code of Canons of the Eastern Churches, Latin-English Edition* (Washington: CLSA, 1992) to take into consideration the critical observations of George Nedungatt, *A Companion to the Eastern Code: For a New Translation of the Codex Canonum Ecclesiarum Orientalium* (Rome: Pontificio Istituto Orientale, 1994).

ple, in connection with marriage it ignores the early church's insistence, expressed in numerous canonical and liturgical texts Western as well as Eastern, that perpetual monogamy is the norm for Christian marriage and that sequential bigamy therefore is at best a concession to human weakness. Further, the *CCEO* at times simply takes for granted and uncritically incorporates concepts that can only be regarded as distinctly "Western"—for example, the Germanic concern for whether a marriage has been "consummated" as a criterion in cases of dissolution/nullity (c. 1367). At the same time, many of the most noteworthy "Eastern" elements in the *CCEO* are by no means exclusively Eastern. They represent part of that return to the authentic sources of the Christian tradition—that creative reappropriation of the bible, the ancient liturgies, the fathers, and the ancient canons—which Vatican II encouraged as part of its effort to renew and revitalize church life today. The same "Eastern" inspiration which can be found in the *CCEO* can also be discerned at a number of points in the *CIC*—for example, in the revised penal law, in which the number of penalties *latae sententiae* is dramatically reduced; in the incorporation of special faculties into the code reducing recourse to "higher authorities" for dispensations (cf. the East's *oikonomia*); in the application of the principle of subsidiarity, etc. It could be argued that, on the whole, the *CCEO* is more successful than the *CIC* at translating the essentially pastoral vision of Vatican II into juridical terms. This may have little to do with its "Eastern" character, however. The *CCEO*'s latinity generally is superior to that of the *CIC* as well. Appearing seven years after the *CIC*, the *CCEO* had the advantage of hindsight.

It would be tempting at this point simply to enumerate the many superior features of the *CCEO*. For example, it is intentionally ecumenical, as is evident especially in its Titles XVII and XVIII, devoted respectively to "Baptized Non-Catholics Coming into Full Communion with the Catholic Church" and "Ecumenism or the Fostering of the Unity of Christians." It provides considerable scope for the various Churches *sui iuris*—potentially including the Latin Church—to formulate their own particular law. It demonstrates due concern for inculturation in its presentation of evangelization and mission (Title XIV). One might go so far as to argue that, with some pruning, adjustment of vocabulary and other minor modifications, the *CCEO* could serve as the common code for all the Churches of the Roman communion, its title being shortened to *Codex Canonum* and the specification *Ecclesiae Latinae* being added to the title of the present *Codex Iuris Canonici*. As such a proposal implies, however, for all its "Eastern" elements and other merits, the *CCEO* re-

mains a code of and for the Roman communion, a new—though improved—edition of the *CIC*.

But if the *CCEO* can be thus characterized, this does not mean that it
is a monolith. Rather, it displays many of the internal tensions, inconsistencies and paradoxes of Vatican II Catholicism itself. This is especially
evident in its treatment of ecclesiological issues, not only in Titles III -
IX, which are devoted to the hierarchical structure of the Church, but
elsewhere as well. In the documents of Vatican II, and even in a single
constitution, *Lumen gentium*, at least two divergent approaches to the
Church have been discerned: the Church as *societas* and the Church as
communio, the institutional model and the sacramental model.[13] With the
skill of a surgeon wielding a sharp scalpel, Eugenio Corecco has shown
how the 1983 *CIC*, in its reception of Vatican II, perpetuated and even accentuated this duality,[14] or rather how it tried to contain the new wine of
the Church understood in sacramental terms as communion in the old juridical wineskins inherited from the preconciliar period. Many of
Corecco's criticisms of the *CIC* apply equally well to the *CCEO*, if only
because the *CCEO* essentially reproduces *CIC* at so many points. Consider, for example, the way that both codes largely fail to take into consideration the ecclesiological significance of the sacraments. Much of
modern Orthodox and Catholic theology has emphasized the sacramental nature and basis of the Church. This approach may be summed up in
the maxim, "the sacraments make the Church." The two codes, however,
return to the old institutional perspective according to which "the Church
makes the sacraments." The Church's power structure is defined (Book II
// Titles III - XIII) and various aspects of its operations (Book III // Title
XIV, "Evangelization of the Nations," and Title XV, "The Ecclesiastical
Magisterium") are explained long before we get to "Divine Worship and
Especially the Sacraments" (Book IV // Title XVI). This obscures the ge-
netic relationship of the sacraments to the Church's norms. So also,
norms for the clerical state (Book II.i.iii // Title X) have no explicit con-
nection to the sacrament of order (Book IV.i.vi // Title XVI.vi); those for
the Church in its various manifestations (particular church/eparchy,
Church *sui iuris*, universal Church) have no explicit connection to the

---

[13]   See, for example, Antonio Acerbi, *Due ecclesiologie: Ecclesiologia giuridica e ecclesiologia di communione nella "Lumen Gentium"* (Bologna: Edizioni Dehoniane,
1975).

[14]   Eugenio Corecco, "Aspects of the Reception of Vatican II in the Code of Canon
Law," in *The Reception of Vatican II*, ed. Giuseppe Alberigo et al. (Washington: Catholic
University of America Press, 1987) 256.

Eucharist (Book IV.i.iii // XVI.iii)—a perspective which of course has been stressed in modern Orthodox eucharistic ecclesiology. The only significant exception in this regard is the welcome connection drawn between baptism and "the rights and obligations of all the Christian faithful" (especially c. 7).[15]

The same criticisms could be made of many other aspects of the two codes. Consider, for example, *CIC* Book V // Title XXIII, "On the Temporal Goods of the Church." Neither code draws attention to "the necessary role of *communio* in the possession and use of material goods." Rather, they formulate "the patrimonial relationship between the faithful and the Church" on the state model. As Corecco observes of Book V of the *CIC*, "It is no accident, therefore, that precisely in this book of the code the Church is still seen (and this not simply by reason of terminology) as a hypostatized entity that, like the state, stands in a relationship of alterity with its subjects."[16] In fairness, it should be noted that at some points the *CCEO* does significantly improve upon the *CIC*. As already has been noted, this is true in its treatment of penalties. Even its organization into some thirty titles rather than into books (seven in the 1983 *CIC*, five in the 1917 *CIC*) might be seen as an improvement. While the division into titles, some brief, some very lengthy, may be less convenient and less logical than the *CIC*'s divisions, this does make the *CCEO* comparatively flexible and open-ended, quite unlike the 1917 *CIC*, which in effect tried to be a comprehensive legal tractate, tightly organized on the basis of certain juridical principles on the model of 19th-century civil law codes and intended to cover virtually every aspect of church life. On the whole, then, the *CCEO* is somewhat more successful than the *CIC* at extricating canon law from the model of the *societas perfecta*. But in its efforts to be practical, to avoid theorizing and theologizing, to be strictly juridical, the *CCEO* prescinds from adopting a more satisfactory model. While words suggesting that the Church is a sacramental communion are repeated frequently in the *CCEO*, they often are cruelly undercut by an essentially institutional and societal view of the

---

[15] Would it have been possible to organize the *CIC* on sacramental lines? For such a proposal, which the Orthodox might find very attractive, see Stephan Kuttner, "Betrachtungen zur Systematik eines neuen Codex Iuris Canonici," in *Ex Aequo et Bono: W. Plöchl zum 70. Geburtstag*, ed. Peter Leisching et al. (Innsbruck: Universitätsverlag Wagner, 1977) 15-21.

[16] Corecco, 256.

Church which is all the more insidious because it is implicit rather than explicit.

Here we begin to touch on some of the more fundamental differences between Orthodox ("Eastern") and Catholic ("Western") ecclesiological conceptions, differences which make it difficult for the Orthodox to recognize the *CCEO* as "our code," "our law," "the voice of our fathers." Certainly for the Orthodox, the mutual interiority which is the essence of communion is expected to be present and to be expressed at all levels and in all aspects of church life. But here, as has been observed so often, the Orthodox have tended to begin with the particular, with the internal life of the local church.[17] Much of modern Orthodox ecclesiology, for example, has taken the local eucharistic fellowship as its point of departure. The Eucharist is seen not just as one of several means of grace at the disposal of the Church conceived as a divinely instituted body politic but as the basis for the Church's life and structures. In the eucharistic assembly, when all the clergy and faithful, with all their diverse spiritual gifts, are gathered in unity under the presidency of the bishop, the very nature of the Church as communion is revealed. In this perspective, the bishop is inseparable from his local/particular church, in a relationship of mutuality which is reflected in the Eastern canonical tradition in a number of ways: in provisions restricting the transfer of bishops from see to see, in provisions restricting the bishop's activities to his own church, and most notably in provisions for participation of the clergy and laity of the local church in episcopal selection.

Quite different is the perspective of the *CCEO*'s Title VII (eparchies and bishops). Canonical provisions like those just mentioned—so "Eastern," so filled with ecclesiological significance—are present only in an attenuated or muted way; for example, in canon 204 (the eparchial bishop's obligation of residency in his eparchy) and in canon 205 (the obligation of canonically visiting the eparchy). Indeed, the eparchy itself

---

[17] Cf. the very apt observations of Archbishop Rembert G. Weakland, Catholic co-chairman of the U.S. Catholic - Orthodox Theological Consultation, "Roman Catholic and Orthodox Dialogue: The Larger Picture," *Ecumenism* 107 (1992) 31: ". . . we Roman Catholics use the phrase 'Universal Church' more often than we realize. It is a phrase that most characterizes our ecclesiological position. . . . Especially since Vatican II, we have evolved an elaborate thinking on how the universal Church is present in the local church and realized there. We Roman Catholics almost always begin with such universalism and then proceed to local manifestations. . . . The Orthodox begin with the local church and the celebration of the Eucharist on the local level. The local eucharistic community—rather than the concept of a universal Church—is their starting point."

is defined in such a way as to abstract the bishop from it, placing him in a relationship of altereity with it:

> The eparchy is a portion of the people of God which is entrusted for pastoral care to a bishop with the cooperation of the *presbyterium* so that, adhering to its pastor and gathered by him through the Gospel and the Eucharist in the Holy Spirit, it constitutes a particular Church in which the one, holy, catholic and apostolic Church of Christ is truly present and operative (c. 177 §1).

Here, as in the corresponding canon 369 in the *CIC*, there is little sense that the particular church is a communion *within which* the bishop and his ministry are situated. Rather, like a precious object, the particular church is "entrusted" to the bishop, who cares for it using the gospel and the Eucharist as his instruments.

This definition, of course, is drawn directly from the documents of Vatican II, but—significantly—from the decree on bishops, *Christus Dominus* 11, and indirectly from *Lumen gentium* 23 (part of chapter 3, "The Hierarchical Structure of the Church with Special Reference to the Episcopate"). How different the definition of particular church/eparchy would have been had it instead taken *Lumen gentium* chapter 2, "The People of God," as its point of departure! That chapter, as has often been observed, constituted a veritable "Copernican revolution" in ecclesiology by situating the hierarchy among the *Christifideles*, within the People of God rather than above them or prior to them. But the council as a whole, including chapter 3, was preoccupied with the issue of episcopal collegiality, with the relationship between primacy and episcopacy, the pope and the council. Its concern was hierarchical communion, the communion of bishops one with another, rather than ecclesial communion, the communion within a local church.[18]

More satisfactory at first glance is the *CCEO*'s treatment of communion within the Church *sui iuris*. Canons relating to the mutual responsibilities and competencies of eparchial bishops and of the patriarch/major

---

[18]   This point is well developed by Nedungatt, *Spirit of the Eastern Code,* 86-88, who points out: "The Church is not only People of God but also the body of Christ, built up with the Eucharist. Hence ecclesial communion is not lost even when hierarchical communion does not exist. But where unequal importance is attached to hierarchical communion, the significance of ecclesial communion risks to be lightly discounted."

archbishop attempt to achieve a proper balance between conciliarity and primacy, in line with ancient canons like Apostolic Canon 34:

> The bishops of every nation must acknowledge him who is the first (*protos*) among them and regard him as their head (*kephale*), and do nothing of consequence without his consent, though each may do those things which concern his own parish and the country places dependent on it. But neither let him who is the first do anything without the consent of all. For thus there will be oneness of mind, and God will be glorified through the Lord in the Holy Spirit.

To be sure, from the perspective of modern Orthodox eucharistic ecclesiology the *CCEO* may appear to accord the institution of the patriarchate undue importance and to give the patriarch "a personal jurisdiction . . . over other bishops, which is alien to the Eastern canonical tradition, where the Patriarch or any other primate is always a *primus inter pares*."[19] The *CCEO* at points does appear to be augmenting patriarchal authority at the expense of eparchial authority simply in order to call attention to the patriarch's exalted position within his Church *sui iuris*.[20] In fairness, however, it must be noted that in actuality a number of Orthodox patriarchs enjoy or have enjoyed rights comparable (or even greater) than those enumerated for the Eastern Catholic patriarchs in the *CCEO* (cc. 82-83, 85-90).

Yet for all this apparent balance, the *CCEO*'s presentation of communion within the Church *sui iuris* does differ from ancient and traditional Eastern patterns in one crucial aspect: the role accorded to the Apostolic See, to the Roman Pontiff. One Eastern Catholic critic has observed, "centralist forces in Rome . . . have succeeded in redefining the Eastern Patriarchs as sharers in the super-episcopal power of the Pope rather than as the apex of the collegial authority of the patriarchal synods."[21] This may be an oversimplification, but certainly the unity, the solidarity, the

---

[19]   Alexander Schmemann, "A Response" to the Decree on the Eastern Churches, in *The Documents of Vatican II*, ed. Walter M. Abbott (New York: America Press, 1966) 387-388.

[20]   For example, according to canon 835, "dispensation from the form for the celebration for marriage required by law is reserved to the Apostolic See or the patriarch, who will not grant it except for a most grave reason," whereas in the Latin Church the local ordinary can dispense.

[21]   Andriy Chirovsky, "Toward an Ecclesial Self-Identity for the Ukrainian Greco-Catholic Church," *Logos* 35 (1994) 121.

"oneness of mind" of the patriarchate's episcopate, patriarch and eparchs together, is potentially undermined when many major decisions (e.g., erection/modification/suppression of eparchies [c. 85 §1], aspects of episcopal discipline [c. 204 §4], approval of candidates for episcopal election [c. 182, cf. c. 185]) require consultation with Rome and when the eparchial bishop in effect is responsible to two superiors (cf. provisions for quinquennial reports [c. 206], *ad limina* visits [c. 208], promises of obedience [c. 187 §2]). The difference in perspective can be seen a liturgical detail with considerable ecclesiological significance. According to the traditional Eastern pattern, in the Divine Liturgy a presbyter commemorates his diocesan bishop, the bishop who is his metropolitan, patriarch or other hierarchical head, and the patriarch or the other heads of Churches in the order of the diptychs;[22] but according to the *CCEO*, the eparchial bishop and indeed all the clergy of the eparchy commemorate both the Roman Pontiff and the patriarch, in that order (cc. 91, 209). Does this not indicate some confusion as to who is "the first among them"?

Provisions relating to the election of a new patriarch reveal another departure from the traditional ancient and continuing Orthodox practice. According to the *CCEO*, synodal letters are to be sent notifying the Roman Pontiff and the patriarchs of the other Eastern Churches of the election, but in addition "the new patriarch must as soon as possible request ecclesiastical communion from the Roman Pontiff by means of a letter signed in his own hand" (c. 76), and he "is not to convoke a synod of bishops of the patriarchal Church nor ordain bishops before he receives ecclesiastical communion from the Roman Pontiff" (c. 77 §2). According to one enthusiastic Eastern Catholic writer, "the relation between the Roman Pontiff and the Patriarch is founded on the communion manifested and requested and the communion conceded and exchanged: perfect communion in faith and full hierarchic communion with the Apostolic See of Rome."[23] But a person familiar with ancient church practice might ask why the new patriarch requests "ecclesiastical communion" only from the Roman Pontiff and not also from the other Eastern Catholic patriarchs and also why a comparable request for "ecclesiastical communion" is not required or expected of a new Roman Pontiff.

---

[22] See Robert Taft, *The Diptychs*, Orientalia Analecta 238 (Rome: Pontificium Institutum Studiorum Orientalium, 1991) 9-21.

[23] Valiyavilayil, 73, quoted by Onuferko, 154 (*supra*, note 10).

298 JOHN H. ERICKSON

As another Eastern Catholic writer, Andrew Onuferko, quite rightly observes:

> The traditional exchange of letters of ecclesiastical communion, as understood in the Orthodox Church, is, in fact, an exchange between heads of particular *Sui Iuris* Churches, and a reaffirmation of the communion that already exists between these Churches. This communion has not ceased simply because the patriarchal See was vacant, just as the Catholic Church does not cease to exist with the death of a Roman Pontiff. It would therefore seem logical that a newly elected patriarch requests ecclesiastical communion from Rome not to receive something he does not yet possess, but to reaffirm the unity of faith and communion that already exists.[24]

Here as in other contexts, the *CCEO* is concerned with hierarchical communion rather than with ecclesial communion, communion between one bishop and another rather than communion between the Churches which they head. But even the word "communion" here seems to be a euphemism. Certainly the text of the canon suggests that the new patriarch's authority to convoke a synod of bishops or to ordain bishops is contingent upon his receipt of "ecclesiastical communion," that his supraepiscopal authority in fact is derived from the supreme authority in the Church and represents a participation in this authority and not something inherent in his position as head of a *sui iuris* Church.[25]

Here, of course, we come to perhaps the most conspicuous obstacle to Orthodox recognition of the *CCEO* as "our code" and "our law": the role of the pope as this is presented in Title III's presentation of "The Supreme Authority of the Church" (// Book II.ii.i.i). As the subject of supreme authority, the pope is also the supreme legislator, whose promulgation in the apostolic constitution *Sacri Canones* gives the *CCEO* itself the force of law.[26] It is not necessary here to review the reasons both

---

[24] Ibid.

[25] Ibid., 155.

[26] Nedungatt, *Spirit of the Eastern Code*, 168, clearly identifies the problems which this legislative aspect of papal authority creates: "*Ecclesia sui iuris*? or *Ecclesia suae gratiae*? The survival in the later papacy of the ancient Roman legal principle that the emperor is above law . . . continues to condition the codes of the Catholic Church. Juridically, the Roman Pontiff as the legislator of CCEO (as of CIC) is not bound by any of its canons; and the same is true also of the ancient sacred canons of the ecumenical councils, which he can change with the power of the Petrine keys of the kingdom. Here diverse opinions from the standpoint of biblical theology, theology of law and ecclesiology criss-cross. Here an ec-

practical and doctrinal which led to promulgation of the *CCEO* by the pope alone rather than in a collegial act with the Eastern patriarchs and other heads of Churches. But as Frederick McManus has observed, "Without weakening in any way the weight of the new code in the abstract, this course of action raises questions in the pastoral order about the collegial consensus of the Eastern Catholic hierarchs and indeed about the future reception of the code of canons by their Churches."[27] This course of action also raises yet another obstacle to reconciliation between Orthodox and Catholics. As the Orthodox certainly will recall, the ancient canons of the universal Church did not emanate from the pope but rather chiefly from local and ecumenical councils, and they were recognized as authoritative in a complex process of reception quite different from that envisioned for the *CCEO*.

Vatican II's *Orientalium Ecclesiarum* 2 spoke of the *aequalis dignitas* of all the Churches of east and west, thus reversing a long history which had insisted on the *praestantia latini ritus*. In principle, the Latin Church is but another Church *sui iuris*.[28] But in fact, as many Eastern Catholics have pointed out, the Latin Church in many respects occupies a privileged position in canon law. The Eastern patriarchal Churches have precise (and exceedingly narrow!) territorial limits, to which their jurisdiction in all but liturgical matters is restricted. But this is not the case with the patriarchate of the west. As Andrew Onuferko tartly observes:

> On the question of equality of rites, because the Roman Pontiff has no territorial limits to his power, the Roman rite has become *de facto* the universal rite of the Catholic Church with no territo-

---

umenical theology is largely at a loss. But both codes furnish the formally juridical certainty that law needs." Is "juridical certainty" worth so great a price? Certainly Eastern Christians whether Orthodox or Catholic would view the basis for their own right of self-governance in a different way. In the stirring words of Ukrainian Catholic Bishop Basil Losten, "Patriarch and Pope: Different Levels of Roman Authority," *Logos* 35 (1994) 211: "in speaking of the autonomy of the Eastern Churches, of the right of the Eastern Churches to govern themselves, we are speaking not of some sort of privilege or exemption, not of a 'special concession' which the Pope might revoke, but of an authentic *right* coming from the Holy Apostles, which the Bishop of Rome is bound to respect, maintain, and even strengthen."

[27] Frederick R. McManus, "The Code of Canons of the Eastern Catholic Churches," *The Jurist* 53 (1993) 37.

[28] Note the many canons that refer to "any Church *sui iuris* including the Latin Church" (c. 696 §1). On the Latin Church as a Church *sui iuris* see, among others, Nedungatt, *Spirit of the Eastern Code,* 102 et passim.

rial limits or restrictions. Allowances are made for other rites because of history and tradition, but always within the restrictions
and boundaries established by the Supreme Authority of the
Church. It would seem that if the Latin Church is the Patriarchate
of the West, then wherever you are on the globe, it is West![29]

The solution to this manifest inequality frequently proposed by Eastern Catholics would free the Eastern Catholic Churches from territorial
restrictions, allowing them freely and directly to minister to their faithful
in "diaspora" according to their own ecclesiastical discipline (e.g., with
a married clergy).[30] More consistent with the ancient canons (e.g., I
Nicaea c. 8) and with the principle of territoriality that the Orthodox up-
hold in principle (but often ignore in practice) would be the delineation
of clear and credible territorial limits for the Latin Church. Provisions
comparable to those which the *CCEO* establishes for Eastern Catholic
eparchs/eparchies in "Western" territory would then apply to Latin bish-
ops/dioceses in "Eastern" territory. But for now, no distinction is made
between the territory of the Latin Church and that of the universal
Church, however much Latin Church and universal Church may be distinguished in theory. That is so because too little attention has been given
to the distinction between the pope's office as patriarch of the west and
his universal "Petrine" office as chief bishop and head of the universal
episcopal college. But practically speaking, can such a distinction be
made? According to Ivan Žužek, "If we speak of the Roman Pontiff as
the 'Patriarch of the West' and the Latin Church as the 'Patriarchate of
the West' we must always remember that within the primatial power conferred by Christ on Peter and his successors, it is not possible to make *adequatae distinctiones* between his powers as Bishop of Rome, Primate of
Italy, and Patriarch of the West."[31] Certainly in practice, as one writer remarks acerbically, this has meant that "whenever the Pope acts, he seems
to act with the Supreme Authority of the Church."[32]

Historical reasons for this confusion are not hard to find, going back at
least to the time of the division of the Churches in the eleventh century.
As Jean-Marie Tillard has observed, "One of the consequences of the

---

[29]   Onuferko, 149-150 (*supra*, note 10).
[30]   See, for example, Philip A. Khairallah, "Melkite Expectations and the Post-Conciliar Church," *Eastern Churches Journal* 2 (1995) 105-134.
[31]   Ivan Žužek, "Presentazione del 'Codex Canonum Ecclesiarum Orientalium,'"
Monitor Ecclesiasticus 115 (1990) 605.
[32]   Onuferko, 151 (*supra*, note 10).

break with the East has been the narrowing of the ecclesial space where bishops preside in communion with the Bishop of Rome, and the quasi-identification of this space with the patriarchate of the West."[33] As a result of this quasi-identification, popes have come to relate to the bishops (and even the patriarchs) of other patriarchates in the same way that they relate to the bishops of their own patriarchate. It is quite understandable why this perspective should have characterized the 1917 *CIC*; it is less understandable why it should still characterize the 1983 *CIC* and the *CCEO* to such a high degree. That a different perspective is possible, that *adequatae distinctiones* can in fact be found, has been argued by both canonists and theologians, including no less an authority than Joseph Ratzinger, who in 1972 wrote:

> The bishop of Rome holds an *administrative office* for the Churches of Italy (and of the West generally) *but not for the Church as a whole*; for that he has a primacy as a direction finder and as a touchstone of unity. It is also true to say that the primates of Alexandria and Antioch are regional primates, while the bishop of Rome holds a regional primacy and in addition a primacy *of quite a different type* in relation to the Church as a whole.[34]

Certainly unless such distinctions are drawn, it is hard to imagine any significant advances towards reconciliation of the Orthodox Churches and the Catholic Church.

But is it enough to appeal to the pastoral and ecumenical reasons why such distinctions should be drawn? In so doing, have we not prejudged or sidestepped the question posed earlier concerning the nature and ecclesiological significance of intermediary entities like patriarchal Churches and other Churches *sui iuris*, with their territorially delimited regional primacies?

Catholic theology sometimes has suggested that the Church *sui iuris* is simply an administrative institution established by ecclesiastical law, in contrast to the papal office and the episcopacy, which exist *iure divino*. Such an approach is evident in the 1917 *CIC*, canon 108 §3: "By divine

---

[33]   Jean-Marie Tillard, *Church of Churches: The Ecclesiology of Communion* (Collegeville, MN: Liturgical Press, 1992) 269.

[34]   Joseph Ratzinger, *Das neue Volk Gottes* (Dusseldorf: Patmos Verlag, 1972) 131, quoted in Jean-Marie Tillard, *The Bishop of Rome* (Wilmington, DE: Michael Glazier, 1983) 50.

institution (*ex divina institutione*). . . the hierarchy of jurisdiction consists of the Supreme Pontiff and the subordinate episcopacy; other degrees have been added by institution of the Church (*ex Ecclesiae institutione*)." The *CCEO* softens this approach somewhat by using phrases like *statuente Domino* (c. 42 // *CIC* c. 330) and *a Domino concessum* (c. 43 // *CIC* c. 331) in reference to the Roman Pontiff and the college of bishops and by stating that the patriarchal institution exists *secundum antiquissimum Ecclesiae traditionem* (c. 55). Yet this still seems to posit a qualitative distinction between two kinds of ecclesiality, one primary and necessary, the other derivative and dispensable. In contrast to the local/particular church and the universal Church, the intermediary entity, the Church *sui iuris*, thus would appear to be only nominally a church. Ontologically as well as historically posterior to both, it may be acceptable for pastoral reasons, but it lacks a properly theological basis.

Curiously enough, Orthodox theology sometimes has suggested much the same thing. Modern Orthodox eucharistic ecclesiology has taken the local church as its point of departure, whereas Catholic ecclesiology more often has started with the universal Church; increasingly both have been emphasizing their simultaneity and mutual interiority. But Orthodox theologians have had little more to say than their Catholic counterparts concerning intermediary ecclesial entities, notwithstanding their prominence in the history of the Orthodox Church, from the ancient patriarchates through the modern autocephalous Church. To be sure, the Interorthodox Preparatory Commission for the Great and Holy Council can affirm that "the institution of autocephaly expresses in an authentic way one of the fundamental aspects of the Orthodox ecclesiological tradition concerning relations between the local church and the universal Church of God," that there is a "profound connection between the canonical institution of autocephaly and Orthodox ecclesiological teaching concerning the local church."[35] But relatively little has been done to elucidate such affirmations. Most often the suggestion has been that church order above the level of the local church, whether intermediary or universal, is determined by the competent authority (the ecumenical council but conceivably also the emperor) in response to particular sociological and political circumstances—in short, it is determined by ecclesiastical law. The main difference, then, between Catholic and Orthodox conceptions would appear to lie simply in their evaluation of the basis for universal

---

[35]   "Autocephaly and the way in which it is to be proclaimed," text adopted Chambésy, November 7-13, 1993.

church order (i.e., papal primacy), Catholics saying *iure divino*, Orthodox saying *iure ecclesiastico*, and not in their evaluation of the basis for intermediary ecclesial entities.

This schematization represents, *grosso modo*, the way that Catholic and Orthodox understandings of ecclesiology have been pitted against each other in past polemics and possibly also in more recent discussions. Is any other approach possible? As a number of modern studies have argued,[36] the concept of *ius divinum* is not very helpful here, even when it is expressed in mitigated form (as in the *CCEO*) or when it is not explicitly invoked (as is the case with the Orthodox position caricatured above). Its implication is always that certain institutions are necessary, and that others, historically contingent, are a matter of relative indifference. But as Tillard has observed, "No clear boundary exists which permits us to say: 'What is on this side has been positively willed by God, what is on that side is entirely dependent on human freedom.'"[37] If the Church were merely a *societas in*stituted long ago by Christ, such a schema might be possible. But the Church is also the living body of Christ, which is always being *con*stituted in history by the Holy Spirit, as the locus for restored communion of men and women with God and with each other. The necessity of a given structure for the Church, be it the intermediary ecclesial entity, the Petrine ministry or even the episcopacy, therefore does not depend simply on whether it was explicitly mandated or established in Scripture but rather on whether it responds to what the nature of the Church itself demands. In this perspective, perhaps, it may be possible for both Orthodox and Catholics to reach a deeper understanding of the ecclesiological significance of the Church *sui iuris* and also of the universal ministry of oversight exercised by the Roman Pontiff.

In *Sacri Canones,* Pope John Paul II indicated that the canons of the *CCEO* will "be in force until abrogated or changed by the supreme authority of the Church for a just cause, of which causes full communion of all of the Eastern Churches with the Catholic Church is indeed the most serious." Is that day likely to come soon? As one whose professional training has been in church history and canon law, I am not qualified to

---

[36] See among others Yves Congar, "Jus Divinum," *Revue de Droit Canonique* 28 (1978) 108-112; Avery Dulles, "Jus Divinum as an Ecumenical Problem," *Theological Studies* 38 (1977) 688-697; Carl J. Peter, "Dimensions of Jus Divinum in Roman Catholic Theology," *Theological Studies* 34 (1973) 227-250.

[37] Tillard, *Church of Churches*, 304.

engage in futuristics. I may, however, be able to identify what Orthodox
and Catholics engaged in the study of canon law and ecclesiology can do
to hasten its coming.

First, we Orthodox should make an effort to wrestle with the many
basic issues in sacramental theology and ecclesiology which the *CCEO*
raises for us, something which we have not done hitherto. We cannot
refuse to recognize the *CCEO* as "our code" and "our law" simply on the
grounds that it is Western rather than Eastern, a somewhat improved version of the Latin Church's *CIC*. The Catholic "position" on these issues
was clearly articulated at Vatican II and is now expressed in the form of
canonical norms in the *CIC* and the *CCEO*. We Orthodox, on the other
hand, have not articulated our "position" in a comparably clear and authoritative manner. What, for example, is the ecclesial status of those outside the visible structures of the Orthodox Church? Would our policies
and practice with regard to baptized non-Orthodox coming into full communion with the Orthodox Church be at all comparable to those expressed in *CCEO* Title XVII with regard to baptized non-Catholics coming into full communion with the Catholic Church? In fact Orthodox
practices in such matters vary wildly, as do the theological explanations
advanced to justify these varied practices. All too often we simply repeat
arguments originally formulated in polemical contexts whose primary
objective was to dissociate the Orthodox East from the "heretical" West
as sharply as possible.[38] The *CCEO* calls us to go beyond polemics to serious theological reflection. On the one hand, we must be willing to listen anew to "the voice of our fathers," whose approach to basic issues in
ecclesiology and sacramental theology was certainly Eastern but not
necessarily anti-Western. But we must not be content simply to repeat
our fathers' words. We must also take seriously the need for "responding
to present-day demands," for applying our fathers' message to new situations. Just as we should not fault the *CCEO* simply for being "Western,"
so also we should not fault it simply for being "new."

Catholics, for their part, need to gain a deeper appreciation for the fundamental and irreducible "differentness" which the Christian East represents. This does not mean simply gaining a deeper appreciation for the
spirituality, liturgy and other characteristic expressions of the various

---

[38]   Cf. some of the theories of sacramental economy which developed in the wake of
the 18th-century controversy over Latin baptism, according to which in principle all con-
verts to Orthodoxy should be baptized, and if they have not been this is simply because the
Church has decided to apply *oikonomia* in their case.

Eastern Churches, important though these are. It means being able to imagine religious mentalities and sensibilities quite different from one's own but at the same time deeply and authentically Christian. For a host of reasons related to its own particular history, the Latin West very often has been insensitive to the particular and the historical. One consequence has been an ahistorical universalist ecclesiology that has been inclined to picture the Church of all ages as a well-regulated, tightly-knit pyramidal institution with the pope at its apex, and to emphasize hierarchical aspects of communion at the expense of others. That this mentality can be transcended is suggested by comments which Cardinal Ratzinger made in 1993 about the Orthodox Churches:

> Their way of guaranteeing unity and stability in the common faith is different from ours in the Western Catholic Church. They do not have a Congregation for the Doctrine of the Faith. But in the Orthodox Church liturgy and monasticism are two very strong factors guaranteeing firmness and coherence in the faith. History shows that these are adequate, secure means in this historical and ecclesial context to fundamental unity.[39]

But are the Eastern Orthodox Churches the only ones, actually or potentially, whose "historical and ecclesial context" provides such secure means to guarantee "firmness and coherence in the faith"? Sometimes Eastern Christians, over against Roman tendencies to monopolize the designation "Apostolic See," have emphasized the apostolic origins of their own Churches in order to justify their autonomy and "differentness," implicitly making of themselves a special case.[40] But apostolicity is not merely a matter of historical foundation. For the Orthodox, at least, apostolicity means above all fidelity to the apostolic faith, something as possible in a relatively new church as in an ancient patriarchate. In that

---

[39] In *30 Days* 2 (January 29, 1993) 66-73, quoted by Losten, "Patriarch and Pope," 228.

[40] On the unfortunate tendency of the *CCEO* to use the expression "Apostolic See" exclusively with reference to Rome, see Jobe Abbass, "Apostolic See in the New Oriental Canonical Legislation," *Studia Canonica* 27 (1993) 173-215. On the significance of apostolic origins for Eastern Catholic identity, see Boniface Luykx, "Thirty Years Later: Reflections on Vatican II's *Unitatis Redintegratio* and *Orientalium Ecclesiarum*," Logos 34 (1993) 370: "The question of the Eastern Catholic Churches' identity is first a *theological* question. Since the Council decrees that they must be treated as real, full-fledged Churches, equal in dignity with the Roman Church because of their apostolic origin and uninterrupted faithfulness to the heritage of Christ (Holy Tradition), their identity is *not constituted* by their ethnic origin or association."

case, however, not only the "newer patriarchates" of the Eastern Christian world but also the newer Churches of Africa, with their increasingly distinctive rites and ethos, fully meet criteria for being a Church *sui iuris*.[41] For the eventual reconciliation of Orthodox and Catholics, recognition of the irreducible "differentness" of such Churches—and their free acceptance in ecclesial communion—may be as important as a deeper appreciation of what is specifically Eastern—or Western.

We are accustomed to dyadic thinking, in which one element is contrasted with or even opposed to a second. When this habit of mind extends to ecclesiology, we at best are left with unhelpful cliches, like *ex oriente lux, ex occidente lex*. But our God is not a dyad, nor is He an all-enveloping monad, but rather a triad, three irreducible persons in one communion of love. If, as apostolic canon 34 suggests, the life of the Church is meant to reflect the life of the Holy Trinity, we cannot think simply in terms of East and West, of "our way" and "their way," "our law" and "their law," "our fathers" and "their fathers." Rather, we must try to discern the workings of the Holy Spirit throughout the fabric of human history, where new ways and new laws and new fathers may yet be emerging unto the renewal of all God's Churches.

---

[41]   See Frederick R. McManus, "The Possibility of New Rites in the Church," *The Jurist* 50 (1990) 435-458.

RESPONSE TO JOHN ERICKSON

CARL GEROLD FÜRST*

It is impossible to give a true "response" to the clear introduction to the theme presented by Professor John H. Erickson. This is all the more so because, at least in regard to principal matters, I share a number of his opinions, and I thank him for his study on the Code of Canons of the Eastern Churches. I do not have enough space to discuss in detail the diversities of ideas existing between us.[1] I have decided, therefore, even at the cost of not using all the space conceded to me, to limit myself to some points which have more general importance but, in my view, are basic.

1. In the first place I think that it would be good to spend a moment on the intentions which they had in elaborating the *CCEO* regarding the Eastern Churches which do not belong to the communion of the Catholic Church. Already in the "Guidelines for the Revision of the Code of Oriental Canon Law," voted during the first plenary meeting of the Commission for the Revision of the Code of Oriental Canon Law of 1974,[2] one reads:

Ecumenical character of the *CICO*

1. The future Code shall declare that it holds good only for those who legitimately belong to an Oriental Catholic Church.

2. It must be a prime concern of the new Code to promote the fulfillment of the desire expressed by the Second Vatican Council that the Oriental Catholic Churches "flourish and execute with new apostolic vigor the task entrusted to them" (*Orientalium Ec-*

---

* Universität Freiburg-im-Breisgau (Germany).

[1] For example I cannot share Professor Erickson's opinion that the *CCEO*, by the fact that it is a codification of the Catholic Church, is only a new edition of the *CIC*. It would be well to have a more indepth discussion of the question (which would also concern the *CIC*) as to the extent—if ever—that the concept of communion can be "translated" into a juridical concept or on whether such a "translation" is needed or not, etc.

[2] *Codex Iuris Canonici Orientalis* (*CICO*) was the "working title" of the future *Codex Canonum Ecclesiarum Orientalium* (*CCEO*).

clesiarum, n. 1), both as regards to the good of souls and as regards the "special office of promoting the unity of all Christians" (ibid., n. 24),—of which unity they are called upon to be faithful witnesses according the principles of the Decree on Ecumenism. . . .

4. Therefore, in all things concerning the Orthodox Churches, the Code must be inspired by the words of Paul VI: on the "sister churches," the "almost full" communion, on the respect due to the Hierarchs of the Churches as "Pastors to whom has been entrusted a portion of the flock of Christ"; inspired also by the Conciliar text on their "right to govern themselves according to their own disciplines, since these are better suited to the temperament of their faithful and better adapted to foster the good of souls" (*Unitatis redintegratio*, n. 16).[3]

But the proposal does not live up to what could have been hoped for, that is, a true and proper collaboration of experts coming from Eastern non-Catholics, because:

3. In virtue of this "special office," referred to in the previous paragraph, due consideration must be given, in the revision of *CICO*, to the "aggiornamento" to which the Orthodox Churches are tending in the hope of an ever greater unity of the Canon Law of all the Oriental Churches.[4]

This final objective, however, could be realized only in part.[5] Aside from the very slow progress of work preparing for the Holy and Great

---

[3] "Guidelines for the Revision of the Code of Oriental Canon Law," *Nuntia* n. 3 (1976) 20.

[4] Ibid.

[5] At the plenary meeting of March 18-23, 1974 the following observers were present: Most Rev. German Timofeev, Bishop of Vienna, Russian; Vartaped Mesrob Krikorian, pastor in Vienna (now archbishop), Armenian; Rev. Salib Sourial, pastor in Cairo, Copt; Prof. Charalambos Frangistas of the University of Thessalonica, Greek. The following were invited to collaborate in the study *coetus*: Most Rev. Iwas Zakka, Metropolitan of Baghdad of the Syrian Orthodox Church (now Patriarch); Most Rev. Panteleimon Kararnikolas, Metropolitan of Corinth of the Greek Orthodox Church; Vartaped Mesrob Krikorian; and Rev. Salib Sourial. Metropolitan Panteleimon and Father Sourial did not attend the meetings. Metropolitan Zakka took part in the sessions of the *coetus* on the sacraments which dealt with the Eucharist, orders, and worship; Vartaped Krikorian participated in the meetings of the *coetus* on the ecclesiastical magisterium.

Synod of the Orthodox Churches, joined with an evermore sensitive tendency to reduce the points to be treated in it, there was already a fundamental obstacle to an exchange of views or at least an update with regard to what was being done on the Orthodox side with respect to an "official" updating. Nevertheless, the idea as such remained alive. Indirectly even Pope John Paul II made reference to it in his discourse on the occasion of the presentation of the *CCEO* to the Synod of Bishops of the Catholic Church:

> I must at least turn my thoughts with respect to all the Orthodox Churches. Even to these I would like to "present" the new code, which right from the start was conceived and elaborated on the principles of true ecumenism and first of all on the great esteem which the Catholic Church has for these as "sister Churches" already "in quasi full communion" with the Church of Rome—as Paul VI affirmed—and for their pastors as those to whom "has been given a portion of the flock of Christ." There is no norm in the code which does not foster the road to the unity of all Christians, and clearly there are norms here for the Eastern Catholic Churches concerning the manner of promoting this unity "first of all through prayers, by the example of life, by religious fidelity to the ancient traditions of the Eastern Churches, by mutual and better knowledge of each other, and by collaboration and brotherly respect in practice and spirit."[6]

Besides the indications already given by professor Erickson, I would like to refer to one canon which for me is most important, which underlines in a very clear manner the obligation of the Catholic hierarchy at least through an "internal collaboration"; i.e., *CCEO* canon 40 §1:

> Hierarchs who preside over Churches *sui iuris* and all other hierarchs are to see most carefully to the faithful protection and accurate observance of their own rite, and not admit changes in it except by reason of its organic progress, *keeping in mind, however, mutual goodwill and the unity of Christians.*[7]

CCEO canon 657 §4 makes direct reference to this canon with regard to liturgical books, a matter of great significance also for the Orthodox.

---

[6] John Paul II, allocution to the Synod of Bishops on the new Code of Canons of the Eastern Churches, October 25, 1990, n. 13: *AAS* 88 (1999) 486-493.

[7] Translation from *Code of Canons of the Eastern Churches, Latin-English Edition* (Washington: CLSA, 1992); emphasis added.

In sum, I think I can say that the *CCEO*, in its development and in its final form, was considered and is effectively a hand extended by the Catholic Church at least as a basis of discussion for a coming closer together between the Catholic Church and the Orthodox Churches.

2. In close connection with these considerations is also the question of the duration of the validity of the *CCEO*. In the final paragraph of the Second Vatican Council's Decree on the Eastern Catholic Churches it is expressly declared: "all these directives of law are laid down in view of the present situation, until such time as the Catholic Church and the separated Eastern Churches come together into the fullness of communion" (*OE* 30). Now it is true that such a norm, even though it was requested,[8] is not found in the *CCEO* itself. In the bull of the promulgation of the *CCEO*, however, it is stated expressly:

> Thus it happens that it is necessary that the canons of the Code of the Eastern Catholic Churches have the same firmness as the laws of the Code of Canon Law of the Latin Church; that is, that they be in force until abrogated or changed by the supreme authority of the Church for a just cause, of which causes full communion of all of the Eastern Churches with the Catholic Church is indeed the most serious.[9]

Here there is again a reference to ecumenism. The accent, however, on the juridical character of the *CCEO* leads immediately to another reflection.

3. I think that one must not forget the question of the "nature" of the *CCEO*, that is, its juridic character. In fact, the guidelines for the revision of the Code of Oriental Canon Law underline:

> In order to hasten the work of codification, it is essential to define the character of the future Code, that is to say, to make clear right from the start whether it is to be a text of a dogmatic or, rather, of a juridical nature.

---

[8] See the observations of the members of the Commission for the Reform of the Code of Oriental Canon Law to the "Schema Codicis Iuris Canonici Orientalis" and the responses of the *coetus de expensione observationum*, n. 7: *Nuntia* n. 28 (1986) 9.

[9] John Paul II, apostolic constitution *Sacri Canones*, October 18, 1990, in *Code of Canons of the Eastern Churches, Latin-English Edition*, xiii. The pope was inspired here by a consideration of the *coetus de expensione observationum* regarding a request relative to an official preface for the *CCEO*: "Comunque si ritiene che il Codice Orientale, per ogni certezza giuridica, non debba essere trattato diversamente dal CIC latino, le cui leggi valgono finchè non sono abrogate." *Nuntia* n. 28 (1986) 12.

Though founded on dogma, as propounded by the Church's authentic magisterium, the Code is not meant to be a body of truths and exhortations on the subject of Faith and Morals but, quite definitely, a body of laws governing the practical life of the faithful.

The juridical character of the Code is recommended, besides, by the fact that it has to establish and define the rights and duties of individuals towards one another and towards society: this result cannot be obtained, if the Code is not juridical in character.[10]

Now, precisely with regard to the nature of canon law, the discussion in Orthodoxy is still in full development, even evident in the practically irreconcilable positions among them.[11] Thus, to evaluate the idea of a possible reception of *CCEO* on the part of the Orthodox, one must first of all, even to avoid delusions, be clear concerning the "ambit" in which such a reception could be possible.

It is evident that outside of this discussion are those who are opposed to a law which would be characterized as a system of law and thus completely extraneous to the spirit of Orthodoxy. Not included also are those who hold as immutable, at least for this time, the sacred canons ordered by an ecumenical council and therefore changeable only by another ecumenical council. There remains, it seems, as interlocutors only those who accept, or even defend, the right of the Church to change, transform, or improve the canons, recognizing that the Church has a true legislative power.

4. Let me now turn to the methodology of the discussion on this theme. But I think that, especially because of the juridic nature of the *CCEO*, we must discuss at least in a certain general line also the question of the relationship between canon law and theology.

Let me say immediately that I doubt there exists "the" theology. I think, rather, that there is some fundamental theological truth which is the object of the interpretive attention of certain theological schools or

---

[10]   "Guidelines," "Juridical Nature of the CICO," *Nuntia* n. 3 (1976) 20.

[11]   See Heinz Ohme, "Zur Diskussion um das kanonische Recht in der neueren orthodoxen Theologie," *Kerigma und Dogma* 37 (1991) 227-256, and Carl Gerold Fürst, "Common Canonical Tradition (Critical Report)," in *Incontro fra canoni d'Oriente e d'Occidente*, Atti del Congreso Internazionale Bari, 23-29 Septembre 1991 (Bari, 1994) 91. John Erickson also has participated in the discussion: "The Orthodox Canonical Tradition," *St. Vladimir's Theological Quarterly* 27 (1983) 155-167.

certain theologians which are quite divergent among themselves. This also goes for Orthodoxy, notwithstanding the efforts of those (among whom, however, is not to be included Professor Erickson) who seek to make us believe that Orthodox theology is monolithic. Let us prescind from the fact that a large part of the norms of canon law, which are of themselves necessary, are simply neutral with regard to theology. But when in fact in a concrete case the theological value is underlined as the indispensable basis for canon law, we must be very cautious in our evaluation of a determined canon as an expression of theology (while it is only an expression of one theological school), or in thinking that it would always be possible to find an univocal, common theology, to be "translated" into the language of canon law.[12]

If we accept these considerations a number of doors are opened to a more humble but more effective evaluation of canon law. I would like to give an example. Professor Erickson has justly noted that the concept "Church *sui iuris*" lacks a theological resonance and an ecclesiological depth. But, at the same time, he admits that there is still lacking a clear ecclesiology of intermediary ecclesiastical organisms between the universal Church and the diocese or eparchy also in Orthodox theology.[13] Now these organisms exist and one cannot simply give up the possibility of a certain regulation of these organisms only because of a still insufficient theological reflection. Thus precisely canon law considered in its juridic nature offers this possibility of regulation and offers also the possibility of a choice of a theologically temporary yet necessarily indistinct concept.

5. Quite briefly, a final point: East and West "aggiornamento."

Already for more than a decade I have expressed the opinion, perhaps without much success, that one of the more urgent topics for historians of Latin canon law is to examine the question of Eastern canon law in the Latin canon law or of the Latin canon law in the Eastern canon law, of the canonical patrimony common between East and West which is indis-

---

[12]   See also Carl Gerold Fürst, "Wesen des Kirchenrects," *Internationale Katholische Zeitschrift Communio* 6 (1977) 496-506.
[13]   Naturally the question was also debated in the meeting of the Eighth Congress of the Society for the Law of the Eastern Churches at Santiago de Compostela, 1987: "The 'Protos' and his Jurisdiction," *Kanon* 9 (1989).

pensable at least in a world subject to rapid changes and "aggiornamento" even in a sense of a convergence of canonical traditions.[14]

Even in regard to this point it is inevitable that there is the danger that here and now we are knocking on one another's heads. I am very grateful to Professor Erickson for having at least in part raised the questions and hope that a discussion even on this point will be able to open the way definitively to further study.

Translation by James H. Provost

---

[14] See Carl Gerold Fürst, "Der Strafrechtsentwurf der Päpstlichen Kommission für die Revision des Orientalischen Codex Iuris Canonici," in *Im Dienst von Kirche und Staat. In memoriam Carl Holböck*, ed. Franz Pototschnig and Alfred Rinnerthaler (Vienna: Verlag der Wissenschaftlichen Gesellschaften Österreichs, 1985) 371, n. 12; and Fürst, "Common Canonical Tradition," note 9.

CLARIFIED POINTS ON "RECEPTION" AND POINTS REQUIRING FURTHER THEOLOGICAL, HISTORICAL, AND CANONICAL CLARIFICATION

These topics, certainly ambitious, were addressed by the discussion groups within the context of ecclesial and canonical reflection following the interventions of Professors Pottmeyer, Carrasco, Redaelli, Krämer, Erickson, Fürst, Beinert, Joncheray, Henn, Tanner, Legrand, and Provost. The contributions are concrete and illuminating in reference both to points of clarification and the need for further in-depth work. These discussions took place on April 12, 1996 and continued to be examined subsequently.

Spanish Language Group

Points Already Clarified

1. The need to foster freedom as a guarantee of real processes of reception: the Church is formed by men and women animated by the Spirit.

2. For its full realization, reception implies freedom and a recognition of the active role of the people of God. In the same line, reception is joined to the *sensus fidei*, which requires openness.

3. The theological complexity of the relationships of communion between the supreme authority of the Church and the totality of the people of God.

4. The analogical character of reception (the very question posed for this session demonstrates it).

5. Necessity for a permanent rereading of history.

6. Distinction between reception and a hermeneutic process, even if the latter is necessary for the former.

7. Reception is more a theological fact than a juridic concept, even if there is a temptation to reduce it to the latter.

8. Reception represents a fundamental process of Christian and ecclesial life.

9. The elaboration of a canonical point of view has been very well thought out, however nothing has been said about the books of the code that Vatican II has not seemed to influence.

10. The historical proposal has been excellent even if it is reduced to a European and Europeanizing vision.

11. There is a need to distinguish between two fundamental levels: reception as a general ecclesiological reality, and particular cases (processes).

Points Needing Further Clarification

1. The identity of the local church as a subject of reception and the determination of different subjects within it.

2. If the subject of reception is an ecclesial subject, what group or community is the real subject, taking into account the tension between the episcopal principle (community around the bishop) and the eucharistic principle?

3. What is the degree of altereity-exogeneity in speaking of reception carried out by the local churches?

4. The unfolding of the autonomy necessary for episcopal conferences.

5. What is the relationship between systematic dissent (understood as a negative phenomenon) and non-reception?

6. It is necessary to probe in depth the relationship between the following realities in principle not excluding:

reception and practice,
reception and obedience,
reception and non-acceptance,
reception and custom.

7. In probing in depth the relationship between reception and communion, various possibilities are possible: reception/ communion, dissent/ communion (in this case negation would not necessarily mean disobedience), and dissent/non-communion. It is necessary to probe this problematic in depth.

8. Reception among other Christian peoples has not been mentioned (this refers to the European and Europeanizing vision of the colloquium). Concretely, from a Latin American viewpoint, nothing has been said about the rich tradition of particular law of Latin America formed by elements of Inca, Aztec, and Spanish origin.

9. It is necessary to consider reception going beyond existing cases of conflict or uneasiness.

10. Reception is often confused with the participation of the people of God, or the *sensus fidei* is confused with public opinion.

11. What are the instances and criteria of objectifying the Church's faith?

French Language Group

1. We all agree that reception pertains to the very life and essence of the Church. At the same time we agree that there are theological epistemologies, as Professor Komonchak suggests, and ecclesiologies, as Professor Schatz illustrates, which preclude making room for reception in the Church or notably diminish its importance. By the same token certain institutional forms, translations, or practices can favor and promote it.

2. Reception is not only a process which takes place between the hierarchy and the faithful, as in the dynamic of the Church teaching and the Church taught, where reception could be erroneously identified with an individualized process of acceptance or rejection of magisterial activity. Reception takes place between churches which are its subjects. These live in history and in societies which oblige them to receive over and over again the essential data of the faith. Such is the case, it seems to us, in the current ecumenical dialogues and in the production of new Christological agreements, e.g., with the Copt and Assyrian Churches.

3. To receive anew the data of faith, reception requires the cooperation of all the faithful and of the ensemble of churches, that is to say in principle:

a. synodality in the local churches (pastors and lay faithful together in the same *conspiratio* according to variable but necessary institutional forms);

b. the conciliarity of the churches (which is not expressed only in ecumenical councils or in episcopal synods, but which could advantageously be expressed regionally through plenary or provincial councils which involve the participation of the lay faithful and their pastors, as the provisions of the Code of Canon Law envision).

Points Requiring Further Clarification

1. All of us agree on the fact that there is a terminus, a closure to the reception of the canon of the Scriptures.

Nevertheless, we ask ourselves if the reception of ecumenical councils itself also arrives at a definitive terminus after which it would become solely the object of hermeneutical work, in which case reception would not be a continuing or "ongoing process," as there is a tendency to define it.

Or rather, would it be necessary to think that historical circumstances can lead to receiving anew (re-receiving) the enunciations of a council or earlier councils all over again or otherwise? Is that not what happened in the case of the Council of Chalcedon? Without formally receiving the enunciations of that council, do not the recent Christological declarations between the Catholic Church and the Coptic and Assyrian Churches constitute a form of reception of the faith of Chalcedon?

2. We note a tension in the use of the word "communion." In effect it happens that the theological vocabulary vindicates a certain originality, e.g., in basing its discourse on the trinitarian mystery in such a manner that the juridical and sociological dimensions of this same Church are seen as having hardly any relevance.

Moreover, all of us know that the verification of communion takes place through concrete institutional operations, procedures, sociocultural conditioning, etc. This is the case also with reception which cannot occur without such concrete, juridical, institutional, and social processes; reception is then at the same time reception of content and of procedures which make it possible.

Instead of opposing approaches which ought neither be excluded nor mutually disqualified, whether they be dogmatic or whether they arise from the human sciences, ought we not develop an ecclesiology where the constitutive elements of the Church (such as the profession of faith, apostolicity, ministries, sacramental life, etc.) would respectfully cohere with all the dimensions of the life and being of the Church?

English Language Group

The discussion of what has been clarified concerning reception also served to identify a number of areas in need of further study.

Reception is an analogous concept, it is closely related to conversion (especially the conversion of the Church), and it varies with the weight of what is being received (in terms of the hierarchy of truths). Even when people say that they have received something (e.g., Vatican II), it may turn out that they understand differently what they have received.

Reception takes time, often involves conflict, and requires patience. It is a complex process, and no single "process" explains it (a situation which is not unlike the diversity of processes encountered in the development of doctrine). How can one determine whether reception has taken place or not? When does one say finally that something has been received or not?

Is de-reception possible? For example, John Paul II has invited the Church to prepare for the third millennium by a three-fold process, the second stage of which is repentance; could this be to repent for what the Church has "received"? Could there be de-reception of non-ecclesial factors which have been received (perhaps unconsciously) from the common culture, secular legal patterns, etc.?

Experience with reception indicates the need for catechesis, continuing formation, and education. This applies to all in the Church. For example, how does the Church help bishops to understand their role in the reception process? How are bishops helped to understand the meaning of "consulting the faithful"? Moreover, if reception is taken seriously as a way of acknowledging the responsibility of everyone in the Church for the life of the Church, and so involves the personal responsibility of each Christian, then it makes a difference in how one tries to teach.

What is the role of obedience in reception? There are various types of obedience: the obedience of Jesus to the Father; obedience as listening and discernment; "blind" obedience; acceptance of a cross which one has not chosen; obedience to unity in truth, which allows for multiplicity; etc. This deserves more study.

Is there, or should there be, a difference in the reception of dogmatic teaching, moral teaching, and law? What is the significance of the lack of reception, for example, of moral teaching: does it mean the doctrine has not been taught effectively, or that in their hardness of heart people have not learned, or that in their sensitivity to the truths of the faith they have not accepted the teaching?

When one teaches and expects reception, there is always the risk that one may be wrong; rational sheep have a duty not to follow a shepherd who would lead them off the cliff! Yet there is a prophetic role in the Church, one which challenges the "received" ways of doing things, and calls for conversion to the gospel. How does one discern the difference?

Italian Language Group

1. At the theological level

The concept of reception is very complex and difficult to define. One could develop in more depth the following points:

a. What is the relationship between "content" and "formal act" in relation to infallibility?

b. On the basis of what criteria can one determine that a law or a dogmatic enunciation has been received?

c. The concept of re-reception emerged numerous times in the reports.

2. At the historical level

Here the evaluation is not easy due to the complexity and vastness of historical processes. One could indicate a more in-depth approach to the reception of the message of Jesus by the disciples (addressed in part by Professors Lanne and Komonchak) as well as reception between the Middle Ages and Vatican I.

3. At the canonical level

We ask ourselves what are the convergences or differences between these three hypotheses regarding the non-reception of a law:

a. non-reception of a juridic norm which is unreasonable and therefore deprived of an essential quality of a law according to the teaching of Suarez;

b. formation of a custom against the law (*contra legem*);

c. the non-observance of a law in light of which authority assumes a posture inspired by dissimulation (*dissimulatio*) or toleration (*tolerari potest*).

German Language Group

It seems clear:

a. "reception" is a vital act in the life of the Church as a concept correlative to "tradition";

b. "reception" is an analogous concept. Hence it is necessary in each case to differentiate it precisely in terms of the level of reception about which one is speaking (dogmatic, moral theological, disciplinary, etc., levels).

Moreover, it seems fundamental that the following points still need to be clarified:

a. the no less significant concept (material or formal) of "non-reception" in terms of the levels mentioned above;

b. "non-reception," even partially, to the extent that it is a criterion, especially in relationship to acts of the Church's teaching authority.

Translation by Thomas J. Green

THE SUBJECTS OF ECCLESIAL RECEPTION

WOLFGANG BEINERT*

THE PROBLEMATIC NATURE OF RECEPTION IN THE CHURCH

Generally speaking, *reception* is the appropriation of an alien good, of the good which is being received, into the domain of the receiver. It corresponds in an exact correlation to the event of transmission (*tradierens*): the intended good is conveyed from the transmitter's own domain to the recipient. Obviously, this presupposes that the received good and the recipient are compatible. Occasions of transmission and reception of this type are present everywhere. In the non-organic sphere, one finds it present in watercourses. In the organic realm, metabolism provides an example. And in the intellectual-personal sphere, every occasion of communication is an instance of transmission and reception. We wish to remain in the last of the three spheres named above because the ecclesiological events of interest to us are found there.

When considering these examples, it immediately becomes clear that fundamentally these events have at least a two-fold character, unfolding in such a way that the roles can change as a matter of principle. This interchangeability is a well known part of the governing circle of communication theory. The sender can become the receiver, the receiver the transmitter. The good being received can change either fully or only in certain aspects. One can exchange topics, or deepen the current topic so as to come to a better understanding of it. This is the case in every true dialogue.

The "object" of events of transmission and reception can also be persons. This is the case with the nomination to an office. The legitimate and competent leader of a community imparts his or her decision that then leads to the conferral of an office on determined persons. Through reception, the members accept the decision as well as the office bearers and the community to which they belong. Practically speaking, this means that

*   Universität Regensburg (Germany).

the members recognize the office holders' authority within the limits of their competence.

These general statements demonstrate first that the discipline of reception has an exceptionally important and fundamental role in all the social sciences and liberal arts. It is also evident that even theology depends in an elementary way on the study of reception. Research into the theory of reception has only recently been conducted within the sphere of theology.[1] But within a short amount of time it demonstrated the important insights it was able to provide for a better reflection on matters pertaining to the faith. Borrowing from a well known advertising slogan, one could say: it has never been more valuable than today. We currently stand in an ecclesial and ecclesiological crisis that seems to be taking on more or less global dimensions, especially in the Northern half of the world of Christian churches. It has shaken the Roman Catholic faith community in a special way. It becomes evident not only in the scandalous number of people leaving the faith, but also more notoriously in the distance that exists between the remaining members of the Church and the official "line" of its office holders. The question arises as to whether there is a vertical schism, a division between the church leadership and the members of the Church. The popular proposals for church reforms (e.g., *Kirchenvolksbegehren* or "We Are Church") that have taken place in several countries in the immediate past certainly signal a clear division between "above" and "below."

On closer view, one sees that the division has not occurred for dogmatic reasons, even though they have often been at the foundation of the division, but due to vital insecurities and uncertainties arising out of the content of instructions (as in the sphere of sexual morality) as well as the forms of instruction used by ecclesial authority (articulated as reproaches against centralization and authoritarianism). It would be too simple, and would contribute very little to healing the division simply to try to reduce the problem to a question of obedience; i.e., by saying that what is actually not functioning in the Church is a humble attitude of the

---

[1]   Actually, theological research into the study of reception began with Alois Grillmeier, "Konzil und Rezeption. Methodische Bemerkungen zu einem Thema der ökumenischen Diskussion der Gegenwart," *Theologie und Philosophie* 45 (1970) 321-352, and now contained in *Mit ihm und in ihm. Christologische Forschungen und Perspektiven* (Freiburg: Herder, 1975) 303-334. More attention was paid, however, to Yves Congar, "La réception comme réalité écclesiologique," *Revue des Sciences Philosophiques et Théologiques* 56 (1972) 369-403.

faithful's "obedience and reverence" in faith toward the jurisdiction of the magisterium of the pope and bishops.

Naturally, this lack of obedience could in fact be the motive, and in seeking the traces of the problem we should consider this possibility. But one cannot close one's eyes beforehand to other possible causes. For example, it could be that pride is not the cause of disobedience, but the fact that someone has better insights into an issue might be. A rather dramatic example can illustrate this point. When it was discovered that spinach contains iron and that iron is good for the human body, generations of mothers wanted to feed their children spinach. Despite the opposition of their children, the mothers knew what was good and nutritional. But with time science discovered that the children's opposition was quite reasonable; spinach did indeed contain iron, but in a form that could damage the delicate bodies of children. Thus disobedience can at times protect life.

Briefly put: What is currently distorted in the ecclesial community today is communication. The critical condition the Church finds itself in is manifested as a problem of reception. The transmission of the content of reception and the assimilation of it on the part of the subjects of the process of reception is lacking. And the suspicion arises that the cause does not reside, or at least not fundamentally, in the content of reception, but in the relation between the persons involved in the process of reception, specifically, between the officials and the remaining members of the ecclesial community. In light of its structure, the body of theologians is to be given special consideration (understood as scientists) to the extent that they have a qualified role and function in the transmission of the deposit of faith. Communication theory further teaches us that in the case of distorted relations between participants in a process of communication, the content of tradition cannot be received or at least not adequately.[2] The more difficult or demanding this becomes, the more importance will be attributed automatically to the personal moment of the process as a whole.

But in a world that is less and less Christian, where the credibility of the Christian message diminishes and is perceived by many Christians as something ever more alien and out dated, the state of relations takes on a greater significance than ever. A microscopic example of this is found in the fact that today for many people a decisive reason for attending Sun-

---

[2]   Wolfgang Beinert, "Wenn Zwei sich streiten. Über die Wiedergewinning des Konsenses," in *Kirche zwischen Konflikt und Konsens. Versöhnung als Lebensvollzug der Glaubensgemeinschaft*, ed. Wolfgang Beinert (Regensburg: F. Pustet, 1989) 13-45.

day Mass, for the choice of a particular celebration of the Eucharist, is *who* is going to preach. The "objectivism" that once characterized the Roman Catholic way of life, that Mass alone was necessary, and that the celebrant did not matter (or only barely), has practically disappeared.

We will develop our observations on the bearers or subjects of the practice of ecclesial reception in the following manner. Following these introductory observations we will address the structure of the ecclesial community in light of communication theory. In order to provide a framework for the current situation, and especially the problems that have taken on particular importance in our day, we will offer a brief historical analysis. Then we will treat the proper subjects of reception. Finally, a few necessarily incomplete remarks will be offered concerning the promotion of ecclesial communication.

THE CHURCH AS A COMMUNITY OF RECEPTION

The basic affirmation of a biblically founded faith is: God offers himself completely to the human person in the gift of the life of Jesus of Nazareth by which he gives people salvation provided that they accept the community of life with the triune God. Even if we do not take the trouble to examine the texts regarding the transmission and reception of the content of salvation history confirmed by the bible (it would be evident that there is a wealth of material available),[3] it can be presented as a process of communication with six important points:[4]

1. It is an event of transmission on God's part. God witnesses to himself in the very act of revelation.

2. It is a process of reception on the person's part. In the act of obedience to faith, the person recognizes God as a saving God and acts from this recognition. Through it the person receives salvation.

3. Therefore, salvation is the content of reception. In the end, it is God himself bringing the complete fulfillment of the human person.

4. To these major elements present throughout the process of communication, another element must be added, a specifically biblical one. Transmission and reception, which in this case are transcendental occurrences, are completed as well through *human means*. Except in excep-

---

[3]   See the appropriate biblical-theological dictionaries.
[4]   See Hans Dombois, *Das Recht der Gnade. Oekumenisches Kirchenrecht I*, 2nd ed. (Witten: Luther Verlag, 1969) 815-836.

tional circumstances, God and the human person do not have direct contact. Rather, they communicate through other people. Primarily, originally, and decisively, the mediator is Jesus Christ through whom God, "many times and in various ways spoke through the patriarchs and the prophets" (Heb 1: 1). And since the gift of God, specifically in the salvation of Christ, had to be communicated to all people of all times in a human fashion, the Holy Spirit was sent to proclaim through his works that the Church was the "mystery of reconciliation" (2 Cor 5: 19). This was concretized first in the apostolic kerygma. As Paul, who considered himself a "co-worker with God" (2 Cor 6: 1), wrote in a moving passage: "We have spoken frankly to you, Corinthians, and our heart has opened out fully to you. We have not closed ourselves to you; you have closed yourselves to us. Let your response be (I speak as to my children) to open your hearts wide" (2 Cor 6: 11-13).

5. The Church as a whole is the catalyst for reception in the event of salvation to such an extent that its *inner structure itself is characterized by communication*. In the text cited above, we encounter a meeting that was primary, original, and decisive for the historical period of the post-Easter Church, between the apostle and the local community.[5] Other pericopes demonstrate that there were other authorities charged with "making the brothers worthy of fulfilling their ministry for the building up of the Body of Christ"; namely, "prophets," "evangelists," "shepherds," and "teachers" (Eph 4: 11f). Along with these "official" tasks, exercised in a permanent way and according to a set function, there were "different gifts according to the grace received," that were in principle given to every member of the community: "For just as we are many members of the one body, even though not all members serve the same function, so we, the many, are *one* body in Christ, but as individuals we are members who belong to one another" (1 Cor 12: 4-6). Every Christian, then, stands *pro modo suo* as a subject in both the transmission and reception of the bestowal of salvation.

6. Finally, the Pauline text of 2 Cor 6 also means that the entire process is not completed automatically or mechanically, but that it takes shape in a fully human connection, that the domain of the recipient is integrated into the transmission. One could say this is a pedagogical act: Paul speaks to the Corinthians, "as to my children" so that they can actually understand him and follow his teaching. In the other letters, he also attends to

---

[5]   This primitive order of operation will be continuously cited to show that the Church was and is essentially apostolic (Credo: *ecclesia apostolica*).

the situation of the concrete community, thereby making his preaching convincing to those listening. The basic presupposition for this type of gospel designed with the people's needs in mind, which can only then become *good* news, was already given by Jesus who said that the Sabbath was meant for man, and not man for the Sabbath (Mk 2: 27).

Moreover, according to the Gospel of John, he said that the process of the transmission of salvation does not wholly coincide with his earthly life, but that thanks to and by the power of his Spirit, it continues without end, not only in the sense of a quantitative presentation of the gospel to subsequent generations, but also in an almost qualitative expansion: "I have much more to tell you, but you cannot hear it now. But when he comes, the Spirit of Truth, he will lead you into the fullness of the truth." This does not mean that there are alternative books of the New Testament. Jesus concluded directly: "For he will not speak for himself, but he will say what he heard, and inform you of what is to come" (Jn 16: 12f). But this does not preclude that there can be discoveries of the Spirit in the course of history that appear to the hearers as quite new and extraordinarily unusual. In this sense, the communication event, and with it the processes of transmission and reception, are co-existent with history and future oriented. No one in the Church can ever maintain: "Now there have been enough innovations. It is demonstrable that we have received the full truth." In modern terminology, one can assert that according to the New Testament there certainly cannot be any modernism that includes a program adding to the Gospels. At the same time, the Church cannot appropriate a traditionalist form of thought that attempts to anchor the ship of the Church in a certain harbor in the current of time (for such a place cannot even exist, as we shall see).

In summary, the following should be stated. Seen from the human perspective, salvation history is a process of reception through which the Word of God is accepted in faith. It is realized in history through the mediation of the Church in such a way that the Church's members, according to their official or unofficial charism, and as contemporary transmitters and receivers of the gift of salvation, become means through whom the creative and salvific faith is witnessed to and thus made credible as content of reception able to be appropriated by them. The members of the faith community are thus *authorities for witnessing* and *subjects of reception*.[6]

---

[6]   In classical theology, ever since Melchior Cano, the phrase *loci theologici* has been used.

Five distinctions can be made:

1. Holy Scripture. Holy Scripture is the repository of the Word of God through the mediation of the sacred writers. And thanks to its special quality as an inspired and unerring medium, it is the first and absolutely normative means of witnessing.

2. Tradition. Tradition here is intended in the theological sense as the normative interpretation of the biblical message in its reception by the ecclesial community in individual historical epochs and their *lebensraum*, and its transmission to subsequent periods. As with the biblical canon, Tradition is closed, and is an unchangeable model. However, insofar as the content of Scripture and Tradition must be received anew by each generation (and according to the presuppositions by which they live) they have a thoroughly vital history of effectiveness not only as sources and norms of faith, but also indirectly as organs of reception. They give a new colorfulness to the Christian life. What quality and what range the bible has, and how it is to be realized cannot be found in the bible itself. Rather, these things are determined from outside the bible. In this sense the bible is an organ of reception. Its concrete value is persistently determined. It is, for example, seen as completely different depending on whether it is given the stamp of verbal inspiration or whether it is considered as an object of historical-critical analysis.

3. The Ecclesial Magisterium. This arises out of the continuity necessary with the authoritative apostolic preaching, and is usually considered in its contemporary function. The exercise of the magisterium in the past is a part of the theological tradition.

4. Academic Theology. By this we understand reflection on the content of the Christian faith which, adjusted according to the object and time, is studied according to scientific methods. The content of theology is also analyzed according to its contemporary relevance. As historical content it is part of tradition in the sense mentioned above.

5. The *Sensus Fidei* of the Faithful. By this phrase we mean the charism of all members of the Church of inner agreement with the content of the faith. This agreement becomes manifest in the consent of the community, perceptible from without, with respect to this content. Proofs of this unanimity can be forms of popular religiosity, literature, art, music, the various forms of expressing the spiritual life, and their acceptance by other believers. Again, the examples are limited to contem-

porary believers. It must be repeated, the witness of faith of the deceased belongs to the sphere of tradition described above.

When we speak in what follows of the subjects of reception, we will limit the field of consideration to the three last authorities for witnessing (magisterium, theology, and *sensus fidei*). These areas contain the problems that arise out of our central concept (reception).

THE RECEPTION OF REALITY

Reception is a vital, foundational process of the Church of the New Testament. More precisely, this means that it does not belong simply to the community existing at the time the Gospels were redacted, but to the Church that always and everywhere receives them as norms. Many texts, and especially the entire *ductus* of the Holy Scripture, supply vast evidence of this. Few texts seem as clear as these. Opposed to them, however, is the already noted fact that the notion of reception has only recently possessed a rightful place in theology. Besides, even within theology it is the object of research by only a few specialists. In no way can it be called the common good of the members of the Church, beginning with the office holders to the last lay member of the faithful.[7] However, at present a change is taking place which does not take into account so much the terminology as it does the thing intended by the terminology. The first paragraph of this article spoke of this. A consequence of this upheaval (along with other causes) has been serious criticisms.

Why was knowledge of the communicative form of the Church buried, and why has it been brought back to life in our day? This question does not have simply an historical interest, but must also be answered objectively. The answer does not clarify only current events, but also clarifies the competence of the bearer of reception. It is evident that we must be satisfied here with a few hasty words of response. But then there are also many good monographs that permit us to leave it at that.[8]

The theological understanding of reception, whether articulated under this concept or another, is always a function of the notion of the Church at work.[9] As we have seen it is a matter of the inner ecclesial mediation

---

[7]   The passage from Augustine, *De praed. sanct.* (*Predestination of Saints*), 14: 37 comes to mind; it was appropriated by Vatican II in *LG* 12.

[8]   Cf., for example, Karl Gabriel, *Christentum zwischen Tradition und Postmoderne* (Freiburg: Herder, 1992).

[9]   See *Kirchenbilder-Kirchenvisionen. Variationen über eine Wirklichkeit*, ed. Wolfgang Beinert (Regensburg: F. Pustet, 1995).

of the message of revelation. Included in this is not only the dogmatic content, but also the ethical, canonical, social developments that occur; in short, the entire theological reality called "Church." This was understood in the first millennium as *communio,* as a pneumatologically anchored community of the faithful that was concretized in the particular churches in the bishop, who was witness of the faith to his own diocese as well as to the entire Church (as a participant in synods and councils). Various forms of communication existed as did an accordingly abundant number of occasions of reception.[10] These forms were self-evident since they took place within a pagan society that was so familiar with them. Roman civil law knew this maxim: "Quod omnes tangit, ab omnibus approbari debet."[11] At the end of the thirteenth century, it made its way (slightly modified) into church law and it is found there today, modestly hidden, in the 1983 version.[12] With the ever more clear-cut elaboration of papal primacy at the end of the Middle Ages, the communal image of the Church changed into an hierarchical one. Its central notion was the New Testament concept of Body of Christ. But contrary to the great Pauline letters, the thought of the reliance of all members on one another no longer dominated. Rather, the body was conceived of from the *head* down. The head, naturally, was Christ. All life in the Church flowed from him, found its source in him. Since he was enthroned at the right hand of the Father, he would act on earth through his *vicarius,* the Roman pope. Thus the pope was the direct source of life for the Church. It is clear that this resulted in the sacralization of the hierarchical office structure, and especially of the office of the pope, almost causing the breakdown of a vital exchange of views in the Church.

Certainly after this change reception existed in the Church in an essential way as it had before. But now it occurred in only one direction, from top down, from the papal head to the subjects of the pope. To the latter now belonged more or less the bishops of the particular churches. Reception, then, became identical with the act through which the precept of the highest ecclesial authority as well as his subordinates was received

---

[10]   Wolfgang Beinert, "Die Reception und ihre Bedeutung für Leben und Lehre der Kirche," in *Glaube als Zustimmung. Zur Interpretation kirchlicher Rezeptionsvorgänge,* ed. Wolfgang Beinert (Freiburg: Herder, 1991) 15-49; Klaus Schatz, "Die Rezeption ökumenischer Konzilien im ersten Jahrtausend—Schwierigkeiten, Formen der Bewältigung und verweigerte Rezeption," in ibid., 93-122.

[11]   Yves Congar, "Quod omnes tangit, ab omnibus tractari et approbari debet," *Revue Historique de Droit Français et Étranger* 36 (1958) 210-259.

[12]   1983 code c. 119.

and carried out in will and action. The element of *approbatio*, which includes the moment of insightful, responsible approval, broke down. Reception was now simply a synonym for obedience. This understanding would be proliferated ever more strongly. It was nourished in a positive form by the adaptation of the concrete ecclesial constitution to the absolute, monarchical civil forms of the European modern era. It gained negative force by standing up against phenomena that appeared to be corrupt, such as the Reformation, the Enlightenment, and secularism. It seemed to present protection against the attacks levied by interpretations of theological "modernism,"[13] the contextual theologies, and the theological appropriation of contemporary hermaneutics.

The Second Vatican Council attempted to bring about an ecclesiological shift in the direction of the ancient Church.[14] The decisive signal was the placement of the chapter on the people of God in the dogmatic constitution *Lumen gentium* before the treatment of the "states of life" in the Church. Inasmuch as these states were to be seen again as *communio*, the moment of reception automatically took on a new significance. This was concretized in the system of consultation enjoined by the council on all ecclesial levels, from the synod of bishops to the parish council. Furthermore, it appears explicitly in different conciliar texts. The *sensus fidei* was recognized again as an authoritative witness (*LG* 12). In the constitution on divine revelation, *Dei verbum*, the transmission of faith is described as a process of transmission and reception: "That which was handed down by the apostles includes all that assists the people of God in living a holy life and for increasing their faith. Thus the Church continues through the ages in teaching, in life, in worship, transmitting to all generations all that was given to it and which it believes"(*DV* 8). In this context, the declaration *Dignitatis humanae* regarding religious liberty is particularly important. It opposes the exercise of automatic obedience in questions of faith and, on the contrary, exhorts a responsible process of reception. Since God gives himself to men and women to be known, "everyone has the obligation, and also the right, of searching for the truth

---

[13]   Recently, an almost exhaustive account of the German situation has appeared: Otto Weiß, *Der Modernismus in Deutschland. Ein Beitrag zur Theologiegeschichte* (Regensburg: F. Pustet, 1995).

[14]   Joseph A. Cardinal Malula, "Die Kirche Gottes, die in Kinshasa ist, spricht zu euch," in *Laien als Gemeindeleiter*, ed. Ludwig Bertsch (Freiburg: Herder, 1990) 34. Malula speaks of an ecclesiological "Copernican Revolution" that occurred at the council. According to it, all the baptized were to possess the right to accept complete ecclesial responsibility in the Church.

in the area of religion, of prudently forming just and true judgments of conscience, using suitable means. But the truth must be sought after in a way that is proper to the human person and his or her social nature; that is, by the path of free investigation with the assistance of the magisterium or instruction, of the exchange of thoughts and dialogue through which men and women share the truth that they have found or that they believe they have found" (*DH* 3).

If one takes into account that even the liturgical constitution, *Sacrosanctum Concilium*, emphasizes the *communio* character of the liturgical community (for example, through the demand for "active participation" [*actuosa participatio*]—*SC* 27, 48) then one must maintain that all the major documents, as well as such a typical conciliar document as *Dignitatis humanae*, stress the principle of transmission-reception and demand its being put back into practice. At the same time, they have still to be fully effective. The conciliar bishops themselves are partly responsible for this inasmuch as they, *together* with Paul VI, the second conciliar pope, were prepared to make "contradictory compromises" in their struggle to reach the broadest possible degree of consensus on the texts.[15] As a result, the models of the ancient and medieval Church, which could be harmonized only with great difficulty, each remained standing next to the other. Consequently, members holding one view or the other could rely on the support of the conciliar assembly.

In addition, there was an ever growing number of serious cases of non-reception of instances of papal teaching in broad circles within the Church. The most recognizable example of this is in the fate of the encyclical *Humanae vitae* of 1968, but also in the discussion about the ordination of women. They cause the Church's leadership to adopt a doctrinally rigid position and a strict reduction of the understanding of the faith to obedience to the magisterium. Again, this is illustrated in the "Instruction on the Vocation of Theologians in the Church," which the Roman Congregation for the Doctrine of the Faith issued in 1990. Franz-Xaver Kaufmann summarized the situation in these words: "It seems to me that the contemporary situation of the Catholic faith in Western Europe can be interpreted along the lines of communication theory in light

---

[15] Max Seckler, "Über den Kompromiß in Sachen der Kehre," in *Im Spannungsfeld von Wissenschaft und Kirche. Theologie als schöpferische Auslegung der Wirklichkeit*, ed. Max Seckler (Freiburg: Herder, 1980) 99-103, 212-215.

of the failure of the mediation of transmission and reception."[16] With that we stand at the personal element of all events. For that mediation is no longer successful because those who do not hold an office, as subjects of reception, as bearers of reception are increasingly critical of the precepts of the magisterium. The *communio* model of the conciliar majority still does not function, while the vertical model of the minority no longer functions at all. Can theology provide assistance in overcoming this tension?

RECEPTION AS THE SELF-PERFECTION OF CHRISTIAN BEING

The core of the content of the ecclesial process of transmission and reception is the gospel, understood not only as the sum total of the historical expressions of the revelation of God, as they are tangible in the Scripture, dogmas, catechisms, creeds, legal sentences, instructions on living, etc., but also as a complex of God's salvific actions in and through Jesus Christ, in whom all things are contained and who is above, and who is characterized by a personal relation with the triune God. The salvific work of God and the human act of faith are (it must be repeated) already essentially a process of transmission and reception, a process that is realized in history through a broad spectrum. Within this spectrum belong (in addition to the content just mentioned) Christians (especially those entrusted with an office), expressions of Christian spirituality, religiosity, and forms of liturgy, etc.; in other words, "everything that (the Church) itself is, everything that it believes" (*DV* 8). In a word, it is a question of a realization and event of faith, that is, of a deeply personal process.

A personal process can only succeed if the personality is respected and taken into consideration. More precisely, this means the subject nature of the recipient as agent is brought into play. Formulated in other terms, every perception of reality must be taken seriously in its relation to the subject. This does not happen extensively, however, when transmission and reception in the Church are reduced to authority and obedience.[17] Naturally, no one would deny that the human person, as a being necessarily requiring a complement, must allow him or herself to listen to others, and that a community can reach its end only in a structured order that

---

[16] Franz-Xaver Kaufmann, "Glaube und Kommunikation: eine soziologische Perspektive," in *Der Glaubensinn des Gottesvolkes—Konkurrent oder Partner des Lehramts?* ed. Dietrich Wiederkehr (Freiburg: Herder, 1994) 135.

[17] Alois Müller, "Ekklesiologische Erwägungen zum Thema 'Gehorsam,'" in *Theologe und Hierarch*, ed. Josef Pfammatter and Eduard Christen, Theologische Berichte 17 (Zurich: Benziger, 1988) 111-144.

includes authority and subordination. This is valid for the Church as well. Thus the Church too should have ecclesial regulations and obedience to them. But when it comes to a faith act, it is a question of something more than general authority. Authority takes on another meaning and quality.

Indisputably, and independently of the dominant ecclesiological notion, intra-ecclesial authority, as an ecclesial dimension, is always ministerial. It does not possess right and validity of itself, but from the mission given it by God. The bearers of authority in the Church are human beings like all others, believers like all believers. Consequently, their authority is human and Christian like all other authority (for example, of theologians, parents) in the faith community. It is distinguished only by the fact that it must show the advantage of divine authority to the community, and in order to do so, it is equipped with the necessary provisions (including the special guidance of the Spirit). Since the actual reference point of Christian obedience can only be God because all people, even Christians and officials, are his children and therefore our brothers and sisters, these authorities can demand Christian obedience only and in so far as they actually and demonstrably show, through their human authority, the validity of divine authority. In other cases, they can have authority under other titles, for instance, based on relevant civil employment law, but this authority is not founded from a Christian perspective. Therefore, the central question of ecclesial authorities should not be: How can we bring the flock to reason? Rather, it should be: How will we best achieve, with the flock, the same goal?

Now, according to revelation, the authority of God is an authority of love. It does not impose itself by force, but seeks free adherents in a familial society. This is expressed fundamentally in the idea of God's covenant with man. Such a relationship includes a partnership of free acceptance. Christian obedience to God is part of a free and mature response of being ready to fulfill his will out of love. Now, if ecclesial obedience is fully derived from divine obedience, then the characteristics of freedom and a mature response arising out of a decision of conscience are also essentially suitable to it. The acceptance and adoption of a good, or of a precept, out of free insight is no longer described as obedience, but as reception. It manifests itself as the genuine form of Christian behavior to a Christian authority.

This general statement is further strengthened when the specific objects of faith are considered. As theological expressions open to reflec-

tion the statements that articulate the substance and content of the Good
News are subject to argumentative questioning. They should and must be
interpreted according to the rules of hermeneutics, and they must be investigated to their core by means of (to name a few examples) historical,
exegetical, and philosophical disciplines; it is a question of the truth that
must be found. The truth, however, cannot be commanded, but only
pointed out. "The truth appears only by virtue of itself. To deny a person
full freedom of conscience, especially the freedom to search for the truth,
or to try to force him or her into a particular way of understanding the
truth, goes against the person's inherent right." This was formulated by
Pope John Paul II in his world peace message of 1991.[18]

Finally, besides the special binary expression in Christianity of authority-obedience, and the characteristic form of doctrinal truth, a third
factor is to be considered: the importance of the subject's environment.[19]
This key notion, introduced into the social sciences by Alfred Schütz
(1899-1959), applies to the structures of the entire spheres of feeling, experience, and action in which the individual exists. One's environment is
precisely the sphere of reality in which one exists, thinks, and acts, and
which one shares with other individuals. One's environment is the indisputable given of the daily sphere of existence in which partial worlds can
first be erected, such as art, science, and also religion. One could compare it best with a current in which the individual rides in a boat all their
life. But the life-current has no dry land with safe shores, no Archi-
medean point, at which one can embark and disembark. Therefore, one
can never perceive the environment at any one time as complete, but only
from one perspective, selectively and in a fragmentary way. Based on
this, it follows that the environment can only be grasped through interpretation.

This environment is also the context of the Christian faith. It appears,
then, that this faith can only reach completion in a personal way when it
is seen in its context as a partial world. This does not happen if ecclesial
models of interpretation are required which arise out of environments

[18]   Message for World Day of Peace 1991, "Ob diem ad pacem in universo mundo
fovendam dicatam," December 8, 1990: *AAS* 83 (1991) 412.
[19]   Alfred Schütz and Thomas Luckmann, *Struckturen der Lebenswelt*, 2 vols. (Frankfurt: Suhrkamp, 1979); *Was der Geist den Gemeinden sagt. Bausteine zu einer Ekklesiologie der Ortskirchen*, ed. Ludwig Bertsch (Freiburg: Herder, 1991); Henning Luther,
Religion und Alltag (Stuttgart: Radius Verlag, 1992), esp. 184-211; Wilfried Härle, *Dog-
matik* (New York: W. de Gruyter, 1995) 168-192.

that are no longer accessible to the normal person. The tragedy of the Catholic Church in the contemporary era consists to a large degree in the fact that it has overlooked the historical character of the environment. As a consequence it clung to models of thought like neo-scholasticism or continued to forbid the use of the historical-critical method in exegesis even when they had long grown obsolete and were no longer compelling. Thus the Modernist crisis at the turn of the last century broke out. When faith in its concrete word and life forms cannot be integrated into the prevailing life context, it cannot be appropriated by the subject. Non-reception is inevitable. On the other hand,

> in order to understand the Christian faith at all, it must be presented with words, pictures, actions, signs, etc., whose *meaning* must be familiar with the prevailing environment or permit itself to be cut off from those who are part of that world. But an understanding of the faith first requires that the significance of the faith for people's life be made visible and comprehensible. And this is possible only when it signifies for the present environment its unconditional trust in God who has revealed himself in Jesus Christ.[20]

Then and only then can the preaching of the faith be received and so become effective.

Christianity as the perfection of life, as we have been able to see, is essentially an occasion of reception. Because no person, whether a church leader, theologian, or a "simple believer," can escape the context of his or her environment; because no Christian is able to live with another faith other than the Christian one; and because ultimately the Christian correlation between authority and obedience carries consequences common to all Christians (for both "superiors" and "subordinates"), the general conditions of communication theory, as well as its typical Christian configuration, apply to all members of the Church. Thus it has already been said that principally the individual authoritative witnesses of the magisterium, theology, and the *sensus fidei* always possess their own legitimacy and are both transmitter and receiver with respect to all others. But since they have their proper task and function, as well as their own importance, we have to take a brief, closer look at these authorities under the aspect assigned them.

---

[20]   Härle, 179.

A. The Ecclesiastical Magisterium

In common awareness, as well as in self-understanding, the magisterium seems clearly to take the part of the transmitter in the communication process of transmission and reception. In classical, neo-scholastic theology this was called simply the *ecclesia docens*, which stood over against the rest of the faith community as *ecclesia discens et oboediens*. But this clear role assignment functioned merely and only in the vertical ecclesial model of the ecclesiology of the Middle Ages and post Middle Ages. It is neither theologically nor empirically correct. There is peace with regards to the assertion that, according to the biblically authorized constitution, there exists an authority in Catholic interpretation that preserves, increases, and safeguards the unity of the Church in truth, and which has received the means necessary to accomplish this. These means are effective from the authentic proposal to the irreformable and infallible proclamation of a revealed matter, and they also include the competence to insist authoritatively on the respect due the proposals. As for the members of the Church, they have the duty to be loyal and obedient to the magisterial instructions in the indicated area.

Nevertheless, relations between the teaching office and the faithful are anything but uni-directional. Theory already provides for this. The magisterium, as we have already once recalled, is first a ministry: its "more" (*magis*) is the "less" (*minus*) of service to the entire faith community. This is so much the case that its powers are theologically derived from it. The primary bearer of truth and the primary subject of the sure proclamation of the truth is the entire Church, the faith community as a whole (*LG* 12). Insofar as the magisterium exists in it and as its organ, these characteristics belong to it in a qualified and specific form.

Since it can do nothing in an authorized and pertinent form except preach and realize the faith of the entire Church, not creating this faith, but encountering, welcoming and witnessing to it, the instrument of transmission pertains to it to the extent that it is faith's receptacle. "The magisterium is not above the word, but serves it by teaching only what has been transmitted. It listens by divine command to the Word of God, and with the assistance of the Holy Spirit, conserves it devotedly and interprets it faithfully. All that it proposes to the faith, as revealed by God, it extracts from this unique deposit of faith" (*DV* 10). The moment of reception cannot be expressed any clearer than this phrase of the Second Vatican Council from the second chapter of the Constitution on Divine Revelation. This phrase must be read together with the description (already alluded to above) of the content of ecclesial reception in the same chapter of this document. If what is to be received—the *recipiendum*—contains "all that (the Church) is in itself, all that it believes" (*DV* 8), then to it belongs as well the living testimony of this faith through the other instances of witnessing. This testimony is also to be received by the magisterium. There are some marks of this doctrine in canon law.[21] Thus, under certain circumstances, customs (*consuetudines*) belong to the matter of reception of the ecclesial legislator.[22]

In canon 337 §2, the free reception of episcopal acts by the pope is provided for. The right of removing bishops also belongs to the matter of free reception even though it has not been codified.[23] Beyond these relatively few references, praxis attests to the fact that the magisterium is both a recipient as well as transmitter of faith and life. One can recall first of all the obvious fact (seldom treated) that the magisterium is not an hypostasis, but comprised of men who grew up in a quite definite environment, and who work in a definite environment as office holders. Whether the pope is Polish or Italian, whether a bishop comes from nobility or the middle class, whether he functioned before ordination as a pastor, a professor of systematic theology, or a Caritas director, what type of spirituality his parents or other guardians gave him, what type of personalities his instructors had, and what type of people his closest advisors are, how much contact he really still has with the "grassroots"—all this flows of its own accord into their thoughts, in their assessment of situations, their emphases on particular teachings, as well as into their character, way of perceiving life, their sensibilities.

It would be simple to demonstrate how in the history of the Church and theology constant impulses from the Church have been taken up by the magisterium and internalized. A few arbitrary examples come to mind. The Christology of the first five ecumenical councils is not imaginable without the reception of Hellenistic philosophy; theology and liturgy of the Eucharist has been influenced by mystics like Julian of Lüttich (the Feast of Corpus Christi); the modern Marian dogmas would hardly have

[21]   Frank Ochmann, "Kirchliches Recht in und aus dem Leben der Communio: Zur 'Rezeption' aus kanonistischer Sicht," in *Glaube als Zustimmung*, 130-138 (*supra*, note 10).
[22]   See 1983 code cc. 23-28.
[23]   Knut Walf and Petrus Huizing, "Was meint 'Recht in und aus dem Leben der Communio'": Zur 'Rezeption' aus kanonistischer Sicht," in Beinert, ed., *Glaube als Zustimmung*, 130-138.

been formulated without the influence of the Marian devotions of the Mediterranean churches; the changes in the magisterium's position with regard to women have been keenly precipitated by the feminist movement in the Church.[24]

B. Scientific Theology

The vertical model of the Church naturally banishes theology entirely to the side of the "hearing" Church; within it theology has at best the task of clarifying the magisterial positions in a positive manner and of preparing simple people for them. The significant expression of this is the presentation of the material of the theological manuals, as was customary in the 1960's and 1970's. The theses were composed, normally with an exact theological qualification, and then exhaustively proven through the demonstration of their place within the magisterium. A reference to other *loci theologici* was not absent, but it was little more than an abundant and thus superfluous confirmation of the position already established. Even the most passing glance at the great Scholastic Summas demonstrates clearly that the entire theological tradition did not stand behind this method. Their smallest element, the *articulus*, is nothing other than the stylized form of the *disputatio*, the examination of an opinion and counter opinion, whose clarification would result from the argument. The famous *distinguo* of the Master demonstrates the receptive valence of the entire process: the truth is not articulated by an external authority; it imposes itself through the acceptance and assimilation of the plausible and coherent moments of argumentation and the refutation and expulsion of inadequate elements of the debate. Theological reflection essentially contains a receptive element inasmuch as it is reflection conducted in a scientific manner, and only by a probing investigation of its subject can it gain knowledge. Inasmuch as it is *theological reflection*, and not the science of religion (which examines the content of faith from outside of the faith), it considers the faith from within the faith community, and also receives the expressions of the other witnesses as acts of faith. Based on this, an exceptionally critical moment belongs to it which, it follows, excludes all positivism, even the positivism of the magisterium.

---

[24] Cf. the document collection of Rudolf Zwank in *Frauenbefreiung und Kirche, Darstellun-Analyse-Dokumentation*, ed. Wolfgang Beinert (Regensburg: F. Pustet, 1987) 113-302. Also, the official positions published to date completely and entirely confirm this fact, especially John Paul II, encyclical letter *Mulieris dignitatem*, August 15, 1988: *AAS* 80 (1988) 1653-1729.

The exegete Thomas Söding, taking dogmatic theology's use of Scripture as an example, has described quite well the contribution of theology to communication:

> On the one hand, it looks to the whole of biblical witnessing to the faith and attempts to demonstrate its unity: it does so by showing, in the history of the transmission and reception of old and new testament theologies, without any harmonizing or leveling, the *oeconomia revelationis* with its central eschatological point in the Christ event. On the other hand, it looks to the ecclesial reception of Scripture and attempts to understand from the standpoint of Scripture itself the discoveries, as well as the deficiencies, the developments, and the changes in the biblical language of God in the formation of creeds, in piety, and in the practice of the faith. It also attempts to mediate these with the contemporary Christian vision. Thirdly, it looks to the reality of people and the world in order to address and interpret them in their truth in a confrontation with Holy Scripture.[25]

In the same way, one must speak of the relation between theology and transmission, between the magisterium and the *sensus fidei* of the faithful. It is hardly necessary to mention that theologians are not robots, but men and women with their contradictions, their characteristics, and the peculiarities unique to their life, no different from those in the magisterium; and that this ensemble of factors out of which one examines the biography corresponding to each theologian, also influences his or her research and teaching.

C. The Sensus Fidei *of the Faithful*

The position of the lay person, of the simple Christian without an office or rank, is described in the German language with expressions that arise out of the ecclesial sphere and the reality of the way the Church acts. These expressions are vast and unequivocal. From the top down, the Christian at the grass roots level is *given a dressing down and duly given a good talking to; he or she is taught ways of behaving, and threatened with hell*; in a word, the Christian is constantly being preached at. The

---

[25] Thomas Söding, "Wissenschaftliche und kirchliche Schriftauslegung. Heremeneutische Überlegungen zur Verbindlichkeit der Heiligen Schrift," in *Verbindliches Zeugnis II. Schriftauslegung-Lehramt-Rezeption*, ed. Wolfahrt Pannenberg and Thomas Schneider (Freiburg: Herder, 1995) 101f.

poor soul is (there is hardly any other conclusion) the recipient par ex-
cellence and nothing other than recipient. *Obedience* describes his or her
ecclesial position most precisely.

An objection must be raised a final time. This occurs only under the
conditions of the vertical-unidirectional church model, and does not coincide with the fully theological and practical reality. Let us begin with the
last point. The religious socialization of every Christian, at least when he
or she is, as usually happens, a Christian from childhood on, occurs
through the handing on of the *sensus fidei* of the faithful. At the beginning,
and not only at the beginning, there are neither papal encyclicals nor vo-
luminous manuals of academic theology, but the mother's prayers, the father's view of the world, the devotion of the family and contemporaries,
custom, the impression of Christian culture in its multiple manifestations:
art, literature, music, liturgy. And since everything in the process of up-
bringing leaves a lasting impression, all these transmissions have a lasting value in life for the recipient, even in those cases when he or she becomes an office holder or theologian. They have an effect even though
they often have little or no conscious influence on official pronouncements and instructions. This has already been mentioned above. Even theological reflection brings considerable differences to the simple image of
the Church that brought about these expressions. The fact that the Church
remains in the truth of the Gospel of Jesus Christ is, as has been shown, a
truth ultimately guaranteed by the Holy Spirit who animates and enlivens
the Church. The Church, however, is the entire people of God, the integral
Body of Christ. All members are stones in the Temple of the Holy Spirit.
Those in the magisterium are obviously not exceptions. They are, as has
been said already, in a certain way entrusted with their task by the Holy
Spirit. But it is not they alone; whoever is baptized and confirmed has the
fullness of the Spirit. The Spirit's character is such that it blows where *it*
wills, and avoids any attempts at canalization. So every bearer of the faith
can be, and must be prepared to be, a recipient of the Holy Spirit.

The early church was well aware of these things, that later were radically forgotten to the extent that it is now apparently up to our generation
to atone for it. Origen speaks of "consent of the entire Church animated
by the Spirit."[26] For him this was much more than a democratic majority.
It was an assertion based on Trinitarian theology. The third chapter of the
Rule of Benedict is significant, "On Convoking the Brothers for Coun-

---

[26]   Origen, *Jes. Nav. hom.* 7: 6: "In uno consensu ecclesia universa conspirans."

sel."[27] The important issues of the cloister are to be discussed by the entire community, under the counsel of the abbot, who, as everyone knows, is given an extraordinary competence by the rule. Why is the decision of the abbot not sufficient according to whatever method he chooses to arrive at it? "Therefore we have determined," the author of the Rule answers, "that all be summoned for counsel because the Lord often revealed to a younger disciple what would be best." This also says something about the quality of reception and, to take a look at the other side of the coin, the non-reception of stipulations of the other instances of witnessing.

The first thing to note is that both means of acting have no jurisdictional meaning, but a confessional one; that is, the consent or non consent of the believers does not touch the validity of a pronouncement of the other official witnesses. This is based on the fact that they are of the law itself and not grassroots determinations. In this lies the essential difference between the community of the faithful and a democracy. Still, in the case of non-reception of a pronouncement of the magisterium or of theology, that pronouncement would lack a vital force, spiritual fruitfulness, and efficacy. The pronouncement can be correct, legitimate, even useful in principle; still, it actually remains dead. This is simply a fact not open for discussion. The fact is that non-reception need not be based on a morally disqualifying disobedience on the part of the recipient; rather, it can also have its own justification, something already spoken of earlier. Denial of consent can also have its cause in the fact that the transmitters were not sufficiently persuasive, not fully objective, not sufficiently credible, or did not do full justice to the plausibility of life in the world.

In light of the above, reception through the believers also takes on a criteriological significance. Together with the assertion of the official infallibility of the pope and bishops' definitions of faith, *Lumen gentium* declares: "Due to the work of the Holy Spirit, by whose power the entire flock of Christ is preserved in unity and progresses, these definitions can never lack the consent of the Church" (*LG* 25). This sentence assuredly seeks first to insure the doctrine already formulated in 1870 and repeated at this point in the constitution on the Church according to which the judgments of the pope are valid "in themselves and not from the consent of the Church" (*ex sese, non autem ex consensu Ecclesiae*); that is, ju-

---

[27] Rule of St. Benedict, 3. See Georg Hozherr, *Die Benediktsregel* (Zurich: Benziger, 1980) 62.

ridical ratification through other authorities is not required. This is the case, however, *because* in cases of infallible proclamations "the charism of the infallibility of the entire Church is given."[28] Such proclamations, then, cannot lack consent.

What happens, though, when this consent is in fact absent and when this defect does not apparently lie in the revolutionary attitude of a few members of the Church, but in the serious and loyal disagreements of sincere Catholics? If the definition can never lack the "consent of the Church," but does in fact lack it in a particular case, does one not have to conclude that in this concrete case it is not a question of a definition at all, even when it carries all the marks of one? Wolfhart Pannenberg, who posed this question, points to a proclamation of Boniface VIII that bore all the formal characteristics of a definition: on the necessity for salvation of being subject to the Roman pope.[29]

Be that as it may, the sentence from the council, inasmuch as it is more than an empty phrase, draws attention to an important fact in the process of reception. This would naturally be all the more serious if it were not a question of definitions, but of other expressions of the magisterium. As always, reflection opens up willy-nilly the fact that, in relation to the grassroots, ecclesial communication is also ecclesiologically multi-directional. Magisterium and theology must take seriously the fact of reception and denial of reception by the faithful. They must also show the theologically justified readiness for the consequences of either reception or non-reception. For the ultimate authority in the Church is not an authority of the Church itself, but of the Word of God. Thus, what can always be received in an obligatory form, and what must be received morally in an obligatory form, is solely and alone that Word. Where it cannot be perceived in a word of ecclesial authorities, whatever the objective and subjective motives, where it is not recognized by the *sensus fidei* of the faithful, the consent of the Church cannot be found there to

---

[28]   See the commentary of Karl Rahner, s.v., "Vat. Konz. I," *Lexikon für Theologie und Kirche* (3rd ed.) 238-241; Hermann-Josef Pottmeyer, "Bleiben in der Wahrheit. Verbindlichkeit des Glaubenszeugnisses der Kirche aus katholischer Sicht," in Pannenberg and Schneider, 151 (*supra*, note 33).

[29]   DS 875; see Wolfahrt Pannenberg, *Systematische Theologie* 3 (Göttingen: Vandenhoeck and Ruprecht, 1993) 46.

the degree that and as long as these reasons are not remedied (or can be remedied). This is a simple statement of the facts.

RULES FOR RECEPTION

Saint Francis Xavier, during his mission in Japan, originally translated the name of God with *Dainichi*, that is, Great Sun. He quickly learned, however, that this expression taken from Buddhism did not coincide sufficiently with the content of Christian theology. So he replaced it with the Latin, *Deus*. But even here he was mistaken; to Japanese ears *Deus* sounded like *Daiuso*, great liar. Francis Xavier was thus mocked and rejected.[30]

This brief history demonstrates again the vital and fundamental meaning of a successful process of communication for the subjects of ecclesial reception. This importance has recently increased greatly. Ecclesiologists and sociologists of religion agree that in the contemporary situation faith can survive only through free acceptance of the one to whom it is addressed.[31] The Catholic subculture in Europe, along with its influence on its environment, has disappeared or, as in Poland and Ireland, is declining. In the relevant literature,

> one sees clearly the problem resulting from a solidly juridical Church with a great bureaucracy and narrow notion of tradition, which is not itself capable of opening those spaces for religious experience that are the condition for the construction of relevant religious structures that allow for the participation in the ecclesial community of communication. Churches without "a praxis of communication" (H.J. Höhn), or "communicative social milieus" (M. Kehl), appear destined for failure under the conditions of late modernity.[32]

One must ask at this point, what is possible in practice, what is there to do in order to enable reception of the Christian faith on the part of the

---

[30]   Elisabeth Gräfin Vitzthum, *Die Briefe des Francisco de Xavier-1545-1552* (Leipzig, 1939) 182, 308.

[31]   Hans-Joachim Höhn, *Kirche und kommunikatives Handeln. Studien zur Theologie und Praxis der Kirche in der Auseinandersetzung mit den Sozialtheorien Niklas Luhmanns und Jürgen Habermas* (Frankfurt: Herder, 1985); Medard Kehl, *Die Kirche. Eine katholische Ekklesiologie* (Wurzburg: Echter, 1992); Kaufmann, 132-160 (*supra*, note 20).

[32]   Kaufmann, 155.

church community? Permit me a few suggestions as a conclusion and as stimulation for further thought. They are complete neither in themselves nor taken altogether.

1. *Theology* has the exceptionally important task of completing and consolidating a theory of theological knowledge which up to this point has been very badly neglected. This is the scientific place for the discussion of the whole complex of questions raised in the foregoing reflections. The insights of communications theory and the results of the sociology of religion as well as, generally speaking, the research of the human sciences, are to be received to a far more intensive degree than has been the case to date. In addition, such reception should be accompanied by further developments in ecclesiological reflection, especially concerning the chapter on the significance of the common priesthood of the faithful and the essence of the Christian lay state.

2. *The official agents of the Church* must, in addition to considering the scientific endeavors mentioned above, assure that the *communio* ecclesiology of the majority of the fathers of the Second Vatican Council be realized in the life of the contemporary Church. A few specific points of such a program would be: (1) a more effective connection between the primatial and collegial teaching offices, and the promotion of forms of more common research for the truth; (2) a strengthening of the competences of the particular churches; (3) observation of the principle of subsidiarity in all relevant ecclesial dimensions; (4) the perception and Christian evaluation of the environment of the faithful and the apparently sudden changes in this world that happen in our day. It will be decisive for this program that the *communio* ecclesiology be also securely anchored in canon law. It is not sufficient to produce a few acts of good will or tolerable privileges; rather, institutional clarification and clarity are much more needed. One cannot forget to install legally complementary forms of communication from the bottom up. One must also reflect on the possibility of development of the subject of the lay Christian. Impulses for this can come from feminist theology. With all of this the hierarchical structure of the Church is in no way brought into question. Rather, forms are sought with which it might be made more reasonable and fruitful.

3. *The particular churches* and their faithful, that is, the well-known "grassroots," have special importance in this context. For here every process of transmission and reception, by which the Church is enlivened, and through which and in which the faith is actually passed on here and

now, either does or does not take place. Since the human person cannot escape his or her environment, the peculiarities of the ecclesial community and its communication of the faith can be expressed, understood, and built on the foundation of the anthropological and cultural conditions of the addressees. Disciples of Christ can only become such *as* Germans, *as* Spaniards, *as* Japanese, etc. The environment does not belong to the *con*text, but already to the *text* of a lived Christian life.[33] Space must be given to legitimate Christian expressions of popular devotion, of art, of doxological forms of veneration of God, just as it is to a determinate selection of magisterial pronouncements that take into consideration the plausible possibilities of the concrete addressees. Obviously, then, a centralist, uniform, authoritarian understanding of the Church which seeks to propagate a uniform, worldwide theology out of a worldwide, unified catechism and a worldwide, unified discipline, would be brought into question. It should be recognized that such a vision does have its advantages. Yet one assumes that it cannot succeed so long as and since the Church of Jesus Christ makes the claim to be a Church for all people.

Within and behind all these questions and problems, visions, and suggestions, which obviously imply an extensive potential for change with regard to the current form of the Church, lies the deep-seated question of the essence of the faith community itself. Is it primarily a legal structure or primarily a place of redeemed freedom and only in this way conceivable as a structure? Does it seek first to promote its own success or does it understand itself foremost as a *communio* of charisms and only then as an ordered presentation of the many gifts directed at a common goal? Is it above all the transmitter of respectable and honorable formulas or a recipient of the divine promise of salvation, and for this reason listening even today to that Word which the Spirit has always spoken to the community and perhaps wishes today to make perceptible in a completely different language and with new content (seen from the perspective of the hearers)? Is the Church primarily uniform unity or polyphonic variety, and thus constrained to unite the differences? A statement of Hans Dombois should stand at the end of all these questions, a statement that

---

[33]   Felix Wilfred, "Anthropologische und kulturelle Grundlagen für die Kirchlichkeit. Reflexionen aus asiatischer Sicht," in Bertsch, *Was der Geist den Gemeinden sagt*, 34 (*supra*, note 19).

can be a guide for all subjects of ecclesial transmission and reception: "Correctly understood catholicity mistrusts its own being-for-self, its own simple will, the *incurvatio* of the intellect and will, and seeks confirmation in free consent."[34]

Translated by Ronny E. Jenkins

---

[34]   Dombois, 832 (*supra*, note 4).

THE AGENTS OF RECEPTION
FROM A SOCIOLOGICAL PERSPECTIVE

JEAN JONCHERAY*

I have been asked to treat the question of the agents of reception "on a sociological level." But the word "level" (*plan* in French) is susceptible to evoking several types of images, some of which would be inadequate.

In the architectural domain the word *plan* evokes a level: the ground floor, the basement, the first or second floor. One can then ask oneself if the level of sociology is superficial and that of theology is in depth or if theology is situated on the surface and sociology in the basement. Numerous images can arise, all of which have in common the inconvenience of letting one believe that these "plans" or levels never meet. But, whether viewed by the theologian or the sociologist, we are dealing with the same agents, the same living persons, who do not change levels in their ecclesial action, as if at certain moments their action arises from sociology and at other moments from theology. Hence this type of image is inappropriate.

However the French word "plan" is also used in cinematographic language: long shot, medium shot, two-shot, close-up. This time one understands better that it is not the actors who change according to the levels but rather the observers who have different points of view.

That is why, in continuity with cinematographic language, it is preferable to consider sociology as an angle of view, different from that of the theologian, but which indeed observes the same ecclesial reality, the same pastoral agents engaged in their action, without reserving to sociology the observation of certain phases of the action or certain particular agents while theology would reserve others to itself.

In viewing a local church from a sociological angle, one observes a particular reality which obeys its own proper laws and which is not in this

* Institut Catholique, Paris (France).

sense reducible to any other organization. But, at the same time, one also sees at work in this reality modes of functioning comparable to what happens in other groups. To perceive it well, everything depends on the tools and instruments that one uses for the analysis.

Thus the sociological analysis or the sociological point of view is likely to offer a particular and useful clarification without, however, representing the only valuable explanation of what happens or a global explanation superior to others.

After these clarifications we can address certain particular questions concerning the processes of reception within a local church.

WHAT INSTRUMENTS OF SOCIOLOGICAL ANALYSIS ARE AT OUR DISPOSAL?

A. Models of Communications

If our instruments of analysis are too limited, we will not have the means of making a precise enough observation. These instruments entail ways of viewing the world. Even "filtered," our techniques never become completely pure. Let us not dream of neutral tools, but let us take care to indicate from the beginning those we are using. Joseph Komonchak has already insisted on this point.

Thus for many, when one speaks of communications, a simple schema is envisioned. The transmitter possesses a message which he or she directs to someone who receives it. Apparently this view takes good account of daily experience. It suffices to listen to the radio or television to receive a message delivered by a transmitting station.

In this case it is a one-way communication from the transmitter to the receiver, and the receiver is viewed as passive. But Gilles Routhier warns us against using this image. What I understand, in effect, of the theological concept of reception in the Church makes me believe that one cannot be satisfied with such an outdated analytical tool even if it evidently bears a certain measure of truth. But this is not proper to what is happening in the Church; there is an ensemble of communications phenomena which would not be correctly analyzed if we used only this model. In effect, it does not take account of the multiple interactions which exist among the agents (or actors) of communications.

That is why it is appropriate, it seems to me, to appeal to field theory. All communications, all social action (and reception is one such action), are to be situated in a social field. And a local church can be considered as a particular social field. The underlying image is that of a magnetic field, i.e., a field of forces. In function of the positions of each point in the field, one notes phenomena of attraction and rejection in the interplay of the positions at which the agents are situated. Thus Pierre Bourdieu indicates that the fields are presented "as spaces structured by positions (or posts)."[1]

To appeal to this theory of fields entails several consequences. First of all, it invites one to analyze the relationships which arise among the agents as strategies (conscious or not) induced by their different positions in the field. And second that invites one to note that the autonomy of each field is both real and relative. The autonomy is real, that is to say that the religious field, for example, functions according to its own proper laws. Thereby one avoids analyzing what happens as if it were a question of a simple enterprise of producing material or even cultural goods. But this autonomy is relative; for the religious field itself is situated in a larger social field, whose cultural, political, and economic dimensions are themselves organized in fields, among which there are established interrelationships which are equally extended to the religious field. It is then important to take cognizance of the socio-historical context in which such processes of reception unfold.

If one refers to the construction of the cultural field which Pierre Bourdieu proposes[2] and which has been adapted by Gérard Defois to the analysis of the religious field,[3] one can note the principal poles which are set off: the pole of the legitimacy, that of the public, that of the mass media, and finally that of the avant garde. Without going into detail on the types of functioning which are proposed by these authors or entering into the technical vocabulary proper to them, we would note that there are established logical systems of alliances and a critical distancing among the different positions in the field, permitting the integration of new developments that arise or their rejection outside the field.

One can thus enumerate the different agents or groups of agents who appear theoretically at different strategic places in the field: instances of reproduction and conservation, agents of transmission, agents which

[1]   Pierre Bourdieu, *Questions de sociologie* (Paris: Minuit, 1980) 113.
[2]   Idem, "Le marché des biens symboliques," *L'Année Sociologique* 22 (1971) 49-126.
[3]   Gérard Defois, "Sociologie de la connaissance religieuse et théologie de la croyance," *Le Supplément* 112 (1975) 101-125.

produce innovations, whether they be avant garde or already on the way to being legitimated, different segments of the public which forge alliances, be it with the instances of conservation or with those proposing innovations or changes.

To be sure, this analysis in terms of "fields" is only one possible instrument of analysis among others. Undoubtedly one can see another way of delineating the three inseparable elements of the ecclesial field according to theologians: magisterium, theology, and the *sensus fidelium*. These three elements are highlighted in the contribution of Wolfgang Beinert.

The question of the modern mass media is not addressed here. It would require an entire line of development by itself. It goes without saying that, in the world in which we live, the processes of reception in the Church cannot be analyzed without taking into account the existence of these mass media, which make a forceful impact in a way which one might judge to be positive or negative, but from which one cannot prescind in implementing such processes.

B. Models of Representation

In the relationships from group to group, one necessarily confronts the question of knowing who represents the group. This is evidently a crucial question in politics. Often two models are opposed. The first is the monarchical model, in which the king is identified with the body of the people. One sees there a representation-identification. That is what Kantorowicz has developed in his book on the two bodies of the king in the medieval west.[4] On the other hand, one speaks of the democratic model as a model in which the representation of the people is organized and controlled in particular by electoral processes. Representation is then perceived as a delegation. Care is taken that one person is not identified with the power; on the contrary, in taking seriously the different points of view that pervade a society, one seeks a balance of powers. The question, in effect, of knowing who is authorized to represent the group, by what means one can be authorized and recognized as its spokesperson, is a question which, if it is not officially treated, risks impairing the life of the group.[5]

---

[4]   Ernst Kantorowicz, *The King's Two Bodies. A Study in Medieval Political Theology* (Princeton, NJ: Princeton University Press, 1957).

[5]   On this point also see the work of Pierre Bourdieu on political representation. See *Actes de la Recherche en Sciences Sociales* 36-38 (1981).

One can also question this widely-accepted typology, distinguishing schematically between monarchical models as opposed to democratic models. Perhaps the question is more complex than it appears. We know well that the English monarchy, for example, has long integrated democratic processes; and no one would think of saying that England is not a democratic country. On the other hand, governments that are so-called "popular democracies" often function in a very monarchical fashion.

In a recent book Marcel Gauchet notes that for a long time people dreamed of a model that would harmoniously integrate monarchical, aristocratic, and democratic dimensions. In this connection he cites a 1789 text of Sieyès: "The three forms monarchy, aristocracy, and democracy, more or less modified, are united in the true constitution."[6]

In reading this work of Gauchet, it would seem that the French Revolution, wishing to be fully democratic but pushing this logic to the point of not recognizing the distinction between the people and its representation, had to transcend much that was wrong, in fact a monarchical type of functioning, with the consequences of which we are aware: the representatives were considered, without any distance, as expressing the popular will, a "virtual substitution of the representatives for the nation."[7] In effect, Gauchet writes,

> The Constituants find within their course of legitimation the logic of the monarchical heritage. They continue what was singular in the development of royal incorporation in France, i.e., its exclusivism.[8]

> Once this national incorporation was installed in the face of royal incorporation, the challenge to the latter could be radicalized only if it entailed an ever more forced identification of representation with the Nation.[9]

If these analyses are correct, if every constitution, at least in becoming totalitarian, forcibly borrows different models of representation of a

[6] Marcel Gauchet, *La Révolution des pouvoirs. La souveraineté, le peuple et la représentation 1789-1799* (Paris: Gallimard, 1995) 220.

[7] Ibid., 267.

[8] Ibid., 265.

[9] Ibid., 266.

group, then the particular case of the postconciliar Church, which strives to reconcile the hierarchical principle with a communitarian principle becomes very much comparable to other situations without, however, losing its particular character. One must attribute this tension not to a lack of coherence with Vatican II, but rather to the search for equilibrium.

Hence one may pose the following question: what procedures are operative in this particular group? As in other groups, in effect, we must avoid taking a person or a fraction of a group for the whole group. The group has then developed original practices to deal with these problems of functioning in fidelity to its charter of foundation. The concept of reception probably takes cognizance of one of these practices.

Recognizing the existence of different points of view seems to be a necessary precondition if one desires to articulate and harmonize them. To recognize the legitimacy, not certainly of all points of view, but of the existence of different points of view, seems equally necessary to conceive of the phenomena of reception as anything other than the application of different points of view and official decisions.

The particular case of the Church is not to be treated as if it had a monarchical dimension in virtue of its divine origins and a democratic or communitarian dimension as a concession to the spirit of the times. One would thus have a curious differentiation of roles between theology, which would work on the divine constitution of the Church, and sociology, which would be concerned about concessions to be made to mentalities which are changing! In fact the observer, sociologist or not, verifies that legitimations of a theological character are advanced for the two dimensions which I have just mentioned: The Spirit guides the ministers ("Who hears you hears me"—Lk 10: 16) but also breathes on the Christian people, sons and daughters, young and old, masters and servants (see the citation of the prophet Joel in Acts 2: 17).

Finally one must note that the term "representation" also entails a connotation of putting on a production. The ecclesial field is also a stage. The group is viewed in its complexity, in its search for equilibrium, in its reference to the message which gives rise to it. For this reason it is as important to observe the procedures employed as the declarations and their content. They say something of the founding message of the group, of its specificity.

SOME PARTICULAR QUESTIONS IN A LOCAL CHURCH

Given the various points to be considered that we have just noted, we now examine the phenomena of reception in a local church in relation to an ecumenical council or a diocesan synod. In this connection one hears expressions such as: "The whole people of God is on the move," or desires such as the following: "All responsible in the Church." Affirmations of convictions, mobilizing slogans, the function of such expressions in the life of a group must be taken seriously, but I cannot take them purely and simply at face value as if these affirmations or these desires were only describing an easily observable reality or one that is easy to attain in the not too distant future. How can the ensemble of agents likely to be concerned by a process of reception be effectively involved or considered de facto as coresponsible for the process?

Theologians invite us to consider that magisterium, theology, and the *sensus fidelium* are three inseparable elements in the functioning of the Church.[10] The ecclesial group in effect is presented as an organic body, in which one can find the structuring function of ordained ministers and the proper role of theologians. Furthermore, this is expressed in canon law through very precise rules. Indeed the third element, the *sensus fidelium*, is equally expressed in the law,[11] but the procedures to implement it and take it into account are less precise. Hence it seems interesting to me to observe in a particular way how the agents evoked implicitly in reference to the *sensus fidelium* can be taken into account in the process of reception.

This second part is divided into three points: a model of functioning of reception, the locating of agents who ought not be neglected, and the description of possible procedures so that the most diverse agents can interact with one another in order that the process of reception might be engaged as broadly as possible.

---

[10] For an expression of these three elements see Jean-Marie Tillard, in *Initiation à la pratique de la théologie*, ed. Bernard Lauret and François Refoulé (Paris: Cerf, 1982) 1: 161-182.

[11] One can find an echo of this, for example, in canon 212 of the Code of Canon Law, which invites the faithful to "make known to the pastors of the Church their needs, especially spiritual ones, and their desires" and to "manifest to their sacred pastors their opinion on matters which pertain to the good of the Church." (But here is it more a question of public opinion than of the *sensus fidelium*?)

A. A Model of Reception at Work

If I take the example of the last ecumenical council, its reception is easily locatable, concretely, through different institutions, groups, or persons who may have been transformed by or, on the contrary, have only been exposed to the council message without it apparently having had any effect on them. A parish, a Catholic Action movement, a catechetical service, a liturgical assembly are all realities which existed before the council. Are they exactly the same after the council? How can one recognize there that the council happened? How has the change been produced if there has been a change?

The example of the liturgical assembly is visible enough and has been frequently mentioned. What one notices first are the effects produced by the change: changes regarding language, the arrangement of places, the structure of the celebration. A postconciliar liturgy is recognizable at first glance. One can then say in a first effort at approximation that the assembly is a place where the council has been implemented or applied.

But logically this easily observable effect which has been produced happens in a third stage, only after two other operations which one cannot neglect. The first operation is this: the liturgical assembly has first been a place carrying change; a place in which change, the conciliar message, has had repercussions. Inquiries have shown that Catholics participating regularly in liturgical assemblies have integrated the conciliar changes more easily than others. Undoubtedly the liturgical assemblies for them have been places where they have been able to hear the conciliar message spoken, take cognizance of it, and become familiar with it.

Furthermore there is another operation, undoubtedly the most important when one speaks of a genuine reception: the persons assembled for liturgy have, one might say, themselves undertaken (especially through the focus of the liturgical teams) the transformation of the assembly because they recognize themselves as the subject of this transformation as the people of God. And they have expressed it in their own way in their own assembly.

It is then that there is manifest what is directly visible as the fruit of the ensemble of the process. The assembly has become a postconciliar liturgical assembly.

A parish can equally be envisioned using this triple approach. In it the change induced by the council has been received, as proposed from without, and that thanks to the agents of the institution: bishop, priests. One of the "orders" could have been to say: "It is necessary to create a parish council." We will be content here with this example.

At a second stage the parish council itself becomes the subject of change, asking itself what it ought to be, giving itself its specifications, interiorizing the change, while setting a direction. In the parish it then finds a function which was not exercised up until then. It can participate in its transformation.

Finally at a third stage, the most visible, the parish sees itself as having a new institution: this parish council, which appears then as one of the fruits of Vatican II.

Thus, like the liturgical assemblies, parish councils can be considered at one and the same time as channels through which change occurs, as subjects of change, and as the fruits of this change.

Undoubtedly what has just been observed regarding groups or institutions can be noted also for persons. A bishop after Vatican II is no longer exactly what he was before it. Indeed he has been an agent of the dissemination of the council's message. But he has not remained external to this operation. He himself is the subject of change. He has changed in his vision of his responsibility, in the way he lives his ministry. And one can say that this "conciliar" bishop is also a fruit of the council.

B. Agents Not to be Forgotten

1. On the Fringes

Among the "agents of reception" the most difficult to take into account are undoubtedly those who are located on the fringes of the group, that is to say precisely in a region where one asks if they are truly part of the group or not. Certainly there exist relatively clear criteria of belonging to the ecclesial group. But to take the simplest among them—baptism—it is necessary to note that the practice of baptizing children at an early age entails a certain ambiguity regarding real attachment to the group on the part of adult persons who, although having been baptized as children and having received some measure of catechesis, minimally participate in the life of the Church, not sharing all its beliefs, not observing all its practices (be they cultic or moral) which ecclesial authorities view as indispensable.

In France, to take an example, it is clear that two-thirds of the French declare themselves to be Catholic when one asks them during a poll, "what is your religion?" while around 12% of the population consider themselves to be regular "practicing Catholics."

Actually the "fringe" is not a thin margin of the population which one could consider as hesitating and which one could liken more or less felicitously to "catechumens" or to persons on the way to becoming such. The ecclesial status of more than half of the population of the country can be considered to be ambiguous or, at least, not responding entirely to the criteria of participation in ecclesial life proposed by church authorities.

The criterion used here is that of regular cultic practice. It is evidently not the only one. It happens then that in ecclesial gatherings, that is to say in groups, movements, or church services, there are people present who, from the point of view of the expression of their faith or their personal ethics, are not in perfect harmony with what church authorities sanction.

However, it would be difficult to suggest radical solutions such as excluding from the group of "agents of reception" all those who do not integrally share official church positions on such and such a point. One can see three problems with that approach. A rigorist attitude would be understood as a practice of exclusion by those who are in the process of envisioning a possible, but progressive, return to more regular participation in the life of the Church. On the other hand, this attitude would be tantamount to considering the group as a group of the "pure," tolerating no departure from the proposed ideal. Finally, if the authorities recognize as worthy of being heard only the opinions of those who in advance share their way of seeing things, the results of any consultation would be known in advance! Only those who would agree with them would have a right to respond. In these conditions one can ask if it is even useful to engage in consultation and the custom of doing so could be lost.

One would have forcibly reshaped the modalities of participation in the processes of reception, for one can no longer purely and simply limit the group without diluting it and making it lose its consistency. But taking cognizance of those agents whose ecclesial status is somewhat ambiguous is indeed a major factor in the process of reception.

2. Persons Formed and Unformed

The question to be addressed now goes a bit farther than the preceding one but in the same direction. It concerns the qualification of the persons participating in the process of reception. In effect there exist persons fully engaged in ecclesial life and seeking to live in full fidelity to the Church's teaching but who do not have a very profound theological formation.

On two occasions during the holding of diocesan synods I had the occasion to observe the reaction of theologians disturbed by the lack of formation of the persons entrusted with the responsibility of voting on dossiers whose theological implications were visibly beyond them. These theologians then proposed either that a minimum of formation necessary for the members of the assembly be offered right within the synod, or that all go through a process of formation before the synod proceeds further. In the first case the synod would be transformed into an instance of formation; in the latter case it would be deferred to a latter date.

But if one wants only theologically formed persons to participate in ecclesial debates, this would undoubtedly delay indefinitely the holding of diocesan synods unless one thinks that only theologians have the right to express themselves along with the ministers. This would be to forget one of the poles which is presented as inseparable from the two others, i.e., the *sensus fidelium*—unless one imagines that all Christians would one day be able to become quasi-professional theologians, which is another way of suppressing the third pole!

It is a question, then, of finding the means to clarify the issues in depth for a public broader than that of specialists, without transforming all the participants into specialists in so doing.

It seems to me that this question is present when one asks who is going to be able to receive the ecumenical agreements which have been negotiated by church authorities or between specialists.

C. Possible Procedures

Several procedures are actually operative in permitting the interaction of a maximum of agents in the processes of ecclesial reception. We will examine some of them.

1. Consultation and Decision-making

If canon law envisions numerous consultations of established councils, it does not envision official consultations of the whole Christian people. It is not then a question of institutionalizing such consultations.

But they often prove to be necessary to permit reception and to measure it. It is necessary then to find adequate forms of consultation.

a. Surveys

Very often in France diocesan synods have been preceded by very broad consultations taking the form of surveys or polls. They have a double effect. They offer valuable indications of how the population has integrated the reforms proposed by the last council, and they also permit one to test the way in which new changes in ecclesial practice would be received, even desired. The results of such consultations can prove valuable for a synodal assembly without, however, being used as norms to guide its choices. In addition they produce among the persons who have agreed to respond the feeling that their opinion has been taken into account. Thus the participation of a large number is itself "represented" in the sense of a theatrical production. But it is useful to take care that it is not only a case of a theatrical production; if not, it risks a cool reaction subsequently.

b. Delegations, Debates

During diocesan synods the implementation of the electoral law leaves a great deal of latitude to diocesan authorities to choose the modality of representation. Elections have taken place in very different ways in numerous places. In one place reflection groups were freely formed, and they in turn sent a delegate. In another place local elections led to the emergence of "significant electors" from whom the synod delegates were chosen. In all cases the members of the synodal assembly were sent by a segment of the members of the diocese to whom they felt particularly responsible. It is then possible to initiate discussions among these different instances, often provisional, which can enrich those of the synod proper. The reception of the synod is thus given impetus from the time it begins to be held by a continual interaction among the synod delegates and the local instances or groups.

c. Votes

It is the very method of making decisions which engages their further reception. We have just clarified the constitution of the synodal assembly. It is the same regarding the process of voting on synodal laws. Decision-making procedures are clear if they do not take place too soon, which risks telescoping a maturing of the consciousness of the group, or too late, which risks giving the impression of letting certain situations decay. If such procedures are clear, reception has a good chance of taking place for a maximum of persons would have been engaged in the decision which is made and they can recognize it as their own even if it does not correspond exactly to what they themselves would have approved.

2. The Discoveries of Practice

When in a diocese or at the level of the universal Church a general decision has been made or a general orientation authorized or when an urgent situation appears, it is interesting to note how local communities react. This heading, "The Discoveries of Practice," seeks to draw our attention to the fact that there is always an unexpected dimension to what happens at the pastoral level. A general law, in effect, or a general orientation cannot take into account particular situations. But, in function of each particular situation, the actors employ their imagination and sense of the Church; and, most of the time, one cannot speak purely and simply of the application of a law but indeed of new forms of ecclesial life which emerge on this occasion or, on the contrary, of resistance, acknowledged or not, to the proposed change.

I have had the occasion to observe, for example, that the proposal of a greater participation of laity in pastoral responsibilities linked to the urgency of certain situations where priests were lacking has given rise in many places to the implementation of original solutions, permitting the utilization of the contribution of many available and competent laity, who are seeing to the fulfillment, in another fashion, of the mission not long ago entrusted to full-time personnel possessing a different ecclesial status. One sees then that it would not be productive to try to decide on high regarding all the organizational details to be implemented because this would not have been applicable. However, in the interaction between diocesan authorities, theologians, and pastoral agents, little by little, appropriate solutions are found which need to be harmonized in the different places of the diocese.

Hence one observes here a relationship of theory and practice which is not only a deductive relationship as if practice could be deduced purely and simply from what the reflection had produced. Reception can then be perceived not as a further step after the elaboration of the principles is completed, but as the practical pole of an interactive action which is progressively realized and in which the magisterial authorities, theological reflection, and the "discoveries of practice" constitute a system and are mutually enriched.

It is interesting to be attentive not only to what thus flourishes, but also to the resistance which takes place and prevents reforms, however seriously considered, from bearing fruit. In effect reality is presented very often as a mixture of initiatives which transform reform projects into real reforms, sometimes at the price of a profound modification of the project itself, and of resistance that cuts short certain projects.

The example of the projected reform of the sacrament of reconciliation is very suggestive of this point of view. The new reforms proposed for France in the celebration of this sacrament have, on the one hand, permitted numerous faithful to be linked again with a practice of the sacrament which they abandoned many years ago. But they have turned to communal celebrations to the point of provoking an outburst of requests for communal celebrations with general absolution, envisioned initially only for urgent cases. But, on the other hand, the reform has not stimulated a perceptible renewal of the individual celebration of the sacrament. One can then reflect on the way in which reform has been "received," using this example as a point of departure.

3. Old and New Structures

At the moment when the decisions of a council or synod enter into the daily life of a local church, it is interesting to observe the way in which they are inserted into the structures of this church. In effect the field is already structured before the council or the synod not only by what the law requires (i.e., parishes, different offices) but also by associative structures such as movements, groups, services which arise thanks to the initiative of ordained ministers or groups of laity and which constitute a part of the image which the Church presents in a given place and moment.

The new decisions often give rise to new structures. Following Vatican II and diocesan synods, for example, one can observe the organizing of parish or presbyteral councils, instances of ecumenical dialogue, interreligious dialogue or dialogue with unbelievers, services of solidarity, etc.

There is a risk of superimposing different strata which are added without planning. Worse still, one can witness a disguised depreciation of old structures in order to promote what appears to be new and thus the bearer of the future, yet which risks aging quickly.

Undoubtedly it would be too easy to measure the reception of a decision solely in terms of the fact that it entails the creation of a new structure. The question would be to know how the whole ecclesial dynamism has been modified. And for that it would be necessary, at the moment when decisions are made, for "representatives" of existing and vital organisms, which give expression to the local church, to be associated with the making of the decision. If not, one attempts to put a new piece on an old garment, and there will be opposition between the new and the old, which would sap the energy of the ecclesial body.

Conclusion

The procedures which are suggested here would merit being completed, supported, and verified in practice. These are only a few examples which do not pretend to be exhaustive.

In conclusion let me only reaffirm that sociology often functions through observations on variations:[12] variations or gaps between what one says and what one does, between what one desires and what one realizes in fact, between what the observer expects to find and what is actually discovered, etc. It is a prefiguring, it is on the way. But in highlighting the variations, the sociologist sometimes appears as someone who can see only what is going wrong, someone who knows only how to criticize. That is not my objective. On the contrary, in highlighting the variations, we can give ourselves a means to facilitate within the ecclesial body the reception of significant decisions made within the Church. This presupposes only that we are willing to recognize these time-lags, these variations, since it is in recognizing the legitimacy of different positions that one can perhaps arrive at harmonizing them rather than choosing to consider only what is a sign of an already realized unity. It is at this price, it seems to me, that the different agents of reception, and especially those one risks forgetting, can truly be considered as authentic ecclesial actors.

Translation by Thomas J. Green

---

[12]   See Michel Crozier and Erhard Friedberg, *L'acteur et le système* (Paris: Editions du Seuil, 1977) 396.

THE RECEPTION OF ECUMENICAL DOCUMENTS

WILLIAM HENN*

The ecclesial process of "reception," whether it has been denoted by this precise term and whether it has been the object of explicit theological reflection, has nevertheless always been an essential aspect of the life of the Church.[1] However, the vigorous theological discussion of reception seems to be largely a product of the last thirty years, owing much of its origin and development to the ecumenical movement.[2] So far, the ecumeni-

---

* Università Gregoriana, Rome (Italy).

[1] See "La realidad de la 'Recepción' presente siempre en la Iglesia," in Angel Antón, "La 'recepción' en la Iglesia y eclesiología," *Gregorianum* 77 (1996) 84-87.

[2] That the discussion of reception is primarily a post-Vatican II phenomenon, see Hermann J. Pottmeyer, "Rezeption und Gehorsam—Aktuelle Aspekte der wiederentdeckten Realität 'Rezeption,'" in *Glaube als Zustimmung: Zur Interpretation kirchlicher Rezeptionsvorgänge*, ed. Wolfgang Beinert, Quaestiones Disputatae 131 (Freiburg: Herder, 1991) 51. On the ecumenical origins of this discussion, see Framz Wolfinger, "Die Rezeption theologischer Einsichten und ihre theologische und ökumenische Bedeutung," *Catholica* 31 (1977) 202-232, especially its first section entitled "Ansätze zu einer Diskussion in der Ökumene," 203-213. Wolfinger, 203, writes: "Erste Versuche, Rezeption als Thema der Theologie zu bedenken, entstehen im Raum der Ökumene; sie verdanken sich alle einem Anlaß, der aus der katholischen Kirche kommt: der Einberufung des II. Vaticanischen Konzils. Die nichtkatholischen Kirchen waren durch die Ankündigung der Ziele, durch die Vorbereitungen, die Vorgänge beim Konzil und durch die Beschlüsse herausgefordert, Stellung zu beziehen." William G. Rusch, *Reception—An Ecumenical Opportunity* (Philadelphia: Fortress, 1988) 16, adds that the Third General Assembly of the World Council of Churches, held in New Delhi in 1961, called for more intensive study of councils, partly in response to the convocation of Vatican II but also partly because of the significant increase in membership of Orthodox Churches in the World Council at the New Delhi Assembly itself. These Churches had always held synods or councils in high esteem. Moreover, some of the earliest divisions between Christians occurred in the East, precisely because of the non-reception of the decisions of councils such as Chalcedon. The earliest studies within the current bibliography on reception derive directly from this ecumenical interest at the beginning of the 1960's. See Rusch, 13-32; Thomas P. Rausch, "Reception Past and Present," *Theological Studies* 47 (1986) 500-501; and Frederick M. Bliss, *Understanding Reception: A Backdrop to Its Ecumenical Use* (Milwaukee: Marquette University Press, 1993). A study which goes back even earlier in ecumenical history, beginning with the "non-reception" of the consensus text on God's Grace from the Second World Conference of Faith and Order in 1937, is Kurt Schmidt-Clausen, "Die Rezeption ökumenischen

cal discussion of reception has unfolded in two phases: the first phase focussed upon the significance of the reception of councils for the ecumenical movement and the second addressed the particular task which is the theme of the present study—the reception of ecumenical documents.

This paper is divided into three parts. The first part sketches the discussion of reception within the contemporary ecumenical movement leading to the assertion that the reception of ecumenical documents, while enjoying a certain continuity with earlier reception of conciliar documents, lays before the Church a genuinely new task. The second part explores the specific nature of this new task, summarizing what may be seen as an emerging consensus about the reception of ecumenical documents which has appeared within some recent statements by dialogue groups and church leaders, and which is also supported by the relevant theological literature. The third part delineates several particularly difficult problems for reception which are related to the fact that ecumenical documents often include points of disagreement. These problems will be treated under the headings "receivability," "receptivity," and "criteria."

THE ECUMENICAL DISCUSSION OF RECEPTION

It is a happy circumstance, no doubt to be attributed to the influence of the Holy Spirit, that ecumenical discussions about reception began with a phase which focussed upon the reception of the decisions of ecumenical councils. This first phase produced a number of excellent historical and systematic studies, thus uncovering within the tradition a solid basis for considering the newer phenomenon of the reception of the results of ecumenical dialogues.[3] A number of themes emerged from the study of

---

Bewegung," *Ökumenische Rundshau* 27 (1978) 1-13. A brief glance at the bibliography concerning reception from the last thirty years clearly shows that ecumenism continued to be one of the dominant forces encouraging the discussion of this theme.

[3] The following are among the ecumenical studies which concerned the reception of the councils: Mesrob Ashjian, "The Acceptance of the Ecumenical Councils by the Armenian Church, with Special Reference to the Council of Chalcedon," *The Ecumenical Review* 22 (1970) 348-362; Jean Coman, "The Doctrinal Definition of the Council of Chalcedon and Its Reception in the Orthodox Churches of the East," ibid., 363-382; Alois Grillmeier, "Konzil und Rezeption: Methodische Bemerkungen zu einem Thema der ökumenischen Discussion der Gegenwart," *Theologie und Philosophie* 45 (1970) 321-352; idem, "The Reception of Chalcedon in the Roman Catholic Church," *The Ecumenical Review* 22 (1970) 383-411; Liviu Stan, "On the Reception of the Decisions of Ecumenical Councils by the Church," in *Councils and the Ecumenical Movement*, World Council of Churches Studies 5 (Geneva: WCC, 1968) 68-75; and Werner Küppers, "Reception, Prolegomena to a Systematic Study," in ibid., 76-98.

councils which would prove useful for considering the reception of ecumenical documents.

First of all, it became clear immediately that councils were not received in a passive or "automatic" fashion. For one thing, the very reality and structure of councils was not given "ready-made," as it were, but had to evolve, so that one can distinguish between various kinds of councils as these emerged historically (local, imperial, medieval, and hierarchical)[4] and between different styles of reception (direct, critical, and formal).[5] Conciliar reception was shown to exclude neither partial reception (the non-reception of some aspects of what is received) nor modifying reception (similar to the acceptance implied in a vote *placet iuxta modum*).[6] Common to all of these findings was the emphasis upon the very "active" nature of the reception of councils, which distinguished it clearly from a simple passive obedience.

Second, the study of the reception of councils demonstrated that a considerable period of time and a wide variety of factors were involved in the process of reception. Regarding the length of time needed for reception, Congar noted: "The faith of Nicea was only completely 'received' after fifty-six years of turbulence punctuated by synods, excommunications, exiles and imperial interventions and violence."[7] Regarding the complexity of factors involved, Grillmeier spoke of three levels at which reception occurs: the "kerygmatic" level, meaning the official promulgation of a doctrine by ecclesiastical authority; the "spiritual" level, referring to the way in which spiritual life is nourished when a doctrine is received in the hearts of the faithful; and the "theological" level, concerning the clarification and enrichment which a doctrine acquires as it is received into the discussions and writings of theologians.[8] Edward Kilmartin summarizes these points, when he writes:

[4]   See Grillmeier, "Konzil und Rezeption," 338-347.

[5]   So Küppers, 84.

[6]   Coman, 371-375, argues that opposition to Chalcedon was actually an important factor in its eventual reception in the East.

[7]   Yves Congar, "La réception comme réalité ecclésiologique," *Revue des sciences philosophiques et théologiques* 56 (1972) 372. For more on the process involved in receiving Nicea, see Wolfinger, 214-217. Indeed, Grillmeier, "The Reception of Chalcedon," 384, wonders whether the process of the reception of such fundamental articles of faith as Chalcedon's doctrine "that Christ is one *hypostasis* (person) in *two* natures" can ever come to an end, adding: "It is far from being a bad thing for a definition of this kind to be the subject of repeated theological discussion." His article traces the reception of Chalcedon through many centuries in the West, just as does Coman's article (*supra*, note 3) in the East.

[8]   Grillmeier, "The Reception of Chalcedon," 386-387.

as in the case of Nicaea I, Chalcedon, and the rest of the so-called ecumenical councils of the first millennium, reception takes place through a more or less complicated process. . . . these cases of reception of conciliar decisions by the church were neither in fact, nor understood by the churches to be, accomplished by a merely juridical act of acceptance by church officials; rather, the juridical act was viewed as initiating a spiritual process of reception by the whole community.[9]

A third point concerns Grillmeier's insistence upon the exogenous nature of reception, a position which was influenced by his reliance upon various analyses of the German reception of Roman law.[10] Congar and others felt that Grillmeier insisted too much on exogeneity; they preferred a wider understanding of the process so as to allow for reception to occur "within" one same community.[11] Nevertheless, Congar's own description of reception includes this aspect of receiving-from-without:

> By "reception" I understand here the process by which an ecclesial body truly makes its own a resolution which it had not given to itself, recognizing in the measure so promulgated a rule which is applicable to its own life.[12]

While in any case of reception one can distinguish a party which gives from a party which receives, nevertheless reception requires the free consent of the receiving party, a consent which is based upon and derived from its own proper life. Thus, whatever may be its exogeneity, reception always implies some degree of prior communion. For this reason Kilmartin remarks that "when significant spiritual goods are involved, which already exist in a vital way in the original spiritual resources of the receiving community, the process of reception takes place smoothly."[13]

---

[9] Edward J. Kilmartin, "Reception in History: An Ecclesiological Phenomenon and Its Significance," *Journal of Ecumenical Studies* 21 (1984) 38.

[10] See Grillmeier, "Konzil und Rezeption," 322-323. This leads him to distinguish reception in a *strict sense*, that is, reception by a community of some good which it has not itself created or of some doctrine which it has not itself originally formulated (324, 331-337), from reception in a *loose sense*, that is, reception within the same community (337-347).

[11] Congar, 370. See also Kilmartin, 38, note 8; and Wolfinger, 228.

[12] Congar, 370.

[13] Kilmartin, 38.

Finally, these early ecumenical studies about councils explicitly pointed out the deep interrelation between reception and ecclesiology.[14] Küppers suggested that the reception of the decrees of the early councils was based not simply upon their "formal authority" but rather upon their intrinsic credibility, which invited assimilation and consent. This reflects a "sacramental, communio-koinonia" understanding of the Church, similar to what was operative at Vatican II when it taught in such a way as to seek to convince by the credibility of its doctrine rather than to compel by the weight of its authority.[15] Congar pointed out that active reception is rooted in a pneumatological view of the Church which sees the Holy Spirit as creating consensus among the whole body of the faithful and which acknowledges "unanimity" to be a sign of the presence of the Holy Spirit.[16] Grillmeier added that the process of reception seen in early councils underlined the fact that all members of the Church had an active role to play and that the Church receives and hands on salvific truth in a fully historical way.[17]

One may say that each of these points which emerged from the discussion of the reception of councils can be applied also to the task of the

---

[14]   The theme of reception proved to be highly congenial to two of the "rediscoveries" of Vatican II, what may be called the principal issues underlying the two "Dogmatic Constitutions" *Lumen gentium* and *Dei verbum*: the ecclesiology of communion, and the understanding of revelation and faith in terms of God's self-manifestation and human existential response. These two themes are in realty two sides of the same coin. *Lumen gentium*'s ecclesiology of communion presupposes and finds its ultimate foundation in the personal, existential, divine and human encounter (giving and *receiving*) which was later expressed in *Dei verbum*'s conception of revelation. And, from the other side, *Dei verbum*'s view of revelation and faith is nothing other than an understanding of these realities in terms of *Lumen gentium*'s vision of communion, God's self-communication being *received* in the faith of the individual believer and of the community as a whole. Thus the theme of reception is intimately related to Vatican II's ecclesiology and doctrine of revelation.

[15]   Küppers, 96. Küppers, 97, adds: "*Communio* is very closely bound up with *traditio* and *receptio*; it 'corresponds' to them." Fifteen years later, Anton Houtepen drew out the relation between these in a much more developed way in his article "Reception, Tradition, Communion," in *Ecumenical Perspectives on Baptism, Eucharist and Ministry*, ed. Max Thurian (Geneva: WCC, 1983) 140-160.

[16]   Congar, 393-396. For Küppers, 83, the distinctively new element about Christian synods, as compared with Jewish or Roman precedents, was precisely the conviction that the former were guided by the Holy Spirit.

[17]   Grillmeier, "Konzil und Rezeption," 347-352.

reception of ecumenical documents. First, the reception of ecumenical documents will be an active process, not merely a passive obedience to statements produced by a dialogue commission or approved in some way by ecclesial authorities. Second, it will unfold over a relatively extended period of time and will entail many factors. Third, it will involve accepting a good which, at least to some degree, originates from outside of one's own community and yet which can be received at all only because it enjoys a profound resonance with the inner life of the receiving community. And fourth, it will reflect an ecclesiology of communion which acknowledges the activity of the Holy Spirit among the whole community as it makes its way through history.

A new phase in the ecumenical discussion of reception occurred when results from ecumenical dialogues began to appear during the 1970's.[18] Already in the mid-seventies, the Lutheran World Federation sponsored a symposium to consider the coordination and aim of the various bilateral dialogues in which it took part.[19] The confusion which could derive from participating simultaneously in many bilateral dialogues, as well as questions concerning the coherence and reception of the results of such dialogues, led to the establishment of a Forum on Bilateral Dialogues, sponsored by the Faith and Order Commission of the World Council of Churches. One of the principal themes of the six forums which have thus far occurred has been the reception of the results of bilateral dialogues. The 1980 meeting of the Societas Oecumenica was devoted to the theme "Theological Consensus and Ecclesial Reception" and other ecumenical study days were also devoted to the results of interconfessional agree-

---

[18] The "council phase" of ecumenical study of reception reached the form of a preliminary summary in a section of the Faith and Order Report from Louvain in 1971, entitled "Problems arising from a study of the reception of Chalcedon by the various traditions," *Faith and Order Louvain 1971: Study Reports and Documents*, Faith and Order Paper 59 (Geneva: WCC, 1971) 28-31. These pages contain a list of fascinating questions about conciliar reception and would provide an interesting context for reflecting upon the various common Christological professions of faith that since have been made between Chalcedonian churches and churches which did not accept the Chalcedonian definition.

[19] Two studies from this symposium were directly concerned with reception: George A. Lindbeck, "Reception and Method: Reflections on the Ecumenical Role of the LWF," in *Ecumenical Methodology*, ed. Peder Højen (Geneva, 1978) 33-48; and Lukas Vischer, "Reception and Method in Interconfessional Dialogue," in ibid., 49-63.

ments.[20] But perhaps the most decisive influence in shifting the discussion of reception toward reflection upon the results of ecumenical dialogues was the decision by the Faith and Order Commission in 1982 to send to the churches its document entitled "Baptism, Eucharist and Ministry," asking for official responses at the highest appropriate level.[21]

[20]   The conferences of the Societas Oecumenica symposium were published under the title *Theologischer Konsens und Kirchenspaltung*, ed. Peter Lengsfeld and Heinz Stobbe (Stuttgart: W. Kohlhammer, 1981), and included many entries relevant to reception, such as Miguel Garijo-Guembe, "Der Begriff 'Rezeption' und sein Ort im Kern der katholischen Theologie," 97-114 (also in Spanish, as "El concepto de 'Recepción' y su enmarque en el seno de la Eclesiología católica," *Lumen* 29 [1980] 311-331); Peter Lengsfeld, "Ökumenische Spiritualität als Voraussetzung von Rezeption," 126-134; Harding Meyer, "Wer ist sich mit wem worüber einig?" 15-30; and Martin Seils, "Die Problematik der Rezeption aus der Sicht evangelischer Kirchenleitung," 110-114. The 41st study day of the "Ökumenischer Arbeitskreis evangelischer und katholischer Theologen," of March 24-28, 1980, held in Friedewald on the topic of "Confession as an historical text and as an ecclesial reality" included several conferences which discussed the reception of the results of ecumenical conversations, such as the two which bore the same title: "Die dogmatische Relevanz der Ergebnisse theologischer Gespräche zwischen römisch-katholischen und evangelischen Theologen," one by Heinrich Fries, *Ökumenische Rundschau* 29 (1980) 261-274, and the other by Reinhard Slenczka, ibid., 440-460.

[21]   Emmanuel Lanne's address given in a plenary session at Lima, "Le problème de la réception par les Églises," *Istina* 27 (1982) 92-99, began a series of published studies and symposia concerned with the reception of BEM. From October 12-14, 1983, in Hyde Park, near Chicago, a congress was held on the reception of BEM, the papers of which were published in the *Journal of Ecumenical Studies* 21 (1984) 1-143, including the following studies: Ratsko Trbuhovic, "Summary of U.S. Churches' BEM Reception Processes," 22-33; Edward J. Kilmartin, "Reception in History: An Ecclesiological Phenomenon and Its Significance," 34-54; Thomas Hopko, "The Lima Statement and the Orthodox," 55-63; Geoffrey Wainwright, "Reception of 'Baptism, Eucharist, and Ministry' and the Apostolic Faith Study," 71-82; David Willis, "*Baptism, Eucharist, and Ministry*, Reception, and the Bilaterals," 96-106; J. Russel Chandran, "Baptism, Eucharist, and Ministry: The Reception of the Text and Third World Concerns," 107-124; Victoria Chandran, "BEM, Reception and the Concerns of Women in the Third World," 125-128; and William G. Rusch, "'Baptism, Eucharist, and Ministry'—and Reception," 129-143.

Hans-Eberhard Fichtner, "Ein großer Beitrag zu einer glaubwürdigen Rezeption. Konsultationen der Konferenz Europäischer Kirchen zur Rezeption der Konvergenzerklärungen 'Taufe, Eucharistie und Amt' (BEM)" *Ökumenische Rundschau* 35 (1986) 198-205, describes four symposia sponsored by the European Conference of Churches on the topics: "The influence of philosophy and culture on the reception of BEM in the various church traditions" (June 25-27, 1984); "The influence of confessional and ecclesial self understanding" (December 10-14, 1984); "The influence of historical, political and economic factors" (June 25-28, 1985); and "A credible reception of BEM at the level of doctrine, worship and praxis" (November 18-22, 1985). In April of 1985, the Lutheran Council of the USA sponsored a "Free Conference on Reception," as reported by Daniel Cattau, *Journal of Ecumenical Studies* 22 (1985) 877-878.

On June 11-18, 1985, a symposium of Orthodox theologians and bishops met at Holy

Thus the appearance of bilateral and multilateral statements provided a sustained impetus for reflecting about the method and theological foundations of their reception.

The very vigorous attention given by theologians and church leaders throughout the 1980's to the theme of the reception of ecumenical documents was governed by two rather universally held convictions. First, practically all voices would agree with what Paul-Werner Scheele stated at the end of the decade, when he wrote: "For better or worse the ecumenical movement of our time to a large degree depends upon the reception of the hard-won results of the dialogues."[22] In stating this, he quoted words from Harding Meyer some sixteen years earlier, when Meyer affirmed, perhaps a bit optimistically at that early point (1973), that what was now needed was not so much additional dialogues on remaining points of doctrine but rather the reception of what had been achieved by the dialogues which had already taken place.[23] This first conviction about the necessity of receiving ecumenical documents was based in part on a very positive assessment of what had been achieved by the dialogues and

---

Cross Seminary near Boston to discuss their response to BEM. The papers of this symposium were published in the *Greek Orthodox Theological Review* 30 (1985) and included the following: Nikos Nissiotis, "The Meaning of Reception in Relation to the Results of Ecumenical Dialogue on the Basis of the Faith and Order Document 'Baptism, Eucharist and Ministry,'" 147-174; Theodore Stylianopoulos, "The Question of the Reception of BEM in the Orthodox Church in the Light of its Ecumenical Commitment," 205-228; K. M. George, "Reception of the BEM Document in the Orthodox Tradition," 229-234; Thomas Hopko, "Tasks Facing the Orthodox in the 'Reception' Process of BEM," 235-247; and Metropolitan Chrysostomos of Myra, "Response to Thomas Hopko: 'Tasks Facing the Orthodox,'" 249-258.

Finally on September 2-6, 1985, the abbey of Chevetogne sponsored a colloquy on reception. Among the papers presented at this colloquy were Giuseppe Alberigo, "La 'réception' du Concile de Trente par l'Église catholique romaine," *Irenikon* 58 (1985) 311-337; Gennadios Limouris, "La 'Réception' du B.E.M. Perspectives et résultats du Colloque inter-orthodoxe (Boston, 11-18 juin 1985)," *Irenikon* 59 (1986) 32-59; Rodger Greenacre, "La réception des textes des dialogues et la réception de la doctrine: deux problèmes pour les Anglicans," *Irenikon* 58 (1985) 471-491; Harding Meyer, "Les présupposés de la réception ecclésiale ou le problème de la 'recevabilité.' Perspectives luthériennes," *Irenikon* 59 (1986) 5-19; and Michel De Montmollin, "Questions posées à une Église réformée par la 'réception' d'un document oecuménique," *Irenikon* 59 (1986) 189-200 and 307-313.

[22]   Paul-Werner Scheele, "Die Rezeption ökumenischer Dokumente als geistliches Geschehen," in *Wissenschaft und Kirche*, ed. Kurt Aland and Siegfried Meurer (Bielefeld: Luther Verlag, 1989) 259.

[23]   Harding Meyer, *Luthertum und Katholizismus im Gespräch* (Frankfurt: Lembeck, 1973) 92.

in part on the perception that the churches, usually here referring especially to those in roles of ministerial leadership, were not doing enough
to utilize the dialogue results in a way which would more effectively
bring about unity.[24] The urgency of the need to do something with dialogue results was expressed by John Hotchkin at the "Free Conference
on Reception," in 1985, where he was quoted as saying that, if the present
opportunity for Christian unity were to be missed, the Church may need
to wait for several hundred years before such favorable ecumenical circumstances come again.[25]

A second conviction which soon gained widespread allegiance was
the acknowledgment that the reception of ecumenical documents could
not be simply equated with that reception which had been the object of
the earlier studies about ecumenical councils. To this effect, the statement of the Inter-Orthodox Symposium on BEM, from 1985, includes
the following affirmations:

> We would like to distinguish between the immediate response of
> the individual Orthodox member churches of the World Council
> of Churches to the BEM document and the long-range form of
> the reception of the text in the Orthodox tradition. We hold that
> the notion of reception of the BEM document here is different
> from the classical Orthodox understanding of the reception of
> the decrees and decisions of the holy councils.

---

[24]   Jürgen Moltmann, on the occasion of the fiftieth anniversary of the Faith and Order
Commission in 1977, wrote: "Now that the theologians have overcome church-divisive
doctrinal differences, it is time for church leaders to carry out their ecumenical responsibility and draw out the appropriate consequences." In Slenczka, "Die dogmatische Relevanz der Ergebnisse theologischer Gespräche," 440, citing Jürgen Moltmann, "Welche
Einheit? Der Dialog zwischen den Traditionen des Ostens und des Westens," *Ökumenische Rundschau* 26 (1977) 288.

[25]   This was reported by Cattau, 877-878 (*supra*, note 21). Another short intervention
which emphasized the urgency of the situation is John Long, "Reception: Ecumenical Dialogue At A Turning Point," *Ecumenical Trends* 12 (1983) 19-21. Long, 20, writes: "Why
does the question of reception present itself with particular urgency now? The answer
seems to lie in the tremendous success which has been achieved in the ecumenical dialogue. . . . This success confronts the Christian churches with the serious problem of further reflection, discernment and action. At every level of their life, they must become
aware of how much they are already engaged by what has been achieved. In their highest
organisms and in their smallest congregations, the churches must face up, concretely and
without sham, to the challenge being offered them by what the Spirit has already said to
them through the multiform ecumenical dialogue."

More positively, the symposium adds,

> Reception of the BEM document means that we recognize in this
> text some of the common and constitutive elements of our faith
> in the matter of baptism, eucharist and ministry so that we may
> stand together as far as possible to bear witness to Jesus Christ in
> our world and to move towards our common goal of unity. Thus
> reception at this stage is a step forward in the "process of our
> growing together in mutual trust . . ." towards doctrinal conver-
> gence and ultimately towards "communion with one another in
> continuity with the apostles and the teachings of the universal
> Church."[26]

It is noteworthy that the Orthodox symposium makes two distinctions
here; one concerns the difference between the official response and the
long-range reception of an ecumenical text, and the other concerns
the difference between the reception of modern ecumenical texts and the
classical understanding of the reception of the councils. Thus the reception of ecumenical documents should be equated neither with the official
response given to those documents nor with the reception of the ancient
councils. Yet an official response surely has *some* important role to play
in the overall reception of ecumenical documents. Moreover, the contemporary process of the reception of ecumenical documents cannot be
thought of as *completely* foreign to the communion-building process of
reception and to the various factors at play in such a process, which were
uncovered in the study of the reception of the early councils.[27]

What precisely is new about the reception of ecumenical documents?
How can this reception be effectively carried out so as to contribute to
full communion? To these questions we must now turn.

THE SPECIFIC NATURE OF THE RECEPTION OF ECUMENICAL DOCUMENTS

The most obvious novelty about the reception of ecumenical documents lies in the fact that such reception aims at reestablishing lost unity

---

[26] Preface, *Greek Orthodox Theological Review* 30 (1985) ix. The text is quoted from
Churches Respond to BEM 1, ed. Max Thurian, Faith and Order Paper 129 (Geneva:
WCC, 1986) 124.

[27] John Zizioulas, "The Theological Problem of 'Reception,'" *One in Christ* 21 (1985)
188, after noting some differences between the reception of ecumenical documents and
the classical idea of reception, adds: "This makes one wonder whether the classical views
would have any relevance for our present situation." The point of Zizioulas' article is to
argue that they do have such relevance.

between divided Christian communities.[28] As Cardinal Willebrands pointed out:

> "Reception" is a word and, indeed, a concept that has assumed a new meaning and a new urgency in the ecumenical movement. The word has its origin in the field of jurisprudence. In theology it is now used to designate the acceptance of a doctrinal statement or a council decision by a local Church or by the Universal Church. But in the ecumenical movement reception now has a new meaning, especially as regards the results of a dialogue between two Churches. In the narrower sense it refers to the formal decision of the competent Church authorities, though in the wider sense it embraces all the phases and aspects of the process by means of which a Church adopts the results of such a dialogue.[29]

Thomas Rausch adds:

> While the classical concept emerged in a church which understood itself as a communion of churches, it was nonetheless a united church. In the ecumenical context, however, a new element appears; for now what is involved is a process of reception between churches separated from one another by differences of history, doctrine and structure. In the absence of communion between the churches, the process of reception is complicated con-

---

[28]   Zizioulas, 188, writes: "In the classical idea of reception (about which students of theology are not very clear anyway), we have to deal with a *united* Church, which knew exactly what the organs of reception were and assumed agreement on this point. Today we have to take into account that there is a variety of views and differences among Christians as to *how* reception operates." While this evaluation is true, nevertheless one should not paint too rosy a picture of the unity which was being preserved during the time of the first ecumenical councils. The Christological and trinitarian differences debated at the early councils were at least as central and crucial to Christian faith as are the doctrines treated by contemporary ecumenical dialogue. A helpful presentation of the contrast between contemporary ecumenical reception and classical conciliar reception is Nissiotis, 147-174 (*supra*, note 21). A Catholic intervention about this difference can be found in Rausch, 499-501 (*supra*, note 2); an Anglican perspective, in Christopher Andrews, "Reception: A Plain Person's Survey," *One in Christ* 27 (1991) 57-76, esp. 59-66. The latter was written under the supervision of Dr. Mary Tanner, who also wrote: "Reception and Provisionality among Anglicans," *Midstream* 29 (1990) 55-61.

[29]   Johannes Cardinal Willebrands, "The Ecumenical Dialogue and Its Reception," *One in Christ* 21 (1985) 220.

siderably; as Anton Houtepen observes, "more theological consensus is needed to restore unity than to preserve unity."[30]

This new finality of trying to reestablish lost unity has consequences both for the form and for the content of ecumenical documents.[31]

Regarding the form, ecumenical documents present doctrines in a language and structure which may be somewhat different from that which is customary in the recent past of the communities engaged in dialogue. At least since Edmund Schlink's famous intervention at the third world conference of Faith and Order at Lund in 1952, ecumenical dialogue partners have tended to adopt a methodology which goes beyond hardened confessional positions and searches the sources of Christian revelation in order to arrive together at a new common expression of the particular doctrine in question. Later, Vatican II (*UR* 11) also proposed such a method when it stated that "the manner and order in which Catholic belief is expressed should in no way become an obstacle to dialogue" and encouraged Catholics to search together with other Christians into the divine mysteries so as to arrive at "a deeper realization and a clearer expression of the unfathomable riches of Christ." Such a methodology implies that the structure and linguistic form of ecumenical documents may at times appear unusual to the wider membership of the communities in dialogue.[32]

Moreover, the "formal" authority of such documents is of a rather peculiar type. On the one hand, dialogue participants are usually officially

---

[30]   Rausch, 500 (*supra* note 2).

[31]   Ulrich Kuhn, "Reception—An Imperative and an Opportunity," in *Ecumenical Perspectives on Baptism, Eucharist and Ministry*, 169 (*supra*, note 15), states that ecumenical documents "differ fundamentally in both form and content from the documents involved in the reception process in earlier church history."

[32]   The Pontifical Council for Promoting Christian Unity, *Directory for the Application of Principles and Norms on Ecumenism* (Vatican City: Libreria Editrice Vaticana, 1993), paragraph 181, states: "In assessing and assimilating new forms of expression of the faith, which may appear in statements issued from ecumenical dialogue, or even ancient expressions which have been taken up again in preference to certain more recent theological terms, Catholics will bear in mind the distinction made in the Decree on Ecumenism between 'the way that Church teaching has been formulated' and 'the deposit of faith itself' (*UR* 6 and *GS* 62). They will take care however to avoid ambiguous expressions especially in the search for agreement on points of doctrine that are traditionally controversial. They will also take account of the way in which the Second Vatican Council itself applied this distinction in its own formulation of Catholic faith; they must also allow for the 'hierarchy of truths' in Catholic doctrine noted by the Decree on Ecumenism (*UR* 11)."

designated to represent their communities. This implies that the church
leaders place a certain amount of trust in the abilities of these representatives and are committed to take seriously the results which they develop together with their dialogue partners. At the same time, however,
these representatives must rely principally on their own faith, intelligence and native abilities in listening and communicating, with the result
that the outcome of their work cannot simply be equated with the faith of
their respective communities. Thus the dialogue results eventually must
be evaluated and accepted by the sponsoring communities. This unique
type of authorship is yet another trait which distinguishes the documents
of ecumenical dialogues from those of ecumenical councils. Along this
line, some have suggested that the ultimate "authority" of ecumenical
documents lies primarily in the intrinsic merit of their content.[33]

Regarding content, the fact that ecumenical texts seek to achieve doctrinal agreement between communities which have separated from one
another precisely for motives of doctrinal disagreement has led to the
consequence that most ecumenical documents are comprised of a mixture of varying degrees of convergence or consensus.[34] This finality usually also implies some lack of agreement or even the presence of some
contradictory positions on particular points. In fact, aside from the failed
union decrees from the Council of Florence, it is probably accurate to
state that there has not yet appeared an ecumenical document which
claimed full agreement on all the specific points treated.[35] This fact cre-

---

[33]   Meyer, "Les présupposés de la réception ecclésiale ou le problème de la 'recevabilité,'" 5-19 (*supra*, note 21), points out the priority of the substance of a teaching over its
formal authority (see esp. 13-14). He writes: "Les résultats des dialogues acquièrent une
recevabilité ecclésiale dans la mesure où ils participent *au contenu* de ce qui, dans nos
Églises, est témoigné et enseigné de manière normative" (14).
[34]   Some of the categories used to describe the range of agreement—convergence,
agreed statement, consensus and substantial agreement—are discussed in Yves Congar,
Diversity and Communion (London: Variorum Reprints, 1984), chapter 14: "Theological
'Agreements,'" 137-144 and 216-218 (these later pages are endnotes and contain some
useful bibliography on this theme). Slenczka, 450-453 (*supra*, note 20), also comments
on the various categories used to express degrees of agreement, warning that the very act
of working for convergence or consensus can carry with it the danger of giving too much
importance to human agreement, thus obscuring the fundamental distinction between the
Word of God and the word of human beings, between Scripture and tradition. (Clearly
Slenczka separates and even contrasts Scripture and tradition here in a way that would be
foreign to some Christian communities).
[35]   Long 19-20 (*supra*, note 25), notes Joseph Gill's study of the Council of Florence,
in which Gill calls its union decrees the "success that failed." Perhaps one of the highest
claims of agreement in the recent ecumenical movement was that made by ARCIC II in
"Salvation and the Church," which stated in paragraph 32: "We find ourselves to be in

ates a special problem for the reception of these documents. How would "receiving" a joint statement which includes the acknowledgment of persistent disagreement on some issues promote communion in faith? Is one not here faced with the most striking difference between ecumenical documents, on the one hand, and the decisions of ecumenical councils, on the other? Conciliar documents are statements of full consensus, expressing the communion in faith of those present at the council. Their "reception" by the whole Church was a process which widened and deepened that consensus. But what is one to do with documents which do not express a full consensus?

I cannot avoid using the adjective "wise" in describing the approach of Günther Gassmann, until recently director of the Faith and Order Commission of the World Council of Churches, to the challenge of the reception of ecumenical documents.[36] Gassmann asks whether the notion of reception correlates to dialogue in the same way that it correlates to councils.[37] His answer is yes, but with a careful nuance. Ecumenical dialogues must be seen within the context of the dynamic nature of the ecumenical movement, which strives to render visible and effective the unity of the Church of Jesus Christ. This cannot happen without the reception of what is achieved in ecumenical dialogue. In this sense reception correlates to the very essence of dialogue; dialogue is essentially incomplete without the reception of its results.

But the shift in perspective proposed by Gassmann is most helpful. The aim of dialogue is not to receive or to ratify documents but rather to

---

agreement that, in this matter, whatever further differences there may be of theological interpretation or of ecclesiological emphasis. . .cannot justify our continuing separation. We believe that our two communions find themselves in agreement on the essential aspects of the doctrine of salvation and on the Church's role in it." As is well known, the Congregation of the Doctrine of the Faith of the Catholic Church offered some observations about this document and, while stating that the document could be interpreted in a way which conforms to Catholic faith and that it contains many satisfying elements especially on traditionally controversial points, nevertheless concludes that because of ambiguities in the text it could not agree with ARCIC II's claim to have achieved agreement on the essential elements of these doctrines.

[36]   Several short works express Gassmann's approach to the reception of ecumenical documents: "Rezeption im ökumenischen Kontext," *Ökumenische Rundschau* 26 (1977) 314-327; "Die Rezeption der Dialoge," ibid., 33 (1984) 357-368; and "The Official Responses to the Lima Document," *Ecumenical Trends* 15 (1986) 186-188.

[37]   In the next two paragraphs I will repeat Gassmann's ideas as presented in "Die Rezeption der Dialoge," esp. 358-362.

realize and manifest unity.[38] In light of this, he proceeds to what I would call a "relativization" of ecumenical documents. First of all, the very fact of entering into dialogue, even prior to the production of any agreed statement, is already an act of reception, recognizing the other community as a sister to one's own community with whom, according to the will of Christ, one should be in full communion.[39] Jean Tillard nicely points out the ecclesiological significance of this when he notes that reception can occur at all only on the basis of a communion that already exists.[40] Gassmann adds that the actual text which results from dialogue should also already be seen as a mutual reception of the parties involved, as well as, in many cases, a reception of the ideas expressed in other bilateral or

---

[38] One could also say "to deepen communion," although Gassmann does not appear to use this precise expression in the present article. J.M.R. Tillard's excellent "Fondements ecclésiologiques de la 'réception' oecuménique," *Toronto Journal of Theology* 3 (1987) 34, states that ecumenism is not about receiving documents but about receiving persons. Zizioulas, 193 (*supra*, note 27), states toward its conclusion: "We must remember that reception is not a matter of *texts* alone, but of *Churches* and *people*. In the very act of reacting to texts the Churches enter a process of receiving each other as *Churches*." The same idea is expressed by Lukas Vischer, "The Reception of Consensus in the Ecumenical Movement," *One in Christ* 17 (1981) 297; Richard L. Stewart, "'Reception': What do the Churches do with Ecumenical Agreements?" *One in Christ* 21 (1985) 195; and William Marrevee, "How do the Churches Read a Convergence Text?" in *Catholic Perspectives on Baptism, Eucharist and Ministry*, ed. Michael A. Fahey (Lanham: University Press of America, 1986) 53.

[39] In agreement is Rausch, 504 (*supra*, note 2): "The process of reception has already begun when two churches, in spite of their separate histories, commit themselves to the search for unity by entering into dialogue. Such a commitment implies not just a willingness to trust each other, but also the recognition of the dialogue partner as a community of Christians also living a Christian life." See also Kuhn, 169; and Stewart, 195.

[40] Tillard, 37-39. It seems to me that the positions of Tillard and Gassmann regarding ecumenical reception are quite similar in viewing it as a global process in which communities come to receive one another on the basis of common faith. I would see a basic difference in the fact that Gassmann, while not excluding explicitly ecclesiological or theological themes from his contributions concerning reception (see, for example, "Rezeption im ökumenischen Kontext," 324-327), nevertheless tends to focus on the process by which ecumenical reception takes place. Tillard, on the other hand, seems always to tune his interventions about reception in an explicitly ecclesiological key. In my opinion, one of the best attempts to weave the theme of reception into a systematic presentation of ecclesiology is the second chapter of Tillard's *Church of Churches: The Ecclesiology of Communion* (Collegeville: Liturgical Press, 1992), especially its subsection "The Church of God, People of Faith," 105-144, a good portion of which is entitled "A Word which is 'received,'" 118-140. See also J.M.R. Tillard, "Reception—Communion," *One in Christ* 28 (1992) 307-322. On the ecclesiological and theological significance of the reception of ecumenical documents, Tillard's writings provide the most thorough treatment.

multilateral dialogues.[41] Thus, elements of mutual reception precede the holding of a dialogue and are woven into the text which emerges from the dialogue process. This leads Gassmann to suggest that Churches in dialogue should seek above all to "receive" the *dialogue event as a whole*, the official response by Church leaders to the *text* and the use of the text in various ways within each community being only part of this broader reception process. Indeed, the text is only "the tip of the iceberg."[42]

By situating the reception of ecumenical documents as only one piece within a broader ecumenical reception, Gassmann opens the roadblock which would result if the whole dynamism toward Christian unity depended solely on the acceptance of dialogue results which do not yet claim to have achieved full agreement on all relevant points. It does not eliminate the problem of disagreement, which still must be addressed, and which I will turn to principally below. But this broader vision of reception as a more comprehensive process opens the path for realistic steps forward, which still will need to utilize the dialogue documents, but which need not grind to a halt should those documents still contain disagreement.

This comprehensive approach has recently gained acceptance in several official or semi-official statements precisely about reception. In 1986, the Anglican-Roman Catholic committees of Southern California produced a short description of and series of recommendations for reception at the level of the local Church.[43] In 1991, a Joint Staff Group of the Pontifical Council for Promoting Christian Unity and the Lutheran World Federation published a document entitled "Strategies for Reception. Perspectives on the Reception of Documents Emerging from the Lutheran-Catholic International Dialogue."[44] 1994 saw the publication of the most

---

[41] Nissiotis, 148-149 (*supra*, note 21) shows that the convergences present in BEM received much from earlier bilateral dialogues. Rusch, "'Baptism, Eucharist, and Ministry'—and Reception," 129-143 (*supra*, note 21) shows how BEM was constructed upon and thus "received" material from earlier Faith and Order multilateral discussions.

[42] A defect of dialogue documents is that they do not sufficiently make clear the extent to which they are rooted in the experience of the particular dialogue and in the wider ecumenical movement as a whole. Gassmann, "Die Rezeption der Dialoge," 362, writes: "Es ist ein Mangel vieler Dialogtexte, daß sie selbst nicht deutlich genug auf diesen breiteren Dialogprozeß hinweisen, dessen 'Spitze des Eisberges' sie sind. Die Dialoge *und* ihre Ergebnisse, und nicht bloß Texte, sind zu rezipieren."

[43] ARC Committees of Southern California, "On the Process of Reception," *Ecumenical Trends* 15 (1986) 188-190.

[44] See Pontifical Council for Promoting Christian Unity, *Information Service* 80/2 (1992) 42-45.

extensive statement to date about reception of ecumenical documents in
the three Group Reports from the Sixth Forum on Bilateral Dialogues.[45]
And, finally, a portion (nn. 80-81) of Pope John Paul II's encyclical on ecumenism, *Ut unum sint* of 1995, took up the theme of reception.[46] The
very appearance of these quasi-official statements about reception testifies to the importance of this theme for the current ecumenical situation.
But even more significantly, their mutual similarity suggests that a certain
convergence may be emerging concerning the way divided communities
are reflecting about the nature and practice of reception.

First, all of these statements see the reception of ecumenical documents within the larger context of the process of growing toward greater
unity. As the Sixth Forum on Bilaterals states:

> Ecumenical reception is the comprehensive process by which the
> churches make their own the whole range of results of their en-
> counters with each other. It is thus far more than the official re-
> sponse to the results of dialogues, although such responses are
> essential. Reception is an integral part of the movement toward
> that full communion which is realized when "all the churches are
> able to recognize in one another the one, holy, catholic and apos-
> tolic Church in its fullness" (Canberra statement on *The Unity of
> the Church as Koinonia: Gift and Calling*).[47]

By distinguishing the official response from the whole range of the results of the encounters between the churches, the report is alluding to the
fact that the situation between divided Christian communities has already irrevocably changed. The production of ecumenical documents
has helped bring about this change. But it is more than the documents
alone, nor can the lack of full consensus in any given document destroy
or render unimportant this new situation.

Second, these statements understand the agents of this comprehensive
process as including all of the members of the Church, specifying the

---

[45]   These three reports are entitled I: "Aspects of Reception," II: "Authority within the
Process of Reception," and III: "Opportunities and Difficulties within the Present Situation of Reception" and are published in *Sixth Forum on Bilateral Dialogues*, ed. Günther
Gassmann, Faith and Order Paper 168 (Geneva: WCC, 1995) 5-21. The second of these reports includes a summary of what the Pontifical Council for Promoting Christian Unity's
Directory for the Application of Principles and Norms on Ecumenism, paragraphs 178-
182, contribute to the discussion of the reception of ecumenical documents.
[46]   John Paul II, encyclical *Ut unum sint*, May 25, 1995: *AAS* 87 (1995) 921-982.
[47]   *Sixth Forum on Bilateral Dialogues*, 5.

particular roles of church leaders, of the whole body of the faithful, and of theologians.[48] This trilogy of the agents of reception has been reiterated by a number of individual authors. Cardinal Willebrands provides one of the best summaries of the various competencies of these subjects when he writes:

> Inasmuch as the entire People of God partakes in the search for and the unfolding of the truth of God's word, all the charisms and services are involved according to their station: the theologians by means of their research activities, the faithful by means of their preserving fidelity and piety, the ecclesial ministries and especially the college of bishops with its function of making binding doctrinal decisions. One can say that ministry and charism, proclamation and theology, magisterial ministry and sense of faith of the People, all act together in the reception process.[49]

It is easy to see in these lines a certain parallelism to the three levels of reception—kerygmatic (ministerial leaders), spiritual (whole community), and theological (professional theologians)—which Grillmeier traced in his study of the reception of Chalcedon in the West.

Third, this plurality of agents is matched by a plurality of means, as the Lutheran-Catholic statement notes:

> the *integration* of dialogue results and insights into the life of the churches occurs in a large variety of ways. The churches' official acceptance and integration of dialogue results will be preceded by a general change of attitude of our churches to each other, as e.g., described in *Facing Unity* (nn. 50-54), and by a growing integration of dialogue insights into liturgical life, pastoral care,

---

[48] "Strategies for Reception," par. 9-13; *Sixth Forum on Bilateral Dialogues*, 6; *Ut unum sint*, nn. 80-81.

[49] Willebrands, 222 (*supra*, note 29). See also Wolfinger, 225 (*supra*, note 2); Marrevee, 45-62 (*supra*, note 38); Rausch, 502 (*supra*, note 2); and Andrews, 71-76 (*supra*, note 28). For the most extensive discussion of the interrelation of ministers, community, and theologians in the process of reception, see the "Ergebnisse und Perspektiven" of the Societas Oecumenica Symposium on Theological Consensus and Ecclesial Reception, *Theologischer Konsens und Kirchenspaltung*, 143-158 (*supra*, note 20). A most interesting attempt to promote the reception of ecumenical documents by the community as a whole is *Twelve Tales Untold. A Study Guide for Ecumenical Reception*, ed. John T. Ford and Darlis J. Swan (Grand Rapids: Eerdmans, 1993). This book presents material from ecumenical dialogues by means of stories from everyday experience, so as to provide an instrument for discussion at the level of the local community.

preaching, theological education and spiritual formation. There can even be occasional changes and modifications in church law and the official teaching of the churches stemming directly or indirectly from the dialogues.[50]

Many authors offer similar lists of various concrete steps which contribute to the integration of dialogue results into the life of the Church as a whole.[51]

Fourth, these statements offer a valuable proposal for addressing the problem posed by the fact that most ecumenical documents contain varying degrees both of agreement and of disagreement. As the Sixth Forum on Bilaterals states:

> where a dialogue has a positive outcome, this represents the discovery of a greater degree of real communion which it may be appropriate to express in some new forms of relationship. As the dialogue is taking place, the dialogue commission ought to give consideration to what practical steps it might recommend to the churches in order to express the agreement they are working out. As the dialogue progresses, the churches themselves should also consider what steps toward deeper communion would be appropriate if they can receive the dialogue positively.[52]

---

[50] "Strategies for Reception," par. 7. Various activities promoting reception at the local level are also mentioned in the ARC Committees of Southern California, 189-190; and throughout the three reports of the *Sixth Forum on Bilateral Dialogues*.

[51] See Vischer, "The Reception of Consensus in the Ecumenical Movement," 300-305 (*supra*, note 38); Gassmann, "Die Rezeption der Dialoge," 363-365 (*supra*, note 36); Thomas P. Rausch, "Reception: A Matter of Perception," *Ecumenical Trends* 15 (1986) 190-192; idem, "Reception Past and Present," 505-508 (*supra*, note 2); and Andrews, 66-71.

[52] *Sixth Forum on Bilateral Dialogues*, 6. Among the steps here envisioned by the report is also the sharing of sacramental life. In this context, the formation of United and Uniting Churches or special agreements which include eucharistic sharing, such as the Leuenberg Agreement of 1973, have been seen as expressions of reception. So, for example, Rusch, *Reception—An Ecumenical Opportunity*, 75-76 (*supra*, note 2), on Leuenberg and on the USA Lutheran-Episcopal Agreement of 1982; and Gassmann, "Rezeption im ökumenischen Kontext," 319 (*supra*, note 36) (Leuenberg), and "Die Rezeption der Dialoge," 362 (the USA Lutheran-Episcopal Agreement) (*supra*, note 36). The history of the Consultation on Church Union in the United States could provide fascinating material for reflection about reception; see Paul A. Crow, Jr., "Ecumenical Lessons from COCU's History, 1960-1995," *Midstream* 34 (1995) 13-41. (This entire issue of *Midstream* is dedicated to COCU and to the new relationship of "covenant communion" into which its member churches are currently entering.)

The Porvoo Common Statement of 1992 merits special attention because of its agree-

The report goes on to state that, even when the parties are not yet able to arrive at that level of communion needed for sacramental sharing, nevertheless practical steps can be taken to express the "greater degree of communion [that] is being discovered . . . . acting on these provisional and intermediate results of dialogue" is not only appropriate but can also help clarify the "ultimate goal of full visible unity."[53] What is important here is that the presence of some level of disagreement should not be allowed to vitiate completely the considerable unity in faith which most ecumenical documents express. Appropriate intermediate steps offer a means to move closer on the basis of the agreement achieved, without disregarding the fact that some important doctrinal points still remain divisive.[54]

A final comment about the specific nature of the reception of ecumenical documents which is mentioned to some degree in these recent statements but which is developed more fully in the contributions of individual authors is the spiritual climate needed for reception.[55] Paul-

---

ment between regional Anglican and Lutheran churches regarding faith, apostolic succession and the episcopacy, and because of the consequences which it draws from this agreement for fuller communion, including eucharistic sharing. Whether sacramental sharing can be seen as an "intermediate" step toward full communion or only as the "final" step which recognizes and, as it were, seals such communion is a point about which various Christian communities differ. Surely all would agree that the ecumenical movement aims eventually toward that fullness of communion which includes also the reception of one another in sacramental and eucharistic sharing.

[53]   *Sixth Forum on Bilateral Dialogues*, 6. This notion of taking appropriate steps even now is also expressed by the ARC Committees of Southern California, 189, when it reaffirms the "Lund Principle" of acting together in all matters except those in which differences of conviction compel communities to act separately, adding a list of suggestions for such intermediate steps. This notion is contained less explicitly in the Lutheran-Catholic "Strategies for Reception," par. 12.

[54]   Houtepen, 153 (*supra*, note 15), writes: "It is important, at this point, to overcome any 'all or nothing' idea of 'communion' and unity, and to learn what it means to speak about 'growing communion.'" Gassmann, "Rezeption im ökumenischen Kontext," 316-322, speaks of many different types of partial and unofficial reception which may precede the institutional finalization of the process. Franz Wolfinger, "Rezeption—ein Zentralbegriff der ökumenischen Diskussion oder des Glaubensvollzugs," *Ökumenische Rundshau* 27 (1978) 17-18, agrees that there are many kinds of reception but criticizes Gassmann for giving too much importance to official reception. The notion of intermediate steps is also implicitly present in Nissiotis, 173-174 (*supra*, note 21), and Vischer, "The Reception of Consensus in the Ecumenical Movement," 304-305, and quite explicitly promoted in Willebrands, 224-225.

[55]   In the two paragraphs of *Ut unum sint* devoted specifically to the reception of ecumenical dialogues, John Paul II does not develop this theme beyond stating that the process, carried forward "in a spirit of faith, will be assisted by the Holy Spirit" (n. 81).

Werner Scheele has argued that if, as Vatican II states, spiritual ecumenism is the "soul" of ecumenism, then without this soul the ecumenical movement will effectively be dead.[56] He goes on to suggest that the considerable mutual recognition of baptism among Christians could provide a foundation for developing a common baptismal spirituality which could help believers to recognize more fully that what unites them is much stronger than what divides them. He encourages the fostering of basic spiritual attitudes such as the effort to listen to others, to be faithful to one's tradition and ancestors, to be open and optimistic. Shared activities in the areas of repentance and conversion, confession of faith and prayer, liturgical celebration and proclamation, catechesis and theology can all help to promote a reception-favorable climate. In this context, Scheele quotes a comment by the "Evangelische Michaelsbruderschaft" describing the virgin Mary as the primordial image (*Urbild*) of the believing Church, her faith being the preparedness to conceive the unexpectedly new by means of the overshadowing of the Holy Spirit.[57]

At the conclusion of this discussion of the distinctive nature of the reception of ecumenical documents, we should not overlook its continuity with the process of conciliar reception, as summarized above. Acknowledging both this continuity as well as the clear difference between conciliar decisions and ecumenical documents, Scheele calls the reception of the latter a "pre-conciliar" process.[58] We now turn to several problems

---

However, the section on reception is followed immediately by some striking passages on "spiritual ecumenism," relating it to what the pope calls the "dialogue of conversion" (nn. 82-85).

[56] Scheele, 260 (*supra*, note 22).

[57]   Scheele, 271. This spiritual climate needed for reception and, in particular, the activity of the Holy Spirit in making reception possible, is a very common theme in the literature. So Wolfinger, "Die Rezeption theologischer Einsichten," 232-233 (*supra*, note 2); Lengsfeld, "Ökumenische Spiritualität als Voraussetzung von Rezeption," 126-134 (*supra*, note 20); Vischer, "The Reception of Consensus in the Ecumenical Movement," 300-301 (*supra*, note 38); Kilmartin, 38 (*supra*, note 9); Rusch, *Reception—An Ecumenical Opportunity*, 63-64; Tillard, "Reception—Communion," 318-322 (*supra*, note 40); and Otto H. Pesch, "Rezeption ökumenischer Dialogergebnisse. Ungeschützte, aber plausible Vermutungen zu ihren Schwierigkeiten," *Ökumenische Rundschau* 42 (1993) 415-417. The Report from the Third Forum on Bilaterals, *The Three Reports of the Forum on Bilateral Conversations*, Faith and Order Paper 107 (Geneva: WCC, 1981) 38-44, is especially strong on the spiritual aspect of reception, stating on 39: "Reception, in both its strict and comprehensive meanings, occurs only as Christ graciously accomplishes it by his Spirit." Section VII of this report, 43-44, devotes four paragraphs to the topic "The Spiritual Dynamic of Reception."

[58]   Scheele, 261.

which characterize the reception of ecumenical documents, precisely insofar as they attempt to overcome doctrinal disagreement.

PROBLEMS CONNECTED TO THE RECEPTION OF ECUMENICAL DOCUMENTS: RECEIVABILITY, RECEPTIVITY, AND CRITERIA

Receivability

This term is borrowed from an article by Harding Meyer, who uses it to speak respectively of the official form and material content of the dialogues.[59] In the latter sense, that is, regarding their content, a particular difficulty for the receivability of ecumenical documents derives precisely from the fact that this content may still include doctrinal disagreements.

For example, in the very impressive Lutheran-Roman Catholic common statement *Church and Justification* of 1994, under the heading of "The Significance of the Doctrine of Justification for the Understanding of the Church," there appears a twenty-nine page section (about one fifth of the text as a whole) entitled "The Areas of Controversy" (nn. 174-241). Four areas are singled out: the institutional continuity of the Church, ordained ministry as institution in the Church, binding church doctrine, and church jurisdiction. One of the great values of this document is that it precedes its discussion of the areas of controversy with a statement of the original consensus and of common basic convictions which Lutherans and Catholics share. Moreover, even in the four areas of controversy, the document is very careful to point out that there is by no means complete disagreement between the two churches about any of the four points. Nevertheless, ultimately it is claimed that "our two churches give in part different and indeed controversial responses to the question of how far and to what degree these ecclesiastical realities which have arisen in history share in the enduring quality of the realities established when the church was founded" (n. 179; for other conflicts, see also nn. 192 and 197 on ministerial structures, 212 on teaching ministry, and 226 on jurisdiction). If there really are diametrically opposed positions here between Lutherans and Catholics on some specific points, as *Church and Justification* attests that there are, how might this document be received? And, further, what ultimate effect may such contradictions have on the prospects for full communion between the two churches?

[59]   Meyer, "Les présupposés de la réception ecclésiale ou le problème de la 'recevabilité,'" 8-18 (*supra*, note 21).

One response could be to say that the differences on these specific points are compatible with full communion and that the extensive unity in faith of which *Church and Justification* gives evidence is all that is required and sufficient. After all, *Ut unum sint*, 78, states that in the process of pursuing the unity Christ wills for the Church, "one must not impose any burden beyond that which is strictly necessary (cf. Acts 15: 28)." Tillard adds that the discernment of what is necessary and sufficient is the key to the ecumenical task of reception:

> Once communion can rest assured of the presence of *id quod requiritur et sufficit*, may we not accept variations in counterpoise as long as these can rest securely on the deposit of faith? . . . In seeking communion today, are we heading for a uniformity even stricter than that which was deemed sufficient by the Church in its earliest days? "Reception" is thus found to be completely dependent on the definition of the phrase *id quod requiritur et sufficit*. As long as we hesitate to take the step of determining its meaning, the future will remain out of focus, the outlook blurred by vacillation between the illusion of a barren uniformity and the lure of an agreeable entente, precarious in the extreme.[60]

Otto Hermann Pesch adds that dialogue commissions should resist pressure to come up with yet further clarifications, especially when all of the relevant aspects of a particular issue have already been examined, because requests for such further clarifications are usually thinly veiled expressions of an unwillingness to take the necessary steps toward unity, based on an ecclesiology of uniformity and an ecumenism of return.[61]

Certainly these points about not imposing what is unnecessary and about legitimate diversity within unity are valid. At the same time, it is difficult to see how doctrinal contradictions could be compatible with unity in faith. For one thing, it is intrinsically unreasonable to hold both sides of a contradiction. The single subject cannot do this. And surely the credibility of the Church could hardly be convincing if, in matters of faith, it countenanced as acceptable two contradictory interpretations of the Word of God. For the ultimate authority which grounds any particular point of Christian faith is the revealed Word of God. Surely the Word of God cannot contradict itself.

---

[60]   J.M.R. Tillard, "'Reception': A Time to Beware of False Steps," *Ecumenical Trends* 14 (1985) 148.

[61]   Pesch, 410-413 (*supra,* note 56).

This being so, it would seem that ecumenical dialogue cannot be said to have achieved its aim if Christians continue to hold contradictory beliefs on specific issues. Of course, the overcoming of contradiction does not occur simply or even primarily by means of ecumenical dialogue. Shared catechesis, education, witness, service and, especially, prayer, all have an important role to play. But it would be a mistake to think that ecumenical dialogue and the attempt to seek greater clarification has no further useful contribution to make.

Consider, if you will, the following very inadequate sketch of the ecumenical situation at the close of the Twentieth Century. The most difficult points of *doctrinal* division concern less the differences between East and West than they do the differences which emerged as the Protestant Reformation unfolded. This reformation began with very legitimate concerns about the need for the reform of church praxis, but in part because of the opposition of Catholic leaders to such reform (cf. *Church and Justification*, n. 192) there soon emerged a deepening conflict concerning ecclesiological doctrine. Moreover, the emerging divisions created a situation in which the Reformers and their communities were not able to continue the ecclesial ministerial structure which they had enjoyed up until that time and which they had no original intention to change. May it not still be possible to get behind this historical sequence of events so as to arrive at a fidelity to both the original intentions of the Reformers and to the ecclesiological vision and structure of the early church?

Church and Justification is a remarkable example of a good use of what Vatican II called the "hierarchy of truths." It presents Christian doctrines regarding the Church and its ministry within the context of that more central doctrine of salvation in Jesus Christ. One wonders if two further steps might not offer hope for deeper unity in those relatively few remaining points of controversy specified by this ecumenical document. A first step could be to appeal once again to the hierarchy of truths, this time bringing the central doctrine of the incarnation more explicitly into relation with the doctrines both about salvation and about the Church and its ministry. A second step could be to examine the historical context of the origins of our divisions so as to see if the difference between the original intentions of our ancestors in faith, on the one hand, and the subsequent sequence of events, on the other, might open possibilities for progress which could be both faithful to those forebears and yet not bound by the historical consequences of their actions. While these suggestions concern principally the Lutheran-Roman Catholic dialogue, a healing of division between those two communities could surely have an impact on a wide range of other interconfessional relationships.

Receptivity

If what we have just said about "receivability" is true, then contradictions would not appear to be compatible with unity in faith and, as such, do not lend themselves to reception. Moreover, it would seem that the overcoming of contradictions between disagreeing parties can only occur if one party changes so as to accept the view of the other or if both parties change so as to adopt some third view. Were only one party to change, such a change obviously would be "one-sided," which does not seem quite fair. Such a situation appeared to take place when the various churches were asked to respond to the Lima document on "Baptism, Eucharist and Ministry." Not a few responses from Reformation churches stated their impression that the Lima text was biased in favor of a Roman Catholic or Orthodox vision of such topics as tradition, sacraments, and the threefold structure of ministry.[62] While it is true that Roman Catholics and Orthodox were not fully satisfied with BEM, nevertheless the overall content of that document appears to be closer to their doctrine and practice than it is to that of many Protestant communities.[63] This situation raises the question: does the need to overcome opposed positions necessarily imply an imbalance, such that some communities are asked to be more "receptive" to change than others?

From a different perspective, the question of receptivity came into focus in the official Roman Catholic response to ARCIC I's *Final Report*. This response was sharply criticized because it did not accept ARCIC's claim to have achieved substantial agreement in the areas of Eucharist and ordained ministry. Analyzing the reasons given for not accepting this claim, Francis Sullivan wrote: "It is clear that for the Vatican, ARCIC

---

[62]   See, for example, the responses of the Presbyterian Church in Canada, in *Churches Respond to BEM 2*, ed. Max Thurian, Faith and Order Paper 132 (Geneva: WCC, 1986) 158; the Waldensian and Methodist Churches in Italy, in ibid., 245; the Seventh Day Adventists, in ibid., 347-348; the United Protestant Church of Belgium, in *Churches Respond to BEM 3*, ed. Max Thurian, Faith and Order Paper 135 (Geneva: WCC, 1987) 177-178; the Presbyterian Church in Ireland, in ibid., 215-216; the Union of Welsh Independents, in ibid., 281; the Evangelical Church in Baden, in *Churches Respond to BEM 5*, ed. Max Thurian, Faith and Order Paper 143 (Geneva: WCC, 1988) 56; and the Evangelical Church of the Rhineland, in ibid., 84.

[63]   Nissiotis, 160 (*supra*, note 21), agreeing with the Catholic author he quotes, concedes: "As Orthodox we must admit that, as Joseph F. Egan, S.J. writes, 'Non-episcopal churches could rightly object that far more is being asked of them than of episcopal churches.'"

will not have achieved 'substantial agreement' on Eucharist and Ordained Ministry until its statements 'fully satisfy' and 'fully correspond'
to Catholic doctrine."[64] If that is the case, it would seem to run against a
point strongly asserted by many authors, who note that one of the conditions for the possibility of reception is that the communities in dialogue
be "receptive," in the sense of being open to accept new doctrinal formulations or ecclesial patterns of life which are not original to themselves.[65]
Tillard states that reception calls each community to be willing to mod-
ify itself, to refuse what he calls the "cheap unity"[66] which

> accepts from the agreed text only "what has always been thought
> and stated" within its own tradition and refuses anything which
> challenges or is alien to it. In this case, the tradition of the group
> becomes the gauge of acceptance, a stand which implies the re-
> fusal to risk becoming seriously involved.[67]

Each of these examples from the responses to the only two international dialogues which have so far called for an official response highlights the question of *receptivity*. In the case of the responses to BEM, it
would appear that some are asked to be more receptive than others. This
raises the question as to whether and how the "receptivity" of *all* participants is engaged in the reception of ecumenical documents. In the case of
the Catholic response to ARCIC, it is more a question of the degree to
which one's own tradition should influence or condition one's receptivity. These examples lead to several reflections about receptivity.

First, if what the study of ecumenical councils demonstrated about the
"active" nature of reception holds true also for the reception of ecumenical documents—and one would think that this would be even more the
rule for ecumenical documents, which, in contrast to conciliar decrees,
do not claim any authority based upon the ministry of teaching—then a
merely passive receptivity and acceptance of the results of dialogue

---

[64]   Francis A. Sullivan, "The Vatican Response to ARCIC I," *Gregorianum* 73 (1992)
492. Also quite critical of the apparent criteria used by the earlier response by the Congregation for the Doctrine of the Faith to ARCIC I is Marrevee, 58-59 (*supra*, note 38).

[65]   Rusch, *Reception—An Ecumenical Opportunity,* 64 (*supra*, note 2) writes: "Genuine reception will not occur if each church keeps judging ecumenical results by how
closely they conform to its own beliefs." See also Gassmann, "Die Rezeption der Dialoge," 365 (*supra*, note 36); Marrevee, 57; Rausch, "Reception Past and Present," 504
(*supra*, note 2); and Tillard, "Fondements ecclésiologiques de la 'réception' oecuménique," 35 (*supra*, note 38). In this last text, Tillard states that to accept texts only on
the basis of one's own tradition changes the process into an act of mere self-reception.

[66]   Tillard, "Fondements ecclésiologiques de la 'réception' oecuménique," 34.

[67]   Tillard, "'Reception': A Time to Beware of False Steps," 146 (*supra*, note 59).

should not be expected. Cardinal Willebrands wrote that "the very nature of the rich fruit of the dialogues calls for a critical reception."[68] Thus, negative comments by official responses need not appear as a complete rejection, but rather can be seen as a contribution by the leadership of a particular community and, thus, a participation in the ongoing discussion of the issue concerned, which aims ultimately at a fuller reception of the dialogue results. Some of the very authors who challenge a methodology which only receives in light of one's own tradition at the same time encourage an active reception which can criticize or call for the modification of a dialogue text.[69] In this regard, a critical or negative response can actually be more "positive" in the long run than a superficial agreement which does not really scrutinize ecumenical documents so as to help them express the truth in the best way possible.

Second, the criticism directed toward churches who wish to receive ecumenical documents solely on the basis of their *own* traditions is grounded on the presupposition that there is some *other* criterion which can serve as a tool for evaluating and receiving these documents. This other criterion is sometimes referred to as "the authentic, apostolic tradition"[70] or even, as stated in the introduction to BEM, "the faith of the Church through the ages." Of course, the crucial question here becomes: to what extent can and in what way should a community differentiate its own tradition from "the authentic, apostolic tradition" or from "the faith of the Church through the ages"? To completely differentiate these two would amount to a virtual rejection of the truth or validity of one's own tradition. What is at issue here is the identity and difference between the apostolic tradition and the various traditions. A careful balance is called for. One cannot completely disjoin one's own tradition from the apostolic tradition; indeed, we only have access to the apostolic tradition by means of its particular expressions. At the same time one cannot completely identify one's own tradition with the apostolic tradition, as if one's own tradition were a complete or perfect expression of Tradition. Those who criticized the Roman Catholic response to ARCIC I seemed to object that it was imposing on the dialogue commission the requirement of using the precise terminology of Trent to speak about the Eu-

---

[68]   Willebrands, 220 (*supra*, note 29).

[69]   So Gassmann, "Rezeption im ökumenischen Kontext," 323; idem, "Die Rezeption der Dialoge," 363-366; Rusch, *Reception—An Ecumenical Opportunity,* 68 and 70-72. On the positive value of a reception which is genuinely "critical," see also Wolfinger, "Die Rezeption theologischer Einsichten," 228; Kilmartin, 36-37; and Stewart, 195 and 199.

[70]   Tillard, " 'Reception': A Time to Beware of False Steps," 145.

charist. But, on the other hand, it surely is not inappropriate to ask what is the relation between the eucharistic terminology of Trent and the apostolic tradition. This comment would apply not only to the Catholic tradition but to the traditions of all of the other churches as well. If there should appear to be a discrepancy between one's own tradition and the expressions used in an ecumenical dialogue, surely it would not be preferable to remain silent about such a discrepancy? Does the difference between an ecumenical document and one's own tradition derive from a deficiency in either one or the other? Or is there some other plausible explanation of such differences? These reflections point to the need for further investigation of the relation between Tradition and the traditions.

A third comment, related to the previous one, finds its inspiration in Cardinal Cassidy's careful reply to the criticisms of the Vatican response to ARCIC I. He wrote:

> one of the dynamics going on in all the official reception processes within the Catholic Church is the conservative desire, in the best sense of the word *conservative*, to ensure that no aspect of the Catholic faith be lost. This conserving tendency is also at the heart of some of the heated discussion in our church about the authentic meaning of terms such as the *hierarchy of truths* and *subsistit in*. A proper explanation of these terms must exclude the loss of any aspects of the authentic Catholic faith.[71]

The desire that no aspect of the faith be lost is surely one that every Christian community can share. At the same time, this desire has a "maximalizing" ring to it, which could seem to be in tension with the commitment of Acts 15: 28, quoted by *Ut unum sint*, 78, not to ask of others more than what is necessary. Are we faced here with an almost unsolvable gordian knot, wanting on the one hand to lose nothing of the truth and on the other to impose no unnecessary burden? Both John Paul II (*Ut unum sint*, 81; see also ibid., 19 and 36) and Cardinal Cassidy are perhaps seeking some way to resolve this conundrum when, in writing about reception, they repeat John XXIII's affirmation of a distinction between the deposit of the faith and the formulations in which it is expressed. If this distinction is valid, then what one wants to preserve, what one must make every effort to assure is not lost, is the deposit of the faith. What could perhaps, however, be "lost," without detriment to the deposit of the faith, is the par-

---

[71]   Edward I. Cardinal Cassidy, "The Measure of Catholic Ecumenical Commitment. Receiving Dialogue Agreements," *Origins* 22/43 (April 8, 1993) 741.

ticular formulation by which the deposit was expressed in some particular historical context. In fact, because of the limitations and imperfection of human language in expressing revealed truth, it may be even beneficial to a more adequate expression of the deposit of the faith that some formulations be "lost," especially if such formulations could be misleading in the new context.

For example, to return to the Catholic response to ARCIC I, the expression "the propitiatory nature of the eucharistic sacrifice" is suggested as valuable for conveying the full content of traditional faith about the Eucharist. At the same time, it would not seem out of place to examine whether the word "propitiatory" may convey also other nuances, even ones in tension with the deposit of faith, such as that of "appeasing an angry God." If that were so, might not one perhaps be more faithful to the deposit by "losing" something conveyed by the expression, that is, by making clear what possible meanings of the expression are *not* intended when the expression is used by the tradition? One wonders whether some expressions from the tradition, such as "sacramental character" or "infallibility," create problems for unity among Christians because of nuances which such language can have but which are quite foreign to the more proper intention underlying the use of such terms. Several authors point out that ecumenical reception leads communities to a greater self-scrutiny and, in that way, to a greater knowledge of themselves.[72] Perhaps this scrutiny of the intentions underlying the traditional language and praxis of one's own community is one of the most important benefits of the process of reception. Moreover, it would seem that this is precisely an area where the principle of not imposing anything beyond what is necessary would come into play. It would seem that a community should insist on using certain traditional expressions only if the language of an ecumenical document is so open to equivocation that contradictory interpretations could be given to the same dialogue statement. When the danger of such equivocation is minimal or non-existent, the insistence on using a particular traditional expression should be scrutinized by the principle of Acts 15: 28 (do not ask more than what is necessary).[73]

---

[72] Tillard, "Fondements ecclésiologiques de la 'réception' oecuménique," 37; and Wolfinger, "Die Rezeption theologischer Einsichten," 233.

[73] Houtepen, 148 (*supra*, note 15), states that what is considered a legitimate diversity of interpretations, when occurring within any given community, at times is labelled an "ambiguity which has to be clarified," when appearing in an ecumenical text. Can one ask for too much clarity? Is some ambiguity tolerable or even unavoidable? The principle of not asking more than is necessary and sufficient also may enter into discerning the answer to these questions.

Fourth, receptivity is to some degree proportionate to the conviction that one has something to learn and to receive from others.[74] The ability to learn does not necessarily imply a repudiation of one's own past. It could mean retrieving some aspects of the tradition which are not foreign but which may simply have been neglected, forgotten, or underdeveloped over the course of time.[75] Receptivity can mean openness to enrichment and the overcoming of onesidedness. It is not a particularly Christian or even religious insight to acknowledge that there is no wisdom in thinking that one has nothing to learn; already Socrates' eloquence about this in Plato's *Apology* is well known. But surely an exaggerated sense of self-sufficiency and self-adequacy is a significant handicap when it comes to participating in ecumenical dialogue and receiving its results. This could be a particular weakness which threatens any Church whose self-awareness includes the conviction that it has faithfully preserved all of the essential features of Christ's Church and is indefectibly, even infallibly, guided through history by the assistance of the Holy Spirit. One might be tricked into thinking that such a Church would have nothing to learn, nothing to receive from any other Christian community. Vatican II's doctrine that the Church of Christ "subsists in" the Catholic Church, while affirming such indefectible preservation of all the essential elements of Christ's Church in the Catholic Church, by no means intends to claim that the Catholic Church is or ever has been the perfect or completely adequate realization of all that God's people is intended to be. A crucial and perhaps decisive step in the process of ecumenical reception will occur only when each and every Christian community humbly recognizes that it has something to receive from the others, when each one seeks to learn from the other.[76]

---

[74] See Wolfinger, "Die Rezeption theologischer Einsichten," 228; Gassmann, "Rezeption im ökumenischen Kontext," 317 and 323; Vischer, "The Reception of Consensus in the Ecumenical Movement," 295 and 300-301; Marrevee, 50 and 55; Tillard, "Fondements ecclésiologiques de la 'réception' oecuménique," 36; and Rusch, *Reception—An Ecumenical Opportunity*, 65-66.

[75] These perspectives are taken from Gassmann, "Die Rezeption der Dialoge," 366.

[76] For example, what might the Catholic Church learn from other Christians about the practice of indulgences, a practice which will no doubt be promoted again during the coming celebration of the jubilee year 2000? Could not a certain willingness to learn from the objections of others to possible abuses of the past regarding this practice be an important gesture on the part of the Catholic Church which could symbolize its ecumenical receptivity? That Vatican II itself was an occasion of much mutual learning and reception among divided Christian communities, see J.M.R. Tillard, "Le Réception de Vatican II par les non-Catholiques," in *Christian Authority*, ed. G. R. Evans (Oxford: Clarendon Press, 1988) 20-39; idem, "Did we 'receive' Vatican II?" *One in Christ* 21 (1985) 276-283; and Fries, 263-267 (*supra*, note 20).

Criteria

The criteria used in evaluating and receiving the results of ecumenical dialogues are intimately related to the two issues which we have thus far been considering: receivability and receptivity. Indeed we have already been speaking about criteria in various ways. While this topic requires much more attention than can be given to it at the close of the present paper, still one would be remiss were one not to address at least a few more direct comments to this complex issue.[77]

First, a document is *receivable* and Christian communities can be *receptive* of it, in the final analysis, to the extent that it expresses the truth of the Word of God, made known in revelation.[78] Ecumenical dialogue strives for communion in faith, which is nothing other than the response to and acceptance of God's self-revelation. Where can the content of this revelation be uncovered? It would appear that the Montreal World Conference of Faith and Order in 1963 achieved a general acceptance among divided Christian communities that revelation is conveyed by means of both Scripture and Tradition, although the precise problem of discerning the apostolic tradition within the various ecclesial traditions was not solved at Montreal. While no one seems to question the validity of Scripture as a conveyor of the Word of God and consequently as a criterion for receiving ecumenical documents, recent developments, especially as evidenced in some of the responses to BEM, raise questions about how widely tradition is accepted as a carrier of revelation and hence as a criterion for reception.[79]

---

[77] Many of the publications about reception call attention to the fact that churches employ varying criteria in evaluating ecumenical documents: Gassmann, "Rezeption im ökumenischen Kontext," 322-324; Wolfinger, "Rezeption—ein Zentralbegriff der ökumenischen Diskussion oder des Glaubensvollzugs," 19-21 (*supra*, note 53); Slenczka, 456-458 (*supra*, note 20); Houtepen, 143; Gassmann, "Die Rezeption der Dialoge," 365-367; Tillard, "'Reception': A Time to Beware of False Steps," 145; Rausch, *Reception—Past and Present*, 504; and Marrevee, 57-59.

[78] Tillard, "Fondements ecclésiologiques de la 'réception' oecuménique," 36, writes: "C'est pourquoi une authentique 'réception' exige le courage de ne pas se satisfaire de compromis nés du désir de ne pas se blesser mutuellement. Il faut savoir—dans l'humilité et la charité—mettre l'autre devant l'exigence de la vérité." See also Wolfinger, "Die Rezeption theologischer Einsichten," 230; and Rusch, *Reception—An Ecumenical Opportunity*.

[79] See, for example, the responses to BEM by the Lutheran Church—Missouri Synod, in *Churches Respond to BEM 3*, 132-133 and 140-141; the Presbyterian Church in Ireland, ibid., 220-221; the Evangelical Lutheran Church in Oldenburg, in *Churches Respond to BEM 4*, ed. Max Thurian, Faith and Order Paper 137 (Geneva: WCC, 1987) 79-80; the Netherlands Reformed Church and the Reformed Churches in the Netherlands, ibid., 107-108. A careful and very helpful analysis of the use of Scripture and Tradition in the re-

The problem seems to stem primarily from the "human-ness" of tradition. How can an unfolding historical process that is so human be considered as normative and, in that sense, on a par with the written Word of God in Scripture? Would not such a supposition appear as almost blasphemous, exalting the human to the level of the divine? Of course, such a line of thinking can easily forget that Scripture is also very human. One believes in it and accepts it as normative for faith and praxis not because of its humanity, in which aspect it would not be different from other human literature, but precisely because in this human word the divine has chosen to express itself. Those who believe that Tradition is a carrier of revelation and a norm of Christian faith and life would say the same thing about Tradition. As in the case of Scripture, its normativity depends on the extent to which the divine expresses itself through and by means of this human tradition. This nuance is crucial when it comes to a question of the Tradition serving as a normative rule for some aspect of faith or structure which is not clearly determined by the explicit testimony of the Scriptures. In such a case it could appear as if the Tradition is even given priority over Scripture, since it seems to make determinative what the Scripture itself has left undetermined. This was the precise problem which many responses to BEM voiced regarding that document's promotion of the three-fold structure of ministry.

One of the great difficulties in fully accepting the Tradition as a bearer of revelation is that, in contrast with Scripture, it is so difficult to define precisely or to locate. In the case of the Scriptures, one has at least the clear limitation of those books which were discerned as belonging to the canon of the Old and New Testaments. Tradition, however, must always be referred to in broader strokes; it includes the writings of the patristic era, liturgical texts and practice, the lives and writings of the saints, and so forth. It seems to me that those churches which believe Tradition to be a carrier of the Word of God have a special ecumenical responsibility to other Christians to develop a more coherent and credible explanation of how that Word can be discerned within the wide range of Tradition.[80]

---

sponses to BEM can be found in Chapter I, "Major Issues Demanding Further Study: Provisional Considerations" under subtitle A, "Scripture and Tradition," in *Baptism, Eucharist & Ministry 1982-1990. Report on the Process and Responses*, Faith and Order Paper 149 (Geneva: WCC, 1990) 131-142.

[80] In my opinion, the comments by the United Reformed Church in the United Kingdom, in *Churches Respond to BEM 1*, 104-105, deserve some coherent response: "it is not clear whether all historical developments are to be regarded as the work of the Holy Spirit, or only some. . . . The question of the criteria for judging which historical developments are to be regarded as theologically significant requires further attention."

What principle of interpretation is used to grasp the normative contribution which Tradition makes on any given point? Are there parallels between the interpretation of Scripture and Tradition, such that, just as one can distinguish with some scientific rationale an exegesis from an eisegesis of Scripture, so too it would be possible to give reasonable grounds for differentiating an accurate from an ideological interpretation of the Tradition?

Even after a more credible approach to interpreting the Tradition has been developed, the Church's communion in faith will require an *evaluation* of the various interpretations offered by individual believers, just as is the case with regard to Scripture. The experience of the Church during the period of the first seven ecumenical councils offers a model of how this process of discernment has worked in the past. Both Scripture and Tradition were interpreted with regard to the Christological and trinitarian doctrines and these interpretations were subsequently tested out in councils by those charged with the office of teaching and received by the people in light of the *sensus fidei*. Pope John Paul includes all of these criteriological factors which enter into the process of the reception of ecumenical documents, when he writes:

> Consequently, for the outcome of dialogue to be received, there is needed a broad and precise critical process which analyzes the results and rigorously tests their consistency with the Tradition of faith received from the Apostles and lived out in the community of believers gathered around the Bishop, their legitimate Pastor (*Ut unum sint,* 80).

It is only reasonable to presume that the process of receiving ecumenical documents can come to full term only after the Christian communities in dialogue have arrived at a rather substantial agreement about the criteria needed for discerning the truth revealed by God. There already is wide agreement about the normative role of Scripture. In addition, important steps have already been taken regarding the respective roles of Tradition and teaching authority in the Church. Obviously more agreement about these latter roles is needed if full reception is to occur. As dialogue continues to seek this agreement, many intermediate steps which express and deepen communion are already possible and should be pursued.

CONCLUSION

The reception of ecumenical documents moves toward its own demise. The greater the reception achieved, the less will be the need for additional ecumenical dialogues and for the reception of documents which would result from them.

But, ironically, ongoing dialogue may turn out to be one of the lasting legacies of the ecumenical movement. As demonstrated at the beginning of this paper, the ecumenical movement was largely responsible for initiating and sustaining the discussion of reception. But this discussion has not only assisted divided Christian communities on the way to fuller communion. In addition, it has greatly enriched ecclesiology, for it has shown that ongoing dialogue and its reception are intrinsic to communion, to Tradition, and to the very being of the Church. Even if the day should come when "ecumenical" dialogues have been superseded, dialogue and reception will remain, just as they always have been, though perhaps in a less explicitly acknowledged or institutionally structured way. Unity in faith is always the result of a process.[81] It involves receiving the Word of God and, at the same time, receiving those companions who also welcomed the Word. This reception of the Word and of those others who have also received it finds efficacious symbolization in the celebration of the sacraments, especially in the Eucharist, a celebration in which all members of the community, ordained ministers and baptized faithful, play an essential role.[82] When we at last can receive the Eucharist together, not only will we receive Jesus Christ; we will also receive one another. This is that for which Jesus himself prayed, when he asked his Father "ut unum sint."

---

[81] I have tried to demonstrate this in William Henn, *One Faith. Biblical and Patristic Contributions Toward Understanding Unity in Faith* (Mahwah, NJ: Paulist, 1995) especially in the final chapter, 195-228.

[82] Tillard, "Reception—Communion," 314 (*supra*, note 40), writes so beautifully: "In Liturgy, *recognition* becomes confession (*todah*); and *reception* is concrete acceptance of the grace of God symbolically made known in the rites. This is especially true of the eucharistic memorial as such. The Liturgy of the Word of God and eminently the Anaphora offer to the gathered community the essential content of the revealed faith. The community *receives* it by proclaiming the AMEN at the end of the Anaphora. It is the same AMEN that will be repeated, with the same connotations, at the communion table, after the declaration by the minister: 'The Body . . . the Blood of Christ.'"

RESPONSE TO WILLIAM HENN

MARY TANNER*

I am grateful to Professor William Henn for his careful and learned paper with its wealth of citations. It is impossible to do justice to the many points raised in the paper. I intend to focus on one point arising from each of the three sections.

A. *The Classical Reception of Conciliar Decisions and Ecumenical Reception*

Professor Henn's paper begins with a comparison of the similarities and dissimilarities of reception in the classical reception of conciliar decisions and ecumenical reception. (He draws out four points of similarity: that reception is active and not passive; it happens over a lengthy period of time; it is exogenous; it involves the whole community of the faithful). Although in a number of places Professor Henn also refers to the differences between conciliar and ecumenical reception perhaps more needs to be made of the fact that conciliar reception took place within a united Church, whereas ecumenical reception today takes place in and among separated churches. Professor Henn quotes from Jean Tillard who makes the point that reception can only occur at all on the basis of a communion that already exists.[1] Those who seek to receive the insights of ecumenical theological dialogue are not out of communion with one another, they already share a profound degree of communion. There is a context of relationship in which reception takes place. The recognition of what already exists is a fundamental element in enabling the process of ecumenical reception. The receiving of the insights of theological dialogues into changed relationships is among those who already recognize a common faith in Jesus Christ, who already share a communion in the life of God the Holy Trinity by virtue of their common baptism, and who are already engaged together in acts of common ser-

---

* Church House, London (England).
[1] Cf. William Henn, "The Reception of Ecumenical Documents," *supra*, 376, note 40.

vice and mission. By acknowledging the context of reception in the communion that already exists, the consensus or convergence of ecumenical dialogue can more effectively be promoted.

The acknowledgement of the degree of communion that already exists between divided ecclesial communities, itself a result of the ecumenical dialogue which followed upon Vatican II, leads to a further question relating to reception. Ought reception today, concerning a pronouncement of faith or order or morals made by one Church, be confined to a process of reception in that ecclesial communion in isolation? Does not the recognition of an already existing degree of communion require involving other ecclesial communities in the discernment of truth?

The pope's invitation in *Ut unum sint* to other ecclesial communities to reflect with him on his ministry seems to recognize that we need each other in the discernment of truth:

> Could not the real but imperfect communion existing between us persuade Church leaders and their theologians to engage with me in a patient and fraternal dialogue on this subject, a dialogue in which, leaving useless controversies behind, we could listen to one another. . . ?[2]

The college of Anglican bishops at the Lambeth Conference in 1988, was insistent that the matter of the ordination of women to the presbyterate and episcopate was given over to what the bishops called "an open process of reception" in the provinces of the Anglican Communion and in the universal Church, before it could be declared, without doubt, to be the mind of Christ for the Church. Does not the state of ecumenical relations today demand that every Church seek to include other churches in its life of discernment and reception of truth?

B. Reception as a Contribution to Full Communion/Visible Unity

In Part II of his paper Professor Henn turns to ask how can reception be carried out so as to contribute to full communion. In relation to this I make three points.

1. The Goal of Ecumenical Dialogue

The relation between the reception of the convergences of ecumenical dialogue and the restoration of "full communion" raises one of the most

---

[2]   John Paul II, encyclical *Ut unum sint*, May 25, 1995, n. 96: *Origins* 25/4 (June 8, 1995) 70.

crucial questions on the ecumenical agenda. What is understood by the churches when they refer to the goal of ecumenical dialogue as "full communion" or "visible unity"? Not all churches engaged in dialogue would agree on an understanding of what is entailed in full communion and yet without some clearer, explicit agreement on the goal of dialogue it is difficult to understand why convergence or consensus is sought on any particular subject. For example, full communion for the Reformed and for some Lutherans is sometimes described as "pulpit and altar fellowship." For Anglicans full communion entails common faith, baptism, Eucharist, a single ministry in the historic succession, and common organs of decision-making and teaching with authority. For Roman Catholics the Petrine ministry belongs with these features of visible communion.[3] We need more agreement on the elements of visible unity and their interrelation if we are to understand what needs to be treated in ecumenical dialogue, what is "sufficient and required" for the establishment of full communion, and what the place of any particular subject is in contributing to the establishment of full communion.

2. Reception and Steps and Stages to Visible Unity

Closely related to this question of the need for greater clarity about the goal of ecumenical dialogue is the need for a clearer understanding of the nature of reception as a dynamic process with room for steps and stages on the way to full communion or visible unity. Professor Henn quotes with appreciation the wisdom of Günther Gassmann who, in distinguishing between convergence and consensus, shows how even a text which represents convergence and not consensus can move churches on the path to unity.[4] Here it is crucial to recognize that the steps of convergence in life which churches are able to take now on the basis of the same theological convergence text are not always identical for the churches involved. For example, on the basis of the convergence on baptism, Eucharist and ministry registered in the Lima document, some churches feel confident in offering and receiving eucharistic hospitality which falls short of a single Eucharist, or of implementing a degree of shared ministry while not yet having a full interchangeable ministry. The degree of convergence in faith required for movement towards unity differs among the churches. It is affected by their different understandings of the

---

[3]   ARCIC II, "Church as Communion, An Agreed Statement by the Second Anglican - Roman Catholic International Commission," *Origins* 20/44 (April 11, 1991) 719-727.

[4]   See Henn, note 36.

goal of visible unity and by their position on the interrelation of the different characteristics of visible unity. This means that it is sometimes the case that a church may share a greater convergence in the expression of faith with another church and yet live more closely with those with whom it has less explicit agreement in faith. We need to recognize this if we are not to entrench new divisions in the process of reception through apparently preferential relationships.

Not all churches feel able to take the same steps at the same time on the basis of the same degree of convergence in faith. Nevertheless, that ought not to lessen the challenge to every church to make changes both in their own lives and in their relationships on the basis of the consensus and convergences of theological dialogue. Unless there is some movement in life then the dialogue texts will risk becoming simply texts on a library shelf.

It was disappointing to note how few churches took seriously the second and third questions put in relation to the Lima document:

> the consequence your church can draw from this text for its relations and dialogues with other churches, particularly with those churches which also recognize the text as an expression of the apostolic faith;

> the guidance your church can take from this text for its worship, educational, ethical, and spiritual life and witness.[5]

Neither Anglicans nor Roman Catholics took seriously the second question addressed to the *Final Report of ARCIC*—"what are the next concrete steps your church can take on the basis of this convergence?"[6] Those in leadership positions need to recognize the despondency of many lay people who were drawn into the response process at the level of the study of texts, and who see little in the way of renewal in their own church's life, or in any tangible change of relationship with their partner churches. If in many places there is a growing impatience with the leadership in some of the churches, it is perhaps hardly surprising.

---

[5] *Baptism, Eucharist and Ministry,* WCC Faith and Order Paper No. 111 (Geneva: WCC, 1982), x.

[6] *The Church of England's Response to BEM and ARCIC* (London: CIO Publishing, 1985).

3. Examples of Reception on the Way to Visible Unity

As we seek to understand the relation between convergence in ecumenical texts and convergence in life, it is useful to reflect upon some of the emerging new models of reception. Anglicans in Britain and Ireland with a number of ecumenical partners from the Lutheran, Reformed, Moravian, and United Churches have taken steps, or are taking steps, on the basis of a new "genre" of text which incorporates the fruits of ecumenical dialogue.

a. The Meissen Agreement[7]

The first example is the agreement between Anglicans in England and Lutherans, Reformed and United Churches in Germany. A synodically made Declaration to move closer to visible unity is made on the basis of an agreement on a shared understanding of the goal of visible unity, on ten explicit agreements in faith (which cover agreements on Scripture, creeds, baptism, Eucharist, ministry, oversight in personal, collegial and communal forms, mission and service). These agreements in faith depend upon the work of the bilateral ecumenical dialogues. Extensive citation from ecumenical texts is made to sum up the degree of agreement in faith which exists now between the churches. There was no need to repeat the theological work. *The Meissen Common Statement* is honest also about where the major remaining difference is, namely in the area of *episcopé* and episcopacy in the service of the apostolicity of the Church. On the basis of a clear statement of the shared faith and an honest acknowledgement of the remaining differences, the churches have made formal acknowledgements of each other and have entered into a number of commitments to share a closer degree of life and witness. Four years after the agreement was ratified, the effect of closer fellowship is being felt and the context prepared for the facing, and overcoming, of the outstanding theological issues without which full communion or visible unity cannot be achieved. What this example of the Meissen Agreement shows is how theological convergence can help to move the churches to convergence in life, a closer life which itself provides a healing context for the next stage of convergence.

---

[7] *The Meissen Agreement, On the Way to Visible Unity*, Conversations between the Church of England and the Evangelical Church in Germany, Occasional Papers of the Council for Christian Unity No. 2 (London: Council for Christian Unity of the General Synod of the Church of England, 1992).

b. The Porvoo Agreement[8]

The second example is the agreement between the British and Irish Anglicans and the Nordic and Baltic Lutheran Churches. Exactly the same dynamic process was used there as in Meissen. A Declaration to move to visible unity, that is to a stage beyond the Meissen Agreement, is made on the basis of a common understanding of the goal of visible unity, twelve agreements in faith (based again on the dialogue texts), and a commitment to live in visible unity. In this example there is no remaining area of difference that is considered church-dividing and which would prevent visible unity. These episcopal churches agreed on episcopacy in the service of the apostolicity of the Church and recognized each other as churches already in the historic succession. The way was open for the restoration of visible unity. (Embedded in this Anglican - Lutheran agreement is an acknowledgement that the Church needs personal, collegial, and communal forms of oversight at every level of the Church's life. Here the agreement acknowledges implicitly the place for a personal ministry of unity at the universal level).

These examples show that visible unity is by no means "an eschatological dream." On the basis of the convergence of ecumenical dialogues a change in relationship can be brought about and different partners can move together at different paces.

These achievements need careful scrutiny within the assessment of reception. They are encouraging signs of progress among some churches. The advantages of this method of receiving the convergences of ecumenical texts through the formulation of another "genre" of ecumenical text represented by the Meissen and Porvoo Common Statements has much to commend itself. It is also a challenge to the Roman Catholic Church to consider the possibility of regional advances in reception.

There are, however, questions that need to be asked. Not least of all, how does a world communion, like the Anglican Communion or the Lutheran World Federation, ensure that a regional form of reception in Europe is consonant with a regional reception in another part of the world? Coherence and consistency relate not only to what one communion says to different ecumenical partners, but also to the steps it takes in

---

[8] *The Porvoo Common Statement*, Conversations between the British and Irish Anglican Churches and the Nordic and Baltic Lutheran Churches, Occasional Papers of the Council for Christian Unity No. 3 (London: Council for Christian Unity of the General Synod of the Church of England, 1993).

different provinces or churches of its own communion. That is a question that Roman Catholics might properly wish to press on these churches. This matter raises the question of whether the existing structures of decision-making within some world communions are sufficient to respond to the demands of the reception process.

C. Problems of Reception

In part III of his paper Professor Henn turns to problems of reception: receivability, receptivity, and criteria. Among the many, many important contributions here is the subject of what should be looked for in ecumenical texts—identity or consonance with one's own tradition. Professor Henn uses as one of his examples the response process to the *Final Report of ARCIC I*. Archbishop Michael Ramsey and Pope Paul VI agreed in 1976 to set up a dialogue "founded upon the Gospels and the ancient common traditions." The members set out "to discover each other's faith as it is today and to appeal to history only for enlightenment, not as a way of perpetuating past controversy."[9] It consciously avoided "vocabulary of past polemic" because of "emotive associations" of that language.[10] The method the Commission used was to go back to Scripture and the early tradition, to take note of separated traditions, and then to re-state afresh together the matter for today.

Although Professor Henn allows that in responding to a text it is proper to ask what is its relation to texts of one's own tradition, nevertheless, with hindsight perhaps a mistake was made when either side was invited to say whether the texts were "consonant in substance with the faith of Anglicans/Roman Catholics." The effect of the question itself was to send some Anglicans to make a comparison with the Thirty-Nine Articles and some Roman Catholics with the language of Trent without asking how today we would wish together to state matters afresh. The official Anglican response from the Lambeth Conference glossed over the question by saying it was asking whether the texts were "in keeping with" or "compatible with" or "in harmony with the faith of Anglicans." The Vatican's response on the other hand interpreted it thus:

---

[9]   *The Final Report of ARCIC*, in *Called to Unity: Documents on Anglican-Roman Catholic Relations, 1966-1983*, ed. Joseph W. Witmer and J. Robert Wright (Washington: USCC, 1986) 229.
[10]   Ibid., 264.

what was asked for was not a simple evaluation of an ecumenical study, but an official response as to the identity of the various statements with the faith of the Church.[11]

The use of the word "identity" seems to suggest a difference in understanding of what the agreements sought in the first place to do.

The official responses in their turn led to the publications by ARCIC II of *Clarifications* intended to answer the question about assurance on identity in particular areas, including propitiatory sacrifice and transubstantiation.[12] Here we see another problem in the process of reception. While clarifications prepared in response to the difficulties of one partner may have satisfied that partner, there is a question for some as to whether *Clarifications* have gone beyond the substantial agreement of the original document itself, thus calling into question the Anglican response of the Lambeth Conference in 1988.

The processes of ecumenical reception are a new feature in the life of the churches in the twentieth century. Churches need together to review this development. The story of the response to ARCIC I invites us to think carefully, as Professor Henn suggests, about receptivity. There are a number of issues here. First, any dialogue needs to make clear the method by which it has reached its own results for only when that is clear can a response be appropriately prepared. Second, any question put to the text needs careful formulation so as to move churches away from looking for identity of language, but put in such a way that allows them to recognize when a text is, or is not, contradictory to what is held to be essential in their own history. The *Report of the Sixth Forum on Bilateral Dialogues*, recognizing this, suggested a question that might appropriately be put by churches to ecumenical texts.[13] Third, the business of elucidation and clarification must make us ask whether it is not wiser to redraft the text rather than to add materials which have to be read cumulatively. Fourth, this example makes it appropriate to ask whether putting precise questions to a text makes reception in fact the more difficult and whether the model of the Meissen and Porvoo Common Statements of taking theological convergence and consensus into another "genre" of text, one which moves from theological convergence to

---

[11] "Vatican Response to ARCIC I Final Report," December 5, 1991: *Origins* 21/28 (December 19, 1991) 447.

[12] ARCIC II, "Clarifications on Eucharist and Ministry" (September 1994), *Origins* 24/17 (October 6, 1994) 301-304.

[13] See Henn, note 45.

change in life, is a more satisfactory and effective way of receiving the convergences of the dialogues. Fifth, it reminds us that each church needs to be sensitive to the different decision-making and authority structures of its partner church. In the case of the Response to the *Final Report of ARCIC* the different timescales for consulting and responding led to frustration and irritation on both sides.

Final Reflections

Finally, Professor Henn makes the important point that reception will always be a part of the Church's life. By examining the nature of ecumenical reception the churches will be helped to understand a part of their own internal life. There will always be matters of faith, order, and morals that threaten to divide the Church as the Church responds to the insights of each age and place. There always will be difference, conflict, tension. If we understand the process of ecumenical discernment and ecumenical reception we may find ways of staying together, even living with contradiction in an on-going process of "open reception" within our own ecclesial community. The on-going and unfinished story of the Anglican engagement with the matter of the ordination of women to the presbyterate and to the episcopate is a story of "open reception" which Anglicans have been helped to understand through pondering both classical reception and contemporary ecumenical reception.[14]

By reflecting more on the processes in which we are currently engaged we learn much about the structures of our own church and not only about the convergence on any particular matters of theology, on Eucharist, on ministry or authority. In the process we learn what structures and processes of decision-making might hold us all together in a visibly united Church in a dynamic and on-going process of discernment and reception.

In conclusion what cannot be stressed too much is what comes through Professor Henn's paper, that is, the importance of the "attitudinal" in the process of reception. Without right attitudes above all of openness to the Holy Spirit and to the otherness of the other, listening, patience and constant *metanoia*, and the desire for unity, there will be no reception and no movement toward that life of full communion and visible unity. To seek that unity is part of Christian obedience.

---

[14]   Anglican Consultative Council, *The Eames Commission*, the Official Report of the Archbishop of Canterbury's Commission on Communion, Women and the Episcopate (Norwich, England: Canterbury Press, 1994).

RECEPTION, *SENSUS FIDELIUM*, AND SYNODAL LIFE: AN EFFORT AT ARTICULATION

HERVÉ LEGRAND*

I. A NECESSARY REFLECTION FOR THE LIFE OF THE CONTEMPORARY CHURCH

Two phenomena, actually heterogeneous, currently make the question of reception particularly urgent for theology: on the one hand progress in the ecumenical dialogues which are proposed for reception;[1] on the other hand, a certain decline of the concept of reception in the actual ebb and flow of Catholicism in Western Europe and North America, which suffers, to put it somewhat crudely, from a "vertical schism" between the hierarchy and the "people" (supported by certain theologians?), a situation often described as a test of reception.[2] Conscious of this double factor

---

*   Institut Catholique, Paris (France).

[1]   The dialogue commissions themselves are preoccupied with the issue. See the working document of the mixed Catholic-Lutheran group "La réception des documents théologiques," *Documentation Catholique* [*DC*] 90 (1993) 140-143. This question has been a concern for all the churches for the past decade. See Roger Greenacre, "La réception des textes des dialogues et la réception de la doctrine, deux problèmes pour les anglicans," *Irenikon* 58 (1985) 471-490; Michel de Montmollin, "Questions posées à une Église réformée par la réception d'un document oecuménique," *Irenikon* 59 (1986) 189-200, 307-313.

[2]   The difficulties experienced by *Humanae vitae*, one knows, are at the origins of a renewal of interest in the whole Church in the reality of reception. See Yves Congar, "La 'réception' comme realité ecclésiologique," *Revue des Sciences Philosophiques et Théologiques* 56 (1972) 369-403: "non-reception . . . of the doctrine of *Humanae vitae* by a part of the Christian people and even by Catholic theologians. 'Non-reception' or 'disobedience' or what?" (388), also in idem, *Eglise et papauté* (Paris: Cerf, 1994) 246. One will find descriptions of the situation in Christian Duquoc, "An Active Role for the People of God in Defining the Church's Faith," in *The Teaching Authority of Believers*, ed. Johannes-Baptist Metz and Edward Schillebeeckx, Concilium 180 (Edinburgh: T & T Clark, 1985) 77: "In recent years theologians have often claimed for themselves the role of spokespersons for the people in dealings with the hierarchy." See also Leo Karrer, "Was ist los mit der Kirche? Das Kirchenvolks-Begehren im Horizont unterschiedlicher Kirchen-Erfährungen," in *Wir sind Kirche. Das Kirchenvolks-Begehren in der Diskussion* (Freiburg: Herder, 1995) 17-30.

and desirous of serving the contemporary Church, our colloquium would like to contribute to the exploration of the reality of reception in order that this fundamental ecclesiological category will not only not be the object of misunderstandings but rather will be adequately implemented.

Much more modestly, after a summary analysis of the ecclesiological factors which have just been indicated, the present contribution would like to test in a colloquium such as this the validity of what might be the principal elements of reception: its primary link to tradition and the *sensus fidei*, its dynamic movement toward the *consensus fidelium* and the *consensio ecclesiarum*, both of which are verified best in synodal life. Is this a question of the fundamental structures of reception in a Church-communion such as are called for in the expectations of the other Christian churches?

A. Progress in Doctrinal Agreements on the Ecumenical Plane and their Reception

In his introduction to the work of our colloquium, Gilles Routhier evoked many reasons explaining the current interest of theologians in the processes of reception in the Church. Among other things he mentioned how the ecumenical movement has generated such interest, and in this context he noted the posing of the question of the modalities of the reception of the results of the ecumenical dialogues. This point is of great importance and its clarification is genuinely urgent.

Indeed our generation has known an exceptional grace in the rapprochement of Christians hitherto separated, which for us Catholics involves the East and the West.

1. Reception of the Dialogues with the Orthodox Churches

Let us look first at the East. During the past twenty years the official Catholic-Orthodox theological dialogue has achieved a doctrinal and practical rapprochement which opens for us a genuinely common future as was manifest in the June 1993 Balamand Accord. In that accord in effect there is a common recognition that "this form of 'missionary apostolate' . . . called uniatism, can no longer be accepted either as a method to be followed nor as a model of the unity our churches are seeking."[3]

---

[3]   Joint International Commission for the Theological Dialogue Between the Roman Catholic Church and the Orthodox Church, "Declaration," Balamand, June 23, 1993, n. 12: *Origins* 23/10 (August 12, 1993) 167.

On the level of principles one turns the page here on more than four centuries of irritation and hostility, whose continuing force is still very painful for both us and the Orthodox in several countries of Eastern Europe.[4] But in this agreement one does more than cope with an ancient difficulty; one equally takes cognizance of the fact that the "rediscovery and the giving again of proper value to the Church as a communion, on the part both of Orthodox and of Catholics, has radically altered perspectives and thus attitudes" (n. 13), a fact which is explicitated in number 14 by a declaration that has been too little noted or commented upon: "The Catholic Churches and the Orthodox Churches recognize each other as sister churches, responsible together for maintaining the Church of God in fidelity to the divine purpose, most especially in what concerns unity."

The recognition of such a partnership, of a responsibility thus shared in fidelity to the plan of God for the unity of the Church, necessarily opens a broad field for reception by the Catholic Church of the ecclesiological values of the Orthodox Church even if any absorption of or fusion between them have been expressly refused. One envisions together "a meeting in truth and love" (n. 14), but truth and love properly produce certain effects which are to be realized: by what procedures will this happen on our side? An analogous question is posed simultaneously and with more likelihood on the Orthodox side since its ecclesial memory is filled by the non-reception of the two reunion councils of Lyons II and Florence, which, it is repeated, were rejected by the people.[5] The place of the active manifestation of the *sensus fidelium* in reception represents a basic question in this context, which Catholic theology cannot ignore. The effectiveness of reception implies a clarity about who must receive.

But what is received is also an issue in the doctrinal and pastoral agreements signed with the ancient churches of the East. The "Common Christological Declaration between the Catholic Church and the Oriental Assyrian Church" of November 1994 is an example. As is known, this Church does not receive the seven sacraments, unlike the other Eastern Churches which agreed on this in the last third of the 13th century. Notwithstanding that, John Paul II and Mar Dinka affirm that "the par-

---

[4]   Hervé Legrand, "Une éventuelle relance de l'uniatisme pourrait-elle s'appuyer sur Vatican II? Quelques enjeux ecclésiologiques de la crise actuelle autour des Eglises unies," *Irenikon* 66 (1993) 7-37.

[5]   John Meyendorff, *The Orthodox Church* (London: Darton, Longman & Todd, 1962) 214: "a council which considers itself formally 'ecumenical' may even be rejected by the Church (examples: Ephesus in 449, Florence in 1438)."

ticular Catholic Churches and the particular Assyrian Churches can recognize each other as sister churches."[6] Could not such a recognition,
made under such conditions, have a significance exceeding its limited
original framework? Could it not assist us in adopting a more flexible approach in dealing with our disagreements with the Reformation churches
who no longer receive the seven sacraments? Certainly full communion
would probably require the reception of the seven sacraments; but if, as
a preliminary step, the churches could accept each other as sisters apart
from the effective reception of the seven sacraments, could not different
theological evaluations be made, e.g., in the line of the medieval theology of greater and lesser sacraments (*sacramenta maiora et minora*),
which would keep one from putting them all on the same level?[7]

Here again the ecumenical dialogue highlights an important dimension of reception: it should neither be confused with obedience nor conceived as a fusion (this is expressly said); it does not entail uniformity,
but favors a pluriformity in ecclesial life even if it is not possible to fore-
see its breadth in advance.

2. Reception of the Dialogues with the Reformation Churches

If we now consider the ecumenical dialogue with the churches arising
from the Reformation, there also we note that more progress has been
made toward a theological consensus in the past thirty years than in the
four preceding centuries. This is true for the Catholic-Anglican dialogue,
which has been the object of an initial evaluation on both sides;[8] the episcopal conferences have been consulted on the results even if not all of
them have responded. Similarly one notes the fact that the Congregation
for the Doctrine of the Faith has desired that its remarks on the matter
reach "the faithful to permit them to be able more easily to appreciate the
Final Report itself in light of the fundamental principles of Catholic doc-

---

[6]   Common Christological Declaration between the Catholic Church and the Assyrian
Oriental Church, Rome, November 11, 1994: *AAS* 87 (1995) 685-687; *Ecumenical Trends*
24 (1995) 167-168.
[7]   Yves Congar, "The Notion of 'Major' or 'Principal' Sacraments," in *The Sacraments in General: A New Perspective*, ed. Edward Schillebeeckx and Bonifac Willems,
Concilium 31 (New York: Paulist Press, 1968) 21-32 (bibliography).
[8]   On the part of Catholics: Congregation for the Doctrine of the Faith, "Observations
on the ARCIC Final Report," March 31, 1982: *Origins* 11/47 (May 6, 1982) 752-756. On
ARCIC II see Congregation for the Doctrine of the Faith, "Observations on 'Salvation and
the Church,'" November 18, 1988: *Origins* 18/27 (December 15, 1988) 429, 431-434. For
an evaluation by the French episcopal conference and that of England and Wales see *DC*
82 (1985) 867-882.

trine,"[9] which implies that the reception of this type of agreement also concerns the lay faithful even if they are not the object of any organized consultation. But wherever such a consultation would be judicious (e.g., in regions where the two churches exist together), would it not be legitimate? According to what procedures?

The international Catholic-Lutheran dialogue has also achieved very important results, not only concerning the historical and theological figure of Luther, but notably concerning the Lord's Supper and ordained ministry, where Lutherans have declared themselves "willing to accept the exigency of entering into communion with the historic episcopate,"[10] and especially on justification, "a church-dividing issue" (*articulus stantis vel cadentis Ecclesiae*), as one says; this last agreement is based on the work of the national German commission which has produced *Lehrverurteilungen kirchentrennend.*[11] It is certainly envisioned that in 1998 the Holy See and the World Lutheran Federation will declare that the question of justification no longer separates us. But nothing has been determined yet on the manner of receiving the other texts of agreement, which presuppose on our side the adoption of a better balanced approach to piety, liturgy, canon law, catechesis, and ecclesiology. The acceptance by the Holy See will be a key element for this reception, but would it not be necessary to reflect now on its complementary forms in order that the results might be integrated into the life of the Church?

On the Lutheran side, doctrinal authority resides in the synods, which encompass a significant proportion of laypeople. A difficulty can be foreseen: texts elaborated by specialists are so foreign to the ordinary culture of synods because of their vocabulary and technical character that in themselves they constitute a barrier to their reception.[12] Probably only

---

[9] "Événements et informations," *DC* 79 (1982) 531.
[10] International Lutheran–Roman Catholic Conversations, "The Ministry in the Church," 1981, n. 80: in *Growth in Agreement*, ed. Harding Meyer and Lukas Vischer (New York/Geneva: Paulist Press and WCC, 1984) 272-273; *Facing Unity: Models, Forms, and Phases of Catholic-Lutheran Fellowship* (Geneva: Lutheran World Federation, 1985) n. 97.
[11] *Lehrverurteilungen-kirchentrennend?*, ed. Karl Lehmann and Wolfhart Pannenberg (Freiburg and Göttingen: Herder, and Vandenhoeck & Ruprecht, 1987); English translation: *The Condemnations of the Reformation Era: Do They Still Divide?*, trans. Margaret Kohl (Minneapolis: Fortress, 1990).
[12] See Armin Kreiner, "Aporien des Konzens-Rezeptions-Schema," *Catholica* 39 (1985) 316. For a concrete example see de Montmollin (*supra*, note 1).

theological faculties would be able to evaluate them in the context in which they are situated.

The process of reception is therefore at an impasse which is not unique to the reformed churches: a fundamental Christian question can require a genuinely technical expression which ordinary people can neither judge nor understand. Whatever may be the view of experts, this question needs to be treated in depth and has consequences in the daily life of the Church.

What is highlighted by the process of the reception of the documents of ecumenical agreements illustrates the larger problem of the reception of formulations of the faith. Certainly one cannot establish as a principle that the teaching church and the Church that is taught are adequately distinct since both are based on the same third reality which is revelation. But in practice, and felicitously so, there is a sophisticated religion, distinct from popular religion; there are catechumens and catechists, etc. Finally, ecclesiologically, if all are responsible for the apostolicity of the faith, some have a ministry, which becomes here a magisterium within the framework of the communion of faith among the local churches. Given these diverse asymmetries, it would be very theoretical to speak in general terms about reception by the people of God, for, as the contribution of Jean Joncheray has shown, there is necessarily a great variety of positions among the agents of reception.

A future colloquium specifically dedicated to the problem of the reception of ecumenical texts ought to deepen this elementary approach much more. For our purpose it suffices to have a concrete vision of the phenomenon of reception, much more realistic than what emerges from its evocation in current pastoral developments.

B. Reception in Current Pastoral Developments: Overly Simplified Perceptions

Initially one can affirm that reception is not merely a binary process simply implying two groups of actors (each too easily viewed as homogeneous): the hierarchy with its decisions on the one side, which is confronted on the other side by the "people" who would receive or refuse these teachings or hierarchic prescriptions, more often making their own selections.

Such an image is widely disseminated in analyses of the Western secular press. It is nurtured by the controversy following *Humanae vitae* a quarter of a century ago and more recently by the refusal to ordain married Christians, by repeated affirmations of the impossibility of ordaining women, by recurrent conflicts involving certain bishops who have not been accepted (e.g., Chur and Sankt-Pölten) and others who, on the contrary, some would like to keep (Gaillot of Evreux).[13] On all these points the media speak of reception and still more of non-reception, and at the same time public opinion in the Church or around it becomes the measure of such reception. This opinion is determined with the assistance of a popular referendum initiative (*Kirchenvolks-Begehren*) first in Austria, then in German-speaking Switzerland and in Germany,[14] and subsequently in several neighboring countries. Hence the complex parameters of reception which the ecumenical dialogue began to clarify for us were reduced to the theme of the democratization of the Church. It even happens that a theologian describing the phenomenon seems to legitimate it. Thus Christian Duquoc writes:

> The movement from a hierarchical society to a community of the people of God does not eliminate a role for leadership; it places it in a different setting, the one created by the new power of public opinion. This term comes from the vocabulary of democratic control. Its use in the Church derives from the new place accorded to the believing people.[15]

C. Some Theological Clarifications Necessary for a Proper Appreciation of the Process of Reception

The brief preceding discussion permits one to clarify the limits of the influence of theological expertise in the current discussions of reception. One notes more than once in these discussions that the concept is linked with the democratization of the Church and with the development of public opinion in its midst. But the link with tradition is noted much more rarely, if at all; yet reception is indissolubly linked to that concept, in which the normative role is played by tradition and not reception. Somewhat differently, however, in these discussions what is received by ecclesial opinion (or para-ecclesial, the distinction not being precise in

---

[13]   Hervé Legrand, "L'affaire Gaillot, une analyseur ecclésial," *Revue de Droit Canonique* 45 (1995) 151-162.

[14]   See the broad debate in *"Wir sind Kirche"* (*supra,* note 2).

[15]   Duquoc, 79 (*supra,* note 2).

our societies) becomes the norm in relationship to which tradition must primarily be interpreted, if not judged. Here then is the first dimension of reception, its relationship to tradition, to which it seems necessary to direct our attention (*infra*, section II). For at the level of faith it would be difficult to give such a priority to reception in relationship to tradition: this explicit relationship of the two poles must never be lost sight of.

A second dimension merits critical examination. The frequent link between reception and public ecclesial opinion, which one nearly always finds in current discussions, suggests an inquiry into the relationship between the *sensus fidei*, the *sensus fidelium*, and public opinion. If the equivalency of these concepts, which results from the successive and unwarranted move from one concept to the other, is not founded, how can one appropriately express the relationship between these three other instances (*infra*, section III)?

A third dimension must also attract our attention. In the current discussion the field of reception is presented first of all as an unequal exchange uniquely involving the pope and the bishops and, to put it briefly, the hierarchy and the people (for whom certain theologians wish to be the spokespersons). Such a limitation of reception implies a number of reductions which must be submitted to analysis: one thereby reduces it practically to obedience and in any case to a very contemporary constellation where one distinguishes the whole of the laity from the whole of the bishops. However, in other historical periods the churches above all are the subjects of reception within the framework of the *communio Ecclesiarum*. In short, must one not express more clearly and decisively reception and ecclesial communion, whose most explicit expression is synodality (*infra*, section III)? That is to say, must not the privileged places and instruments of the process of reception be the different councils where the churches' communion in faith is expressed, be it regionally or universally? Or again, do not diocesan synods and analogous organs explicitate the local communion of all?

Such is the principal suggestion proposed for discussion in the present contribution: theologically and practically would it not be better to link much more clearly the fate of reception and synodality than has been done until now? At the same time, would it not make the ecumenical journey more satisfying? Would it not also give us an instrument to govern that inculturation which has become a necessity experienced nearly everywhere in the Church?

Let us not get ahead of ourselves but rather take up each of these three issues one by one without worrying about giving them a strictly equal treatment.

II. Tradition and Reception: Two Correlative Processes, but Tradition is First

For St. Paul the actions of transmitting and receiving are correlative. On the subject of the Eucharist he says typically that he has received from the Lord what he transmits (1 Cor. 11: 23), a formula which one finds in an absolutely identical fashion regarding the subject of the kerygma of the Resurrection (1 Cor 15: 1) and in nearly the same terms on the subject of the proclamation and reception of the gospel (Gal 1: 11-12). Congar has quite properly written:

> Paul makes of the acts of transmitting and receiving, holding and preserving, the very fiber of the rule of faith by which communities are built up.[16]

The apostolic witness has thus been given once for all. Others will have to build on this foundation, as the pastoral epistles insist.

Tradition is thus the process by which God gives himself to us. His gift is not only a message. Certainly there is indeed a message, for revelation is presented as a conversation between God and human beings. *Dei verbum* begins by recalling that:

> Thus in this revelation, the invisible God (see Col 1: 15; 1 Tim 1: 17) from the abundance of his love speaks with humankind as to friends (see Ex 33: 11; Jn 15: 14-15); he moved among them (see Bar 3: 38) to invite them to share his own life and to admit them to it. (*DV* 2)

The Word transmitted far surpasses the message: it establishes the human community as a partner in dialogue with God, and it is completely oriented toward a sharing which is grace, the gratuitous gift of new relations with God and with brother and sister Christians, access to the truth, justice, holiness, in short *koinonia* with God and others. Finally "what eye has not seen nor ear heard, what has not entered into the heart of the human person, God has prepared for those who love him" (1 Cor 2: 9).

---

[16]   Yves Congar, *La Tradition et les Traditions. Essai historique* (Paris: Fayard, 1960) 20.

Thus to tradition, which is primary, corresponds reception, which, as has been indicated, is of another nature than the obedience which was insisted on during the last century in emphasizing the authority of God who reveals himself, the obligatory character of revealed truth, and the resulting submission to God.

We are right in no longer recognizing ourselves in these authoritarian expressions of Christian life. Nonetheless, there is no reversibility in the correlation between tradition and reception. Reception is a present reality in relationship to tradition which comes from the apostles. Reception does not produce what it receives, but on the contrary it conceives of tradition as normative. Reception is a fruit which blossoms in *redditio*, to use an ancient liturgical language; it leads to thanksgiving vis-à-vis God and to a confession of faith vis-à-vis the world.

This primacy of the pole of tradition in relationship to that of reception is essential to the faith. Neither as a Christian subject nor as a local church nor as the whole Church can we exercise the slightest pretension of sovereignty in relationship to what is transmitted to us, the gift which is given to us.

This primacy is essential to a proper faith and to the vitality of the process of reception in the Church. In effect, if no local church gave rise to itself, if no such church coincides perfectly with the tradition, each must refer itself to other churches, which themselves have also received the tradition and experience the indwelling of the Spirit, in order to be certain of being in the Church of the true faith. And even when a church has founded others, it cannot arrogate to itself a permanent and universal decisional power over them; their relationship to their mother church will be a relationship of free reception for the same reasons.

As Hermann Pottmeyer has often illustrated, this absence of sovereignty is a condition for the health and vitality of the process of reception among the churches, to say nothing of their very condition.[17]

In short, to remain faithful to the very structure of the tradition of faith when confronted with a temptation to emphasize the sovereignty of the human conscience, and to assure the very vitality of reception among the

---

[17]   Hermann J. Pottmeyer, "Rezeption und Gehorsam, Aktuelle Aspekte der wieder-entdeckten Realität 'Rezeption,'" in *Glaube als Zustimmung*, ed. Wolfgang Beinert, Quaestiones Disputatae 131 (Freiburg: Herder, 1991) 51-91.

churches, is it not essential in the doublet *traditio-receptio* to maintain the primacy of the *traditio*?

III. *SENSUS FIDEI, CONSENSUS FIDELIUM,* PUBLIC OPINION

In the current debates on reception, or on what one calls such more or less correctly, it is to the *consensus fidelium* that one most often has recourse. Unfortunately such an expression is somewhat equivocal in its current usage, for sometimes it is understood in the technical sense of *sensus fidei*, and at other times it is viewed as almost equivalent to public opinion. Should not the theological community do what it can to clarify these equivocations if its legitimate efforts to give a certain consistency to the fundamental process of reception are not to be too easily disregarded? There is no lack of examples, for instance, to the tendency to inflate the concept in the repeated recourse to *consensus fidelium* and the confusion which accompanies it.

One might realistically object to the repeated recourse to *consensus fidelium* in theological discourse that there does not exist in the life of the Catholic Church a structural possibility of verifying such a consensus, be it on a regular basis or in exceptional circumstances. Besides bishops and theologians, how can it be expressed? Such recourse surfaces only in somewhat idealistic discourse. The best illustration of this would be the fact that the ordinary faithful in our parishes would not believe their ears if the clergy approached them with the intention of verifying what is truly the content of the faith among them.

And if this discourse were not idealistic, it would be ideological. Such an ideology would be "conservative" in legitimately appealing to popular religion or "progressive" if one were to identify with the sentiments of the people the positions taken by the most intellectual lay segments close to theologians.

Taking into account these suspicions of idealism and ideology, it would still be necessary to dissipate the confusion which has been indicated. Hence does the term *sensus fidei* have exactly the same sense as the *consensus fidelium*? In particular who are the faithful in this latter expression: all the faithful or only the laity? Certainly no theologian would risk endorsing the overly simplified dialectic of the media, which oppose the majority consensus of the lay faithful to the "isolated" and "out of touch" teaching of the magisterium of pastors. One notes, however, certain desires to attribute to the simple faithful a magisterium which, without being independent of that of pastors, would have a certain autonomy vis-à-vis them. The title of a segment of the international review *Concilium* entitled *The Teaching Authority of Believers* probably bears witness to this development.[18]

Properly understood, there are relationships between the *sensus fidei*, the *consensus fidelium*, and public opinion. We have tried to show that the care with which theologians try to articulate them can only benefit the process of reception. This is the point of what follows: these strengths and weaknesses must surface in the discussion.

A. "Sensus Fidei" ("Sensus Fidelium")

Despite the current ambiguities concerning vocabulary and definitions, the Catholic theological community commonly agrees on the meaning which *Lumen gentium* 12 gives to the sense of the faith (*sensus supernaturalis fidei*):

> The whole body of the faithful, having the anointing of the Holy Spirit (see 1 Jn 2: 20 and 27), cannot be mistaken in believing; it shows this special property by means of a supernatural sense of faith of all the people, when "from the bishops to the last of the lay faithful," it shows its universal consent about matters of faith and morals. (*LG* 12)

This meaning was restated twenty-five years ago in a quasi-definition of Wolfgang Beinert, which has been broadly accepted in the theological community. He wrote:

> The sense of faith is a free charism belonging to all the members of the Church, a charism of internal agreement with the object of faith, in virtue of which the Church in its totality, which is expressed in the consent of faith, recognizes the object of faith and confesses it in the unfolding of its life in constant consonance with the ecclesial magisterium.[19]

---

[18] See *supra*, note 2. See also Claude Geffré, "Les enjeux actuels de la théologie pour nos Eglises," *Cahiers Universitaires Catholiques* (May-June 1990) 27: "The magisterium of theologians, which has always existed, must take cognizance of three other magisteria. . . . First of all, there is what one may legitimately call in a broad sense the magisterium of the faithful themselves, the *sensus fidelium*."

[19] Wolfgang Beinert, "Bedeutung und Begründung des Glaubensinnes (*sensus fidei*) als eine dogmatischen Erkenntniskriterium," *Catholica* 25 (1971) 293.

Thus one sees that all the Christian faithful (including ministers) are the beneficiaries of faith *in credendo*, which one must understand as "something active, by which the faith is vigorously preserved and attested, penetrated ever more profoundly and made the formative element in life."[20] Unfortunately there is no historical monograph which would describe the evolution of the concept of *sensus fidei*. The reality of that *sensus fidei* was already present in the consciousness of the Church before the expression of it was forged. It is clearly expressed, for example, in the adage of Vincent of Lérins: "(that we hold) what has been believed everywhere, always, and by all" (*quo ubique, quod semper, quod ab omnibus creditum est*) (*Commonitorium* 2). There is the same persuasion of the correlation of faith with the whole Church in Thomas Aquinas, who justifies the fact that we gather together the articles of faith in a creed because "the Church in its universality can never be mistaken, governed as it is by the Holy Spirit, who is the Spirit of truth," so that it is inexact to say, formally or materially, that the Christian believes in the Church. In this context St. Thomas remarks: "it is preferable and more customary not to put there the word 'in' but rather to say simply 'I believe the holy catholic Church.'"[21] Möhler has an identical perception of the *sensus fidei*. For him there is an organic link between a living tradition and the *sensus fidei*:

> Tradition is the expression of the Holy Spirit who inspires the collectivity of the faithful; it passes through all times, lives in every moment, but is incarnated at the same time.[22]

In effect,

> the Spirit of God, which governs and vivifies the Church, generates in the human person with whom he is united an instinct . . . which leads the person to all true doctrine. . . . this sense proper to Christians . . . is perpetuated by education . . . but it cannot be understood without its content; rather it is constituted around that content and by it, so that one can speak of an accomplished

---

[20] Alois Grillmeier, in *Commentary on the Documents of Vatican II*, ed. Herbert Vorgrimler (New York: Herder and Herder, 1966) 1: 165.

[21] IIa IIae q. 1, art. 9 ad 5um.

[22] Johann Adam Moehler, *Die Einheit in der Kirche oder das Prinzip des Katholizismus*, ed. Johannes R. Geiselmann (Cologne: Hegner, 1957) 51.

sense. Tradition is the Word who lives continually in the heart of the faithful.[23]

Thus one briefly illustrates the correlation between tradition and reception which the great tradition has always made. From this one draws two points and one question:

First point: the subject of the *sensus fidei* cannot be the individual Christian; faith cannot be the product of efforts which one expends; on the contrary, faith is necessarily to be referred to the faith of the Church as such.

Second point: the *sensus fidei* refers to the content of faith; as regards this content, one is not to distinguish pastors and the laity. The content of faith is the same for the two groups (if it is legitimate to speak thus), and pastors themselves can receive the faith only from the Church's tradition and from no other source. That is also to say that the adherence of people to the faith envisions directly "the faith transmitted to the saints once for all" and not what is expressed by the magisterium as such.

A question is posed relative to the genesis of the *consensus fidelium*. Vatican II speaks of it only as a reality that may be verified without describing its genesis, which can be complex. On this issue a reference to Newman's analysis of the Arian crisis could be profitable.[24]

B. "Consensus Fidelium"

In passing from the *sensus fidelium* to the *consensus fidelium*, one passes from the content of faith to the determination of the persons who are competent to interpret its content in order to safeguard it. Concretely, can one theologically always attribute that role to pastors alone as distinguished from their people? Or rather to pastors with their people? Or even to the people distinguished from their pastors? The Arian crisis shows that the question is not solely a theoretical one. The non-reception of the Council of Florence shows equally that it is not merely a theoretical a question for a number of Orthodox theologians either.

---

[23]   Idem, *Symbolik*, ed. Johannes R. Geiselmann (Cologne: Hegner, 1958) 415.
[24]   As is known, his famous essay *The Arians of the Fourth Century* played a role in his passage to Catholicism.

At the time of Arianism, the consciousness of the problem was evident in the remark of Hilary of Poitiers for whom "the ears of the people are purer than the heart of bishops."[25] For Newman it is the people, as distinguished from their pastors, who saved the faith at the time: "I see, then, in the Arian history a palmary example of a state of the Church, during which, in order to know the tradition of the Apostles, we must have recourse to the faithful."[26] He draws the conclusion "that the voice of tradition may in certain cases express itself, not by Councils, nor Fathers, nor Bishops, but the 'communis fidelium sensus.' "[27]

However, Newman draws another ecclesiologically normative conclusion from this situation, which is this:

> Yet each constituent portion of the Church has its proper functions, and no portion can safely be neglected. Though the laity be but the reflection or echo of the clergy in matters of faith, yet there is something in the "pastorum et fidelium *conspiratio*," which is not in the pastors alone.[28]

Furthermore, for Newman, as well as for Perrone, on whom he comments in the same article, the *sensus Ecclesiae* is found above and beyond Scripture and the councils, thanks to various indications among which one can name the liturgy, feast days, pious formulae, theological controversies, preaching, etc.

Newman's contribution to our subject is to draw attention to the intrinsic and inalienable value of the *consensus fidelium* and to the necessity of the *conspiratio* of pastors and the faithful. If one overemphasizes or minimizes the role of pastors, they would be situated externally outside the body of the Church. But in the expression of faith the magisterium cannot properly be separated from the *consensus fidelium*, which in certain exceptional circumstances can be more authentic than the precise teaching of the magisterium of the bishops. No more, no less. The process of reception is then part of the very essence of the life of the Church.

---

[25] *Contra Arianos vel Auxentium* 6, in *Patrologia Latina* 10: 615.
[26] *Rambler* (July 1859) 213; John Henry Newman, *On Consulting the Faithful in Matters of Doctrine*, ed. John Coulson (London: Geoffrey Chapman, 1961) 76.
[27] *Rambler* (July 1859), 214; *On Consulting the Faithful*, 77.
[28] *Rambler* (July 1859), 228; *On Consulting the Faithful*, 103-104.

However, Newman, and Vatican II after him, do not tell us the ways in which one passes from the indefectibility of the Church and the *sensus fidei* to the *consensus fidelium*. All the texts of Vatican II which touch the question (*LG* 12, 25, 35; *GS* 52) express themselves as if it were a given, as if the *consensus fidelium* were not characterized by ambiguities and tensions!

However, there remains one last step to take before we come to our proposal in this regard, which is to highlight synodal life; first of all, we need to distinguish the *consensus fidelium* from public opinion.

C. Public Opinion

Newman defined opinion in continuity with the Greek philosophical tradition as "an assent to a proposition, not as true, but as probably true, that is, to the probability of that which the proposition enuntiates."[29]

Obviously one cannot make public opinion thus understood equivalent to the sense of faith. Furthermore, it would be rare to see public opinion linked with the *consensus fidelium*. Thirty years ago Paul VI reflected more of a pastoral lucidity than a complaining spirit in remarking: "Certain people tend to adapt the message of faith to the mentality, tastes, and sensibility of contemporary people, going so far as sometimes altering the authenticity of this message and confusing the 'sense of faith' with the current opinion, not always that of a formed and conscious Christian community but of the world such as it is."[30]

However, despite these pessimistic statements of fact, when they are justified,[31] pastors and theologians ought to adopt two lines of conduct:

1. Support the existence of public opinion in the Church in the fashion desired by Pius XII.[32] Better still, foster debates for two things are proven in Western societies: all debate stifled in the Church will reappear in the public press and under worse conditions if it takes place without

[29]   John Henry Newman, *A Grammar of Assent* (London: Burns, Oates, & Co., 1874) 58.

[30]   Paul VI, Allocution to *Pro Civitate christiana*, November 4, 1966: *DC* 63 (1966) 2026.

[31]   Congregation for the Doctrine of the Faith, instruction "On the Ecclesial Vocation of the Theologian," May 24, 1990, nn. 32 and 39: *Origins* 20/8 (July 5, 1990) 123-125, draws attention to the influence of public opinion on the positions taken by certain theologians.

[32]   Pius XII, allocution to participants in the international convention of Catholic news reporters, February 17, 1950: *AAS* 42 (1950) 256: "The Church is a living body, and some-

our participation; the poor quality of the Church's communications with the surrounding society often reflects the mediocre character of communications within the Church.

2. Participation in public debates is essential because the gospel is for the people: it must then be present in the public arena. Besides, the channels of public opinion also offer resources. Undoubtedly the excellent press coverage of Vatican II greatly facilitated its reception. For all that no one would make the press a locus of normative theological value.

After thus distinguishing the interplay of public opinion and reception, we need to propose for discussion the thesis according to which reception and synodality are not only linked, but also that manifestations of the Church's synodal life are the privileged way of reception. This is because it is only in councils and synods that one finds the most explicit *conspiratio* among the churches as well as between pastors and the faithful in the midst of the local churches.

IV. COUNCILS AND SYNODS: EXPRESSIONS OF THE LIFE OF FAITH AND COMMUNION OF THE CHURCHES, PRIVILEGED INSTRUMENTS OF RECEPTION

A. Council and Reception

A reference to ecumenical councils, to their role in the reception of tradition, and to the manner in which they are received is necessary as an entry point for reflection on synodal life as an instrument of reception.

1. Councils Receive

The purpose of councils is always to assure the reception of the faith transmitted in expressing it anew. That is seen and understood: in effect one enthrones the book of the Gospels in the assembly and one rereads the decisions of prior ecumenical councils to receive them anew.[33] Hence councils conceive their role as a service of the faith transmitted.

---

thing would be lacking in its life if there were no public opinion, a defect to be blamed on pastors and the faithful."

[33] Heinrich J. Sieben, *Vom Apostelkonzil zum Ersten Vatikanum. Studien zur Geschichte der Konzilsidee* (Paderborn: Schöningh, 1996) 73-76.

2. Councils Are Received

Evidently councils await the reception of their decisions in all the churches but not by the laity as such. In effect only the bishops or their representatives, priests or deacons, sign the acts, if they are personally present; and if they are absent, only they must receive the acts.

The only layperson who had to receive these acts was a very special one: the emperor who assured the decisions the force of law in the empire.[34]

The fact that the laity as laity are not considered to have received councils is explained by the most classical ecclesiology, such as one finds in the adage of St. Cyprian: "You ought to know that the bishop is in the Church and the Church is in the bishop."[35] Representing the communion of the churches through the bishops who presided over them, councils never envisioned that because of that fact their acts needed reception to be valid. The eighteenth century Jansenists affirmed the contrary, but Heinrich Sieben, who certainly knows the conciliar life of the ancient church better than anyone and who has just recovered this body of material, assures us that there is not the least support for this position in the sources.[36]

In reality certain councils were received, and others were not, even though they were declared ecumenical (Seleucia/Rimini [359-360]; "Robber Council of Ephesus" [449]). There are no criteria that one can isolate positively to explain such discernment; the sole valid criterion is the very content of tradition.

In this case one sees in effect that non-reception is not an act of disobedience toward higher authority but an active participation in the process which a council thought it was achieving in its essence, the act of tradition. To receive a council is then to be integrated in a process of transmission of the faith, such as is accomplished between apostolic times and the return of the Lord.

---

[34] Constantine gave himself the title *episcopos tôn ektos*. See Eusebius, *Vita Constantini*, 4: 24; *Patrologia Graeca* [*PG*] 20: 1172. De facto he gave the force of imperial law to conciliar decisions and also to the *episcopalis audientia*. See ibid., 4: 27; *PG* 20: 1176.

[35] Cyprian, Ep. 66: 8, in *Corpus scriptorum ecclesiasticorum latinorum* 3: 733.

[36] Sieben, 93, 551-576.

3. Synodality and Reception: Two General Remarks

a. The conciliar character of a decision accords it a presumption of legitimacy and reception.

As a representation of the *communio ecclesiarum*, councils are credited with the assistance of the Holy Spirit, the spirit of truth and communion.[37] Their legitimacy and reception are presumed; never has anyone seen a need to formalize this reception before the royal *placet* of Bourges and Mainz, imposed by political authorities on a somewhat weak council.[38]

Although their legitimacy is presumed, the acts of councils are nonetheless found vis-à-vis the local churches. This explains the fact that their authority grows when they are broadly received. It also explains the fact that they can be more or less fruitful. It also explains the fact that exceptionally they may lack any authority: a sign that they have not been found faithful to tradition.

b. The refusal of reception is based on the lack of conformity to tradition, of which the decisive indication will be the absence of the "consensus ecclesiarum."

For the ancient church the refusal of a council was based on a rejection of innovation. Indeed this process would be guided by persons such as theologians and bishops basing their position on popular reactions. However, in this regard, it was not a matter of submitting "the decisions of the hierarchy" to a critical examination, no more than receiving the same council would have signified that the laity were submissive to hierarchic authority. No, the subject of reception is the Church, most often a group of churches, who were preoccupied with the transmission of what had been received. In today's language the reception of a council is not vertical, or from on high; rather it is horizontal, i.e., from church to church, so that in case of difficulties one verifies if the message received has been faithfully transmitted from the first witnesses to the present day, according to Paul's vocabulary (1 Cor. 11: 23; 15: 3).

---

[37]   Yves Congar, "Remarques sur le concile comme assemblée et sur la conciliarité foncière de l'Eglise," in *Le Concile au jour le jour. Deuxième session* (Paris: Cerf, 1964) 9-39.

[38]   Sieben, 9, 233-239.

One must agree with Wolfgang Beinert when he remarks that "reception is a given reality which concerns the Church in nearly all its dimensions and a complete theology of reception cannot fail to appeal to anything less than an integral ecclesiology."[39]

However, for an ecclesiologist it is less arbitrary, which one would not have considered a priori, to place the accent above all on synodality as a condition of reception. In effect synodal life is a place where things happen, a place of transformations, a place of experimentation, which in turn accentuate the capacity of reception.

As regards this synodal life, we will develop our suggestions in two stages: it will be necessary to make progress in understanding the relationship of the bishop and the Church, at the same time as we develop the very life of the synods and councils.

B. The Bishop as Point of Contact of Reception among the Churches

The foundation of the process of reception is found in the communion and mutual relations between the local churches and the whole Church according to the logic on this subject affirmed by *Lumen gentium* 23: "particular churches formed in the likeness of the universal Church, in which and from which the one and unique Catholic Church exists" (*LG* 23).

All Christians are responsible for the vitality and correctness of these relations, but the bishops have a specific ministry from the very fact of their special place in the Church. The bishop represents his church vis-à-vis all the others and he represents the whole Church in his own church, which makes him the official organ of the process of reception.

However, in contemporary Catholic ecclesiology this equilibrium has been broken.[40] Vatican II, for example, did not situate the diocesan bishop within his own church; it only enumerated his duties on its behalf. Actually, at least according to the language of institutions (for fortunately the reality is different), the Catholic bishop is "a member of a high ranking corps of personnel directing the universal Church" (according to

---

[39] Wolfgang Beinert, "Die Rezeption und ihre Bedeutung für Leben und Lehre der Kirchen," in *Glaube als Zustimmung*, 36 (*supra*, note 17).

[40] For an ecclesiological and canonical analysis see Hervé Legrand, "Collégialité des évêques et communion des Eglises dans la réception de Vatican II," *Revue des Sciences Philosophiques et Théologiques* 75 (1991) 545-568.

the expression of Karl Rahner). He is directly chosen by the pope after consultation with other bishops and certain private persons regarding his suitability. But the church to which he is sent will not be consulted as such in ninety-five percent of cases (there are exceptions in German-speaking dioceses and in the Eastern Churches). Furthermore, if he is promoted, neither the church he leaves nor the church to which he goes will be consulted.

1. The Current Idea of Collegiality needs to be Deepened

The factual situation which has just been described is legitimated among other things by a concept of collegiality of bishops which has been articulated without taking account of the communion of churches. In effect, according to certain decisive texts of *Lumen gentium*, the bishop is conceived above all as a member of a college of persons of whom the pope is the head. It is only subsequently that his relationship to the local church is envisioned, if one is entrusted to him. *Lumen gentium* 22 describes how one becomes a member of the college without mentioning his presiding over a church:

> One is constituted a member of the episcopal body in virtue of sacramental consecration and hierarchical communion with the head of the college and its members.

More important from a practical standpoint, the system of the 1983 code shows well that the concept of the college poses a dilemma for the *communio ecclesiarum* as a structuring element. In material fidelity to *Lumen gentium*, the code envisions successively in Book Two the status of the lay faithful and the clergy (first part), supreme power in the Church, the college of bishops (second part, section one), and finally *after the college of bishops*, the particular churches or dioceses (second part, section two). But before one knows what a local church is and what the communion of churches represents, how can one establish institutionally and even theologically who are the laity and the clergy, a pope, a bishop and the college of bishops, the synod of bishops, the cardinals, the Roman Curia, and the nuncios?

2. Some Legitimate, Opportune and Limited Expectations concerning the Involvement of Local Churches in the Choice or Reception of their Bishop

The process of reception in the *communio ecclesiarum* would gain something in vitality or at least in clarity if the participation of the local churches in the choice and reception of their bishop were developed. In manifesting better the fact that the bishop belongs to his church and in clarifying his role in the process of reception, such a doctrinally legitimate development would be pastorally fruitful if it were conducted prudently.

a. A Doctrinally Legitimate Development

In the current ritual for the ordination of a Catholic bishop, a representative of the church for which the ordination is being carried out speaks the first word in its name and addressing the presiding bishop states: "Most Reverend Father, the church of N. asks you to ordain this priest, N., for service as a bishop."[41] In fact, in entrusting the choice of nearly all the bishops to the pope since the 1917 code, the *ius vigens* does not respond to a doctrinal necessity.[42] Furthermore, the custom of election continues to be operative for certain churches of the Latin Church,[43] and election by the patriarchal synod often remains the rule in the Eastern Catholic Churches.[44]

b. Visible Indication that the Bishop Belongs to his Church

Such a development would permit us to rediscover the unity of election, the imposition of hands, and the assumption of the episcopal task, a unity which has been broken since the early Middle Ages with the negative consequences of which we are aware. One would also transcend unilateral interpretations tending to reduce ordination to the imposition of hands (among Catholics) or to the installation in the episcopal task (as for the bishops of certain Protestant churches). Thus one would no longer

---

[41] *Roman Pontifical for the Ordination of a Bishop*, n. 16.

[42] *Lumen gentium* 24 is explicit on this point: "The canonical mission of bishops can be given either by means of lawful customs which have not been revoked by the supreme and universal power of the Church, or by means of laws made or recognized by that same authority, or directly by the successor of Peter himself; and if the latter opposes the appointment or refuses apostolic communion, bishops cannot be admitted to office."

[43] See the list in Jean Louis Harouel, *Les désignations épiscopales dans le droit contemporain* (Paris: PUF, 1997) 23-40; text in Angelo Mercati, *Raccolta di Concordati* (Vatican: Libreria Editrice Vaticana, 1954).

[44] *CCEO* cc. 181 and 947-957. See Marco Brogi, "Elezione dei vescovi orientali cattolici," in *Il processo di designazione dei vescovi. Storia, legislazione, prassi. Atti del X Symposium canonistico-romanistico*, ed. Domingo J. Andrés Gutiérrez (Rome: Libreria Editrice Vaticana and Libreria Editrice Lateranense, 1996) 597-613.

dissociate the power arising from the task (ex officio) and that arising from ordination (*ex Spiritu*).

In practice there is also a small hope of reducing the number of cases of non-reception of bishops by their diocese, of seeing diminished the number of bishops ordained absolutely, a custom which conveys a questionable concept of apostolic succession among the reformed churches, and finally of reassuring the other churches that in case of reunion with us they would preserve the possibility of choosing their bishops.

c. A Reform to Undertake Prudently

The participation of the churches in the choice of their bishop would be introduced prudently if one decided on it. The bishop's ministry, like all ministry, comes from God; it is not a delegation of the community. The procedures and symbols ought to communicate clearly the two aspects according to which the bishop is in the Church and also of it.

Furthermore, the strength of nationalist sentiments, to which the past and present testify, shows how important it would be always to reserve the final decision to the Holy See for the good of the episcopal ministry. In this regard the customary procedures of certain German dioceses seem to prove this.[45]

C. Importance of the Principle and Fact of the Development of Synodal Life for the Process of Reception

1. The Vitality of the Process of Reception Partly Linked with Synodal and Conciliar Life

Reception would have no place in the life of the Church and one would replace it with obedience if the magisterium alone expressed the faith and Christian life, as Wolfgang Beinert has written[46] and as Hermann Pottmeyer notes in expressing certain reservations regarding the idea of sovereign authority in the Church.

At the level of principle, it is necessary then to revitalize synodal life as the place for the expression of the faith and Christian life. There are

---

[45]   Bruno Primetshofer, "La nomina dei vescovi nell'Austria, Germania e Svizzera," and Pier V. Aimone Braisa, "Elezione e nomina dei Vescovi in Svizzera," in Andrés Gutiérrez, 533-559.

[46]   Beinert, "Die Rezeption und ihre Bedeutung," 28 (*supra*, note 39).

many methods that may be indicated to proceed in this way. Here we choose to be supported by recent ecumenical developments which precisely ask of the Catholic Church a clearer acceptance of synodal authority in its midst.

Since the sixteenth century a genuine misunderstanding has developed between the Catholic Church and Reformation churches on the subject of the respective place of the hierarchy and other Christians in ecclesial life. Fearing that the concept of the hierarchy removes the bishops from the faith of the Church, Melancthon formulated the difficulty in the following terms:

> Perhaps our adversaries would like the Church defined as follows: it is an external monarchy whose supremacy extends over the whole earth and in which the Roman Pontiff must have an unlimited power which no one has the right to question or judge. . . . But, for us, in the Church as defined by Christ . . . it is not necessary to apply to pontiffs what belongs to the Church as a whole.[47]

Such a misunderstanding is being transcended today. Proof of this is in the 1983 Lima document *Baptism, Eucharist, Ministry*, produced by Faith and Order, of which the Catholic Church is officially a member and where one can read the following recommendation in the part on ministry:

> The ordained ministry should be exercised in a personal, collegial and communitarian way.

This point is developed further as the three aspects are elaborated, and there is added the following:

> An appreciation of these three dimensions lies behind a recommendation made by the first World Conference on Faith and Order at Lausanne in 1927: "In view of (*i*) the place which the episcopate, the council of presbyters and the congregation of the faithful, respectively, had in the constitution of the early Church, and (*ii*) the fact that episcopal, presbyteral and congregational systems of government are each today, and have been for centuries, accepted by great communions in Christendom, and (*iii*) the fact that episcopal, presbyteral and congregational systems

---

[47] "Non est ad pontifices transferendum quod ad veram ecclesiam pertinet, quod videlicet sunt columnae veritatis, quod non errent." Philip Melancthon, *Apologie de la Confession d'Augsbourg*, 1531, art. VII, in *La foi des Eglises luthériennes. Confessions et catéchismes* (Paris: Cerf, 1991) 159, n. 188.

are each believed by many to be essential to the good order of the Church, we therefore recognize that these several elements must all, under conditions which require further study, have an appropriate place in the order of life of a reunited Church. . . ."[48]

Such a position is an invitation to Reformation churches to accept the episcopate, but it also indicates a precise request made of the Catholic Church to permit the Church to be expressed by all its members, which means the necessity of developing synodal life.

Concretely this synodal life opens the door for reception among the churches, for no one can be the sovereign authority expecting only obedience from the others. The authority of witness of each church is linked with the freedom of the others through the slant of the *consensus ecclesiarum* expressed in council.

Such a perspective is no longer totally utopian if the approach taken at Balamand becomes an effective commitment involving the Catholic and Orthodox Churches who recognize themselves in this text as "responsible together for maintaining the Church of God in fidelity to the divine purpose, most especially in what concerns unity" (14).

At the more modest level of the local churches, this rearticulation of the relationship between the faithful and the bishop needs to be deepened. We have just seen that nothing blocks this. At the level of principle, the way is even open since *Lumen gentium* 37 does not hesitate to say that "pastors, for their part, helped by the experience of the laity, are able to make clearer and more suitable decisions both in spiritual and in temporal matters" and "the whole church, strengthened by all its members, is able to fulfill more effectively its mission for the life of the world." One sees here the role which synodal life must play in inculturation.

2. The Vitality of the Process of Reception Linked with the Reality of Synodal Life to be Developed by Experimentation

This is not the place to offer an institutional overview of the different forms of synodal life which have flourished since Vatican II or to stress the frequent restrictiveness of its generally consultative canonical status.

For our purpose, because they are fundamental, three points of clarification will suffice to illustrate the potential fruitfulness for reception of

---

[48]   *Baptism, Eucharist and Ministry* (the so-called Lima document) (Geneva: WCC, 1982), n. 26.

these instances which one finds at all levels of church life, from parish councils to synods of bishops with the pope.

These instances, diversified in their ecclesiological status, correspond to the level of ecclesial communion where they gather the principal actors who are capable of being the bearers of reception.

They will be particularly valuable for the fruitful reception of ecumenical agreements. Besides the official reception by the authorities of the universal Church, these agreements in effect will need a diversified regional reception.

Finally, their current limitations are not necessarily a handicap. In effect, how could they acquire a more consistent status without experimentation? It is evident: it is not after only one or two synods in a diocese that synodality become a dimension of diocesan life. Several are necessary before such experimentation is a success.

V. CONCLUSION

We now focus attention on non-synodal ways of reception.

The ecumenical concern which was constantly on the horizon of the present contribution explains the specific emphasis on synodal ways of reception to the detriment perhaps of the explicitation of its pneumatological-trinitarian foundations[49] and undoubtedly also the discussion of the convergences and divergences between synodality and democracy.[50]

The reason is that as Catholics we do not simply have to find a vitality in the process of reception but we have to receive synodal life in the global equilibrium of our ecclesiology.

Being concentrated on this perspective, it is appropriate now in conclusion to draw attention to non-synodal ways of reception. For this happens largely through legislation but not always, e.g., in the case of receivability.[51] It often happens effectively also through public opinion,

---

[49] On the importance of the trinitarian structure of the Church see Hervé Legrand, "L'Eglise se réalise en un lieu," in *Initiation à la pratique de la théologie*, ed. Bernard Lauret and François Refoulé, 3rd ed. (Paris: Cerf, 1993) 210-219.

[50] Hervé Legrand, "Democrazia o sinodalità per la Chiesa? Convergenze reali e divergenze profonde," *Ricerca* 12 (1996) 4-5, n. 5; 5-9, n. 6.

[51] Receivability is the judgment rendered on an expression of the faith or more often on a liturgical, canonical, disciplinary practice, to which a particular church does not object, but which it does not intend to adopt for itself.

even if in a partial fashion. It happens especially in the word of theologians, prophets, experts, and saints. They do not express themselves daily in our synods, our committees, our councils. Perhaps it is more important to hear them, for they can significantly contribute to the correspondence between *traditio* and *receptio*, i.e., the faithful reception of the word that is transmitted, which is alone what counts.

Translation by Thomas J. Green

RESPONSE TO HERVÉ LEGRAND

JAMES H. PROVOST*

Professor Legrand, with his usual clarity and insight, has provided us with an opportunity to focus on suggestions for the methods for reception in and among the local churches, as well as some key concepts for understanding the reality of reception. I am very much in agreement not only with his analysis of the situation but also with many of his suggestions for addressing it. Perhaps the following comments will assist us to "receive" his thoughts more fruitfully.

Ecumenical concerns at Vatican II helped the Roman Catholic Church to rediscover some of its own tradition, and to place it in a more appropriate perspective. Similarly, at our colloquium, as evidenced in the presentation we have just heard, ecumenical concerns are helping us to recapture significant aspects of our tradition today. My emphasis will be on how these insights are rooted in our own tradition, even though I recognize the importance of the ecumenical dimension which has occasioned them and which helps to keep them in focus. Moreover, I will concentrate on the reception of the reforms of Vatican II, the second phenomenon of Professor Legrand's introduction.

Synodality

Episcopal conferences have already been addressed by a previous colloquium. I will not repeat the important work already published.[1] Rather, let me turn to another dimension of synodality, particular councils and diocesan synods. A traditional process in the reception of councils has been to hold councils at a less general level. Prescinding from the legislation concerning the holding of particular councils (which has a rather mixed history in practice), ecumenical councils have often been followed

---

*   The Catholic University of America.
[1]   *The Nature and Future of Episcopal Conferences*, ed. Hervé Legrand et al. (Washington: CUA Press, 1988); see also *The Jurist* 48 (1988) 1-412.

by provincial councils; provincial councils have often been followed by diocesan synods.[2]

After the Second Vatican Council there was a notable increase in diocesan synods, but not in particular councils.[3] Many of these diocesan synods were preceded by surveys and soundings of opinion to discern the needs and current state of religious life. These are a precious witness to a process underway. While most of the surveys do not meet technical scientific standards, this whole body of material merits more study.

A similar experience of synods has been verified after the promulgation of the code, perhaps sensing (whether wisely or not) that the code is a step in the council's implementation rather than in its reception strictly speaking.

Many of these synods were marked by remarkable candor in the exchange of views and desires. Despite their various problems, including a number of canonical ones, these synods are perhaps a sign of readiness in the local churches to receive the council by moving beyond the letter of the conciliar documents. Regrettably, many have been followed by an experience of disillusionment, shattering the hopes of local churches in the face of current church discipline. This, too, merits attention as an experience in the process of reception; will this disillusionment weaken the reception of renewal in the Church, or is it a stage in the difficult process which seems to be a part of reception? To a canonist, the disillusioning experience also raises the question of the need for further reform of canon law, but a reform which this time listens to the experiences and needs of the local churches.

As Professor Legrand mentioned toward the conclusion of his paper, the new code provides for a limited number of consultative bodies within the local church, and also a limited role for these bodies. A presbyteral council, college of consultors, and finance council are all mandatory bodies within a diocese today; diocesan pastoral councils are a possibil-

---

[2] See, for example, Silvio Cesare Bonicelli, *I Concili Particolari da Graziano al Concilio di Trento: Studio alla evoluzione del diritto della Chiesa latina* (Brescia: Morcelliana, 1971); José Orlandis, "Función historica y eclesiologica de los concilios particulares," in *La Synodalité. La participation au gouvernement dans l'Église. Actes du VIIe congrès international de Droit canonique* (Paris: L'annèe canonique, 1992) 289-304.

[3] See James H. Provost, "The Ecclesiological Nature and Function of the Diocesan Synod in the Real Life of the Church," in *La Synodalité*, 537-558.

ity even within the law.[4] It was probably not appropriate to legislate in more detail about these new diocesan structures; they need time to mature and to develop in keeping with the possibilities and needs of local churches. Yet it is increasingly difficult to conceive of a diocese in the Catholic Church today without such consultative bodies, some of which must give their consent for the diocesan bishop to act in various matters.

There is a process here of building a new way of interaction within the local church. We are still learning how to do this, but the process can eventually produce that richer synodality which Professor Legrand desires. This apprenticeship, however, can be cut short by a poor selection of a new bishop. It seems to be a truism that it is easier for a bishop to stop the development of the life of the local church than it is for a bishop to stimulate it. It is therefore all the more essential that bishops be selected with care, that they might foster the reality of reception in the local churches.

Selection of Bishops

This is not the time or place to engage in a lengthy discussion of the selection of bishops; the topic merits a colloquium all its own.[5] However, I cannot pass over in silence the careful and important analysis of Professor Legrand on this subject. Selection of leadership is crucial if the Tradition is to be passed on, and received effectively in the local churches and by succeeding generations.

Regrettably, the present practices in the Latin Church reflect an over-centralization which is a relatively recent innovation. Even the post-conciliar norms for the selection of bishops called for greater consultation than seems to be the practice today in many parts of the world.[6] Moreover, despite the dedication and best intentions of those responsible, the results of the present system indicate the need for a change. If selection leads to division within dioceses and countries, and to a disturbance of the "peace of the Church"—and the present system has done that to a regrettable extent—then something needs to be done both to protect the

---

[4]   See cc. 495 (presbyteral councils), 502 (college of consultors), 492 (finance councils), and 511 (pastoral council).

[5]   The Canon Law Society of America conducted such a study over twenty-five years ago. See *The Choosing of Bishops*, ed. William W. Bassett (Hartford, CT: CLSA, 1971).

[6]   See S. Council for the Public Affairs of the Church, decree, March 25, 1972: *AAS* 64 (1972) 386-391.

function of the Apostolic See as center of unity within the communion of churches, and to safeguard the life of the Church.

I am not speaking about pressure coming from various fringe groups. It is the concern of local churches—their pastors and people—which leads to this conclusion.

Caution Against Confrontational Approach

Underlying these practical suggestions, Professor Legrand cautions us against a simplistic, confrontational approach to reception. His observations are well taken, and if I offer some comments these are intended as further reflections occasioned by what I welcome as sound advice.

1. Tradition has priority over reception. Yet the process by which the tradition is received and put into practice is itself an important consideration, as the comments concerning synodality have already demonstrated. This process is not a strictly democratic one. True, the Church is not a democracy. But where is sovereignty in the Church? It is not located in the hierarchy, or in the people, or in the institution of the Church itself. The Lord Jesus and his Spirit hold the sovereignty in the Church. Even so, we still have much to learn how *quod omnes tangit ab omnibus tractari debet*; the processes for this are embedded in our tradition. Can these not respond to the experience and expectations of Catholics today—even to their democratic experiences—leading to greater participation in a church as subject?

2. To a canonist, *sensus fidei*, *consensus fidelium*, and public opinion are familiar concepts, even if they are not fully developed in the present law.

Canon 750 presents the ordinary and universal magisterium not as only the episcopal college headed by the pope, dispersed around the world (as in *Lumen gentium* 25), but as the common adherence of the Christian faithful under the leadership of the sacred magisterium (as in *Lumen gentium* 12). This is the common way in which the deposit of faith is proposed. In both *traditio* and *receptio*, the Christian faithful have a canonically sanctioned role.

Consensus fidelium is at work in canon 127, which governs the consultation even by bishops of the consultative bodies in their dioceses. Acting against a consensus requires an overriding reason. Again, the role of *consensus fidelium* is already structured in canon law, albeit in a very limited fashion.

Public opinion is presented in canon 212 in a nuanced fashion, respecting the role of tradition (§1) while encouraging the expression of needs and opinion on what is for the good of the Church (§§2-3). This is also a limited expression, but provides the basis for further growth through experience and attention to the guidance of the Spirit.

These canons mark a limited but important building block on which to construct a more effective process of reception. Even the reception of ecumenical documents, as Professor Legrand observes, will rely on such structures within the Roman Catholic Church. But the law does not implement itself, and the scholar's task, in the opportunities open to each, is to foster an intelligent and sensitive implementation even of canon law if the work of reception is to move forward.

EVALUATION OF COLLOQUIUM
SUGGESTIONS FOR IMPROVEMENT
FUTURE TOPICS

Towards the end of the colloquium the working groups were asked to evaluate it as a whole with an indication of those aspects which could be improved in subsequent experiences. The responses manifest a desire for a continuation of the experience. Suggestions were also sought regarding topics for the next colloquium. These are the contributions of the groups.

Spanish Language Group

Evaluation of Colloquium and Possible Improvements

1. There is a notable consensus on praising the colloquium for the climate of fraternity and openness, for the rigor and seriousness of the presentations and the reflections, for the hospitality. In short the first reaction is satisfaction.

2. The liturgy: the majority opinion affirms that it is good as it stands with the prevalence of Latin. The minority proposes enriching it more with other languages.

3. The presence of colloquium members from Latin America is most welcome. The organizers (of the colloquium) are encouraged to follow through in this line by seeking as much as possible the participation of theologians of other continents or significant cultural areas.

4. Suggestions as regards methodology: more pedagogic expositions without being reduced to the reading of an article. Would it be possible to rely on two versions, one for publication and the other for presentation and debate, reading the written one? Clarifying dialogue between presentations; time for personal work (prior reading, preparation of questionnaires); request for presence until the end (important above all for group reflections).

Suggestions for the Next Colloquium

Method: valid even if somewhat subject to improvement as noted above.

437

Topics: ecumenism, synodality, Church from the perspective of mission: evangelization.

As regards the first topic (ecumenism), possible aspects: reception of ecumenical documents, dialogue with world religions, dialogue with Orthodoxy, choice of a central topic, e.g., ministry and ministries, primacy, etc.

French Language Group

The participants in our working group first of all highlight the respect for the schedule which has permitted attention to the study of the topic. It is equally necessary to mention the exceptional work of the secretariat in printing and translating the text of the communications. It is also appropriate to express our gratitude to those responsible for the quality of the overall organization of the colloquium (including the material organization). Finally, we have appreciated the dynamic of the linguistic working group where we have found different cultural dimensions which have greatly contributed to the enrichment of the exchanges.

On the other hand we would like to make three proposals to improve the functioning of the colloquium:

1. The first concerns the presidency role during the work of the colloquium. Those presiding at the sessions could not only present the speakers but also situate their interventions within the general dynamic of the colloquium and the study of the topic.

2. After the response which follows a presentation, it would also be very interesting to engage immediately in dialogue with all the participants for fifteen to twenty minutes. This would permit the specification of certain elements or the raising of certain questions.

3. We believe that it would be possible to improve the quality of the work during the plenary sessions. To achieve this the facilitator could pick up certain questions raised in the reports of the working groups and submit them to public debate, based on two or three persons who have raised these questions or expressed an opinion on the subject. Technically speaking, it would be desirable for the reports of the secretaries to be printed and distributed to all before the plenary session.

Suggestions for the Next Colloquium: Topics and Methodology

In a perspective of continuity with the first three colloquia devoted to episcopal conferences, the catholicity of the local churches, and reception and communion among the churches, the majority judges the topic of the primacy of the bishop of Rome to be a priority. This topic would equally respond to the desire expressed by John Paul II in *Ut unum sint* to pursue the theological study of this question in a spirit of dialogue and in an ecumenical perspective.

As regards this topic the participants have proposed what follows regarding the method of work. It would not be necessary to repeat what has already been done on this topic and what one must hold as a given; the colloquium ought to be a research enterprise. In this regard, one could prepare in advance a bibliography which could constitute the point of departure without having to take up those questions again. If this topic were undertaken, we think it would be absolutely necessary to treat it by taking into account the ecumenical dimension of the question. For that it would certainly be necessary to have a much broader participation of our sisters and brothers from other churches.

A second topic, that of the reception of ecumenical documents, elicited the support of a majority of the members of the working group. In this case there would be an immediate continuity with the topic of this colloquium.

Some other topics were proposed without, however, eliciting the support of a majority of the participants: the episcopate, synodal life, membership in the Church.

English Language Group

Evaluation of the Colloquium

This colloquium has gone better than the previous two, perhaps because the number of participants was smaller. The lectures were very good, and the secretariat did an excellent job. The involvement of other Christians was substantial, which was more valuable than only providing reflections toward the end of the colloquium (as in previous colloquia). We also valued the presence of the Archbishop, head of the episcopal conference; in the future, it would also be worth while to have some bishop-theologians as participants.

At this colloquium there was less overlapping in the papers than at the previous Salamanca colloquium. It would help, however, to provide some additional explanation to the authors in advance, so they would have a better idea of where each one's paper fits within the overall scheme of the program.

Some consultation among participants in advance, perhaps by people within the same geographic area, could help to prepare for the colloquium more effectively.

Ways need to be found to involve people from other parts of the world; e.g., Central Europe, Latin America, etc. This colloquium suffered from the low number of women participants, and the absence of anyone from the Reformed Church tradition. We recognize there is a problem in funding, since the sponsoring universities are to pay for two or three participants.

In terms of the topic of the colloquium, several other aspects of reception remain to be addressed. Reception of the liturgy was not discussed, yet it is an area where there has been a lot of reception between the churches (e.g., adoption of the Roman Lectionary). Reception of cults of saints from other local churches could also be explored, especially in a Salamanca colloquium with the example of the early church here dedicated to St. Thomas of Canterbury. Here are some other aspects of reception which have not yet been addressed: reception of non-institutional means for unity and union; related questions of inculturation and its limits; the relationship between dissent and *obsequium* in the context of reception; and how individual churches go about receiving ecumenical documents, including the patterns of decision making in the various churches.

Suggestions Toward Future Colloquia

1. Method. The balance between plenary and small group sessions could be examined. More time in small groups could be used to discuss the various papers. There is also a need for more time for discussion in the large group after the main papers. Even when this occurred at this colloquium, only a few intervened. Good keeping of time with the speakers could permit time for discussion in both the large group and, so that others can enter the discussion, in the small groups.

Designing the small groups along linguistic lines is easiest, but it can become parochial. We noted that all the participants from other churches were in our English-speaking group, which enriched our discussions but may have denied other small groups the benefit of this ecumenical presence.

The role of questions posed to the small groups might be reviewed. They seemed to keep us from addressing the papers themselves. The questions may be needed to keep the various groups focused on the same topics, but could be more integrated with the papers. The timing of the reports from the small groups should be adjusted so that reports from groups are at the next plenarium instead of being delayed, as happened this time.

Only a few responses to the papers were really "responses." Others were separate papers. One suggestion is to drop the responses, in order to permit time for more discussion. An alternative, which would respect the value of the responses but also put them to greater use for the group, would be to require each response to pose one or more questions which could lead to discussion by the group.

To facilitate continued exchanges even after the colloquium, an updated list of addresses and phone numbers would be helpful.

2. Topics. The following topics are suggested for a future colloquium; they are not ranked in order of preference:

a. Catechesis and evangelization
b. Primacy and the fashion in which it is exercised (or, primacies in the Church)
c. Ecclesiastical authority and spiritual power (includes both the question of the Primacy or primacies, and the sources of "spiritual power" outside of "office")
d. Episcope
e. Inculturation
f. Local church as parish (in the sense that the life of the Church is lived in the family and parish, or even smaller ecclesial units)
g. Nature of the unity we seek

The group was not in favor of dedicating an entire future colloquium to the theme of the procedures for the reception of ecumenical documents. Some of this has already been done at this colloquium; the familiarity with the topic varies according to language groups; the theological questions relate more to issues of the nature of the Church and the role of primacy and collegiality within the communion of churches, while the practical dimensions of these procedures is not a question for a colloquium. The issues should be incorporated into a larger theme, such as a study of primacy.

Italian Language Group

1. The evaluation of the colloquium is very positive. In recent years the Salamanca colloquia have become a fundamental gathering place for theological-canonical research at an international level. The organization of the activities is substantially balanced even if it strictly follows the proposed rhythm of the sessions. The cultural half day (visit to a city or historic places) is appreciated also as a time for fraternal communion.

We make some suggestions from a general point of view:

a. It would be desirable, if possible, to have the participation of other non-Western cultural orientations at the colloquium.

b. Trim the time for discussion for all the reports.

c. It should be more clear what is the link between the different reports, and between them and the general topic of the colloquium. It would be good to have a "moderator" who could synthesize the development of the topic (points of agreement, problematic points, questions, etc.).

d. The linguistic criterion for the constitution of the groups seems inadequate and reductive because it can lead to numerical imbalances and imbalances in terms of expertise in the various areas envisioned, i.e., historical, canonical, theological.

e. It is suggested that there be a greater correspondence between the topics of the reports and the questions addressed to the working groups.

f. Insertion of a biblical report.

2. The following proposals are made for the next colloquium:

a. Synodality at the level of the local church (among the different possible questions one might note the selection of the bishop);

b. "Rethinking" the petrine ministry within the perspective of different modalities of its exercise;

c. Reflection on "ordained ministry" in its biblical, historical, theological-canonical, and ecumenical dimensions even in relation to the current context;

d. "Salvation" in the interface/dialogue between the Christian churches and other religions.

At the methodological level it would be useful to send in advance the text of the presentations to the individual participants in the colloquium to enable them to read them before hand. This would permit the exposition of the reports to be limited to a few essential points so as to leave adequate space for exchange and discussion in the general assembly.

3. If ecumenical documents are to be received, it is fundamental above all that they be known. There is a problem in specifying the ways and modalities of facilitating contact and the study of such documents. There ought to be more room for them and a more effective role for them in ecclesial practice and in the local community.

German Language Group

Evaluation of the Symposium

In a positive sense:

a. The topic was well chosen.
b. Through the presentation of so many aspects of the topic, and indeed both formal and material aspects, at least a fundamental consensus was achieved on the importance of reception as a vital act in the Church —this despite different points of departure.
c. The schedule envisioned by the program could be observed.

In a negative sense:

There were too many presentations in comparison with the time allotted for discussion. Ultimately still (too) many questions were left open (see the detailed references in the position papers of the other language groups which we will not repeat here).

Proposals for Future Symposia

Only one presentation in the morning and one in the afternoon (eventually with a response), introduction of the discussion by a specialist prepared in the material, concrete questions.

Topics:

The highest authority in the Church (primacy, ecumenical council, and. . . ?)

Proposals in relation to the reception of ecumenical documents: The greatest problem still seems to be the often experienced difficulty of having access to these documents so that as a result a fundamental basis for reception is impeded, if it is not entirely precluded.

Translation by Thomas J. Green

CLOSING SESSION

FERNANDO SEBASTIÁN AGUILAR*

The colloquium's organizers have offered me the honor and responsibility of speaking a few words to close your scientific reflections on "Reception and Communion among Churches." I will not add anything significant to what you have already said with professional competency within each of the fields: history, theology, canon law, and ecumenism. From outside and afar, we have expected from you an attempt, first, to give an overview of the conceptual clarifications of the word and idea of reception; then to turn your gaze on what a non-specialist sees when looking at the dynamism at work in the Church from 1870 to our days; then to endeavor to decipher how the logic of "gift-welcome" worked in the three phases of salvation history: the time of the first covenant, the time of Christ, and the time of the Church; finally, to suggest from this what attitudes should guide both theological work and our pastoral responsibility in the coming years.

1. You have selected a fruitful, complex, and difficult theme. "Fruitful," because it shows and recalls the vitality of a Church in which all the members acted as subjects with full responsibility in obedience and in leadership, in faithful listening and creative response, in recognition of the gratitude for God's revelation and in the search for his mediations from the heart of history. "Complex," because nevertheless we did not have the time to discern and clarify all the realities implied or designated with this word, which could embrace very diverse things partly irreducible among themselves, and each one of which requires a distinct treatment. "Difficult," because it presumed to have clarified what is the specific authority of the apostles in the Church, the material and formal conditions for its exercise, and at the same time the nature of the Spirit's action in each believer, and in each group or small community in regard to the respective authority: what collaboration to look for with one another, what limits bind all, and what general criteria is to guide their joint

* Archbishop of Pamplona (Spain); Grand Chancellor, Universidad Pontificia de Salamanca.

activity at the same time as the necessary internal activities in case of collision. Life is not made of limit situations, but it can come to that. What does the bond of charity mean, and what does it mean to serve each one, and to submit oneself to one's neighbor? Reception is located in the middle of the road, on one side between obedience, acceptance, and application; and on the other, between collaboration, critical reflection, enlarging the word and decision of authority, explicating what is implicit, interrogating what is not clear, rejecting what is false. Between mechanical and mimetic acceptance, unworthy of rational beings and children of God on one side, and, on the other, a type of autonomy of individual conscience, of groups or local church which would lead to distance, dissent, and finally to schism which would put one outside the Church and the means of salvation left by Christ—this is the space of true reception, of increasing interpretation and Catholic communion.

It is necessary to be rigorously precise in each case with the use the term "reception" in order to extract the fruit of the idea and not to succumb to fuzziness, or to a melange of totally diverse things. Reception can be a constitutive structure of Christianity, in so far as revelation is positive, is realized in history as a gift of a personal God, who in his liberty directed his word to us through the prophets until he gave us his Son incarnate. To receive him is the first reaction of people, once they discover God speaking and acting. We do not invent revelation, but receive it; we do not create the incarnation, we welcome it; but it is God who first speaks to us as friends, who invites us into his company and welcomes us.[1]

This primordial meaning is continued in the binomial "transmission-reception," of the apostolic kerygma as well as of tradition, which comes from the apostles' successors in the sees they established. Later, it concerns the reception of the great councils with their two types of documents, dogmatic-doctrinal and juridical-practical. Finally, it is reception of documents of popes, bishops, and their respective synods. In a slightly different sense we find it in dealing with ecumenical dialogue, in which we speak of the reception or recognition of the faith traditions and vital institutions of some churches by others. Finally, within the Catholic Church, there are two major facts which we are still receiving in the complex sense of listening, interpreting, applying, integrating in ecclesial consciousness, and articulating with cultural, theoretical, and practical expressions of each of the churches. I am referring to the Second Vatican

---

[1] *Dei verbum* [*DV*] 2: "ad societatem secum invitet in eamque suscipiat."

Council on one hand, and on the other—although they are not objectively comparable—to some documents of recent popes which have received an acceptance which goes beyond direct obedience to questioning perplexity, from meditative dubitation to partial rejection or explicit dissent. There is a more distant sense or quasi-equivocal use of the word when speaking of reception on the part of ecclesiastical authority of theological documents in general or ecumenical ones in particular, which were prepared by technical groups either with or without prior commission.

It is necessary to distinguish also the distinct logical and chronological moments of reception of documents coming from a person or apostolic organisms: (1) *religious acquiescence* with which the word of apostolic authority itself is to be received, without suspicion or prior misgivings; (2) the slower process of *intellectual appropriation* and of integration in the universe of thought and experience both of each Christian and of the community; (3) the *theological interpretation* which professionals give to this, relating it to the Bible, to the Church's normative tradition, to earlier theology and contemporary culture in reference to which the apostolic word must be spoken; (4) *practical application* with its translation into institutional forms and reforms, and regulations for the juridical and canonical order.

Consequently, initial volitive consent, intellectual reception, theological interpretation, practical application and juridical translation of the doctrine or decision of authority, are distinct aspects and moments, each with its own exigencies, phases, and protagonists.

2. Reception expresses an historical fact which you have verified and analyzed as essential to the Church's life from the beginning. For us today this is the fruit of a rediscovery of essential elements for God's plan of salvation, for the Church's order and proper Christian experience, which begin to be explicated through the clashes and frights which the decades following Vatican I provoked. Its texts on the supreme jurisdiction of the pope and his infallible magisterium as supreme pastor of the universal Church affirm that his decisions are valid in themselves and do not depend on the Church's consent. Although the conciliar affirmations were very nuanced, certain interpretations led to a simplification of complex processes and to forgetting elements which are also essential in the Church. The authority of the pope and bishops exists in the Church, from the Church, and for the Church. The fact that they are prior to the faithful and are based on the grace of the sacrament of order cannot mean that they are exercised at a distance or in forgetting what belongs to the entire

believing community. Such a restrictive interpretation of Vatican I is
silent about this dimension of Christian life and opposes the pope's authority, at times explained in an authoritarian sense, to a Christian who is
isolated and alone. Authoritarianism and individualism are opposed to
each other, and mutually reinforcing. The word of the apostle appears
only to require obedience from the believer.

The theology of the last fifty years has helped in recovering other dimensions: the community as an integral subject of ecclesial action; the
necessary participation of each of its members in the responsibility of listening, obeying, witnessing, and incarnating the gospel; the special responsibility of lay persons in temporal tasks. This responsibility presupposes a personalizing of the faith, an integration in culture with what
people say of our world, think of action, and anticipate for the future.
How is all this to be realized without a personal process of discernment,
understanding, and interpretation of divine revelation, of apostolic tradition, of the conciliar teaching? Between absolute authority on one side,
and the individual merely obeying and applying an earlier word from
someone else, has been born the responsible person, active in a Christian
way in both the intellectual and volitive orders. A Church which is a community and mission in so far as it is a universal Church which integrates
and is constituted from the local churches at the same time as it is realized in them, today has the need and the difficulty of carrying out each of
these processes of listening, personal appropriation, and coherent response. It is in the communitarian order what Newman called "the realization of faith" in the personal order.[2] This is to realize the faith as discernment, integration in one's own life, and expression with one's own
concepts within the culture of each place. The old spiritual tradition of
the East spoke of a soul or of a "dioratic attitude" (penetration, contem-
plation), of a "dialogic attitude" (communication, exchange both with
God in prayer and with humans in dialogue), and of a "diacritical attitude" (discernment, judgment). Through these the entire being of a person was integrated in the word heard, carrying it to the heart, the eyes,
and the hands. It is necessary to recognize at the same time that there is a
difference between the supernatural meaning of the faith, the consent of
the faithful, public opinion of the Church, and the opinion of the culturally and politically dominated media which interject themselves into the

---

[2]   See Werner Becker, "'Realisierung' und 'Realizing' bei John Henry Newman,"
Newman Studien 5 (1962) 269-282; Josef Goldbrunner, *Realization: Anthropology of Pastoral Care* (Notre Dame, IN: University of Notre Dame Press, 1966).

Church and even sometimes set themselves up, according to their special view, as authentic interpreters of what according to them is necessary to be a modern church, culturally and politically correct. This goes far beyond simple obedience, dry observance, or mere application. It goes much farther, it does not remain much closer. John Paul II repeated in Spain that only that faith is living faithfully which realizes itself as culture.[3] More, for this to be possible, requires that it be personalized by a process of joining together with what went before, and of confrontation with the universe of truths and experiences in the midst of which each human community expresses itself. The difficulties which arise for us in this process of "reception" derive from many factors, but not in the final place from a cultural break with respect to the formulas in which the faith has crystallized up to now, from an almost unrecognizable pluralism of forms of life and thinking, from the pressure which the Church lives in each national, social, and political sphere, or from the lack of experience on the Church's part in the functioning of participative structures.

All these are difficult realities, but they cannot keep us from seeing the need for active, personal, and communitarian participation by each believer and by the respective churches in the task of receiving the gospel, of accepting the apostolic word, of welcoming all the previous history, of listening to the Spirit, and of aiding initiatives to perceive the first word of the gospel given once and for all and eternally new.

3. When one looks at the history of divine revelation in its constitutive moments, we can encounter there the call to a bipolarity of elements which are included mutually and which reciprocally interact, or if one prefers another image, we encounter an ellipse with two foci, a biunivocal relationship. *Dei verbum* affirmed expressly that "divine revelation is realized by deeds and words intrinsically bound to one another" (*DV* 2). There are objective facts of human history and prophets inspired by God who offer the interpretation of events which in themselves can have diverse meanings. The prophet, in turn, welcomes from God the word in order to interpret these facts. Yet there are no facts without prophets, nor prophets without basic facts.

If we examine the New Testament we encounter another constitutive bipolarity: revelation which comes about by the word of Christ, who is the last, the definitive, the one time for ever, *ephapax*. Christ cannot be

---

[3]   John Paul II, discourse to the recently created Pontifical Council of Culture, June, 1982; and discourse to university personnel at the Universidad Complutense, November 3, 1982.

surpassed by another prophet. Nevertheless, Christ's word has to be interpreted by the Spirit, who is to bring out of them all that his immediate hearers could not comprehend until it brings truth to its completion, making perfect in them and making them perfect in it. The Holy Spirit takes what Jesus said; it does not invent, but interprets. Jesus' word is thus bound more tightly to the Spirit's interpretation, and the Spirit's interpretation to Jesus' word. Jesus did not depend on the Holy Spirit, but was awaiting it.

Finally, in the Church we have the binomial: apostle-community. The apostle has his authority from Christ, but he holds it from the community and in the community. He holds *eksousía* from the resurrected Lord, and each one of the members of the community has the anointing of the Holy One. The pneumatic and sacramental realities which are at work in the apostle are also at work in each of the faithful. The apostle has the first word when he establishes the community and the last when this does not find *koinonía* among its members. But to have the first and last, in this sense, does not mean to have it all. Believers have their matrix and permanent foundation in the apostle's word, without which they cannot exist.

The existence of these two elements—facts-prophets, Christ-Holy Spirit, apostle-community—is a source of tension in the Church's history, but it is also a guarantee of God's freedom and of human participation in the historical processes of discovery and realization of Christian life. God continues to speak in human history, with reference to the Word which he spoke once, which if it was definitively given is not definitively exhausted.

Thus to speak of reception in its primordial sense in the light of which any other sense must be understood, is equivalent to the full integration of a person, in personal and communal expression, in the act of welcoming, responding, and realizing the word of God, which comes giving itself and speaking itself in history through the apostle, as its authorized witness and interpreter. This word comes also incrementally to the extent that generous and perspicacious readers, listening and obeying, read and practice it. Thus, with full reason and anticipating new theories of communication and information, Saint Gregory said: "Divine words grow with reading" (*Divina eloquia cum legente crescunt*).[4]

4. What attitudes should guide us in situations in which we do not yet have full clarity in the matter of reception and interpretation before real

---

[4] St. Gregory, *Homilia super Exechiel* I, 7, 8, 9: *Patrologia Latina* 76: 843.

problems, which evidence aspects which are difficult to reconcile among themselves? In these moments what is needed is a will for truth at the same time as a disposition of love, all persons speaking their own word with anticipation, aware at the same time that each believer is by definition a member and that each one's vitality, thinking, and reasons are not absolute, separated reasons, because each is joined to others forming one family and are part of one body or organism. The will for total truth is not the same as integralism; the disposition of love is not the same as accepting everything that one's neighbor does, as if there were no objective rule by which all of us measure and let ourselves be measured; the courage to sustain the perspective which one sees does not mean that if other words appear one cannot open up to them and expand oneself with them. The love of one's own time and place, of one's own local church or special group, cannot make us forget catholicity in time and space. We need today to develop criteria for true and false reception in the Church which will be equivalent to what at one time Congar formulated for a reform without schism. Do you recall what he said?

a)   Primacy of charity and pastoral.
b)   Remaining in the communion of all.
c)   Patience. Respect for delays.
d)   A true renewal by means of a return to the principle of tradition, not to the introduction of a "novelty" by means of a mechanical adaptation.[5]

Without seeking to make a rigorous exposition at this time, I dare to suggest some fundamental attitudes to remain faithful and creative while putting up with difficulties, so that we do not succumb to laziness, impatience, radicalism, or mutual blackmail.

1. Broadening the view of normative tradition and the concrete history of the earlier Church in order to learn from it and to overcome the narrowness of place (*angustia loci*) and the tightness of time (*angor temporis*).

2. Explicit acceptance of the special authority given by Christ to the apostles to build up and not to destroy. This has to be exercised in a community of brothers and sisters which, if they are faithful, can count on the anointing of the Holy Spirit, who teaches all.

3. Courage to integrate everyone, and leadership in what affects everyone, holding in esteem with greater love and service, the greater in-

[5]   Yves M. Congar, *Vraie et fausse réform dans l'Église* (Paris: Cerf, 1969) 211-230.

terest and the greater claims. The negative and redemptive cross accompanies any mission of the Kingdom: that of Jesus himself, of the Church, and of each one of his members.

4. Permanent attention to ecumenical listening, for what affects one church immediately has repercussion on all the other churches or communities; one and all are responsible for unity, as guarantee of the apostolic mission to the end of the created world.

5. Effort and expectation for knowledge, at the same time as patience for ignorance. Truth will increase with time and time will reveal the truth. Tertullian glossed the famous affirmation of Aulius Gelius, "Truth is the child of time" (*Veritas est filia temporis*) in the following words: "Bene autem quod omnis tempus revelat, testibus etiam vestris proverbiis atque sententiis, ex dispositione divinae naturae quae ita ordinavit ut nihil diu lateat, etaim quod fama non distulit."[6] Thus, we are not filled with anguish when we do not see with full clarity in basic questions, nor encounter efficacious solutions immediately. The obsession for clarity at whatever price and the educated dreams of reason can sometimes produce monsters.

No lesser figure than Saint Augustine shows that one form of wisdom is patience, when speaking of the difficulties of knowing nature and the human body in order to heal it when sick, writing: "Cum vero eis ignoratis, medicos quaerimus, quis non videat quod de secretis coeli et terrae nos latet, quanta sit patientia nesciendum?"[7]

6. At the end of the span of a theologian's reflection there is always a believer, who must bring before God in prayer one's work, one's difficulties, one's drama of truth and fidelity. Every search for truth about God must end in prayer to God. And just as we ask for our daily bread, we have to ask for the light to advance the necessary daily steps; not for the whole route, but for what we try to walk today, without forgetting the advance of each moment and without seeking to anticipate all that remains for tomorrow. In a situation of personal obscurity in the journey of his life, Newman wrote that admirable prayer, "Lead, Kindly Light." I believe that what he sought personally from God is what we must seek ourselves as well, for each one of us and for the whole Church:

> Lead, Kindly Light, amid the encircling gloom
> Lead Thou me on!

---

[6] Tertullian, *Apologeticum*, 7: 13.
[7] St. Augustine, *Enchiridion*, 5: 16.

The night is dark and I am far from home —
Lead Thou me on.
Keep Thou my feet; I do not ask to see
The distant scene—one step enough for me.[8]

I hope that your work has clarified the step which today we have to take in the Church and in theology; not all the future, which is in the hands of God, but that of today which God has given as our charge and our glory. This is my desire, my prayer, and my hope. Thank you very much.

Translation by James H. Provost

---

[8]   John Henry Newman, *Prayers, Poems, Meditations* (New York: Crossroad, 1990) 147.

PARTICIPANTS

Most Rev. Braulio Rodríguez, Bishop of Salamanca, Spain

Most Rev. Fernando Sebastián Aguilar, Archbishop of Pamplona and Grand Chancellor of the Universidad Pontificia, Salamanca, Spain

Most Rev. Elías Yanes Alvarez, Archbishop of Zaragoza and President of the Spanish Episcopal Conference

Dr. Angel Antón-Gómez, Pontificia Università Gregoriana, Rome, Italy

Dr. Joseph Avril, CNRS, Paris, France

Dr. Gaëtan Baillargeon, Université de Québec, Trois-Rivières, Canada

Dr. Wolfgang Beinert, Universität, Regensburg, Germany

Dr. José Eduardo Borges de Pinho, Universidad Católica, Lisbon, Portugal

Dr. Nuno Brás, Universidad Católica, Lisbon, Portugal

Dr. Claude Bressolette, Institut Catholique, Paris, France

Rev. Pierluigi Cabri, Edizioni Delhoniane, Bologna, Italy

Rev. Denis Carlin, Real Colegio de Escoceses, Salamanca, Spain

Dr. Alfonso Carrasco Rouco, C.E.T. San Dàmaso, Madrid, Spain

Dr. Arturo Cattaneo, Facoltà di Teologia, Lugano, Switzerland

Dr. Santiago del Cura Elena, Facultad de Teología, Burgos, Spain

Dr. Luc De Fleurquin, Katholieke Universiteit, Leuven, Belgium

Dr. Nelson Carlos Dellaferrera, Facultad D. Canónico, Buenos Aires, Argentina

Dr. José María Díaz Moreno, ICADE, Madrid, Spain

Dr. John Erickson, St. Vladimir Seminary, Crestwood, NY

Dr. Michael Fahey, University of St. Michael's College, Toronto, Canada

Dr. Joseph Famerée, Université Catholique, Louvain-la-Neuve, Belgium

Dr. Giorgio Feliciani, Università Santa Cruore, Milan, Italy

Dr. José Román Flecha Andrés, Universidad Pontificia, Salamanca, Spain

Dr. Gerald Fogarty, University of Virginia, Charlottesville, VA

Dr. Carl G. Fürst, Universität, Freiburg-im-Breisgau, Germany

Dr. Angel Galindo García, Universidad Pontificia, Salamanca, Spain

Dr. Antonio García y García, Universidad Pontificia, Salamanca, Spain

Dr. Miguel María Garijo Güembe, Katholische-Theologische Fakultät, Münster, Germany

Dr. Pablo Gefaell, Pontificio Ateneo Romano della Santa Croce, Rome, Italy

Dr. Gianfranco Ghirlanda, Pontificia Università Gregoriana, Rome, Italy

Dr. Olegario González de Cardedal, Universidad Pontificia, Salamanca, Spain

Dr. Adolfo González Montes, Universidad Pontificia, Salamanca, Spain

Dr. William Henn, Pontificia Università Gregoriana, Rome, Italy

Dr. Jesús Hortal Sánchez, Río de Janeiro, Brazil

Dr. Jean Joncheray, Institut Catholique, Paris, France

Dr. Joseph A. Komonchak, Catholic University of America, Washington, DC

Dr. Peter Krämer, Katholische Universität Eichstätt, Germany

Dr. Emmanuel Lanne, Abbaye de Chevetogne, Belgium

Dr. Hervé Legrand, Institut Catholique, Paris, France

Dr. José María Lera, Bilbao, Spain

Dr. Julio Manzanares Marijuán, Universidad Pontificia, Salamanca, Spain

Rev. Antonio Martín Olivera, Guijelo, Spain

Dr. Juan Antonio Martínez Camino, Conferencia Episcopal, Madrid, Spain

Dr. Frederick R. McManus, Catholic University of America, Washington, DC

Dr. Arnaldo Pinho, Facultade de Teologia, Porto, Portugal

Dr. Hermann-Josef Pottmeyer, Universität, Bochum, Germany

Dr. James H. Provost, Catholic University of America, Washington, DC

Dr. James Puglisi, Centro Pro Unione, Rome, Italy

Dr. John A. Radano, Pontificio Consiglio Unità dei Cristiani, Rome, Italy

Dr. Julio Ramos Guerrerira, Universidad Pontificia, Salamanca, Spain

Dr. Carlo Maria Redaelli, Facoltà Teologica del Norte d'Italia, Milan, Italy

Dr. Lawrence T. Reilly, Wapato, WA

Dr. Fernando Rodríguez Garrapucho, Universidad Pontificia, Salamanca, Spain

Dr. Pedro Rodríguez, Universidad de Navarra, Pamplona, Spain

Dr. Gilles Routhier, Université Laval, Ste-Foy, Québec, Canada

Dr. José Manuel Sánchez Caro, Universidad Pontificia, Salamanca, Spain

Rev. Javier Santa Clotilde, Arcos de Jalón, Spain

Dr. Mariano Sanz González, Universidad Pontificia, Salamanca, Spain

Dr. Josè Ignacio Saranyana, Universidad de Navarra, Pamplona, Spain

Dr. Klaus Schatz, Theologische Fakultät St. Georgen, Frankfurt-am-Main, Germany

Dr. Bernard Sesboüé, Centre Sévres, Paris, France

Dr. Mary Tanner, Church House, London, England

Dr. Joaquín Tapia, Obispado, Salamanca, Spain

Dr. Robert D. Turner, Okanogan, WA

Dr. Angel M. Unzueta, Bilbao, Spain

Dr. Laurent Villemin, Institut Catholique, Paris, France

Dr. Lionel Wickham, The Divinity School, Cambridge University, England